Our Common Lands

OUR COMMON LANDS

Defending the National Parks

Edited by David J. Simon

Washington, D.C. ☐ Covelo, California

ABOUT ISLAND PRESS

Island Press, a nonprofit organization, publishes, markets, and distributes the most advanced thinking on the conservation of our natural resources—books about soil, land, water, forests, wildlife, and hazardous and toxic wastes. These books are practical tools used by public officials, business and industry leaders, natural resource managers, and concerned citizens working to solve both local and global resource problems.

Founded in 1978, Island Press reorganized in 1984 to meet the increasing demand for substantive books on all resource-related issues. Island Press publishes and distributes under its own imprint and offers these services to other nonprofit organizations.

Funding to support Island Press is provided by The Mary Reynolds Babcock Foundation, The Ford Foundation, The George Gund Foundation, The William and Flora Hewlett Foundation, The Joyce Foundation, The John D. and Catherine T. MacArthur Foundation, The Andrew W. Mellon Foundation, The Northwest Area Foundation, The Jessie Smith Noyes Foundation, The J.N. Pew, Jr. Charitable Trust, The Rockefeller Brothers Fund, and The Tides Foundation.

For additional information about Island Press publishing services and a catalog of current and forthcoming titles, contact Island Press, P.O. Box 7, Covelo, California 95428.

© 1988 National Parks and Conservation Association

Cover photograph: Canyon de Chelly National Monument by Ansel Adams. Courtesy, National Archives.

Cover design: Studio Grafik.

Island Press gratefully acknowledges permission to reprint "Glacier National Park and Its Neighbors: A Study of Inter-Agency Cooperation" by Joseph L. Sax and Robert B. Keiter. © 1987 *Ecology Law Quarterly*

Island Press gratefully acknowledges permission to reprint in Appendix C material originally published in *Legal Research: How to Find and Understand the Law* by Stephen Elias. © 1986 Nolo Press

Library of Congress Cataloging-in-Publication Data

Our common lands : defending the national parks / edited by David J. Simon.

"National Parks and Conservation Association, Washington, D.C."
Bibliography
Includes index.
ISBN 0-933280-58-0   ISBN 0-933280-57-2 (pbk.)
1. National parks and reserves—Law and legislation—United States. 2. Environmental law—United States. 3. Conservation of natural resources—Law and legislation—United States.
I. Simon, David J., 1963- . II. National Parks and Conservation Association.
KF5635.O95 1988
346.7304'6783—dc19
[347.30646783]   88-16977
                                                                                 CIP

MANUFACTURED IN THE UNITED STATES OF AMERICA

CONTENTS

PART III PROTECTING SPECIFIC PARK RESOURCES

Preface

On the evening of August 17, 1886, Troop M, First United States Cavalry, rode through the Great Arch at Yellowstone National Park, packing law and order in their saddlebags. Since 1872, when the world's first national park was established, thousands of elk, deer, bighorn sheep, and antelope had been slaughtered in the park. The law establishing the park did not provide for enforcement against poachers. Despairing of operating funds, staff, and the regulatory power needed to protect the park, the first superintendent of Yellowstone at one point returned to his previous job as a bank examiner in Minnesota. For thirty years, therefore, the Army wound up running the national park. Not until it passed the Lacey Act in 1894 did Congress bolster protection of the park's wildlife.

Protecting natural processes through statute is a lot like a small boy capturing the wind in a mason jar. Yet we have achieved some remarkable successes. Since the Yellowstone Act in 1872, a body of law has grown up around the concept of environmental protection and wise stewardship of the earth. These laws, some of which are discussed in this volume, are a line of defense in an dynamic world that seems to continually challenge our nation's commitment and ability to preserve our natural and cultural heritage for future generations.

As we approach the twenty-first century, the potential for conflict between park values and the world's need to sustain its population will increase. Parks are facing increasing encroachment and impacts because we simply cannot separate them from society as a whole, nor insulate them entirely from our ability to foul our own nest. More than ever, park defenders must employ every legal tool available to protect these priceless resources held in the public trust. The national park system must stand foremost for preservation while other lands feel the pressures of multiple-use.

Although this is a book about law, it is not for lawyers alone. It was intended to serve a broad spectrum: park managers, activists, students, and other interested citizens. The book explores the strengths and weaknesses of the laws which are the protective net for the National Park System. It is divided into four parts: Part I is an overview which argues forcefully for a greater degree of Park Service independence in policy formulation and legal representation. Part II focuses on general authorities which affect the federal land management agencies. Part III discusses the protection of specific park resources and Part IV addresses development issues that affect the parks. Finally, we have included an appendix chapter which contains a primer on case law and legal research. By no means, however, have we been all-inclusive; state and local statutes, for example, are important elements of park protection that are generally not treated here.

For myself, three key messages emerge from these essays:

First, both citizens and the National Park Service have substantial existing authority to act on behalf of the parks in protecting them from diverse types of threats. The Park Service and supporters of the parks have no reason to back away from insisting that the parks remain unimpaired--that they receive the very highest level of protection possible. The parks are a commitment not only to succeeding generations of Americans, but to the world and its fragile biosphere as a whole. The lessons of the past teach that we must be proactive in defense of those things we hold most dear.

Second, existing authority permits--and requires--the Park Service to be a very active player in the land management decisions of private citizens, local governments, and other federal authorities. This authority is frequently overlooked, underutilized, or untested. Citizens have a responsibility to push at the frontiers of park protection law, to help it evolve in conjunction with the growing value our society is placing on conservation and historic preservation.

Third, litigation should be used as a last resort; it essentially reflects the failure of the planning process. Litigation can cajole, command, or compel. It can force analysis where analysis has been cursory. Litigation sometimes resolves an issue when negotiation fails, but frequently it does not; the courts are simply not suited to make complex land use choices. Ultimately, decisions on how to protect our parks must be made elsewhere-- in boardrooms, offices, legislatures, and schoolrooms--all across this land. Attitudes and values, not merely judicial decisions, must be influenced.

In the wake of the bicentennial year of the United States Con- stitution, the national park system stands out as one of the highest expressions of our constitutional and democractic principles. Yet, can we truly say that we are doing a good--even an adequate --job in educating our children about the critical importance of conservation to the fate of the earth? About the unestimable value of preserving the physical presence and atmosphere of historic places, not just their photographs and reconstructions? Can we feel self-satisfied about how well we are protecting our heritage?

As I write these words, bulldozers are tearing up the site of Robert E. Lee's headquarters at the Manassas Battlefield, in prepara- tion for the construction of a 1.2 million sq. foot mall adjacent to the national battlefield park; a religious cult is threatening to drill for geothermal energy on the margin of Yellowstone National Park; a new beauty parlor has been proposed for construction in Yosemite Valley; and a movement is afoot to drill in the Arctic National Wildlife Refuge--which would sacrifice a majestic arctic ecosys- tem on the altar of America's energy gluttony.

There's my answer. And that is why this book may offer a tiny contribution to parks, and ultimately, to people. Parks are cul- tural creations; ideas spun from our laws and the social values they reflect. If we can strengthen a strand here and there, we're making progress. John Maynard Keynes once said, "We will do the ration- al thing--but only after exploring all other alternatives." Strong en- vironmental laws keep us focused on long-term costs, on values, on alternatives--not just on the easy way out.

Credit for this book rests only marginally with the editor, though its defects squarely do. The book evolved during the National Parks and Conservation Association's work on a blueprint for the future of the National Park System. At NPCA, Susan Buffone got the project off the ground. Destry Jarvis kept it there, indulging the editor with advice and support far past his due. Each of the authors gave freely of their thoughts, but also of their already over-budgeted time and patience; they are a unique group of dedi- cated citizens. Particular thanks should go to Joseph Sax and Robert Keiter for graciously allowing the reprint of their article which

appears as Chapter 7, and to Stephen Elias and Nolo Press for permitting the use of selections from their primer in Appendix C. The
skilled work by Mary Medland, Ruth Blau, and Allison Porter
at Island Press was also essential to the project.

Special recognition is due Bill Lockhart. His steady guidance
and impeccable sense of moral purpose about the importance of
the parks shaped the entire book. He stands in the front ranks of
the friends of the national park system. Perhaps now I might be
ready to tackle one of his classes!

In an oft-quoted phrase, Wallace Stegner referred to the national parks as "the best idea we ever had." He is correct; we can
be self-congratulatory. But we must never fail to continue to contemplate and care about the parks--in policy, in law, and in
our hearts.

David J. Simon
Washington, D.C.
May 1988

Foreword

The early national parks were established as enclaves of spectacular natural beauty. They were not meant to be, and they were not, integral ecological preserves. Parks were often managed essentially as wildlife zoos and boundaries were often ecological jokes. Nonetheless, because of their size and isolation, and because the lands around them were commonly uneconomical to develop, many parks in fact constituted the core of essentially pristine ecosystems, biological as well aesthetic treasures.

The modern environmental movement is both more knowledgeable and more scientifically oriented than its precursors. Park defenders demand not only that there be wildlife in the parks for visitors to see, but that there be sufficient habitat to sustain wildlife populations in more or less natural conditions. The environmental movement's legislative program has produced the Clean Air Act and the Endangered Species Act, for example, laws that demand recognition of the interrelatedness of natural systems.

The difficulty is that the National Park System, indeed the whole system of public and private lands, is not organized to produce the results these and similar ecologically sophisticated laws require. Parks are not, with occasional exceptions, ecologically integral in any respect. They do not encompass entire habitats for their animals, or whole watersheds, or even viewsheds, to say nothing of the airsheds by which acid deposition must be accounted for. Indeed, as one of the authors in this book points out, even the huge Yellowstone National Park does not include sufficient land to protect its geysers--the very symbol of American national parks --from geothermal mining beyond its boundaries.

From the perspective of preserving biological and genetic integrity, by which contemporary environmental opinion measures

xiii

success, the parks (for all their wonders) are seriously deficient. If our parklands are to provide, in any degree, what we are now asking of them, far-reaching changes will have to be made. A great deal of land, both public and private, the use of which affects the parks and their resources, is going to have to be managed more sensitively. Traditional boundaries, between park and national forest, or between park and private land, must become less important, and "resource boundaries" must loom much larger. We already talk about the "Greater Yellowstone Ecosystem," which is essentially a euphemism for the habitat of the Yellowstone region's grizzly bear population. This is the first resource region of the sort that should be the basis of future land management.

So far neither Congress nor any agency of government has been willing to face up to the far-flung consequences of moving from traditional enclave management to the challenge of resource-based, natural system management. It is not difficult to see why there is reluctance. A great many people, interest groups, and public agencies have a lot invested in the traditional boundary lines, which define their turf. Thus, efforts to obtain enactment of park protection legislation, which would generally take account of transboundary impacts, languish in Congress. At the same time, paradoxically, Congress has moved forward with a great deal of modern environmental legislation that is, almost by definition, ecosystem-based and resource-oriented. The result is that, piece by piece, we have accumulated a considerable quantity of *de facto* park protection legislation, despite congressional unwillingness to enact anything with that label.

*Our Common Land*s is a book about that legislation, both its possibilities and its inadequacies. There are great gaps in protection, but there is also a great deal more coverage than one might think. Some of the book's contents will come as a revelation even to experts, and certainly to many Park Service officials. Among the most interesting and novel discoveries are Jim Banks's discussion of the strong provision in the nondegradation regulations under the Clean Water Act, Brian Gray's comprehensive discussion of the powerful protective provisions of the Wild and Scenic Rivers Act, and William Lockhart's analysis of the political and institutional contraints that frustrate effective defense of the parks and argue for greater autonomy for the Park Service. Every chapter contains valuable information, much of it never published before.

In addition to the storehouse of information the book provides on a wide range of subjects, from geothermal development to historic preservation to the possibilities of international treaties, it also contains a message to officials of the Park Service that needs to be taken to heart. While probably no federal agency is as well regarded by the public as the National Park Service, its lofty standing can be, and is being, eroded to the extent that it remains passive in the face of damaging assaults on the parks. A number of the authors observe that park officials have been less than avid in using the tools already available to them. For example, the dismal performance of the Park Service in dealing with mining in Alaska, for which it was roundly chastised by a federal court, is noted by several authors. Another author describes Park Service stewardship as "unimaginitive, inconsistent . . . and ponderously bureaucratic."

Since 1919, the National Parks and Conservation Association has been a strong voice for the development and stringent enforcement of laws that defend our park system, the finest in the world. But NPCA is to be especially commended for this publishing effort. The following pages constitute a virtual recipe for the protection of our parks. It's time to get cooking.

Joseph L. Sax
Boalt Hall
Berkeley, CA

PART I

THE REALITIES OF PARK PROTECTION

Chapter 1

EXTERNAL PARK THREATS AND INTERIOR'S LIMITS: THE NEED FOR AN INDEPENDENT NATIONAL PARK SERVICE

William J. Lockhart[*]

Any sound study of the effectiveness of legal protections for our national parks must begin by examining the institutional and political framework in which the law must be applied. But the pervasive threats and increasing imminence of irreversible damage to our parks give special urgency to that inquiry. The author of this first chapter demonstrates that the Park Service response to these threats is severely limited by political and institutional constraints that stymie protective action and impede evolution and application of needed legal standards. Exploring the possibilities for more effective protection under existing laws, the author argues that adequate long-term protection is unlikely unless the Park Service is given substantial independence in policy formulation, administration, administrative initiatives, and legal representation.

--ed.

I. INTRODUCTION

Americans deeply value the natural and cultural heritage preserved for their inspiration and enjoyment in our national parks and monuments. Almost universally, Americans want their national parks vigorously protected. Yet it is increasingly evident that unless we better protect our parks, a mounting accumulation of internal abuse and external threats will degrade and impair the landscapes, resources, values, and experiences that embody "the best idea we ever had."[1]

Assuring the protection of our parks, however, has increasingly become a legal problem. Legal and regulatory solutions must be adequate to prevent damaging impacts from a wide range of land uses and activities not only within the parks, but also those generated on adjacent lands or, sometimes, at great distances. This book offers a detailed review of the scope and application of the diverse legal protections available for national parks. As the contributions to this book make clear, effective park protection depends upon applying an expanding and eclectic body of law involving a variety of statutes, regulations, guidelines, and judicial or administrative precedents.

Americans wishing to preserve their parks must become familiar with this diverse body of law because no single system of legal protections or institutions is adequate to avert the engulfing accumulation of threats. Statutes designed specifically for park protection--particularly the National Park Service Organic Act[2]--set promising standards for protection, but their reach and effect remain uncertain because of a paucity of interpretive precedents.[3] For that reason, it may frequently prove more helpful to rely on statutes requiring broad environmental review or public land planning,[4] because comprehensive consideration of resources and impacts may provide context and focus for the application of basic park protection standards.[5]

Similarly, the protection offered by comprehensive planning requirements may often be strengthened by the application of specialized statutes that require special planning attention or impose concrete standards for protection of particularly vulnerable[6] or significant resources or values.[7] Still other laws may aid park protection by imposing procedures or standards designed to reduce the impacts of specific types of intrusions.[8] Finally, important legal tools to protect specific resources or to supplement statutory remedies may be found in other statutes or common law concepts not necessarily designed for protection of parks or related resources.[9]

Review of these legal protections available for our parks, however, also highlights disturbing and fundamental inadequacies of the current legal framework:

- The basic laws protecting our national parks use general language, which can be given specific content and application only through interpretation in judicial precedents, agency regulations, or operating guidelines that recognize fundamental protective standards and priorities. Yet development of that needed body of park protection law has been stunted because the National Park Service confronts institutional and political constraints that seriously restrict its role in the litigation or rulemaking that could generate concrete legal standards.

■ The lack of detailed, specific, and concrete interpretive precedents and standards seriously handicaps the National Park Service (and other park advocates) in asserting the priority that Congress intended for park protection. Those limitations frequently hobble park protection in the face of conflicting state or private development. But the problem may be even more serious where external threats are generated by other federal resource development programs on adjacent lands. The result, too often, is that Park Service officials may politely question, but seldom directly challenge, those conflicting programs or their impacts--even where intrusions threaten at the very borders of the parks.

To a major extent, these inadequacies of the legal structure are both caused and compounded by institutional and political obstacles in the Department of the Interior that severely handicap effective response to the increasing external threats that face our national parks. Those obstacles, their impact on park protection, and possible solutions are explored in this essay.

Beginning with exploration of the pervasive and serious threats facing our parks, particularly as summarized by the Park Service's 1980 *State of the Parks* report, this essay focuses on obstacles to effective park protection revealed by the institutional response to those threats. While some important preliminary steps have been taken, the Park Service has been handicapped in translating those steps into specific programs or initiatives that could strengthen the legal and institutional defenses available to protect our parks.

Too often, the Park Service responses are characterized by constrained, inward-looking strategies that are the predictable result of the limited role permitted the Park Service within the Department. Particularly during the Reagan years, from 1980-88, Department of the Interior officials have discouraged or resisted management or regulatory initiatives that would control, avoid, or minimize threatened impairments or promote development of more rigorous park protections standards. Confronted with threats generated by the conflicting missions and politically-supported demands of other agencies, the Park Service is confined to addressing those threats through low-key efforts at "conflict avoidance and resolution." Yet that approach virtually guarantees that any solutions will reflect the lowest common denominator that can be negotiated with competing agencies.

Without a departmental priority for park protection and without the ability to enhance or enforce park protection standards, it will be impossible for the Park Service to resist the engulfing tide of development that threatens continuing, incremental, serious impairment of our national parks. Inevitably, then, America's future generations will inherit parks whose well-defined boundaries cannot protect their own captive geography.

Is the Interior Department's lack of support for park protection based on legitimate legal doubts--doubts about the protective reach of the governing statutory and case law that preclude it from implementing effective initiatives for park protection? Surprisingly, in view of Interior's reluctance to take park protection initiatives, even the Department, sometimes, acknowledges that it has adequate authority to provide the needed protection.

This essay argues that fundamental institutional change is essential if we are to fulfill our commitment to preserve our national parks. The Park Service must have a substantial measure of independence to establish protective policies and pursue remedies for park threats free of the intradepartmental political demands and conflicts of interest that are endemic in the Department of the Interior. Furthermore, it is critical to recognize that remedies for park threats necessarily must be sought in a complex legal environment involving local, state, Indian, and federal jurisdictions and programs, as well as a multitude of private legal interests. For that reason, and to assure effective advocacy uncompromised by conflicting loyalties, the Park Service must have independent legal counsel. Finally, that advocate must have resources and authority to conduct administrative and court litigation to challenge park threats and to seek protective interpretation and application, or revision, of basic legal standards.

These changes are urged in the belief that most Americans will demand better protection for their national parks when they understand the serious inadequacy of the current legal structure. We hope this book will aid that understanding and will stimulate a national call for more effective legal protection.

II. THE BASIC PROBLEM: A NEED FOR EFFECTIVE INSTITUTIONAL AUTHORITY TO AVERT THREATS TO OUR PARKS ARISING OUTSIDE THEIR BOUNDARIES

A. The Reality of Cumulating Threats Beyond Effective Reach of the National Park Service

This collection of legal essays is grounded in an obvious premise. If we are truly committed to preserving "the scenery and the natural objects and the wildlife" in our national parks, leaving them "unimpaired for the enjoyment of future generations,"[10] the legal and institutional framework for protecting our parks must reflect reality.

The reality is that our parks are being impaired, and are increasingly threatened with impairment, by a wide range of activities and projects occurring both within the parks and on other public or private lands. Ordinarily, of course, impairing activities inside the parks are within the established authority of the Park Service to control.[11] But it is not yet widely understood that the external threats, which arise from activities on adjacent (or sometimes, distant) lands, are often beyond the present legal or political capacity of the Park Service to resolve. Protection of our parks requires solutions for external threats that are ubiquitous, diverse, and often severe. The threats range from the familiar problems of logging or oil and gas drilling on adjacent lands to a gargantuan proposal for a nuclear waste disposal facility; from dam construction and water rights disputes to strip mining, water pollution, scenery-obscuring plumes, regional haze, and acid rain; from road construction and off-road vehicle damage to insecticide spraying, condo developments, and TV transmitter stations at the very boundaries of the parks.

It is the cumulative effects of these threats, even more than their individual impacts, that most endanger our parks. For example, Canyonlands National Park, a pristine wilderness park in southeastern Utah, has recently faced a combination of threats including (at least):

■ A complex proposal for a huge nuclear waste disposal
  facility near the entrance road and less than a mile
  from the park boundary.[12]

■ Proposals for massive drilling and in situ development
  of tar sands near the most remote and scenic part
  of the park.

■ Unrestricted oil and gas leasing, with high probability
  of exploratory drilling and potential field development
  in vulnerable viewsheds along other boundaries.

■ Continuing demands by local boosters for an expanded
  network of roads both within the park and through
  adjacent de facto wilderness.

■ Potential expansion of tourist facilities and services,
  including an airport and runway for "scenic flights,"
  in the immediate scenic foreground to the park on
  adjacent state property.

■ Significant visibility reductions from haze caused by
  distant sources of man-made pollution, now occurring
  in all Colorado Plateau parks more than 90 percent of
  the time.[13]

Any of those projects could have severe impacts on the
park. Yet all are serious proposals or are at various stages of processing for approval. All have a strong special-interest constituency;
all are based on arguable, though seldom invincible or controlling
legal positions; and all are potentially vulnerable to appropriate
legal challenges. Their complexity and diversity are not unusual
among external threats.

Unfortunately, it also is not unusual, particularly in the
West, that every one of these threats arises from activities that are
promoted by, or significantly involve, programs or decisions of
other federal agencies--including sister agencies of the Park Service in the Department of the Interior.[14] While certain of the threats
are unique or may have doubtful prospects, some or all of them
could be approved and begin the inevitable degradation of a park
that is now relatively free of serious impacts.

Effective park protection against such external threats requires
aggressive administrative action by the responsible agency--the Park
Service--and a capacity to back up those steps with inde-

pendent legal action. This book suggests that a wide range of administrative steps or legal defenses may be available to protect the parks. But though the Park Service often takes some initial steps, those steps tend to be tentative or politically constrained, and seldom involve invocation of available legal remedies.

To a substantial degree, the reasons for that hesitancy lie in restraints imposed by the internal politics and conflicting missions of the Department of the Interior.

B. The Severity and External Origin of Many Park Threats

The extent, complexity, and seriousness of the external threats to our parks have been fully acknowledged and broadly documented by the Department of the Interior and the National Park Service. In its *State of the Parks--1980* report to Congress, the Park Service explained the results of a comprehensive, park-by-park survey of the threats they confronted. The report concluded that "without qualification, it can be stated that the cultural and the natural resources of the parks are endangered both from without and from within" by a broad range of threats "which have the potential to cause significant damage to park resources or to seriously degrade important park values or park experiences."[15]

The *State of the Parks* report emphasized the expanding scope and severity of the threats:

> Many previously pristine areas today have become surrounded by and exposed to an ever growing array of incompatible and threatening activities on adjacent lands . . . ranging from trespassing livestock which trample vegetation to acid rain from remote industrial facilities which causes severe damage to park terrestrial and aquatic systems and historic structures.

> It is clear that events are taking place that are causing demonstrable and severe damage to the natural and the cultural resources of the nation's national parks, monuments, historic sites and other units. The survey suggests that no area is immune. Although some impacts are subtle and not immediately obvious, long-term consequences can be disastrous.[16]

The Park Service analysis of the sources of those threats also showed that more than half were traceable to external origins:

[M]ore than 50 percent of the reported threats were attributed to sources or activities located *external* to the
parks, [particularly] industrial and commercial development projects on adjacent lands; air pollutant emissions,
often associated with facilities located considerable distances from the affected parks; urban encroachment; and
roads and railroads.[17]

Although the report traced many threats to external sources, it
did not attempt to determine what federal or state agencies may
have been responsible for specific threatening activities, or
under what legal authority they may have been conducted. Yet, as
this book repeatedly demonstrates, the jurisdiction or authority
under which specific threats arise may significantly affect the
availability of, and the need for, legal or institutional remedies.

No systematic survey or analysis has yet catalogued the legal
authorities or agencies responsible for the various identified sources of external threats.[18] But the examples and problems analyzed
in the following essays, as well as the experience of the National Parks and Conservation Association (NPCA) and of this
author in challenging park threats, demonstrate that:

- A substantial portion of the most serious external threats
  arise from activities on other public lands,
  authorized or promoted by other federal agencies,
  and conducted by both public and private entities.[19]

- A significant portion of the remainder of the external
  threats *involve incompatible land use or zoning practices*
  encouraged or permitted by local or state government
  with little regard for their park impacts.

These conclusions about the jurisdictional origins of the threats
are also well supported by summaries of significant threats recited
by a group of Park Service regional directors and park superintendents who testified in 1982 at oversight hearings following
up on the *State of the Parks* report.[20]

Finally, concentration in these essays on external threats
does not imply that internal threats may be safely disregarded.
While the Park Service does have well established authority to deal
with most internal management issues,[21] even that authority is
sometimes qualified or uncertain.[22] Furthermore, the Park Service
authority over internal park management does not necessarily assure that management decisions will be based on park protec-

tion concerns where upper-level Interior Department officials respond to special-interest demands or where state congressional delegations choose to play an aggressive role in critical decisions affecting specific parks.[23]

While internal management problems can be serious, the increasingly severe impacts and threats from external activities, and the need to develop a more protective legal framework to deal with those threats, demand prompt solutions. Furthermore, any strengthening of the legal framework to address external threats also will almost certainly aid in addressing internal management issues. Unfortunately, the converse is not true.

C. Park Service Programs to Address Park Threats: Progress and the Limitations of an Inward-Looking Focus

The Park Service response to these serious threats has taken the general approach suggested by the conclusions summarized in the *State of the Parks* report:

> To deal with the wide range of pervasive and complex problems facing the parks today will require a comprehensive science and resource management program that addresses sound resources management planning, the development of an information data base for each park unit, a carefully structured and well documented monitoring program, and a resources management plan that adequately addresses not only the many threats that exist Service-wide, but additionally the steps to be taken to mitigate these problems.[24]

Under these recommendations, some important steps have been taken to improve the development and analysis of information about park resources and the mitigation of impacts from both internal and external activities:

> ■ In 1981, the Park Service proposed and reported to Congress a "servicewide strategy" that, for "mid-term" solutions, proposed to rely on more effective development and use of comprehensive resource management plans (RMPs) for each unit of the park system.[25] After initiating a program to implement that strategy,[26] the Park Service has continued to emphasize resource management planning as a central feature of its response,[27] with increased emphasis on training and assignment of resource management

specialists,[28] regional resource management assessments
and programs,[29] and a new and better-focused survey
that promises to provide new and additional data about
park threats, including better data about sources of
external threats.[30]

- In 1981, the Park Service proposed, as part of its
"servicewide strategy," a shorter-term program intended
to provide a more immediate response to "significant
resource problems" (SRPs) by establishing a priority list
of SRPs to receive special budgetary and management
attention. While the Park Service believed that many
threats could be addressed by "a change in management
style" or revised "programming of funds and personnel,"
the SRP program was intended to address "some of the
most severe and pervasive problems . . . that
require additional funds or personnel."[31] By identifying,
documenting, and prioritizing those problems, the Park
Service hoped to obtain budgetary support to deal with
issues that "warrant special attention and
emphasis."[32] That program, now redesignated the
Natural Resources Preservation Program (NRPP),
continues to provide a mechanism by which Park Service
regional directors prioritize resource protection
needs for special budgetary consideration. Most of the
prioritized needs, however, involve specific internal
projects at specific parks, and do not propose broader
resource protection programs or address external
threats.[33]

- The 1981 "servicewide strategy" also proposed to
undertake ten (later, eleven) further initiatives designed
to support or strengthen key elements of Park Service
resource management planning. Those initiatives
included a number of projects that highlighted the need
for a more effective Park Service science program,
particularly development of baseline inventories of park
resources and of guidelines for monitoring the condition
of resources. [34] The science program was subsequently
restructured and strengthened by creating and obtaining
budget support for the addition of special servicewide
divisions of air quality, water quality, and energy,
mining, and minerals to improve Park Service analysis
and response to threats.[35]

All of these programs offer potentially valuable additions to the Park Service's ability to respond to both external and internal threats. Unquestionably, the development of adequate baseline information on resource conditions and data on specific threats, as well as structured resource management programs, would significantly strengthen the Park Service's capacity to identify, assess, and respond to park threats.

Furthermore, if properly integrated with broader park protection strategies, these programs could lay the groundwork for challenging park threats. Expanding the parks' scientific data base can provide solid evidence that will highlight the potential impacts of specific threats. Better resource management practices, guided by better resource data, can set standards that support challenges to careless or intentional deviations. To the extent these programs generate credible resource data or establish foundations for better management practices, they facilitate more effective legal protection. Park protection legislation and other environmental protection laws and regulations are likely to be interpreted by federal courts to require agencies sponsoring potentially impairing activities to show that they have dealt adequately with environmental or resource threats that are demonstrated with credible data.[36]

Important as they are, however, it is doubtful that these improving Park Service programs can assure the needed protection for our parks, particularly protection from external threats. Some serious reasons for doubt, discussed below, arise from continuing inadequacies in the programs. But the developing data, however imperfect, could be used to support, clarify, and focus the application of existing park protection standards. The fundamental problems, rather, lie in the constraints imposed on specific, concrete initiatives and planning for compliance strategies that could effectively use the data. Those basic problems are discussed in subsequent sections of this essay.

Some reasons for doubt also relate to continuing inadequacies in Park Service programs. The U.S. General Accounting Office (GAO), reporting on its program audit of these Park Service programs, recently concluded that important aspects of the servicewide strategy have yet to be implemented:

> Some parks do not have an approved resource management plan even though they were required to be completed by the end of 1981, others have not updated their

plans, and the plans that have been prepared are not being used in formulating the Park Service's annual budgets.[37]

GAO also points out that although the staff training initiatives have been undertaken, the Park Service has not followed through on most of the other resource management support initiatives, including important baseline inventory and research.[38]

In addition, NPCA's recent "Research Needs Assessment" of the Park Service science program shows a serious lack of commitment to the use of scientific research in management decision making, and states that "weak managerial commitment may result from a lack of understanding about the value of research in the decision making process."[39] NPCA's analysis concluded:

> NPS resource management decisions are increasingly challenged in the courts, the Congress and in the National Environmental Policy Act (NEPA) public involvement process. Yet, this study found that scientific information is not being consistently utilized in the decision making process.[40]

In light of these assessments of Park Service programs following the *State of the Parks--1980* report, it remains doubtful that improved resource management or expanded science programs will be strengthened sufficiently to provide an adequate basis for response to the serious and mounting challenge of external threats. Furthermore, these doubts are intensified because current park planning and action programs are oriented primarily to addressing in-park threats. With some exceptions,[41] they are not designed to focus research and management planning on data and requirements that can assist regulatory protection from external threats, or to expand or complement legal remedies against those threats. Thus, in the absence of a dramatic shift in the basic Park Service policies and authority for dealing with those threats, it is highly unlikely that the servicewide strategy will make a meaningful difference in remedying them.

D. The Ability of the Park Service to Protect the National Parks is Severely Handicapped by Reluctance to Confront the Sources of External Threats, and by Political Constraints in the Department of the Interior

> *(1) Effective response to external threats arising on adjacent federal lands is seriously handicapped by Park Service hesitancy to press for legal remedies.*

In assessing the institutional response to the problem of external threats, it appears that the Department of the Interior and the Park Service, so far, have metaphorically thrown up their hands. The servicewide strategy, the Park Service's fundamental blueprint for responding to the *State of the Parks--1980* report, offered no focused or systematic response to those threats, saying only:

> Problems associated with sources located *outside* the park boundaries are considerably more complex and much more difficult to deal with. . . . [A]ny real mitigation of adverse impacts to the parks resulting from external threats will require a substantially expanded program within the Service augmented in many instances by favorable zoning, land use and regulatory control actions on the part of local and State governments.[42]

Despite that acknowledged need for a "substantially expanded program," the overriding fact about external threats is the lack of any meaningful program for improved federal protection against those threats--a critical deficiency reflecting consistent refusal, at the national level, to confront those "much more difficult" legal and institutional problems.

Both the tone and substance of the Department's approach to the problems of external threats are captured by its response to a recent GAO report that had raised serious doubts about the Department's legal authority to regulate or control external threats. GAO had contrasted its analysis with the Interior Department's earlier claims, in opposing proposals for strengthened park protection legislation, that it has adequate legal authority.[43] Yet, given prepublication opportunity to comment on the GAO report, Interior enthusiastically took the occasion to endorse and reiterate GAO's conclusory rejection of possible "public trust" concepts for park protection. Far from contesting GAO's questionable legal assessment, the Department recommended deletion of any discussion of the legal problems on the ground that the extremely negative GAO analysis essentially duplicated a solicitor's opinion on the scope of park protection authority (though the Solicitor's opinion was not quite so stingy).[44] And it concluded with a death-knell reminder that legal remedies would, in any event, "require the support of the Department of Justice."[45]

That reluctance at the upper levels of the Interior Department to support adequate park protection authority is not lost on Park Service management and park superintendents. Park managers can hardly be blamed for hesitating to assert or pursue legitimate concerns about activities going on beyond park boundaries; undoubtedly that is the safest way to avoid the turf battles and political sanctions that would be the price for challenging the activities of other land management agencies or their client groups.

The strong tendency of park managers to avoid or minimize confrontation with other agencies over the basic policy conflicts that may result from development on adjacent lands was emphasized in a case study of serious external threats to Glacier National Park by Professors Sax and Keiter in this volume. Focusing on threats arising from Forest Service authorization of development on lands adjacent to Glacier, the study concludes: "the evidence suggests that the park makes case-by-case judgments on just how much opposition is prudent and proceeds accordingly." [46] In taking that cautious approach, park officials characteristically disregarded potential legal remedies:

> Glacier could acquire significant leverage over activities on neighboring lands through laws of general application like NEPA and the federal air and water pollution acts as well as other statutes. Accordingly, we predicted that invocation of those statutes would be a principal tool for influencing external conduct.

> We could not have been more mistaken. Glacier officials rarely mentioned the law in discussing their dealings with neighboring national forests.

* * * *

> Glacier officials do sometimes invoke the law in very limited ways. For example, Glacier called for a full .

> . . . EIS [environmental impact statement] . . . on the en-
> tire cycle of oil and gas development in [adjacent na-
> tional forests] rather than assessments limited to the im-
> pacts of particular exploration proposals. But Glacier does
> not follow up its official comments by seeking to enforce
> compliance, despite the availability of a formal administra-
> tive mechanism for pursuing such a strategy.[47]

While avoiding legal confrontation over the park impacts resulting from specific adjacent-land projects, Park Service officials also
tend to opt out of the broader policy conflicts that generate those
impacts:

> Glacier has clearly rejected a search for structural solu-
> tions in favor of case-by-case negotiation. For example,
> despite their aversion to oil and gas development on the
> edge of the park, Glacier officials have not taken a general
> position against mineral leasing of peripheral lands. . . .
> Nor has the park played a role in proposals for wilder-
> ness designation of lands around the park's borders, though
> such designation would limit or prohibit mineral develop-
> ment.[48]

A similar reluctance to confront the issues raised by other agencies' activities on adjacent lands appears to inhibit effective use of
park management planning. Despite the emphasis in the Park Service's "servicewide strategy" on development and use of comprehensive resource management plans, most park management plans tend
to reflect an inward focus, emphasizing management and protection of the parks within their boundaries. As a result, except
for occasional acknowledgement of particularly dramatic threats,
the plans generally fail to address the need for compatible uses on
adjacent federal lands important to protection of park resources.
And the plans are seldom used to lay the foundation for strategies
to encourage compatible uses or to resist potential threats.[49]
    The failure of park planning to address these threats effective-
ly is particularly unfortunate, because emphasis in park plans
on the importance of adjacent lands and the impacts of adjacent development could lay a strong legal foundation for demanding compatible management. Agencies managing adjacent lands are
specifically obligated under NEPA and/or their own organic legislation to coordinate their decision making and planning with
that of the Park Service (as well as other federal and state agen-

cies).[50] Unfortunately, Park Service guidelines for preparation
of General Management Plans do not explain that role of park
planning; nor do they require planning to assess the park impacts of activities on adjacent lands, or to develop plans or strategies
to avoid or minimize those impacts.[51] Apparently, those failures
are attributable, at least in part, to politically imposed restrictions.[52]

   *(2) The Interior Department weakens park protection by permit-
      ting sister agencies to disregard or minimize any legal
      priority for park protection.*

   A major influence contributing to Park Service reluctance to
confront the problems of external threats is the Interior Department's passive or indulgent acceptance of other agencies' disregard
of park protection obligations--particularly by other Interior Department agencies.
   Repeatedly, in the face of serious threatened impairments from
activities by other agencies on adjacent lands, Interior has declined
to assert, demand compliance, or otherwise apply or test the protective requirements of existing law. Not only does that failure undermine Park Service planning and resolve by raising doubt about
the reach or applicability of the established statutory protections; it also directly weakens the Park Service legal position. Any
effort to invoke park protection statutes in litigation is almost certain to be met with a defense of Interior Department inconsistency or inequity, based on the demonstrable failure of the Interior Department itself to construe or apply the statutes to control
impairing activities, even on its own adjacent lands. More subtle, but of equal or greater substantive importance, is the fact that
in failing to implement park protection standards in interagency
conflicts, the Department has relinquished crucial opportunities to
define and expand the scope of protective interpretation of governing statutes.
   The Department's failure to give effect to park protection standards, of course, has an immediate practical impact on Park Service effectiveness in the inevitable bureaucratic and turf battles
between agencies--particularly other Interior agencies--whose activities on adjacent lands may threaten the parks. *Where the governing legal standards are so thoroughly undermined that even Interior Department sister agencies freely disregard park protection
obligations, even the best resource management programs are not
likely to protect the parks from external threats.*

As may be expected, then, neither the various Interior Department agencies nor other federal agencies appear to recognize any controlling legal obligation to avoid activities on the lands they manage that may impair adjacent parks. Possibly extreme, but apparently within the realm of indulgence permitted by the Interior Department, are the following responses of Interior's Bureau of Land Management (BLM) to Park Service requests for protection of adjacent lands. Commenting on a BLM draft resource management plan generated pursuant to the land-planning process mandated by the Federal Land Policy and Management Act,[53] the Park Service submitted an unusually direct request for park protection from potential external threats. Specifically, the comment requested that scenery on adjacent BLM lands viewed from two scenic parks be designated for protection under BLM's most protective "visual resource management Class I designation." BLM replied:

> The inventory of visual resources did not identify any Class I areas on BLM administered lands. . . . The Class I designation is normally given to areas managed under special designations, such as Wild and Scenic Rivers. *The public lands surrounding the national parks are managed for multiple use.*[54]

In commenting on the same land plan, the Park Service noted that, under the plan, certain BLM wilderness and state park areas would be buffered from the impacts of potential oil and gas leasing by designating adjacent BLM lands under management categories that impose more rigorous protective stipulations. Citing those examples, the Park Service suggested that similar protective leasing categories should be applied as buffers against oil and gas development adjacent to Arches and Canyonlands National Parks. BLM replied: "The oil and gas leasing category system is oriented toward protecting site-specific resource values. The categories are not designed to act as protective buffers."[55]

Similarly, in the preplanning process for identification of issues to be addressed by another BLM resource management plan, NPCA had requested BLM to identify and plan for issues relating to "conflicts between mineral development and the scenic, recreational, aesthetic and cultural values of the area, particularly as those conflicts may affect Canyonlands National Park." And in subsequent comments on BLM's draft plan, NPCA had

sought protections for adjacent lands whose scenic and cultural
resources were integral to the significance, experience, or preservation of related park resources.

It is reasonable to assume that the state director's response,
if not necessarily definitive, at least reflects a position well-ac-
cepted at the upper echelons of BLM, since he was recently chosen
as deputy director of the agency:

> BLM does not have the authority to plan for lands within
> Canyonlands National Park. *We do not manage public
> lands as a "buffer zone" to the park.*

* * * *

> The NPS Organic Act, as amended, states that NPS is to
> leave [parks] "unimpaired for the enjoyment of future
> generations." This law does not address the administra-
> tion of [BLM] public lands, whether in proximity to
> an NPS unit or not; *it does not require the Secretary
> to leave public lands unimpaired to preserve park values.*
> To the contrary, Congress provided that public lands are
> to be managed for multiple use and sustained yield,
> whether in proximity to an NPS unit or not.[56]

Essentially similar rejection of buffer protections on adjacent
lands is also common from Forest Service officials.[57]

Other federal agencies can be even more explicit in rejecting any obligation to avoid impairment of park values where their
programs threaten to conflict with park protection. A dramatic example is reflected in the Department of Energy's explanation of
its nomination of a site less than a mile from Canyonlands National Park as "suitable" for a high-level nuclear waste repository. Applying a legally questionable balancing test that it had previously promulgated,[58] the Department of Energy (DOE) acknowledged that serious impacts would impair the experience of visitors
in portions of the park, but concluded that the "projected environmental impacts are acceptable when balanced against programmatic
and technical, social, and economic considerations." [59]

In explaining its selection decision, DOE expressly declined to
accept the authority of the Park Service conclusion that the impacts would be unacceptable. Rejecting the Park Service's judg-

ment "that repository siting, construction, operation, closure, and decommissioning would be in irreconcilable conflict with its duty to protect the Park," DOE explained its decision as follows:

> The DOI [Interior Department] has a stated inability, because of its statutory mandate, to balance environmental impacts against the DOE's programmatic objectives . . . . DOE has conducted this balancing and concluded that the impacts are acceptable.[60]

Obviously, DOE's position rested specifically upon an essential legal premise: that, as a matter of law, its "programmatic objectives" may disregard Interior's "duty to protect the park" under the National Park Service Organic Act. BLM's position that the lands around parks are managed "for multiple use" and are not managed "as a 'buffer zone' to the park" reflects essentially the same legal position: that the statutory authorities under which BLM operates owe no deference to park protection requirements. Despite that essential premise for their similar conclusions, *neither DOE nor BLM made any effort to offer a legal analysis or justification for its conclusions.*

(3) The Department of the Interior resists or undermines efforts to strengthen park protection from adjacent-land threats.

Any inclination of Park Service officials to act aggressively in confronting park threats generated by other agencies is bound to be discouraged by the consistent rejections received from the top levels of the Department of the Interior. Although there are substantial legal grounds for recognizing the primacy of park protection policies, particularly in "turf" battles within the Department,[61] the Secretary and high-level Department officials have repeatedly rejected or severely watered down important initiatives designed to strengthen park protection.[62]

A unique but important example is offered by the Park Service efforts to avert selection of a site close to Canyonlands National Park for the huge industrial project involved in testing for, and possibly constructing, a repository for disposal of high-level nuclear waste. The project would have required Interior Department approval for withdrawal and transfer to the Department of Energy of BLM lands less than one mile from the park. Because of the severe impacts to the park if the site were selected

and the apparent seriousness of the threat, Park Service Director
William Penn Mott, Jr., sought intervention by Secretary of the Interior Donald P. Hodel. Mott submitted a memorandum asking
Hodel to send a letter to Secretary of Energy Herrington opposing
selection of the site and asserting strong legal grounds for probable Interior Department disapproval of any DOE request for
the land.[63] Despite the significance and urgency of that request in
view of the explicit disregard of park impacts shown by other DOE
officials,[64] Secretary Hodel declined to comply with the Park Service request.[65]

A more central, important, and disturbing demonstration of the
Department of the Interior's refusal to strengthen park protection is illustrated by its calculated dilution of an internal initiative
originally begun to seek remedies for the increasing threats to park
resources. Recognizing public concern about external threats to the
parks resulting from sister agencies' activities on adjacent lands,
the Department had been under pressure to deliver on its 1982
claims that no new legal authority was needed to protect the national parks.[66] As a result, the Under Secretary of the Interior con-
vened a "park protection working group" in late 1984, consisting
of senior officials from all Interior Department bureaus and the
Forest Service. The "working group" was to consider the issues
raised by external threats to the parks and determine what measures
could be taken to address those issues.

After more than six months, the "working group" returned with
a report that barely mentioned park protection. Rather, it redefined
the problem as one of "resource conflicts" among the various Interior agencies, to be addressed by better management through "anticipation, avoidance and resolution." Despite explicit acknowledgment that "differences in statutory mandates and resources
management philosophies" require resolution,[67] the working
group report recommended that resource conflicts be addressed
"within the existing framework of legal authorities and organizational arrangements."[68] No supporting legal analysis or other explanation was offered.

The report received severe congressional criticism. Focusing on
the fundamental failure of the working group report to address the
central problem of park protection, the Chairman of the House
Subcommittee on National Parks and Recreation commented that
the working group erroneously "perceived the issues involving conflicts between land and resource uses to be . . . based on equal

weight of law," while Congress intended existing law to afford parks "the highest possible level of protection."[69] But the Interior Department declined to affirm that basic standard--or take responsibility for any other--as the basis for resolving agency conflicts identified in the course of management steps to "anticipate, avoid and resolve" threats to the parks. It purported to find no legal basis, "pending judicial clarification," for taking a position on the degree to which--or whether--park protection policies should have priority in resolving conflicts arising from the impact of other agencies' programs on adjacent parks.[70]

While the Department thus appeared to accept at least case-by-case determination of appropriate park protection priorities, its implementation of the working group recommendations belies this theoretically noncommittal position. In responding to a Park Service "action plan" to implement the working group recommendations, the Assistant Secretary for Fish, Wildlife and Parks approved a proposal for periodic compilations of external actions that may impact park resources--but only on the condition that the list *"identify the comparative significance of the resources involved*, their condition, degree of potential impact and so forth."[71] While that position did not purport to be justified by any legal analysis, it obviously rested on a crucial, if unstated, legal premise: that the Department may determine the relative significance of threatened park resources and "balance" them against the objectives of other agency programs that may impair those resources. In effect, then, the Department's implementation of the working group report reflects a controlling policy viewpoint that gives little or no priority to park protection.

The Assistant Secretary's response to other aspects of the Park Service "action plan" reveals the Department's lack of commitment to fulfill even the limited objectives of "anticipation, avoidance and resolution" ultimately endorsed by the working group.

Recognizing that "anticipation" and "avoidance" of potential resource conflicts with other agencies would be aided by identifying areas where incompatible activities could have serious impacts on the parks, the Park Service had proposed that a first step include:

> identification and documentation of discrete areas adjacent to park units that contribute in a significant way to park resource values or visitor use and enjoyment (i.e., critical external resource areas such as migration

routes, habitats, scenic views, watersheds, and complementary historic districts) . . . [to be] shared with other Federal
agencies and bureaus . . . and . . . to help identify management and resource issues to be addressed in NPS planning documents.[72]

Apparently unwilling to authorize any explicit recognition of a
Park Service interest in activities on lands adjacent to the
parks, the Assistant Secretary curtly responded that "this activity
is inappropriate and must be removed [from the plan]."[73]

Recognizing that the policies and regulations of other agencies
often promote or authorize activities that may generate park threats,
the Park Service "action plan" had sought to implement "conflict
avoidance" by proposing to

. . . identify regulations, policies and legislation of other
bureaus/agencies which have the potential to cause conflicts with park resources or visitor enjoyment and propose
specific changes that would reduce the potential for causing conflict.[74]

Determining that "if . . . such an activity is appropriate it
should be done at the Departmental, not bureau [Park Service]
level," the Assistant Secretary also required removal of this
proposal from the action plan,[75] but has taken no steps to provide
for that crucial review.

Even more disturbing is the continuing failure of Department officials even to consult with the Park Service on important
issues affecting the parks, despite its theoretical commitment to
continuing consultation under the working group recommendations
to "anticipate, avoid and resolve" resource conflicts. Thus, on May
27, 1987, the Park Service Director found it necessary to direct a
memorandum to the Department's Assistant Secretary for Fish,
Wildlife and Parks, noting that the Park Service had been "overlooked or excluded in the development of . . . several issues being
addressed by other Department of the Interior Bureaus."[76]

III. THE FUTURE OF PARK PROTECTION: EXPANDING OUR LAW TO PROTECT OUR VISION

The converging picture of the future for our national parks is not encouraging: while external threats accumulate, the Department of the Interior repeatedly declines to take an aggressive role in park protection.

Undeniably,[77] the parks are increasingly besieged by external threats--accumulating developments and activities encroach on their borders, threatening both their resources and their basic character. Yet the Department of the Interior refuses to acknowledge or give meaningful effect to existing legal obligations that grant priority to park protection, including significant, if not yet fully defined protection from external threats. The Department declines to approve meaningful programs that would establish protective standards for control of external threats--even threats generated by other Interior agencies. Rather, the Department insists on maintaining its discretion to weigh the "comparative significance of the resources involved" in every "resource conflict," "case by case" and, presumably, impact by impact.

Under these circumstances, it is understandable that the National Park Service program for responding to park threats continues to be confined to a traditional nonregulatory, in-park focus. Some new and creative programs have significantly improved the Park Service's technical capacity to assess and manage park resources, as well as its potential for assessing the consequences of external threats. But, constrained by politically imposed limitations that stunt more protective initiatives, the Park Service is hesitant to use its existing authority and is foreclosed from developing programs that could directly and effectively redress the external sources of park threats.

The fundamental question posed by these circumstances is whether our laws, and the commitment and creativity with which they are being applied, are adequate to fulfill our national vision of parks created

> . . . to conserve the scenery and the natural and historic objects and the wild life therein and to provide for the enjoyment of the same in such manner and by such means as will leave them unimpaired for the enjoyment of future generations.[78]

Is the Interior Department's reluctant response to external park threats based on legitimate doubts about the adequacy of its legal authority under existing statutes and case law? Is its insistence on "balancing" park values against competing resource values based on legitimate doubt about legal authority to prioritize park protection? Is existing law inadequate to support creation of more effective programs and initiatives that could buffer our parks against the accumulating impacts of external threats?

Or is the Interior Department's reluctance grounded more in politics, institutional bias, or competition than in legal constraints? Could existing law, with a change of political priorities or of institutional structure, provide the basis for more adequate park protection?

The essays collected in this volume demonstrate that, if effectively applied, substantial legal authority is available to protect our parks. These essays explore a wide array of existing statutory and common law sources of authority that could be invoked if the Department were seriously inclined to use available legal tools. That legal framework includes a basic core of statutes that directly establish standards for park protection; and those standards could be creatively elaborated by internal practices and directives, by rulemaking, and by aggressive selection of precedent-setting litigation.[79] In addition, the pertinent legal framework includes a wide range of other environmental, land planning, and resource protection laws that could also be invoked to provide further protective standards or procedural requirements.

These essays demonstrate that creative and effective implementation of existing law could provide significant protection, despite some troubling uncertainty about the reach of the applicable legal standards and basic statutory policies. Undoubtedly, legislative improvements such as the "Park Protection Act" proposed in 1982 would provide needed additional protection.[80] It is possible, too, that aggressive administration of existing law may disclose the need for specific improvements in the basic statutory framework. But the crux of the problem lies elsewhere: in failure to exert, or even to test, the reasonable reach of existing authority to avert or minimize external threats.

Surprisingly, a similar conclusion emerges from the following analysis of the Interior Department's own conflicting views about the adequacy of existing law. That analysis, however, brings into focus another central question: can there be any real hope of creative and effective implementation of existing law--or of any improved legal standards--without significant institutional change? Given its own acknowledgement of the need for legal initiatives, Interior's failure to utilize available opportunities under existing law resoundingly demonstrates the need for institutional change.

A. While Opposing New Statutory Protections, the Department of the Interior Admits that the Adequacy of Current Park Protection Authority Depends on the Effectiveness with Which it is Implemented

Claiming that existing law is adequate for park protection, Interior has repeatedly opposed proposals for new legislative authority that would strengthen protection from external threats, despite the gloomy picture painted by the *State of the Parks* report.

In opposing the proposed "National Park System Protection Act of 1982," former Park Service Director Russell E. Dickinson testified on behalf of the Department that existing authority is adequate because the National Park System Organic Act

> requires the Secretary to avoid or modify any proposed action that would, in any way, degrade those park resources which have been set aside for preservation and protection.[81]

When asked directly whether "current authority" is adequate to address the threats revealed by hearings on the *State of the Parks* report, Dickinson replied, *"I believe that we have sufficient existing authority."* [82] Following up on Dickinson's testimony, then–Acting Secretary of the Interior Hodel reiterated the Department's opposition on the ground that "we have the authority, and are using it, to coordinate land use activities and avoid or mitigate harmful effects." For that reason, Hodel said, the proposed act "is unnecessary, duplicates existing laws and administrative programs."[83]

Similarly, when more recently asked at oversight hearings "what additional tools are necessary to avoid critical external threats?" the Park Service responded: "We believe existing authorities provide us with sufficient tools to continue to successfully fulfill the mandate of the National Park Service."[84]

But when proposed initiatives require exercise of the Department's "sufficient existing authority," it takes a different posture. When the Park Service proposed to initiate a planning program that would help resolve intra-Departmental "resource conflicts" by identifying adjacent lands where conflicting uses may impair park values, the Assistant Secretary for Fish, Wildlife and Parks curtly rejected the suggestion as "inappropriate."[85] And when asked whether the Park Service can utilize its Organic Act as one basis for protecting the parks from external sources of air pollution, the Interior Solicitor's office responded by emphasizing what he characterized as an "administrative concern" based on "the Secretary of the Interior's long standing interpretation of his regulatory power under the Organic Act *as relating to activities within the boundaries of NPS units."* [86] Needless to say, in opposing the "Park Protection Act" as "unnecessary," the Department had not mentioned that "long standing interpretation."

That limiting interpretation of park protection laws is undoubtedly reflected in the Interior Department's refusal to establish policies or adopt procedures that would give priority to resolving park threats ("resource conflicts") generated by other agencies--even its own agencies. Undoubtedly it is that reluctance to recognize any priority for park protection that permits BLM summarily to reject Park Service requests for adjacent land protections on the ground that the National Park Service Organic Act

> . . . does not address the administration of [BLM] public lands, whether in proximity to an NPS unit or not; *it does not require the Secretary to leave public lands unimpaired to preserve park values.*[87]

Yet, even as BLM was rejecting the extra-park reach of park protection laws, the Park Service was responding to a congressional inquiry, saying that it has adequate tools to address "critical *external* threats" through "utilization of injunctive and other legal tools [that] can prevent others from conducting activities that are demonstrably harmful to park resources." [88]

More to the point than Interior's conflicting postures on the adequacy of existing law, the Solicitor's recent air pollution opinion recognized that important questions about interpretation of existing law have not yet been addressed by judicial precedents. Recognizing that judicial interpretation of park protection statutes simply has not yet confronted key questions about their reach and application to external threats (as explained by Professor Keiter's essay in this volume),[89] the Solicitor's air pollution opinion acknowledged that existing case law

. . . logically would appear to be as supportive of the Secretary's efforts to protect NPS units from external threats as it has been found applicable to internal threats.[90]

Recognizing that the logic of existing case law should be applicable to extend protection from external threats, the Solicitor's conclusions highlighted the need for initiatives that can expand that body of law:

> Under the circumstances, the utility of . . . administrative reinterpretation of the Organic Act to support new regulation of park-threatening activities . . . outside the boundaries of NPS units remains untested and uncertain.

> * * * *

> To a certain extent the effectiveness of existing law to deal with this problem will be determined case by case in the litigation process. Statutory mandates will have to be interpreted by the Secretary in the context of specific problems. Ultimately, those judgments will be tested and resolved in the courts, where the Justice Department is responsible for defending the interests of the United States. How those actions are prosecuted and defended will play a role in the development of the law for the protection of NPS units from [external threats].[91]

The solicitor's opinion understates a conclusion that emerges forcefully from this book: whether existing law is adequate or whether new and more explicit statutory protections should be sought depends heavily on how effectively--and whether--the Department's existing authority is used.

Secretary of the Interior Hodel probably focused the basic problem more clearly than intended when, as Acting Secretary opposing the "Park Protection Act of 1982," he objected that it "attempts to impose statutory mandates on what are properly discretionary administrative functions." [92] There is serious doubt about the lawfulness of Interior's continuing effort to retain maximum discretion at the expense of park protection.[93] The fundamental question, however, is whether new "statutory mandates" for park protection are needed because the Department

of the Interior consistently refuses to exercise its "discretionary administrative functions" to utilize and expand the protective
reach of existing law.

**B. Interpretation of the "Core" Park Protection Statutes
Demonstrates a Substantial Legal Basis for Initiatives that Would
Protect National Parks from External Threats**

In recognizing that logical extension of existing case law would
provide protection for our national parks against external threats,[94]
the Interior solicitor's air pollution opinion implicitly recognized
that the basic park protection laws invite that protective interpretation. That conclusion was more directly supported by a carefully cautious, but well-supported legal opinion rendered by the Library
of Congress's Congressional Research Service in 1985. It assessed the solicitor's opinion and concluded:

> On balance, although the issue is not free from ambiguity,
> it appears the [Redwoods Amendments were] intended to
> clarify that the values and purposes for which the
> Park Service System was established were intended to
> provide the basis for their management and protec-
> tion, *including protection from external threats.*[95]

Close scrutiny of the text, structure, and legislative history of the
core park protection legislation strengthens that conclusion.

*(1) The extra-park reach of the National Park Service Organic
Act and its 1978 Redwoods Amendments.*

The fundamental starting points for identifying the legal standards that protect our national parks are the original 1916 National Park Service Organic Act, together with the 1978 "Redwoods
Amendments," which strengthened and extended the protective reach
of that Act.[96] The relevant provision of the original Organic
Act provided that the Park Service was to "regulate the use" of national parks, monuments, and reservations by means that "conform
to" their "fundamental purpose":

> . . . to conserve the scenery and the natural and historic
> objects and the wild life therein and to provide for
> the enjoyment of the same in such manner and by such
> means as will leave them unimpaired for the enjoy-
> ment of future generations.[97]

On its face, this provision of the Organic Act creates a powerful, sweeping priority for park protection, unqualified in its protection against *any* impairments, *external* as well as internal. The only real question would seem to be whether its sweeping standard is framed in terms that can be given enforceable legal effect.

Did Congress intend that those rigorous standards be *applied*, even in the face of competing statutory programs that may encourage impairing activities on adjacent lands? Is the Act's legal effect weakened by its quaintly hortatory tone, leaving an implication of mere unenforceable aspiration? Is the reach of the Act confined by the mandate to "regulate the use" of parks, thus redressing only impairments whose origins and effects are traceable to in-park "use"?

If enforceability of the Organic Act standard was ever in doubt, those doubts should have been erased by the 1978 Redwoods Amendments. The amendments were prompted by Park Service difficulty in protecting Redwood National Park from the consequences of erosion and silting generated by heavy logging of adjacent private lands, and by related litigation whose unsuccessful conclusion had left doubt about the efficacy of existing law.[98] While major aspects of the amendments dealt with specific issues affecting Redwood National Park, the amendments also included an important provision that prohibited "derogation" of park values, made generally applicable to all units of the National Park System.

The prohibition against "derogation" is important not only because it reiterated a rigorous standard of protection, but also because it imposed those restrictions in terms designed to impose regulatory prohibitions:

> *The authorization of activities* shall be construed and the protection, management, and administration of these areas shall be conducted in light of the high public value and integrity of the National Park System and *shall not be exercised in derogation of the values and purposes for which these various areas have been established,* except as may have been or shall be directly and specifically provided by Congress.[99]

The regulatory tone and thrust of that language was intended expressly to reassert and effectuate the high standard of protection prescribed by Congress in the original Organic Act. To that end, the prohibition against derogating park values not only reiterates and emphasizes the rigorous nonimpairment theme of the original Act; it also explicitly provides that "the promotion and regulation of all areas of the National Park System . . . shall be consistent with and founded in the purpose established by section 1"[100] (the nonimpairment provision of the 1916 Organic Act). Furthermore, the legislative history is also explicit in asserting that the amendment was intended "to refocus and insure that the *basis for decision making* concerning the System continues to be the criteria provided by 16 U.S.C. § 1."[101]

In addition to refocusing and reemphasizing the rigorous park protection intended by the Organic Act, the provision of the amendments that prohibits derogation of park values strongly invites interpretation that can provide important further support for protection of parks from external threats.

Literally read, the prohibition against derogating parks' values and purposes is applicable to *any* "authorization of activities," and hence should apply generally to bar any agency from authorizing activities on adjacent lands that would cause any derogation of park values.[102] That interpretation is well-supported by the legislative history of the Redwoods Amendments. Without contest from dissenting senators, the key committee report explicitly indicated that the amendments were designed to resolve legal disputes about "competing private and public values" in *areas surrounding* the national parks:

> This restatement of these highest principles of management *is also intended to serve as the basis for any judicial resolution* of competing private and public values and interests *in the areas surrounding* Redwood National Park *and other areas of the National Park System.*[103]

Despite the explicit transboundary reach suggested by that legislative history, a contrary argument is sometimes offered suggesting that the derogation provision is directed only to park administration, and thus prohibits only impacts from activities within parks. But that limiting interpretation is inconsistent with the independent phrasing and literal generality of the "authorization of activities" provision. Furthermore, it fails to address any of the interpretive considerations that strongly support transboundary application of the amendment.[104]

As a matter of construction, moreover, limiting the derogation provision to protect only against the consequences of in-park administrative actions would be clearly inconsistent with its parallel structure. The provision prohibits any derogation of park values that may result *from either or both of two separate types of actions:* any "authorization of activities" and any actions for "protection, management, and administration of these areas." Since the conjunctive phrasing of the latter provision obviously establishes an independent prohibition that amply covers in-park activities, a narrow reading of the former provision, also limiting its effect to in-park activities, would render it entirely surplus.

Thus, at a minimum the "authorization of activities" provision should be read to reach external activities that may "derogate" park values. Furthermore, a similar analysis suggests that protection against external threats is also afforded by the second clause, which requires that "the protection" as well as the "management and administration of these areas" must be conducted to avoid derogation of park values. Since derogation resulting from in-park activities is amply covered by "management and administration of these areas," the "protection" provision is most reasonably read as also referring to external sources of threats to park values.

Finally, in view of the clear congressional purpose of reinvigorating the application of the original Organic Act, a cribbed reading of that Act to constrain the natural reading of the derogation provision of the Redwoods Amendments would be inappropriate. The only interpretive impediment to giving full transboundary effect to the original Act arises from the clumsy framing of the impairment prohibition, because a literal reading makes it applicable as the criterion under which the Park Service is directed to "regulate the use" of the parks. There is nothing in the original Act, however, implying that "use" does not include the many forms of intrusions and impacts generated within parks by activities outside of park boundaries.

The above interpretation is particularly appropriate in view of the comprehensive protective purpose of the Organic Act, reinvigorated by the Redwoods Amendments. Surely that interpretation is no less appropriate than the strikingly parallel holdings of the many courts that have so construed former Section 4(f) of the Department of Transportation Act (now recodified).[105] That provision prohibited approval of any federally supported highway project "which requires the *use* of any publicly owned land from a public park" (or other preserves) unless there is "no feasible and prudent alternative."[106] Although the textual context of that

statute might have been narrowly construed more readily than the
Organic Act, the courts have repeatedly interpreted that statute,
consistent with its protective purpose, to recognize that impacts
arising from activities on adjacent land constitute "use." Thus:

> . . . a highway which either encircles or even comes very
> close to parklands, and thereby blocks the view or causes
> noise, air pollution, etc., is in fact use of the area
> even though there is no physical intrusion on the
> parklands.[107]

Like this comparable interpretation of the Department of
Transportation Act, then, the presence of intruding impacts or
"use" from external activities should trigger application of the more
rigorous protective standards of the Organic Act and the Redwoods Amendments.[108]

(2) The "exceptions clause."

An exceptions clause enacted as a part of the Redwoods Amendments qualifies the protections afforded by the "derogation"
provision, making it applicable "except as may have been or shall
be directly and specifically provided by Congress."[109] Professor
Keiter recognizes that the clause has provoked questions about
whether it may be triggered by the existence of the general statutory
authorities on which the major resource development programs are
based. Keiter, however, persuasively argues for a narrow interpretation of the clause that would apply the exception only where
legislation authorizes activities in terms that expressly contemplate
specified types of intrusions and explicitly authorizes them to
be conducted within parks.[110]

So interpreted, it remains true that the exceptions clause permits limited impairments of park values in narrowly specific situations. In permitting those exceptions, however, the clause also carries helpful implications that the derogation provision should be
interpreted to reach at least those external threats that result from
the activities of other land-management agencies on lands adjacent
to the parks.

Although the clause obviously preserves a narrow realm of permitted derogations that result from activities explicitly
authorized by Congress, the logic of the exceptions clause also serves to define the wider field in which the general prohibitions
were intended to apply. There would have been little need or call

for the exceptions clause if Congress had intended that the exceptions authorize derogating activities conducted only *within* the parks. The Park Service was already authorized to conduct a wide range of in-park management activities that could be potentially impairing. In view of the Park Service's statutory hegemony over the parks, there was no prospect that other agencies would exercise their general statutory authorities to initiate impairing activities within the parks. Only highly explicit statutory grants sufficient to overcome the general Park Service protective obligation and jurisdiction could conceivably have been the basis for in-park activities that might conflict with the derogation prohibition. But in those cases, the exceptions clause would obviously have been unnecessary.

Thus, the only truly viable realm of applicability for the exceptions clause arose from the potential effect of the Redwoods Amendments upon the mandates of other agencies to conduct their usual activities in areas *external* to the parks. A viable function or field of operation for the exceptions clause is apparent only if the Redwoods Amendments were otherwise perceived to bar *all* external activities that would impair the parks or "derogate" their values. Only with that understanding does the exceptions clause play a meaningful role, by carving out a carefully confined exception that, in narrow circumstances, permits external activities to proceed despite their derogating impact on the values and resources of an adjacent park.

(3) National park "values and purposes."

While it may seem obvious, it is important to recognize the statutory logic that extends the protection against impairment or derogation of park values to *all* park units, protecting the values, resources, and purposes identified by the 1916 National Park System Organic Act, as well as any other values or resources identified by the enabling legislation for a specific park. Under the 1916 Organic Act, the values and resources to be preserved unimpaired included "the scenery and the natural and historic objects and the wild life therein."[111] As the National Park System grew to embrace parks with a wide variety of purposes, the Park Service developed different management policies for parks in different management categories: "natural," "historical," and "recreational."

That management approach raised congressional concern about the need to assure protection of basic park values and purposes in all park units.[112]

In response to that concern, the 1970 General Authorities Act made clear that the Organic Act values and purposes were to be protected in all areas of the park system. All units were specifically declared to be part of the "national park system," and the Organic Act was made "applicable to all areas within the national park system."[113] Previous statutory references to narrower categories of parks (national parks, monuments, recreation areas, etc.) "shall . . . not be construed as limiting such Acts to those areas." Each area, however, was also to be administered in accordance with "any statute made specifically applicable to that area."[114]

Finally, the 1978 Redwoods Amendments, in reemphasizing and refocusing[115] the original preservation purposes of the 1916 Act, explicitly provided that its protection against derogation of "the values and purposes for which these various areas have been established" is applicable to *all* of the areas of the National Park System as earlier defined by the General Authorities Act.[116]

In summary, then, proper application of the protective requirements of the amended Organic Act explicitly requires protection of all park units against impairment or derogation of any of the fundamental resources or values preserved by that Act, and of any specific values, resources, or purposes identified by the enabling legislation for specific parks.

C. The Department of the Interior Declines to Exercise a Variety of Initiatives that Could have Expanded the Reach and Effectiveness of Existing Park Protection Law

The Interior solicitor's air pollution opinion discussed above--though relied on by the Interior Department to limit the scope of park protection initiatives[117]--actually emphasized the need for those initiatives in order to clarify the interpretation of existing statutes to provide better protection. Because application of the National Park Organic Act to regulate external threats is "untested and uncertain," the solicitor emphasized that "statutory mandates will have to be interpreted by the Secretary in the context of specific problems" in order to provide for "development of the law for protection of NPS units."[118]

The solicitor did not specify the "specific problems" or "contexts" in which creative "development of the law" might have assisted park protection. But a wide range of obvious initiatives has been available. Although most of these initiatives have been expressly or impliedly rejected by the Department of the Interior, no substantive reasons for the rejection have ever been offered or explored. Yet the failure to take needed initiatives raises important questions, about either the adequacy of the existing laws or the institutional capacity of the Interior Department to implement those laws, or both. Those important questions demand careful inquiry into the reasons for Interior's failure to take meaningful initiatives, an inquiry best conducted by detailed congressional oversight hearings.

The following sections discuss some of the obvious initiatives that could have been taken.

(1) Internal administrative practices could require identification of park protection needs and emphasize park protection priorities prior to authorizing activities on adjacent lands that may adversely affect park resources and values

(a) Department of the Interior rejection of Park Service action plan initiatives that would have focused and improved administrative management to avert park threats.

As discussed above, Interior has recently rejected or severely qualified several internal procedural initiatives suggested by the Park Service as part of an action plan to implement Interior's vague policy of "anticipation, avoidance and resolution" of "resource conflicts." The Park Service proposals, which would have facilitated identification and protection of park resources vulnerable to impacts from activities on adjacent Interior lands, included:

■ Periodic compilation of external actions proposed by other Interior agencies that may have impacts on park resources.

■ Identification and documentation of adjacent land areas that are integral or important to park resource values and visitors' experiences, such as migration routes, habitats, scenic views, watersheds, and complementary historic districts.

■ Identification of regulations, policies, and legislation administered by other agencies having potential for conflict with park values, with proposals for changes to reduce conflict.

These initiatives were summarily rejected or severely cut back as "inappropriate" or "more appropriate at the Department level" by the responsible Assistant Secretary.[119] Yet there is no indication that comparable initiatives have been developed or encouraged by the Department.

Most troubling about the rejection of these initiatives is the strong indication that the Department's decision was based on a dominating policy view that resolution of every resource conflict should be based on a discretionary assessment of the comparative value of the conflicting resource opportunities.[120] Not only does that approach appear to deny any special priority for park protection, but it assures--and is obviously designed to assure--maximum discretion to "weigh" competing values without committing to meet any controlling standards.

Thus, far from acting to give protective content to existing law, the Department has sought simply to maximize its uncontrolled discretion to protect or decline protection for our national parks.

(b) Interior rejection of more formal "action forcing" directives designed to force review of all proposed actions likely to impact park resources.

Shortly before the "park protection working group" generated Interior's "policy" of addressing "resource conflicts" through "anticipation, avoidance and resolution," an internal proposal for a more formal, rigorous, and far-reaching approach was apparently discouraged without ever receiving serious consideration. The proposal sought adoption of a "Model Bureau Directive" for Interior agencies that would have established an "action forcing" process, requiring identification and review of the potential impacts of every activity on adjacent lands that might result in impairment of park resources or values, and focusing decision on the appropriateness of proceeding and the adequacy of mitigation.[121] Although final disposition of the proposal is unknown, it was obviously rejected, presumably because its rigorous approach implied a priority and emphasis on park protection not shared at the upper levels of the Department, for no alternative action forcing mechanism appears to have been considered.

*(2) Formal internal directives or instructions to other Depart-
ment of the Interior agencies could establish standards and
procedures to implement resource-protective policies incorporated in the statutes governing those agencies.*

(a) The failure to develop the statutorily-required protections
for "areas of critical environmental concern."

A clear example of Interior's institutional inability to implement clear statutory priorities for protection of park or other sensitive resources is disclosed by the fate of a recent internal proposal
to amend the *Bureau of Land Management Manual* to improve
protection of "areas of critical environmental concern" (ACECs).

BLM's organic legislation, the Federal Land Policy and Management Act, is explicit in designating the identification and protection of ACECs as the only specific priorities in BLM's land planning function.[122] An ACEC is defined as an area on BLM lands
where

> . . . special management attention is required (when such
> areas are developed or used or where no development is
> required) to protect and prevent irreparable damage to
> important historic, cultural, or scenic values, fish and
> wildlife resources or other natural systems or processes.[123]

It is obvious that the ACEC definition, combined with the explicit
statutory priority, demands special attention to protection of
resources such as those integral to the values of an adjacent park.
Clearly, the ACEC provision offered an ideal opportunity for
the Interior Department to demonstrate its willingness to utilize
existing law--law that invites recognition of a priority for park
protection.

In September 1986, BLM released draft revisions of the
BLM Manual to clarify the standards and procedures governing
identification and protection of ACECs through BLM's resource
management planning function.[124] Although the revisions were dis-
appointing in their failure to utilize ACECs more explicitly for
park protection, they did offer guidance that invited park-protec-
tive interpretation.[125] More than a year and one-half later, however,
BLM has not only failed to strengthen its proposal; it has failed
to take any further action to adopt it.

(b) The discretion-maximizing vagueness of the interagency "memoranda of understanding."

Apart from the yet-unknown results of the most recent survey of park threats,[126] it appears that Interior's primary effort to implement its "working group" recommendation of "anticipating, avoiding and resolving" resource conflicts has focused on development of memoranda of understanding (MOUs) between potentially conflicting agencies.

Conceptually, it seems apparent that MOUs could provide a useful tool for establishing interagency obligations based on recognition and implementation of governing statutory standards. As currently implemented by the Interior Department, however, most aspects of the current crop of MOUs amount to little more than agreement to consult and attempt to reach agreement where disputes arise, an obligation already imposed at least as specifically by existing statutes.[127]

A recently signed "Memorandum of Understanding Between The Bureau of Land Management (BLM) and The National Park Service (NPS) for Planning and Program Coordination," for example, calls for various improvements in cooperation and anticipation of potential conflicts. With respect to the critical issue of conflict resolution, the agencies pledge to "anticipate . . . conflicts early, avoid them if possible, and resolve them promptly."[128]

Far from offering initiatives that will establish better standards for recognition of statutory priorities, however, this MOU-- apart from its milktoast generality--reflects standards of doubtful consistency with park protection requirements. The conflict resolution provision, for example, goes on to provide that the agencies will resolve their disputes based on recognition of "the national interest in the mission of each agency,"[129] a standard that, in its vague suggestion of an equal weighting of statutory policies, impliedly rejects any priority for park protection.

Equally unacceptable is the MOU's adoption of a slightly more specific agreement that the agencies will "experiment . . . with innovative dispute resolution techniques such as mediation by neutral parties."[130] However useful in other contexts, mediation by neutral parties can hardly substitute for substantive legal initiatives designed to give more explicit content and scope to the law of park protection. Furthermore, to the extent it implies the Department's relinquishment of responsibility for establishing park protection standards, mediation may be of doubtful legality.

(3) Rulemaking authority could be utilized to adopt regulations establishing basic procedures and standards for anticipation and avoidance of potentially impairing activities on adjacent federal lands.

It has long been recognized that rulemaking procedures offer both the fairest and most effective way to clarify, develop, and assure application of the general statutory standards administered by federal agencies.[131] However, despite the acknowledged need[132] and clear authority,[133] the Department of the Interior has declined to undertake rulemaking initiatives that could clarify and strengthen application of park protection statutes to the problem of external threats. To the contrary, while there have been revisions of the basic in-park administrative regulations,[134] the only significant initiatives addressing the application of park protection laws to external threats have been rejected, discouraged, or sidetracked.

Interior has not only failed to develop or offer any rulemaking proposals of general application to the problem of external threats; it has also failed to take advantage of explicit and well-focused opportunities that have virtually dropped into its lap.

(a) The "integral vista" fiasco: avoiding the needed development of precedents urged by the Solicitor.

Ironically, despite the Solicitor's recognition in his clean air opinion of the need for development of the law through interpretation, application, and litigation "in the context of specific problems," one of the clearest examples of Interior's refusal to use available authority arose in the context of visibility protection.

Environmental Protection Agency (EPA) regulations implementing the Clean Air Act had provided a ready regulatory mechanism specifically designed to protect "integral vistas"--scenic views of specific landmarks or panoramas located outside of park boundaries which are viewed from points within the parks.[135] The EPA regulations, while far from ideal,[136] were substantial and clearly legitimate examples of creative use of rulemaking authority to effectuate statutory policy. Congress had declared a policy of "prevention of any future, and the remedying of any existing, impairment of visibility" in parks and other selected areas where "visibility is an important value."[137] All that was required to implement those protections was for the Secretary to effectuate the EPA regulations by designating specific views by December 31, 1985.[138]

On October 25, 1985, Secretary Hodel announced his decision *declining* to make any use of this ready mechanism: he declined to designate *any* integral vistas for protection in any of the 162 qualified areas.[139] Despite substantial Park Service investment in development of data and technology designed to apply such protections, the "policy" reasons offered for the decision can fairly--even objectively--be characterized as laughable. Hodel argued, for example, that the regulations may engender in park superintendents and other federal land managers "a false sense of security," causing them to feel that "I don't have to be as alert."[140]

In view of the Solicitor's explicit recognition of the need for case-by-case elaboration of protective standards, the only more or less substantive reason offered by the Secretary for declining integral vista protection is troubling: he asserted that "prolonged litigation" prompted by "State resentment" would leave vista protection "in doubt" until resolved.[141]

The Secretary did not explain how his failure to act improved the level of certainty for vista protection. Nor did he explain how vista protection could be implemented without such interim doubts. More fundamentally, if the Secretary's explanations are to be taken as anything more than rhetoric, his rationale would seem to preclude *any* effort to generate protective interpretations at *any* of the boundaries of existing law, since similar litigative uncertainties would inevitably accompany virtually any kind of significant legal initiative.

(b) The Tar Sands significant adverse impacts rule.

One rulemaking proposal--until sidetracked--did make a substantial attempt to grapple with the problem of defining prohibited impacts to parks in the specialized context of proposed tar sands developments on adjacent lands. Compelled to address the problem by the Combined Hydrocarbon Leasing Act of 1981, which allows development only upon a finding of no "significant adverse impacts" to adjacent parks,[142] Interior published in 1984 a notice of proposed rulemaking that would have established a rigorous standard for that determination.[143] After the Director of BLM voiced his opposition on the ground that the proposal "represents unilateral programmatic decisions not in the best interest of the Department,"[144] the proposal was apparently sidetracked at the upper levels of the Department. There has been no further public notice of action on or amendments to the proposal which presumably will languish until the current administration's final days.

(4) Park Service or Department of the Interior litigation or participation in administrative procedures.

In view of the Interior Department's obvious reluctance to take less aggressive initiatives, it may seem futile to suggest that the Park Service could undertake to implement and elaborate park protection standards through judicial or administrative litigation. Yet, because litigation has been a primary mechanism by which government agencies in this country have defined the reach and limits of their authority,[145] it should be considered within the realm of available Park Service initiatives.

To some extent, Park Service litigation challenging park intrusions generated by other agencies would fall within the vague limitations of a traditional taboo against intragovernmental litigation. But, as this chapter later suggests, there is little legal compulsion supporting that taboo, and good reason to disregard it in the context of the Interior Department's built-in conflicts of interest.[146] Indeed, it is those very conflicts of interest that make it necessary to consider litigation that would challenge the taboo.

Like other agencies,[147] on at least one occasion the Park Service took initial steps in disregard of that taboo. In a 1979 dispute with the Federal Communications Commission (FCC) over licensing of a complex of broadcast towers on a peak within the wilderness viewshed of Saguaro National Monument, the Department of the Interior initially sought judicial review of the FCC's order in the Court of Appeals for the District of Columbia. After that appeal was dismissed as premature, the FCC persisted in its position. But Interior, under the current administration, declined to go back to court and limited itself to presenting informal argument to the Commission.[148]

Without confronting the complications involved in taking another agency to court,[149] however, existing authority would permit the Park Service to pursue its concerns through the variety of administrative contest procedures available under statute or regulation. In a typical contest with BLM or the Forest Service over land-planning decisions to permit leasing or other development on adjacent lands, for example, procedures for formal protest or administrative appeal would permit the Park Service to specify issues for argument or briefing and decision.[150] Similarly, many other agencies' procedures would permit the Park Service to contest, by both legal argument and factual evidence, the failure to give appropriate priority to national park values impacted by adjacent-land activities.

For example, in its recent dispute with the Department of Energy over the lawfulness of DOE's selection of a nuclear waste repository site less than a mile from Canyonlands National Park, the Park Service and Interior limited their opposition to technical criticism in comment letters and informal meetings. An important area of dispute concerned DOE's adoption of regulations establishing criteria that permitted selection of sites in proximity to national parks regardless of significant park impacts.[151] Despite the effect of that rule, however, no effort was made to invoke more rigorous statutory procedures governing DOE rulemaking, which would have permitted the Park Service an opportunity to raise the profile of the park protection issues, to obtain more extensive consideration of those issues, and to demand that DOE provide "an explanation responding to the major comments, criticisms, and alternatives offered."[152]

A similar procedural opportunity, also generally disregarded in park protection, is available under the regulations of the Council on Environmental Quality (CEQ), which provide for referral of "interagency disagreements concerning proposed major Federal actions that might cause unsatisfactory environmental effects."[153] Although rigorous park protection may not be encouraged by the variety of negotiation or settlement steps prescribed by its regulations, the Council also has authority to make "findings and recommendations . . . that the submitted evidence does not support the position of an agency."[154] Alternatively, the Council may submit the matter, with its recommendation, for action by the President.[155]

While the history of referrals to the CEQ indicates little use of that process in connection with park threats,[156] it would appear to offer a forum in which those issues could be focused for creative review and development of legal standards for park protection.

IV. CONCLUSION

A. Meaningful, Long-term Protection Requires an Independent Park Service with Independent Legal Authority and Litigating Capability

The performance of the Department of the Interior in its administration of legal protections for our national parks convincingly demonstrates that the National Park Service must be given substantial independence, unrestricted by the conflicting demands and political constraints endemic to the Department.

Despite acknowledgment of the substantial statutory basis for administrative and legal steps that would strengthen park protection, the Department has repeatedly declined available initiatives and rejected specific opportunities to generate a protective body of law consistent with the congressional intent that our parks be preserved unimpaired. As a result, it has become increasingly clear that those responsible for preserving our parks must have the authority to develop and utilize the legal tools necessary to stand up to the institutions and forces that increasingly threaten impairment. Political pressures and turf rivalries guarantee that the Department will otherwise continue to reject or divert critical park protection initiatives. In seeking to accommodate its competing bureaus and missions, it is inevitable that the Department will continue to dilute the high statutory priority that Congress intended for park protection.

Without a largely independent institutional advocate, it is extremely unlikely that the statutory priority for park protection can be meaningfully and consistently implemented. Even in administrations less allied with development interests than the Reagan administration, the entrenched roles and conflicting missions of the various Department bureaus and agencies assure that every judgment--particularly the important early judgments about possible initiatives, or options for resolving park threats--will be made in an atmosphere of conflict of interest and compromise that foredooms effective protection.

Concern about the Interior Department's conflicts of interest and tendency to dilute legal standards requiring resource protection is not a new phenomenon. A striking and instructive parallel, for example, is found in the experience of Indian tribes with Interior Department management of their lands.

Through the Bureau of Indian Affairs, the Interior Department has long supervised the management of Indian tribal lands, exercising final authority to approve or disapprove permits, leases, and other claims or uses, primarily by non-Indian applicants. That authority has been subject to a legally imposed fiduciary or trust obligation to manage tribal lands and resources in the best interest of the tribes. Thus, the Department of the Interior is under a specific legal obligation to give priority to protection of Indian lands and resources--an obligation comparable to the similar statutory priority required in its management of national parks.[157]

In 1972, a report and study by the Administrative Conference of the United States[158] was prompted by the "institutional conflict-of-interest faced by Federal agencies," primarily the Interior and Justice Departments, "in dealing with the natural resources of Indian tribes."[159] The study emphasized the Department's repeated compromise of the legal priority protecting Indian interests in response to the powerful demands that place Indians "in competition, in their claims for land and water, with burgeoning cities, industries, ranching and farming interests."[160]

Based on a detailed study that concluded that protection of Indians' interests under Interior's "trust" obligation" is at present greatly diminished because . . . the federal trustee is tarnished, in many cases, with conflicting interests,"[161] the Administrative Conference report characterized the basic problem in terms readily applicable to the problem of park protection:

> The problem is particularly acute in the Department of the Interior, which has administrative responsibility for carrying out trust responsibilities to the Indians and for promoting the development of the nation's public lands and natural resources. A reclamation project . . . , for example, may affect the water, fishing or other rights of Indians. The dispute may be mediated by the Solicitor's office, which functions as an attorney for the Bureau which wants to build the project as well as for Indian interests. If the Department's decision is adverse to the affected Indians, the Department of Justice is unlikely to seek judicial review . . . , even though an in-

dependent advocate might well do so in the not infrequent situations in which the answers to legal questions are unclear. Furthermore, an independent advocate would have the leverage in departmental or inter-agency negotiations that come from the ability ultimately to seek court relief.[162]

* * * *

Agency officials have tried to be conscientious. But they are being asked to carry out an awkward and inconsistent role. . . . [U]nder principles of good administrative procedure, an agency should not have an institutional responsibility for representing both sides in a dispute, particularly when it is also the decision-maker.[163]

To avoid the consequences of the Department's conflicting roles and to assure effective advocacy commensurate with the legal priority intended to protect Indian resources, the Administrative Conference recommended establishment of an independent Indian Trust Counsel Authority, "to provide Indians with an independent, effective voice to speak for their land and resource claims."[164] The primary function of the proposed Authority would be to provide legal representation "in any formal or informal administrative or judicial proceedings before any agency or court of a State or of the United States."[165]

Obviously, the Department's trust obligation to protect Indian resources has different legal roots than its park protection obligations. But both obligations involve legal priorities for resource protection that, in the absence of effective advocacy and empowered negotiation, will inevitably be compromised and diluted in the face of conflicting and powerful demands. The analysis in this chapter strongly suggests that a solution similar to that recommended for protection of Indian lands is essential if preservation of our national parks is to remain a national priority.

Like the protection of Indian interests, or of any other institutional priorities, adequate protection of our parks demands the ability to initiate and obtain administrative and judicial applications of the protective standards intended by Congress. Conflicts with other agency missions are inevitable; but the inability to initiate and pursue effective legal remedies assures the continuing institutional weakness of the National Park Service as protector of our national parks.

If the national parks are to be preserved, their institutional protector--presumably the National Park Service--must have capabilities equal to its mission. Its authority, institutional position, and resources must permit it to take initiatives that can establish the legal and factual foundation for concrete applications of park protection standards and procedures. It must have the tools by which our legal system transforms nascent interpretations into governing law. It must be authorized to adopt regulations that fairly implement the basic statutory standards. And it must have authority and a legal staff that can, and will, initiate and pursue administrative proceedings and conduct court litigation designed to elaborate, clarify, and apply evolving legal standards that can protect our parks.

B. Independent Park Service Litigating Authority Would be Consistent with Constitutional and Administrative Practice.

Vesting the National Park Service with a degree of independent authority for legal representation would hardly be a radical step. As of 1982, some thirty-five federal agencies, in both the executive departments and the independent agencies, were empowered to conduct at least some of their own civil litigation[166] --authority often sought because of the ineffectiveness of Justice Department legal representation in fulfilling statutory goals.[167]

Undoubtedly, any suggestion of vesting independent litigating authority in an independent National Park Service, particularly authority to challenge external threats generated by other agencies, will evoke opposition grounded in the traditional taboo against intragovernmental litigation. Yet that taboo is often disregarded.[168] Furthermore, neither the basis for nor the legal contours of the taboo are well defined.

Former Attorney General Griffin B. Bell, for example, asserted rather than explained the taboo, as follows:

> I think it is unseemly for two governmental agencies to sue each other. It requires the judicial branch to decide questions of government policy, a role never envisioned by our country's Founding Fathers.[169]

The "unseemliness" of intragovernmental litigation, of course, is likely to depend on the beholder's political viewpoint, institutional loyalties, or interest in the specific issues. But Bell's substantive objection--that courts should not decide "questions of government policy"--seems contrived in the face of the broad constitutional and statutory grants of jurisdiction to federal courts to decide "all cases . . . arising under this constitution, [and] the laws of the United States."[170] In other contexts, the Supreme Court of the United States has found no obstacle to judicial implementation of a congressional directive that the federal courts "fashion" federal law "from the policy of our national labor laws";[171] or, in the absence of statutory rules for liability on government checks, that they "fashion the governing rule of law according to their own standards."[172] In the face of those more expansive examples of judicial law making, more traditional judicial interpretation and application of park protection laws can hardly be objectionable merely because the Park Service may be contending with another government agency.

Similarly, Bell offers no support from the Founding Fathers for his view that interagency disputes can be "resolved more easily and better though the mediation of the Department of Justice," because

> . . . the Department of Justice can exercise a review and supervisory function . . . to bring uniformity to government legal positions and still recognize the independence of the regulatory agencies' enforcement efforts.[173]

Presumably, that claim, and similar claims by other departmental secretaries, of authority to resolve interagency disputes about conflicting legal authority, are grounded in the executive branch duty to "take care that the laws be faithfully executed,"[174] and in claims of the need for presidential political accountability.[175] But those contentions are poorly supported where the executive fails to take responsibility for effective execution of the laws,[176] and where the President declines any process for appeals from departmental decisions that could effectuate his claim of accountability.[177] Furthermore, as one thoughtful analyst has emphasized, the Justice Department's claim to the role of gatekeeper of agency access to the courts raises the serious separation of powers problem of "distinguishing the role of advocate from the role of judge"; and "the agencies tend to see the Justice Department's gatekeeping role as edging too far into the judicial role."[178]

Undoubtedly, the basic constitutional power of the executive branch to "take care that the laws be faithfully executed" vests in the President and his appointees a realm of authority to allocate enforcement resources, to establish related priorities, to seek en-

forcement consistency, and to exercise judgment within the scope
of granted discretion. But recent cases have recognized that executive branch interference with proper agency implementation of
statutory requirements "is incompatible with the will of Congress and cannot be sustained as a valid exercise of the President's
Article II powers."[179] Surely, then, Congress can rearrange existing legal authorities to provide an advocacy mechanism that will
assure the faithful implementation of its park protection policies.

**C. The Challenge of Restructuring Park Service Authority: Divorce,
or a Live-in Relationship?**

Recognition of the need for a National Park Service with independent authority in policy formation, administrative initiatives and legal representation inevitably compels debate about
the range of possible institutional structures.

Should the Park Service become a fully independent agency
with policy and management set by its own collegial body of commissioners, appointed under requirements for partisan balance, and
removable by the President only for misconduct, but arguably not
for policy differences?[180] Alternatively, should authority be centered
in a Director of the Park Service with similar tenure protections? And if authority is concentrated in the Director, would it
be desirable to provide for an oversight body to guide policy
development, to assure open and professional internal practices,
and to moderate external political conflicts? Under any approach,
should independence include insulation from other realms of executive branch control and supervision commonly exercised over
even the "independent" agencies, such as control over budget[181] and
other legislative proposals[182] to Congress? And under any structure, what appointment standards and other mechanisms can
help to assure professional management that is sensitive to the park
protection and visitor enjoyment mandates of the National Park
Service Organic Act?[183]

These fundamental questions obviously implicate difficult judgments about the nature of any continuing relationship between the
Park Service and the Department of the Interior. Certain advantages,
as well as the drawbacks, of a continuing relationship with that
Department must be considered in structuring the extent and form
of independence.

Unquestionably, there are significant advantages in maintaining a continuing, though modified, relationship with the Depart-

ment. When inclined to assist, the Department can play an important role in buffering the Park Service against parochial demands by members of congressional delegations seeking to exercise their claimed prerogative of interfering in the management of their home-state parks. And executive branch support also can play a similar role in moving a reluctant Congress to support critical legislative needs, despite the drawbacks of intra-Departmental conflicts over budget and other needed legislative proposals.

Furthermore, in the context both of major land-planning initiatives and in day-to-day public land management, there are significant advantages in maintaining a supportive working relationship with the Department of the Interior. Those advantages are most dramatically illustrated by the crucial role played by a sympathetic Department in 1968 and in 1978 in protecting vast tracts of Alaskan wildlands from imminent parcelling out through private land selections or mineral development. Comprehensive executive branch "withdrawals" of those lands[184] assured their protection for eventual inclusion in parks and other preserves in the Alaska National Interest Lands Conservation Act.[185]

Apart from such dramatic and singular interventions to protect public lands, however, the need for a supportive working relationship is also suggested by other public land management authorities vested in the Department that can be extremely important to park protection. Examples include the Secretary's authority to withdraw public lands from mineral or other development;[186] to deny applications by other federal agencies for withdrawal of public lands adjacent to parks for incompatible uses;[187] to designate sensitive areas adjacent to parks as "areas of critical environmental concern";[188] to establish and enforce rigorous protective management requirements for adjacent lands, including "no surface occupancy" or other protective stipulations in development leases;[189] and to impose protective conditions or deny various types of rights of way in park-sensitive areas.[190]

Also important in any restructuring of the Park Service role is the need to determine where authority will reside for decisions regarding disposition of the public lands that are presently assigned to the Secretary by statute. An important example is the Secretary's authority to acquire park inholdings by conveying other public lands in exchange.[191] Although that authority involves an important issue of park management, its exercise would seem to require the Department's umbrella authority over the agency relinquishing the land to be exchanged (presumably the BLM), as well as over the Park Service. Equally important is the need to assure that the Department's role and responsibility for the health of the national parks is sufficient to encourage support for such beneficial land exchanges.

Finally, while park protection should be measurably strengthened by an independent National Park Service that can take aggressive administrative and legal initiatives, it is obvious that the conflicting demands on the public lands will continue and are likely to intensify under population pressure and increasing resource demands. In view of those continuing demands, it would be unfortunate if new independence for Park Service initiatives were accompanied by a design or perception that minimized the Department's preservation and conservation role in favor of unrestrained commodity and resource development. For that reason, any new institutional arrangements should assure that the Secretary continues to bear a legal and institutional responsibility for protecting the parks as well as other legally-protected lands.

These institutional and political issues obviously pose a difficult challenge. A workable design must strike a balance between Park Service independence and authority to take legal and policy initiatives, while preserving a working relationship with the Department that can put the protective umbrella and ultimate power of the executive branch in service of park protection.

One response to this challenge, of course, could be to yield to the political ruckus likely to arise from more far-reaching proposals, and merely strengthen the hand of the Park Service by imposing new procedural requirements to govern inter/intra-agency rivalries. An approach such as that designed by a 1982 proposal for a "National Park System Protection and Resource Management Act" would impose procedural obligations requiring notice from agencies proposing to undertake activities on or adjacent to park lands that may degrade park resources. Notice would trigger opportunity for the Park Service to investigate proposed impacts, followed by specific requests to the sponsoring agency for any changes necessary to avoid adverse effects. The Park Service request would have had some legal effect: projects otherwise authorized by law on park lands would be required to comply with the Secretary's recommendations; and projects on other federal lands would be required either to comply or briefly to defer action pending notice to the relevant congressional oversight committees.[192]

Procedural mechanisms such as those proposed by the 1982 "Park Protection Act" can undoubtedly have some impact when judicial review tests the validity of justifications offered to meet procedural and substantive requirements.[193] But in the absence of a strong legislative commitment of authority to the Park Service to seek effective enforcement, it is doubtful whether such procedural devices can have significant effect in diverting the mission-oriented, clientele-supported projects of other agencies, despite serious prospects of damage to park resources. Indeed, the planning and appeal procedures of the Park Service's most frequent potential adversaries, the Bureau of Land Management and the Forest Service, already offer a forum where the requirements of the National Environmental Policy Act and other procedural statutes, as well as the National Park Service Organic Act, may be invoked. Yet, those avenues remain unexplored by the Park Service, largely because of inability to take independent initiatives with the assistance of effective advocacy.[194]

In the absence of a grant of clear and concrete policy-making and enforcement authority, "the redemptive quality of procedural reform" is likely to offer little more than the "nine parts myth and one part coconut oil" that Professor Sax long ago found in agencies' procedures for NEPA compliance.[195] While procedural mechanisms can undoubtedly play a helpful role in the context of more fundamental institutional change, if Congress is serious about wanting to protect our parks "unimpaired" for the enjoyment of living as well as "future generations," only restructuring to confer adequate authority can send the kind of clear legislative message that will be heard.

NOTES

*Professor of Law, University of Utah College of Law. Extensive assistance in exploring many of the issues discussed in this chapter was provided by Terri Martin, Rocky Mountain Regional Representative for the National Parks and Conservation Assocation, and by Dave Simon of NPCA's Washington office. Thoughtful editorial comments were also offered by Don Baur, formerly an attorney in the Office of the Solicitor, Department of the Interior. The author draws on experience in representing NPCA and other conservation groups in addressing park protection issues, particularly in Utah and other Western public land states.

1. W. Stegner, *The Best Idea We Ever Had*, 46 WILDERNESS 160 at 4 (1983).

2. 16 U.S.C.A. §§ 1 and 1a-1 (Act of Aug. 25, 1916, 39 Stat. 535). *See* Keiter, *National Park Protection: Putting the Organic Act to Work, infra* at 79-89; Sax & Keiter, *Glacier National Park and Its Neighbors: A Study of Federal Inter-Agency Cooperation, infra* at 181-246; Barnett, *The Mining in the Parks Act: Theory and Practice, infra* at 423-432; Magraw, *International Law and Park Protection: A Global Responsibility, infra* at 149-179.

3. *See infra* note 89 and accompanying text.

4. *See* Futrell, *NEPA and the Parks: Use It Or Lose It, infra* at 111-130; Harvey, *The Federal Land Policy and Management Act: The Bureau of Land Management's Role in Park Protection, infra* at 131-147; Hocker, *Oil, Gas, and Parks, infra* at 397-422.

5. It is seldom a matter of choosing one statutory protection to the exclusion of another. More often, statutes establishing parks, or protecting parks or other resources, play a significant role in the application of statutory planning procedures because they authoritatively identify the subjects, values, or standards that must be considered or protected in fulfilling those planning requirements. *See, e.g.,* Citizens to Preserve Overton Park v. Volpe, 401 U.S. 402 (1971); Northwest Indian Cemetery Ass'n v. Peterson, 565 F. Supp. 586 (N.D. Cal. 1983), *aff'd in part and partially vacated as moot*, 795 F.2d 688 (9th Cir. 1986); Sierra Club v. Corps of Engineers, 23 ERC 1153 (2d Cir. 1985); Sierra Club v. Peterson, 717 F.2d 1409 (1983); Stop H-3 Ass'n v. Coleman, 533 F.2d 434 (9th Cir. 1976).

6. *See, e.g.,* King, *Park Planning, Historic Resources, and the National Historic Preservation Act, infra* at 283-300; Bean, *The Endangered Species Act: Protecting the Living Resources of the Parks, infra* at 261-268; Gray, *No Holier Temples: Protecting the National Parks through Wild and Scenic River Designation, infra* at 339-394.

7. *See, e.g.,* Banks, *The Clean Water Act: Still Vital to the Parks, infra* at 249-259; Fayad, *The Clean Air Act: New Horizons for the National Parks, infra* at 301-338.

8. *See, e.g.,* Dodd, *The Geothermal Steam Act: Unlocking its Protective Provisions, infra* at 433-457; McGinley, *The Surface Mining Control and Reclamation Act: Ten Years of Promise and Problems for the National Parks, infra* at 477-510; Bodi, *Hydropower, Dams and the National Parks, infra* at 459-475.

9. *See* Squillace, *Common Law Protection for our National Parks, infra* at 91-109; Wilkinson, *Water Rights and the Duties of the National Park Service: A Call for Action at a Critical Juncture, infra* at 269-282.

10. National Park Service Organic Act of 1916, 39 Stat. 535, 16 U.S.C.A. § 1 (1974).

11. *See* Keiter, *supra* note 2.

12. The threat of a nuclear waste repository has receded as a result of 1987 amendments to the Nuclear Waste Policy Act of 1982, which specifically selected Nevada's Yucca Mountain site for the first repository, subject to successful preliminary testing. Nuclear Waste Policy Amendments Act of 1987, 133 CONG. REC. H12168-12176 (daily ed. Dec. 21, 1987).

13. The air pollution threat is summarized in a letter dated Nov. 14, 1985, from the Assistant Secretary of the Interior for Fish, Wildlife and Parks to Charles L. Elkins, Acting Assistant Administrator for Air and Radiation, Environmental Protection Agency (EPA), responding to an EPA inquiry about air pollution impacts on parks.

14. The nuclear waste repository, if developed, would have required Department of the Interior approval for use of the Bureau of Land Management (BLM) lands for the Department of Energy project through "withdrawal" of the lands from other uses; the tar sands developments and oil and gas leasing are both directly administered by BLM; the road construction proposals involve related BLM determinations of whether to grant or recognize a right of way; expanded airport operations adjacent to the park would require approval by the Federal Aviation Administration under statutes that specifically require consideration of impacts on national parks; and identification and control of the sources contributing to regional haze are handicapped by the Environmental Protection Agency's refusal, to date, to initiate a program for attribution to and regulation of those sources.

15. U.S. DEPARTMENT OF THE INTERIOR, NATIONAL PARK SERVICE, STATE OF THE PARKS -1980, at vii (hereinafter STATE OF THE PARKS--1980).

16. STATE OF THE PARKS--1980 at 34. Those conclusions are well supported by an earlier NPCA survey of park superintendents. *See, NPCA Adjacent Lands Survey: No Park Is an Island,* NATIONAL PARKS AND CONSERVATION MAGAZINE, Vol. 53, No. 3, at 4-9 (1979). Also see, National Parks And Conservation Association, *To Preserve Unimpaired: The Challenge of Protecting Park Resources,* in THE NATIONAL PARK SYSTEM PLAN: A BLUEPRINT FOR TOMORROW, Vol. 1 (1988).

17. STATE OF THE PARKS--1980, at vii-viii (emphasis added).

18. Although the STATE OF THE PARKS--1980 report did not identify the jurisdictional origins of threats, it analyzed activities generating the threats in a manner that permits broad inferences. For example, an analysis of "aesthetic degradations" attributed threats to a number of subcategories that strongly suggested jurisdictional origins, including "land development," "utility access-powerlines, pipelines, etc.," "urban encroachment," "mineral surveys, development, extraction," "grazing or agriculture," and "timbering." STATE OF THE PARKS--1980, at 13. A new "threats" assessment, however, will provide some data on the jurisdictional entity owning or managing land on which identified threats arise. *See infra* note 30.

19. Those conclusions are fully supported by NPCA's experience and that of the author in attempting to respond as park advocates to specific park threats. For example, even a quick and partial tabulation of fourteen current issues that present significant threats to Utah parks shows that twelve of those threats are primarily promoted or supported by other federal land use and development programs or (in two cases) by the accommodating position taken by federal regulatory programs. *See also* the author's summary of seven major threats to Utah parks, all of which arise out of programs administered by the Bureau of Land Management, in Lockhart, BLM Land Planning and Consistency Obligations to Provide for Protection of Natural Values on Adjacent Protected Lands, 3-6 (Conference Paper, Natural Resources Law Center, University of Colorado School of Law, June 8-10, 1987).

20. *Oversight Hearings Before The Subcomm. on Public Lands and National Parks of the Comm. on Interior and Insular Affairs, House of Representatives,* 97th Cong., 2d Sess. at 254 *et seq.* and 726-788. *See* particularly the testimony and prepared statements of Park Service regional directors Chapman and Mintzmeyer and of Park Service park superintendents Townsley (Yellowstone), Lancaster (Glen Canyon), and Herriman (Chaco Culture).

21. National Park System Organic Act of 1916, 39 Stat. 535, 16 U.S.C.A. §§ 1, 1a-1 through 1a-8, 1b and 3 (1974 and West Supp. 1987); Clark v. Community for Creative Non-Violence, 468 U.S. 288 (1984); Keiter, *supra* note 2.

22. Particularly where specific intrusions are permitted by statutes within the scope of the "exceptions clause" in the "Redwoods Amendments" to the National Park Service Organic Act, 16 U.S.C.A. § 1a-1 (West Supp. 1987), discussed *infra*, notes 109-110 and accompanying text. *See, e.g.*, authorization for tar sands leasing within Glen Canyon National Recreation Area "if the Secretary finds that there will be no resulting significant adverse impacts on the administration of such area, or on other contiguous units of the national park system." Section 11 of Combined Hydrocarbon Amendments to the Mineral Leasing Act, 95 Stat. 1072, 30 U.S.C.A. § 181 (1986) ("Historical Note" on "Construction and Applicability of 1981 Amendments").

23. *See, e.g.*, discussion of the Department's crucial role in refusing to implement park visibility protection under EPA's integral vista regulations, and its stalling of the "adverse impacts" rule proposed for protection against the impacts of tar sand development, notes 135-144 *infra* and accompanying text. *See also* former Park Service Director Everhardt's description of the role of Senator Frank Moss and the Utah congressional delegation and governor in forcing abandonment of an established plan to phase out tourist accommodations in the narrow Virgin River canyon of Zion National Park. W. EVERHARDT, THE NATIONAL PARK SERVICE at 66-68 (1983); Nick D'Alesandro, Concessions In Our National Parks--Are They Necessary and Appropriate, at 13-14 (unpublished student seminar paper, 1985). In the author's personal experience, examples from Utah are dramatic and instructive, though hardly unique. Utah Senator Jake Garn, for example, is unquestionably responsible for extension of the statutory phase-out period for controversial grazing privileges within Capitol Reef National Park, 16 U.S.C.A. § 273(b) (West Supp. 1987), and for continuing efforts to impose an unrequested paved road on the "Burr Trail" through the heart of a wilderness portion of the same park. *See* H.R.J. Res. 465, 131 CONG. REC. at H12038 (daily ed. Dec. 16, 1985) (Continuing Appropriation Resolution for Fiscal 1986).

24. STATE OF THE PARKS--1980 at 35.

25. NATIONAL PARK SERVICE, STATE OF THE PARKS: A REPORT TO THE CONGRESS ON A SERVICEWIDE STRATEGY FOR PREVENTION AND MITIGATION OF NATURAL AND CULTURAL RESOURCES MANAGEMENT PROBLEMS, 6-7 (1981) (hereinafter, SERVICEWIDE STRATEGY).

26. Memorandum dated Sep. 11, 1980, from Park Service Director Russell E. Dickinson to all regional directors. The Resource Management Plans (RMPs) were to summarize the condition of each park's resources; identify, rank, and explain the significance of the most important and urgent resource management problems; and determine the research needed to address the high-priority resource management problems.

27. Only about one out of three Park Service areas had approved resource management plans in 1980. While progress in developing the RMPs was initially slow and depended heavily on oversight from Park Service regional offices, current data compiled from the "NPS Common Data Base" show that by May 6, 1987, of the 251 parks required to have an RMP, 198 were approved and current, while 39 previously approved plans had not been currently updated.

28. Beginning in 1982, special funding was obtained for the Park Service's Natural Resources Trainee Program, which in the years 1985-86 was funded as a servicewide natural resource program and is now an established part of the training programs offered by the Employee Development Division. In the years 1984-1987, seventy-four natural resource specialists were trained by this program. Telephone interview, Katherine P. Kitchell, natural resources trainee and Park Service resource management specialist, with Bill Walker, natural resource specialist, Employee Development Division, Washington, D.C. office, National Park Service, February 1988. Beginning with fiscal year 1987, the Park Service sought to reduce the expense of the program by making it a part of its Servicewide Training Program.

29. Memorandum dated Oct. 22, 1986, from acting director, National Park Service to Park Service regional directors regarding "procedures for developing the regional natural resources assessment and action program," following up on a program of the previous year for establishment of a Regional Natural Resource Management Plan.

30. See Memorandum dated Dec. 18, 1986, from associate director, natural resources, National Park Service to regional directors regarding "natural resources assessment and action program," with accompanying "threats questionnaire" for response from each park. The questionnaire seeks useful information about the jurisdictional entity that owns or manages the land on which the threat arises. Unfortunately, it seeks no information about the program responsible for generating the threat. A key reason for that failure may be the politically imposed constraints on such inquiries. See infra notes 71-75 and accompanying text.

31. SERVICEWIDE STRATEGY, supra note 25, at 3-4.

32. Id. The original "significant resource problems" (SRPs) were suggested by park superintendents, and reduced to a priority list by Park Service regional directors, applying sixteen "SRP Criteria," which, in descending order, included: actions mandated by court order or specific legislation; situations where a "nationally significant resource" is being damaged in parks designated as a Biosphere Reserve or Research Natural Area, or in "older national parks"; legislative or executive directive; public or political sensitivity; situations where the resource will be irreversibly damaged and impossible to restore; etc. (The last three categories dealt with resource data development and monitoring.) Source: undated Park Service memo from SRP program entitled "SRP Criteria."

After review of 266 problems, the regional directors established priorities for 38 "minimum essential projects" in four categories, including: "direct remedial action" (19 projects); wildlife and fish research and monitoring (9 projects); water quality research and monitoring (10 projects, including Park Service-wide identification/assertion of water rights throughout the Park Service); and air quality/pollution projects (5 projects, unranked). A diverse list of an additional 22 SRPs were identified but not designated as "minimum essential projects." Source: undated Park Service memorandum from SRP program entitled "Summary of Natural Resource SRP Priorities."

33. One Natural Resource Preservation Program (NRPP) list shows priorities for a total of 209 projects, the first 66 of which are prioritized region by region (including three Park Service-wide projects for the Washington, D.C., office.) While it is difficult, from the summary listing, to assess the content or scope of some of the listed projects, a rough analysis suggests that 50 of the 63 regional office priorities are directed to specific needs at particular parks. Of the 13 priority projects characterized as having region-wide applicability, only four appear to be directed to institutional or resource problems of potentially broad application. See Park Service memorandum dated Apr. 24, 1985, entitled "NPS Natural Resource Multi-Year Program Formulation System (MYPFS) File, Approved Servicewide NRPP Project Priority List." See also related discussion infra note 49 and accompanying text.

34. The initiatives included four other science-related projects: determining special protection zones for fragile or unique resources; developing a program to store and share natural resource and science data; and two projects to review Park Service and related university-based science and management programs. SERVICEWIDE STRATEGY, supra note 25, at 8.

35. Park Service director's memorandum dated Mar. 3, 1983, and memorandum dated Mar. 17, 1983, from associate director, science and technology, to science and technology employees; Department of the Interior Manual, Ch. 7, 145 DM 7.1; letter dated Dec. 16, 1986, from Assistant Secretary William P. Horn to J. Dexter Peach, U.S. General Accounting Office (GAO), commenting on GAO's review of the Park Service programs developed in response to STATE OF THE PARKS--1980.

36. See infra note 94.

37. U.S. GENERAL ACCOUNTING OFFICE, LIMITED PROGRESS MADE IN DOCUMENTING AND MITIGATING THREATS TO THE PARKS, 2-3 (GAO/RCED-87-36; 1987). (Hereinafter, GAO PROGRESS REPORT.)

38. Id. at 3. On the other hand, GAO noted that the Park Service has undertaken new initiatives to establish a national air quality monitoring program and a national inventory of mining and mineral development threats.

39. NATIONAL PARKS AND CONSERVATION ASSOCIATION, *Research in The Parks: An Assessment of Needs*, at 14 in THE NATIONAL PARK SYSTEM PLAN: A BLUEPRINT FOR TOMORROW, Vol. 2 (1988).

40. *Id.* at 103.

41. The Park Service's specialized scientific divisions (Air Quality, Water Resources, Mining and Minerals) do provide substantial analysis of specific, high-profile issues for regulatory application. The author has had considerable contact with the work of those divisions regarding, *e.g.*, hydrology and "night sky" impacts relating to the proposed nuclear waste repository near Canyonlands National Park; air quality and noise impacts relating to designation of portions of the Alton coal field next to Bryce Canyon National Park as "unsuitable" for strip mining; and natural flow requirements for park streams such as the Virgin River in Zion National Park. The work of these divisions also seeks to develop a data base essential to effective response to external threats, particularly through, *e.g.*, visibility monitoring and streamflow quantification. But even those effective programs are severely constrained in initiating the use of legal remedies to address potential threats arising beyond park boundaries, both because of the lack of access to an independent legal or enforcement arm and because of the Interior Department's reluctance to permit resolution of intra-Departmental disputes on the basis of adjudicated application of legal standards.

42. SERVICEWIDE STRATEGY, *supra* note 25, at 13.

43. GAO PROGRESS REPORT, *supra* note 37, at 13. *See also, infra* notes 81-84 and accompanying text.

44. *See infra* note 90 and accompanying text.

45. Letter dated Dec. 16, 1986, from Interior Assistant Secretary William P. Horn to J. Dexter Peach, U.S. General Accounting Office, responding to GAO summary of Park Service programs for response to the STATE OF THE PARKS--1980 report, GAO PROGRESS REPORT at 68. Secretary Horn offered no suggestions to improve the Park Service legal position. He merely asserted that the Secretary's duty to protect the parks "must be exercised on a case-by-case basis," and emphasized that certain Interior Department efforts have sought to encourage greater cooperation among its agencies. *Id.* at 65. For an assessment of those efforts, *see infra* notes 66-76 and accompanying text.

46. Sax and Keiter, *supra* note 2 at 211.

47. *Id.* at 187. Sax and Keiter demonstrate that the failure to utilize available legal tools limits the Park Services's role at crucial early stages--not merely in last-ditch resistance to imminent projects:

> [A] study of the stipulations imposed on [adjacent oil and gas leases] reveals a clear assumption that development will be allowed unless there is some legal reason to restrain it . . . . Yet, park officials, perhaps because they disfavor legalistic behavior, did not seek a role in the original formulation of lease stipulations to make them conform more fully to Glacier's concerns.

> *Id.* at 231.

48. *Id.* at 213.

49. This tendency is reflected in the "significant resource problems" identified by the park superintendents for prioritization as part of the servicewide strategy, which were almost wholly directed to in-park problems within the institutional grasp of the superintendents. *See supra* note 33 and accompanying text. That approach is understandable when broader vision is discouraged at the upper levels of the Interior Department. *See infra* notes 66-76 and accompanying text.

Serious threats from external activities are likely to be treated summarily in the basic planning documents, with only vague recognition of probable impacts, even by parks noted for aggressive resource protection. *See, e.g.*, NATIONAL PARK SERVICE, CANYONLANDS NATIONAL PARK, STATEMENT FOR MANAGEMENT, (Aug. 1985). Despite significant concerns about unrestricted oil and gas leasing along vulnerable park boundaries (*infra* note 55 and accompanying text), the issue was not mentioned in the required discussion of "land uses and trends" on adjacent lands. *Id.* at 13. Threats from possible tar sands development at the park's western boundary and a nuclear waste repository at the eastern boundary were summarily acknowledged with the comment that "the industrial scope of these proposals has raised questions concerning impacts upon the park." *Id.* And even where more detailed planning documents forthrightly described the scope of those projects, impact descriptions were minimal ("could have a major impact"), and planning recommendations were cautiously noncommittal (develop "good baseline information" in order "to assure that decisions are made on the best information available"). NATIONAL PARK SERVICE, CANYONLANDS NATIONAL PARK, NATURAL RESOURCES MANAGEMENT PLAN AND ENVIRONMENTAL ASSESSMENT, at 53 (1985).

50. National Environmental Policy Act, 42 U.S.C.A. §§ 4321, 4331(b) (1977) and implementing Executive Order No. 11514, 25 Fed. Reg. 4247 (1970); Federal Land Policy and Management Act, 43 U.S.C.A. § 1712(c)(9) (1986) and implementing regulations at 43 C.F.R. §§ 1610.3-1 and 1610.3-2 (1987).

51. *See* NATIONAL PARK SERVICE, PLANNING PROCESS GUIDELINE (NPS-2), Ch. 5, titled *General Management Plan* (Release No. 3, Sept. 1982). Under the heading "The Affected Environment," NPS-2 requires a plan to "provide the information necessary to understand the issues, the proposal, and the alternatives." NPS-2, Ch. 5, p. 17. That is, to include information on "other agency programs and private sector activities" such as "increasing intensity of development adjacent to the park" or "nature and intensity of use on adjacent lands." *Id.* at 19. Except for those vague instructions, however, nothing in the planning guidelines specifically requires park officials to assess the impacts of those adjacent actions or to formulate plans or establish objectives designed to contest, avoid, or minimize the impacts.

52. *See infra* notes 66-76 and accompanying text.

53. Federal Land Policy and Management Act of 1976, § 202, 43 U.S.C.A. § 1712 (1986). *See* particularly § 202(C)(9), 43 U.S.C.A. § 1712(c)(9), requiring BLM to "coordinate the land use inventory, planning, and management activities . . . with the land use planning and management programs of other Federal departments and agencies."

54. U.S. DEPARTMENT OF THE INTERIOR, BUREAU OF LAND MANAGEMENT, GRAND RESOURCE AREA PROPOSED MANAGEMENT PLAN, FINAL ENVIRONMENTAL IMPACT STATEMENT, at 4-55, 4-56 (1983) (Emphasis added).

55. *Id.*

56. Response by BLM State Director Roland Robison, dated Mar. 6, 1985, to author's comment on BLM preplanning analysis of issues for the resource management plan, San Juan Resource Area; and response by Moab District BLM, in FINAL SAN JUAN RESOURCE MANAGEMENT PLAN AND ENVIRONMENTAL IMPACT STATEMENT, Sept. 1987, at 2-10, to NPCA's detailed comments on the earlier draft plan insisting on BLM's obligation to treat consistency with national park plans and policies as a planning issue. *Id.* at 2-8 to 2-19 (emphasis added). *See also* the BLM response in the final RMP to a Park Service request that the plan "recognize that the public lands adjoining Canyonlands . . . and Natural Bridges . . . are integral to the reasons these two areas were established as units of the National Park System." BLM replied:

> [C]ongress did not provide that [Organic Act standards] be applied to public lands, nor that NPS would authorize uses on public lands. FLPMA provides that all public lands (including those adjacent to or seen from NPS units) will be managed to provide for multiple use and sustained yield [and does] not require a different, more protective level of management for public lands adjacent to NPS units. *Id.* at 2-258.

57. *See* Sax and Keiter, *supra* note 2 at 197.

58. 10 C.F.R. § 960.5-2-5(d) (1987). The guideline provided that a site would not be disqualified, despite anticipated severe impacts from initial site-testing and construction activities, unless environmental quality in the area "could not be adequately protected"

or impacts in the area "could not be mitigated to an acceptable degree taking into account programmatic, technical, social, economic, and environmental factors." *See infra* note 151 and accompanying text.

59. U.S. DEPARTMENT OF ENERGY, ENVIRONMENTAL ASSESSMENT, DAVIS CANYON SITE, Vol. II, at 6-67 (1986).

60. *Id.*

61. *See* discussion *infra* notes 90-91, 94-116, and accompanying text.

62. In addition to the key issues discussed above, *see infra* notes 121, 135-144, 148, and accompanying text.

63. Memorandum dated Oct. 31, 1985, from the Director, National Park Service to the Secretary, Department of the Interior, with accompanying draft letter to Secretary of Energy Herrington.

64. *See supra* notes 58-60 and accompanying text.

65. The arguments asserted in the Director's proposed letter to the Secretary of Energy were similar to, though more explicit and comprehensive than those later asserted in a comment letter to DOE from the Department's Director of Environmental Project Review. Those comments contended that statutory park protection standards prohibited activities that would result in derogation or degradation of the area, and prohibited "balancing" or "trade-offs" that would compromise park resources or values, concluding:

> In summary, the Department . . . cannot sanction the required withdrawals or a cooperative agreement for use of public lands adjacent to Canyonlands National Park that would cause derogation of park values and purposes.

Letter dated Jan. 21, 1986, from Bruce Blanchard, Director, Environmental Project Review, Department of the Interior, to Ben C. Rusche, Director, Office of Civilian Radioactive Waste Management, Department of Energy. The Secretary, however, never intervened directly to exert the authority cited in that letter, and DOE formally designated the site as one of five nominated sites on May 28, 1986. While NPCA's lawsuit challenging that selection was pending along with other challenges to DOE's selections, the Nuclear Waste Policy Act of 1982 was amended in late 1987 to designate Nevada's Yucca Mountain as the sole repository site, rendering NPCA's suit moot. Nuclear Waste Policy Amendments Act of 1987, 133 CONG. REC. H12168-76 (daily ed. Dec. 21, 1987).

66. The Department of the Interior under the current administration has consistently opposed legislation to strengthen standards and procedures for protection of the national parks, claiming that existing legislative authority is fully adequate. *See infra* notes 81-84 and accompanying text.

67. U.S. Department of the Interior, Report of the Subgroup of the Park Protection Working Group, at 3 (1985).

68. *Id.* at 7. The substance of the working group report was incorporated into Ch. 4 of the *Departmental Manual* of the Department of the Interior, 301 DM 4.1, which states as policy that "it is an objective of the Department . . . to resolve resource threats among land and resource management agencies through emphasis on threat anticipation, avoidance and resolution." The policy statement is followed by a list of nine vaguely worded descriptions of "existing agency and interagency structures and processes" to be used to address that objective.

69. Letter dated Oct. 9, 1985, from Representative Bruce F. Vento to Ms. Ann Dore McLaughlin, Under Secretary, Department of the Interior. For another example of the same refusal to recognize any priority for park protection, *see* discussion of the "cooperation" memorandum between the Park Service and the Bureau of Land Management, *infra* note 129 and accompanying text.

70. In response to Chairman Vento's letter, note 69 *supra*, Under Secretary McLaughlin responded that legal conflicts between park protection standards and the law governing other agencies "can be most successfully interpreted on a case by case basis." She relied on an opinion from the Solicitor, Department of the Interior, that declines to take a position on the primacy of the park protection statutes and recommends "resolution of conflicts . . . on an *ad hoc* basis pending judicial clarification." Letter dated Nov. 1, 1985, from Under Secretary of the Interior Ann McLaughlin to Representative Bruce F. Vento, relying on Memorandum dated Sept. 20, 1986, from Associate Solicitor Keith E. Eastin, U.S. Department of the Interior, to Director, National Park Service, addressing available legal grounds for protecting parks from encroaching air pollution, discussed *infra* notes 86, 90-91, and accompanying text.

71. Memorandum dated Sept. 25, 1985, from William Horn, Assistant Secretary for Fish, Wildlife and Parks to Director, National Park Service, responding to memorandum on "Proposed National Park Service Park Protection Action Plan" dated Aug. 19, 1985, from the Director, through Assistant Secretary for Fish, Wildlife and Parks, to Assistant Secretary for Policy, Budget and Administration. (Emphasis added.) (Hereinafter, Horn Memorandum" and Park Service Action Plan.)

72. Park Service Action Plan, *supra* note 71.

73. Horn Memorandum, *supra* note 71.

74. Park Service Action Plan, *supra* note 71.

75. Horn Memorandum, *supra* note 71. While the memorandum merely noted approvingly "that you have already removed this activity" from the plan, personal inquiry by the author disclosed disagreement with that assertion, indicating that the change was made in the Assistant Secretary's office.

76. Memorandum dated May 27, 1987, from Director, National Park Service to Assistant Secretary, Fish, Wildlife and Parks. The issues of concern included: a proposed BLM rulemaking proceeding on its coal leasing program that could affect leasing adjacent to parks; a proposed rulemaking by the (coal) Office of Surface Mining Reclamation and Enforcement defining "valid existing rights" that could significantly affect the right to strip mine adjacent to parks; and reexamination of Interior's position on EPA regulation of surface coal mining.

Most troubling are the indications that a variety of sanctions, from canceling speaking engagements to manipulation of personnel performance ratings for career Park Service officials, may have been used to enforce the political agenda of senior Department officials. *See* R. Cahn and P. Cahn, *Disputed Territory*, NATIONAL PARKS 5-6, at 28, 32-33 (1987).

77. The following summary is drawn from the circumstances and events described in Part II of this chapter.

78. National Park Service Organic Act, 16 U.S.C.A. § 1 (1974) (Act of August 25, 1916, 39 Stat. 535).

79. *See infra* notes 94-116 and accompanying text.

80. *See infra* note 81 and accompanying text.

81. *Hearings on Public Land Management Policy before the Subcomm. on Public Lands and National Parks of the House Comm. on Interior and Insular Affairs,* 97th Cong. 2d Sess., Mar. 30, 1982, at 436. The proposed "National Park System Protection and Resource Management Act of 1982," H.R. 5162, included a requirement that other agencies' activities must "not significantly degrade the natural or cultural resources or values for which any [adjacent] . . . unit [of the park system] was established"; provided for (1) a process for "federal program review," requiring notification of any proposed federal agency action on park or adjacent lands that may degrade park resources and (2) a response to such notice by the Secretary, with recommendations for any changes necessary to avoid adverse effects; and required that the agency comply fully with the Secretary's recommendations for activities on park properties, or, for other ac-

tivities, fully consider the recommendations and defer action for thirty days following submission of notice of any disagreement to the Senate Committee on Energy and Natural Resources and the House Committee on Interior and Insular Affairs.

82. *Id.* at 451. (Emphasis added.)

83. Letter dated Sept. 28, 1982, from Donald Paul Hodel, Acting Secretary of the Interior to Rep. Morris K. Udall, Chairman, House Committee on Interior and Insular Affairs, in H.R. REP. NO. 97-881, 97th Cong., 2d Sess. 20, 22.

84. *Hearings On Department of the Interior and Related Agencies Appropriations for 1987 Before the Subcomm. on the Department of the Interior and Related Agencies of the House Comm. On Appropriations,* 99th Cong., 2d Sess. 801 (Mar. 12, 1986). (Written questions and answers accompanying hearing transcript, question 3e.)

85. *See supra* note 73 and accompanying text and notes 67-70 and text.

86. Opinion letter dated Sept. 20, 1985, from Associate Solicitor Keith E. Eastin to Director, National Park Service, at 18. (Emphasis added.) Similar contradictory positions are reflected in a more current solicitor's opinion. When recently confronted with EPA proposals for new regulations to control "fugitive dust" affecting the parks, Interior again vigorously asserted that it has "adequate existing authority." But in contending that adequate authority is available under a variety of laws, including the Park Service Organic Act, the solicitor heavily qualified his opinion, without explanation, *limiting that Act's reach to in-park activities* ("[T]he Organic Act is available to DOI to protect NPS units *from activities within NPS units* should the need arise.") Draft comment letter dated Oct. 14, 1987, from Ralph G. Tarr, Solicitor, U.S. Department of the Interior to General Counsel, U.S. Environmental Protection Agency, at 22. (Emphasis added.) The unexplained confinement of the opinion to in-park activities seems gratuitous, since the issues addressed by the opinion were not so confined.

87. *See supra* note 56 and notes 54-57 and accompanying text. (Emphasis added.)

88. *Hearings on Department of the Interior and Related Agencies Appropriations for 1987 Before the Subcomm. on the Department of the Interior and Related Agencies of the House Comm. On Appropriations,* 99th Cong., 2d Sess., part 8, 800-01 (Mar. 12, 1986). (Emphasis added.) (Question 3e in written questions and answers accompanying hearing transcript.)

89. Several decided cases have involved application of park protection requirements to avert the consequences of activities on state or private holdings within the parks. Because these cases may be viewed as involving an analogous reach beyond park boundaries, they invite logical extension to address "external" threats. *See* Keiter, *supra* note 2 at 79-89.

90. Opinion letter dated Sept. 20, 1985, from Associate Solicitor Keith E. Eastin to Director, National Park Service, at 13.

91. *Id.* at 18 and 31. Inexplicably, the opinion in the fourth quoted line above referred to park threatening activities "on nonfederal land" outside park boundaries. In context, however, the solicitor's analysis clearly dealt with the general scope of authority for protection of parks from external threats, without distinguishing between threats arising on federal and nonfederal lands. Similarly, although the concluding line referred to external air pollution, the context and the Department's broader reliance on the opinion (*supra* notes 44-45, 70 and accompanying text) supports the broader reference to external threats.

92. Letter dated Sept. 28, 1982, from Donald Paul Hodel, Acting Secretary of the Interior to Rep. Morris K. Udall, Chairman, House Committee on Interior and Insular Affairs, *supra* note 83.

93. *See* discussion of *Sierra Club v. Andrus* in Keiter, *supra* note 2.

94. *See supra* notes 90-91 and accompanying text. Applicability of the statutory standards discussed below would provide a substantial basis for park protection. Federal agencies must comply with governing statutes by weighing the factors identified by those

statutes (or by regulations) as relevant to their application. They must show that they have taken a "hard look" at the facts about those "relevant factors" and that their decisions comply with the statutory standards. Citizens to Preserve Overton Park, Inc. v. Volpe, 401 U.S. 402 (1971); Motor Vehicle Manufacturer's Ass'n of the United States, Inc. v. State Farm Mutual Automobile Ins. Co., 463 U.S. 29 (1983); National Lime Ass'n v. EPA, 627 F.2d 416 (D.C. Cir. 1980); Portland Cement Ass'n v. Ruckelshaus, 486 F.2d 375 (D.C. Cir. 1973); Sierra Club v. Block, 615 F. Supp. 44 and 622 F. Supp. 842 (D. Colo. 1985). *See also* cases cited *infra* note 107.

In prohibiting "impairment" or "derogation" of the resources and values of the national parks, therefore, 16 U.S.C. §§ 1 and 1a-1 (1974 and West Supp. 1987) require identification of resource impacts and, potentially, land management requirements necessary to avoid "impairment." To the extent data and standards on those issues have been developed, they must be adequately addressed by any agency decisions affecting the parks. Thus, for example, the Secretary of the Interior was held not to have met those requirements when he failed to take steps recommended by several National Park Service studies to prevent or minimize damage to Redwood National Park from logging operations on adjacent lands. Sierra Club v. Department of the Interior, 376 F. Supp. 90, 96 (N.D. Cal. 1974); Sierra Club v. Department of the Interior, 398 F.2d 284 (N.D. Cal. 1975). Similar standards require agencies to give weight to specific data bearing on the application of other environmental statutes. *See, e.g.,* Foundation for North American Wild Sheep v. United States Department of Agriculture, 681 F.2d 1172, 1178-82 (9th Cir. 1982) (National Environmental Policy Act).

95. Memorandum dated Nov. 19, 1985, from the American Law Division, Congressional Research Service, Library of Congress to House Committee on Interior and Insular Affairs, titled "Comments On Department of Interior Memorandum of Sept. 20, 1985 entitled 'Protection of National Park System Units from the Adverse Effects of Air Pollution,'" reproduced in *Hearings on Impacts of Air Pollution on Units of National Park System before the Subcomm. on National Parks and Recreation, House Comm. on Interior and Insular Affairs,* 99th Cong., 1st Sess., 575 (1985).

96. It is important to recognize that the basic protections against "impairment" in the Organic Act are given further content by the identification of specific protected values recognized in the enabling legislation creating specific parks. *See infra* note 114 and accompanying text.

For discussion of case law applying these provisions in contexts pertinent to external threats *see* Keiter, *supra* note 2.

97. 16 U.S.C.A. § 1 (1974) (Act of Aug. 25, 1916, 39 Stat. 535).

98. *See* Sierra Club v. Department of the Interior, 424 F. Supp. 172 (N.D. Cal. 1976).

99. 16 U.S.C.A. § 1a-1 (West Supp. 1987) (emphasis added) (Pub. L. No. 95-250, Title I, § 101(b), Mar. 27, 1978, 92 Stat. 166). Other amendments dealt with specific issues affecting disputes about clearcut logging at the borders of Redwood National Park.

100. 16 U.S.C.A. § 1a-1 (West Supp. 1987); *see infra* note 103.

101. S. REP. NO. 95-528, 95th Cong., 1st Sess. 7-8 (1977) (Emphasis added.)

102. The original author of the portion of the Redwoods Amendments that prohibits authorizations of activities that may derogate park values was James D. Webb, Associate Solicitor for Conservation and Wildlife, Department of the Interior, at the time the amendments were enacted. Webb has explained that the purpose of the provision was to embody the public trust doctrine advanced by Professor Joseph L. Sax in *The Public Trust Doctrine In Natural Resource Law: Effective Judicial Intervention,* 68 MICH. L. REV. 471 (1970). The concept was developed in cooperation with the amendments' chief proponent, the late Congressman Phil Burton, and developed in exchanges between the solicitor's office and counsel for President Carter (Bob Lipschutz) and the Assistant Attorney General for the Lands Division (Jim Moorman). Because of concerns about the legal quagmire involved in applying the concept of U.S. trust responsibilities to Indian tribes, Webb was instructed to redraft the provision to incorporate the essential ele-

ments of Sax's concept, but without expressly using the words "trust" or "trustee." And because of concerns about provoking opposition from the State Department or Department of Defense, he drafted the introductory phrase ("authorization of activities"), "leaving open the question whether the inhibitions of the statute would extend beyond the authorities of the Secretary of Interior." Letter dated Sept. 17, 1986, from James D. Webb to Prof. Robert Keiter and letter dated Oct. 8, 1986, from James D. Webb to William J. Lockhart.

103. s. REP. NO. 95-528, *supra* note 101, at 7-8 (1977) (emphasis added). The general applicability of the standards established by the Organic Act to all decisions, and to all park units, was further emphasized by the Committee in its "Section-By-Section Analysis" of the derogation prohibition of § 1a-1:

> The committee has been concerned that litigation with regard to Redwood National Park *and other areas of the system* may have blurred the responsibilities articulated by the 1916 Act creating the National Park Service.

> Accordingly, this provision suggested by the administration would appear to be particularly appropriate. The Secretary is to afford the highest standard of protection and care to the natural resources within Redwood National Park *and the National Park System. No decision* shall compromise these resource values except as Congress may have specifically provided.

Id. at 14 (emphasis added). The committee's specific emphasis that "no decision" shall compromise park resources indicates intent to impose a regulatory prohibition of general application. Certainly, in view of the direct committee reference to the Secretary, the provision must be read as barring any decisions (with the prohibited effect) made by or on behalf of the Secretary of the Interior.

104. The contrary argument is based on the immediately preceding sentence, which reads: "Congress further reaffirms, declares, and directs that the promotion and regulation of the various areas of the National Park System . . . shall be consistent with and founded in the purpose established by section 1 of this title." 16 U.S.C.A. § 1a-1 (West Supp. 1987). It has been argued that this language limits the scope of the derogation provision to activities involving the "promotion and regulation" of areas *within* the park system. *See, e.g.,* GAO, LIMITED PROGRESS MADE IN DOCUMENTING AND MITIGATING THREATS TO THE PARKS, Report to the Chairman, Subcommittee on National Parks and Recreation, House Committee on Interior and Insular Affairs, GAO/RCED-87-36, at 54 (1987).

That interpretation, however, rests heavily on a narrowly literalistic interpretation of the vague words "regulation of the various areas" and fails to address the comprehensive "purpose established by section 1" which the very language in question is designed to reaffirm. *See supra* notes 100-101, 103, and accompanying text. It also fails to explain the parallel structure of the derogation provision; fails to recognize that the amendment was adopted in response to external threat problems (impacts from logging of adjacent lands); and fails to explain the explicit and uncontested legislative history emphasizing that the amendments were to provide a basis for "judicial resolution" of conflicts "in areas surrounding" the parks.

105. Now recodified at 49 U.S.C.A. § 303(c) (West pamphlet 1987); 4(f) was previously codified at 49 U.S.C.A. § 1653(f) (1976).

106. 49 U.S.C.A. § 1653(f) (1976) (emphasis added). The statute also prohibited approval in those circumstances unless "all possible planning" had been done "to minimize harm" to the park or other preserve. As recodified, the current version of this section now provides that the Secretary of Transportation "may approve" a project "requiring the use of publicly owned land of a public park [etc.] only if . . . there is no prudent and feasible alternative to using that land" and "the project includes all possible planning to minimize harm to the park . . . resulting from the use." 49 U.S.C.A. § 303(c) (West pamphlet 1987).

107. Louisiana Environmental Society, Inc. v. Coleman, 537 F.2d 79, 85 (5th Cir. 1976), *rehearing and rehearing en banc denied* (1976). *See also* Citizen Advocates for Responsible Expansion v. Dole, 770 F.2d 423, 441 and cases cited at n. 23 (5th Cir. 1985); Adler v. Lewis, 675 F.2d 1085, 1092 (9th Cir. 1982); Brooks v. Volpe, 460 F.2d 1193 (9th Cir. 1972); Conservation Society v. Secretary of Transportation, 362 F. Supp. 627 (D. Ver. 1973), *aff'd* 508 F.2d 927 (2d Cir. 1974).

108. It is important to recognize that this interpretation merely establishes the *applicability* of the relevant statutory standards for evaluating activities whose impacts within the park constitute "use." That determination is made under the Transportation Act in order to determine whether the Secretary must assess the availability of any "prudent and feasible" alternatives before going ahead with a project, subject to "all possible planning to minimize harm." Under the Organic Act and Redwoods Amendments, however, the protective standards triggered by that interpretation comprehensively prohibit any "impairment" or "derogation" of park values, under 16 U.S.C.A. §§ 1 and 1a-1 (1974 and West Supp. 1987). Thus, even though the Transportation Act imposes a rigorous standard requiring clear justification for such spillover "use" of a park, the park protection laws impose even higher standards of protection, approaching an outright ban, wherever intruding impacts or consequences to park values may be found to impair or derogate those values.

109. 16 U.S.C.A. § 1a-1 (West Supp. 1987).

110. *See* Keiter, *supra* note 2. Keiter's interpretation is generally supported by the court in National Rifle Ass'n v. Potter, 628 F. Supp. 903 (D.D.C. 1986). The court emphasized the exceptions clause in ruling that the Park Service validly adopted regulations barring hunting and trapping in all but a few park units. Although specific parks' establishing legislation was frequently silent on the issue, the Park Service prohibited those activities except "in park areas where such activity is specifically mandated by Federal statutory law." 36 C.F.R. § 2.2 (1985).

111. 16 U.S.C.A. § 1 (1974).

112. *See* discussion of these developments in National Rifle Ass'n v. Potter, 628 F. Supp. 903; 905-06 (D.D.C 1986).

113. 16 U.S.C.A. § 1c (1974), enacted by the Act of Aug. 18, 1970, Pub. L. No. 91-383, § 2(b), 84 Stat. 826.

114. *Id.* In addition to specific protections arising from the purposes or resources preserved by particular park enabling acts, it has also been suggested that the Park Service has long recognized a congressionally ratified policy of preserving natural flora and fauna in their primitive state. *See* book review, Baur, *Playing God in Yellowstone: The Destruction of America's First National Park*, 22 LAND WATER L. REV. 49, at 56 (1987), citing, *e.g.*, DIXON AND THOMAS, FAUNA OF THE NATIONAL PARKS OF THE UNITED STATES, A PRELIMINARY SURVEY OF FAUNAL RELATIONSHIPS IN NATIONAL PARKS at 147 (National Park Service, 1932).

115. *See supra* note 101 and accompanying text.

116. The amendment's prohibition against "derogation of the values and purposes for which these various areas have been established" is drafted with explicit reference to "the various areas of the National Park System, as defined in section 1c of this title," thus referring specifically to the inclusive definition of the "National Park System" enacted by the General Authorities Act. 16 U.S.C.A. § 1a-1 (West Supp. 1987).

117. *See supra* notes 44, 70, and 86 and accompanying text.

118. Solicitor's opinion discussed *supra* note 91 and accompanying text.

119. *See supra* notes 71-75 and accompanying text.

120. *See supra* note 7 and accompanying text. *See also* instructions for the conduct of "Regional Natural Resource Assessment And Action Program," accompanying Memoran-

dum dated Oct. 22, 1986, from acting director, National Park Service to regional directors, instructing that the condition of park resources should be assessed by categorizing the significance of all resources as "primary," "secondary," or "other."

121. Draft "Model Bureau Directive" dated Sept. 14, 1984, entitled "DOI Bureau-Level Directive to Regional and Field Offices Regarding Actions Impacting Resources Within Units of the National Park System." The directive would have required officials of every Department of the Interior agency to give notice to the appropriate Park Service manager prior to approving any activities meeting certain criteria designed to identify potential impacts. No approval could be granted unless the Park Service determined that there would be no significant adverse park impacts, or unless adequate mitigation was agreed upon through a detailed conflict resolution process designed to elevate continuing differences to higher levels of decision.

122. Federal Land Policy and Management Act, §§ 201(a) and 202(c)(3), 43 USC §§ 1711(a) and 1712(c)(3).

123. Federal Land Policy and Management Act, § 103(a), 43 U.S.C.A. § 1702(a) (1986).

124. BLM release dated Sept. 4, 1986, accompanied by draft entitled "Proposed Revisions to Guidance for Identification, Evaluation and Designation of Areas of Critical Environmental Concern and Changes to BLM Manual Section 1617."

125. The proposed revision included criteria that identified an ACEC as an important resource because it "possesses more-than-locally significant qualities which give it special worth" or make it "fragile, sensitive, rare . . . or vulnerable to adverse change." *Id.* at 1-4. The revision also specified that ACEC designation is the principal BLM tool for designating public lands "where special management is required," explaining the relationship of such designations to "designations made by other agencies," including the National Park Service. *Id.* at 1-11.

126. *See supra* note 30 and accompanying text. The survey was conducted during the winter/spring of 1986-87; and though the reported data has been available to the Park Service since at least July 1987, no summary, report, or analysis is available at this writing.

127. *E.g.,* National Environmental Policy Act, 43 U.S.C.A. § 4332(C) (1977), Executive Orders 11514 and 11991, and implementing regulations at 40 C.F.R. §§ 1501.1(b), 1501.5-1501.7, 1502.19(a), 1503.1-1503.3 (1987); Federal Land Policy and Management Act, 43 U.S.C.A. §§ 1712(c)(9) and (f) (1986), and implementing regulations at 43 C.F.R. §§ 1610.3-1 and 1610.3-2 (1987).

128. Paragraph V of MOU executed Jan. 29, 1987, between the Directors of the Bureau of Land Management and the National Park Service. Probably the most useful cooperation provisions call for exchange of schedules for major planning projects to be undertaken in each fiscal year. *Id.* at paragraph IV-C.

Even less specific is a "Memorandum of Understanding Between the Rocky Mountain Region, National Park Service and the Northern, Rocky Mountain and Intermountain Regions, Forest Service," executed Sept. 24, 1986, agreeing to a range of general aspirations for cooperation and coordination that should characterize any good faith effort to "execute the laws" in related fields.

129. *Id.* Even where an MOU establishes a more specific procedure for identification and disposition of potential conflicts, it is likely to leave decision to undefined discretionary judgments without addressing the applicable standards of park protection. For example, an "'Umbrella' Memorandum of Understanding Between Bureau of Land Management and National Park Service" regarding BLM management of grazing within the Glen Canyon National Recreation Area, executed Aug. 20 and Sept. 4, 1984, established procedures for the Park Service to respond to any grazing plans by providing a "written determination . . . regarding the potential effect . . . on the values and purposes of the area." But without specifying any criteria for the decision, any conflict that cannot be settled at the regional level is to be referred "to the next level of management for resolution."

130. *Id.*

131. The informal "notice and comment" rulemaking process established by the federal Administrative Procedure Act, 5 U.S.C. § 553, heralded by Prof. Kenneth Culp Davis in 1970 as "one of the greatest inventions of modern government," has, through intervening development, "been vastly improved." *See, e.g.,* K.C. DAVIS, ADMINISTRATIVE LAW TREATISE, Vol. 1, 6.1, 6.39 (1978); and K.C. DAVIS, DISCRETIONARY JUSTICE, A PRELIMINARY INQUIRY, 56-57 (1969):

> The typical failure in our system that is correctable is not legislative delegation of broad discretionary power with vague standards; it is the procrastination of administrators in resorting to the rule-making power to replace vagueness with clarity.

Also see President Nixon's ASH COUNCIL REPORT, *infra* note 175, at 21-22.

132. *See supra* notes 90-91 and accompanying text.

133. The National Park Service Organic Act mandated the Secretary of the Interior to "make and publish such rules and regulations as he may deem necessary or proper for the use and management of the parks, monuments, and reservations under the jurisdiction of the National Park Service." These rules are enforceable by criminal sanctions. 16 U.S.C.A. § 3 (1974) (§ 3 of the Act of Aug. 25, 1916, 39 Stat. 535). The original Organic Act, as expanded and refocused by the General Authorities Act of 1970 and the Redwoods Amendments of 1978, should provide ample rulemaking authority to protect the parks. *See supra* notes 94-116 and accompanying text. In addition to Clark v. Community for Creative Non-Violence, 468 U.S. 288, 289-90 (1984), key cases affirming Park Service's rulemaking authority include, *e.g.,* National Rifle Ass'n v. Potter, 628 F. Supp. 903, 906 (D.D.C. 1986); United States v. Brown, 552 F.2d 817, 821-23 (8th Cir. 1977); and Free Enterprise Canoe Renters Ass'n v. Watt, 711 F.2d 852, 855-56 (8th Cir. 1983).

134. General and Special Regulations for Areas Administered by the National Park Service, 48 Fed. Reg. 30252 (1983).

135. 40 C.F.R. § 51.301(n) (1987). Upon designation, the integral vistas would have been subject to protection under procedures and standards required to be included in EPA-mandated "state implementation plans." 40 C.F.R. §§ 51.304-51.307 (1987).

136. The regulations did not give unqualified protection to the integral vistas. They permitted, for example, administrative review of emissions by new sources, to consider a variety of economic and energy-related factors without any concrete guide to decision making other than a vague mandate for "reasonable progress" toward the congressional goal. 40 C.F.R. § 51.307(c) (1987).

137. 42 U.S.C.A. §§ 7491(a)(1) and (2) (1983). That mandate was applicable in "mandatory class I Federal areas," *id.,* which are defined as all international parks, national parks exceeding 6000 acres, and national wilderness areas and memorial parks exceeding 5000 acres. 42 U.S.C.A. §§ 7472(a)(1)-(4) (1983).

138. 40 C.F.R. § 51.304(a) (1987).

139. EPA had designated 162 qualifying areas in those categories where "visibility is an important value." 40 C.F.R. §§ 81.400-437 (1987).

140. Equally laughable were his contentions that he did not want to send the message to park personnel at other park units "that *their* vistas are not important;" or that acting on vista protection "might falsely suggest that . . . vistas [have] higher priority than pollution, crowding, development and the like". *See* press statement released Oct. 25, 1985, by Secretary of the Interior Donald P. Hodel. (Emphasis in original.)

141. *Id.*

142. Pub. L. No. 97-78, 95 Stat. 1070 (Nov. 16, 1981), which provided in § 11 that:

> The Secretary of the Interior shall apply the provisions of this Act to the Glen Canyon National Recreation Area, and to any other units of the na-

tional park system where mineral leasing is permitted . . . if the Secretary finds that there will be no resulting significant adverse impacts on the administration of such area, or on other contiguous units of the national park system.

143. The proposed regulation delegated that determination to the Park Service regional director under standards that defined an impact as "any quantitative or qualitative change in environmental, ecological, historic, cultural, aesthetic or visitor experience factors or indicators," and defined "significant adverse impacts" as any impact whose "magnitude, scope, location, timing, extent, frequency or duration . . . conflicts with the preservation of the resources, values, or attributes of a park unit, or portion thereof, for present or future visitors." 49 Fed. Reg. 19438, 19439 (1984).

144. Undated Memorandum from Director, BLM, to Director, National Park Service, through Interior Assistant Secretary for Fish, Wildlife and Parks and Assistant Secretary for Land and Minerals Management, at 1, offering comments on the *Federal Register* notice of proposed rulemaking. The BLM director complained that the proposed rule did not reflect either the legislative and administrative history of the Act and of Glen Canyon National Recreation Area or "the agreements and commitments reached between the [BLM] and the [National Park Service] in the planning and development of the Federal tar sand program." *Id.*

145. A distinguished court of appeals judge has observed that "historically, [agency] policy has evolved mainly from a case-by-case approach." H. J. FRIENDLY, THE FEDERAL ADMINISTRATIVE AGENCIES 143 (1962). *See also* Report of the [Attorney General's] Committee on Administrative Procedure, *Administrative Procedure In Government Agencies*, S. DOC. NO. 8, 77th Cong., 1st Sess. at 29 (1941): "[A]dministrative agencies, like the courts, must often develop their jurisprudence in a piecemeal manner, through case-by-case consideration of particularized controversies."

146. *See infra* notes 149, 168-179, 160-164, and accompanying text.

147. *See, e.g.,* United States v. FPC, 345 U.S. 153 (1953); United States v. ICC 337 U.S. 426 (1949); North Carolina v. United States, 56 F. Supp. 606 (E.D.N.C. 1944) (Office of Price Administration intervened against ICC), *rev'd on other grounds*, 325 U.S. 507 (1945). (Cited in report supporting recommendation for creation of a federal "Indian Trust Counsel Authority" to represent Indian interests against the United States in R. Chambers, *Conflicts of Interest in the Administration of the Federal Trust Responsibility*, 2 RECOMMENDATIONS AND REPORTS OF THE ADMINISTRATIVE CONFERENCE OF THE UNITED STATES.) *See also* report of 1979 survey by the U.S. Office of Management and Budget showing up to 237 cases involving disputes between two or more federal agencies in fiscal year 1977, note 68, *supra*, Note, *Judicial Resolution of Administrative Disputes Between Federal Agencies*, 62 HARV. L. REV. 1050 (1949); *but see* FTC v. Guignon, 390 F.2d 323 (8th Cir. 1968).

148. Case Nos. 80-2559 and 80-2560, U.S. Court of Appeals for the District of Columbia, dismissed July 2, 1981, on motion of the FCC for lack of ripeness because the agency's comparative hearing process had not been completed; and letter dated Dec. 16, 1982, from G. Ray Arnett, Assistant Secretary of the Interior for Fish, Wildlife and Parks, to Mark Fowler, Chairman, Federal Communications Commission. Apparently reflecting a more limited view of park protection statutes, even Interior's informal arguments failed to assert any claim under the National Park Service Organic Act for legal protection for the park from external threats.

149. A significant complication arises in attempting to provide for legal representation of conflicting agencies in the face of the requirement of 28 U.S.C. § 519 that "the Attorney General shall supervise all litigation to which the United States, an agency, or officer thereof is a party." However, that requirement is applicable "except where otherwise provided by law," and it has frequently been modified, by statute or by formal arrangements with the Department of Justice, to provide for direct representation in civil

matters by attorneys employed by a variety of federal agencies. *See* S. Olson, *Challenges to the Gatekeeper: The Debate Over Federal Litigating Authority,* 68 JUDICATURE 71, 73 (1984-85); and discussion *infra* notes 166-179 and accompanying text.

150. As a party that typically participates in the BLM planning process for development of Resource Management Plans for adjacent lands, 43 C.F.R. § 1610.3, the Park Service would be entitled to file a protest with the BLM director raising any issues properly framed by its earlier comments on the adequacy of the plan as it affects adjacent park lands. 43 C.F.R. § 1610.5-2. A similar process could be invoked in contesting the potential impacts of forest plans approved by a regional forester, 36 C.F.R. § 211.18, with prospects for further appeal to the Secretary of Agriculture, 36 C.F.R. §§ 218(f)(3) and (4).

151. DOE's regulation permitted site selection to proceed in spite of the massive impacts of its testing (or "site characterization" program) unless DOE found that impacts from the development could not be "mitigated to an acceptable degree, taking into account programmatic, technical, social, economic, and environmental factors." It also permitted assessment of the suitability of a site as a location for the later-constructed repository so long as its presence "would not conflict irreconcilably with the previously designated resource preservation use of a component of the National Park System [and other preserves]." DOE, Nuclear Waste Policy Act of 1982; General Guidelines for the Recommendation of Sites for the Nuclear Waste Repositories," 49 Fed. Reg. 47714, 47784-85 (1984), 10 C.F.R. §§ 960.5-2-5(a), (d)(1), and (d)(3) (1987).

152. 42 U.S.C. §§ 7191(c)(2) and (d). Also troubling was the Park Service's failure to recognize and challenge the serious effect of the rule, either when it was adopted or in later application, despite the fact that it purported to balance the impacts of repository site testing and construction against the values preserved by a particularly pristine national park.

153. 40 C.F.R. § 1504.1(a).

154. 40 C.F.R. § 1504.3(f)(6).

155. 40 C.F.R. § 1504.3(f)(7).

156. *See Special Report: Agency Referrals to CEQ,* in CEQ FIFTEENTH ANNUAL REPORT--1984, at 524-557. The report shows only three referrals by the Department of the Interior in the period Jan. 1974-Jan. 1981, with no referrals since 1981 relating to potential impacts on national parks.

157. R. Chambers, *Conflicts of Interest in the Administration of Federal (Indian) Trust Responsibility,* REPORT OF THE COMMITTEE ON CLAIMS ADJUDICATIONS OF THE ADMINISTRATIVE CONFERENCE OF THE UNITED STATES, 2 REPORTS OF THE ADMINISTRATIVE CONFERENCE OF THE UNITED STATES 659, 668-75 (1972). (Hereinafter, ACUS CONFLICTS OF INTEREST STUDY.)

158. The Administrative Conference of the United States is a federal administrative agency established to study and make recommendations concerning "the efficiency, adequacy and fairness of the administrative procedure used by administrative agencies in carrying out administrative programs." 5 U.S.C. § 574.

159. ACUS CONFLICTS OF INTEREST STUDY, *supra* note 157, at 659.

160. ACUS CONFLICTS OF INTEREST STUDY, *supra* note 157, at 666.

161. ACUS CONFLICTS OF INTEREST STUDY at 667.

162. ACUS CONFLICTS OF INTEREST STUDY at 660.

163. ACUS CONFLICTS OF INTEREST STUDY at 661. For further parallels remarkably relevant to the problems of national park protection, *see id.* at 674-75.

164. ACUS CONFLICTS OF INTEREST STUDY at 661 (report), 57-58 (formal recommendation adopted by the Administrative Conference of the United States, June 9, 1972).

165. ACUS CONFLICTS OF INTEREST STUDY at 57. The Administrative Conference recommended enactment of S. 2035, 92d Cong., 1st Sess., proposed by the Nixon administration.

166. S. Olson, *supra* note 149 at 73.

167. *Id.* at 80-82.

168. A 1979 study conducted by the Office of Management and Budget surveyed "how much litigation that occurred during Fiscal Year 1977 involved disputes between two or more Federal agencies." OMB reported that the Department of Justice litigating divisions identified 99 cases; U.S. Attorneys identified 237 such cases; and selected agencies' general counsels and headquarters offices identified 122 such cases. OFFICE OF MANAGEMENT AND BUDGET, PRESIDENT'S REORGANIZATION PROJECT, DATA ON THE FEDERAL LEGAL SYSTEM 46 (1979).

169. G. Bell, *The Attorney General: The Federal Government's Chief Lawyer and Chief Litigator, or One Among Many?* 46 FORDHAM L. REV. 1049, 1058 (1978).

170. U.S. Const. art. III, § 2; 28 U.S.C. § 1331.

171. Textile Workers Union v. Lincoln Mills, 353 U.S. 448, 456 (1957). The Court went on to state that problems lying "in the penumbra of express statutory mandates . . . will be solved by looking at the policy of the legislation and fashioning a remedy that will effectuate that policy. The range of judicial inventiveness will be determined by the nature of the problem." *Id.* at 457.

172. Clearfield Trust Co. v. United States, 318 U.S. 363, at 367 (1943); *cf.* United States v. Kimbell Foods, Inc., 440 U.S. 715, 727 (1979). ("It is precisely when Congress has not spoken [on] 'issues substantially related to an established program . . .' that *Clearfield* directs federal courts to fill the interstices of federal legislation 'according to their own standards;'" and the decision "whether . . . to fashion a nationwide federal rule *is a matter of judicial policy* [that depends on] the nature of the specific governmental interests and . . . the effects upon them of applying state law," citing United States v. Standard Oil Co., 332 U.S. 301 (1947) (emphasis added).) For the view of a distinguished judge that the federal courts have been empowered to develop "truly uniform federal common law on issues of national concern," *see generally,* H. Friendly, *In Praise of Erie --and of the New Federal Common Law,"* 39 N.Y.U. L. REV. 382, 384, 405-422 (1964).

173. Bell, *supra* note 45, at 1058.

174. U.S. Const. art. II, § 3.

175. A NEW REGULATORY FRAMEWORK, REPORT ON SELECTED INDEPENDENT REGULATORY AGENCIES BY THE PRESIDENT'S ADVISORY COUNCIL ON EXECUTIVE REORGANIZATION, at 14-16 (1971) (the ASH COUNCIL REPORT, commissioned by President Nixon).

176. The Department of the Interior's failure to utilize effective policy-making procedures certainly falls within the general condemnation of the ASH COUNCIL REPORT'S, criticism of agencies' excessive reliance on case-by-case decisions because it fosters "development of ad hoc policies often limited to the particular fact situation" and fails to provide "early, comprehensive statements of policy through rulemaking proceedings and other informal policymaking procedures." ASH COUNCIL REPORT, *id.* at 21.

177. W. GELLHORN, C. BYSE, P. STRAUSE, T. RAKOFF AND R. SCHOTLAND, ADMINISTRATIVE LAW, CASES AND COMMENTS 159 (8th ed. 1987), cite a series of opinions of attorneys general establishing the position that there is no appeal to the President from departmental decisions.

178. S.M. Olson, *supra* note 149 at 74. Olson recites the ambivalent histories of the federal centralization of litigation responsibility in the Department of Justice and parallel statutory grants of litigating independence to federal agencies.

179. Environmental Defense Fund v. Thomas, 627 F. Supp. 566, 570 (D.D.C. 1986). The court held that the President's Office of Management and Budget, acting under Executive Order 12,291, 46 Fed.Reg. 13193 (1981), had no authority to delay and seek changes in the substance of regulations adopted by the Environmental Protection Agency

to implement statutory controls on hazardous waste. *See also* C. Sunstein, *Cost-Benefit Analysis and the Separation of Powers,* 23 ARIZ. L. REV. 1267, 1278 (1981): "Nothing in the Constitution authorizes the President to decide, contrary to an instruction from Congress, that a particular statute should not be enforced."

180. Myers v. United States, 272 U.S. 52 (1926). *See* discussion in 1 DAVIS, ADMINISTRATIVE LAW TREATISE § 2:8, at 88 (1978).

181. The Budget and Accounting Act of 1921 subjects even independent agencies' budgets to review and revision by the President through his Office of Management and Budget. 31 U.S.C.A. §§ 1104, 1108 (1983). BREYER & STEWART, ADMINISTRATIVE LAW AND REGULATORY POLICY at 124-25, notes that few agencies are excepted from that requirement, citing only the Consumer Product Safety Commission, 15 U.S.C. § 2076(k).

182. GELLHORN ET AL., ADMINISTRATIVE LAW, CASES AND COMMENTS, at 129 (8th ed. 1987), emphasizes that, except for a few agencies required by law to transmit their recommendations directly to Congress, all other agencies are required to submit both draft legislation and comments on proposed legislation for prior clearance by the President's Office of Management and Budget pursuant to "Circular A-19," an internal regulation implementing the President's powers under Art. II, §§ 2 and 3, Constitution of the United States.

183. Most of the issues raised in this concluding discussion, with the exception of independent legal representation, are addressed by H.R. 3964, 100th Cong., 2d Sess., introduced by Representative Bruce Vento, Chairman of the Subcommittee on National Parks and Public Lands of the House Committee on Interior and Insular Affairs.

184. *See* discussion of the Department's role in the "superfreeze" withdrawals that preserved those lands in 1968 and 1978 in COGGINS & WILKINSON, FEDERAL PUBLIC LAND AND RESOURCES LAW, at 165-68, 249-57 (2d ed. 1987), and *Stall Prompts Administrative Actions to Protect the Alaska National Interest Lands,* 8 E.L.R. at 10245 (1978).

185. 16 U.S.C.A. § 3101 (1985), Pub. L. No. 96-487 (Dec. 2, 1980).

186. FLPMA § 204, particularly § 204(e) (emergency withdrawals, 43 U.S.C.A. § 1714(e)) (1986).

187. FLPMA § 204(b)(1)(a), 43 U.S.C.A. § 1714(b)(1)(a) (1986). *See* discussion of the now-moot proposals by the Department of Energy for withdrawal of BLM lands adjacent to Canyonlands National Park for a nuclear waste repository at notes 63-65 *supra,* and accompanying text.

188. FLPMA §§ 103(a), 201(a), and 202(c)(3), 43 U.S.C.A. §§ 1702(a), 1711(a), and 1712(c)(3) (1986), discussed at notes 122-125 *supra,* and accompanying text.

189. Though generally developed in the BLM land planning process, authority to require protective stipulations prior to leasing is of general application. *See, e.g., BLM Manual* part 1624, §§ 1624.21-1-2b and .22 (Supplemental Program Guidance For Energy and Mineral Resources, dated Nov. 14, 1986) (lease stipulations for fluid minerals where, *e.g.,* even a single well might cause unacceptable impacts); BLM Instruction Memorandum No. 84-415 on "Environmental Protection Stipulation Policy for Oil and Gas Leasing (Apr. 17, 1984; expired 9/30/85).

190. FLPMA §§ 501(b)(1), 504(a) and (d), 505(a) and (b)(v), 43 U.S.C.A. §§ 1761(b)(1), 1764(a) and (d), and 1765(a) and (b)(v) (1986).

191. 16 U.S.C.A. § 460 1-22(b), § 5(b) of the Land and Water Conservation Fund Amendments, Act of July 15, 1968, Pub. L. No. 90-401, 82 Stat. 356.

192. H.R. 5162, 97th Cong., 2d Sess., § 11 (Federal Program Review), reprinted at *Hearings on Public Land Management Policy before the Subcomm. on National Parks and Public Lands of the Comm. on Interior and Insular Affairs,* House of Representatives, Mar. 30, 1982, at 1-9. In addition, projects sponsored by a federal agency for action on state or private lands would also be required to comply with the Secretary's recommendation unless the sponsoring agency determines that "the public interest in the proposed action is greater than the public interest in avoiding the adverse effects" on park resour-

ces. *Id.* at § 11((f)(1)(B). Yet another substantive standard was prescribed by the introductory section of the federal program review provisions, which would have required that other agencies' activities on or adjacent to the parks "shall, to the extent practicable, undertake to insure that those activities will not significantly degrade the natural or cultural resources or values for which the [adjacent park] unit was established." *Id.* at § 11(a). In applying that standard only "to the extent practicable," and in encouraging other agencies to assess impacts on the basis of a balancing of competing public interests, the Act might actually have undermined more rigorous standards that may be derived from the National Park Service Organic Act and its Redwoods Amendments. *See* notes 94-116 *supra,* and accompanying text. After overwhelming approval by the House of Representatives, Sept. 29, 1982, H.R. 5162 died in the Senate Energy Committee. 34 CONGRESSIONAL QUARTERLY 348 (1983). A similar bill, H.R. 2379, was again overwhelmingly approved by the House on Oct. 4, 1983, but again died after referral to the Senate Energy Committee. *Id.*

193. *See* note 94, *supra.*

194. *See* note 150 *supra,* and accompanying text.

195. Sax, *The Unhappy Truth About NEPA,* 26 OKLA. L. REV. 239 (1973).

PART II

General Authorities

Organic Act of 1916

Common Law

National Environmental Policy Act

Federal Land Policy and Management Act

International Law

Glacier National Park and Interagency Cooperation

Chapter 2

NATIONAL PARK PROTECTION: PUTTING THE ORGANIC ACT TO WORK

Robert B. Keiter[*]

I. INTRODUCTION

The National Park Service Organic Act[1] is a logical starting point for understanding the parks' legal position in the external threats controversy. Besides creating the National Park Service, the Organic Act establishes the standard under which the Secretary of the Interior is to manage national parks. The Act requires the Secretary to administer the National Park System to conserve scenery, natural and historic objects, and wildlife, and to provide for public enjoyment, while ensuring that the parks are left "unimpaired for the enjoyment of future generations."[2]

The Secretary is, therefore, confronted with the sometimes conflicting responsibilities of managing the national parks to protect their resources while assuring public access. But since the Act's "public enjoyment" mandate is qualified by such strong preservation language, the Secretary's first responsibility must be to assure that park resources are not damaged or irretrievably lost. Unless the parks are protected, public enjoyment will not be possible.

II. A DUTY TO PROTECT THE PARKS

While the Organic Act does not specify how the Secretary is to fulfill the preservation responsibilities, Section 3 of the Act provides general regulatory authority over park lands and activities occurring on them. The Secretary has relied upon this authority to adopt administrative regulations governing such diverse matters as

75

backcountry travel, boating, fire management, and snowmobile use. The Secretary has also promulgated regulations limiting activities occurring on nonfederal lands located within the national parks. The courts have consistently sustained these uses of the Secretary's authority so long as there is a reasonable connection between the regulation and the preservation-enjoyment mandate.[3] And recently in *Clark v. Community for Creative Non-Violence*,[4] the Supreme Court confirmed the Secretary's broad regulatory power over the national parks by rejecting a free speech challenge to an Interior Department regulation prohibiting sleeping in Lafayette Park in Washington, D.C. Thus, to the extent that threats to park resources involve internal activities by visitors, concessionaires, inholders, or others, the Secretary has considerable authority under the Organic Act to respond and limit access or use.

By definition the external threats problem involves activities originating outside the parks--where the Secretary lacks clear jurisdictional authority. Under the Organic Act, however, the Secretary has a legal duty to protect the parks against activities threatening their resources.[5] The Secretary's responsibility was clarified in 1978 when Congress amended the Organic Act to provide: "The protection, management and administration of those areas [national parks] shall be conducted in light of the high public value and integrity of the National Park System and shall not be exercised in derogation of the values and purposes for which these various areas have been established."[6] Congress adopted the Section 1a-1 amendment in response to the Redwood National Park crisis and the litigation it spawned. In *Sierra Club v. Department of the Interior*,[7] a federal district court had ruled that the Secretary of the Interior had a statutory duty and common law trust responsibility to protect Redwood National Park from environmental damage caused by intensive logging activity on adjacent lands. The amendment was intended to clarify that the Secretary's Organic Act responsibilities included protecting the national parks from harmful external activities.

Since 1978 the courts have held that under Section 1a-1 the Secretary has an absolute duty to protect park resources. For example, in *Sierra Club v. Andrus*,[8] the district court recognized that in the event of a threat to Grand Canyon National Park's water resources, the Secretary has a responsibility under the amended Organic Act to take appropriate actions to protect the park's waters from depletion. Similarly, the court in *National Rifle As-*

sociation v. Potter,[9] concluded that Section 1a-1 read in conjunction with the Organic Act reflects a clear "protectionism" philosophy, providing a basis to sustain Park Service regulations prohibiting hunting and trapping in the national parks. But the court in *Andrus* also held that the Secretary's park protection responsibilities are defined solely by the statute, rejecting the argument--earlier accepted in the *Redwood* litigation--that the Secretary has a common law public trust responsibility to conserve park resources under his jurisdiction.[10]

The strong protection mandate reflected in Section 1a-1 is qualified by an exceptions clause modifying the Secretary's obligation to protect the national parks. The statute provides that the protection and management of the national parks "shall not be exercised in derogation of the values and purposes for which the various areas have been established, *except* as may have been or shall be directly and specifically provided by Congress."[11] The unresolved legal question is whether the exceptions clause should be interpreted broadly or narrowly. To be more specific, does the Bureau of Land Management's organic legislation sanctioning multiple use activity on BLM land constitute a "direct and specific" congressional action relieving the Secretary of the Interior of the responsibility to protect adjacent park lands from these activities? If the exceptions clause is broadly construed, a general statutory provision like the BLM's multiple use mandate would obviate any protection responsibilities the Secretary has under the amended Organic Act. On the other hand, if the exceptions clause is narrowly interpreted, then unless Congress explicitly authorized the threatening activity, the Secretary would violate his Section 1a-1 responsibility if he permitted it to proceed.

Several compelling arguments can be advanced to support a narrow construction of the exceptions clause. First, the statutory language of Section 1a-1 strongly suggests that Congress was primarily concerned with protecting the parks. The exceptions clause is written in very limiting terms; it relieves the Secretary of the protection responsibility only if Congress has "directly and specifically" authorized an incompatible activity. This language indicates that Congress must individually authorize a particular project or activity before the clause applies. Second, the legislative history reflects a clear congressional concern that the Secretary assure protection for park resources against activities such as those threatening Redwood National Park at the time of the legislation.[12] Third, the Secretary has adopted a narrow construction of the clause, as evidenced by the recent regulations banning hunting from the parks unless specifically authorized by Congress.[13] Finally, the only cases construing the provision have interpreted it in a manner consistent with this analysis.[14] Indeed, unless the exceptions clause is given a narrow construction, the Secretary may have no legal duty to protect the parks from threatening activity arising on adjacent federal lands, since most of these activities are undertaken pursuant to general statutory powers vested in other public land management agencies. Hence, a broad construction that embraced those general powers among the "exceptions" would leave little room for operation of the preservation mandate.

III. IMPLEMENTING THE PROTECTION DUTY

Given the Secretary's duty to protect park resources, what action is he legally obligated to undertake in defense of the parks? Though the courts have held that the Secretary's actions are subject to judicial review under an abuse of discretion standard,[15] they also have consistently ruled that the Secretary has broad discretion in deciding how to respond to external threats. In *Sierra Club v. Andrus*,[16] the district court held that under the amended Organic Act, the Secretary did not act unreasonably when he refused to initiate litigation to determine the extent of federal water rights in waterways affecting Grand Canyon National Park. And in *Clark v. Community for Creative Non-Violence*,[17] the Supreme Court observed that the judiciary does not have "the authority to replace the Park Service as the manager of the Nation's parks or . . . the competence to judge how much protection of park lands is wise and how that level of conservation is to be attained."[18] Moreover, the courts have not required the Secretary to accomplish the politically impossible to protect the parks. In the *Redwood* case, for example, the district court eventually dismissed the suit after the Secretary demonstrated that he had approached Congress in good faith--albeit unsuccessfully--for additional statutory authority and funds to respond to the park's external threats problems.[19]

Park protection advocates who are unhappy with how the Secretary is fulfilling his park protection responsibility can take little solace from these decisions. They indicate that the courts are reluctant to compel the Secretary to undertake particular actions on behalf of the parks, unless the Secretary is virtually ignoring the matter and thus seriously imperiling park resources. Indeed, only once--in the *Redwood* litigation--has a court found the Secretary in violation of the park protection duties, and in this case it was shown that he had essentially overlooked the recommendations in five separate reports prepared for him, failing to take any meaningful action on behalf of the park.[20]

Yet it is nevertheless clear that when external activities threaten a park's resources, the Secretary must take reasonable steps within available authority to protect them. In the *Redwood* litigation the court suggested some possible actions the Secretary might pursue, including attempting to acquire peripheral lands or entering into cooperative agreements limiting use of these lands.[21] And, in *Sierra Club v. Andrus*, the court suggested that the Secretary might institute common law trespass or nuisance suits, or otherwise assert recognized federal rights.[22] But the Secretary's litigation options are somewhat limited. While it is firmly established that the Secretary has the legal authority to initiate litigation to protect the parks,[23] he may not be able to rely upon the Organic Act to limit the activities of adjacent public or private landowners over whom the Department of the Interior has no jurisdiction. The Secretary also can probably invoke the federal common law as a legal basis for securing park protection only in certain narrow circumstances.[24] In most cases, therefore, the Secretary may be forced to rely upon federal or state environmental control statutes to establish a cause of action.[25] Furthermore, in the absence of congressional authorization, the Secretary has only limited ability to exercise the eminent domain power, or to purchase lands adjacent to the parks.[26]

The primary problem confronting the Secretary in meeting park protection responsibilities is the lack of clear jurisdictional authority over lands external to the parks. While the amended Organic Act imposes a duty on the Secretary to respond to external threats, courts have not yet held that the Act extends this authority beyond park boundaries or provides a cause of action against neighboring landowners whose activities threaten park resources. In the case of such federal lands as the national forests, Congress has mandated that they are to be managed under a multiple-use standard, which sanctions development activity such as timber harvesting, oil and gas exploration, mining, and road building that could prove harmful to an adjacent national park. The Secretary might argue that, with its 1978 amendments, the Organic Act reflects Congress' intent to protect the parks, and that it would, therefore, be unreasonable for the Forest Service to permit incompatible activities that jeopardize park resource values. Unless the Organic Act trumps the Forest Service's organic legislation--a view that has not yet been endorsed by any court--the Secretary will probably be forced either to rely upon the goodwill and cooperation of the Forest Service or to invoke other federal environmental control statutes, such as the National Environmental Protection Act or the Endangered Species Act, as a means of limiting threatening activities in the national forests.[27]

The Secretary's problems can be even more difficult when the threatening activity originates on nearby state or private lands. By definition these lands are not under federal control and, with the exception of such statutes as the Clean Air and Clean Water Acts, there is very little federal regulatory legislation governing the use of such lands. While it may be possible to argue that the protective mandate of the Organic Act should be treated as preemptive federal legislation limiting incompatible adjacent developments sanctioned by state law, it is doubtful that the courts would accept such an argument in view of the strong tradition of local land use control and the absence of clear congressional intent to infringe on this state prerogative. The Secretary is, therefore, left with only limited options: establish cooperative relationships with landowners and seek to persuade them to alter their plans, or rely upon local land use planning, environmental, or zoning laws to challenge incompatible activities on these adjacent lands. (A recent noteworthy example of an innovative cooperative approach to the problem of adjacent private lands is the North Fork Interlocal Agreement, signed by Glacier National Park, other area land management agencies, the county, and local landowners committing themselves to consult regularly on matters relating to the North Fork region adjacent to the park.)

Nonetheless, a credible argument can be made that the Organic Act provides the Secretary with the legal authority to promulgate regulations controlling activities on lands adjacent to the parks. Although the Secretary has never aggressively attempted to extend jurisdiction in this manner, the case law suggests that the Secretary's powers can be construed to authorize regulations directly related to the parks' welfare.[28] Several cases have sustained regulations governing activities on state or private property within the parks, and their reasoning would support regulations limiting activities on nonfederal lands beyond park boundaries.[29] While the decisions also might support regulations limiting activities on adjacent federal lands, the Secretary may be understandably reluctant to intrude upon the administrative prerogatives of other federal agencies. Moreover, Congress' cool reaction to the parks protection bill, as well as the remote possibility that the Section 1a-1 exceptions clause might be given an expansive interpretation, may further explain the Secretary's reluctance to promulgate such regulations. In view of the court rulings recognizing that the Secretary has broad discretion in deciding how to protect the parks, it is unlikely that an action to compel the exercise of such regulatory power in this fashion would be successful.

Congress clearly has the authority, however, to regulate and control developments occurring on federal, state, and private lands adjacent to the national parks, relying either upon its property power or its commerce power.[30] Occasionally Congress has protected the parks directly by limiting activities on adjacent lands in the establishing legislation for certain new parks. For example, the statute creating the Cape Cod National Seashore established minimal federal zoning requirements that local governments must meet; otherwise the Secretary is authorized to invoke eminent domain power to protect the park against nonconforming adjacent property uses.[31] In the interest of achieving desirable national environmental goals, Congress has also indirectly protected the parks, passing such federal statutes as the Clean Air Act and the Endangered Species Act to regulate environmentally harmful activities with consequences transcending ownership boundaries. Thus, if Congress can be persuaded to act on behalf of the parks, it can afford them meaningful protection from threatening adjacent activities.

IV. CONCLUSION: A BASIS FOR ACTION

Several conclusions respecting the Organic Act as an instrument of park protection can be drawn. The Act sets forth an impressive, unambiguous resource preservation mandate. It has been consistently construed by the courts as legally obligating the Secretary to protect the national parks against externally threatening activities. Unfortunately, however, the Act is ambiguous regarding the Secretary's legal authority over adjacent nonpark lands, making attainment of its resource preservation goal difficult. While the Secretary might invoke the Organic Act to challenge threatening activity or as a basis for promulgating regulations to control such activity, it is uncertain whether either of these approaches would prove successful. Ordinarily, therefore, the Secretary is left with the options of relying upon limited land acquisition and exchange authority, securing the cooperation of neighboring landowners, or invoking environmental laws other than the Organic Act as a means for protecting the parks. Additionally, in a few limited instances, the Secretary could look to an individual park's establishing statute for authority to respond to an external threats problem.

The logical question, therefore, is how might Congress revise existing park legislation to better protect the parks? At one extreme, Congress might conclude that each park is unique and devise individual responses by amending park establishing statutes to expand or clarify the Secretary's authority over specific adjacent lands or threatening activities. At the other extreme, Congress might perceive that the external threats problem is endemic to the entire National Park System and respond comprehensively by broadly extending the Secretary's authority over adjacent lands. This type of response might take the form of the proposed Parks Protection Act, which would have mandated consultation between the Interior Department and other federal agencies before threatening developments on federal lands adjacent to the parks could proceed.[32]

On a more modest scale, Congress might tinker with the Organic Act and related statutes to clarify the Secretary's responsibility and authority in dealing with external threats issues. In the interest of avoiding federal interagency conflict, Congress should provide the Secretary and other federal land management agencies with some guidance as to how park threats issues are to be resolved. Congress could accomplish this by clarifying the Section 1a-1 amendment and indicating clearly whether the Organic Act trumps the multiple-use mandate of other federal land management agencies when their activities threaten park resources. Alternatively, Congress could adopt some variation of the Parks Protection Act consultation scheme to assure that park protection is recognized as an important national goal meriting the consideration of all federal agencies. Congress also should clarify the extent of the Secretary's authority to promulgate administrative regulations governing activities on adjacent federal, state, or private lands that directly and immediately threaten substantial harm to park resources. This could probably be accomplished by amending 16 U.S.C. § 3 to provide that the Secretary can adopt regulations "for [the] use, management and protection" of the national parks. Furthermore, Congress should consider expanding the Secretary's presently limited authority to purchase adjacent lands as a means of alleviating some external threat problems. By granting additional land acquisition authority, Congress would provide the Secretary with an effective tool for dealing with particularly serious problems arising on nonfederal lands immediately adjacent to the parks.

While none of these proposals is sufficient alone to deal with the complexities of the external threats problem, each would afford the parks some additional protection that they presently lack under the Organic Act. If Congress could be persuaded to embrace any of them, then the inspirational preservation goals of the Organic Act would be brought closer to realization.

NOTES

*Professor of Law, University of Wyoming; J.D. 1972, Northwestern University; A.B. 1968, Washington University.

1. 16 U.S.C. § 1 *et seq.*

2. 16 U.S.C. § 1.

3. *See, e.g.,* Free Enterprise Canoe Renters Ass'n. v. Watt, 711 F.2d 852 (8th Cir. 1983); United States v. Brown, 552 F.2d 817 (8th Cir. 1977), *cert. denied,* 431 U.S. 949 (1977).

4. Clark v. Community for Creative Non-Violence, 104 S. Ct. 3065 (1984).

5. National Rifle Ass'n v. Potter, 628 F. Supp. 903 (D.D.C. 1985).

6. 16 U.S.C. § 1a-1.

7. Sierra Club v. Department of the Interior, 376 F. Supp. 284 (N.D. Cal. 1974), 398 F. Supp. 284 (N.D. Cal. 1975).

8. Sierra Club v. Andrus, 487 F. Supp. 443 (D.D.C. 1980).

9. National Rifle Ass'n v. Potter, 487 F. Supp. 443 (D.D.C. 1980), 628 F. Supp. 903 (D.D.C. 1985).

10. 487 F. Supp. at 449.

11. 16 U.S.C. § 1a-1 (1978). (Emphasis added.)

12. *See* Sierra Club v. Andrus, 487 F. Supp. 443, 448 (D.D.C. 1980).

13. *See* National Rifle Ass'n. v. Potter, *supra.*

14. *See* Sierra Club v. Watt, 566 F. Supp. 380 (D. Utah 1983) (rejecting an Organic Act challenge to mining in the Lake Mead National Recreation Area because Congress had specifically authorized mining in the Lake Mead Act); National Rifle Ass'n. v. Potter, *supra* (sustaining National Park Service regulations prohibiting hunting except when authorized by Congress).

15. Sierra Club v. Department of the Interior, 376 F. Supp. 90 (N.D. Cal. 1974), 398 F. Supp. 284 (N.D. Cal. 1975); Sierra Club v. Andrus, *supra.*

16. Sierra Club v. Andrus, 457 F. Supp. 443 (D.D.C. 1980).

17. Clark v. Community for Creative Non-Violence, 104 S. Ct. 3065 (1984).

18. *Id.* at 3072.

19. Sierra Club v. Department of the Interior, 424 F. Supp. 172 (N.D. Cal. 1976).

20. Sierra Club v. Department of the Interior, 398 F. Supp. 284 (N.D. Cal. 1975).

21. *Id.* at 294.

22. 487 F. Supp. at 448.

23. Cappaert v. United States, 426 U.S. 128 (1976); United States v. Arlington County, 487 F. Supp. 137 (E.D. Va. 1979).

24. *See* City of Milwaukee v. Illinois, 451 U.S. 304 (1981) (rejecting a federal common law nuisance claim because the Clean Water Act preempted the claim); United States v. Arlington County, 487 F. Supp. 137 (E.D. Va. 1979) (denying an aesthetic nuisance claim). *See generally,* Squillace, *Common Law Protection for Our National Parks,* Chapter 3, *infra.*

25. For a discussion of how federal and state laws might be used by the National Park Service to respond to external threat problems, *see* Keiter, *On Protecting the National Parks From the External Threats Dilemma,* 20 LAND & WATER L. REV. 355 (1985); Hiscock, *Protecting National Park System Buffer Zones: Existing, Proposed, and Suggested Authority,* 7 J. ENERGY L. & POL'Y 35 (1986). *See also* other chapters in this volume.

26. *See* Land & Water Conservation Fund Act of 1965, 16 U.S.C. §§ 460L-9(b), 460L-10(b).

27. *See generally,* Sax and Keiter, *Glacier National Park and Its Neighbors: A Study of Federal Interagency Relations,* 14 ECOL. L.Q. 207 (1987), reprinted *infra* as Chapter 7.

28. *See,* Free Enterprise Canoe Renters Ass'n. v. Watt, 711 F.2d 852 (8th Cir. 1983); United States v. Brown, 552 F.2d 817 (8th Cir. 1977) *cert. denied,* 431 U.S. 949 (1977). *Cf.* Comment, *Protecting National Parks from Developments Beyond Their Borders,* 132 U. PA. L. REV. 1189 (1984).

29. *Cf.* Kleppe v. New Mexico, 426 U.S. 529 (1976) (sustaining congressional legislation regulating activity on nonfederal lands to protect federal lands).

30. Kleppe v. New Mexico, 426 U.S. 520 (1976); Sax, *Helpless Giants: The National Parks and the Regulation of Private Lands,* 75 MICH. L. REV. 239 (1976).

31. 16 U.S.C. § 459b-3(b)(2).

32. *See* Keiter, *supra.*

Chapter 3

COMMON LAW PROTECTION FOR OUR NATIONAL PARKS

*Mark S. Squillace**

Despite the many laws enacted by Congress to protect our national parks, none seems wholly adequate against threats to the parks from activities that occur outside their borders. The insufficiency of statutory law, however, does not necessarily deprive the government or other interested parties of the tools they need to protect the parks; in some circumstances, the common law may provide an appropriate remedy. This chapter considers the two common law actions that are most likely to afford protection from external threats to the parks: nuisance law and the public trust doctrine.[1]

I. NUISANCE LAW[2]

Commentators usually distinguish between a private nuisance --an unreasonable interference with the use and enjoyment of land- -and a public nuisance--an unreasonable interference with rights that are common to the general public.[3] In applying nuisance law to the national parks, either analysis works well; that is, the outside activities that interfere with park purposes may be viewed either as an interference with the lands that consitute the park or as an interference with rights to federal park lands that are common to the general public.[4]

While either analysis should work, the public nuisance action is preferable, to the extent it is available, because it may increase the prospects for an injunction rather than damages.[5] Unfortunately, a private citizen who does not suffer any injury different from that of the general public may lack standing to sue on behalf of the public on a public nuisance theory.[6] Although this rule has been criticized, and can be circumvented on a statutory theory in some states, it has yet to be abrogated by an court decision.[7] Thus, while the public nuisance action remains the common law action of choice for protecting park resources, private citizens who want to bring such an action must be certain to allege some special harm to them that is not common to the general public.

A. Elements of a Nuisance Action

In order to maintain a nuisance action, one must establish an intentional and *unreasonable* interference with the use and enjoyment of public or private property rights. The interference must result in *substantial* physical harm.[8] The test for reasonableness is essentially a balancing process. The gravity of the harm is balanced against the utility of the conduct sought to be enjoined.[9] The *Restatement (Second) of Torts* describes the elements on each side of the equation as follows.[10] First, in determining the gravity of the harm, the court should consider the extent and character of the harm, the social value that the law attaches to the type of use invaded, the suitability of the particular use or enjoyment invaded to the character of the locality, and the burden to the person harmed of avoiding the harm. In assessing the utility of the conduct that is alleged to cause the nuisance, the court must assess the social value of the invading use, the suitability of the invasive conduct to the character of the locality, and the impracticability of preventing or avoiding the invasion.[11] In the context of external threats to the national parks, the parks would appear to have the upper hand under this balancing process. While the extent and character of the harm will vary according to the facts, the social value of the park lands will certainly be high, and the need for maintaining the park at that particular location indisputable. Further, it is unlikely that the government could take any reasonable action to mitigate the harm, given that most park land is managed to preserve its *natural* beauty. The social value of the invading use may be correspondingly high, but it is unlikely that the use will be immobile, or that the harm it causes cannot be mitigated. Several examples of how the nuisance doctrine might apply to national park resources in particular cases are described in greater detail below.

Although nuisance law varies by jurisdiction, the applicable law in any dispute involving interference with national park resources will likely be the federal common law. This conclusion follows from two distinct attributes of any such dispute: (1) its interjurisdictional quality and (2) the overriding federal interest in a case involving park resources.[12]

In most circumstances where the federal common law is invoked to resolve an interjurisdictional problem, the controversy involves two states. Either state might reasonably object to being made subject to the law of the other state, and it thus seems more fair to apply uniform principles of a federal common law. A dispute involving national park resources and private resources has an interjurisdictional quality similar to a dispute involving two states.[13]

Even more compelling is the argument that federal common law principles apply because of the overriding federal interest in protecting national park resources. The overriding federal interest was the basis for the Supreme Court's application of federal common law in *United States v. Little Lake Misere Land Company, Inc.*[14] There the land company had claimed mineral rights underlying a federal wildlife refuge under Louisiana state law. The Court held that where the land acquisition to which the United States was a party "is one arising from and bearing heavily upon a federal regulatory program," the federal common law provides the rules for decision.[15]

The Supreme Court's decision in *Utah Power and Light Co. v. United States*[16] further supports the application of federal common law principles to disputes over the protection of park resources. There the power company claimed to have acquired a right to use national forest lands for generating and distributing power based on the government's knowledge and acquiescence in that use. The power company further claimed that the court's determination of its right to use this public land must be based on state law. The Court disagreed:

> [T]he settled course of legislation, congressional and state, and repeated decisions of this court, have gone upon the theory that the power of Congress [to dispose of and make all needful rules and regulations respecting the lands of the United States] is exclusive . . . . True, for many purposes a state has civil and criminal jurisdiction over lands within its limits belonging to the United States, but this jurisdiction does not extend to any matter

that is not consistent with full power in the United States to protect its lands to control their use, and to prescribe the manner in which others may acquire rights in them.[17]

The application of the federal common law should not change the nuisance analysis dramatically, but it may tip the scales in favor of park protection, and it may increase substantially the prospects for obtaining injunctive relief rather than money damages. In analogous Supreme Court cases where federal common law principles were applied, the Court accorded the complaining party considerable deference. For example, in *Illinois v. City of Milwaukee*,[18] the court considered a motion by Illinois to invoke the original jurisdiction of the Supreme Court. The action was brought to abate a nuisance alleged to have been caused by sewage disposal into Lake Michigan by Milwaukee. Although the Court declined to accept jurisdiction, remanding instead to an appropriate district court, it affirmed the availability of a federal common law remedy and suggested an analysis that strongly favored the complaining party. Speaking to the merits of Illinois' claim, Justice Douglas indicated that the federal common law should protect the party seeking to maintain a high quality of life. "A State . . . may well ask that its strict standards be honored and that it not be compelled to lower itself to the more degrading standards of a neighbor."[19]

A similar conclusion was reached by the Court years earlier in *Georgia v. Tennessee Copper Co.*[20] In that case, Georgia complained that the discharges from the smelters of the defendant copper companies were fouling the air and damaging the state's forests. In entering an injunction against the companies for maintaining a public nuisance, the Court stated:

> This is a suit by a state for an injury to it in its capacity as a quasi-sovereign. In that capacity, the state has an interest independent of and behind the titles of its citizens, in all the earth and the air within its domain. It has the last word as to whether its mountains shall be stripped of her forests and its inhabitants shall breathe pure air.[21]

In discussing the "peculiarities" of a lawsuit brought by a state against the citizens of another state, the Court further found that a state has a much stronger claim for injunctive relief than would a similarly situated private party:

If the state has a case at all, it is somewhat more certainly entitled to relief than a private party might be. It is not lightly to be required to give up quasi-sovereign rights for pay; and apart from the difficulty of valuing such rights in money it may insist that an infraction of them be stopped. The states by entering the Union, did not sink to the position of private owners subject to one system of private law. This Court has not quite the same freedom to balance the harm that will be done by an injunction against that of which the plaintiff complains that it would have in deciding between two subjects of a single political power.[22]

If the National Park Service is accorded "the last word" as to whether park resources may be compromised by outside forces, and if it is assured access to an injuctive remedy where necessary to protect those resources, it will indeed have a powerful tool at its disposal.[23]

B. Application of Nuisance Law to Our National Parks

One can imagine at least three different circumstances in which external factors may interfere with the preservation of national park resources. First, a building, structure, or other development outside the park but visible from inside the park may create an aesthetic intrusion on the park resources. Second, some development near the park may cause air, water, or noise pollution harmful to the natural resources of the park. Finally, some development outside a park that is neither visible from the park nor directly threatening to any park resources may nonetheless attract so many people or so degrade the character of the park environment as to deprive park visitors of the opportunity to experience and enjoy the resources that the park has to offer.[24] Each of these potential circumstances is explored below in the context of a federal common law nuisance analysis.

1. Aesthetic Intrusions

Having established that the federal common law of nuisance is available for park protection, it remains to be shown that the scope of that law extends to aesthetic intrusions.[25] The courts have frequently shown a sensitivity toward protecting aesthetic resources. The Supreme Court, for example, has recognized that "cities may enact land use restrictions or controls to enhance the quality of life by preserving the character and desirable aesthetic features of a city."[26] As with many of the other cases involving aesthetic injuries, the *Penn Central* case concerned the legality of land use legislation. An aethetic nuisance doctrine is a logical extension of aesthetic land use law, since the general zoning and land use laws were the progeny of the common law nuisance doctrine.[27]

State court decisions have been generally supportive of the notion that aesthetic considerations alone may form the basis for a nuisance action.[28] To the extent that courts have rejected nuisance claims based on aesthetic considerations, however, those decisions appear to be based on a sense that aesthetic judgments are too subjective to form the basis for a legal doctrine.[29]

This does not seem an adequate justification for rejecting the doctrine. Rather, it merely suggests that the burden of demonstrating that the interference is an unreasonable one is a substantial burden in the context of an aesthetic nuisance claim. Most would agree that the courts should not tread on private preferences that are acceptable as a matter of differing tastes. At some point, however, an aesthetic intrusion may so interfere with the use and enjoyment of the lands or resources that are sought to be protected as to leave no doubt that a nuisance exists. Consider, for example, a proposal to locate an automobile junkyard at a point visible from a scenic vista within a national park. Few would disagree that an aesthetic intrusion of this kind should constitute a nuisance.

At least one case has raised the prospect of an aesthetic nuisance claim involving national park resources. In *United States v. County Board of Arlington County*,[30] the government alleged that the construction of high-rise office buildings that would tower over the memorial core of the Nation's Capital constituted an aesthetic nuisance.[31] The government introduced evidence that Washington had been planned from its inception as a "horizontal" city, with no building to exceed the height of the Capitol. The proposed high-rise buildings were to be located just across the Potomac River in an area originally designated as part of the capital city, and would form the backdrop for views of the Lincoln and Jefferson Memorials and other Washington historic landmarks. The government claimed that the high-rise buildings would interfere with visitors' experience and enjoyment of these historic landmarks. In rejecting the government's aesthetic nuisance claim, the court appeared also to reject the idea that aesthetic intrusions are actionable in nuisance. Unfortunately, the court relied on Virginia state law and did not consider the federal common law arguments that had been made. Further, the Virginia case cited by the court did not hold, as suggested by the court, that aesthetic considerations alone may never form the bases for a nuisance action.[32] Thus, it cannot be considered dispositive of that legal theory.

To be sure, the facts in *Arlington County* do not present a clear case of aesthetic intrusion. Reasonable persons might differ as to whether high-rise office buildings that form a backdrop to Washington vistas are unsightly. Indeed, the thousands of tourists who continue to throng to Washington, D.C., annually seem unperturbed by their now-established presence. But a balancing test that followed the principles of the *Restatement of Torts* and the federal common law nuisance doctrine might easily support a finding of a nuisance on a claim not unlike that made in *Arlington County*.[33]

2. Air, Water, and Noise Pollution

Allegations that activities outside the park are polluting and damaging resources within the park fit the classic pattern of a nuisance action. Alternatively, such pollution might be deemed a trespass as was found in *United States v. Atlantic Richfield Co.*[34] As noted previously, a pollution action on trespass grounds is the functional equivalent of a nuisance action for such pollution, and the two claims can be analyzed in the same manner.[35]

In *Atlantic Richfield*, the National Park Service and the U.S. Forest Service sought to enjoin fluoride emissions from the defendant's aluminum reduction plant that were allegedly damaging the resources of Glacier National Park and the Flathead National Forest. The court granted the injunction notwithstanding the fact that the defendant's facility was complying with applicable requirements of the Clean Air Act.

While *Atlantic Richfield* may seem to afford a useful remedy for activities that pollute park resources, the Supreme Court appears to have undermined that holding with its second decision in *Illinois v. City of Milwaukee*.[36] Addressing Illinois' claim that Milwaukee's discharges into Lake Michigan should be enjoined under federal common law nuisance, the Court found that Congress had so completely occupied the field of water pollution through the Clean Water Act that the federal common law had been preempted.

It is important to recognize that some forms of air, water, and noise pollution may not be covered by the federal pollution statutes and accordingly, some federal common law nuisance actions may not have been preempted.[37] Consider, for example, the water pollution problems caused by timber companies in the Redwood National Park cases described below in conjunction with the discussion of the public trust doctrine. The erosion caused by the timber harvesting activities involved in that case is not encompassed by any specific provision of the Clean Water Act.

An even stronger case against preemption exists where air pollution affects the national parks. For example, the visibility standards of Section 169A of the Clean Air Act apply only to Class I areas.[38] Yet many units of the national parks are not listed as Class I areas and thus receive no visibility protection under the Clean Air Act. Furthermore, many of the Act's requirements apply only to new sources or to very large point sources of pollution.[39] Minor sources adjacent to or near national parks, however, can cause serious damage to park resources. Finally, the failure of the Clean Air Act to address the acid rain phenomenon suggests another area where federal common law principles might be applied fruitfully to protect national park resources.[40]

Despite these examples of polluting activities not covered by federal laws, the availability of a federal common law remedy for air, water, and noise pollution that adversely affects the national parks remains in doubt following the Supreme Court's second *Illinois v. City of Milwaukee* decision.[41] Thus, any action on these grounds must be approached with caution.

Even where the federal common law has been preempted, a state common law remedy may be available. In *International Paper Co. v. Ouellette*,[42] the Supreme Court unanimoulsy held that a private nuisance action alleging pollution of Lake Champlain could be maintained under state nuisance law.[43] A majority of the Court, however, limited the cause of action to a claim brought under the law of the source state, that is, the state where the pollution was generated. The majority considered this limitation necessary to insure that a company would not be subject to competing (and perhaps conflicting) statutes from two different states.

The limits set by the Court's decision in International Paper may be important in situations where a pollution source is in a different state than the affected park resources; but most pollution that affects a park will probably originate in the state where the park is situated. In these circumstances, *International Paper* should impose no limits on state common law actions. Furthermore, while nuisance law will vary from state to state, it should not be assumed that state courts will be any more tolerant than federal courts of pollution that adversely affects park resources. Indeed, many states depend substantially on tourist revenues that are generated indirectly by these great scenic wonders. Thus, the states have a strong financial incentive in seeing their park resources preserved.

3. Development Outside the Parks

Take a drive through Estes Park, Colorado, just outside Rocky Mountain National Park some warm summer afternoon. Along the way you will likely be overwhelmed by merchants beckoning park visitors to experience all forms of manufactured stimuli. Traffic will be bumper-to-bumper, and the streets will be filled with people, virtually all of whom have ostensibly come to visit not Estes Park, but rather to visit Rocky Mountain National Park. Some, I suspect, never make it. To be sure, it is fairly easy to escape the crowds and find the serene pleasures of the park; but to what extent does the development in and around Estes Park detract from the visitors' experience of the national park? Is unlimited development for the tourist trade always compatible with the national park resource and national park purposes?[44] Few would suggest that private lands outside the park must be free from all development. Some development is inevitable and may in fact aid the Park Service in keeping population pressures within the park more manageable. But can development ever reach levels that make it vulnerable to an action in a nuisance--an unreasonable interference with the use, enjoyment, and resources of the park?[45]

The proof for such a claim, even under the favorable balancing test of the *Restatement of Torts* will be difficult to muster. The impact of these outside activities on the character of Rocky Mountain National Park itself cannot be measured readily. But it is not difficult to understand how the carnival atmosphere that exists in the shadow of Long's Peak may offend those who cherish the natural beauty of the park. The words of the Wisconsin Supreme Court in 1923 may yet presage a time when such a claim will be enjoined as a nuisance. Speaking in support of a city zoning ordinance alleged to have been based solely on aesthetic grounds, the court stated:

> It seems to us that aesthetic considerations are relative in their nature. With the passing of time, social standards conform to new ideals. As a race, our sensibilities are becoming more refined, and that which formerly did not offend cannot now be endured. That which the common law did not condemn as a nuisance is now frequently outlawed as such by the written law. This is not because the subject outlawed is of a different nature, but because our sensibilities have become more refined and our ideals more exacting. Nauseous smells have always come under the ban of the law, but ugly sights and discordant surroundings may be just as distressing to keener sensibilities. The rights of property should not be sacrificed to the pleasure of an ultra-aesthetic taste. But whether they should be permitted to plague the average or dominant human sensibilities well may be pondered.[46]

Future courts may well ponder whether development outside our national parks may be enjoined as a nuisance. Changing times and "keener sensibilities" may yet afford relief for our parks from the more offensive kinds of development.

II. PUBLIC TRUST DOCTRINE

Much has been written in recent years about the public trust doctrine and its application to public land resources.[47] Simply stated, the doctrine holds that certain public resources are so essential to the public weal as to be incapable of alienation. The doctrine has its roots in the Roman and English concepts of *res communes*, the notion that certain property was held by the Crown for the benefit of all the people. The doctrine was historically limited in scope to rights of access to and use of water courses. It did not apply to all public property.

The most celebrated public trust case in American jurisprudence is *Illinois Central Railroad v. Illinois.*[48] The *Illinois Central* case involved a statute enacted by the Illinois legislature conveying title to the submerged lands underlying Lake Michigan to the railroad. The land conveyed encompassed the Chicago shoreline and the submerged land one mile out from the shore.

Several years thereafter, the Illinois legislature had second thoughts about the conveyance and enacted legislation to repeal the original grant. In an action brought by the state of Illinois to have that original grant declared invalid, the Court found for the state. Title to the submerged lands was held by the state of Illinois "in trust for the people of the state that they may enjoy the navigation of the waters, carry on commerce over them, and have the liberty of fishing therein freed from the obstruction or interference of private parties."[49] Thus, the state could not divest itself of the responsibility to govern the area for the benefit of the public.[50]

While the public trust doctrine has gained wide acceptance in its application to waterways, the extension of the doctrine to public lands has had a rougher journey. Nonetheless, the analogy between waterways and national parks as public resources remains too strong to ignore. Further, the public trust doctrine seems particularly suited to protecting public land resources against encroachments by executive branch officials lacking specific legislative authority. A leading case is *Gould v. Greylock Reservation Commission.*[51]

In *Gould*, five citizens brought suit as trustees for the public to block an agreement between the Greylock Reservation Commission and a private developer to lease 4,000 acres of Mount Greylock Reservation land to the developer for development of a ski resort. The state legislature had approved construction of ski facilities and associated development on the reservation but had not specifically authorized a commercial venture of the sort arranged by the Commission. The court held the agreement with the private developer outside the scope of the Commission's authority: "[W]e find no express grant to the [Commission] of the power to permit use of public lands . . . for what seems, in part at least, a commercial venture for private profit."

Rather than striking down state legislation as in *Illinois Central*, the *Gould* case takes a more moderate approach, construing any legislative authority involving trust properties in a manner protective of public rights. But a judicial rule that favors protection of public land resources against encroachment by private interests would surely benefit the national parks.

Also instructive of the public trust doctrine's application to public lands is a series of cases involving Redwood National Park.

In *Sierra Club v. Department of the Interior*,[52] the Sierra Club challenged the Department of the Interior's failure to prevent logging operations upstream from the park from causing damage to the park's resources by soil erosion and stream siltation. Relying on the Supreme Court's opinion in *Knight v. United States Land Ass'n*,[53] the court held that the Secretary of the Interior had a trust obligation to protect the parks. This obligation was found to be supplemental to the Secretary's responsibilities under the National Park Organic Act and the Redwood National Park Act. In a second opinion, however, the court appeared to back away from the trust language contained in its first opinion. Without speaking to the trust responsibility, the court ordered the Secretary to protect the park's resources in accordance with *statutory* powers.[54] Finally, in a third opinion, the court held that despite the Secretary's failure to ameliorate the damage from the logging operations, the Secretary had attempted in good faith to meet the statutory obligation and that nothing further was required.[55] In this third opinion, the court held that "[T]he primary responsibility for the protection of the Park rests no longer upon Interior, but squarely upon Congress to decide . . . to what extent new legislation should be passed to provide additional regulatory powers or funds for protection of the Redwood National Park."[56] The trust responsibility, so prominently featured in the court's first opinion, was largely ignored by the third opinion.[57]

A final case that must be considered in the context of applying the public trust doctrine to national park lands is *Sierra Club v. Andrus*.[58] The case arose on a claim by the Sierra Club that the Secretary of the Interior had violated his statutory and trust responsibilities to assert reserved water rights alleged necessary for the protection of various public land resources, including national parks. Relying on the legislative history of the National Park Service Organic Act Amendments of 1978, the court held that the Secretary's trust obligation was indistinguishable from his statutory obligation. The court refused to impose on the Secretary any responsibility beyond that imposed by Congress, and held that the Secretary had not violated his statutory duty in failing to assert federal water rights.

While the holding in this case might at first blush seem a defeat for public trust principles, a closer look at the court's discussion of the Secretary's obligations under the National Park Service Organic Act suggests otherwise. Indeed, quoting from the Senate report

on the 1978 Amendments to the Organic Act, the court noted that
"[t]he Secretary has an *absolute duty*, which is not to be compromised . . . to take whatever action and seek whatever relief as
will safeguard the units of the National Park System."[59] The court
concluded from this duty that "in the event of a real and immediate
water supply threat to the scenic, natural, historic or biotic resource
values of the [national parks] the Secretary must take appropriate action."[60] While the Secretary's discretion to take appropriate action is broad, it is limited by the congressional mandate that the protection, management, and administration of national park resources "shall not be exercised in derogation of
the values and purposes for which these areas have been established."[61] Thus, even if *common law* notions of public trust are in-
applicable to the national parks, a congressional directive to manage
the parks consistent with public trust principles remains. Time will
tell whether the public will be able use this directive to demand
greater protection for park resources.[62]

   The extension of public trust doctrine to public lands generally and to national parks in particular has received a mixed review
in those few cases in which it has been addressed. Indeed, its application to the national parks may no longer rest on common law
principles but may be limited by the salutary language of the National Parks Organic Act. Nonetheless, the doctrine remains, at
a minimum, as a backstop against the most egregious actions by
the government; and as in *Mount Greylock*, it may yet find useful
applications where the statutory directives are ambiguous and
the actions of a public land administrator are without a clear public
benefit.

III. CONCLUSION

   Despite their infrequent use for this purpose, common law principles of nuisance may afford a substantial means for protecting
park resources, particularly where statutory law is inadequate. The
public trust doctrine may offer a further remedy against park
degradation. Although the authority to apply this doctrine to public
lands generally, and to national parks in particular, may now derive
from a statute rather than the common law, the principles that
define the doctrine remain unchanged.

The explosion of statutory environmental law over the past two decades has been accompanied by increased reliance on these statutes by persons committed protecting our natural resources. But our current laws are not adequate to protect fully the resources of our national parks. Common law principles may help to fill the gaps that now exists in our statutory law.

NOTES

*Associate Professor of Law, University of Wyoming, Laramie, WY. The author wishes to thank Molly Ross, Assistant Chief, Air Quality Division, National Park Service, for her helpful suggestions and comments.

1. Another common law principle, that of "custom," has been used by the Oregon Supreme Court to protect the public's right to use the dry sand area of Oregon's coastal lands. State *ex rel.* Thornton v. Hay, 254 Or. 584, 462 P.2d 671 (1969). In *Thornton*, the court identified seven requirements for establishment of a "custom." Usage must be ancient, without interruption, peaceable, and reasonable. The custom must be established with certainty and must be obligatory, i.e., not left to the option of each landowner. Finally, the custom must not be inconsistent with other customs or other law. While it is conceivable that such a common law doctrine might find application to one or more national parks, the test for "custom" is sufficiently narrow as to preclude its application in all but the most unusual cases.

2. This discussion of nuisance law will encompass the related concept of trespass law to the extent applicable. The distinction between the two doctrines has become "wavering and uncertain," and for the purposes of this article is not significant. *See* PROSSER & KEETON, TORTS, Section 87, at 622 (5th Ed. 1984).

3. *Id.*, Sections 86-91.

4. Comment, *Protecting National Parks From Developments Beyond Their Borders*, 132 U. PA. L. REV. 1189 (1984).

5. RESTATEMENT (SECOND) OF TORTS, Section 942 ("With increased public awareness of the importance of environmental protection the individual plantiff seeking to enjoin a nuisance created by an industrial operation that extensively pollutes the atmosphere or waterways may rely on the factor of community interest so as to tip the balance in favor of injunctive relief"). *See also*, Georgia v. Tennessee Copper Co., 206 U.S. 230 (1907), discussed in greater detail, *infra*.

6. RESTATEMENT (SECOND) OF TORTS, Section 821C (1979).

7. PROSSER & KEETON, TORTS, § 90, n. 41 (5th ed. 1984).

8. It may also be necessary to show that the interference was intentional rather than accidental, or that it was unintentional but otherwise actionable, such as with abnormally dangerous activities for which a person is strictly liable, *Id.*, Section 821B. This requirement should pose no problem in an action to protect park resources. Virtually any activity from outside a park that is likely to threaten park resources will involve intentional development activity of some kind.

9. The RESTATEMENT discusses the balancing process in the context of private nuisance actions, *Id.*, Sections 827-831. It suggests that a public nuisance may be found where one of three circumstances is met: (a) the conduct involves a significant interference with the public health, the public safety, the public peace, the public comfort, or the public convenience; (b) the conduct is proscribed by statute, ordinance, or administrative regulation; or (c) the conduct is of a continuing nature or has produced a permanent or long-lasting effect, and as the actor knows or has reason to know, has a significant effect on the public right, *Id.*, Section 821B. With the possible exception of subsection (b), which should, presumably, be otherwise actionable, it seems unlikely that a court would find that a nuisance exists without some sort of balancing of the interests involved. Perhaps this is implied by the reference in the RESTATEMENT to the *significance* of the interference. In any event, the RESTATEMENT appears to recognize that some form of balancing may be necessary even for public nuisance actions, *see*, discussion, Section 821B.

10. Case law supports the use of the RESTATEMENT OF TORTS in determining the scope of the federal common law of nuisance. *See, e.g.*, National Sea Clammers Ass'n.

v. City of New York, 616 F.2d 1222, 1234 (3d Cir. 1980), *rev'd on other grounds*, Middlesex County Sewerage Authority v. National Sea Clammers Ass'n. 453 U.S. 1 (1981).

11. RESTATEMENT (SECOND) OF TORTS, Sections 82*i*, 828 (1979).

12. *See* Illinois v. City of Milwaukee, 406 U.S. 91, 105, n. 6 (1972), wherein the Court found that a federal common law remedy should be fashioned "where there is an overriding federal interest in the need for a uniform rule of decision or where the controversy touches basic issues of federalism."

13. The extent to which Congress has accorded the national parks jurisdiction independent of that of the states may, however, vary depending on the park. *See Jurisdiction Over Federal Areas Within the United States: Report of the Interdepartmental Committee for the Study of Jurisdiction over Federal Areas Within the United States* in PART II: THE TEST OF THE LAW OF LEGISLATIVE JURISDICTION, U.S. G.P.O., (June 1957). For this reason alone, federal common law principles should probably apply.

14. United States v. Little Lake Misere Land Company, Inc., 412 U.S. 580 (1973).

15. *Id.* at 592-94. *See also* Clearfield Trust Co. v. United States, 318 U.S. 363 (1943).

16. Utah Power and Light Co. v. United States, 243 U.S. 389 (1916).

17. *Id.* at 404.

18. Illinois v. City of Milwaukee, *supra.*

19. Nine years after this decision, the case returned to the Supreme Court on a claim that the federal common law remedy had been preempted by the Clean Water Act. The Court held that Congress had so completely occupied the field of water pollution law under the Clean Water Act that the federal common law had been preempted. The Court nonetheless remanded the case to the lower court to determine whether state common law might apply. Illinois v. City of Milwaukee, 451 U.S. 304 (1981). On remand, the Court of Appeals for the Seventh Circuit held that an interstate dispute over contamination of interstate waters "is a controversy of federal dimensions, implicating conflicting rights of states and inappropriate for state law resolution." Illinois v. City of Milwaukee, 731 F.2d. 403 (7th Cir. 1984), *cert. denied*, 469 U.S. 1196 (1985). Despite the outcome in this case, its impact on a controversy concerning national park resources should be limited. Congress has not directly addressed the question of external threats to the parks and no one can reasonably claim that the field has been preempted, except perhaps with respect to certain claims involving air and water pollution of park resources.

20. Georgia v. Tennessee Copper Co., 206 U.S. 230 (1907).

21. *Id.* at 237.

22. *Id.* at 238.

23. The cases are split as to whether private litigants may invoke the federal common law of nuisance. In support of private party standing *see* National Sea Clammers Ass'n v. City of New York, *supra* 616 F.2d at 1234 ("In order to give full effect to the federal common law of nuisance recognized in *Illinois*, private parties should be permitted and indeed, encouraged to participate in the abatement of such nuisances."); Byram River v. Village of Port Chester, 394 F. Supp. 618 (S.D.N.Y 1975). Opposing private litigant standing are Township of Long Beach v. City of New York, 445 F. Supp. 1203 (D.N.J. 1978); Parsell v. Shell Oil Co., 421 F. Supp. 1275, 1281 (D. Conn. 1976), *aff'd*, 573 F.2d 1289 (1st Cir. 1977); Committee for Jones Fall Sewage System v. Train, 375 F. Supp. 1148, 1153-54 (D. Md. 1974), *aff'd on other grounds*, 539 F.2d 1006 (4th Cir. 1976).

24. As Professor Sax argues: "Crowds diminish the opportunity for visitors to set their own pace. It may be said that millions of people want to visit these places, and that no one should be denied the opportunity. True enough. Yet it is impossible to provide unlimited visitation and the essential qualities of an unconventional non-urban experience simultaneously." SAX, MOUNTAINS WITHOUT HANDRAILS 82 (1980). *See also*, Sax,

America's National Parks: Their Principles, Purposes, and Prospects, NATURAL HISTORY (October, 1976).

25. At least one case states flatly that the federal common law is limited to interstate pollution of air and water resources. Reserve Mining Co. v. EPA, 514 F.2d 492, 520 (8th Cir. 1975). This aspect of the court's decision, however, turned on the lack of any interstate dispute over alleged air and water pollution caused by the defendant company. It did not arise in the context of an aesthetic nuisance claim and would not control the outcome of any possible future action brought on this ground.

26. Penn Central Transportation Co. v. City of New York, 438 U.S. 104, 129 (1978).

27. *See* Village of Euclid v. Ambler Realty, 272 U.S. 365, 387-88 (1926); *See also*, Note, *Aesthetic Nuisance: An Emerging Cause of Action*, 45 N.Y.U. L. REV. 1075, 1082. (1970).

28. Cases supporting an aesthetic nuisance doctrine include: Hay v. Stevens, 271 Or. 16, 530 P.2d 37 (1975) (hogwire fence between private property and beach enjoined as an aesthetic nuisance); Obrecht v. National Gypsum Co., 361 Mich. 399, 105 N.W.2d 143 (1960) (gypsum loading dock located in a scenic summer cottage area enjoined as a nuisance); Martin v. Williams, 141 W.Va. 595, 93 S.E.2d 835 (1956) (operation of a used car lot enjoined as a nuisance because the location and manner of operation were incompatible with residential character of area); Yeager v. Taylor, 306 Pa. 530, 160 A. 108 (1932) (construction of parking ramp restricted on nuisance theory as necessary to hide its "unsightly appearance").

29. *See* United States v. County Board of Arlington County, 487 F. Supp. 137 (E.D. Va. 1979); Livingston v. Davis, 243 Iowa 21, 50 N.W.2d 592 (1951). A number of other cases refuse to find a nuisance based on aesthetic considerations, but few cases hold that such concerns may *never* constitute a nuisance. *See* 58 AM. JUR. 2D, *Nuisances*, Section 44 and cases cited therein.

30. United States v. County Board of Arlington County, 487 F. Supp. 137 (E.D. Va. 1979).

31. The memorial grounds and many other park resources in Washington, D.C. are managed by the National Park Service in the Department of the Interior.

32. *See* City of Newport News v. Hertzler, 210 Va. 587, 221 S.E.2d 146 (1976).

33. A problem similar to that in *Arlington County* arose several years earlier at Gettysburg National Military Park in Gettysburg, Pennsylvania. A private developer proposed to build a tower that would overlook the battlefield on private land. The National Park Service, which manages the battlefield, was strongly opposed to the tower but decided that it had no legal authority to prevent the construction. It eventually decided not to oppose the tower in exchange for an agreement by the developer that it would move the tower to a less intrusive site. Pennsylvania filed suit seeking to block construction of the tower under a state constitutional provision that purported to give the citizens of Pennsylvania a right "to the preservation of the natural, scenic, historic and aesthetic values of the environment," PA. CONST., Art 1, § 27. The plurality opinion of the court failed to reach the merits of Pennsylvania's claim, holding instead that the constitutional provision was not self-executing, Commonwealth of Pennsylvania v. National Gettysburg Battlefield Tower, Inc., 311 A.2d 588 (Pa. 1973). *See also*, Roe, *The Second Battle of Gettysburg: Conflict of Public and Private Interests in Land Use Policies*, 2 ENV. AFFAIRS 16 (1972).

34. United States v. Atlantic Richfield Co., 478 F. Supp. 1215 (D. Mont. 1979).

35. Under either theory, the analysis will be similar, and federal common law principles applicable. *See, e.g.*, Renken v. Harvey Aluminum Co., 226 F. Supp. 169 (D.Or. 1963), wherein the court treated allegations almost identical to those in the *Richfield* case as making out claims in either nuisance or trespass. *See also* PROSSER & KEETON, TORTS, Section 87 (5th Ed. 1984).

36. Illinois v. City of Milwaukee, 451 U.S. 304 (1981).

37. In Middlesex County Sewerage Authority v. National Sea Clammers Ass'n, 453 U.S. 1 (1981), the Court stated that "the federal common law of nuisance in the area of water pollution is *entirely* preempted by the more comprehensive scope of the Federal Water Pollution Control Act," *Id.* at 22. (Emphasis added.) This statement appears not to set precedent since the *Sea Clammers* case involved ocean discharges that are covered directly and specifically by the Clean Water Act and the Marine Protection, Research, and Sanctuaries Act. A substantial argument can yet be made against preemption where the applicable pollution statute does not address the pollution problem encountered. *See* Bleiweiss, *Environmental Regulation and the Federal Common Law of Nuisance: A Proposed Standard of Preemption,* 7 HARV. ENVTL. L. REV. 41, 55-58 (1983). This is particularly so in the context of national park protection, to which Congress has spoken as follows: "[T]he protection, management, and administration of these [National Park System] areas shall be conducted in light of the public value and integrity of the National Park System purposes for which these various areas have been established, *except as may have been directly and specifically provided by Congress,*" 16 U.S.C. § 1a-1. (Emphasis added.) *See also* H.R. REP. NO. 95-581, 95th Cong., 2d Sess. at 21 (1978).

38. 42 U.S.C. § 7491. Class I areas are those areas designated by Congress or the EPA for greatest protection from air degradation.

39. *See, e.g.,* §§ 111, 165(b)(2), 172(a); 42 U.S.C. §§ 7411, 7475(a), 7491(b)(2), 7502(a).

40. *See* Bleiweiss, *supra* at 66-8.

41. *See also*, City of Burbank v. Lockheed Air Terminal, Inc., 411 U.S. 624 (1973) wherein the Court held that state and local controls over airplane noise were preempted by federal statutes vesting responsibility over such problems in the Federal Aviation Administration and the Environmental Protection Agency.

42. International Paper Co. v. Ouellette, ___U.S.___,107 S.Ct. 805 (1987).

43. In so holding, the Court took notice of the fact that in enacting the Clean Water Act Congress had specifically preserved state statutory and common law, at least to the extent that such laws were not preempted by any provisions of federal law, *Id.* at 812. Such "savings clause" provisions are commonplace in environmental legislation.

44. Professor Sax has explored these questions in MOUNTAINS WITHOUT HANDRAILS, *supra,* n. 16. He makes a compelling case against activities and development that interfere with a contemplative recreational experience.

45. Any ad hoc effort to control development through a nuisance action would, no doubt, generate considerable controversy. Thus, it would seem preferable to provide the Park Service with explicit authority to control development through legislation or administrative regulation. Such an approach would allow Congress or the National Park Service to adopt reasonable standards for protecting the parks from external threats before such threats materialize. It might further deter prospective developers from taking action that would run afoul of those standards. This argument assumes that no such authority is forthcoming.

46. State *ex rel.* Carter v. Harper, 196 N.W. 451, 455 (Wisc. 1923).

47. Sax, *The Public Trust Doctrine in Natural Resources Law: Effective Judicial Intervention,* 68 MICH. L. REV. 471 (1970); Sax, *Liberating the Public Trust from Its Historical Shackles,* 14 U.C. DAVIS L. REV. 185 (1980); Stevens, *The Public Trust: A Sovereign's Ancient Prerogative Becomes the People's Environmental Right,* 14 U.C. DAVIS L. REV. 195 (1980); Wilkinson, *The Public Trust Doctrine in Public Land Law,* 14 U.C. DAVIS L. REV. 269 (1980); Jawetz, *The Public Trust Totem in Public Land Law--Ineffective and Undesirable Judicial Intervention,* 10 ECOLOGY L. Q. 455 (1982).

48. Illinois Central Railroad v. Illinois, 146 U.S. 387, 460 (1982).

49. *Id.* at 452.

50. *See also*, Prieve v. Wisconsin State Land and Improvement Co., 93 Wisc. 34, 67 N.W. 918 (1896), wherein the Wisconsin Supreme Court using reasoning similar to that found in *Illinois Central* struck down a legislative disposition of submerged lands.

51. Gould v. Greylock Reservation Commission, 350 Mass. 410, 215 N.E.2d 114 (1966).

52. Sierra Club v. Department of the Interior, 376 F. Supp. 90 (N.D. Cal. 1974).

53. Knight v. United States Land Ass'n, 142 U.S. 161 (1891).

54. Sierra Club v. Department of the Interior, 398 F. Supp. 284 (N.D. Cal. 1975).

55. Sierra Club v. Department of the Interior, 424 F. Supp. 172 (N.D. Cal. 1976).

56. Id.

57. Perhaps the Sierra Club and/or the Department of the Interior should have proceeded under a nuisance theory. While the timber companies might have argued that the federal common law was preempted by the Clean Water Act, citing Illinois v. City of Milwaukee II, the plaintiffs might still have succeeded under a state law theory. Further, the Clean Water Act does not treat timber harvesting as a point source under its National Point Discharge (NPDES) program and thus, as is argued earlier in the test, there is a strong argument that there has been no preemption whatsoever. See 40 C.F.R. 400-469 (1985).

58. Sierra Club v. Andrus, 487 F. Supp. 443 (D.D.C. 1980).

59. Id. at 448. (Emphasis added.)

60. Id.

61. Sierra Club v. Andrus, supra at 448. See also 16 U.S.C. § 1a-1.

62. The court also recognized that the Federal Land Policy and Management Act imposed on the Secretary a trust-like responsibilty to protect all public domain lands. Id. at 448. This responsibility may be particularly useful in protecting the resources on public lands surrounding national parks and in protecting lands being considered for park status.

Chapter 4

NEPA AND THE PARKS: USE IT OR LOSE IT

*J. William Futrell**

I. INTRODUCTION

The National Environmental Policy Act[1] (NEPA) has been described as the Magna Carta of environmental law and as legislation of constitutional dimensions. It is ironic that NEPA's importance flows out of the mundane requirements of Section 102, which calls for reforms in administrative procedure, rather than the sonorous goals of Section 101, which declare a national policy on the environment. The courts have chosen to make the procedural requirements of NEPA the workhorse of environmental litigation. Park defenders should carry this emphasis one step further by putting renewed efforts into the NEPA process to influence better agency decision making without losing sight of NEPA's powerful courtroom tools.

A series of dramatic court cases in the early 1970s established the power of local citizen groups and individual environmentalists in using NEPA to stop harmful projects. This chapter is a brief introduction to how NEPA affects the national parks. Other sources can provide a more complete discussion of the history and development of NEPA case law.[2] The early cases opened new doors to citizen participation in planning for a better environment. But while these legal victories ensure that the door is open, they do not guarantee a good result unless citizens use their NEPA opportunities.

This chapter outlines the points of the NEPA process that should be of special interest to park defenders. Unless they use their rights, however, they will lose the benefits of NEPA and be barred from being fully effective at a later date. Judicial doctrines such as laches, undue delay on the part of the plaintiff in bringing the action, may bar later court action no matter how meritorious the claim.

The legal victory that caused the greatest shock to government officials who wanted to treat NEPA as a paper tiger was *Wilderness Society v. Hickel*,[3] in which the district court enjoined the TransAlaska Pipeline project because of an inadequate environmental impact statement (EIS). The decision underscored the fact that courts would halt even important government projects unless there had been full compliance with NEPA.

Almost all of the more than two thousand lawsuits filed under NEPA have arisen out of Section 102's requirement that the lead agency file an environmental impact statement for "each federal action significantly affecting the human environment." The EIS must include a detailed description of the proposed action, a discussion of its direct and indirect effects, a description of the cumulative and long-term effects, alternatives to the proposed action (including a no-action alternative), and an identification of any irreversible commitment of resources that might result.

Because one of the most important requirements for comprehensive land use planning is the gathering of an adequate data base, NEPA makes a giant contribution to planning law. The Act requires the gathering of a data base as a prerequisite to the planning of any major federal action. This can be an important opportunity to ensure that the science and resources management programs of the National Park Service receive full consideration. NEPA activities should reinforce the ongoing activities needed in baseline monitoring and data collection.

Furthermore, the Act requires that this information be published in an official document that receives wide distribution to all interested parties, to whose comments the lead agency must respond. This works to build a cadre of concerned scientists and professionals actively concerned about the parks. The promise of the law will not be fulfilled, however, unless park defenders use the NEPA process.

Critics of the National Park Service in environmental organizations express concern that agency officials may cut corners. Many EISs have been faulted for inadequate data and failure to consider alternatives. Park defenders approach a draft EIS warily.

Citizens participating in the NEPA process need to verify and insist that the data be reliable and that the agency has considered alternatives and assessed the impacts.

Land use planning in the United States is a democratic process that requires action by citizens. Often in the past citizens were at a disadvantage because they lacked basic information, which was closely held by the authorities bent on developmnt, and because they lacked access to networks of allies who shared their values. By reviewing the EIS documents they get access to the information and by participation in the scoping and commenting processes they become part of the network. These processes are discussed in detail later in this chapter.

NEPA has been the single most useful development in opening up federal agency decision making to local environmental groups which do not have the budgets or staff of the national groups based in Washington to investigate projects. Local groups find environmental impact statements particularly useful because they include key information about projects in one easily accessible document. The EIS is furthermore a trustworthy document because of the legal requirement to make full disclosure about the project. An agency that withholds or falsifies information risks an injunction halting the project. NEPA documents can serve as the eyes and ears of park allies. The political reality, though, is that all too many EISs--and environmental assessments--do not live up to the promise of NEPA. Citizen groups catch a number of the worst of these, with the result that the proposed agency action is halted by an environmental lawsuit.

As important as NEPA is to environmental litigation, environmentalists should look first to the significant advantages the NEPA process gives them in being more effective lobbyists within the Park Service. By participating early in the NEPA process, they get a seat at the table and can become full participants in the planning process. More often than not they will find themselves on the side of Park Service professionals resisting political pressure to relax the law. Public lands decisions are laced with influence and political pressure to relax the law. The files of the National Parks and Conservation Association show many instances in which the NEPA process has been swayed by political pressure and in which the countervailing pressure of park defenders is needed if the parks are to be well managed. It should be emphasized that this participation does not allow them to substitute their judgment for that of the decision maker--the Secretary of the Interior--but it does allow them to get their evidence on record. Citizen participation is ensured both by a long string of court decisions and by the 1978 Council on Environmental Quality regulations.[4]

II. THE NEPA PROCESS

In 1978 the Council on Environmental Quality (CEQ) issued final regulations for implementation of the National Environmental Policy Act. These rules are binding on all federal agencies and establish a set of uniform and streamlined procedures for the NEPA process. The rules codify the court victories of the 1970s and outline the procedural rules for the NEPA process. These have been restated by the National Park Service in its own informal agency guidelines known as *NEPA Compliance Guidelines.* These are referred to by Park Service employees as NPS-12.[5] These guidelines have never been published in the *Federal Register* or the *Code of Federal Regulations* and do not have the force of law. Citizens who wish to read a copy must contact local or regional offices of the National Park Service or seek the assistance of one of the national environmental organizations. It would make things easier for citizens of all persuasions--environmentalists, the recreation and tourism industry, and local governments--if the Park Service would publish these guidelines in the *Federal Register* so they would be available to all.

An important threshold question is whether NEPA applies at all to a proposed action. In many cases, agency officials would like to avoid compliance with NEPA because the full-blown EIS process is expensive and time consuming. In the appropriate circumstances they can comply with the law by filing a shortened, simplified environmental review, an environmental assessment (EA), or claim an exemption from NEPA because of a categorical exclusion (CX).

The threshold of agency action that requires the preparation of an EIS is low; the crucial test is whether the federal action significantly affects the environment. Hundreds of lawsuits by conservation organizations have given substance to the statutory framework, and courts have ordered agencies to file EISs on such diverse undertakings as barge canals, construction of a federal jail in an urban area, the granting of offshore oil leases to private parties, and the filing of railroad tariffs. While the federal activity in each case might appear to be minimal, as in the case of issuing a permit, the test has been whether the consequences that flow from the activity have a significant effect on the environment. If so, then an impact statement must be prepared.

Two early cases against the National Park Service emphasized the courts' insistence that even local efforts could so significantly affect the environment as to require the filing of an EIS.[6] In *Biderman v. Morton*, the court prohibited the Park Service from granting permits for motor vehicles within the Fire Island National Seashore until it filed a master plan for the park and an accompanying EIS. In *Berksen v. Morton*, the court enjoined local construction in the C&O Canal National Historical Park until the Park Service had complied with NEPA.

Fewer than a dozen of the more than two thousand NEPA lawsuits have been aimed at the National Park Service. The rich body of case law on NEPA has been made in suits against other agencies, primarily the Army Corps of Engineers, the Federal Highway Administration, and the Forest Service. Nonetheless, the holdings of these cases govern the Department of the Interior and are available as precedents to park defenders.

Currently park defenders are using NEPA to protect the national parks of Alaska from the ravages of placer mining.[7] In *Northern Alaska Environmental Center v. Hodel*, the plaintiffs secured an injunction halting mining in all the national parks of Alaska until the Park Service had complied with NEPA. Significantly, no environmental analyses had been undertaken and the Park Service had sought to avoid compliance with NEPA on the ground that the mining activities did not significantly affect the environment. The Park Service has halted these mining operations while it prepares an environmental analysis on the cumulative impact these activities have on the parks.

The *Northern Alaska Environmental Center* case illustrates the potential wide-ranging impact of a NEPA injunction. One lawsuit and one district judge's decision has resulted in a sweeping review of the way mining operations are carried on in hundreds of thousands of acres of Alaskan parklands. On appeal by the mining companies, the court held that the NEPA claim was mooted by the Park Service's voluntary compliance with the district court order.[8]

NEPA will always apply to major actions that significantly affect the human environment. The Park Service guidelines state that the following types of Park Service proposals will normally require the preparation of an EIS:

1. Wild and Scenic River proposals;

2. National Trail proposals;

3. Wilderness proposals;

4. General Management Plans for major National Park System units;

5. Grants, including multi-year grants, whose size and/or scope will result in major natural or physical changes, including interrelated social and economic changes and residential and land use changes within the project area or its immediate environs.

6. Grants which foreclose other beneficial uses of mineral, agricultural, timber, water, energy or transportation resources important to National or State welfare.[9]

The Park Service regulations require that if for any of these proposals it is initially decided not to prepare an EIS, an environmental assessment will be prepared and made available for public review.

The NEPA guidelines establish the classification of categorical exclusions to make it easier to decide just which actions are so minor in impact as to not require NEPA consideration. The categorical exclusion classification established in the CEQ regulations cuts delay by creating an entire category of agency actions that will not be considered for either environmental assessment or an environmental impact statement. The Park Service guidelines on categorical exclusions include actions related to activities such as general administration; plans, studies, and reports; and development that does not affect the environment. Examples of these three categories include land acquisition and boundary surveys, renewal of permits, interpretative plans, and routine maintenance and repair. It should be emphasized that the decision not to prepare an EIS or EA is based on the facts of each proposal; if the project does have a significant effect on the environment, the NEPA process should be triggered.

The actual determination as to whether an action is appropriate for a categorical exclusion is an informal decision that is not published. NEPA watchers worry about the potential abuse of categorical exclusions whose wholesale application could result in an end run around the NEPA process. Here again is another instance where local monitoring of the NEPA process by friends of the parks is necessary. The categorical exclusion approach is a reasonable way to streamline the bureaucratic process. The answer to abuse of this practice is better oversight. Often it is a decision that is not monitored by higher authorities, nor is it one to which the public is privy. If a categorical exclusion does not apply, however, an environmental assessment must be prepared.

The environmental assessment ends in either a finding of no significant impact (FONSI) or a decision to prepare an EIS. If the decision is made to prepare an EIS, the Park Service publishes a Notice of Intent in the *Federal Register*. Agencies vary sharply in their handling of FONSIs; some publish a notice in the *Federal Register*, while others restrict their handling of the FONSI to publication in the local newspaper. In many agencies, there is little opportunity for participation in the environmental assessment process, and again public awareness of what is happening is minimal. The Alaska mining case is a sobering warning that important actions may proceed without NEPA compliance. It is a mistake to assume that silence means all is well on the NEPA front. NEPA can be eroded through not-so-benign neglect. Citizen groups need to work with the National Park Service to find ways to open up the environmental assessment process.

After a decision to prepare an EIS is made, however, the process generally involves the public and other agencies in a meaningful manner. Following the filing of the notice to prepare an EIS, the scoping process begins. The scoping process usually involves a meeting of affected federal, state, and local agencies, and interested members of the public to identify key issues that will receive in-depth treatment in the EIS. Park defenders should strive to be present at all scoping sessions and following public meetings. Many agencies hold scoping meetings in the evening and use mailing lists to generate interest. Citizens interested in park planning decisions, therefore, should be on the park's mailing list.

The importance of the scoping process can not be overestimated. This is where park defenders can make significant contributions. They should prepare for the meeting and enter the process armed with data and a proactive attitude that seeks to help the Park Service reach the best decision for the parks.

The Park Service regulations state:

> Scoping is an early and open process to determine the range of actions, alternatives and impacts to be addressed in an EIS. Scoping for all NPS proposals should also include a determination of permits and other entitlements which must be obtained from Federal, State, or local sources prior to implementation of the NPS proposal. Scoping is a process and not simply a single event or meeting, although scoping meetings are sometimes held. Public participation may provide input to the scoping process, but is not the only element of it. The scoping process sifts all input for critical environmental/decision significance, decides upon the issues and alternatives to be documented in the EIS and provides the reasons for dropping lesser environmental issues and alternatives from further consideration.[10]

The scoping process is open to the public and state and local governments, as well as to affected federal agencies. The openness of the scoping process gives rise to important new opportunities for better and more efficient NEPA analyses and simultaneously places new responsibilities on public and agency participants alike to present their concerns early. Scoping helps ensure that real problems are identified early and properly studied, that issues that are of no concern do not consume time and effort, and that the delays occasioned by redoing an inadequate draft are avoided. A comment raised for the first time after the draft EIS is finished will not be accorded the same serious consideration it would have merited if the issue had been raised during scoping. Thus park defenders have a responsibility to come forward early with known issues.

The general consensus among federal officials is that the scoping process is useful. It identifies issues and interested parties at the outset. Early in the development of the project, federal planners can see the depth of community feeling and learn the chief areas of concern. This can serve as an opportunity for the Park Service to identify needed changes and is a major opportunity for citizens to shape the project. When an agency has not fully committed its resources, its learning capacity and responsiveness to public concern is greater. This early involvement of those most concerned with a project avoids the situation in which the community is presented with the shock of an advanced agency plan. Such a shock is more likely to lead to litigation and wasted time and effort.

The work product of the scoping process, the draft EIS, seeks to provide an accessible information resource for users. Most statements have an executive summary, a list of the preparers (setting forth their professional disciplines and qualifications), and a list of all required federal permits and licenses. The main body of information should contain a scientifically accurate description of the environment, detailed information on what the government plans to do, and how the agency thinks the environment will be affected. The reader should be able to determine the environmental effects and merits of the project because of the full disclosure in the EIS. Interested members of the public should ask whether the EIS is adequate: Are the environmental qualities and values of the resource identified and assessed? Is there a full discussion of the planned action and how it will affect the parks? Has the most protective alternative been addressed? Does the agency acknowledge gaps in the information?

Citizen groups should cooperate with one another and with professional environmentalists in responding to the EIS. The EIS is a complex document and the time for commenting is short. Organizations such as the National Parks and Conservation Association and the Sierra Club can help coordinate and improve responses. After circulation of the draft EIS to other officials and interested members of the public, comments and agency responses are collated and included as part of the final EIS, prepared and filed by the responsible federal agency. The EPA's Office of Federal Activities has the duty (under Section 309 of the Clean Air Act) to file comments on each EIS, giving two grades: one on the environmental merits of the project and another on the quality of the disclosure in the EIS document.[11] The lead agency has the duty to respond to those who comment and explain its decision.

Concerned citizens should never neglect the commenting process. The Park Service takes comments very seriously. It reprints each substantive comment in the final EIS and publishes agency replies to criticisms and explanations of questions. A study of other groups' comments can alert citizens to problems they may have missed. This is another place for park defenders to advance their arguments and present their best evidence.

These comments can be an important source of support for Park Service plans as well as an opportunity for criticism. The July 1985 final EIS for the Lake Mead National Recreation Area contained 303 pages of analysis and 110 pages of comment. Some of the comments were simple statements of opposition by mining companies to the plan and others were uncomplicated appeals by individual citizens for ecological protection. But most important were the sophisticated comments from the National Parks and Conservation Association on the need to balance tourism and recreational needs with ecological protection, and the Sierra Club Legal Defense Fund's comments calling for a more painstaking wilderness management evaluation.[12]

The National Park Service in turn is required to comment on proposed actions by other federal agencies that may affect the parks. This is an opportunity for Park Service staff to take the lead in marshaling arguments and evidence against unwise development that may spill over onto parkland.

III. COMMENTING ON OTHER AGENCY PROPOSALS

Some of the most important environmental threats to the parks arise not from Park Service actions but as a consequence of other federal agencies' plans for projects in areas neighboring the parks. The Park Service has a duty to comment on proposals by other agencies that may have an impact on parks. For instance, Park Service comments would be called for on an EIS written by the Corps of Engineers on a proposed dam upstream from a park boundary, or on an EIS written by the Federal Highway Administration on proposed highway changes near a park, or by the Federal Aviation Administration on an airport in or near a park.

NEPA can play a large role in addressing what many believe is the greatest threat to park integrity in the coming decades, the spillover of impacts from incompatible uses on neighboring lands. For example, the designation of an area as a national park often acts as a magnet that attracts a rash of unsightly developments on the surrounding lands. The entrances to the Great Smoky Mountain and Rocky Mountain National Parks exhibit carnival-type developments, and the suburban sprawl of second homes threatens the integrity of park resources. In other places, inconsistent actions by other federal agencies, such as EPA's failure to control upriver water pollution or the advance of federal funds to assist construction of a high-rise structure overlooking a historic monument, may be the threat. Regional planning tools are essential to prevent such unfortunate occurrences.

NEPA can be an important regional planning tool for both Park Service employees and their citizen allies if they use the commenting process effectively. Park Service and EPA comments are frequently sources for a good summary of the environmental protection concerns on the proposed project. This is not always the case, however, because political pressures or bureaucratic considerations may lead to Park Service staff concerns being softened or muted. In such instances, private citizens should be ready to assume the role of lobbyists for the Park Service. They should be in touch with the Park Service commentators and urge them to make their comments as strong as possible. If the other federal agency ignores the Park Service's valid comments, these may be used as evidence of arbitrary and capricious behavior by the government.

NEPA works as a coordinating device to get federal and state agencies to work together. While the environmental field overall is often characterized by regulatory gridlock, NEPA has acted as a consensus-building tool to ease these impasses.

The Record of Decision

One of the consistent concerns of the 1970s was the variance between the procedural requirements of NEPA to make full disclosure and the substantive requirements under Section 101 to protect the environment.[13] The NEPA regulations attempt to bridge this gap by requiring the filing of a Record of Decision, which is a concise public statement explaining how the environmental considerations were factored into the decision-making process. The Record of Decision (ROD) normally is completed no earlier than thirty days after the filing of the final EIS. In the ROD, the decision maker must identify the alternatives considered and list both the environmentally preferred alternative and the agency's preferred alternative. The agency must identify and discuss all relevant factors, including any essential considerations of national policy that were balanced by the agency in making its decision. This provision could lead a reviewing court, in order to assure that the actual balance struck was not arbitrary and capricious, to inquire into the agency's substantive decision not to adopt that choice. If litigation ensues, the lawyer's attack will focus on defects in the NEPA process and on whether evidence in the EIS supports the government's Record of Decision.

IV. NPS PLANNING AND NEPA

The passage of NEPA in 1970 presented the NPS with a major challenge. The Park Service was immediately faced with the requirement of bringing the planning process for the then slightly less than three hundred units of the National Park System into compliance with the Act. NEPA requires an EIS to accompany a federal action. For the Park Service, the "action" that most often triggers an EIS is the adoption of a General Management Plan (GMP). The appropriate NEPA document, EIS or EA, accompanies the General Management Plan or Resource Management Plan to the official who makes the final approval in the Record of Decision. Every effort is made to fully integrate the ongoing Park Service planning effort and NEPA. As of 1986, General Management Plans are in effect for 280 of the 337 units. A current major activity in 1987 is the preparation of GMPs for the fourteen park units in Alaska. In addition, the Park Service has the duty to prepare NEPA documents on proposed additions to the National Trails System and the Wild and Scenic Rivers System.

The table in Appendix A lists draft EISs (DEIS) and final EISs (FEIS) by year of publication. It dramatically illustrates the bulge in the pipeline from 1973 to 1975 caused by the Park Service's initial push to comply with NEPA. Since then the pace of activity has significantly lessened. Currently only five draft EISs are out for comment. The list was obtained from the Office of the Secretary of the Interior and is the first time a list of National Park Service EISs has been published.

No similar lists exist for environmental assessments or for findings of no significant impact. In fact, National Park Service officials are not even sure of the total number of environmental assessments because the Washington office does not maintain records on them. Park superintendents can sign off on environmental assessments. If the environmental assessment ends in a finding of no significant impact, the report must be forwarded to the Regional Superintendent, who has the final authority to sign off on FONSIs. Their decisions are not forwarded to Washington headquarters either for review or recordkeeping.

The environmental compliance office of the National Park Service in Washington estimates that in 1987 approximately 150 environmental assessments will be written on actions in the National Park Service and another 500 will be written on Park Service grants (primarily relating to the Land and Water Conservation Fund programs). Headquarters officials in Washington express confidence in the integrity of the regional handling of environmental assessments. Their confidence would be more reassuring, however, if they had records and a means of monitoring local activity. The absence of reports on local and regional EA and FONSI actions means that staff of national environmental organizations cannot assist in this monitoring effort. The Park Service should establish a central registry and monitoring point for EA activity so that it will have the facts and the basis to assure itself and the public that projects that really need environmental impact statements are not being handled with environmental assessments.

Citizens concerned about park resources should not only look carefully at the quality of information and analysis in the EISs but also at the proposals being treated with EAs to make sure that these are being handled in a satisfactory manner. This is a case where vigilant local chapters and affiliates are the only line of defense for citizen monitoring of the national parks and the NEPA process.

NEPA is a powerful tool for intergovernmental coordination among federal agencies. As environmental protection statutes proliferated in the 1970s, so did the responsibilities of federal agency environmental offices. Legislation on clean air, clean water, historic preservation, and other subjects added specific new issues and requirements to the more general NEPA concerns. NEPA provides a mechanism for coordinating most of the responsibilities imposed by the other statutes.

NEPA has a large and supportive constituency in state and county planning offices. They perceive NEPA not as an environmental law but as a device that allows local governments to interact with federal officials on projects designed for their areas. Frequently state planners and county commissioners first learn about a project's scope and impact when they receive the early notice for the scoping session required by the NEPA regulations. For example, the first concrete information the local planning agency for southeast Georgia received about the Kings Bay Trident Submarine Base, planned for St. Mary's County adjacent to Cumberland Island National Seashore, came in the form of informal notices required by NEPA. The notices triggered local government planning to deal with the impacts of the base.

Citizens should cooperate with regional Park Service officials in ensuring that potentially harmful proposals by other agencies are fully disclosed. Some of the most important environmental threats to park resources arise from external threats growing out of other federal agency plans.

Referrals to CEQ

The referral process is another important resource that NEPA provides to park defenders. When other federal agency plans conflict with Park Service protection efforts, it may be appropriate to seek a referral to the Council on Environmental Quality (CEQ), especially when the final EIS is unsatisfactory.

The referral process allows federal agencies to bring to the Council on Environmental Quality interagency disagreements concerning proposed major federal actions that may cause unsatisfactory environmental effects. CEQ often attempts to resolve the disputes through mediation, sometimes assisted by its own independent fact-finding efforts. CEQ normally issues findings and recommendations on referrals, although its recommendations are not legally binding on the parties to a dispute.

There are two routes by which referrals come to CEQ. First, under Section 1504 of CEQ's NEPA implementation regulations, any federal agency or department may refer a proposed major federal action to CEQ within twenty-five days after a final EIS on the action has been made available to EPA, commenting agencies, and the public. A second referral route is provided by Section 309 of the Clean Air Act. Under Section 309, the EPA Administrator may refer to CEQ any proposed major federal action deemed to be environmentally unsatisfactory. Whichever referral route is applicable, the following criteria will be pertinent to an agency's decision on whether to refer a federal action to CEQ:

(1) possible violation of national environmental standards or policies

(2) severity of impact

(3) geographic scope of impact

(4) duration of impact

(5) importance as precedent

(6) availability of environmentally preferable alternatives

A referral is initiated by the delivery of a letter of referral from the head of the referring agency to CEQ. The referring agency must inform the agency proposing the action (lead agency) about its intentions at the earliest possible time. Other interested parties, whether federal agencies or members of the public, may submit written comments in support of the referral to CEQ up until the time the referral letter is received by the Council. The lead agency then has twenty-five days from the Council's receipt of the referral to make its response in writing. During that period, other agencies or members of the public may submit written comments in favor of the lead agency's position. After CEQ has received the lead agency's written response to the referral, the Council may intervene to seek to resolve the impasse.

The Department of the Interior has called on CEQ's assistance to help protect national parks twice, in 1978 for a beach erosion proposal at Fire Island National Seashore and in 1981 for a proposed jetport in Grand Teton National Park. The experience with referrals is mixed. The Fire Island referral receives good ratings; the jetport, negative ones.

In 1978, the Army Corps of Engineers proposed to rebuild the southern edge of Long Island by creating a twenty-five-by-sixteen foot dune along eighty-three miles of barrier beach. The purpose of the project was to slow the pace of erosion and to shield developed and underdeveloped areas. Following publication of the project's EIS, the Department of the Interior took immediate action to stop the project and referred the proposal to CEQ in March of the same year. In the official referral letter, Interior cited the irreversible adverse impacts on the natural resource values of the barrier islands and beach. It also feared that the tremendous scale of the project would have a precedent-setting nature for numerous similar projects pending around the country. Finally, Interior found the proposal in conflict with the congressional authorization establishing the Fire Island National Seashore. Interior's referral was supported by the Department of Commerce and EPA, but, according to an ex-CEQ staff member, these two agencies did not participate actively in the case.

According to CEQ files, the Council followed its standard procedure of first reviewing the cases of the opposing agencies. After being briefed by the Corps and Interior representatives, CEQ held a meeting of the involved agencies in an attempt to reconcile the concerns of Interior, Commerce, and EPA.

In a formal letter of response to the Corps' Chief of Engineers three months after receiving the referral, CEQ agreed with the objectives of the proposal, but questioned whether the proposal would actually resolve the problem and whether it was the best available alternative. CEQ recommended that the Corps revise its overall project plan to give more attention to the potential adverse impacts of the proposal. The Council also recommended that the Corps work more closely with EPA and the Departments of Commerce and Interior in the revision process.

No construction has been initiated along the proposed project route, and the Corps is still examining possible ways to slow the pace of erosion in the area. Officials from Interior and CEQ have attributed the redirection of the project to the CEQ referral. It appears that this case is a particularly good example of CEQ's successfully examining a project with significant adverse effects and stopping the project until the lead agency conducts a more substantive analysis of environmental impacts.

The Jackson Hole airport referral did not fare as well for the Park Service. Beginning in the early 1970s, a series of proposals was made by the Jackson Hole airport authorites for facilities located within the Grand Teton National Park. Following a draft EIS, draft development plans, and public meetings, the Department of Transportation (DOT) published a final EIS calling for, among other things, expansion of the airport and certification for the first time of jet aircraft service to the airport. On January 9, 1981, the Department of the Interior, which had once supported the project, and EPA referred the proposal to CEQ. The primary concern was the potential impact of jet noise on the park.

EPA recommended that the certification be denied and that further studies be undertaken to ascertain the environmental impacts of the proposal as well as to identify alternative sites for the jet service.

Boeing 737 jet service began at Jackson Hole Airport in June 1981 and has continued since then. This is despite three Sierra Club lawsuits, the last of which is still pending. To date, all suits have found in favor of the DOT position. In late 1982 Secretary of the Interior James Watt changed the agency's position in terms of the possibility for relocation of the airport and ruled that the airport was necessary for carrying out the functions of the Department of the Interior. Following that decision, DOT in early 1983 made the Boeing 737 certification permanent and deleted many of the provisions of the earlier Record of Decision (concerning, for example, the importance of relocation). Some of the noise mitigation provisions were apparently retained. In April 1983 the National Park Service reached a management agreement with the airport control board to improve noise control, but no reference to relocation was made. This agreement is the subject of the third Sierra Club suit.

The effectiveness of CEQ's role in the referral process is a matter of some dispute and reflects the bitter divisions between environmentalists and Secretary Watt. Interior officials said CEQ in the late 1970s had been effective in bringing the three agencies together and working out a mutually satisfactory resolution to remove the airport from the park. Interior said the basic issues of the referral were later undercut by politics. An official from an environmental group was much less complimentary. He said CEQ was not helpful: "CEQ was not interested in advancing principle, but in role playing." The dispute underscores that NEPA does not operate in a political vacuum and the referral process--like other aspects of NEPA in action--requires political will and skill on the part of park defenders.

V. THE ROAD AHEAD: MORE AND BETTER CITIZEN PARTICIPATION

The career staff of the National Park Service is made up of dedicated professionals who have chosen to make the national parks their life's work. Citizen groups can be partners in that work. For instance, local citizen groups are in the best position to gather data and make informed judgments about possible subversion of the NEPA process by overreliance on environmental assessments.

The NEPA process calls for informed citizen participation. What the Park Service NEPA process needs is not more law, but more life. Park Service officials themselves say that the NEPA process may be 100 percent complied with, and still environmental degradation may occur. NEPA opens up the process but it does not guarantee the best result. There is no substitute for politics.

The current legal and regulatory structure is underutilized. National and local environmental groups should put their staff energies into training local members to interact with Park Service park planning efforts. The state chapter or local affiliate where the park is located is the best place to assist National Park Service environmental activities.

Every state conservation society should have in its offices a library of the EISs written on projects in the state. For instance, The Georgia Conservancy office in Atlanta has dozens of EISs on projects in that state. These serve as an important information resource for volunteers. Georgia Conservancy members working on Georgia coastal issues have in the Kings Bay Trident Submarine Base and the Outer Continental Shelf offshore oil leasing EISs a superb information resource on the Georgia coastal environment. In addition, the alternatives sections gives citizens insight on possible other options. These older EISs provide citizens with the historical background of past agency actions--something that might otherwise be difficult to obtain. In the comments sections of final EISs they can discover the responses of EPA, state environmental agencies, and private groups who participated in these earlier efforts. This is an information resource on possible allies and coalition partners.

Participation requires alertness and preparation to make informed comments. Past efforts by hard-working citizens opened up the planning and NEPA processes so we can fully participate in shaping the future of the parks. This opportunity calls for effective participation by competent citizens.

There is no better way to ensure an increased level of effective citizen participation than by cooperation between local and national environmental organizations concerned with park protection. Together they can ensure that the NEPA process works well and can forge an alliance for better park protection with the Park Service's professionals.

NOTES

*President, Environmental Law Institute, Washington, D.C.; LL.B. Columbia University, 1965; B.A. Tulane University, 1957.

1. National Environmental Policy Act, 40 C.F.R. § 1500.

2. *See* legal treatises such as Rodgers, ENVIRONMENTAL LAW (1977).

3. Wilderness Society v. Hickel, 1 ENVTL. L. REP. 20042 (1970), 325 F. Supp. 422 (D.D.C. 1970).

4. 40 C.F.R. §§ 1500-1508.

5. U.S. Department of the Interior, National Park Service,*NEPA Compliance Guideline*, NPS-12, September 1982 (amended October 1984).

6. Biderman v. Morton, 5 ENVTL. L. REP. 20027 (1975), 505 F.2d 396 (2nd Cir. 1974); Berkson v. Morton, 2 ENVTL. L. REP. 20659 (1972).

7. Northern Alaska Environmental Center v. Hodel, 17 ENVTL. L. REP. 20015 (1986).

8. Northern Alaska Environmental Center v. Hodel, 17 ENVTL. L. REP. (9th Cir. 1986).

9. *NEPA Compliance Guideline*, NPS-12, *supra* note 5.

10. *NEPA Compliance Guideline, NPS-12, supra,* at Chapter 2, p. 5 (516 DM 2.6).

11. Clean Air Act, 42 U.S.C. § 1857, §§ 309(a) and (b).

12. *See* U.S. Department of the Interior, National Park Service, *Final Environmental Impact Statement, Lake Mead National Recreation Area, Volume II* (1985).

13. 42 U.S.C. § 4331. NEPA, § 101 reads, in part:

> The Congress, recognizing the profound impacts of man's activity on the interrelations of all components of the natural environment . . . and recognizing further the critical importance of restoring and maintaining environmental quality to the overall welfare and development of man, declares that it is the continuing policy of the Federal Government, in cooperation with State and local governments, and other concerned public and private organizations, to use all practicable means and measures . . . to create and maintain conditions under which man and nature can exist in productive harmony, and fulfill the social, economic, and other requirements of present and future generations of Americans.

Chapter 5

THE FEDERAL LAND POLICY AND MANAGEMENT ACT: THE BUREAU OF LAND MANAGEMENT'S ROLE IN PARK PROTECTION

*D. Michael Harvey**

I. INTRODUCTION

Although many of the threats confronting our national parks are generated by activities on park lands, the *State of the Parks* report indicated that more than 50 percent of the threats to the parks' natural and cultural resources originate outside park boundaries.[1] Inevitably, then, efforts to avoid or minimize park threats must address the resource development and utilization activities carried out on adjacent public lands managed by other federal agencies--primarily the Bureau of Land Management (BLM) and the Forest Service.

Because a major portion of public land is managed by BLM, many potential park threats arise from development activities on adjacent BLM lands, either through permits granted to private promoters or government entities, or through private acquisition of those lands by sale or exchange. Development permits may include authorization for exploration and development of oil, gas, coal, uranium, and other minerals; grant or recognize rights-of-way or use permits for roads, transmission lines, or pipelines; and a variety of uses by federal or state agencies, including dams and reservoirs, toxic and radioactive waste disposal sites, and military activities.

These and many similar activities on lands adjacent to national parks can have major impacts on an equally wide range of park values: scenery and vistas, silence and solitude, wildlife and fish, water levels and flows, air and water quality, and many other subtle or aesthetic elements that may affect park resources or a visitor's park experience.

Many of these development activities were once conducted under an assortment of statutory authorities that gave little or no consideration to their environmental consequences. However, under the Federal Land Policy and Management Act of 1976[2] (FLPMA), BLM's basic authority for management of the public lands now includes important environmental protections that can and should be invoked to protect national parks from the consequences of development on adjacent public lands.

FLPMA was a landmark achievement in the management of U.S. public lands. For the first time in the long history of the public lands, one law provided comprehensive authority and guidelines for the administration and protection of those vast tracts of federal lands and resources under the jurisdiction of the BLM-defined by FLPMA as the "public lands."[3] It enunciated a federal policy of retention of these lands for multiple-use management and repealed many obsolete public lands laws that had hindered effective land use planning for, and management of, public lands. Some of its provisions also apply to national forest lands managed by the Forest Service.

FLPMA replaced over 2,500 individual laws and was the first definitive, comprehensive federal statement of public lands management policy. It formally reversed long-standing assumptions about the eventual disposal of the public domain lands. It mandated that they be retained in federal ownership for the benefit of the entire nation, unless it was in the public interest to dispose of a particular parcel.

FLPMA established that the public lands are to be managed under principles of "multiple use and sustained yield."[4] In so doing, it expressly recognized that the many and varied resources of the public lands are important but not limitless. They require balanced use to realize their many potential benefits. Congress declared as national policy that:

> [T]he public lands be managed in a manner that will protect the quality of scientific, scenic, historical, ecological, environmental, air atmospheric, water resource, and archaeological values; that, where appropriate, will preserve and protect certain public lands in their natural

condition; that will provide food and habitat for fish and wildlife and domestic animals; and that will provide for outdoor recreation and human occupancy and use.[5]

FLPMA did not specify which uses would be allowed on which areas. Rather it set out a planning process to be used for making land use decisions and general principles to be followed in those decisions.

These basic principles include:

(1) explicit recognition that the resources to be managed and protected include "recreation," "wildlife and fish," "natural scenic, scientific and historical values;"[6]

(2) decisions based on complete and current resource inventories and land use planning with broad public participation;[7]

(3) protection of the environment,[8] with the cost of preventing or minimizing damage paid by users;[9]

(4) receipt of fair market value for private use of public resources;[10] and

(5) cooperation with other federal agencies, state and local governments, and local citizens and consistency with state and local land use plans.[11]

This chapter discusses FLPMA and its implementation, describing how FLPMA can be used for park protection, and identifies several features of FLPMA that are currently underutilized for park protection. In this discussion, "park protection" means preventing or minimizing damage or degradation of natural and cultural resources of the National Park System caused by activities on public lands or on lands transferred out of federal ownership by BLM.

II. GENERAL PROVISIONS OF FLPMA

FLPMA contains a wide variety of provisions that could be used to implement a park protection policy. While many provide discretionary authority, others are mandatory congressional directives for public land management. The most important for park protection purposes are the mandatory inventory and planning requirements of Sections 201, 202, and 603, which include a priority for designation and protection of "areas of critical environmental concern," and a mandate for review and recommendation of areas qualified for wilderness designation.[12]

One of the most important is the prohibition against impairing the suitability of areas under wilderness review.[13] In the discussion of the FLPMA authorities that follows, it is important to bear in mind that the managers of the national parks--the National Park Service--and the managers of the public lands--the BLM--both report to the Secretary of the Interior. Indeed, because the authority and responsibility for management of both land systems are assigned by law to the Secretary, difficult tensions arise from the very composition of the Department of the Interior. As a result, the success of any park protection program depends heavily on the sensitivity and commitment of the Secretary and those who serve as directors of the National Park Service and the Bureau of Land Management.

A. Inventory and Protection of Wilderness

The impact of the Secretary's attitudes toward park protection has been apparent since FLPMA's enactment in 1976, as the Department of the Interior has gone about implementing FLPMA's provisions. In terms of the statute's potential to contribute to park protection, the BLM wilderness review process is a critical focal point.

Section 201(a) of FLPMA directed the Secretary to "prepare and maintain on a continuing basis an inventory of all public lands and their resource and other values (including, but not limited to, outdoor recreation and scenic values), giving priority to areas of critical environmental concern."[14] As part of this inventory process, by 1991 the Secretary must complete a review of all roadless areas of five thousand acres or more and roadless "islands" of the public lands (i.e. smaller tracts detached from other BLM holdings) having wilderness characteristics[15] as described in the Wilderness Act.[16] The Secretary must complete the review and periodically report recommendations to the President on the suitability or nonsuitability of each area for inclusion in the National Wilderness Preservation

System. Within two years following each report, the President, in turn, must make recommendations for ultimate designation by Congress, which reserves final judgement.

For obvious reasons, wilderness designation and management of BLM lands adjacent to national parks can contribute substantially to protecting the parks themselves. In ten western states undergoing wilderness review, ninety-two of the "wilderness study areas" (WSAs) identified by BLM, comprising 3.6 million acres, have contiguous boundaries with National Park Sytem units.[17] Designation of those wilderness areas would reinforce National Park Service park protection objectives by improving management of adjacent BLM lands to better emphasize the protection of cultural, scientific, wildlife, and other natural values. And designation may eliminate whole categories of adjacent land threats by foreclosing or confining the threatening uses. Thus, as part of a comprehensive park protection strategy, the Secretary of the Interior should strive to improve such coordinated management by recommending wilderness designation for all appropriate areas adjacent to National Park System units.

Although initial Interior Department policies promised to expand the scope of park protection through proper recognition of adjacent wilderness, the BLM wilderness review process later reflected policies that undermined its potential benefit to parks. Initially, BLM policy called for inventorying, with certain exceptions, all public lands administered by the agency. All contiguous roadless areas of greater than five thousand acres were eligible for WSA status.[18] In addition, areas of fewer than five thousand acres that had wilderness characteristics were to be eligible if they were either contiguous with land managed by another agency that had been formally determined to have wilderness or potential wilderness values or contiguous with an area of fewer than five thousand acres of other federal lands administered by an agency with authority to study and preserve wilderness lands, and the combined total is five thousand acres or more.[19]

The wilderness review process itself, even prior to designation, offers substantial management protection for areas determined suitable for wilderness study because FLPMA Section 603 also mandates that the Secretary of the Interior protect the wilderness qualities of those areas until Congress decides which WSAs will be designated wilderness.[20] BLM has implemented that requirement through adoption of an "Interim Management Policy," which

prescribes detailed requirements designed to assure that WSAs
are managed so as not to impair their suitability for wilderness.[21] In recent years, Congress has also imposed a leasing ban in
all WSAs, renewing this ban in each of the past several years.[22]
Clearly Congress desired to preserve its right to decide which areas
should be permanently protected and intended that candidate areas
not be degraded or destroyed in the interim, which would surely reduce their prospects for becoming wilderness areas. During
the wilderness study process, the interim management of WSAs and
BLM-Park Service cooperative planning should, in theory, provide
buffer protection for any nearby parks.

   In December 1982, however, a new Secretary of the Interior, James Watt, published an order that changed the scope and
direction of the wilderness review process. The Secretary ordered that three actions be taken:

- Lands in which the United States did not own the
  subsurface mineral rights (so-called "split-estate" lands)
  were to be deleted from the wilderness inventory and
  no longer managed under the nonimpairment
  Interim Management Policy guidelines. After this
  adjustment, all WSAs were to be reexamined. If the
  remaining acreage was less than five thousand acres,
  the WSA was to be deleted entirely.

- All WSAs of fewer than five thousand acres were to
  be deleted from WSA status, the Secretary having
  determined that these lands need not be considered
  under FLPMA.

- All areas larger than five thousand acres found to have
  wilderness characteristics only in association or in
  conjunction with contiguous wilderness or
  wilderness candidate areas administered by other federal
  agencies were to be deleted unless they were determined
  to have wilderness attributes of their own.[23]

   The Secretary based his decision, in part, on three interpretations of FLPMA made by the Interior Board of Land Appeals
(IBLA).[24] In *Santa Fe Pacific Railroad Co.*,[25] the IBLA ruled that
split-estate lands could not be included in the wilderness inventory, reasoning that their inclusion would violate Section 701(h) of
FLPMA, which provides that "[a]ll actions by the Secretary concerned under this Act shall be subject to valid existing

rights."[26] In *Tri-County Cattleman's Association*,[27] the IBLA had ruled that BLM did not have authority to designate a roadless area of fewer than five thousand acres as a WSA pursuant to Section 603(a) of FLPMA. The Board held, however, that wilderness management was authorized by Sections 202 and 302. Finally, in *Don Coops, et al.*,[28] the IBLA ruled that to the extent that BLM had assessed an inventory unit's wilderness characteristics "in association with" a contiguous area of federal lands not administered by BLM, it had exceeded its statutory authority.

The impact of the Secretary's order was substantial. More than 1.2 million acres were removed from wilderness inventory, exempted from further wilderness study, and released for multiple uses other than wilderness. However, in a suit filed to contest Watt's administrative order, *Sierra Club v. Watt*,[29] the federal court ruled that FLPMA did *not* exempt split-estate lands from wilderness review because Section 603 and the Wilderness Act were intended to preserve Congress' option to designate wilderness wherever the surface characteristics of the public lands had wilderness qualities. The court also ruled that the Secretary, while possessing the authority to delete WSAs of fewer than five thousand acres, had failed to develop any reasons for doing so and could not simply ignore the administrative determination of his predecessor. Thus, the court required that all of the BLM lands "dropped" by the Secretary be reinstated to wilderness review (though the smaller areas and areas adjacent to other federally-managed lands were to be reviewed under Section 202, not Section 603), and that they be managed under the nonimpairment guidelines pending congressional decisions on the future of these lands. As a result, possible wilderness designation of these lands still offers substantial opportunity for park protection.

B. Management Authority and Obligation to Protect Adjacent Park Lands

In addition to providing the opportunity to "buffer" the parks with designation of wilderness areas, other FLPMA provisions impose obligations and grant power to manage adjacent BLM lands in a manner consistent with park protection.

A key provision imposing protective obligations requires BLM to develop and apply park land use plans that "give priority to the designation and protection of areas of critical environmental concern" (ACECs).[30] While the FLMPA definition of ACECs does not explicitly refer to park lands, it specifically protects land values that are especially characteristic of national parks. Section 103(a) defines ACECs as

> areas within the public lands where special management attention is required (when such areas are developed or used or where no development is required) to protect and prevent irreparable damage to important historic, cultural, or scenic values, fish and wildlife resources or other natural systems or processes, or to protect life and safety from natural hazards.[31]

Furthermore, nothing in FLPMA or in its legislative history suggests that the values or resources to be protected by the ACEC designation are limited to those found on the ACEC itself or on other BLM lands. Thus, there is substantial basis for arguing that BLM must give priority to identifying and designating areas adjacent to national parks where special management practices are necessary to prevent damage to the unique qualities of sensitive park lands. That management obligation is strongly supported by related FLPMA provisions governing BLM's land planning and management duties.

A key illustration is FLPMA's definition of "multiple use." While BLM is required to develop its land use plans under "principles of multiple use and sustained yield," the definition of that concept unquestionably authorizes (and can reasonably be construed to require) ACEC management designed to protect adjacent park lands. Thus "multiple use" is defined in Section 103(c) in terms that authorize prohibitions on incompatible development within adjacent lands--particularly where they may qualify as ACECs. While management for resource utilization is one major goal, the definition clearly contemplates conservation-oriented management on appropriate areas of the public lands by providing for: (1) "the use of some land for less than all of the resources," (2) "a combination of balanced and diverse resource uses that takes into account the long-term needs of future generations for renewable and non-renewable resources, including, but not limited to recreation . . . wildlife and fish, and natural, scenic, scientific and historical values" and (3) management "without permanent impairment of the . . . quality of the environment . . . and not necessarily to the combination of uses that will give the greatest economic return of greatest unit output."[32]

BLM's authority and obligation to give enlightened consideration to long-term and noneconomic values in its management planning is further emphasized by other management mandates. Thus, "in the development and revision of land use plans," BLM is instructed to "consider the relative scarcity of the values involved and the availability of alternative means (including recycling) and sites for realization of those values," and "to weigh long-term benefits to the public against short-term benefits."[34]

Finally, any doubt about the appropriateness of applying these land management principles to require BLM to protect parks from incompatible activities on adjacent lands should be erased by FLPMA's "coordination" and "consistency" provisions: "to the extent consistent with the laws governing the administration of the public lands, [BLM shall] coordinate the land use inventory, planning, and management activities of or for such lands with the land use planning and management programs of other Federal departments and agencies." [34]

The coordination requirement is further implemented by the obligation to "allow an opportunity for public involvement" and to "establish procedures, including public hearings where appropriate, to give Federal, State, and local governments and the public adequate notice and opportunity to comment upon and participate in the formulation of plans and programs relating to the management of the public lands." [35]

These provisions of FLPMA in effect mandate that management plans for and actions on public lands must consider park protection needs. As will be seen in the following section, there are a wide variety of other specific authorities in FLPMA available to implement this objective. No changes in the law are needed to allow the Secretary of the Interior to implement park protection as a management consideration on public lands. Not only does the Secretary have ample authority, but certain of the above provisions impose protection obligations that should be enforceable where the park protection importance of key adjacent lands is clear.[36]

It is possible, of course, that authority for park protection under FLPMA could be strengthened by adding a specific directive to protect the parks. But any effort to insert such language will surely be resisted as an attempt to authorize administrative expansion of park boundaries already established by Congress. For these reasons, instead of seeking to modify FLPMA, it may be preferable to initiate a vigorous campaign to get the Secretary of the Interior to make effective use of existing authority.

C. Other FLPMA Provisions

There are many other FLPMA provisions that could be used for park protection purposes.

1. Withdrawals

Section 204 authorizes withdrawals of public lands. These could be made to prevent activities that would be threats to parks, particularly location of claims under the Mining Law of 1872.[37]

2. Exchanges

Section 206 authorizes exchanges of public lands for private lands.[38] This authority can be used to acquire private inholdings within parks or lands outside parks in order to prevent activities that might threaten park values. Conveyances out of federal ownership can contain provisions protecting the public interest. These could include restrictive covenants or scenic easements designed for park protection.

3. Conveyances

Section 208 directs the Secretary to include in all other conveyances of land out of federal ownership authorized by FLPMA "such terms, covenants, conditions and reservations as he deems necessary to insure proper land use and protection of the public interest."[39] These could also be designed for park protection.

4. Reservation and Conveyance of Minerals

Section 209 provides authority to reserve minerals when lands are conveyed out of federal ownership, thereby precluding private mineral development.[40]

5. Management of Use, Occupancy, and Development

In addition to the broad obligation to manage in compliance with land use plans based on an inventory of public land values,[41] Section 302 provides broad authority to regulate "use, occupancy and development" of public lands.[42] That section includes a specific directive that "the Secretary shall, by regulation or otherwise take any action necessary to prevent unnecessary or undue degradation of the lands." [43] This is particularly significant because it is specifically made applicable to activities on public lands conducted by persons who file mining claims under the Mining Law of 1872.

6. Cooperative Agreements

Section 307(b) authorizes cooperative agreements "involving the management, protection, development, and sale of public lands." [44] Park protection would clearly be an appropriate purpose of such an agreement.

7. Grazing Leases and Permits

Section 402(a) applies to grazing leases and permits on public lands and in national forests.[45] It authorizes, among other things, inclusion in leases and permits of "such terms and conditions as the Secretary [of the Interior or Agriculture] deems appropriate and consistent with the governing law, including, but not limited to . . . authority . . . to cancel, suspend or modify a grazing permit or lease, in whole or in part, pursuant to the terms and conditions thereof." A similar provision in Section 402(e) authorizes the inclusion of such terms and conditions where grazing is managed without an applicable allotment management plan.[46] This provision clearly invites inclusion of terms and conditions designed for park protection, at least where there are substantial grounds to believe such terms are necessary to avert damage to park values.

8. Rights-of-Way

Title V provides broad authority for the granting of rights-of-way over public lands and national forest lands for virtually every conceivable purpose except oil and gas pipelines.[47] Oil and gas pipeline rights-of-way are covered by Section 28 of the Mineral

Leasing Act of 1920.[48] Like other management decisions, all rights-of-way must be consistent with land use plans under FLPMA or the National Forest Management Act (NFMA).[49]

Title V gives the Secretaries of Agriculture and the Interior broad power to condition rights-of-way grants. Section 503 authorizes requiring common sharing of rights-of-way corridors in order to "minimize adverse environmental impacts," and further allows corridor designation to be governed by "natural and state land use policies" and by consideration of "environmental quality." [50] Section 504 sets out a number of provisions allowing the imposition of terms and conditions designed to prevent environmental damage.[51]

Finally, Section 505(a) requires each right-of-way to contain terms and conditions that, among other things, "minimize damage to scenic and esthetic values and fish and wildlife habitat, and otherwise protect the environment." [52] Section 505(b) also provides for additional terms and conditions where necessary to (1) protect federal property and economic interests, (2) require location of the right-of-way along a route that will cause the least damage to the environment, taking into consideration feasibility and other relevant factors, and (3) otherwise protect the public interest in the lands traversed by the right-of-way or next to it.[53]

III. CONCLUSION

FLPMA contains a wide variety of statutory mandates and discretionary authorities that could be used to achieve park protection objectives. Potentially the most important of these is the directive to give priority to designation and management of areas of critical environmental concern. In a recent "Instruction Memorandum," BLM has recognized that its implementation of this congressional directive has been "uneven and inconsistent" and is "a growing source of criticism." [54]

The memorandum includes a draft BLM plan to "assure improved use of ACECs and . . . achieve a consistent approach Bureauwide to designation." The BLM plan states that FLPMA and its legislative history give "clear guidelines" for implementation of the ACEC provisions. It recognizes that "designation of ACECs during resource management planning is an affirmative requirement," and that "priority is afforded to ACECs." It also points out that "the ACEC provision demands *two* specific actions for areas requiring special management attention. They are designation *and* protection."[55] BLM's memorandum recognizes that "ACECs are fully supportive of and compatible with BLM's multiple-use mandate and mission," reminding agency officials that "the ACEC provision conveys a unique and explicit designation authority. It is the only existing authority for BLM managers to specifically designate public land areas."

Under BLM procedure, a State Director's approval of a Resource Management Plan that includes an ACEC accomplishes ACEC designation. The plans must be developed in accordance with the Department of the Interior's regulations[56] and the *BLM Manual.* (A major draft revision of the manual was recently promulgated to implement the policies discussed in the ACEC memorandum.[57] The planning process expressly requires coordination and consultation with other federal agencies, including, of course, the National Park Service.)

It is important to note that there is nothing in the law that precludes ACEC designations prior to completion of a Resource Management Plan. In fact, beginning in 1977 the *BLM Manual* and BLM directives to field offices have indicated that nomination and designation of ACECs could take place at any time and that special management was authorized prior to formal designation.[58] In addition, ACEC nominations (if supported by justifying data) can be made by interested private individuals or groups.

Clearly FLPMA provides the authority for managing public lands so as to assure park protection. Whether actual on-the-ground actions will achieve that result depends in large measure on the attitude of the Secretary of the Interior, the Directors of the National Park Service and BLM, and their senior managers in the field. In the absence of effective action by BLM, there are numerous provisions inviting oversight and enforcement by concerned parties and by Congress.

NOTES

*Chief Counsel for the Majority, Committee on Energy and Natural Resources, United States Senate.

1. U.S. Department of the Interior, National Park Service, STATE OF THE PARKS--1980: A REPORT TO CONGRESS, at pp. viii and 4 (1980).

2. 43 U.S.C. §§ 1701-1782, Pub. L. No. 94-579, 90 Stat. 2745 (1976).

3. FLPMA § 103(e), 43 U.S.C. § 1702(e).

4. FLPMA § 103(c), 43 U.S.C. § 1702(c).

5. FLPMA § 102(a)(8), 43 U.S.C. § 1701(a)(8).

6. FLPMA § 103(c), 43 U.S.C. § 1702(c).

7. FLPMA §§ 201(a), 202(a), and 302(a), 43 U.S.C. §§ 1711(a), 1712(a), and 1732(a).

8. FLPMA §§ 102(a)(8) and (11), 103(a) and (c), 201(a), and 202(c)(3), 43 U.S.C. §§ 1701(a)(8) and (11), 1702(a) and (c), 1711(a) and 1712(c)(3).

9. FLPMA § 504(h) and (i), 43 U.S.C. § 1764(h) and (i).

10. FLPMA §§ 102(a)(9) and 504(g), 43 U.S.C. §§ 1701(a)(9) and 1764(g).

11. FLPMA §§ 102(a)(2), and 202(b), (c)(9) and (f), 43 U.S.C. §§ 1701(a)(2) and 1712(b), (c)(9), and (f).

12. FLPMA § 603, 43 U.S.C. § 1782.

13. FLPMA § 603(c), 43 U.S.C. § 1782(c).

14. 43 U.S.C. § 1711(a).

15. FLPMA § 603(c), 43 U.S.C. § 1782.

16. 16 U.S.C. §§ 1131-1136.

17. *See infra* Appendix B.

18. U.S. Department of the Interior, Bureau of Land Management, WILDERNESS INVENTORY HANDBOOK (1978).

19. *Id.*

20. FLPMA § 603(c), 43 U.S.C. § 1782(c), provides, with defined exceptions for existing uses and for continuing mineral location, that "during the period of review . . . and until Congress has determined otherwise, the Secretary shall continue to manage such lands . . . in a manner so as not to impair the suitability of such areas for preservation as wilderness."

21. U.S. Department of the Interior, Bureau of Land Managment, INTERIM MANAGEMENT POLICY AND GUIDELINES FOR LANDS UNDER WILDERNESS REVIEW, (1979).

22. *See*, Pub. L. No. 98-473, 98 Stat. 1871 (1985). Despite the nonimpairment guidelines for management of WSAs, and the congressionally-imposed leasing ban, there have been numerous reported incidents of violations of these policies, including leasing of WSAs adjacent to National Park System units. *See generally, Oversight Hearings on Bureau of Land Management Wilderness Management Program, Subcomm. on Public Lands and National Parks, House Comm. on Interior and Insular Affairs*, 98th Cong., 1st Sess. (1984). *See also, Oversight Hearings on the Bureau of Land Management Wilderness Review Process, Subcomm. on Public Lands and National Parks, House Comm. on Interior and Insular Affairs*, 98th Congress, 2d Sess. (1985).

23. 47 Fed. Reg. 58,372 (1982).

24. The Interior Board of Land Appeals (IBLA) decides appeals from Interior Department officials' decisions relating to the use and disposition of public lands, mineral

resources, and the conduct of surface mining, 43 C.F.R. § 4.1(b)(3) (1984). The Secretary has authority to review and reconsider any decision rendered by the Board, 43 C.F.R. § 4.5 (1984).

25. 64 IBLA 27 (1982).

26. 43 U.S.C. § 1701, note subparagraph (h).

27. 60 IBLA 305 (1981).

28. 61 IBLA 300 (1982).

29. Sierra Club v. Watt, 608 F. Supp. 305 (E.D. Cal. 1985).

30. FLPMA § 202(c)(3), 43 U.S.C. § 1712(c)(3).

31. 43 U.S.C. § 1702(a). For an excellent discussion of the ACEC provisions of FLPMA and their implementation *see*, Charles H. Callison, AREAS OF CRITICAL ENVIRONMENTAL CONCERN ON THE PUBLIC LANDS: PART I--ORIGINS OF THE CONCERT AND LEGISLATIVE HISTORY (1984) and Charles H. Callison, AREAS OF CRITICAL ENVIRONMENTAL CONCERN ON THE PUBLIC LANDS: PART II--RECORD OF PERFORMANCE BY THE BUREAU OF LAND MANAGEMENT (1986).

32. FLPMA § 103(c), 43 U.S.C. § 1702(c).

33. FLPMA § 202(c)(6) and (7), 43 U.S.C. § 1712(c)(6) and (7).

34. FLPMA § 202(c)(9), 43 U.S.C. § 1712(c)(9). The same provision also extends these coordination requirements to "states and local governments within which the lands are located."

35. FLPMA § 202(f), 43 U.S.C. § 1712(f).

36. In Sierra Club v. Department of the Interior, 398 F. Supp. 284 (N.D. Cal 1975), the federal court held that the Secretary of the Interior had acted unlawfully and abused his discretion by failing to utilize the legal tools available to him to seek protection for Redwood National Park from the consequences of logging on adjacent lands.

37. 43 U.S.C. § 1716.

38. 43 U.S.C. § 1716.

39. 43 U.S.C. § 1718.

40. 43 U.S.C. § 1719.

41. *See, supra*, at notes 7, 12, 15, and 35 and accompanying text.

42. 43 U.S.C. § 1732.

43. 43 U.S.C. § 1732(b).

44. 43 U.S.C. § 1737(b).

45. 43 U.S.C. § 1752(a).

46. 43 U.S.C. § 1752(e).

47. 43 U.S.C. §§ 1761-1771. Title V rights-of-way include provisions for (1) impoundment, storage, and transportation of water; (2) pipelines and other systems for transportation, distribution, and storage of liquids and gases (other than oil or natural gas); (3) pipelines and other systems for transportation, distribution, or storage of solid materials; (4) systems for generation, transmission, and distribution of electric energy; (5) systems for communication; (6) roads, trails, highways, and other transportation facilities; and (7) "other necessary transportation or other systems or facilities which are in the public interest."

48. 30 U.S.C. § 185.

49. FLPMA § 302(a), 43 U.S.C. § 1732(a).

50. 43 U.S.C. § 1763.

51. 43 U.S.C. § 1764.

52. 43 U.S.C. § 1765(a).

53. 43 U.S.C. § 1765(b).

54. BLM Instruction Memorandum No. 86-299, Mar. 6, 1986.

55. Draft "guidance statement" entitled "Areas of Critical Environmental Concern in Resource Management Planning," at p. 1, accompanying BLM Instruction Memorandum No. 86-299, and accompanying text. (Emphasis added.) BLM's memorandum recognizes that "ACECs are fully supportive of and compatible with BLM's multiple use mandate and mission," reminding agency officials that "the ACEC provision conveys a unique and explicit designation authority. It is the only existing authority for BLM managers to specifically designate public land areas," *supra* note 54.

56. *See* 43 C.F.R. § 1600 in general and 43 C.F.R. § 1610.7-2 in particular.

57. *See* BLM MANUAL, Section 1600 series; ACECs at Section 1617.81, subparagraph B.1; and draft revisions accompanying BLM Instruction Memorandum No. 86-712 (Sept. 24, 1986).

58. *See* Organic Act Directive No. 77-77, Change No. 2, July 8, 1980.

Chapter 6

INTERNATIONAL LAW AND PARK PROTECTION: A GLOBAL RESPONSIBILITY

*Daniel Barstow Magraw**

I. INTRODUCTION

National parks and other areas administered by the National Park Service (hereinafter referred to jointly as "national parklands") currently face a variety of threats from outside their borders. Such threats are commonly referred to as "external threats."[1] Many, probably most, external threats are domestic threats, that is threats to national parklands originating in the United States.

Others, however, are international threats to national parklands that originate outside the United States. International threats can be either continuous and long-term, such as acid rain resulting from ongoing industrial activity, or instantaneous or short term, such as radioactive fallout from the accident at the Soviet Union's Chernobyl nuclear power reactor. Some national parklands adjoin a U.S. boundary with another nation and are threatened by sources in that nation. Glacier National Park, which is threatened by water pollution from the proposed Cabin Creek coal mine in British Columbia, Canada, and by logging in Canada, is one example.[2] Approximately twenty-four national parklands immediately adjacent to U.S. borders with Canada and Mexico may be so affected.[3] Four of those national parklands and sixty other national parklands are on U.S. seacoasts and thus face possible threats from pollution occurring in international or foreign waters.[4]

A larger number of national parklands are not on a U.S. boundary but nevertheless face threats emanating from foreign sources. Rocky Mountain National Park, which could be threatened by air pollution from a copper smelter in Mexico, and the national

143

parklands in Alaska, which are threatened by air pollution originating in northern nations such as the U.S.S.R., typify this subcategory of international threats.[5]

A probably more ominous example is the phenomenon of global warming caused by increasing atmospheric concentrations of "greenhouse" gases such as carbon dioxide and methane, and the effects of chlorofluorocarbons on the ozone layer. Much uncertainty exists regarding the overall rate of increase and the location-specific temperature, air circulation, and precipitation effects that global warming is likely to cause. If significant global warming does occur, as seems probable, the resulting changes will likely affect many national parklands. Particularly hard hit will be parklands whose raison d'etre is the preservation of natural rather than cultural features, because weather changes are probably more likely to affect natural features, for example, waterfalls at Yosemite National Park, than such cultural features as cliff dwellings at Mesa Verde National Park. Because of the probable rise in sea level, parklands along seacoasts are also endangered.

The array of international threats is particularly ominous. International threats are likely to intensify as the world industrializes, as the demands on the world's resources increase, and as the global ecosystem's ability to assimilate the various pressures placed on it is exceeded.[6] In addition, international threats involve "externalities": the nation in which a threatening activity occurs does not experience the transboundary damage caused by the activity and thus is unlikely of its own accord to regulate that activity.[7] Further, the activities giving rise to international threats cannot, by definition, be regulated by the United States unilaterally. Some solutions can be bilateral (or binational), for example, eliminating the threats confronting Glacier National Park alluded to above. But many must be regional or even global in breadth.

The need for multinational cooperation and regulation poses differing degrees of difficulty depending on, among other things, the number of foreign sources of a particular threat and on the United States' relations with the nations in which those sources are located. External threats that emanate from a combination of domestic and foreign sources pose particularly sensitive questions, especially when neither the domestic nor the foreign component is objectionable standing alone. Similarly, external threats coming from, or influenced by, the participation of more than one foreign nation present difficult issues.

The goal of this chapter is to suggest the rough outlines of an analytic framework for examining whether international law provides rights to, or imposes obligations on, the United States with respect to international and domestic threats to national parklands. In the course of developing that framework, I comment on specific threats to particular parklands, but do not undertake to investigate fully the implications of international law for any one threat or parkland.

Part I below examines specific sources of international law that may already provide some protection against international threats to national parklands. Part II discusses the possibility that international law may impose obligations on the United States with respect to domestic threats. Part III presents tentative conclusions regarding the current state of international law in relation to external threats and makes recommendations regarding future action in this area.

The following four points provide an analytic perspective: First, international law may serve two roles in controlling external threats to national parklands. It may provide substantive rules governing particular threats, and it may provide procedural mechanisms or frameworks for resolving disputes and making rules about external threats.[8] International law's potential in both of these roles should be kept in mind when considering alternative approaches to dealing with international threats to national parklands. Second, it is important to recognize that just as activities in other nations can endanger U.S. national parklands, activities sponsored by the United States both internally and externally can threaten other nations' protected areas. For example, activities in Alaska reportedly threaten Canadian parks. Quite apart from the issues of whether the United States is obligated by international law or U.S. domestic law[9] to prevent or mitigate such threats, the fact that threats to other nations can, and sometimes do, arise in the United States as a result of U.S. activities abroad obviously affects international negotiations regarding threats to national parklands (and to other U.S. resources). Third, although this chapter focuses on areas administered by the National Park Service, the international law under discussion also applies to other protected areas within the United States.[10] Fourth, my research is at an early stage regarding many of the issues discussed in this chapter. My conclusions thus are preliminary in nature.

II. INTERNATIONAL THREATS TO NATIONAL PARKLANDS

In analyzing the relevance of international law to international threats to national parklands, it is essential to recognize that these threats can arise from both lawful and unlawful acts and that the international law implications vary accordingly. If the threat involves an act by a foreign nation that is unlawful under international law, that nation will be required to make reparations. Such reparations might take three forms, depending on the situation: restitution of the status quo; satisfaction (for example, an apology by the offending nation); and indemnification, (that is, compensation for damages in the form of monetary payments). None of these forms is particularly helpful regarding many types of damage to national parklands. For example, aesthetic damage may be impossible to quantify in monetary terms. Similarly, a mere apology will not suffice. Finally, restitution may not be possible for damage to an ecological system. The emphasis, thus, should be on preventing harm before it occurs, not in trying to undo or compensate for harm.

Putting aside the question of the form of reparations, it is obvious that a wide variety of international law rules defining lawfulness are potentially relevant to the international threats question. Many such violations are unlikely, or the interest violated generally would not concern parklands. For example, Mexico might invade the United States through Big Bend National Park and thus violate the international law norm against aggression. The focus in the following discussion is on those norms that are most likely to be violated and to cause harm to national parklands or that are specifically relevant to national parklands.

If behavior is lawful but nevertheless harms or threatens to harm a national parkland, it is still possible that the acting foreign nation may be accountable under international law. Because the rules are evolving, great certainty is not possible. The closest analogy under U.S. domestic law is strict liability. For example, if an engine part falls from an airplane in flight and strikes someone on the ground, the airline will be liable for the damages without the necessity of proving negligence on the airline's part. If lawful activity gives rise to transboundary harm to a national parkland, separate international law rules of liability may apply, as will be discussed in Part I.C.2. Perhaps confusingly, if those rules are violated, an international wrong occurs, and the analysis may revert to the reparations rules already described.[11]

The discussion in this part is organized according to the two major sources of international law: international agreements (variously referred to by terms such as treaties, conventions, etc.) and customary international law.[12] More precisely, the discussion is organized as follows: (A) multilateral treaties (treaties to which three or more nations are parties); (B) bilateral treaties (treaties to which only two nations are parties); (C) general customary international law (customary law that applies globally); and (D) regional customary international law (customary law that applies only within a specific region).

A. Multilateral Treaties

There is no multilateral treaty pertaining to national parklands per se. Other multilateral treaties or multilateral cooperative arrangements, described below, may, however, provide some protection.

The World Heritage Convention, effective December 17, 1975, provides some protection for cultural heritage (including monuments, buildings, and sites) and natural heritage (including biological, geological, and physiographical formations and natural areas of "outstanding universal value from the point of view of science, conservation or natural beauty").[13] Ninety-two countries are parties to the Convention, including Canada and the United States; Mexico is not a party.[14]

Twelve national parklands (and two other U.S. sites) are designated as World Heritage sites on the World Heritage List.[15] Chaco Culture National Historical Park, Glacier National Park, and Hawaii Volcanoes National Park have been nominated as World Heritage sites by the United States but have not yet been approved for such status by the international body authorized to maintain the World Heritage List. Worldwide, the list contains 247 sites. The nomination of Glacier National Park is interesting because of the Cabin Creek coal mine controversy. The United States' original nomination of Glacier was not approved, but the United States renominated Glacier, with supplemental information. The designation might not be approved on the international level, however, unless Canada joins in the application, which it appears reluctant to do in part because of the Cabin Creek controversy.

The legal effect and meaning of the World Heritage Convention is not entirely clear. The only case to analyze the Convention is an Australian case, *Australia v. Tasmania.*[16] It is beyond cavil that the Convention is binding (on the United States, Canada, and the other states that are parties to it) as international law. Nevertheless, there is no international forum that automatically has jurisdiction to hear disputes arising under the Convention, and none appears likely. Thus, it might be impossible for a nation alleging that another nation is violating the Convention might not be able to obtain an international adjudicatory determination of that allegation.

With respect to enforceability in U.S. domestic courts, a crucial question is whether the Convention requires implementing legislation in order to be effective, that is, whether the Convention is "self-executing." The *Tasmania* case did not address that question because under Australian law, treaties cannot be self-executing. If it is not self-executing, it will not be effective as domestic law within the United States (although it remains in force as international law and binding on the countries that are parties to it) unless implementing legislation is passed.[17] The Solicitor of the Department of the Interior has concluded that the World Heritage Convention is not self-executing.[18] That result is not free from doubt, however. The Secretary of the Interior has been designated to direct and coordinate U.S. participation in the Convention,[19] and the Secretary has issued rules setting forth policies and procedures in that regard, which may give rise to enforceable domestic legal rights.[20]

As discussed in greater detail in Part II, below, Articles 4 and 5 of the Convention place obligations for protecting cultural and natural heritage sites on the nation in which those sites are located. In addition, Article 6.2 imposes an obligation on parties to the Convention to aid in "the identification, protection, conservation and preservation of the cultural and natural heritage" identified in the World Heritage List, if the nation in which the site is located so requests. The extent of that obligation is not clear from the face of the Convention, and research has revealed no source that analyzes that question. Nevertheless, vis-a-vis other nations that are parties to the Convention, Article 6.2 offers protection of some sort to national parklands that are on the World Heritage List.

Article 6.3 of the Convention imposes an obligation on parties "not to take any deliberate measures which might damage directly or indirectly the cultural and natural heritage referred to in Articles 1 and 2 situated on the territory of other" parties to the Convention. The meaning of Article 6.3 is subject to debate. For instance, the important term "damage directly or indirectly" is subject to widely differing interpretations. Further, Article 6.3 applies by its terms regardless of whether the heritage site has been placed on the World Heritage List, an interpretation that is supported by the structure of the Convention as a whole and by several opinions in the *Tasmania* case.[21] If that interpretation is correct, Canada may be obligated to prevent British Columbian approval of the Cabin Creek coal mine, even though Glacier National Park, which would seem to qualify easily as a natural area of "outstanding value from the point of view of science, conservation, or natural beauty," has not yet been approved at the international level for placement on the World Heritage List. The constitutional powers of the Canadian provinces complicate the analysis, however. Article 34 of the Convention provides that if the federal government has the authority to prevent the prohibited action, it must do so; but if the federal government does not have that authority, it is obligated only to inform the competent authorities at the provincial level with its recommendations. I am not informed regarding which alternative applies to the Cabin Creek situation.[22]

Another possible source of international obligations is the Man and the Biosphere Program, which operates under the auspices of UNESCO (the United Nations Educational, Scientific and Cultural Organization). Perhaps the primary component of that program is the biosphere reserve project, which began in the early 1970s and is not based on an international agreement per se. Each participating country, of which there are now 104, voluntarily establishes its own national autonomous committee. The activities of those committees are coordinated to some degree by UNESCO, but UNESCO does not control their operations.[23] Two hundred fifty-two biosphere reserve sites now exist in sixty-six nations.

The United States, which continues to participate in the Man and the Biosphere Program even though it has withdrawn from membership in UNESCO, has designated all or part of twen-

ty-six national parklands as biosphere reserves.[24] Preliminary research has not revealed any basis for concluding that the biosphere
reserve project creates binding legal obligations for the participating nations with respect to biosphere reserves in other nations.
Nevertheless, the project may give rise to expectations that warrant some legal protection and contains, at the very least, an element of moral suasion. That result might particularly follow where
two adjacent parks are both biosphere reserves, as is the case with
the United States' Glacier National Park and Canada's Waterton
Lakes National Park. Recently proposed legislation would direct
the Secretary of the Interior to give priority attention to biosphere
reserves.[25]

The Solicitor of the U.S. Department of the Interior reportedly is, at the time of this writing, preparing a legal memorandum analyzing the Cabin Creek situation in light of international law, including the World Heritage Convention and the biosphere
reserve program. That analysis will be highly important not only
with respect to Cabin Creek, but also as it will, for the first time,
establish official U.S. positions on these international law issues.

The sixty-four national parklands located on U.S. seacoasts face
a variety of threats from marine pollution. Particularly threatened
are marine parks, such as Key Biscayne National Park and Virgin
Islands National Park, which include marine resources and underwater environments as primary features. Several international agreements are pertinent to the seacoast parklands.

The recently negotiated Law of the Sea Convention
prohibits marine pollution under certain circumstances.[26] Such pollution could eventually damage national parklands on U.S. seacoasts
and thus would be an unlawful activity, as defined in the Convention, giving rise to an international threat. The United States is
not party to this Convention (which is not yet in force) and has
declared that it will not be a party. Thus the United States may
not be able to take advantage of the Convention. However, it is
likely that the United States eventually will find it advisable to
become a party. Moreover, the Reagan administration has taken
the position that the Convention embodies customary international law except with respect to the deep-seabed mining
provisions. To the extent that the argument prevails, the United
States would have the protection (as well as the obligations) of the
relevant rules contained in the Convention even though it is not a
party.

A variety of multinational conventions regarding marine oil pollution and waste disposal that might be relevant to obtaining compensation for water-borne oil pollution to national parklands also exist.[27] There is also a convention regarding marine nuclear pollution.[28] The 1958 Convention on the High Seas might also provide protection regarding marine pollution.[29]

Furthermore, multilateral conventions for the protection of wildlife might be relevant to international threats to national parklands. Examples include the Convention on International Trade in Endangered Species of Flora and Fauna and the Convention on Nature Protection and Wildlife Preservation in the Western Hemisphere.[30]

In addition, the 1979 Convention on Long-Range Transboundary Air Pollution might offer some protection with respect to international threats involving air pollution.[31] Thirty nations (including Canada, the U.S.S.R., and the United States, but not including Mexico) and the European Economic Community are parties to that convention. If damage to national parklands was caused by pollution that violated any of these conventions, the United States would be justified in demanding cessation of the pollution-creating activity and demanding reparations.

Finally, the Environmental Law Center of the International Union for the Conservation of Nature and Natural Resources is circulating a draft convention on international protected areas. If that convention eventually comes into force and if the United States becomes a party, it would be relevant to international threats.

B. Bilateral Treaties

The United States has entered into a number of international agreements and treaties with a single other nation--usually Canada or Mexico--that might protect certain parklands from external international threats.

1. Parkland-specific treaties

Research has not revealed any binding international agreements that specifically apply to individual national parklands. Such agreements might exist, however, with respect to parklands such as Glacier National Park, which is part of an "international peace park" with Canada's Waterton Lakes National Park.[32] Such an agreement might have been entered into in the 1930s when the inter-

national peace park was formed or when the two parks were designated as biosphere reserves; inquiries and research thus far have
not uncovered any such agreement, however. Even if no such agreement explicitly requires ameliorating an international threat,
such an obligation--at least in a moral sense and possibly in a legal
sense, depending on the situation--might be inferred from the purposes underlying the formation of the international peace park, including conducting joint education and wildlife-monitoring activities. Other national parklands that might be protected by
such agreements include the San Juan Island National Historical
Park (Washington), the Roosevelt Campobello International Park
(which is administered jointly by Parks Canada and the U.S. National Park Service and is located in Canada), the Rio Grande Wild
and Scenic River (Texas), the Amistad National Recreation Area
(Texas), and the Chamizal National Memorial (Texas). If an international agreement exists with respect to a parkland, it might impose protection obligations that could be used with respect to
an international threat.

2. *United States-Canada boundary area agreements*
    In 1909, the United States and Great Britain (on behalf of
Canada) entered into the Boundary Waters Treaty,[33] which establishes certain obligations with respect to boundary waters and also
provides a mechanism--the International Joint Commission (IJC)-
-for helping resolve boundary water disputes. Notably, Article IV
of the Treaty provides: "It is further agreed that the waters herein
defined as boundary waters and waters flowing across the boundary shall not be polluted on either side to the injury of health or
property on the other." That language, which is (probably unrealis-
tically) absolute and unyielding on its face, is nowhere in the Treaty
defined more precisely, and research has not disclosed any detailed
analysis of such terms as "polluted," "injury," "health," or "property."[34] The force of Article IV may be reduced considerably by the
inclusion in Article II of a provision akin to the "Harmon Doctrine,"
which holds that a nation has the unqualified sovereign right to
utilize and dispose of the waters of an international river flowing
through its territory.[35]
    The fact that Glacier National Park is a biosphere reserve may
affect the application of Article IV, on the theory that the term
"property" includes that biosphere reserve status. According to that
argument, any interference with biosphere reserve goals or uses

would constitute an injury to property within the meaning of Article IV and thus would constitute a violation of the Boundary Waters Treaty.

The IJC, which is composed of three members from each nation, is a quasi-judicial body with mandatory jurisdiction and binding authority to approve or disapprove the quantitative--but not qualitative--aspects of projects such as boundary water diversions or obstructions.[36] In addition, Article IX of the Boundary Waters Treaty provides that either or both nations may refer matters to the IJC for its nonbinding recommendation. Such references tend to be handled in an ad hoc fashion, often involving (as in the case of the Cabin Creek controversy) a joint investigative board with the directive to conduct scientific studies. The recommendations have not always been followed strictly, but have generally been followed in spirit. Article X of the treaty permits both parties to refer a dispute to the IJC for a binding decision, but that has never been done.[37]

In 1972, the United States and Canada also entered into an agreement regarding Great Lakes water quality, based on a report of the IJC.[38] A more detailed supplemental agreement specifying measures for achieving water-quality objectives was entered into in 1978.[39] Those agreements may provide protection regarding the water quality of national parklands located in or adjacent to the Great Lakes system.[40]

3. *United States-Mexico boundary area agreements*

Mexico and the United States have entered into a long series of boundary area agreements over the past century. Most recently, a 1983 executive agreement provides a framework for negotiations to establish air pollution regulatory standards within one hundred kilometers on either side of the border.[41] That agreement was preceded by a 1978 agreement regarding cooperation on the environment.[42] Negotiations under the 1983 Environmental Agreement resulted in another (apparently nonbinding) agreement dated July 19, 1985, to control emissions from the recently opened smelter in Nacozari, Mexico, and from the smelter in Douglas, Arizona, each of which pollutes the other country.[43] The 1983 Environmental Agreement might also prove useful with respect to any international threats involving air pollution in the border area (for example, to Big Bend National Park) and possibly other types of international threats (such as the threat from Mexico's use of DDT and other pesticides, which are reportedly affecting animal species in the United States (including those at Organ Pipe Cactus National Monument in Arizona[44]) and the threat from Mexico's increased irrigation activities (which is reportedly lowering the groundwater table in the same park).[45]

A 1944 treaty[46] established the International Boundary and Water Commission (IBWC) to replace the old International Boundary Commission (created by treaty in 1889 to settle boundary demarcation disputes[47]) to plan, build, and manage border waterworks, to enter into further agreements regarding international waters, and to settle disputes regarding interpretation of the Agreement if both parties consent. The IBWC, which has been quite active, might provide a forum for investigating international threats, though it has not been used for that purpose thus far.[48]

4. Others

The United States has bilateral environmental cooperation treaties with the Soviet Union (1972), West Germany (1974), Japan (1975), Panama (1979), France (1984), and the Netherlands (1985).[49] These treaties might provide assistance with respect to particular international threats, although I have not had the opportunity to investigate that possibility in detail. Bilateral treaties regarding migratory wildlife and fish might also provide some protection, although time constraints have not allowed identification of such agreements.

C. General Customary International Law

Determining whether a rule of customary international law exists is a difficult task. The test is whether there has been a general, consistent, and representative practice of nations taken or done under the belief that such practice was required (or, in some instances, permitted) by international law.[51] That inquiry is complex, and the standards that have been applied are less than crystal clear. The situation is complicated because a rule of special custom or regional custom may exist between two or more nations even if a worldwide rule of customary international law on the same topic does not and because a customary international law norm does not bind a nation that has persistently and notoriously objected to the norm.

1. Protected areas generally

There does not appear to be any general customary international law regarding protected areas or national parklands per se that would provide protection to national parklands.

2. Transboundary harm generally

A substantial body of state practice has led some commentators to conclude that there exists general customary international law imposing accountability with respect to serious transboundary harm caused by otherwise lawful activities, that is, that a nation may be held liable for lawful activities in its territory that cause injury in or to the territory of another nation. An excellent study of the relevant state practice has been conducted by the Secretariat of the United Nations General Assembly.[51] In summary, this state practice consists of a wide variety of treaties (including those discussed above) and is supported[52] by arbitral decisions such as the *Trail Smelter*[53] and the *Laq Lanoux*[54] awards, court decisions such as the *Corfu Channel*,[55] United Nations declarations such as the 1972 Stockholm Declaration on the Human Environment (particularly Articles 21, 22, and 23) and General Assembly Resolutions 2995 and 3281 (Charter of Economic Rights and Duties of States).[56] Also supporting accountability is the general principle of *sic utere tuo ut alienum non laedas*, that one has the duty to exercise one's rights in ways that do not harm the interests of other subjects of law, which may be a "general principle of law" within the meaning of Article 38(1)(c) of the Statute of the International Court of Justice,[57] and international law principles and concepts such as the common heritage of mankind, due diligence, equity, good neighborliness, shared natural resources, and solidarity.

The principle imposing international accountability for causing serious transboundary harm reflects a tension between potentially competing aspects of sovereignty. On one hand is the state's right to engage freely in activities within its own territory and to regulate its own nationals. On the other hand is a state's right to exercise its rights without interference from other states. Given the many interrelationships--economic, ecological, political, and cultural--of today's world, activities within the territory of one state frequently affect activities in another state, which in turn requires balancing the rights of the states involved and restricting, either directly or indirectly, the activities of those states. The principle thus derives from the dual-faceted nature of sovereignty and the inevitable interdependence of the global community.

There is currently a lively debate regarding the existence and nature of the rule imposing international accountability for causing serious transboundary harm. Some commentators take the view that causing such harm--at least if it is caused negligently or by an ultrahazardous activity--is prohibited by international law and thus requires reparations as described in Part I. Others take the view that causing such harm is not unlawful but nevertheless gives rise to a type of international accountability referred to as "international liability," which requires reparations to be determined by a different set of rules.[58]

The main development regarding international liability is occuring in the International Law Commission of the United Nations, which is currently attempting to develop rules regarding transboundary harm.[59] In summary, the Commission's approach thus far has been to propose rules that encourage establishing conventional (treaty) regimes to deal with specific transboundary injury situations and that assert, in the absence of such a regime, a fourfold duty to prevent, inform, negotiate, and repair.[60] The duty to inform requires an acting nation to provide the affected nation with all relevant and available information when an activity occuring within the acting nation's territory or control gives or may give rise to harm to the affected nation. The duty to negotiate requires, under certain circumstances, the acting and affected nations to enter into negotiations regarding the necessity and form of a conventional regime to deal with the situation, taking into account a variety of enumerated criteria. If a conventional regime is not arrived at and if injury occurs, the duty to repair requires the nations to negotiate in good faith to determine the rights and obligations of the nations with respect to the injury. Reparations must be made unless they are not in accordance with the "shared expectations" of the nations involved. Reparations are to be determined according to a balance-of-interest test, taking into consideration the shared expectations of the nations, the enumerated criteria referred to above, and possibly the nations' actions with respect to the duties to prevent, inform, and negotiate. The duty to make reparations thus is not the same as a rule of strict liability, but it approaches, and may be identical to, strict liability if the harm is unpredictable or if the harm is predictable and the acting nation completely ignores the first three duties.[61]

The ultimate failure to make the required reparations in the event of harm is a wrongful act. Only at this point, therefore, has a nation committed an act prohibited by international law.

The concept of "shared expectations" in the Commission's approach seems closely related to the notion of regional customary international law. Consideration of the shared expectations of the United States and Canada, and the United States and Mexico, respectively, thus would presumably be affected by the same types of factors relevant to determining whether a norm of regional customary international law exists between those two sets of countries.[62] If that is the case, one would anticipate being able to identify fewer shared expectations between the United States and Mexico than between the United States and Canada.[63]

The scope of international liability, that is, under what circumstances the fourfold duty applies, has been the subject of ongoing debate. One aspect that remains largely unanswered is what actually constitutes transboundary harm. This aspect is particularly important because international liability potentially extends to the large universe of lawful activities and because so many activities have effects of some kind in other of these nations. It seems fairly clear that the injury resulting from the activity must be serious or significant,[64] a criterion that many injuries to natural habitat, for example, would meet, at least if there is a substantial adverse impact on a national parkland. But presumably not all threats to or pollution of a national parkland would qualify.

A second aspect concerns the degree to which nations are to be accountable for the activities of private persons. Thus far, it seems that nations are to be accountable for virtually all private activities within their territory or control. Canada, for example, would thus be accountable for effects resulting from such private activities as the Cabin Creek coal mine.

A third critical aspect concerns what types of activities are to be covered (assuming there is transboundary harm and that the actor is one for whose activities the nation is accountable). The Commission's current approach is to limit international liability to physical activities giving rise to physical transboundary harm. More specifically, the activity or situation giving rise to the harm must have a physical effect and a physical quality, and the effect

must flow from that quality by way of a "physical linkage,"
that is, natural physical media such as atmosphere, water, or earth,
rather than economic, political, international-trade, or cultural
media. Most international threats would satisfy this set of physical criteria.

A final point is that the Commission has not yet grappled with
the complexities arising from situations in which a joint activity
of two or more nations causes harm to a third nation,[65] or the activity of one nation combined with activity in another nation causes
harm in that other nation. International threats could obviously involve such situations. For example, pollution from the Nacozari
Smelter in Mexico might combine with pollution from Los Angeles
to pollute Grand Canyon National Park.

Because the Commission's deliberations carry only limited weight
standing alone and because, in any event, those deliberations
are still in process and substantial questions remain unanswered,
the rules just discussed do not offer concrete assistance at present
with respect to international threats. Nevertheless, they offer some
promise for the future.

As indicated above, some commentators take the view that,
quite apart from the Commission's deliberations, international environmental law of an enforceable nature already exists, based on
the state practice alluded to earlier in this part. It is not clear that
any general customary environmental law exists, but that does not
mean that a nation is entirely free under customary law to pollute
as it wishes without considering the interests of other nations.
Phrased differently, there are general international law principles (for example, *sic utere tuo ut alienum non laedas*)[66] that place
restrictions on behavior by nations, and those principles encompass, among other things, behavior affecting the environment.[67] It
is useful in examining that question to consider the *Trail Smelter*
case.[68] That case involved transboundary pollution from an iron
ore smelter in British Columbia that caused damage to private
property in the state of Washington. Canada and the United States
agreed to submit the dispute to arbitration. The tribunal stated:

> [U]nder the principles of international law, as well as of
> the law of the United States, no state has the right to
> use or permit the use of its territory in such a man-
> ner as to cause injury by fumes in or to the territory of

another or the properties or persons therein, when the case is of serious consequence and the injury is established by clear and convincing evidence.[69]

The arbitral tribunal, among other things, imposed a regulatory regime on Canada with respect to the smelter and held, significantly, that even after complying with those regulatory controls, Canada would still be liable to make reparations to the United States if any harm occurred, that is, Canada would have to make reparations for harm arising from wholly lawful activity.

No other international tribunal, to my knowledge, has applied such a rule to a transboundary pollution question (possibly because very few such disputes have been submitted to arbitration or to adjudication). In a case involving the destruction of two British warships by mines placed in Albanian waters, however, the International Court of Justice held that a nation was obliged "not to allow knowingly its territory to be used for acts contrary to the rights of other States."[70] Moreover, a significant embracing of the *Trail Smelter* rationale is found in Principle 21 of the nonbinding Stockholm Declaration, which reads as follows:

> States have, in accordance with the Charter of the United Nations and the principles of international law, the sovereign right to exploit their own resources pursuant to their own environmental policies, and the responsibility to insure that activities within their jurisdiction or control do not cause damage to the environment of other States or of areas beyond the limits of national jurisdiction.[71]

International law rules such as those just described obviously could be very important in determining accountability for international threats to national parklands, even when the activity giving rise to the threat is otherwise lawful and non-negligent.

3. *Non-navigational uses of international watercourses*

A number of commentators have concluded that there exists a norm of general customary international law to the effect that a riparian (or basin) nation has an obligation to consult and negotiate in good faith with other riparian (or basin) nations if that nation proposes to affect an international watercourse (for example, a river flowing between two nations) in a manner that might cause serious injury to those other nations.[72] Such a duty, assuming it exists, would provide some protection against international threats involving watercourses, but that duty might not prevent the threat from occurring or make that occurrence unlawful even if the duty of prior consultation and negotiation had been complied with.

The Helsinki Rules,[73] drafted by the private International Law Association in 1966, are regarded by some commentators as a comprehensive statement of the international law of rivers.[74] Article X of the Helsinki Rules provides that no nation has the right to pollute an international drainage basin so as to cause "substantial injury" to a co-basin nation. If that proposition is law, it may be useful in protecting against international threats involving pollution of international watercourses or international drainage basins more generally.

The International Law Commission of the United Nations is currently studying the non-navigational uses of international watercourses, and its deliberations may be useful in the future. The Commission has approached this topic in a manner similar to its approach to international liability, described above. Both are based on the potentially conflicting rights of sovereigns to be free to engage in activities in their own territory and still be free from interference from other states; both include duties to negotiate and to notify and inform; both encourage the formation of conventional regimes to deal with specific situations; both prescribe a balancing test that is not well defined; and both entail international accountability for failure to fulfill their respective obligations.[75] The prospects for progress in this area, however, are dimmed by the fact that the issue is extremely political due to the conflicting, and to some degree irreconcilable, interests of upstream and downstream nations.

D. Regional Customary International Law

As indicated above, the United States and Canada have a long tradition of cooperation with respect to boundary and environmental issues. It is possible that those activities have created a norm of regional customary international law regarding transboundary pollution or the environment more generally. If such a norm does exist--and I emphasize that my thinking on this topic is especially embryonic--it seems likely that the norm would provide protection against pollution to some degree and thus might be helpful with respect to protecting national parklands against international threats emanating from Canada. The behavior of the two nations on which such a regional norm might be based include the 1909 Boundary Waters Treaty; activities in connection with the *Trail Smelter* arbitration; the IJC investigations and responses thereto; cooperation regarding the Waterton-Glacier International Peace Park in the 1930s; the other jointly operated or established national parklands or similar areas identified above,[76] and the biosphere reserve activities more recently; the 1972 and 1978 Great Lakes Agreements; a 1980 Memorandum of Intent Between the Government of Canada and the Government of the United States Concerning Transboundary Air Pollution;[77] the 1986-87 discussions between the two nations about cooperating on an acid rain study; the 1985 Pacific Salmon Treaty regarding salmon management off the coasts of Washington, British Columbia, and Alaska;[78] and a common legal tradition with respect to issues such as nuisance.[79] In this respect, it is interesting that in the *Gulf of Maine* case (concerning the maritime boundary between the two nations in the Gulf of Maine area), the panel of the International Court of Justice based its reasoning in part on the long tradition of cooperation between the two nations.[80]

One might also attempt to identify a norm of regional customary international law regarding pollution between the United States and Mexico. Relevant behavior by the nations in this respect would include the many bilateral agreements identified in Part I.B.3 above; the activities of the IBWC and responses thereto; the ongoing dispute about the quality of the Colorado River; and the fact that the Douglas Smelter in the United States sent pollution into Mexico for many years with no compensation and little or no amelioration by the United States.[81] The fact that Mexico is a less developed country might also ffect the contents of any regional norm.[82] That Mexico has a civil law system whereas the United States has a common law system might lessen the likelihood that a regional norm exists. As with the possibility that there exists a regional norm between the United States and Canada, my research here is at a very early stage.

It might also be possible to establish the existence of other regional or special customary international laws relevant to protecting national parklands. I raise two possibilities, neither of which I have had the opportunity to investigate. First, several national parklands are located in, or on the rim of, the Caribbean Basin, where regional initiatives have occurred. Perhaps regional customary law exists in that regard. Second, it is sometimes argued that special customary international law may exist among nations that are grouped according to similarities other than geographic proximity. Perhaps a special norm relevant to national parkland preservation exists among industrialized countries or among countries with similar environmental protection strategies or laws.

III. DOMESTIC THREATS

We turn now to the question of whether international law requires the United States to protect national parklands against domestic threats, that is, threats originating from within the United States. I have encountered no evidence of customary international law that would require the United States to protect national parklands against domestic threats. With respect to international agreements, if any parkland-specific agreement exists, as is hypothesized in Part I.B.1, it may require the United States to protect a particular national parkland. Similarly, if the United States is required by an international agreement, such as a migratory bird or wildlife treaty, to protect the breeding grounds or other habitat of a particular species and such breeding ground or habitat is in a national park, international law could be relevant.

The World Heritage Convention[83] obligates participatory nations in which outstanding natural or cultural resources are located to engage in some activities, although the extent of that obligation is uncertain. Article 4, for example, states that each party to the Convention:

> recognizes that the duty of insuring the identification, protection, conservation, presentation and transmission to future generations of the cultural and natural heritage referred to in Articles 1 and 2 and situated on its territory, belongs primarily to that State. It will do all it can to this end, to the utmost of its own resources and, where appropriate, with any international assistance and cooperation.

The inclusion of the word "duty" is reassuring; the qualification implied by the terms "do all it can," "to the utmost of its own resources," and "where appropriate," reduce the strength of that obligation considerably.

Similarly, Article 5 provides that each party to the Convention "shall endeavour, insofar as possible, and as appropriate for each country" to take a number of enumerated measures, including "the appropriate legal, scientific, technical, administrative and financial measures necessary for the identification, protection, conservation, presentation and rehabilitation of [the cultural and natural heritage situated on its territory]." It is not obvious that the promise to "endeavour, insofar as possible, and as appropriate for each country" entails any obligation other than one of good faith. The judges in the *Tasmania* case disagreed on that issue.[84] A 1981 Interior Department legal memorandum (summarizing a 1980 memorandum) states that "the Convention . . . established a general good faith responsibility for each signatory to protect heritage properties, but left latitude for implementation to each country."[85] (The 1981 memorandum further says that 16 U.S.C. § 470a-1 "implements these provisions . . . and [restricts] that latitude" in such a way that "the Secretary [of the Interior] must be satisfied that each nominated site has adequate legal protection to ensure its preservation.") There does not appear to be a definitive answer at present regarding the extent of the obligations imposed by Articles 4 and 5 of the Convention, but it is clear that the obligations exist and that they at least require good faith efforts.

Finally, it is possible that either customary international law or international agreements could provide a type of indirect protection to national parklands against domestic threats. For example, the United States' boundary agreements with Canada and with Mexico possibly could provide a basis for protecting a national parkland from a domestic threat if the existence of that threat also resulted in prohibited harm in Canada or Mexico, and thus caused the United States to be in violation of any of those international agreements.

IV. CONCLUSIONS AND RECOMMENDATIONS

A growing body of international practice exists that is evolving to--and may already have formed, in particular instances--general customary international law with respect to transboundary harm, even where the activities giving rise to the harm are not unlawful in any way. At present, except possibly with respect to the United States' immediate neighbors, that body of law does not offer much assistance in terms of international threats to national parklands, although there is a duty that a state should not allow its territory to be used in such a manner as to cause serious injury to or in the territory (including the parklands) of another state. Customary international law regarding international watercourses may require prior consultation and good-faith negotiation about international threats involving international rivers or bays, but it is doubtful that that general custom provides much additional assistance.

It is also possible that regional customary law which exists between Canada and the United States and between Mexico and the United States might provide some protection against international threats. Other relevant regional or special customary norms might also exist.

A set of treaties--and possibly some customary international law--concerning pollution at sea is relevant to national parklands threatened by pollution from the high seas. In addition, the United States has bilateral agreements with Canada and Mexico that may either protect a specific parkland or provide a framework for negotiations regarding international threats. More generally, the long experience of the international legal system in negotiating treaties and resolving disputes offers some guidance in dealing with international threats. Furthermore, a handful of national parklands are World Heritage sites or international biosphere reserves, and those programs may offer some protection, either directly or indirectly.

With respect to the future, the first step is to recognize the international dimension of the external threats situation. The United States may have international obligations, which should not be ignored, with respect to preventing or alleviating domestic threats. Conversely, the United States may have rights under international law vis-a-vis another nation from which international threats to national parklands are emanating. Serious international threats exist now and are certain to intensify. Moreover, international threats almost certainly will not be removed spontaneously by the foreign nations in which they arise, and they cannot adequately be dealt with unilaterally by the United States. Bilateral or multilateral action and cooperation are imperative, and it is equally imperative that U.S. legislative and executive leaders recognize that reality.

Second, the United States needs to understand more precisely the nature and dimensions of the international threat facing national parklands. We need to inventory, quantify, and evaluate the sources of threats and their likely effects on specific national parkland resources. The National Park Service should prepare a report analyzing and documenting those issues of concern to the Service, to be used as the basis for policy making and management. We also need to put into place a permanent monitoring system for continuously surveying the existence and impact of international threats. That type of information is necessary not only for policy making and for planning and implementing specific domestic remedial measures (to the extent they can be taken), but also for use in negotiating with other nations and in possible dispute settlement procedures if negotiations do not resolve the issue.

Third, to the extent domestic remedial and protective measures are appropriate, they should be implemented, if necessary through the U.S. criminal code. Fourth, the United States must evaluate the present relevance of international law to external threats and take steps within the international legal framework to strengthen the international rules and procedures for dealing with external threats. This process will almost certainly involve give and take, because U.S. activities threaten protected areas and other resources in foreign nations. The United States' relationships with Canada and Mexico are certainly the most important aspects of this effort and deserve careful and sustained attention. Past involvement with boundary issues and other environmental matters will undoubtably prove relevant in those endeavors. The National Park Service, as the U.S. agency with the most relevant experience managing and protecting national parklands and implementing solutions negotiated at the international level, should play a significant role. Nongovernmental organizations and the public at large should also be invited to participate in meaningful ways.[86]

Fifth, in establishing rules and procedures, attention should be paid not only to national parklands but to environmental protection and interdependence more generally. In addition, the focus should be on preventing harm before it occurs, because of the frequent inadequacy of remedial measures. Nevertheless, reparation rules should also be clarified and strenthened, because it is unfortunately probable that they will be called upon with increasing frequency unless the nations of the world act in a more enlightened manner regarding transboundary impact than has heretofore been the case.

NOTES

*Associate Professor of Law, University of Colorado. This chapter is dedicated to Tom Lucke, National Park Service, whose enthusiasm and dedication were an inspiration to us all. I would like to thank Jim Chandler, Rick Collins, Rick Cook, Alan Fitzsimmons, Bill Gregg, Bob Keiter, Dan Kimball, Howard Klemme, Laurie Lambrix, Tom Lucke, Randall Luthi, Larry MacDonnell, Gary Machlis, David Mastbaum, Terry Parsons, Joe Sax, and David Simon for commenting on or otherwise adding perspective to earlier drafts of this chapter; Lucky Smith for research assistance; and the Natural Resources Law Center, University of Colorado School of Law, for funding that research.

1. *See, e.g.,* U. S. DEPARTMENT OF THE INTERIOR, NATIONAL PARK SERVICE, STATE OF THE PARKS--1980: A REPORT TO THE CONGRESS [hereinafter cited as STATE OF THE PARKS].

2. *Id.* at 48-50; Keiter, *On Protecting the National Parks from the External Threats Dilemma,* 20 LAND & WATER L. REV. 355, 361-69 (1985); Wilson, *Cabin Creek and International Law--An Overview,* 5 PUB. LAND L. REV. 110 (1984).

3. Those twenty-four are as follows: Amistad National Recreation Area, Apostle Islands National Lakeshore, Big Bend National Park, Chamizal National Memorial, Coronado National Memorial, Coulee Dam National Recreation Area, Glacier National Park, Glacier Bay National Park and Preserve, Grand Portage National Monument, Isle Royale National Park, Klondike Gold Rush National Historical Park, North Cascades National Park, Organ Pipe Cactus National Monument, Palo Alto Battlefield National Historic Site, Perry's Victory and International Peace Memorial, Pictured Rocks National Lakeshore, Rio Grande Wild and Scenic River, Ross Lake National Recreation Area, Saint Croix Island International Historic Site, San Juan Island National Historical Park, San Juan National Historic Site, Voyageurs National Park, Wrangell-Saint Elias National Park and Preserve, Yukon-Charley Rivers National Preserve. *See also infra* note 41. The STATE OF THE PARKS, *supra* note 1, at 52-57, identifies 386 threats to those national parks, although it is not clear how many are international threats. For additional national parklands on the Great Lakes, *see infra* note 40; these parklands could also be considered to be on the United States-Canada border, depending on one's definition.

4. Those sixty-four are as follows: Acadia National Park, Aniachak National Monument and Preserve, Assateague Island National Seashore, Bering Land Bridge National Preserve, Big Cypress National Preserve, Biscayne National Park, Boston National Historical Park, Buck Island Reef National Monument, Cabrillo National Monument, Canaveral National Seashore, Cape Cod National Seashore, Cape Hatteras National Seashore, Cape Krusenstern National Monument, Cape Lookout National Seashore, Castillo de San Marcos National Monument, Channel Islands National Park, Christiansted National Historic Site, Cumberland Island National Seashore, De Soto National Memorial, Everglades National Park, Fire Island National Seashore, Fort Caroline National Memorial, Fort Clatsop National Memorial, Fort Frederica National Monument, Fort Jefferson National Monument, Fort Matanzas National Monument, Fort McHenry National Historic Site, Fort Point National Historic Site, Fort Raleigh National Historic Site, Fort Sumter National Monument, Gateway National Recreation Area, George Washington Birthplace National Monument, Glacier Bay National Park and Preserve, Golden Gate National Recreation Area, Gulf Islands National Seashore, Haleakala National Park, Hawaii Volcanoes National Park, Jean Lafitte National Historical Park, Kalaupapa National Historical Park, Kaloko-Honokohau National Historical Park, Katmai National Park and Preserve, Kenai Fjords National Park, Lake Clark National Park and Preserve, Minute Man National Historical Park, Muir Woods National Monument, Noatak National Preserve, Padre Island National Seashore, Pu'uhonua O Honaunau National Historical Park, Puukohola Heiau National Historic Site, Redwood National Park, Saint Croix Island International Historic Site, San Juan Island National Historical Park, Santa Monica Mountains National Recreation Area, Sitka National Historical Park, Statue of Liberty National Monument, U.S.S. Arizona Memorial, Virgin Islands National Park, War in the Pacific National Historical Park, Wrangell-Saint Elias National Park and Preserve, and Wright Brothers Na-

tional Memorial. The STATE OF THE PARKS report, *supra* note 2, at 52-57, identifies 698 threats to those national parklands, although again, it is not clear how many are international threats.

5. *See, e.g.*, CONGRESSIONAL RESEARCH SERVICE, LIBRARY OF CONGRESS, THE NACOZARI, MEXICO, COPPER SMELTER: AIR POLLUTION IMPACTS ON THE U.S. SOUTHWEST (1985): Magraw, *The International Law Commission's Study of International Liability for Nonprohibited Acts as it Relates to Developing Countries*, 26 WASH. L. REV. 1041 (1986); Denver Post, Dec. 4, 1986, at 4A, col. 1.

6. *See, e.g.*, R. FALK, THIS ENDANGERED PLANET (1971); J. SCHNEIDER, WORLD PUBLIC ORDER OF THE ENVIRONMENT (1979); I. VAN LIER, ACID RAIN AND INTERNATIONAL LAW (1980).

7. *See generally*, F. KIRGIS, JR., PRIOR CONSULTATION IN INTERNATIONAL LAW 1-2 (1983).

8. *See, e.g.*, Bilder, *International Law and Natural Resource Policies*, 20 NAT. RESOURCES J. 451, 480-84 (1980).

9. *See, e.g.*, 16 U.S.C. § 470a-2; Exec. Order 12114, 44 Fed. Reg. 1957 (1979); International Environmental Protection Act of 1983, Pub. L. No. 98-164, §§ 701-704, 97 Stat. 1045-1047 (1983) (international wildlife resources); Endangered Species Act, Pub. L. No. 97-301, § 8, 87 Stat. 892-893 (1981); note 24, *infra*, and accompanying text. This chapter does not investigate the requirements of domestic law in the context mentioned in the text accompanying this note.

10. The U.S. federal government's constitutional authority to enter into treaties with respect to federally-owned lands (which total nearly 730 million square acres, *see*, THE WORLD ALMANAC AND BOOK OF FACTS: 1987, at 436) is clear. The federal government's constitutional authority to prescribe rules for protected lands regulated by state or local governments also appears clear, at least if appropriate political procedures are followed and it does not appear that the majority of states are picking on one state or a few states. *See* Garcia v. San Antonio Metropolitan Transit Authority, 469 U.S. 528, 552 (1985); *see also* Missouri v. Holland, 252 U.S. 416 (1920). Similarly, the federal government's constitutional authority to regulate or otherwise affect, via treaties with foreign governments, protected lands under the control of Indian tribes (*see, e.g.*, 19 Navajo Trib. Code § 1 (1969); *cf.* 16 U.S.C. §§ 445, 445a (1982) (Canyon de Chelly National Monument is administered by the federal government pursuant to Navajo consent) is less clear, although (as with a treaty applying to state-owned land) the treaty's applicability to lands owned by Indian tribes must be clearly stated. *See* United States v. Dion, 106 S. Ct. 2216, 2220 (1986). Applicable customary international law (*see, infra,* text accompanying note 49) would bind the United States regardless of the nature of the lands affected, unless the customary-law norm related to that nature.

11. *See, infra*, text accompanying notes 42-59.

12. According to Article 38(c) of the Statute of the International Court of Justice (ICJ), there is a third source of international law: "the general principles of law recognized by civilized nations." That source has rarely been used, but it might be significant for present purposes. *See, infra*, text accompanying notes 61 and 68. Regarding the possible law-creating effect of international organizations such as the United Nations, *see, infra*, note 21.

13. Convention Concerning the Protection of the World Cultural and Natural Heritage, Nov. 16, 1972, art. 1 & 2, 27 U.S.T. 37, T.I.A.S. No. 8226.

14. U.S. Dep't of State, Office of the Legal Advisor, TREATIES IN FORCE 318-319 (1986).

15. *See* World Heritage Convention, *supra*, note 13, at art. 11 (authorizing the list). The national parklands on the list are: Everglades National Park, Grand Canyon National Park, Great Smoky Mountains National Park, Independence National Historical Park (Independence Hall), Mammoth Cave National Park, Mesa Verde National Park, Olympic National Park, Redwood National Park, San Juan Island Historic Site, Statue of Libery National Monument, Yellowstone National Park, and Yosemite National Park. The other U.S. sites on the list are Cahokia Mounds State Historic Site and La Fortaleza, Puerto Rico.

16. 57 A.L.R. 450 (1983).

17. *See, e.g.,* Iwasawa, *The Doctrine of Self-Executing Treaties in the United States: A Critical Analysis,* 26 VA. J. INT'L L. 627 (1986); ALI, RESTATEMENT FOREIGN RELATIONS LAW OF THE UNITED STATES (REVISED) § 131; Frolova v. USSR, 761 F.2d 370 (7th Cir. 1985).

18. *See* Memorandum from Assistant Solicitor, Parks and Recreation [Dep't of the Interior], to Director, Heritage Conservation and Recreation Service, Aug. 22, 1980 (copy on file with the author).

19. 16 U.S.C. § 470a-1.

20. 36 C.F.R. 73 (1985); Memorandum from Associate Solicitor, Conservation and Wildlife [Dep't of the Interior], to Assistant Secretary for Fish and Wildlife and Parks, regarding implementation of the World Heritage Convention and Pub. L. No. 96-515, Jan. 21, 1981.

21. *See* Australia v. Tasmania, 57 A.L.R. 450, 470 (Gibbs, C.J.), 534 (Brennan, J.), 546 (Deane, J.) (1983).

22. *See generally* Lucas, *Acid Rain: The Canadian Position,* 32 KAN. L. REV. 165, 171-75 (1983).

23. *See* UNESCO, *Action Plan for Biosphere Reserves,* 20 NATURE & RESOURCES (Oct.-Dec. 1984). For a description of the U.S. approach to biosphere reserves, *see* DEP'T OF STATE, U.S. MAB SECRETARIAT, GUIDELINES FOR IDENTIFICATION, EVALUATION AND SELECTION OF BIOSPHERE RESERVES IN THE UNITED STATES (OES/ENR(MAB)) First Revision (1983). A final point to be made with respect to the sources of law is that the existence of the United Nations General Assembly and the practice of the General Assembly to pass resolutions (and declarations) have raised a significant controversy with respect to the effect of such resolutions. It seems clear that a unanimous General Assembly resolution that states that it embodies international law will be given great, and probably conclusive, weight in establishing that an international law norm does in fact exist. Resolutions that do not contain such a statement or that are not unanimous raise more difficult questions, on which commentators differ widely. Actions or declarations by other parts or agencies of the United Nations or by other international organizations are less persuasive as sources of international law than are General Assembly resolutions. Thus, for example, statements by UNESCO regarding the meaning of the biosphere reserve program or the World Heritage Convention do not, by themselves, constitute international law.

24. Those twenty-six are: Big Bend National Park, Big Thicket National Park, Cape Lookout National Seashore, Channel Islands National Park, Congaree Swamp National Monument, Cumberland Island National Seashore, Death Valley National Monument, Denali National Park, Everglades National Park, Gates of the Arctic National Park (part), Glacier National Park, Glacier Bay National Park, Great Smoky Mountains National Park, Haleakala National Park, Hawaii Volcanoes National Park, Isle Royale National Park, Joshua Tree National Monument, Kings Canyon National Park, Noetek National Preserve, Olympic National Park, Organ Pipe Cactus National Park, Redwood National Park, Rocky Mountain National Park, Sequoia National Park, Virgin Islands National Park, and Yellowstone National Park. In addition, Big South Fork National Recreation Area, Shenandoah National Park, and Voyageurs National Park have been recommended as reserves by the U.S. Man and the Biosphere Panel.

25. *See* S. 2092, 99th Cong., 2d Sess.; 132 CONG. REC. S1561 (Feb. 25, 1986). Such legislation, if perceived as an attempt to force participation by state and local authorities, might discourage cooperation by those authorities and thus prove detrimental to the program.

26. Convention on the Law of the Sea, opened for signature Dec. 10, 1982, U.N. Doc. A/CONF.62/122, arts. 1, 192-195, 207-212, reprinted in 21 INT'L LEGAL MAT. 1261, 1271, 1308, 1310-11 (1982).

27 *See, e.g.,* International Convention for the Prevention of Pollution of the Sea by Oil, May 12, 1954, 12 U.S.T. 2989, T.I.A.S. No. 4900, 327 U.N.T.S. 3; Convention on the Prevention of Marine Pollution by Dumping of Waste and Other Matter, Dec. 29, 1972,

26 U.S.T. 2403, T.I.A.S. No. 8165; *cf.* International Convention on Civil Liability for Oil Pollution Damages, Nov. 29, 1969, 973 U.N.T.S. 3 (United States not a party); International Convention on the Establishment of an International Fund for Compensation for Oil Pollution Damage, Dec. 18, 1971, 1978 Gr. Brit. T.S. No. 95 (Cond. 7383), U.N.T.S. ___ (United States not a party).

28. *See* Convention Relating to Civil Liability in the Field of Maritime Carriage of Nuclear Material, Dec. 17, 1971, 974 U.N.T.S. 255 (United States not a party); *cf.* Convention on the Liabiltiy of Operators of Nuclear Ships, May 25, 1962 (not yet in force), reprinted in 57 AM. J. INT'L. L. 268 (1963). For a discussion of the recent negotiations to revise the oil pollution conventions and to develop a new compensation regime for ocean pollution incidents involving hazardous and noxious substances, *see* Comment, *Dead in the Water: International Law, Diplomacy and Compensation for Chemical Pollution at Sea,* 26 VA. J. INT'L L. 485 (1986).

29. 13 U.S.T. 2312, T.I.A.S. 5200, 450 U.N.T.S. 82 (arts. 24 & 25). The rules in the 1985 Convention might be superseded by the rules in the new Law of the Sea Convention, however.

30. Mar. 3, 1973, 27 U.S.T. 1089; Oct. 12, 1940, 56 Stat. 1354, T.S. No. 981. For other examples, *see* F.P. GRAD, TREATISE ON ENVIRONMENTAL LAW, ch. 13 (1983).

31. March 16, 1983, ___ U.S.T. ___ ; T.I.A.S. 10541.

32. *Cf.* Pub. L. No. 72-116, 45 Stat. 145 (May 2, 1932).

33. Boundary Waters Treaty, Jan. 11, 1909, United States-Great Britain, 36 Stat. 2448, T.S. No. 548.

34. Accord Arbitblit, 8 ECOLOGY L. Q. 339, 348-49 (1979).

35. The Harmon Doctrine was enunciated in the course of an 1895 boundary water dispute between Mexico and the United States. *See* 21 Op. Att'y Gen. 281-82; MCCAFFREY, SECOND REPORT ON THE LAW OF THE NON-NAVIGATIONAL USES OF INTERNATIONAL WATERCOURSES, U.N. Doc. A/CN.4/399, paras. 79-87 (1986). The United States did not adhere to that doctrine in the dispute in which the doctrine was asserted, however, and it is not evident that the United States has ever followed the doctrine. *See* MCCAFFREY, PROTECTION OF THE TRANSBORDER ENVIRONMENT BETWEEN MEXICO AND THE UNITED STATES (1986) (unpublished) [hereinafter cited as MCCAFFREY, PROTECTION].

36. *See generally* J. CARROLL, ENVIRONMENTAL DIPLOMACY: AN EXAMINATION AND A PERSPECTIVE OF CANADIAN-U.S. TRANSBOUNDARY ENVIRONMENTAL RELATIONS 47 (1983).

37. *See* Wilson, *Cabin Creek and International Law--An Overview,* 5 PUB. LAND L. REV. 110, 118 (1984); Comment, *Who'll Stop the Rain: Resolution Mechanisms for U.S.-Canadian Transboundary Pollution Disputes,* 12 DEN. J. INT'L L. & POL'Y 51, 69-70 (1982); IJC, 1983-1984 ACTIVITIES REPORT. For a report expressing dissatisfaction with certain aspects of the IJC's powers, *see* AMERICAN BAR ASS'N & CANADIAN BAR ASS'N, SETTLEMENT OF INTERNATIONAL DISPUTES BETWEEN CANADA AND THE USA (1979) (discussed in Mingst, *Evaluating Public and Private Approaches to International Solutions to Acid Rain Pollution,* 22 NAT. RESOURCES. J. 5, 10 (1982)).

38. Agreement Between the United States of America and Canada on Great Lakes Water Quality, April 15, 1972, 23 U.S.T. 301, T.I.A.S. No. 7312. *See* J. BARROS & D. JOHNSTON, THE INTERNATIONAL LAW OF POLLUTION 71 (1974). See generally *Seminar Papers--Great Lakes Legal Seminar: Diversion and Consumptive Use,* 18 CASE W. RES. J. INT'L L. 1 (1986).

39. *See* Agreement Between the United States and Canada on Great Lakes Water Quality, Nov. 22, 1978, United States-Canada, 30 U.S.T. 1383, T.I.A.S. No. 9257.

40. Those national parklands include: Apostle Islands National Lakeshore, Indiana Dunes National Lakeshore, Isle Royale National Park, Perry's Victory and International Peace Memorial, Pictured Rocks National Lakeshore, and Sleeping Bear Dunes National Lakeshore.

41. *See* Agreement Between the United States of America and the United Mexican States on Cooperation for the Protection and Improvement of the Environment in the Border Area, 19 WEEKLY COMP. PRES. DOC. 1137 (Aug. 14, 1983) [hereinafter cited as the 1983 Environmental Agreement]. Article 2 of that Agreement provides:

> the Parties undertake, to the fullest extent practical, to adopt the appropriate measures to prevent, reduce and eliminate sources of pollution in their respective territory which affect the border area of the other. Additionally, the Parties shall cooperate in the solution of the environmental problems of mutual concern in the border area, in accordance with the provisions of this Agreement.

See also art. 7. For a discussion of that Agreement, *see* Note, *The Environmental Cooperation Agreement Between Mexico and the United States: A Response to the Pollution Problems of the Borderlands*, 19 CORNELL INT'L L. J. 87 (1986).

42. Agreement for Cooperation on Environmental Programs and Transboundary Problems, June 19, 1978, 30 U.S.T. 1574, T.I.A.S. 9264 (exchange of notes).

43. See *U.S. and Mexico Plan to Curb Pollution by Copper Smelters*, N.Y. Times, July 23, 1985, at A8, col. 1.

44. *See* STATE OF THE PARKS, *supra* note 1, at 21.

45. *See* U.S. DEPARTMENT OF THE INTERIOR, NATIONAL PARK SERVICE, ORGAN PIPE CACTUS NATIONAL MONUMENT NATURAL AND CULTURAL RESOURCE MANAGEMENT PLAN (1983), at 55-68.

46. Treaty Relating to the Utilization of Waters of the Colorado and Tijuana Rivers and of the Rio Grande, Feb. 3, 1944, 59 Stat. 1219, T.S. No. 994, 3 U.N.T.S. 313.

47. Convention Between the United States and Mexico, Mar. 1, 1889, 26 Stat. 1512, U.S.T.S. 232, 9 Bevans 877.

48. For a discussion of some of the IBWC's activities and of other United States-Mexico agreements and activities (including at the local government level) regarding transboundary environmental issues, *see* MCCAFFREY, PROTECTION, *supra* note 35; Bath, *U.S.-Mexico Experience in Managing Transboundary Air Resources: Problems, Prospects, and Recommendations for the Future*, 22 NAT. RESOURCES J. 1147 (1982); Bath, *Environmental Issues in the United States-Mexico Borderlands*, 1 J. BORDERLANDS STUD. 49 (1986).

49. *See* U.S. DEP'T OF STATE, OFFICE OF THE LEGAL ADVISOR, TREATIES IN FORCE (1986).

50. *See, e.g.*, RESTATEMENT OF FOREIGN RELATIONS LAW OF THE UNITED STATES (Revised) § 102(2) (1986).

51. *See* SURVEY OF STATE PRACTICE RELEVANT TO INTERNATIONAL LIABILITY FOR INJURIOUS CONSEQUENCES ARISING OUT OF ACTS NOT PROHIBITED BY INTERNATIONAL LAW (prepared by U.N. Secretariat), U.N. Doc. ST/LEG/15 (1984).

52. As indicated by Article 38 of the ICJ's Statute, judicial decisions and the teachings of the most highly qualified publicists of the various nations are "subsidiary means for the determination of rules of law," although they are not, strictly speaking, sources of law themselves. Thus, for example, the 1941 *Trail Smelter* award holding Canada liable under international law for lawful transboundary pollution in the United States did not create a rule of international accountability in such circumstances, but it does serve as evidence that such a rule exists. *See* Trail Smelter (U.S. v. Can.), 3 R. Int'l Arb. Awards 1905 (1938 & 1941).

53. *Supra* note 52.

54. Laq Lanoux (Fr. v. Spain), 12 R. Int'l Arb. Awards 281 (1957) (French), 24 I.L.R. 101 (1957) (English).

55. Corfu Channel (U.K. v. Alb.), Merits, 1949 I.C.J. Rep. 4 (Judgment of Apr. 9).

56. REPORTS OF THE UNITED NATIONS CONFERENCE ON THE HUMAN ENVIRONMENT, Stockholm, June 5-16, 1972, Pt. 1, ch. I (UN Pub. Sales No. E73.II.A.14), *reprinted in* 11

I.L.M. 1416 (1972); G.A. Res. 2995, 21 U.N. GAOR, Supp. 30, U.N. Doc. A/8730, at 42 (1972); G.A. Res. 3281, art. 3, 29 U.N. GAOR, Supp. 30, U.N. Doc. A/9030, at 50 (1974). For a discussion of the weight to be given to United Nations declarations and resolutions in determining the existence of a particular international law norm, *see supra* note 23.

57. *See, e.g.*, OPPENHEIM, INTERNATIONAL LAW 291, 346-47 (8th ed., H. Lauterpacht, ed., 1950) (stating that principle is a general principle of law applicable by virtue of article 38(1)(c)); RESTATEMENT OF FOREIGN RELATIONS LAW OF THE UNITED STATES (Revised), pt. IV, Intro. Note (1986). Statute of I.C.J., art. 38(1)(c), 59 Stat. 1055, T.S. 993, 3 Bevans 1179; *see supra* note 11.

58. *Compare* Akehurst, *International Liability for Injurious Consequences Arising Out of Acts Nots Prohibited by International Law*, 16 NETH. Y.B. INT'L L. 3 (1985) and I. BROWNLIE, SYSTEM OF THE LAW OF NATIONS: STATE RESPONSIBILITY (PART I) 50 (1983) with Handl, *Liability as Obligation Established by a Primary Rule of International Law*, 16 NETH. Y.B. INT'L L. 49 (1985) and Magraw, *Transboundary Harm: The International Law Commission's Study of "International Liability,"* 80 AM. J. INT'L L. 305 (1986).

59. For a detailed description of that work, *see* Magraw, *supra* note 58. *See also* FIRST REPORT ON INTERNATIONAL LIABILITY FOR INJURIOUS CONSEQUENCES ARISING OUT OF ACTS NOT PROHIBITED BY INTERNATIONAL LAW, U.N. Doc. A/CN.4/402 & Corr. 1 & 2 (1986).

60. The Commission's approach can change, of course. A new special rapporteur, Julio Barboza, was appointed for this topic in 1985. Barboza has referred to the series of duties in several ways, at times in a manner that suggests that he does not think there is separable duty to prevent but only duties to inform or to negotiate. *See, e.g.*, FIRST REPORT ON INJURIOUS CONSEQUENCES ARISING OUT OF ACTS NOT PROHIBITED BY INTERNATIONAL LAW, at 8-10, 17 (Þ37), 34, U.N. Doc. A/CN.4/402 & Con. 1 & 2 (1986). The nature of the component duties will undoubtedly be resolved as the Commission continues its study.

61. *See supra* text preceeding note 11.

62. *See infra* Part I.D.

63. *See id.,* Magraw, *supra* note 5, at 1058.

64. For a discussion of some of the IBWC's activities and of other United States-Mexico agreements and activities (including at the local-government level) regarding transboundary environmental issues, *see* MCCAFFREY, PROTECTION, *supra* note 35; Bath, *U.S.-Mexico Experience in Managing Transboundary Air Resources: Problems, Prospects, and Recommendations for the Future,* 22 NAT. RESOURCES J. 1147 (1982); Bath, *Environmental Issues in the United States-Mexico Borderlands,* 1 J. BORDERLANDS STUD. 49 (1986).

65. For a brief discussion of that issue, *see* Magraw, *supra* note 58, at 329-30.

66. *See supra* text accompanying note 62.

67. *See* Brownlie, *A Survey of International Customary Rules of Environmental Protection,* 13 NAT. RESOURCES J. 179, 191 (1973); Johnston & Finkle, *Acid Precipitation in North America: The Case for Trans-boundary Cooperation,* 14 VAND. J. TRANSNAT'L L. 787, 818-19 (1981).

68. *Trail Smelter, supra* note 52.

69. *Id.* at 1965.

70. *See also Laq Lanoux* award, *supra* note 54.

71. *Supra* note 55. The same language appears in article 7.5 of the International Law Association's Declaration of the Progressive Development of Principles of Public International Law Relating to a New International Economic Order, 29 Aug. 1986.

72. *See, e.g.,* Bourne, *Procedure in the Development of International Drainage Basins: The Duty to Consult and to Negotiate,* 1972 CAN. ₄.B. INT'L L 212, 233. For an excellent discussion of that and related literature, *see* F. Kirgis, Jr., *supra* note 7, at 17-87.

73. International Law Ass'n, *Helsinki Rules on the Uses of the Waters of International Rivers* (1966), *reprinted in* J. Barros & D. Johnston, *supra* note 18, at 77-82.

74. *See* G. WETSTONE & A. ROSENCRANZ, ACID RAIN IN EUROPE AND NORTH AMERICA: NATIONAL RESPONSES TO AN INTERNATIONAL PROBLEM 157 (1983).

75. *See* Magraw, *supra* note 58, at 322.

76. *See supra,* text preceding note 34.

77. Dated Aug. 5, 1980, Canada-United States, U.S. Dept. State Bull., No. 2043, at 21 (Oct. 1980).

78. Treaty Concerning Pacific Salmon, entered into force March 18, 1985, United States-Canada, U.S.T. ___ , T.I.A.S. No .___.

79. *See* McCaffrey, *Private Remedies for Transfrontier Pollution Damage in Canada and the United States: A Comparative Survey,* 19 W. ONT. L. REV. 35 (1981).

80. For a thoughtful discussion of dispute settlement between Canada and the United States, *see* AMERICAN BAR ASS'N & CANADIAN BAR ASS'N, SETTLEMENT OF INTERNATIONAL DISPUTES BETWEEN CANADA AND THE U.S.A. (1979). For a discussion of resource issues between these two nations, see *U.S.-Canada Transboundary Resource Issues,* 26 NAT. RESOURCES J. 201-376 (1986).

81. *See* Magraw, *supra* note 5, at 1048.

82. *See id.* at 1049-59.

83. *See supra* text accompanying notes 13-22.

84. *Compare* Australia v. Tasmania, 57 A.L.R. 450, 489 (Mason, J.), 509 (Murphy, J.), 531 (Brennan, J.), & 546 (Deane, J.) (1983) (finding affirmative duties imposed by the Convention), *with id.* at 471 (Gibbs, C.J.), 514 (Wilson, J.) & 556 (Dawson, J.) (finding no such obligation).

85. *See supra* notes 19-21 and accompanying text.

86. The role of nongovernmental actors in protecting the environment is well known generally. An interesting example in the context of national parklands is that the idea to link Glacier National Park and Waterton Lakes National Park as the International Peace Park originated in a meeting between the Alberta and Montana Rotary Clubs in 1931, and those clubs lobbied effectively for the necessary legislation. R. SHARF, GLACIER NATIONAL PARK AND WATERTON LAKES NATIONAL PARK 8 (1967).

Chapter 7

GLACIER NATIONAL PARK AND ITS NEIGHBORS: A STUDY OF FEDERAL INTERAGENCY RELATIONS*

*Joseph L. Sax** and Robert B. Keiter****

I. INTRODUCTION

This Article grew out of simple curiosity about how neighboring federal agencies resolve land use conflicts among themselves - -a practical, difficult subject to which little attention has been given.[1] Most of the western national parks are bordered by federal lands administered by the United States Forest Service and the Bureau of Land Management (BLM)--agencies with multiple use mandates including mining, timber harvesting, grazing, and oil and gas development.[2] Activities on those neighboring lands frequently threaten harm to nearby parklands managed by the United States National Park Service for conservation of natural conditions.[3]

At one time, boundary lines all but defined the way public lands were managed. Foresters pursued their mission within the national forest limits and, across the border, national park officials prosecuted their quite different mission. Neither group paid much attention to what happened beyond their boundary line. This arrangement stirred little controversy in an era when less was known about wildlife management and when impacts on a common watershed or airshed, then less well understood, seemed less menacing. But modern environmental knowledge and concerns increasingly reveal conventional borders to be dangerous irrelevances, mocked by acid rain and the tragedies that befall migratory wildlife. Because traditional land management builds fundamentally on the idea of a defined boundary--good fences make good neighbors--and rights and responsibilities are defined with respect to such boundaries, the question arises: What happens when, and to the extent that, the boundary concept ceases to be functional?

Congress has been asking this question in oversight hearings on national parks, but so far has obtained only vague and general answers.[4] Traditionally, federal agency neighbors had no parallel to the protection that the common law of nuisance gives private land owners, who unlike federal land managers do sue each other.[5] Congress has usually dealt with its land agencies as if they were islands, each insulated from the other.[6] Indeed, the island is one of the most familiar metaphors for the national parks: islands of preservation, of beauty, and of solitude.[7] As a result, Congress has enacted legislation addressing the problem of incompatible missions among adjacent federal land agencies on only a few occasions.[8] Despite repeated urgings in recent years to enact new legislation to protect parks against external threats, Congress has so far declined to do so.[9] The Park Service, which presumably would benefit from such laws, asserts that no new legislation is needed, although it considers the national parks to be seriously imperilled by activities on neighboring lands.[10]

In light of this background, we wondered how park officials dealt with incompatible activities on nearby federal lands.[11] It seemed to us likely that some basic and important changes were taking place, and we set out to discover them. In 1980, the Park Service formally recognized the adverse effects on parks of external activities by issuing a *State of the Parks* report, which enumerated and categorized threats to every unit of the national park system.[12] We chose Glacier National Park for this case study[13] because it reported more threats than any other major park[14] and because of its physical setting, the diversity of its neighbors, and the issues presented by activities on neighboring lands.[15] In this Article, we describe some of what we learned about Glacier's relationships with its neighbors, we evaluate the Park's success in influencing external activities, and we draw some broader lessons that seem relevant to park protection legislation.

II. EXTERNAL THREATS TO GLACIER NATIONAL PARK

A wilderness-like buffer of undeveloped lands surrounds Glacier. But there are pressures to develop these areas. The park is bordered by two national forests--the Flathead and the Lewis & Clark--each largely leased for oil and gas development and subject to extensive timber harvesting.[16] To complicate matters, Glacier's western border is delineated by the North and Middle forks of the Flathead River, both of which are "designated" under the Wild and Scenic Rivers Act.[17] This Act requires that the river's watershed and shoreline be maintained in a "largely primitive" condition,[18] a mandate that is not easily achieved on the forest side where commercial timber harvesting is conducted.[19]

Glacier's northern border is the international boundary with Canada. North and west of Glacier, in Canada, but also within the watershed of the Flathead River, is the site of a proposed surface coal mine known as Cabin Creek. Lying west of Glacier in the North Fork region around Polebridge is largely undeveloped private land with considerable development potential. A state forest, managed under state law for maximum economic return,[20] also borders Glacier just across the Flathead River. On the park's southern boundary lie a highway, a railroad track, and a strip of private lands.

The Blackfeet Indian Reservation abuts the park on the east. The reservation, severely depressed economically and suffering from high unemployment, is divided on the issue of development--one faction wishes to develop the land, others desire to preserve it.[21] Relations between the Blackfeet and Glacier have long been strained, we were told, largely because the Blackfeet see adjacent lands within the park as an extension of their traditional religious and economic turf. A typical source of friction is cattle that wander from the reservation onto parklands and compete with park wildlife. The Blackfeet also resist interference by neighboring federal officials in decisions relating to tribal economic development. One result is the presence of oil and gas development on the reservation very near to Glacier's border. The Blackfeet claim rights of use under an 1896 agreement both in the park and in areas of the Lewis & Clark Forest, where oil and gas exploration is proposed.[22]

Glacier is home to the grizzly bear and the gray wolf,[23] as well as other wildlife species that roam between the park and wilderness areas in the two adjoining forests,[24] over lands that are valuable for timber harvesting and oil and gas prospecting. The grizzly and gray wolf are "listed" animals under the Endangered Species Act (ESA),[25] which is administered by the United States Fish and

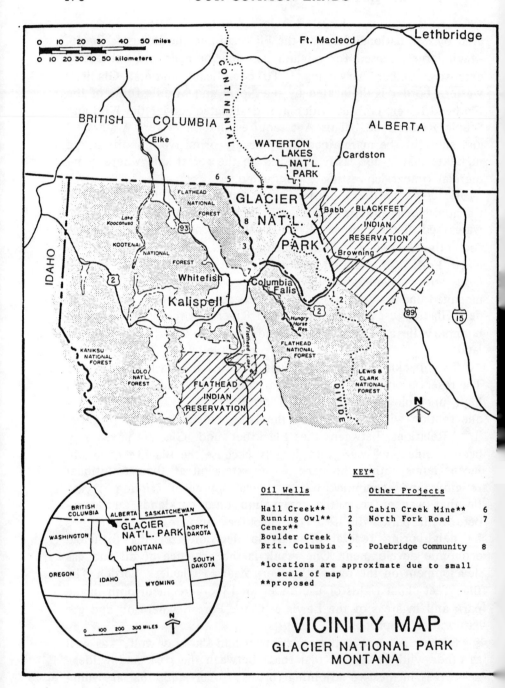

KEY*

Oil Wells   Other Projects

Hall Creek**   1   Cabin Creek Mine**   6
Running Owl**   2   North Fork Road   7
Cenex**   3
Boulder Creek   4
Brit. Columbia   5   Polebridge Community 8

*locations are approximate due to small
    scale of map
**proposed

VICINITY MAP
GLACIER NATIONAL PARK
MONTANA

Wildlife Service (FWS). The FWS is responsible for initially determining which species are to be listed as threatened or endangered[26]
and then for reviewing federal agency activities that might adversely affect protected species.[27] Any proposed activity, wherever
conducted, that poses a possible threat to the survival of a
listed species or its critical habitat can go forward only if the
proponent can obtain a so-called "no jeopardy" opinion from
the FWS.[28] Thus, as long as some park species are listed, the ESA
occupies a powerful place in the arsenal of park protection.

At Glacier, the grizzly bear makes the ESA an influential but
tenuous weapon. The grizzly is probably the most popular of all
protected animals, and every developmental decision in the region
inevitably raises the question: What will it do to the grizzly? Because the grizzly's habitat radiates out broadly beyond Glacier, and
because bear experts view any additional human impact as putting
stress on grizzly populations, the prospect of a jeopardy opinion
serves as a potential veto on any developmental activity in and
around the park. So long as the bear remains listed under the ESA,
it will be (at least in law) protected from threats to its survival
and to the integrity of its habitat. But species can be "delisted"
from the ESA if their survival is no longer threatened, and this
may happen to the grizzly in the Glacier ecosystem.[29]

In this Article, we focus primarily on Glacier's relations
with its two principal fellow-agency neighbors--the Flathead
and Lewis & Clark National Forests.[30] These forests are
managed by different types of supervisors with quite different
perspectives on their relationship to Glacier. The Supervisor of the
Flathead is a young, Ivy-League-educated landscape architect.[31]
The Lewis & Clark Supervisor is from the old school, which is
strongly oriented toward traditional commodity uses of the forest.[32]

The relationship between the Forest Service and the Park Service is a crucial one because national forest lands adjoin or sur-
round much of the national park lands in the American West.
Despite their proximity, forests and parks traditionally have
been managed independently (with notable exceptions such as
cooperative law enforcement or fire management). For example,
forests sometimes have been cut right up to the boundary line
of a park. Forest officials also have assumed in their planning that

they shoulder no responsibility for the park next door, despite a shared river or viewscape, or wildlife that freely crosses boundary lines.

Given the proximity and uncoordinated management of forest and park lands, one might expect frequent transboundary conflicts. However, such conflict has been relatively uncommon because much of the forest land is remote and has lain largely undeveloped for many years. Nevertheless, there has been a long, deep rivalry between the two agencies, arising in part from the fact that conservationists persuaded Congress to save some of the most spectacular forest lands from the forester's axe by turning it over to the parks.[33] The two agencies also embody the two competing branches of the conservation movement-- utilitarianism and preservation.[34]

In order to study relations between Glacier and its Forest Service neighbors, we decided to look at the park's responses to threats emanating from neighboring lands. We asked Glacier officials to identify what they considered to be the most serious of the fifty-six external threats that they had reported in 1980.[35] They named: oil and gas development in both of the national forests, on state land, and on the Blackfeet Reservation; timber harvesting, especially clearcutting in Canada to salvage lumber subjected to beetle infestation; the proposed Cabin Creek coal mine in Canada; and developmental activity, such as road improvement, in the remote North Fork area of the Flathead Basin. Glacier officials feared that oil and gas activity would intensify human impact in critical corridors for park wildlife, directly through mineral work itself and indirectly by increasing road access for hunters (especially poachers) and recreationists. The Cabin Creek mine and stream siltation from timber harvesting could exacerbate water pollution.[36] Timber harvesting also creates unsightly cutover areas that are visible from the park.[37] In addition, Glacier officials worry that a proposal for paving a road parallel to the North Fork of the Flathead River is the first step toward development adjacent to the most remote region of the park,[38] where solitude and pristineness are still primary values.[39]

III. PARK PROTECTION STRATEGY

A. An Early Surprise: The Unimportance of Law

Initially, we assumed that Glacier officials would vigorously assert legal protection available to the park. Glacier is not in a favorable negotiating position because it has little to give the forests in return for the restraint it seeks over commercial activity on forest lands.[40] However, Glacier could acquire significant leverage over activities on neighboring lands through laws of general application like NEPA[41] and the federal air and water pollution acts,[42] as well as other statutes.[43] Accordingly, we predicted that invocation of those statutes would be a principal tool for influencing external conduct.[44]

We could not have been more mistaken.[45] Glacier officials rarely mentioned the law in discussing their dealings with neighboring national forests. Indeed, the only "law" they wanted to talk about was something we would not even have considered as an element of their legal position, the designation of Glacier as an international biosphere reserve under a United Nations program.[46]

During the entire time we spent at Glacier, not one park official brought up the private citizen litigation that thus far has enjoined much of the oil and gas activity on the park's borders and has caused the Forest Service to redesign several timber sales. A lawyer who filed several of these cases told us:

> The park makes no real effort to develop any constituencies. No superintendent has made any effort to develop relations with environmental groups that would carry their sword. If you say 'I'm going to get involved,' they'll help, but the Park Service doesn't reach outside, stroke, build alliances. That's one reason why they are in so much trouble in Yellowstone.

Glacier officials do sometimes invoke the law in very limited ways. For example, Glacier called for a full NEPA "environmental impact statement" (EIS) on the entire cycle of oil and gas development in the Flathead and the Lewis & Clark, rather than assessments limited to the impacts of particular exploration proposals.[47] But Glacier does not follow up its official comments by seeking to enforce compliance, despite the availability of a formal administrative mechanism for pursuing such a strategy.[48]

Our impression is that Glacier officials do not cite NEPA to assert legal obligations, but rather to emphasize the importance of a full consideration of the cumulative effects of oil and gas development. Park comments treat legal and non-legal issues in the same muted tone--as ways to express concern and to urge greater protection for Glacier.[49]

Upon reflection, we are not so surprised by the failure of park officials to seize upon legal standards for leverage with the Forest Service. Because park and forest officials don't use lawyers in their day-to-day interactions,[50] and don't have ready access to legal advice, they are hardly in a position to press complex legal demands, even if they wanted to do so.[51]

Park officials also lack sophistication about the legal system and how it interacts with what they do. A Glacier executive told us, "Sometimes we have to go to court . . . [but] the attorneys settle out of court on economic grounds, or bring in issues unrelated to land management, and get us bad precedents." Park managers have trouble understanding that legal decisions are constrained by procedural requirements, statutes with specific and limited scope, and difficult problems of proof that may engender compromises. They are unnerved, for example, when a decision rests on a point that they consider irrelevant and that ignores the substantive resource management issue they wanted resolved. "The grizzly bear's fate," one expert told us, "is hanging upon ever finer points of law." In short, Glacier officials seem to have difficulty perceiving the law as a tool by which they can gain leverage over decisions that will affect park resources.

In addition, park and forest officials (like business people with continuing relations)[52] do not want to deal with each other in a formal legal manner. Indeed, Glacier officials are self-consciously aware of the dynamics of a continuing, mutually dependent relationship.[53] We were told by an official primarily involved in working with neighboring agencies on external threat problems: "[A]nytime one is forced into something, he will find other things to fight you on. We can lose, rather than gain, ground with hard legislation. It is better to work together with neighbors, and try to understand each other."

In one respect, Glacier's reluctance to deal formally with its national forest neighbors comports perfectly with its long-term strategy on external threats. As we shall see, Glacier's central goal is to legitimize the idea of regional land management and move its neighbors away from traditional boundary or enclave consciousness.[54] To do so, Glacier officials feel that they must keep pressing the notion of a common enterprise with shared interests and goals, and avoid conflict and confrontation. Asserting formal legal rights against their neighbors would undermine this long-term strategy by underlining separateness and reaffirming the significance of boundary lines.[55]

Beyond all this, however, we sensed a more profound reluctance to use law, a sense that resort to the legal system was an admission of failure. In one revealing example, a ranger recited to us something he had no doubt learned from his superiors: There are three elements to dealing with park management problems-- data, policy, and legal--"and," he told us, "our goal is to try to deal with the data and policy, and to avoid the legal."

B. Glacier As A Sacred Cow

1. The Park's Moral Capital

Because Glacier officials do not rely on formal legal restrictions or litigation to protect the park, on what do they rely? "The park is a kind of sacred cow," one Glacier manager told us, and park officials think they are pretty good at milking it.[56] He explained:

> The Forest Service knows they have to work with us; we have a watchful constituency. We have a strong congressional delegation. We could probably get congressional support, if we had our information in order, even if we said there should be absolutely no oil and gas development within one mile of the park.

He offered as examples: Glacier once persuaded the local congressman to support a bill to control noisy helicopter overflights,[57] and the park used the media extensively to publicize its case on the Hall Creek oil well in the Lewis & Clark Forest, the Cenex oil well on state lands, and water rights in the Flathead River.[58]

All our informants outside the park agree that Glacier has a strong public constituency and that the Park Service enjoys high status and great respect. One knowledgeable observer said:

The park has enormous moral capital, and if they waded
in to do battle, they could make things very difficult for
the Forest Service. If the Park Service simply wrote a
letter saying 'this is wholly inconsistent with the mission
of the park,' it would be seized on politically and legally. Glacier National Park is the crown jewel of Montana,
and if the park was to 'come unglued' about some project,
like an oil well, they could make it a running fight even
with the best that industry could muster . . . .

The question is whether Glacier can and does effectively
use its considerable reservoir of good will. We recalled the conditional way in which a park official spoke: "We could stop oil and
gas work if we had our information in order" and "if we said there
should be . . . no oil and gas development." Though park officials
identified oil and gas activity near Glacier's boundaries as one
of the most serious threats,[59] they do not in fact have their information in order, and they have never explicitly come out for an
oil free zone around the park.

2. Glacier's Unexpended Moral Capital

We were quite surprised to discover that Glacier, while it
has a small scientific staff, does not produce detailed studies to
back up its administrative comments on the potential harm from
oil drilling or other activities. The park limits its technical work
to monitoring existing situations and provides only its conclusions
to other agencies like its national forest neighbors. Although Glacier
sometimes has the benefit of work by others (such as the Fish and
Wildlife Service when the grizzly is involved), the park's administrative comments don't include or refer to that data, even when it is
strongly supportive.[60] Moreover, Glacier officials don't prepare
technical reports on potential adverse effects even when there is
no one else to do the work.

As one Glacier official told us, the park "does not provide
documentation; it communicates park values, not formally, but on
every occasion. We do not have data or studies, we have an overall strategy." For example, when we asked whether Glacier had
a technical position on the adequacy of the Flathead Forest's "best
management practices"[61] for controlling the impact on water quality
of timber harvesting, we were told that the park simply does
not do that sort of work.[62]

Nor does Glacier explicitly come out against development. Traditionally, the park has been loath to speak out on issues beyond its own borders. Glacier's policy is "never say never" to its neighbors.[63] "I've always used guarded terms," a top Glacier manager told us, "for example, even with the Lewis & Clark Forest [whose support of oil and gas development is extremely troublesome to Glacier],[64] I said only, 'We're very concerned.'" A former superintendent told us, "I never felt comfortable taking a 'no' position." "The most they [Glacier] will do formally," an official of an environmental organization observed, "is to send a letter saying, 'Gee, we hope . . . .'"

Moreover, Glacier officials are reluctant to use their access to sources of influence.[65] For example, they consider ongoing clearcutting in Canada a severe threat to a park watershed.[66] Nevertheless, they decided not to seek help from the U.S. State Department, even though their own efforts with the provincial government had been fruitless. We were told, "There is a limit to how frontal we can be. Timber is not major enough to move up the ladder. It is hard to go to the mat on these smaller issues. If there were really a clear-cut issue, we would go through the State Department." Also, a former high level official, speaking of oil drilling in the Lewis & Clark Forest, told us:

> The issue is not *that* important. It's not as important as the North Fork since it is out of the park drainage. . . . I did do something my predecessor would not, I spoke out on issues outside the park [including oil and gas in the Lewis & Clark], but [beyond speaking out I decided], 'let's save our chips for the real zingers.'

Is Glacier simply too timid? Issues like timber cuts and oil and gas exploration may be "real zingers," their true danger obscured by sequential development patterns--a well here, a well there, one timber contract at a time. Glacier officials identified these threats as the most serious that they face, and wildlife experts told us that a major developmental activity puts intense pressures on park wildlife. Nevertheless, as we shall see, the Lewis & Clark Forest is proceeding full-speed with its plan to meet court-imposed procedural requirements for permitting oil exploration in that area of the forest nearest Glacier.[67] And everyone we interviewed is resigned to the prospect that drilling is inevitable

despite the park's objections. Perhaps current exploration will
not yield a discovery, as park officials devoutly hope. Even if there
is a discovery, mitigation measures may work, as BLM officials
claimed to us. But it seems puzzling to us that Glacier has not
taken stronger steps to forestall the developments the park itself
has identified as the most serious threats on its borders.

C. Some Preliminary Observations

Glacier's management is openly neither optimistic nor pessimistic. They told us that in the Flathead Forest circumstances are ripe
for a kind of cross-agency zoning that would ban major developments from a corridor extending about five miles out along the
park border. But they recognize that such a corridor is unlikely in
the Lewis & Clark Forest, where oil and gas prospects are quite
promising and forest officials are committed to allowing such
development to go forward. Park officials are fully alert to this
situation, and they are looking for a way around the recal-
citrant officials in the Lewis & Clark Forest.[68] They also told
us that some day Glacier may be able to engage its neighbors
in a regional approach to managing resources.

One problem with Glacier's approach to park protection is that
there is a tension between its short-term and long-term goals.
In the short-term, the park is trying to push development back
from its borders and to create a sort of low intensity use, or compatible use, buffer zone around the park. As we shall see, this
sometimes requires strong, confrontational stands. In the long-term,
Glacier hopes to bring about a commitment to regional land management in which, for example, the river basin rather than traditional boundaries will be the focus for decisionmaking, and the
main substantive goals will be maintaining genetic integrity and
biological diversity.[69] Successful regional management, at least
in Glacier's view, rests in part on the ability of repeat players
to cooperate with one another and to avoid stepping on each other's
toes.

Our field work has left us with the sense that Glacier is feeling its way intuitively--groping, to put it more bluntly--as to both
of these goals, and that it has given only casual thought to how it
expects to effectuate them. We observed that, while park officials
accurately perceive progress in deterring some immediate threats
(such as a proposed road paving or oil well) and in moving toward

"regional thinking," they don't seem able to come to terms with all the forces at work on Glacier. Part of the problem, we think, is that the park does not find congenial some of the reality around it. For example, we have already noted that Glacier officials want to stay as clear as they can of the law and legalism (and for reasons that make some sense for them). But one result is that they blind themselves to the role that law plays in decisions that affect the park.

Similarly, as we shall see, Glacier officials view the Fish and Wildlife Service almost as an intruder, and the Endangered Species Act as a "slender reed" on which to rest the park's protection. Yet it seems plain that, given the presence of listed species like the grizzly, Glacier has no more powerful tool than the ESA with which to obtain concessions from its neighbors. In a similar vein, Glacier officials do not ask themselves what has motivated the changing attitudes of officials such as the managers of the Flathead. Surely NEPA, the planning provisions of the National Forest Management Act, and the policies of the Wilderness Act and the Endangered Species Act--all of which have led to court challenges to traditional national forest management --have been instrumental in inducing sensitivity to resource protection among forest managers. Yet, Glacier officials exhibited a kind of amnesia in matters where the law has been the key to controlling development across their borders.

What this suggests is that Glacier so far has been unable to reconcile the tensions between it short-term and long-term goals. Our sense is that Glacier officials are caught up in a very complex web of perceptions about what is going on around them. At one level, because law and lawyers and the confrontational legal style is uncongenial to them, they seriously downplay its significance. Similarly, they see legal solutions (courts, administrative appeals, jeopardy opinions) as taking control and discretion out of their hands, so that they no longer are in charge of their own parks. Their desire to maintain discretion makes them averse to the sort of structural, rule-determined, consistent results that a legal approach, at its best, promises.

Even if the park accurately believes that to achieve its larger goals it should avoid confrontation, it needs to ask how much this approach will cost it in the short run. If, due to lack of capacity and power to stop harmful developments, serious damage is done to the park before cooperation leads to regional management, then the cooperative approach will have sacrificed the very thing that Glacier managers seek to protect. Park officials seem to think that this dilemma can be resolved through their capacity to expend moral capital if and when a crisis arises. But external threats to Glacier tend to develop incrementally, one oil well at a time, in a way that never presents the park with the kind of discrete, dramatic crisis it stands ready to avert. And, the park's distaste for confrontation makes it timid in invoking the power of the "sacred cow."

In the remainder of this Article, we explore the accuracy of these perceptions and the effectiveness of Glacier's approach to park protection.

IV. GLACIER AND ITS TWO NATIONAL FOREST NEIGHBORS

Here we examine the recent history of several major development proposals on the borders of Glacier, focusing principally on proposals in the Flathead and Lewis & Clark Forests (but also noting Glacier's response to threats from Canada, a state forest, and the Blackfeet Reservation). We hope to illustrate how the park has sought to influence its federal neighbors and to venture some tentative conclusions about the effectiveness of its strategy.

A. The Flathead National Forest

1. An Emerging Sensitivity to Glacier

Park officials, local residents, and environmental activists all speak favorably, some even enthusiastically, of the new Flathead managers: Supervisor Edgar Brannon; and District Ranger Tom Hope, who has charge of the North Fork area of the forest. Unlike their predecessors, who apparently turned a deaf ear to outside pressures, Brannon and Hope embrace a new, open management style. They have invited Park Service officials to participate on planning teams, kept citizens informed about ongoing decisions, and listened willingly and patiently to residents and organizational representatives. Brannon understands that people want to be heard and to be treated as if their opinions matter, and that such

treatment increases their tolerance for a manager who faces competing constituency interests.[70] In describing his relationship to
Glacier, he told us:

> Traditionally we treated each component of the
> federal lands as an island. I don't see the Flathead as an
> island. . . . I view protecting Glacier as within my man-
> date. . . . [The law] gives me fairly broad discretion--to
> maximize net public benefit, including non-economic
> considerations. Forest policy has a strong intent and some
> specific language authorizing us to cooperate with our
> neighbors.[71]

What does this mean in practice? On "low stakes" issues--ter-
minable annoyances rather than permanent threats to Glacier's
ecosystem--the Flathead has been very accommodating and evi-
dently considers Glacier to be one of its constituents. For example,
at the park's request, Flathead officials worked assiduously to control noise from oil company seismic activities,[72] thereby mitigating an annoying problem and, we were told, earning intense gratitude
and admiration from Glacier staff members. In addition, we were
told that the Flathead has agreed to shape several timber cuts to
reduce visual impact on the park and, at the behest of environmental groups, has modified the intensity of some timber harvest plans on lands adjacent to Glacier.[73]

The Flathead also has made changes on some bigger issues.
Most importantly, its *Forest Plan* sets aside the northern third
of the North Fork region as the Trail Creek Grizzly Bear Management Area, to be managed exclusively to promote grizzly bear
recovery and to enhance the opportunity for resettlement of the
endangered gray wolf.[74] Timber harvesting and further oil and gas
leasing in the Trail Creek Area are prohibited for the next ten
years.[75] And, the originally scheduled timber harvesting for this
area has been removed from the total amount of timber the forest
considers harvestable, a significant act of self-denial for the Forest
Service.[76]

The *Forest Plan* further adopts a set of interagency guidelines
for grizzly bear management, under which some eighty percent of
the Flathead is designated as "essential" habitat to be managed
so as to assure the bear's recovery. The guidelines do not bar timber and mineral development,[77] but they require such uses to yield

to the needs of the bear where there is conflict.[78] The *Flathead Forest Plan* is also innovative in establishing a quantitative range for annual timber harvest, which gives the Forest Service increased flexibility to respond to resource-protection issues, rather than limiting it to a fixed quota, as in other forests.[79]

These policies manifest a growing concern for Glacier, but they no doubt also reflect the Flathead's response to economic forces and to legal pressures from players other than Glacier. To date, a proposed road development in the forest was vetoed by a FWS jeopardy opinion under the ESA,[80] further oil and gas leasing remains enjoined by a federal court injunction under NEPA,[81] and a number of appeals of the *Forest Plan* have been filed.[82] Moreover, in the Trail Creek Area there is little promise of oil and gas,[83] and timber harvesting is not sound, at least in the current market.[84] Whatever the combination of motives, the most striking fact is that the Flathead has bound itself for the future as little as possible.[85]

2. The Primacy of Managerial Discretion

However accommodating they have been in certain individual cases, the Flathead managers have consistently acted to maximize their own discretion and flexibility. They still decline to commit themselves to a set of regional management priorities, and they still hold to tradition by retaining sole authority over matters with regional implications--for example, the extent to which timber harvesting should yield to wildlife or to aesthetics, or the appropriateness of oil development next to Glacier.

In a number of actions, the Flathead managers have tenaciously preserved their discretion. For example, the Trail Creek designation is an entirely discretionary category that the forest can change if its management goals change, as happened, according to one of our sources, with a grizzly bear management unit that it had set up previously.[86] The same is true of the forest's sliding-scale annual timber harvest.[87] Similarly, the Flathead refused to propose a wilderness designation that would have imposed a legal barrier to commercial activity within the Trail Creek Area.[88] Yet another example of discretionary management is the Flathead's commitment to water quality, which takes the form of "good management practices" that are articulated and defined under the Forest Service's own administrative judgment, rather than objective effluent limits or ambient water quality standards.[89] Also, the forest has resisted joint management initiatives,[90] and declines to establish any formal buffer zones which would in effect legitimate joint park-forest areas.[91] In sum, the Flathead management apparently views the protection of park resources as something they are permitted, and even encouraged, but not obliged to do.[92]

3. Glacier's Tactics: Three Case Studies

The Park Service understands very well how strongly its Forest Service and other neighbors feel about controlling turf. Perhaps this is why Glacier has been reserved in pressing its "real goal"-- recognition of the region as the relevant entity for management. Even when responding to specific development proposals that it acknowledges to be serious threats, the park has been more than a little timid.[93] For example, Glacier has not explicitly opposed the forest's decision to authorize oil and gas exploratory activity in the North Fork region. Sometimes, though, the park speaks out more forcefully-- for example, in opposition to the proposed paving of the North Fork Road in the Flathead and against the plan for a coal surface mine (Cabin Creek) in Canada on the upper reaches of the North Fork. These three cases--oil and gas exploration in the North Fork region, the proposed paving of the North Fork Road, and the proposed Cabin Creek mine--reveal how Glacier operates when confronting proposed developments that it views as a danger to the park.

a. Oil and Gas Development

Despite Glacier's aversion to any oil and gas activity on its borders, the park has never taken a stronger stand than urging the Forest Service to prepare a comprehensive environmental impact statement at the initial leasing stage[94] and to consider all the potential effects if a valuable discovery leads to full field production.[95] The park is concerned that unless environmental effects are fully considered at the outset, by the time a discovery is made the economic pressure to go forward will be too great to resist, and any limiting lease stipulations will be inadequate to control the momentum.

The Forest Service resolutely opposes a comprehensive impact analysis and insists on segmenting the evaluation process by treating each stage of development separately and site-specifically as it arises.[96] Accordingly, in 1980 the Flathead authorized the leasing of forest lands on the strength of an Environmental Assessment[97] (a less comprehensive document than an EIS), which did not address the question of full field development in the event of a big discovery. Glacier inexplicably took no steps against this leasing proposal (indeed, the park did not even officially comment on it),[98] and the park appears reconciled to the prospect of oil and gas exploration on its flanks.[99]

Both the Park Service and the Forest Service urge the propriety of their own approach. Because neither the Forest Service nor the BLM[100] has ever denied a leaseholder's exploratory drilling application,[101] Glacier's concerns are not simply hypothetical. The Flathead, on the other hand, claims that so few leases ever reach the production stage that a full environmental analysis at the time of leasing is unnecessary.[102] More importantly, the Flathead argues that natural resource protection can be assured by inserting stipulations in leases authorizing the Forest Service to impose whatever conditions are necessary, even to the extent of prohibiting extraction.[103] In theory at least, the same level of protection is possible whether decisions are made comprehensively, or step-by-step in a segmented fashion. Predictably, the Forest Service's approach--segmented, site-specific evaluations and broadly worded lease stipulations--maximizes its discretion in determining the future of mineral development in the Flathead.

Local environmentalists successfully challenged the leases in court. In *Conner v. Burford*,[104] a federal district court rejected the Forest Service position, holding that oil and gas leasing decisions require preparation of a full EIS because the leasing decision is the first, and potentially irreversible, step in a cumulative process.[105] This is precisely Glacier's view.

It is too early to predict how the oil and gas issue will finally be resolved, because the district court's NEPA injunction is under appeal and the oil market is currently quiescent. But the lawsuit has heightened the Forest Service's sensitivity to the regional nature of the oil and gas question, and it might move the Flathead managers to view other development proposals from a regional perspective.[106] The lawsuit also should send Glacier two important messages: The park's regional planning strategy is legitimate; and Glacier might effectively advance its agenda by recognizing the help it gets from private organizations that share its concerns and that are willing to go to court.

b. Paving the North Fork Road

Forest Highway 61 is a dirt road that runs through the Flathead, parallel to Glacier, and connects the populated area of the Flathead Valley with the remote North Fork region of the park, and with Canada to the north. In 1982, Flathead County, which maintained Highway 61,[107] proposed a plan to widen and pave a ten-mile stretch adjacent to Glacier.[108] The County argued that the road had deteriorated badly and was causing safety problems and substantial maintenance costs. In addition to the County Commissioners, the Flathead National Forest and the Federal Highway Administration (FHA) supported the paving plan. As a major federal action significantly affecting the environment, an EIS was required.[109] The FHA was also required to consult with nearby federal land agencies[110] and the Fish and Wildlife Service about the plan's impact on wildlife protected under the Endangered Species Act.[111]

From the outset, Glacier officials feared that paving Highway 61 might stimulate timber harvesting in the Flathead, development of private lands along the Flathead River, and recreational use in the remote North Fork Region.[112] Nevertheless, consistent with Glacier's traditional reluctance to speak out on issues beyond the park's borders, park officials initially took no position on the paving proposal.[113] Eventually, they asserted that paving "must be viewed as incompatible with the park's management objectives and philosophy."[114] Mild as this statement may seem to outsiders, explicit opposition to developments outside park boundaries represents a radical departure from standard Park Service practice. As soon as the park spoke, it heard sharp criticism, as it still does today.[115]

Undoubtedly, Glacier was emboldened by the broad coalition that developed to defeat the road proposal. Opposed were a majority of local residents,[116] environmental organizations,[117] the Montana Department of Fish Wildlife and Parks, those United States Department of the Interior officials charged with environmental review responsibilities,[118] and the Fish and Wildlife Service. The Fish and Wildlife Service advised the FHA that increased human presence in the North Fork threatened wildlife populations and important habitats,[119] and it issued a jeopardy opinion under the Endangered Species Act finding a threat to both the grizzly bear and the gray wolf.[120] This constellation of forces stalled the paving project, at least for the present.[121] Because a jeopardy opinion is effectively a veto, it alone was sufficient to stop the project, although the breadth of opposition may well have strengthened the resolve of Fish and Wildlife officials.

The park, typically, let others lead the opposition. As one Glacier official put it, "We were a second line player, and we hid behind the grizzly bear." It did, however, seize the opportunity to promote regional cooperation by supporting an effort to coordinate land planning in the North Fork.[122] Local officials from the Forest Service and county government were receptive to the idea, and local citizens and officials, along with federal officials in the region, began meeting informally as the North Fork Coordinating Committee.[123] North Fork residents have also developed an area land use plan which they intend to submit to County officials,[124] and they have entered into an Inter-Local Agreement with the Park Service and other land management agencies, arranging to meet regularly to coordinate their plans and to share mutual concerns.[125] This represents a significant step for these private landowners, most of whom are independent people by nature who purposefully moved to the North Fork area to escape the trappings of civilization, including government regulation.

The Flathead has softened its stand on the paving proposal. Originally, the forest supported paving to promote timber harvesting and mineral development. Today, however, the Forest Supervisor takes no position, and he says that he will deal with the issue on a site-specific basis should it arise again. Characteristically, his stance maximizes the Flathead's future discretion. Reminded of the park's unambiguous opposition, and of his own assertion that he sees protecting park values as one of his responsibilities, he replied that the paving "was not a big issue for the Park Service. They preferred that it not be paved, but that was all." That conclusion certainly is not the one we would draw from the oral and written record on the North Fork road controversy. But, it is perfectly consistent with our sense of the approach of the Flathead management: Cool controversy down, try to be accommodating, participate in voluntary cooperative activities, but yield as little authority and discretion as possible in the management of forest lands.

No one believes that the road improvement issue is finally settled. Pressures to pave Highway 61 could be renewed by successful oil and gas exploration, by an improvement in the timber market, or by coal development in the North Fork watershed across the Canadian border. Although Glacier's strategy did not secure the future against such pressures, it did advance the park's agenda, and Glacier has weathered public criticism of its opposition to development beyond park borders.[126] The park has set a precedent for involvement in transborder issues and has taken advantage of an opportunity to promote regional cooperation by bringing together various public and private agencies to consult and cooperate on the future of the North Fork.

Thus, the road paving dispute plainly provided a success for the park. No doubt it is to some extent a success in the sense of raising regional consciousness, which is surely how Glacier likes to see it. But it would be a serious error to overlook the crucial roles played by the jeopardy opinion and environmental coalition politics or to view the current equipoise as a permanent victory.

c. The Cabin Creek Mine[127]

In British Columbia, a few miles north of the international boundary, lies Cabin Creek--a tributary of the North Fork of the Flathead River. Millions of tons of coal lie in the hills near where Cabin Creek meets the North Fork, and a concern called Sage Creek, Inc. wants to develop a coal surface mine there. Glacier officials told us that they consider this project the gravest external threat to the park. They fear not only the human impacts of industrial development but also sediment loading in the Flathead--a particularly ominous possibility should waste-containing earthen settlement ponds collapse.[128]

Although the Cabin Creek project is Glacier's most serious peril, it is also the park's greatest success in securing a regional approach to resource management. At the present time, a high level international study board of technical experts is investigating water quality conditions in the Flathead, the effects which the proposed mine would have on the River, and the steps that would be required to maintain fisheries and certain specified levels of water quality. Upon completion, the study will likely be presented as a recommendation to the federal governments of Canada and the United States. Its standards for Flathead Basin users will not be legally binding, but the technical expertise and prestige of the

Study Board members will put strong pressure on British Columbia authorities to conform.[129] If the Province imposes limits on its side of the border, there surely will be pressures for similar controls on the United States side, because the Canadians will be restricting themselves to protect downstream uses of the Flathead across the border. Such self-restraint is unlikely if American users go ahead and pollute the river.

Thus, the study might lead to controls that will be adopted throughout the basin of the North Fork of the Flathead--a real triumph of regional management. How has such an extraordinary possibility come about? Paradoxically, the North Fork's international status, usually a source of extra difficulty in controlling pollution, in this instance has facilitated protective action. The reasons are geographic, diplomatic, and legal.

Because Canada will receive all the benefits of coal mining at Cabin Creek, and the United States will feel only harms, a natural coalition of allies arose in the North Fork, including parties who otherwise are sometimes in conflict--Glacier, the Flathead, state and local officials, and private landowners.[130] With such unanimity, and the support of those with whom they repeatedly deal, park officials were uncharacteristically outspoken in trumpeting dangers to the North Fork environment. They joined with local officials and citizen groups in a successful lobbying effort to secure federal funding for a regional environmental study.[131] The EPA funded the study, which was published in 1983 as the *Flathead River Basin Environmental Impact Study.*[132] This five-year, interdisciplinary investigation documented the environmental, demographic, and economic characteristics of the Flathead Basin and examined the potential impact of the Cabin Creek mine on the region's natural resources. It also provided the basis for extensive technical comments submitted by the United States and the State of Montana to the British Columbia government (which favored the Cabin Creek proposal) criticizing the Province's environmental assessment of the coal mine project.[133]

The Boundary Waters Treaty of 1909 between Canada and the United States served as the vehicle for securing review of the project.[134] The Treaty provides for a joint reference by the two governments to the International Joint Commission (IJC) for recommendations regarding transboundary water problems.[135] Glacier solicited the aid of the then local congressman--Max Baucus--

to urge the State Department in Washington to seek an IJC referral. Such a dramatic step is quite unusual. But the Park Service was in the happy situation of being allied with every other interest group on the United States side, and it considered the Cabin Creek issue to be very serious. Everything came together. The State Department, initially reluctant, decided to pursue the reference because it saw an opportunity to point its finger at Canada as the bad guy for a change.[136] Canada, yet more surprisingly, agreed to the reference, probably perceiving an opportunity to make some modest concessions to United States concerns and to improve its position in seeking concessions on acid rain.[137]

At the time of this writing, the Study Board's recommendations have not yet been issued. However, they promise to be a standard-setting precedent that will influence activities in the North Fork on both sides of the border.[138] Whatever the precise outcome, the North Fork area has been identified as an interdependent region. The detailed Basin Study has laid a technical foundation; the Treaty reference on Cabin Creek provides an example of transboundary working relations; and the State of Montana has given its blessing to the regional concept by establishing by law a permanent Flathead Basin Commission with membership from the governor's staff, the Department of State Lands, the Flathead County Commission, the Forest Service, and the Park Service.[139]

Glacier officials are understandably pleased to have come this far in obtaining recognition of the region as the appropriate unit of management in the setting of Cabin Creek. They may already have reaped some specific benefits. The moderation shown in the *Flathead Forest Plan,* discussed above, and restrictions imposed on development by a state forest in the North Fork,[140] suggest sensitivity to the need to "keep things clean" on the United States side in order to keep the pressure on Canada. Such sensitivity is itself a modest triumph of regionalism.

B. The Lewis & Clark Forest

On the Flathead side of Glacier, circumstances have pretty much favored the park. There are progressive forest managers, aggressive and visible constituencies united on behalf of resource protection, and no heavy pressures for commodity development. On the Lewis & Clark side, almost the opposite situation prevails. A high pressure, high stakes situation is created by very promis-

ing oil and gas lands lying right on the wildlife corridor between Glacier and the Bob Marshall Wilderness.[141] The Forest Supervisor's stated position is that oil and gas development is entitled
to go forward unless it can be shown to be illegal, and the district
ranger is widely said to be an active and enthusiastic proponent of
that development.[142] Moreover, there is no strong, vocal, environ-
mentally-oriented local constituency in the Badger-Two
Medicine area of the Lewis & Clark, which adjoins Glacier.
The area is almost unpopulated except for the small community of
East Glacier and the nearby Blackfeet Reservation, whose members have been ambivalent about nearby oil and gas development.[143]
How has the park behaved, and how has it fared, in the face
of this unwelcoming atmosphere?

1. The Ineffective Tactic of Silence

Although Glacier officials oppose oil and gas development close
to Glacier's borders and in critical wildlife corridors extending
from the park, they have been no more willing to speak out in the
hostile milieu of the Lewis & Clark than they were on the Flathead.
Their reticence has made it easier for oil and gas exploration to
proceed. For example, in an administrative appeal of the grant of
an oil drilling permit, the appeals board, in rejecting some of the
appellant's environmental objections, expressly noted that Glacier's
official position was "no opposition" and that the park had only
expressed concern that effects be adequately studied.[144] Also, Lewis
& Clark officials are emboldened by the park's failure to assert
opposition to oil and gas drilling on their borders. The District
Ranger told us that "certain elements within the Park Service who
only want wilderness" are the ones who convey the impression that
Glacier is against oil development, but that opposition is not
the park's policy.

The park has made itself vulnerable to such misperceptions. In
December 1983, the Forest Service solicited public comments on
the Hall Creek drilling application, which proposed a test well very
close to Glacier. Although the forest received numerous public
comments, Glacier officials, who were specifically contacted by
BLM (which has official charge of oil development on the national forests), chose not to respond. The park did not comment until
the draft EIS was issued, when it suggested that the EIS should
consider the full cycle of development. Glacier officials did not,

however, express clear opposition to the project, and they have not done so even today.[145] Nor have they offered detailed technical data to support the positions they have taken, thereby permitting Lewis & Clark officials to deny any adverse effects from drilling.

The park has left it to others--usually the Fish and Wildlife Service and private environmental groups--to carry the ball for them. This strategy can work satisfactorily, as in the North Fork paving controversy. But it is probably failing in the recent battle over drilling in the Lewis & Clark Forest.

The Fish and Wildlife Service simply has not been able to bear the burden. In the first round of controversy over the expected wildlife impacts of the Hall Creek drilling proposal, FWS issued a jeopardy opinion finding that arrangements for access to the well and the location of production facilities nearby would put too much pressure on the already depressed grizzly bear population.[146] But after Lewis & Clark and oil company officials modified their production and access plans somewhat, the FWS reluctantly issued an amended no-jeopardy opinion, conditioned on the forest limiting access and thus human impact.[147]

A key FWS official described to us the agency's official position in support of its revised assessment: Without "ironclad data" demonstrating harm, the agency had little choice but to issue a no-jeopardy opinion.[148] However, we learned that the FWS still harbors considerable doubt that full-scale oil development will not jeopardize the grizzly bear. We also learned that the FWS is not convinced that the oil companies can be adequately controlled by lease stipulations that give the Forest Service formal power to regulate access and other pressures. Because a FWS official told us of these concerns in a formal interview, we took his comments as a not very subtle way of emphasizing that everyone knowledgeable about oil development in the Lewis & Clark knows how reluctant the FWS was to issue a no-jeopardy opinion, and that pressure was imposed on it to obtain that result.[149]

Private environmental groups also have had only modest success. First, they filed an administrative appeal of the decision to permit oil drilling to the Interior Board of Land Appeals.[150] The Board found several deficiencies in the permit, particularly uncertainty as to whether the Forest Service had the means adequately to restrict access to the area from the Blackfeet Indian Tribe, and it remanded the matter to determine that question.[151] The matter is now back in the hands of Lewis & Clark officials, who are actively attempting to meet the requirements for access control.[152]

Also, as in the Flathead Forest, private environmental groups successfully challenged the Lewis & Clark's environmental review of the oil and gas leasing process as inconsistent with NEPA. They obtained an injunction against further leasing in the forest until an EIS is prepared that evaluates the full cycle of development.[153] But we were told that forest officials interpret the decision as applying only to pending lease applications, not to existing leases that were not challenged.[154] Thus, their working assumption is that the injunction has no effect on the several controversial drilling proposals that are now pending, including those very near the park border.

The outcome of all this is that Lewis & Clark officials are pretty much continuing with business as usual. They were delayed on Hall Creek by the possibility of a jeopardy opinion under the ESA, and temporarily set back by lawsuits and administrative appeals. However, they apparently see those decisions as imposing only procedural or managerial obstacles which can be overcome. For example, they are now preparing a full EIS for a new drilling proposal, rather than a briefer environmental assessment as before. But, their oil and gas development agenda has not changed, even though they know perfectly well that Glacier, despite its formal reticence, opposes drilling at Hall Creek and elsewhere on the edge of the park.[155]

So far, neither Glacier's timid opposition, nor the Endangered Species Act, nor litigation under NEPA has stopped developmental momentum in the Badger-Two Medicine area. Park officials now are reconciled, though unhappily, to the likelihood that exploratory drilling will go forward.[156] They rest their hope on the chance that commercial quantities of oil and gas will not be discovered in environmentally critical areas and that the most serious damage--which occurs at the full field development stage--will never come to pass.

2. Is Regionalism Inevitable?

Paradoxically, pressure for regional management arises from the very recalcitrance of Lewis & Clark officials to consider Glacier's needs, and from the park's own position as one element in the regional ecosystem. The Lewis & Clark's unyielding traditional stance in favor of commodity development has earned them strong disfavor, even among their natural allies. For example, noticeably upset with the Lewis & Clark are BLM officials, who have formal authority over mineral development in national forests, but who routinely go along with what the forest managers want. At the forest's behest, the BLM put its stamp of approval on plans for oil and gas development and then was hit with an administrative appeal which it lost.[157] Local BLM officials have been chastised for not doing what the law requires of them, and they look bad. Furthermore, there is a blot on the BLM's professional reputation for technical work, and it must go back and redo a substantial amount of work. "I spent 18 months on the Hall Creek matter," a BLM official told us, "and it's all down the tubes."

More significantly, the problems on the Lewis & Clark have generated dissension and instability among its fellow federal agencies, an atmosphere that is not favored in federal land management. BLM ordinarily attempts to bring everyone into agreement before proceeding with an oil and gas project on lands for which they are responsible.[158] But on the Lewis & Clark, environmental groups have brought appeals and lawsuits (even if their effects are only temporary). The Fish and Wildlife Service is not at all happy with the outcome: It has felt pressure to go along and complains quite openly about it.[159] The discontent of the Park Service is manifest, and Glacier officials talk about bringing their unhappiness with the Lewis & Clark management before the Regional Forester. A well-informed observer told us that "the regional office [of the Forest Service] was 'pissed off' at Gorman and Swanger [the Supervisor and District Ranger, respectively] because every time they turned around there was controversy, and they were getting beat up. . . . The Forest Service feels quite beleaguered, at least some days of the week." This is not the way the federal bureaucracy likes to do business.

Apparently, Lewis & Clark managers feel the sting of disapproval from their BLM colleagues and recognize that they are out of step with the tendency toward greater interagency cooperation and greater environmental sensitivity. They are making changes, at least in their procedures. For example, in responding to a new drilling application--the so-called Running Owl well[160]--the forest managers are proceeding quite differently. Recognizing that the area is grizzly bear and mountain goat habitat, they plan to do a full environmental study rather than a more limited assessment as before. They also propose to consult with Glacier during the environmental study process,[161] having identified "the effects on Glacier National Park and adjacent wilderness" as one of the issues to be addressed in the environmental analysis.[162] And they indicate that they will examine the area's roadless condition and wilderness character, as well as its intangible values, including aesthetic values.[163]

The recently-issued *Lewis & Clark Forest Plan* also reflects awareness of Glacier's concerns. It does not withdraw any proposed oil and gas development, but it does provide that special leasing stipulations are required.[164] It also reduces timber harvesting in areas close to Glacier and shifts those timber quotas to the southern part of the forest.[165] Some twenty-thousand acres formerly designated for commercial logging will now be managed largely to maintain their natural appearance.[166] And, as the Flathead did,[167] the Lewis & Clark adopted the interagency grizzly bear management guidelines, designating ninety-eight percent of the forest adjacent to the park as Situation 1 lands.[168]

So, even on the Lewis & Clark, change is taking place. Even the most traditional, most inward-looking forest managers no longer assert that every effort to get them to respond to park needs is simply an indirect way of expanding park boundaries de facto or "locking up" vast additional tracts of public land. Perhaps this thought is unspoken,[169] but it is significant that such thoughts remain unspoken. However grudging it may seem, there is change when even the Lewis & Clark management says: "We recognize that other entities exist and we try to protect other entities, for example, by screening sights or noise . . . ."

Many knowledgeable observers still insisted to us that the Forest Service is "timber driven," despite its public assertions, and that commodity goals still prevail over every other goal. But we see real and irreversible pressures away from such institutional single-mindedness: laws that legitimate and demand transboundary planning; litigation pressures of citizen groups; growing local constituencies with environmental and recreational demands; and the quiet influence of neighbors like the national parks.

V. DRAWING UP A BALANCE SHEET

The full test of how much change has taken place is yet to come. Our study took place during a particularly quiescent period, when both the timber and oil markets were depressed and there was little immediate developmental pressure. On the Flathead, we heard, three years of timber lay sold but still uncut, so local residents dependent on the timber industry had no present basis for complaining about wood harvesting limits. It remains to be seen whether the Flathead will maintain discretionary designations like the Trail Creek Bear Management Area against stronger economic pressures.[170] And, no one thinks the North Fork road improvement issue is permanently decided. It also remains to be seen how the Lewis & Clark will finally resolve the Hall Creek project and the Running Owl proposal. As for the Cabin Creek mine proposal and the Cenex well, our informants told us that both are poor investments and may well die of their own economic infirmities.

A. Is Glacier's Position Uniquely Strong?

At one level, what we learned is specific to Glacier and its distinctive situation. At the least, we hope that our field study will reveal how one national park deals with threats from beyond its borders, and will add some useful information to the debate over proposed park protection legislation. We hope we have also added a little to our understanding of administrative behavior. We would be surprised to find that what we have observed in attitudes about using the law, avoiding confrontation, and maintaining discretion differs measurably from one national park or region to another.

Nevertheless, we want to emphasize that Glacier enjoys a more favorable position than most other national parks, and its difficulty in controlling external threats is likely to be experienced even more keenly elsewhere in the national park system. Not only can Glacier take advantage of the potent Endangered Species Act, but along with Yellowstone it is the only park outside Alaska to have important grizzly bear populations,[171] the most highly visible and politically important animal listed under the Act.[172] It might fairly be said that the entire land management scheme surrounding Glacier is built on the grizzly. The bear's presence has mobilized citizen watchdog groups,[173] forced other federal agencies to cooperate in management planning that crosses boundary lines, and provoked the development of a program of cumulative effects modelling that encourages forest service managers to adopt an expansive, long-range perspective in their planning processes.

Glacier also benefits from political and legal factors that promote cooperative joint action. For example, in the case of the proposed Cabin Creek coal mine, the Boundary Waters Treaty provided a framework for regional, interagency, and intergovernmental participation that will not be easy to duplicate in other settings. The presence of a jointly managed wild and scenic river strengthens cooperative activity between Glacier and the Flathead Forest. Glacier is also one of only twenty-five biosphere reserves managed by the National Park Service.[174]

Moreover, Glacier's neighbors may be unusually sensitive to their national park neighbor. True, few park managers would choose as neighbors the present staff of the Lewis & Clark or the troubled Blackfeet Reservation. But Glacier is fortunate in that it primarily deals with the Forest Service, whose multiple-use mission substantially overlaps that of the parks, and whose mandate under laws like the National Forest Management Act encourages collaboration with the parks. Working with national forest supervisors is undoubtedly easier than developing relations with the military.[175] Moreover, little private land adjoins Glacier, and the private tracts in the sensitive North Fork area are largely held by proprietors who share Glacier's goal of retaining a remote, "end-of-the-road" area.

B. An Evaluation of Glacier's Strategy

1. Short-Term: Rearguard Actions

Glacier's short-term goal is to identify a defensive perimeter that includes the park's watersheds, some adjacent critical wildlife corridors, and a buffer of several miles from the border,[176] and within this perimeter to prevent industrial (mines and oil wells) and infrastructural (highway) development. But Glacier does not pursue a consistent pattern of action. The evidence suggests that the park makes case-by-case judgments on just how much opposition is prudent and proceeds accordingly. Though Glacier took a firm, rather confrontational stand over the proposed Cenex well on state forest lands in the North Fork region,[177] and received some concessions,[178] Glacier is reluctant to take as strong a position against development proposals in the Flathead and the Lewis & Clark. And it has been even more reticent with the Blackfeet, though a well was drilled on the Reservation at Boulder Creek very near the park border.[179]

The problem with Glacier's individualized approach is that it opens the park to charges that political judgments temper its concerns for the regional environment--a charge that Forest Service officials have been quick to level.[180] It may prove impossible for Glacier to work out a comprehensive and consistent position on commercial oil and gas development that satisfies each of its neighbors. But without some such position the park is seriously undercutting its regional agenda. Also, the park is undermining the position of its natural allies whose efforts have thus far been largely responsible for saving the park from drilling on its borders, and who may prove instrumental in persuading the Forest Service to take seriously a regional perspective.

If the case-by-case strategy described here is likely to work anywhere, it ought to work at a park like Glacier with visible, dramatic resources like the grizzly bear and the bald eagle. But even at Glacier, park officials have adopted a high-risk approach that forces them into fighting a series of rearguard actions, challenging one proposal after another.

Their position is actually more fragile because the weapons in this rearguard action are unpredictable and outside Glacier's control. At Hall Creek in the Lewis & Clark, for example, once the forest complies with NEPA requirements the only constraint on drilling is the requirement in the FWS's no-jeopardy opinion that access to the drill site be controlled. Whether that is possible depends on whether the Blackfeet (who claim rights of access under a treaty) can be kept out, a question that the forest and the Blackfeet will probably litigate.[181] At Cabin Creek, the Canadian government has so far saved the day by agreeing to a study board reference under the United States-Canada Boundary Waters Treaty, apparently because Cabin Creek is a useful pawn in the larger international maneuvering on acid rain. Oil and gas leasing on both forests has been halted by NEPA litigation, but not necessarily for good, because NEPA requirements can be met by more extensive EIS's.[182] Furthermore, while NEPA regulates wells on the national forests, it does not protect the park against developments on state forest lands; today such developments are constrained only by a title defect and poor economics. And, not even NEPA litigation has restrained oil exploration on the Blackfeet Reservation. Finally, the protection of the ESA, as park officials repeatedly note, depends on the uncertain listing of the grizzly bear and the pertinacity of beleaguered FWS officials.[183]

Under such circumstances, it is risky to fight threats one by one as they arise. The practical question, of course, is not whether Glacier's situation is desirable, but whether there is a preferable alternative. Although no one can say with confidence that a different approach would be more effective, Glacier has clearly rejected a search for structural solutions in favor of case-by-case negotiation. For example, despite their aversion to oil and gas development on the edges of the park, Glacier officials have not taken a general position against mineral leasing of peripheral lands. To date, virtually all the non-wilderness lands in the adjoining forests have been leased.[184] Nor has the park played a role in wilderness proposals for lands around the park's borders, though such designation would limit or prohibit mineral development. Indeed, we got the distinct sense that park officials had never really paid attention to the Forest Service wilderness process, nor thought it bore on them.[185] And, of course, the Park Service position that it needs no additional protective legislation against external threats helps assure that it will get none.

Granted, it is far more difficult, both technically and politically, to take a position on oil leasing or wilderness designation outside the park than it is to focus on damage from a particular site-specific development. However, the case-by-case approach contributes to a momentum that favors development. For example, once leases are issued, oil company lessees understandably assume that they will be permitted to go forward with development. Leasing is taken as a signal that mineral development is permissible.[186] Once a lease is signed, the companies spend money--first on surveys, then on seismic activity, then on exploration. And, they hire experienced lawyers (as at Hall Creek) to represent them in each stage of the permit proceedings.

Moreover, a study of the stipulations imposed on leases reveals a clear assumption that development will be allowed unless there is some legal reason to restrain it--such as a requirement of the Endangered Species Act or a wilderness designation.[187] Because Glacier's objections to development are broader than these formal legal constraints, there is a certain misfit between the park's agenda and the lessees' perceived legal rights. Yet, park officials, perhaps because they disfavor legalistic behavior, do not seek a role in the formulation of lease stipulations to make them conform more fully to Glacier's concerns.

We are not claiming that Glacier's strategy of rearguard actions is bound to fail. Prediction is difficult, principally because Glacier's sacred cow status is such a wild card. But surely the odds are against it in a war of attrition fought against powerful and determined economic interests. "Money can always wait."[188]

2. Long-Term: A Vision of the Future

Glacier's short-term strategy seems best characterized as a mixture of optimism, good luck, and confidence in the power of public opinion to prevent ruinous development on Glacier's borders. But does the park have a broader vision of what an adequately protected park would be, and how such a park would relate to its neighbors, both public and private? In short, does the concept of regional land management--which Glacier invokes so frequently--have any specific content? The answer seems to be "yes": Glacier's vision builds on an international program of "biosphere reserves."

Biosphere reserves are one element of the United Nations Educational, Scientific and Cultural Organization's (UNESCO's) "Man in the Biosphere" program, which began in 1970. The idea for a biosphere reserve system originated at an international conference sponsored by UNESCO and others to establish a program for rational use and conservation of the earth's living natural resources.[189] Participating countries establish a national committee to nominate biosphere reserve designations, which are then submitted for approval and acceptance by UNESCO.[190] Designated places are not simply reserves, they are also places for ecological research and for education.[191]

We remarked earlier that Glacier officials have used the park's biosphere reserve designation to persuade others of its international status. The park does "wave the biosphere reserve flag" for tactical advantage, but it also takes the concept more seriously--as the basis for a theory of regional resource management. Indeed, our impression is that Glacier has adopted the biosphere reserve concept as its central policy idea for park protection and as its guidepost for understanding the implications of policies that protect the park from activities beyond its borders.

a. The Biosphere Reserve Concept

The biosphere reserve concept is twofold. First, it is a scientific program for the designation of representative ecosystems, including well-preserved natural systems, to be managed for the protection of their biological diversity and integrity and the maintenance of the variety of species they contain and their genetic diversity.[192] Second, it contemplates management of nearby areas on an economically viable, sustained-yield basis. This dual aspiration apparently arose from concern about less developed countries, where people sometimes destroy the very resource base that sustains them.[193]

The goals of the biosphere program are as attractive as they are all- encompassing: identifying representative ecosystems, maintaining their biological integrity,[194] promoting research and education, and providing for the well-being of nearby human populations. One element of the program anticipates "socio-benefits that flow from the sustainable productivity of rational systems, rather than protection per se. Biosphere reserves, in principle, are flexible enough to accommodate both perspectives."[195]

The biosphere reserve also offers a rare example of a true regional conception of land management aspiring both to resource preservation and to community sustenance.

> Unless the much larger area outside of such reserves is subject to sound land use policies and practices, resource values cannot be sustained over the longer term. That is one of the basic axioms of the Man and the Biosphere Program of which the biosphere reserve is the *in situ* component.[196] . . . In the final analysis, the biosphere reserve is a new, overarching concept aimed at welding together a combination of land uses to the common purpose of conserving representative ecological areas.[197]

b. Glacier's Use of Its Biosphere Reserve Designation

Glacier has taken up the biosphere concept as precisely the mandate it needs.[198] The park's enthusiasm is not surprising. Designation bestows international status and importance, and the biosphere reserve program states a scientific agenda[199] that can garner general support. This is not to suggest that scientific data is a substitute for policy preferences and choices. Plainly it is not.[200] It is only to say there are some goals--such as maintaining biological diversity--that will doubtless garner broad public and governmental support. Insofar as the Park Service is promoting such a goal, its agenda will likely trump the traditional commodity program of neighboring agencies. Thus, from a Park Service perspective, the biosphere reserve concept could be a way out of prospective stalemates where the park's preservation goals come into direct conflict with the competing goals--such as commodity development--of its neighbor federal agencies.

Unfortunately, Glacier's enthusiasm is a little premature. First, biosphere reserve designation is not a legal mandate, but simply a United Nations program in which the United States participates.[201] Officially, Glacier knows this,[202] but park officials still repeatedly talk of reserve designation as creating legal obligations.[203] The neighboring forests take a much narrower view of the significance of biosphere reserve designation, and apparently see the park's broader interpretation as a threat to their autonomy. The Flathead Forest Supervisor told us:

> A biosphere reserve is not a legal designation of anything. There is no inherent legal sanction on doing anything. It is just a label saying they are participating in a very broad program. You can have a mine in the biosphere program. You can have junkyards. People have an emotional view about the biosphere. There is nothing in it about preservation. We recently read all the biosphere documents. If you read the documents you'll see it's more of a network, including a variety of lands, managed and unmanaged, for research. It is an effort to learn about the effects of various kinds of management on ecosystems. It is a question of what role management chooses to play. Our Coram Experimental Forest is in the program.

Second, the biosphere reserve concept is still at the conceptual stage. There is so far no concrete notion of how biological preservation in a core reserve area is to be integrated with sustainable productive use of resources for the people in the peripheral areas.[204]

The biosphere reserve concept, however evocative an idea, remains a vague one. It is not surprising, as Glacier officials themselves recognize, that there is "presently little local or Regional understanding of the concept and suspicion that this is another lock-up program under a different name."[205]

Park officials are nonetheless making valiant efforts to bring the biosphere reserve idea to life within the Glacier region. They are identifying and actively seeking to protect essential elements of Glacier's biological integrity (such as wildlife corridors beyond park boundaries for genetic exchange), while reconciling themselves to losing some amenities that are not vital from a biological perspective (such as scenic vistas). They also appear to be shifting toward a more science-directed perspective in defining the purpose of national parks. Indeed, there is a certain irony in Glacier yielding on scenic amenities which, irrelevant from a scientific perspective, helped establish the parks in the first place[206] and are still a primary attraction for visitors to them.[207] The reason for the change is clear enough. As external effects become more and more important, the parks will be able to limit external development only if park values can override the multiple-use values of neighboring agencies, particularly the Forest Service. A potential vehicle for such an override is a deep scientific mission that focuses on preventing irreversible harm to basic resource stocks.[208]

c. Other Initiatives for Regional Cooperation

Glacier officials also appreciate that the national parks cannot limit the uses of neighboring lands until they begin taking some affirmative responsibility for the well-being of adjacent communities. The park is beginning to think about its responsibility to people and to the local economy. We were told that "each agency becomes more involved in issues that previously were only the concern of the other. Now there is a greater tendency to understand, empathize, compromise, than if you stayed back behind your own boundary." Insofar as this is the case, it betokens a radical revision of perspective for a notoriously insular agency.

There is considerable evidence that Glacier officials no longer, as the saying goes, "see the world only from the back of their own entrance signs." As we noted earlier, Glacier encouraged the negotiation of an agreement with a number of landowners in the

North Fork area to maintain large-lot, low-intensity use. It helped form an "interlocal agreement" among public agencies and associations of North Fork landowners, and it cooperated in the drafting of a proposed North Fork land use plan. Glacier also helped spearhead the lobbying effort that secured funding for the Flathead River Basin EIS Study and ultimately convinced the Montana legislature to create the Flathead Basin Commission.

Moreover, Glacier is making some concessions regarding its own interests. While none of them are major changes, they at least symbolize the park's recognition that it must affirmatively attend to the needs of neighboring human communities and that it cannot concern itself solely with protection of Glacier's natural features. For example, in negotiating for the park's water rights in the North Fork, Glacier does not demand maintenance of virgin flow, but agrees that water may be appropriated sufficient to support future compatible private uses such as stock watering, irrigation, and domestic supply.[209] We were told that Glacier has agreed to accept some visual disamenities to the park and is reconciled to protecting the quality of park resources, rather than demanding a pristine buffer for the park.[210]

Glacier is still far from solving its community relations problems, but it is trying to implement the sustaining-without-destroying concept even with its most difficult neighbor, the Blackfeet.[211] For example, the park has been urging the tribe to eliminate cattle grazing near the boundary because cattle trespass into the park, compete for forage with Glacier's wildlife, and transport into the park seeds of exotic plants on their hooves. Trespassing cattle have long been a troublesome problem for Glacier, and for years Glacier and the Blackfeet have disputed over installing and paying for a fence to restrain the cattle. For all the trouble they cause, the grazing cattle do not provide the Blackfeet much income. Glacier is now proposing to the Blackfeet that they substitute for grazing a trophy-hunting industry on the reservation, which would rely on exiting migratory park animals.[212] Park officials contend that their proposal substitutes for an economically marginal and ecologically destructive activity a more economically profitable and ecologically acceptable one.

VI. FINAL REFLECTIONS

A. The High Price of Discretion

Though they are in a sense adversaries, the park superintendent and the forest supervisor understand each other very well. They are professional managers who want to maximize their own judgment, discretion, and inventiveness, and to be free of outside forces dictating what shall happen on their turf. They do not seek to determine the fundamentals of forest or park policy; rather, they accept without hesitation the authority of Congress to set mandates for the public lands. But they want broad mandates so that they aren't reduced to mere pawns mechanically applying rules. If there were a managerial motto at Glacier, and indeed throughout the public domain surrounding Glacier, it might well be: Law is a shackle, only discretion liberates.

In this light, what at first seemed paradoxical and unlikely becomes more coherent. We wondered, for example, why Glacier officials oppose park protection legislation even when they seem to be losing out on issues like oil development on neighboring national forests. Now we know: As land managers, they resist being more rule-bound. Seeking maximum discretion themselves, they are acutely conscious that their Forest Service counterparts likewise value such autonomy, and they don't feel comfortable having veto power over decisions on another manager's turf.

We also think that we know why Glacier officials seem ungrateful to Fish and Wildlife Service officers who have helped them by issuing, or threatening to issue, jeopardy opinions under the ESA. The Fish and Wildlife Service is an outsider, and its intervention threatens a loss of discretion. For the same reason, we now understand Glacier's lack of contact with citizen environmental groups, and the virtual amnesia of Glacier officials about lawsuits, injunctions, and administrative appeals.

But the Glacier management's commitment to discretion generates a serious problem for them: It makes impossible consistent solutions for problems. Accordingly, a species of political judgment tends to dominate results. For example, because it is hard to put pressure on the economically depressed Blackfeet, Glacier officials keep silent while the Tribe installs a precedent-setting, potentially destructive well on Glacier's boundary. When decisions are discretionary, there is no objective basis for saying "no" to the

Blackfeet. Having once said yes to peripheral development, it is difficult to say no to essentially identical proposals on the ground of grave damage to basic park resources.

Indeed, it almost appears that the park managers' abstract commitment to maintaining managerial authority hinders park protection. This may explain why they have adopted an unyielding stance against any legislative solution to problems of peripheral development despite the fact that no other approaches seem to be working. In a sense, Glacier's Superintendent summed up this perspective when he observed, "Congressional legislation never comes on a silver platter."

We were surprised that Glacier officials, facing what seems to us to be, at best, a difficult situation, continue to believe in the talismanic force of the national parks and to feel confident that they can mobilize the press, public opinion, and the Congress to protect the park from grave perils. They may be right about a visible, dramatic danger like the Cabin Creek mine.[213] But they may be dead wrong when, like oil and gas development, the threat develops incrementally, without discrete dramatic episodes.

B. The Role of Law

The progress that has been made so far involves a good deal more legal coercion than park officials are willing to acknowledge. They believe that left to their own devices, and in light of changing public values about such matters as wildlife protection and clean water, park managers and their counterparts in neighboring agencies will be able to work out reasonable solutions like those emerging in the North Fork area. But Glacier officials also are quite aware that what seems "reasonable" to national forest managers is shaped by public values and, most importantly for their purposes, by congressional recognition of those values. They know perfectly well that their neighbors' attitudes and behavior are affected by laws mandating species protection and clean air and water, and by more general pro-environmental laws like NEPA, Federal Lands Policy Management Act (FLPMA), and National Forest Management Act (NFMA). We were astonished at how little weight Glacier officials attached to the coercive aspects of those statements of national policy, and at how resolutely they ignored the fact that NEPA produces injunctions, that NFMA gives rise to administrative appeals of forest plans, and that the ESA generates jeopardy opinions.

We could not imagine any Glacier official saying to us what a local reporter observed as if it were the most obvious thing in the world: "The Forest Service only fears the jeopardy opinion and prosecution under NEPA."

C. A Race With Time

Glacier is constrained by bureaucratic prudence and timidity. It is reluctant to use the law; highly deferential to the traditional turf prerogatives of its neighbors; and heistant to subject itself to criticism by speaking out forcefully on transboundary issues. It is not that Glacier's officials lack a vision of what the future should be, nor that they are wrong in believing that their vision of regionalism and commitment to biological and genetic conservation will eventually prevail. As we have emphasized, events are in motion that set the stage for important long-term changes in federal land management, and Glacier is affirmatively trying to shape that future.

But Glacier is in a race with time where present dangers threaten irreparable, incremental harm. The question is how much Glacier will sacrifice in the short run before some new and enlightened conception of land protection prevails. Glacier officials seem unable to bring themselves to do what is necessary to mobilize effective means to their admirable ends. One of our most striking findings was the central role of private groups that used the legal system to control threatened damage to the park. We were surprised at how often outside organizations held the critical leverage in the resolution of conflict between Glacier and its national forest neighbors. Having seen how the park operates, what we learned is not so surprising. Whether Glacier officials lack understanding of the power relationships that are at work around them, or they cannot energize themselves to work with those realities, the result is that Glacier has become largely a bystander as decisions are made that will determine its destiny.

POSTCRIPT

On April 13, 1987, the BLM Great Falls Area Office issued a Decision Notice reauthorizing the American Petrofina drilling permit application for the Hall Creek site in the Lewis & Clark National Forest.[214] The BLM concluded that the Forest Service has adequately addressed each of the remand points in the Interior Board of Land Appeals' 1985 decision, specifically finding that the Forest Service has adequate authority to enforce its road closure orders against the Blackfeet and thus can insure compliance with the terms of the FWS "no jeopardy" opinion.[215] Eleven appeals--initiated by the Blackfeet as well as by environmental groups --have been filed with the BLM challenging this decision.[216] Meanwhile, the Lewis & Clark is continuing with its environmental impact study of the Running Owl drilling application, and will address the cumulative environmental impacts of the Hall Creek and Running Owl wells on the Badger-Two Medicine region.

List of Individuals Interviewed

1. Kathy Athenslager (Seasonal Naturalist, Glacier National Park)
2. Bill Barmore (National Park Service Biologist, retired)
3. Arnold Bolle (Dean, Forestry School, University of Montana, retired)
4. Edgar Brannon (Supervisor, Flathead National Forest)
5. Wayne Brewster (United States Fish and Wildlife Service)
6. Mark Brunson (Reporter, Daily Interlake, Kalispell, Montana)
7. Bill Bryan (Environmental Activist, Bozeman, Montana)
8. Chuck Carr (New York Zoological Society)
9. Tim Clark (Wildlife Biologist)
10. Buzz Cobell (Ranger, Glacier National Park)
11. Nancy Cotner (Area Manager, Bureau of Land Management, Great Falls, Montana)
12. Bob Dunkley (Planner, Glacier National Park)
13. Keith Fellbaum (Chief of Maintenance, Glacier National Park)
14. Tom France (Attorney, National Wildlife Federation, Missoula, Montana)
15. Bob Frauson (Ranger, Glacier National Park, retired)
16. John Frederick (North Fork Resident, Polebridge, Montana)
17. John Gatchell (Montana Wilderness Association, Helena, Montana)
18. John Dale Gorman (Supervisor, Lewis & Clark National Forest)
19. Gary Gregory (Resource Specialist, Glacier National Park)
20. Robert Haraden (Superintendent, Glacier National Park, retired)
21. John Heberling (Attorney, Kalispell, Montana)
22. Phil Hocker (Environmental Activist, Jackson, Wyoming)
23. Joe Jessupe (Environmental Activist, East Glacier, Montana)
24. Charles Jonkel (Professor, University of Montana, Missoula)
25. Randy Kaufman (Ranger, Glacier National Park)
26. Loren Kreck (Environmental Activist, Columbia Falls, Montana)
27. Dave Lange (Ranger, Glacier National Park)
28. Bernard Leiff (Superintendent, Waterton Lakes National Park)
29. H. Gilbert Lusk (Superintendent, Glacier National Park)

30. Leo Marnell (Scientist, Glacier National Park)

31. Bob Martinka (Montana Fish, Wildlife & Parks Department, Helena, Montana)

32. Clifford Martinka (Scientist, Glacier National Park)

33. Ernie Nunn (Assistant Supervisor, Bridger-Teton National Forest, Wyoming)

34. Lance Olsen (Great Bear Foundation, Missoula, Montana)

35. Alan O'Neill (Assistant Superintendent, Glacier National Park)

36. Kenneth Pitt (Attorney, United States Department of Agriculture)

37. James A. Posewitz (Chairman, United States Section, Flathead River International Study Board)

38. Matt Reid (Wyoming Wildlife Federation)

39. Bill Rohrer (Environmental Engineer, Chevron, Casper, Wyoming)

40. Don Schwennesen (Reporter, Missoulian, Missoula, Montana)

41. Chuck Sigler (Chief Ranger, Glacier National Park)

42. Gary Slagel (Environmental Specialist, Bureau of Land Management, Great Falls, Montana)

43. Dick Smith (Land Management Planner, Lewis and Clark National Forest)

44. Lloyd Swanger (District Ranger, Lewis and Clark National Forest)

45. Jim Tilbe (Manager, Drilling Operations, Western Canada Shell Oil)

46. Tom Thompson (Businessman, Glacier Highlands, West Glacier, Montana)

47. John Warne (Consulting Geologist, Billings, Montana)

NOTES

*Copyright 1987 by ECOLOGY LAW QUARTERLY. Reprinted with permission of the authors and publisher.

**Professor of Law, Boalt Hall School of Law, University of California, Berkeley; J.D. 1959, University of Chicago; A.B. 1957, Harvard College.

***Professor of Law, University of Wyoming; J.D. 1972, Northwestern University; B.A. 1968, Washington University.

1. *See generally* Finn, *Interagency Relationships in Marine Resource Conflict: Some Lessons From OCS Oil and Gas Leasing,* 4 HARV. ENVTL. L. REV. 359 (1980) (discussing interagency coordination in marine resource exploitation); Sirico, *Agencies in Conflict: Overlapping Agencies and the Legitimacy of the Administrative Process,* 33 VAND. L. REV. 101 (1980) (analyzing multiagency decisionmaking from political science and constitutional perspectives); Comment, *Small Hydro in the Forest: Interagency Conflict Over Environmental Regulation,* 18 U.C. DAVIS L. REV. 321 (1984) (discussing conflict between the Forest Service and the Federal Energy Regulatory Commission over licensing of small hydroelectric plants); Note, *Interagency Conflict: A Model for Analysis,* 9 GA. J. INT'L & COMP. L. 241 (1979) (discussing multi-agency conflict with respect to national export policy).

2. The Forest Service multiple use mandate is codified at 16 U.S.C. §§ 523, 529, 531(a), (b), 1601(d)(1) (1982).

3. For background, *see* THE CONSERVATION FOUNDATION, NATIONAL PARKS FOR A NEW GENERATION: VISIONS, REALITIES, PROSPECTS 141 (1985); *see also infra* note 4 (park oversight hearings).

4. *See, e.g., Greater Yellowstone Ecosystem: Oversight Hearing Before the Subcomm. on Public Lands and the Subcomm. on National Parks and Recreation of the House Comm. on Interior and Insular Affairs,* 99th Cong., 1st Sess. 23, 25, 28, 59 (1985) [hereinafter *Yellowstone Ecosystem Hearing*]; *see also To Reform the Federal Onshore Oil and Gas Leasing Program, Hearings on H.R. 1960, H.R. 4741 and H.R. 4826, Before the Subcomm. on Mining and Natural Resources of the House Comm. on Interior and Insular Affairs,* 99th Cong., 2nd Sess. (1986) [hereinafter *Onshore Leasing Hearing*] (oversight hearings to reconcile oil and gas leasing on public lands with the goals of environmental protection). UNITED STATES GEN. ACCOUNTING OFFICE, GAO/RCED-87-36, PARKS AND RECREATION: LIMITED PROGRESS MADE IN DOCUMENTING AND MITIGATING THREATS TO THE PARKS (1987) [hereinafter GAO REPORT].

5. *See* Note, *Judicial Resolution of Inter-Agency Legal Disputes,* 89 YALE L.J. 1595 (1980) (urging that suits should be permitted).

6. Although some laws explicitly govern transboundary effects, *e.g.,* Clean Air Act, 42 U.S.C. §§ 7472(a), 7491 (1982), and others require consideration of environmental impacts wherever they may occur, *e.g.,* National Environmental Protection Act (NEPA), 42 U.S.C. §§ 4321-4370(a) (1982 & Supp. III 1985), no federal law of general application explicitly accommodates the differing missions of neighboring agencies. The Coastal Zone Management Act recognizes a need for consistency between federal and state managers. 16 U.S.C. § 1456(c), (d) (1982). *See generally* Keiter, *On Protecting the National Parks from the External Threats Dilemma,* 20 LAND & WATER L. REV. 355 (1985) (discussing application of the various pieces of existing federal and state environmental legislation to the external activities threatening Glacier National Park).

7. *See, e.g.,* W. BROWN, ISLANDS OF HOPE: PARKS AND RECREATION IN ENVIRONMENTAL CRISIS (1971); R. MCINTYRE, DENALI NATIONAL PARK: AN ISLAND IN TIME (1986).

8. *See, e.g.,* 16 U.S.C. § 230a(b) (1982) (establishing a park protection zone around Jean Lafitte National Historic Park); *id.* § 410ff-4 (requiring comment and consideration for a "proposed Federal or federally assisted undertaking . . . within or adjacent or related to the [Channel Islands National] park"); *id.* § 410ii-5(b) (mandating protection of outlying sites at Chaco Culture National Historic Park); 43 U.S.C. § 1636 (1982) (making

federal benefits available to Alaskan landowners who agree to manage their land in a manner consistent with federal management of adjoining or "directly affect[ed]" federal land, pursuant to Alaska National Interest Lands Conservation Act (ANILCA), 16 U.S.C. §§ 3101-3233 (1982 & Supp. III 1985)). The Federal Water Pollution Control Act gives the Environmental Protection Agency authority to veto a Corps of Engineers Permit. 33 U.S.C. § 1344(c) (1982); *see* Newport Galleria v. Deland, 618 F. Supp. 1129 (D.C. Cir. 1985); *see also* Federal Power Act, 16 U.S.C. § 797(e) (1982) (giving federal land managers authority over the issuing of licenses by the Federal Power Commission).

9. *See infra* note 10 (bills, hearings, and committee reports); Keiter, *supra* note 6, at 357 nn.6-7; *see also* Hiscock, *Protecting National Park System Buffer Zones: Existing, Proposed, and Suggested Authority,* 7 J. ENERGY L. 35 (1986) (recommending amendments to park legislation to force federal action protecting the parks from both internal and external development); Comment, *Protecting National Parks from Developments Beyond Their Borders,* 132 U. PA. L. REV. 1189 (1984) (urging legislative broadening of the Secretary of the Interior's authority to deal with external threats to the parks).

10. *See Yellowstone Ecosystem Hearing, supra* note 4, at 15-17, 44 (statement of William P. Mott, Director, National Park Service). The Bureau of Land Management (BLM) and industry representatives take the same view. *Id.* at 17-18, 20, 156, 159; *see also Public Land Management Policy: Hearings on H.R. 999, H.R. 2379, H.R. 2014, H.R. 2107, Before the Subcomm. on Public Lands and National Parks of the House Comm. on Interior and Insular Affairs,* 98th Cong., 1st & 2d Sess., p. 10, at 97, 115, 116 (1983-1984) [hereinafter 1983-1984 Public Land Management Hearings] (statement of Russell E. Dickenson):

> As I indicated earlier . . . we believe that the existing numerous legislative authorities that are available to us for dealing with outside influences are sufficient . . . .
>
> • • • •
>
> . . . [T]hrough consultation and negotiation, even though sometimes it takes a little bit longer, we can achieve those [park protection goals] without having coercive legislation to help bring it about.

Id.; Public Land Management Policy: Hearings on H.R. 5162, H.R. 5552, H.R. 5973 and H.R. 5976 Before the Subcomm. on Public Lands and National Parks of the House Comm. on Interior and Insular Affairs, 97th Cong., 2d Sess., pt. 3, 435-52 (1982) [hereinafter 1982 Public Land Management Hearings] (statement of Russell E. Dickenson, Director, National Park Service); HOUSE COMM. ON INTERIOR AND INSULAR AFFAIRS, NATIONAL PARK SYSTEM PROTECTION AND RESOURCES MANAGEMENT ACT OF 1982, H.R. REP. NO. 881, 97th Cong., 2d Sess. 20-22 (1982) (Letter from Donald Paul Hodel, Acting Secretary of the Interior); HOUSE COMM. ON INTERIOR AND INSULAR AFFAIRS, PROVIDING FOR THE PROTECTION AND MANAGEMENT OF THE NATIONAL PARK SYSTEM, AND FOR OTHER PURPOSES, H.R. REP. NO. 170, 98th Cong. 1st Sess. 12-15 (1983) (Letter from J. Craig Potter, Acting Assistant Secretary of the Interior).

11. For the current policy of the Department of the Interior regarding reconciling interagency conflicts over external threats, *see* Report of the Subgroup of the Park Protection Working Group (Submitted to the Under Secretary of the Interior) (June 12, 1985) (recommending interagency notification of ongoing planning activities, good faith efforts to avoid conflicts, increased formal and informal communications among land managers, and improved personnel management to encourage anticipation, avoidance, and resolution of conflicts). Interior's policy has been called into question. *See, e.g.,* Letter from Rep. Bruce Vento, Chair of the Subcomm. on National Parks and Recreation of the House Comm. on Interior and Insular Affairs, to Ann McLaughlin, Under Secretary

of the Interior (Oct. 9, 1985) (Commenting on the Working Group proposal, Rep. Vento said, "We are very disappointed with what we believe to be ineffective and inappropriate results.").

12. OFFICE OF SCIENCE AND TECHNOLOGY, NAT'L PARK SERV., U.S. DEP'T OF THE INTERIOR, STATE OF THE PARKS 1980: A REPORT TO THE CONGRESS (1980) [hereinafter STATE OF THE PARKS 1980].

13. We conducted formal and informal interviews with various individuals in May and June 1986, and again in late July and August 1986, at Glacier National Park; Flathead National Forest; Lewis & Clark National Forest; Yellowstone National Park; Waterton National Park (Canada); Bureau of Land Management Area Offices in Great Falls, Kalispell, Polebridge, Choteau, and Missoula, Montana; Yellowstone National Park, Wyoming.

The names and associations of our interviewees are listed in the Appendix at the end of this Article. A number of interviewees did not wish to be identified, so we usually refer to our sources generally--for example, as "a BLM official" or "a Glacier employee." Sometimes we simply say, "We were told . . . ." We have in our files verbatim notes of all our interviews.

We also reviewed a great deal of documentary materials, which are in our files or available from the agencies.

14. Strictly speaking, two national recreation areas--Chattahoochee River and Cuyahoga Valley--and Prince William Forest Park, with 64, 58, and 57, respectively, reported more than Glacier's 56 threats. STATE OF THE PARKS 1980, *supra* note 12, at 52.

15. For a description of Glacier Park and its problems, *see* NATIONAL PARK SERV., U.S. DEP'T OF THE INTERIOR, NATURAL RESOURCES MANAGEMENT PLAN AND ENVIRONMENTAL ASSESSMENT: GLACIER NATIONAL PARK (1983) [hereinafter GLACIER RESOURCES MANAGEMENT PLAN]; NATIONAL PARK SERV., U.S. DEP'T OF THE INTERIOR, GLACIER NATIONAL PARK STATEMENT FOR MANAGEMENT 1-13 (1981) [hereinafter GLACIER MANAGEMENT STATEMENT]; NATIONAL PARK SERV., U.S. DEP'T OF THE INTERIOR, GLACIER NATIONAL PARK, MONTANA: FINAL MASTER PLAN (1977).

16. Both forests have issued final plans that set out management directions for the next 10-15 years. FLATHEAD NAT'L FOREST, FOREST SERV., U.S. DEP'T OF AGRIC., FOREST PLAN (1985) [hereinafter FLATHEAD FOREST PLAN]; LEWIS & CLARK NAT'L FOREST, FOREST SERV., U.S. DEP'T OF AGRIC., FOREST PLAN (1986) [hereinafter LEWIS & CLARK FOREST PLAN]. These plans are required by the National Forest Management Act (NFMA). 16 U.S.C. § 1604(a) (1982). They are accompanied by Environmental Impact Statements (EIS's), as required by 16 U.S.C. § 1604(g). *See* FLATHEAD NAT'L FOREST, FOREST SERV., U.S. DEP'T OF AGRIC., ENVIRONMENTAL IMPACT STATEMENT ON THE FLATHEAD NATIONAL FOREST LAND AND RESOURCE MANAGEMENT PLAN (1985) [hereinafter FLATHEAD PLAN EIS]; LEWIS & CLARK NAT'L FOREST, FOREST SERV., U.S. DEP'T OF AGRIC., LEWIS AND CLARK NATIONAL FOREST PLAN ENVIRONMENTAL IMPACT STATEMENT (1986) [hereinafter LEWIS & CLARK PLAN EIS].

17. 16 U.S.C. § 1271 (1982). On the North Fork of the Flathead, the middle of the stream is the boundary line between the park and the Flathead National Forest. On the Middle Fork, the northern stream bank marks the park boundary. GLACIER NAT'L PARK, U.S. DEP'T OF THE INTERIOR, NATURAL RESOURCES MANAGEMENT PLAN AND ENVIRONMENTAL ASSESSMENT 51 (1983) [hereinafter GLACIER EA].

18. 16 U.S.C. § 1273(b)(2).

19. *See infra* note 43.

20. MONT. CODE ANN. § 77-1-601 (1985) (stated policy for state land is to "[s]eek the highest development of state-owned lands in order that they might be placed to their highest and best use and thereby derive greater revenue").

21. Because these factions alternately capture control of the Tribal Council in annual elections, park and forest officials told us that they are often frustrated by inconsistent, shifting positions on resource issues of mutual concern.

22. Agreement with the Indians of the Blackfeet Indian Reservation in Montana, Sept. 26, 1895, ch. 398, § 9, 29 Stat. 321, 353-354 (1896) [hereinafter Blackfeet Treaty], *quoted in* 1 LEWIS & CLARK PLAN EIS, *supra* note 16, at 3-4 to 3-5. The current Blackfeet position is set out in 2 LEWIS & CLARK PLAN EIS, *supra* note 16, at app. F-109 to F-119.

23. NATIONAL PARK SERV., U.S. DEP'T OF THE INTERIOR, DRAFT LAND PROTECTION PLAN: GLACIER NATIONAL PARK 7-8 (1985) [hereinafter GLACIER DRAFT LAND PROTECTION PLAN].

24. *See, e.g.,* FLATHEAD FOREST PLAN, *supra* note 16, at II-25, II-35 (descriptions of grizzly bear and gray wolf distribution in the Northern Rockies); GLACIER MANAGEMENT STATEMENT, *supra* note 15, at 10 (describing wildlife influences within the park).

The Bob Marshall and Great Bear wilderness areas lie south of the park in the Flathead and Lewis and Clark National Forests. Adjacent to the Bob Marshall Wilderness is the Scapegoat Wilderness, managed by the Helena and Lolo and Lewis and Clark National Forests. Together with Glacier National Park these national forest wilderness areas form a nearly contiguous complex of designated wilderness along the northern Rocky Mountain Crest. GLACIER EA, *supra* note 17, at 1; FLATHEAD FOREST PLAN, *supra* note 16, at VI-6, VI-7; LEWIS & CLARK FOREST PLAN, *supra* note 16, at 6-6.

25. 16 U.S.C. §§ 1531-1543 (1982 & Supp. III 1985); 50 C.F.R. § 17.11, at 74, 82 (1986); *see* GLACIER DRAFT LAND PROTECTION PLAN, *supra* note 23, at 7. Two other listed species, the bald eagle and the peregrine falcon, also inhabit or pass through Glacier. *Id.* at 8.

26. 16 U.S.C. § 1533.

27. *Id.* § 1536(a).

28. *Id.* The Endangered Species Act provides that every federal agency is required to consult with the Secretary of the Interior (Fish and Wildlife Service) to assure that none of its actions is likely to jeopardize the continued existence, or adversely modify or destroy the habitat, of an endangered or threatened species. *Id.* § 1536(a)(2). The Secretary, following such consultation, is required to provide "a written . . . opinion . . . detailing . . . [i]f jeopardy . . . is found." *Id.* § 1536(b)(3)(A). That is what is familiarly known as the jeopardy opinion. Because the ESA prohibits action that jeopardizes listed species, a jeopardy opinion operates as a veto on the proposed action. The statute does provide a procedure by which exemptions may be obtained from a jeopardy opinion. *See id.* § 1536(e)-(k).

29. The Department of the Interior Fish and Wildlife Service (FWS) cooperates with the Montana Department of Fish, Wildlife, and Parks (FWP) on wildlife matters, and the FWP is presently investigating whether the grizzly bear should be "delisted" from the Endangered Species Act (ESA) as a threatened species in the Glacier region. *See* MONTANA DEP'T OF FISH, WILDLIFE & PARKS, FINAL PROGRAMMATIC EIS: THE GRIZZLY BEAR IN NORTHWESTERN MONTANA, SUMMARY 29 (1986) [hereinafter MONTANA FINAL PROGRAMMATIC EIS] ("The review in this EIS indicates that the continued classification as threatened [in the northern continental divide ecosystem] needs to be evaluated and the possibility of delisting explored."). Several bear experts and advocates to whom we talked tend to favor delisting, seeing continued delisting as a measure of the Act's success. But, we were told, environmental lawyers doubt it will occur soon, or they are preparing to fight delisting on the ground that it is essential to the grizzly's survival to maintain protection under the ESA. For a sense of the local situation, *see* Robbins, *A Town Divided By The Grizzly,* N.Y. Times, Aug. 31, 1986, § 6 (Magazine), at 22.

Other federal and state agencies also figure in development issues. Subsurface mineral development (such as oil drilling) on national forest lands is under the authority of the federal Bureau of Land Management. 43 C.F.R. §§ 3100.0-3, 3101.1-2, 3101.7 (1986); *see generally,* Wilkinson & Anderson, *Land and Resource Planning in the National Forests,* 64 OR. L. REV. 1, 242-72 (1985). An important controversy over proposed road paving in the Flathead National Forest involved the Federal Highway Administration as well as Flathead County, which maintains the road. *See infra* notes 107-126 and accompanying text.

30. The limited scope of this Article should not suggest that private activity does not pose dire threats. For discussion of those threats, *see, e.g.,* Sax, *Buying Scenery: Land Acquisitions for the National Park Service,* 1980 DUKE L.J. 709, 711-31; Sax, *Helpless Giants: The National Parks and the Regulation of Private Lands,* 75 MICH. L. REV. 239, 239-41 (1977).

31. An interview with the Flathead Supervisor, Edgar B. Brannon, appears in the N.Y. Times, Apr. 16, 1986, at A-22, col. 1; *see also infra* notes 70-71 and accompanying text.

32. *See infra* notes 141-143 and accompanying text.

33. *See* H. STEEN, THE U.S. FOREST SERVICE: A HISTORY 113-22, 157-59, 209-13 (1976); B. TWIGHT, ORGANIZATIONAL VALUES AND POLITICAL POWER: THE FOREST SERVICE VERSUS THE OLYMPIC NATIONAL PARK (Pa. State Univ. Studies No. 48, 1983).

34. For discussion, *see* Sagoff, *Where Ickes Went Right or Reason and Rationality in Environmental Law,* 14 ECOLOGY L. Q. 265 (1987).

35. Not all the reported threats were external, but external threats were by far the most common ones. STATE OF THE PARKS 1980, *supra* note 12, at 4.

Park officials talked almost exclusively about *potential* harm to Glacier, no doubt because we indicated an interest in their efforts to protect the park from current threats. This focus on potential threats does not mean that Glacier has so far escaped actual harm. In fact, Glacier officials have learned to accept a certain amount of damage which they have been unable to control. For example, we were told that the most serious recent pressure arose from large clearcuts in the Kishenehn drainage in Canada designed to harvest beetle- infested trees before they lost their economic value. However, we were also told that the park has not yet been able to document any serious impact from stream sedimentation related to the logging, which began in 1980-1982 and still continues to some extent. Another example, considered under control, is a long-standing controversy over fluoride emissions from a nearby aluminum refining plant. *See* Keiter, *supra* note 6, at 379. Other ongoing problems include trespassing cattle from the Blackfeet Reservation (which compete with park wildlife and transport an exotic weed on their hoofs), wildlife poaching from nearby access roads installed to promote oil exploration, and sulphur dioxide emissions from Canadian wells north of Glacier. By far the greatest effect on the historic natural environment, a park scientist told us, comes from suppressing fires that traditionally burned in neighboring forests. Nevertheless, there are not yet reports of grave impairment to Glacier's resources, and Glacier may be the most ecologically intact national park in the contiguous forty-eight states.

36. *See* 1 FLATHEAD PLAN EIS, *supra* note 16, at VI-41; 2 LEWIS & CLARK PLAN EIS, *supra* note 16, at app. F-14.

37. *See* 1 FLATHEAD PLAN EIS, *supra* note 16, at VI-41; 2 LEWIS & CLARK PLAN EIS, *supra* note 16, at app. F-16.

38. It is amusing to recall that several decades ago Glacier was pressing for the North Fork Road, and for recreational development there, to relieve visitor congestion within Glacier. A. Bolle, The Basis of Multiple Use Management of Public Lands in the North Fork of Flathead River, Montana 198, 210 (1959) (Ph.D. diss., Graduate School of Public Administration, Harvard Univ.).

39. *See* FLATHEAD RIVER BASIN EIS STEERING COMM., FLATHEAD RIVER BASIN ENVIRONMENTAL IMPACT STUDY: FINAL REPORT (1986) [hereinafter FLATHEAD BASIN STUDY]. Glacier officials also worry that opening the Canadian Cabin Creek mine will make paving the North Fork road inevitable, with the same effects on presently remote areas. *See* CENTRAL DIRECT FED. DIV., FED. HIGHWAY ADMIN., DEP'T OF TRANSP., DRAFT ENVIRONMENTAL IMPACT STATEMENT FOR RECONSTRUCTION OF MONTANA FOREST HIGHWAY ROUTE 61, FLATHEAD COUNTY, FHWA-FPMT-EIS-82-1-D, at 105, 114 (1982) [hereinafter NORTH FORK ROAD DRAFT EIS]; *see also* CENTRAL DIRECT FED. DIV., FED. HIGHWAY ADMIN., DEP'T

OF TRANSP., FINAL ENVIRONMENTAL IMPACT STATEMENT, FHWA- FPMT-EIS-82-1-F, at 83 (1983) [hereinafter NORTH FORK ROAD FINAL EIS] ("The remoteness of the North Fork has contributed to a historically low level of activity and impacts.").

40. Flathead and Lewis & Clark officials would like Glacier to help when noxious weed, beetle infestation, or wildfire problems cross the borders. In fact, in the 1950's and 1960's, Glacier applied chemicals to protect the neighboring forests against disease and sprayed DDT on land along the Going-to-the-Sun Highway. C.W. Buchholtz, The Historical Dichotomy of Use and Preservation in Glacier National Park 95-96 (1969) (M.A. thesis, Univ. of Montana). However, as forest officials recognize, "There isn't much [Glacier officials] can do with their constituency. They get hell for anything they do-- a tiny timber cut, a burn to control insect infestation . . . ."

41. 42 U.S.C. §§ 4321-4370(a) (1982 & Supp. III 1985).

42. 42 U.S.C. §§ 7401-7642 (1982 & Supp. III 1985); 33 U.S.C. §§ 1251-1376 (1982 & Supp.III 1985).

43. *See* Keiter, *supra* note 6, at 376-77. Glacier has available to it several interesting, but unexplored legal arguments. For example, the National Forest Management Act requires the Forest Service to provide for diverse plant and animal communities. 16 U.S.C. § 1604(g)(3)(B) (1982). Glacier has not, however, tried to hold the Forest Service to that requirement, even though management of land to protect species diversity is precisely one of the issues on which the park differs with the forests.

Another unexplored legal possibility arises from the fact that stream siltation may result from timber harvesting in the Flathead River basin. The North Fork of the Flathead River has been designated a scenic river under the Federal Wild and Scenic Rivers Act. 16 U.S.C. § 1274(a)(13) (1982). Section 12 of the Act, 16 U.S.C. § 1283, provides that where national forest land is adjacent to a designated river, the officials in charge of the forest "shall take such action respecting management [of such adjacent lands] as may be necessary to protect such rivers in accordance with the purposes" of the Act, which, as to scenic rivers, is to maintain them "with shorelines or watersheds still largely primitive . . . ." *Id.* § 1273(b)(2). Section 12 further provides that "particular attention shall be given to scheduled timber harvesting, road construction, and similar activities which might be contrary to the purposes of this [Act]." *Id.* § 1283(a). If it could be shown that timber harvesting will necessarily prevent the maintenance of a "largely primitive watershed" (a phrase that the Wild and Scenic Rivers Act does not define), Glacier could find itself in a very strong legal position. For wild rivers like the Middle Fork the standard is even stronger--"primitive and waters unpolluted." *Id.* § 1273(b)(1). There are also questions as to whether the forest's water quality management practices for timber harvesting are adequate. *See infra* note 51. Glacier has not yet pursued any of these possibilities.

Nor, apparently, has Glacier considered traditional legal remedies for damage from clear-cutting across the border in Canada. Whatever the vagaries of international law, article II of the U.S.-Canada Boundary Waters Treaty, *infra* note 134, does provide that if use of a transboundary river causes injury downstream, the courts of the upstream country are open to the downstream country. *See* LeMarquand, *Preconditions to Cooperation in Canada-United States Boundary Waters,* 26 NAT. RESOURCES J. 221, 233 (1986). For a discussion of possible international liability for harmful transnational environmental effects, *see* Magraw, *Transboundary Harm: The International Law Commission's Study of "International Liability,"* 80 AM. J. INT'L. L. 305 (1986).

44. Indeed, one of the authors had prepared a report for the park two years earlier outlining its legal rights vis-a-vis its neighbors. *See* R. Keiter & W. Hubert, An Assessment of Research Needs to Develop Legal Bases for Challenging External Threats to Glacier National Park (July 5, 1984).

45. We are not the first to discover Park Service reluctance to invoke legal remedies. "I think the National Park Service should be using the legal tools that are available. We had extensive hearings on air pollution and threats to the parks, and it's clear the Park Ser-

vice is not pursuing its lawful remedies." *Vento Takes Charge*, NAT'L PARKS, Mar.-Apr. 1986, at 11, 13 (Interview with Rep. Bruce Vento, Chair, U.S. Congress, House of Representatives, Subcomm. on National Parks).

46. *See infra* note 53. The biosphere reserve concept is discussed *infra* notes 189-208 and accompanying text. The concept is what international lawyers call "soft law"--agreements to a principle, or nonenforceable commitments, that may be made through designation in an international program. Gold, *Strengthening the Soft International Law of Exchange Arrangements*, 77 AM. J. INT'L. L. 443, 443-44 (1983).

Glacier officials exhibit some awareness of the actual status of the biosphere reserve designation:

> Biosphere reserve designation in concert with various existing legal designations . . . and the pending World Heritage nomination would seem to provide collectively the legal and ethical basis for the highest degree of protection for the North Fork
>
> • • • •
>
> Biosphere reserve designation provides a symbolic and practical framework for voluntary efforts . . . . Its voluntary nature--and, specifically, the lack of legal constraints--has been a major factor in the willingness of an increasingly diverse array of Federal, state, and private land administrators to participate in biosphere reserve linkages.

Memorandum from Bill Gregg, Man and the Biosphere Program Coordinator, Nat'l Park Serv., U.S. Dep't of the Interior, to Dan Kimball, Water Resources Div. 1-2 (Feb. 25, 1986) (Ref. No. N16(498)).

47. *See infra* notes 94-95 and accompanying text.

48. 40 C.F.R. §§ 1504.1-.3 (1986) (providing for referral of interagency disagreements over projects covered by NEPA to the Council on Environmental Quality); *see also* notes 94-98 and accompanying text (Glacier's decision to comment on Flathead drilling proposal but refusal to oppose in NEPA proceedings).

49. *See, e.g.*, 1 FLATHEAD PLAN EIS, *supra* note 16, at VI-40 to VI-41 (Glacier's letter commenting on Flathead's Plan).

50. The only time the law came into play during our interviews at Glacier was when park and forest officials met to discuss the treaty access claims of the Blackfeet. *See supra* note 22. Even on this sensitive issue, which both park and forest officials assumed would go to litigation, no Park Service lawyer was present. Of course, the park headquarters in West Glacier are 415 miles from the nearest solicitor in Billings, Montana. A Forest Service attorney came up from Missoula to East Glacier for the meeting.

Apparently, lawyers are brought in only when there is an obligation to participate in legal proceedings, as in the settlement of Glacier's federal reserved water rights. *See* MONT. CODE ANN. §§ 85-2-217, -233, -702, -703 (1985) (proscribing procedures for negotiating and adjudicating federal reserved water rights).

51. Determining what the law requires can be very complicated. For example, what are the water quality requirements that govern timber harvesting in the Flathead River basin? Because the runoff from lumbering is a "nonpoint" source, no federal quantitative standards govern it. *See* 33 U.S.C. § 1311 (1982). But *see* 40 C.F.R. § 131.20(a)(3) (1986) (federal nondegradation standards for national park waters). *See also* 33 U.S.C. § 1344(f) (1982) (excepting discharge of dredged fill from timber harvest and forest road construction from permit requirements of the Clean Water Act). There are state water quality standards, and the State of Montana has set its highest standard, nondegradation, for waters within or bounding national parks. Under Montana's regulations, though, runoff from timber harvesting is not considered degradation if "all reasonable . . . conservation practices have been applied." Montana Water Pollution Control Regulations, 16 Mont. Admin. Reg. § 16.20.701(1)(b)(i) (1986), *reprinted in* Env. Rep. (BNA), 2 State

Water Laws 831.0501. However, we were told that Montana does not explicitly define these "reasonable practices," but instead incorporates as its criteria the practices the Forest Service wants to meet. The upshot is that the Forest Service defines for itself its "best management practices." FLATHEAD FOREST PLAN, *supra* note 16, at II-40 note. Moreover, those practices are set with reference to timber harvest goals that the Forest Service sets for itself. 1 FLATHEAD PLAN EIS, *supra* note 16, at II-94 to II-100. For other examples of complex legal questions, *see supra* note 43.

52. *See* Macauley, *Non-Contractual Relations in Business,* 28 AM. SOC. REV. 55 (1963) (study finding that resort to legal sanctions in business dealings may have undesirable consequences and thus this tactic is rarely used).

53. As a top park official put it:

We start with common interests and shared goals . . . . I use various means to 'sell' what needs to be done. The various cooperative organizations, like the Flathead Basin Commission [MONT. CODE ANN. § 75-7-301 to -308 (1985)] are useful. They dealt with phosphates and detergents, not too big an issue. But we can [through the Commission] put important issues on the table to be responded to, such as water quality and the Cabin Creek [Canadian] coal mine. . . . Then, if necessary, we may have to invoke legal standards, like the biosphere reserve.

54. This idea has been around for quite a while. Arnold Bolle proposed joint "planning units" so that the Flathead and Glacier could "work together toward a continuing solution over time" of their mutual problems. A. Bolle, *supra* note 38, at 220 (At that time, conflict was between timber harvesting and recreation in the North Fork area.).

55. Surely this is one major reason why Glacier doesn't want a park protection act, which would be seen as a bill-of-rights for national parks, and--inevitably in its view--against its neighbors. One park executive told us, "The legislation that has been most helpful is that which doesn't relate specifically to parks, but which focuses on protection of the resource, such as the Clean Air Act." Of course, he meant that he did not want any legislation suggesting that the Forest Service was losing turf to the Park Service, a long-standing sore point between the two federal services. *See e.g.,* H. STEEN, *supra* note 33, at 113-22, 157-59, 209-13; B. TWIGHT, *supra* note 33.

A noteworthy exception to Glacier's reluctance to assert formal legal rights is in its dealings with the Blackfeet. A top park manager told us:

The Blackfeet won't interact with us [the park]. . . . I welcome a court case. I want these issues [access and fencing] off the [bargaining] table. . . . As far as we are concerned the [access] issue is dead. There is a court decision that decides there is no right of access and our management will be based on that. If they want to litigate, so be it. I would welcome clarifying litigation. . . . It will be easier to have a court case. I don't think we've had a very good record in negotiations.

Park conflict with the Blackfeet goes back at least sixty years. *See e.g.,* C.W. Buchholtz, *supra* note 40, at 45-46 ("unauthorized" hunting by the Blackfeet of elk "which occasionally wandered from the park onto the Blackfeet Indian Reservation").

56. In regard to the Cabin Creek mine, we were told by a Glacier executive, "We played on the theme of the park as a national, international treasure, as an inviolate sanctuary." An official of the Bridger-Teton National Forest in Wyoming, explaining why he yielded to a demand from the National Elk Refuge that he close a road in the forest, said, "Elk have national significance, that's why we had to accommodate."

57. The most recent version of this bill, H.R. 921, S. 451, 100th Cong., 1st Sess., 133 CONG. REC. S1592 (daily ed. Feb. 3, 1987). The bill would restrict low level flights at Grand Canyon, Yosemite, and Haleakala National Parks, and would mandate a study of

aircraft noise throughout the national park system. We were told that planned military overflights have also been prevented, as a result of congressional intervention, at the behest of both Glacier and national forest officials. *See also infra* note 175.

58. The water rights issue, currently under negotiation with the State of Montana, involves how much water Glacier is entitled to have flow past the park as a federal reserved water right. *Cf.* Sierra Club v. Block, 622 F. Supp. 842 (D. Colo. 1985) (Federal water rights are impliedly reserved, but federal authorities have the duty to claim such rights.); United States v. City and County of Denver, 656 P.2d 1 (Colo. 1982) (Federal government reserved water rights equal the amount necessary to achieve the primary purpose of the reservation.); *see also* J. SAX & R. ABRAMS, LEGAL CONTROL OF WATER RESOURCES 493-572 (1986) (discussing the history and legal implication of federal reserved water rights); *supra* note 209 and accompanying text.

59. "Our goal is to start edging [development] away from [nearby] parts of the forest."

60. *See, e.g.*, Hall Creek APD, American Petroleum Co. of Texas, Federal South Glacier 1-26, Lease # M53322 (affidavit of Keith Aune, Wildlife Biologist, Mont. Dep't of Fish, Wildlife, and Parks) [hereinafter Keith Aune Affidavit], *reprinted in Onshore Leasing Hearing, supra* note 4, at 181-88 (Exhibit A to the statement of Lou Bruno, President, Glacier-Two Medicine Alliance). *See also* GAO REPORT, *supra* note 4, at 26 (noting Park Service awareness that it lacks "factual data on which to base and to support [its] position").

61. *See supra* note 51.

62. We were also told, "We don't have in-house capability. Region [the Regional Office] has--I think--one person." The lack of specificity weakens Glacier's effectiveness in the eyes of Forest Service officials: "[Glacier's comments] raise questions; they have concerns that they bring up. . . . A lot of concerns they have are not site-specific, but relate to what long term development means to an area." Officials from the Lewis & Clark flatly denied that Glacier had data to support its misgivings about oil and gas development adjacent to the park.

63. We discovered only one case of open, unambiguous opposition. In 1947, "Park officials confronted the Army Corps of Engineers with an unalterable position opposed to [proposed] dam construction" on the North Fork that would have flooded over 20,000 acres in the park. C.W. Buchholtz, *supra* note 40, at 74-75; *see also infra* note 93.

64. *See infra* notes 141-142 and accompanying text.

65. A former superintendent remarked, "The only time I went outside to get action was on B-52 overflights. I heard about it from the Fish and Wildlife Service, leaked it to the local press, and then Williams [congressional representative for the district] got involved."

66. A well-informed citizen told us that the clearcutting virtually decimated the native trout population in several important spawning streams tributary to the North Fork.

67. *See infra* text accompanying note 155. However, it may not be possible to drill at the Hall Creek site because the no-jeopardy opinion rests on being able to control access, to which the Blackfeet claim a treaty right. *See infra* note 152.

68. We were told by a top Glacier official, "There must be some people in the forest who share our views--we need to find out who they are." Glacier intends to make sure the regional forester "can't turn a blind eye to the issue" by insuring that there will be "more public concern than would ordinarily be brought to bear on those oil wells. . . . The park will stay in the background but push hard."

69. These goals will be discussed when we describe the biosphere reserve concept. *See infra* notes 189-208 and accompanying text.

70. We were told that, during the forest planning process, the Flathead ran a citizen alternative plan through its computers.

71. Brannon was referring principally to the National Forest Management Act, 16 U.S.C. §§ 1601-1687 (1982), which mandates interagency consultation and broad public invol-

vement as part of the forest planning process. Because the *Flathead Forest Plan* establishes the future direction of forest management, and because park officials commented extensively on the draft *Plan*, we drew heavily upon the *Plan* as an objective indication of current relations between the Flathead and Glacier National Park. *See* 1 FLATHEAD PLAN EIS, *supra* note 16, at VI-37 to VI-46.

72. Letter from Robert Haraden, Superintendent, Glacier National Park, to Dick Call, Glacier View District Ranger, Flathead National Forest (July 13, 1983).

73. *See* Letter from J. Lamar Beasley, Deputy Chief of the Forest Service, to Jon Heberling, Attorney, Kalispell, Mont. (May 22, 1986) (discussing stay of Akinkoka Mountain Timber Sale). We were also told, "If ever there was a good timber sale, that was it."

74. FLATHEAD FOREST PLAN, *supra* note 16, at IV-150.

75. *Id.*

76. 1 FLATHEAD PLAN EIS, *supra* note 16, at I-13. If the forest declares an area out of bounds to harvesting, but doesn't reduce the total timber quota, it simply shifts the impacts of lumbering from one part of the forest to another. Reducing the overall quota cuts against the Forest Service's traditional emphasis on timber production as a primary activity on forest lands, one that generally dominates other multiple-use responsibilities. *See* Wilkinson & Anderson, *supra* note 29, at 117-18.

77. The Fish and Wildlife Service has given the *Plan* a no-jeopardy opinion. 1 FLATHEAD PLAN EIS, *supra* note 16, at VI- 29 to VI-36. But see ROCKY MOUNTAIN REGION, FOREST SERV., U.S. DEP'T OF AGRIC., SHOSHONE NATIONAL FOREST LAND AND RESOURCE MANAGEMENT PLAN app. H (1986) (prohibiting oil and gas leasing on essential (Situation 1) grizzly bear habitat lands).

78. FLATHEAD FOREST PLAN, *supra* note 16, at II-26; *see also* LEWIS & CLARK FOREST PLAN, *supra* note 16, at app. K-1 (describing the categories of land management for grizzly bear management in the northern Rocky Mountains); *id.* at app. I-1 (the wildlife management guidelines).

79. 1 FLATHEAD PLAN EIS, *supra* note 16, at IV-73 to IV-81. We were told that the lumber industry is appealing the *Plan* on the ground that it does not provide for enough timber harvesting.

80. *See infra* notes 119-121 and accompanying text.

81. Conner v. Burford, 605 F. Supp. 107 (D. Mt. 1985), *appeal filed,* No. 85-3929 (9th Cir. June 17, 1985); *see* FLATHEAD PLAN EIS, *supra* note 16, at III-37. Subsequently, the same court relied on the same grounds to invalidate oil and gas leases issued in the Deep Creek area of the Lewis & Clark National Forest. Bob Marshall Alliance v. Watt, 16 ENVTL. L. REP. (Envtl. L. Inst.) 20759 (D. Mont. 1986), *appeal filed,* No. 86-4019 (9th Cir. July 22, 1986).

82. There have been 39 separate appeals of the *Flathead Forest Plan.* Telephone interview with James Gladen, Appeals & Litigation Coordinator, Forest Service, Department of Agriculture (May 4, 1987).

83. Unlike the Lewis & Clark, we were told, the Flathead is not generally attractive for oil and gas development.

84. Several timber sales in the area reportedly have gone unbid.

85. One constraint is that the *Forest Plan* would have to be amended were a "significant change" to occur, and the Forest Service would most likely have to prepare a new EIS. *See* 16 U.S.C. § 1604(f)(4) (1982).

86. The designation is part of the *Forest Plan. See supra* note 74 and accoompanying text. *See also supra* note 85.

87. *See supra* note 79 and accompanying text.

88. *See* FLATHEAD NAT'L FOREST, FOREST SERV., U.S. DEP'T OF AGRIC., DRAFT ENVIRONMENTAL IMPACT STATEMENT--SUPPLEMENT II-26 (1984). The only wilderness land proposed

is well south of the park, adjoining the existing Bob Marshall Wilderness. *Id.* at II-25. California v. Block, 690 F.2d 753 (9th Cir. 1982), obliged the Flathead to reevaluate roadless areas for wilderness classification in the forest planning process.

89. *See supra* note 51.

90. 1 FLATHEAD PLAN EIS, *supra* note 16, at VI-38. Only the river designated as wild and scenic on the Flathead is jointly managed.

91. *Id.* On buffer zones, *see infra* note 176. This refusal is consistent with Forest Service policy in general. FOREST SERV., U.S. DEP'T OF AGRIC., FOREST SERVICE MANUAL § 2320.3-2 (Amendment No. 97, Apr. 86).

92. Supervisor Brannon spoke positively to us of laws such as the National Forest Management Act that empower him to consider effects on wildlife and environmental values in a form that actually enlarges his discretion. On the other hand, he expressed no positive feelings about the Endangered Species Act and NEPA, which have parallel goals but cut away at his autonomy and seem to obliterate the importance of "turf" boundaries.

Similarly, Brannon chastised the Park Service for repeatedly emphasizing Glacier's designation as a biosphere reserve. The park was using that designation to suggest--as he saw it--the establishment of a region-wide, ecosystem-based management area. That, he said most emphatically, entirely misunderstands what a biosphere reserve is meant to do, which is *not* to create an ecosystem as a management entity. *See infra* text following note 203.

93. *See, e.g.,* Letter from Alan O'Neill, Assistant Superintendent, to John Dale Gorman, Supervisor, Lewis & Clark National Forest (Apr. 8, 1986) ("[W]e have some concerns . . . [about Running Owl Application for Permit to Drill]"); *see also* 2 LEWIS & CLARK PLAN EIS, *supra* note 16, at app. E-13 ("The National Park Service supports a more protective classification . . . ."). The strongest statement we found was former superintendent Robert Haraden's comment on the North Fork road paving in NORTH FORK ROAD DRAFT EIS, *supra* note 39, at xxii ("Therefore, improved accessibility . . . must be viewed as incompatible with the park's management philosophy and objectives."). But *see supra* note 63.

94. *See, e.g.,* 1 FLATHEAD PLAN EIS, *supra* note 16, at VI-40; *see also* Letter from Robert Haraden, Superintendent, Glacier National Park, to Lloyd Swanger, District Ranger, Lewis & Clark National Forest (May 10, 1984) ("[A]pproval of the permit to drill constitutes a major Federal action which should be thoroughly considered in an Environmental Impact Statement.").

95. Oil and gas development is a multiple step process, ordinarily beginning with leasing, and followed by seismic exploration, exploratory drilling, production, and full field development. NEPA requirements assure some degree of environmental analysis at each stage, 42 U.S.C. § 4332 (1982), though there is currently debate over how much analysis is required at the initial leasing stage. *See* Sierra Club v. Peterson, 717 F.2d 1409 (D.C. Cir. 1983); Conner v. Burford, 605 F. Supp. 107 (D. Mt. 1985), *appeal filed,* No. 85-3929 (9th Cir. June 17, 1985).

96. 1 FLATHEAD PLAN EIS, *supra* note 16, at VI-40. This is a regional Forest Service policy, we were told.

97. FLATHEAD NAT'L FOREST, FOREST SERV., U.S. DEP'T OF AGRIC., ENVIRONMENTAL ASSESSMENT OF NON-WILDERNESS NATIONAL FOREST LANDS: OIL AND GAS LEASING, FLATHEAD NATIONAL FOREST (1980) [hereinafter 1980 FLATHEAD ENVIRONMENTAL ASSESSMENT]. After reviewing the proposal, the Fish and Wildlife Service granted a no-jeopardy opinion, conditioned on the inclusion of lease stipulations to control access and activity in critical habitat areas. *Id.* at 109.

98. There is no evidence in the 1980 FLATHEAD ENVIRONMENTAL ASSESSMENT that Glacier offered any comments on the leasing proposal. However, during the mid-1970's, when the Flathead initially contemplated oil and gas leasing in the forest, the Park Service urged a thorough environmental analysis before leases were issued. Letter from Stanley Doremus, Deputy Assistant Secretary of the Interior, to E.L. Corpe, Supervisor,

Flathead National Forest (Nov. 11, 1975); *see also* C. Fauley, Glacier National Park Briefing Statement 2 (Dec. 15, 1977) ("It is imperative that the effect of development be evaluated. Once oil and gas are discovered, it will be too late.").

99. *See* Letter from Alan O'Neill, Acting Superintendent, Glacier National Park, to Bernie Lieff, Superintendent of Waterton Lakes National Park, Canada (Mar. 12, 1986) [hereinafter O'Neill Letter]. A Glacier official responsible for resource management told us that a well was drilled recently on British Columbia provincial forest lands, less than two miles north of the park boundary and within the North Fork watershed, and another exploratory well was drilled within one-half mile of the park's eastern boundary on the Blackfeet Reservation.

100. The Bureau of Land Management, Department of the Interior, has formal responsibility for oil and gas leasing on national forest land, 16 U.S.C. § 508(b) (1982); 43 C.F.R. § 3101.7-4 (1986), but in practice it routinely follows Forest Service recommendations. *Yellowstone Ecosystem Hearing, supra* note 4, at 25-26 (testimony of Robert Burford, BLM Director).

101. Environmental Quality Council, Public Hearing, Oil and Gas Tour of the Rocky Mountain Front (Aug. 4, 1986) (statement of Chuck Laakso, BLM employee). The same "no denial" record exists in the Yellowstone region. *Yellowstone Ecosystem Hearing, supra* note 4, at 26. The *Flathead Plan EIS* observes that conflicts over oil and gas activity in the forest center around "where," not "if," the activity will occur. 1 FLATHEAD PLAN EIS, *supra* note 16, at IV-69.

102. According to a Forest Service executive:

> It's sort of like worst case analysis--worrying about the one-in-a- million chance. . . . It requires too much effort and cost to do the whole thing in advance. Also we need to be site-specific. . . . An exploratory drill would happen on one to five percent of these leases. Exploratory wells going into production reflect one-tenth of one percent of total leases.

103. A policy issue of profound importance is whether resources are adequately protected by the mere presence of lease stipulations that empower the Forest Service to protect them, or whether there should be additional assurance that the authority will be effectively exercised. Increasingly, courts are demanding assurance that the authority provided will actually be effectively exercised. *See, e.g.,* Wyoming Wildlife Fed'n v. United States, 792 F. 2d 981 (10th Cir. 1986); *see also* Glacier-Two Medicine Alliance, 88 Interior Bd. Land App. 133, 152-55 (1985) (requiring assurance that access to the site will in fact be prevented). A similar issue figures in the proposed coal mine at Cabin Creek, where an International Study Board is examining the mine proposal under two alternative assumptions: A "most desirable" case assumes that the mine will be operated in accordance with its design as specified in regulations; and an "operational case" assumes failure to achieve full and consistent compliance. *See* Flathead River Int'l Study Bd., Second Progress Report 6 (Jan. 31, 1986) [hereinafter Second Progress Report]; Flathead River Int'l Study Bd., Directive: The Mine 1 (Aug. 27, 1985), *reprinted in* Flathead River Int'l Study Bd., Progress Report app. B-1 (Oct. 9, 1985) [hereinafter Flathead Int'l Study Bd. Directive]; *see also infra* note 138.

104. 605 F. Supp. 107 (D. Mt. 1985), *appeal filed,* No. 85-3929 (8th Cir. June 17, 1985); *see also* Bob Marshall Alliance v. Watt, 16 ENVTL. L. REP. (Envtl. L. Inst.) 20,759, 20,762 (D. Mont. 1986), *appeal filed,* No. 86-4019 (9th Cir. July 22, 1986) ("The [Forest Service] violated NEPA by failing to prepare an EIS for the Deep Creek Area oil and gas leasing program [in the Lewis & Clark Forest]."). *Contra* Park County Resource Council v. United States Dep't of Agriculture, 817 F.2d 609 (10th Cir. 1987).

105. According to the court, the leasing decision is critically important because it represents a preliminary determination that the lands are suitable for oil and gas activities, which perforce may preclude later consideration of them for wilderness or other noncommodity uses. 605 F. Supp. at 109. This actually represents the second time that the Flathead has been stopped by local opposition in its efforts to lease forest lands for

oil and gas activity. During the mid-1970's, after the Flathead released a draft EIS on leasing, local and national opposition rose to such a level that Congress passed a law temporarily prohibiting the BLM from processing any lease applications. *See* 1980 FLATHEAD ENVIRONMENTAL ASSESSMENT, *supra* note 97, at 7.

106. The *Flathead Forest Plan* contemplates oil and gas activity in much of the North Fork region, but this is dependent upon the outcome of the *Conner* litigation. 1 FLATHEAD PLAN EIS, *supra* note 16, at II-109, III-137, IV-65.

107. Although located on Forest Service land, the road was originally built by Flathead County and has been maintained primarily by the County. NORTH FORK ROAD DRAFT EIS, *supra* note 39, at 2.

108. The portion of the road in question runs between Canyon Creek and Camas Junction.

109. 42 U.S.C. § 4332(C) (1982).

110. 23 U.S.C. § 138 (1982).

111. 16 U.S.C. § 1536(a)(2) (1982) (grizzly bear and gray wolf).

112. *See* NORTH FORK ROAD DRAFT EIS, *supra* note 39, at xxi, 105.

113. NORTH FORK ROAD DRAFT EIS, *supra* note 39, at 105, 114.

114. *Id.* at xxii.

115. "Where is the park boundary? . . . [W]hy do you have a statement for this road?," Glacier officials were asked when they testified critically on the North Fork paving. Corridor/Design Public Hearing: Montana Forest Highway 61, County Road 486, North Fork Flathead Road, Canyon Creek-Camas Junction at Columbia Falls, Mont., at 20-21 (Mar. 17, 1982) (transcript prepared by Preconstruction Bureau, Dep't of Highways); *see also id.* at 23 ("Glacier Park officials haven't made too many bright decisions inside the park, let alone trying to tell us how to do on the outside of the park."); *Wilson: Manage Park Bears First,* Hungry Horse News, July 30, 1986, at 10, col. 4 (strongly criticizing Glacier Superintendent's claim that "the grizzly is doomed unless development *outside the Park* is controlled").

116. NORTH FORK ROAD FINAL EIS, *supra* note 39, at 101.

117. *Id.* at 142, 162.

118. At one point, Interior officials were sufficiently concerned that they contemplated seeking a referral to the Council on Environmental Quality (CEQ) under NEPA regulations. *See supra* note 48. We secured from park files a draft of a Department of the Interior letter to the Federal Highway Administration (FHA) Division Administrator threatening a possible referral. The letter apparently was never sent; a similar letter without reference to the referral appears in the NORTH FORK ROAD DRAFT EIS, *supra* note 39, at 109-10.

119. *Id.* at xviii, 117-22.

120. *Id.* at A-1 to A-8. Following a review of the *North Fork Road Draft EIS,* the FWS again concluded that paving would jeopardize the grizzly bear and the gray wolf. NORTH FORK ROAD FINAL EIS, *supra* note 39, at vii, 69, app. A-1 to A-9.

121. "Based primarily on this biological opinion [FWC's jeopardy opinion], and secondarily on the concerns of Glacier National Park, the Montana Department of Fish, Wildlife, and Parks, and input from other agencies and the public, the Forest Highway Program agencies now recommend [an improved gravel road] as the preferred alternative . . . ." NORTH FORK ROAD FINAL EIS, *supra* note 39, at 69.

122. *Id.* at 51, 109. At this time, area land managers were already consulting on interregional matters through the Flathead Basin Commission, which was preparing a Flathead Basin Environmental Impact Study. Authority for the Commission is found in MONT. CODE ANN. §§ 75-7-301 to -308 (1985).

123. Interlocal Agreement, North Fork Flathead River Drainage, Flathead County, Montana 1-2 (Sept. 23, 1985) [hereinafter Interlocal Agreement] (between Flathead County Board of Commissioners, Montana Department of Fish, Wildlife and Parks, Glacier National Park, and Flathead National Forest, and Private Landowners (North Fork Improvement Association, North Fork Compact, and North Fork Preservation Association)).

124. North Fork Land Use Planning Comm., Draft North Fork Flathead River Valley Land Use Plan (Summer 1986); *see also* The North Fork Compact 2 (Aug. 1, 1971), *recorded in* Flathead County, Book 550, at 835, 836 (signed by several North Fork landowners establishing five-acre minimum residential sites).

125. Interlocal Agreement, *supra* note 123.

126. *See supra* note 115.

127. Although it lies outside the forest, we include the Cabin Creek mine here because it lies within the Flathead River basin and the issue is integral to relations between Glacier and the Flathead Forest.

128. Such a collapse occurred at a nearby mine in the summer of 1986. High Country News, June 23, 1986, at 7, col. 2. Ironically, this collapsed mine site was being touted as a state-of-the-art example of mining engineering technology that could be utilized in the Cabin Creek mine.

129. The Study Board report will go to the International Joint Commission (IJC), which will then make recommendations under the U.S.-Canada Boundary Waters Treaty, *infra* note 134, to the Canadian and United States governments; *see also infra* note 135 (containing language of the treaty).

130. For a description of the evolution of the controversy, *see* Arbitblit, *The Plight of American Citizens Injured by Transboundary River Pollution,* 8 ECOLOGY L.Q. 339, 339-42 (1979); Wilson, *Cabin Creek and International Law: An Overview,* 5 PUB. LAND L. REV. 110 (1984).

131. Wilson, *supra* note 130, at 113-14.

132. FLATHEAD BASIN STUDY, *supra* note 39.

133. United States Technical Review of Sage Creek Coal Limited's Stage II Environmental Assessment and Specific Comments (n.d.).

134. The Boundary Waters Treaty of 1909, Jan. 11, 1909, United States-Canada, 36 Stat. 2448, T.S. No. 548 (effective May 13, 1910) [hereinafter U.S.-Canada Boundary Waters Treaty], provides that "waters flowing across the boundary shall not be polluted on either side to the injury of health or property on the other." *Id.* art. IV. Though article II of the Treaty states that nations have exclusive jurisdiction and control over the use of all waters within their boundaries, other language of the article provides that a downstream user injured by an upstream user is entitled to the same rights and remedies he would have if the injury had occurred in the source nation.

135.

The High Contracting Parties further agree that any other questions or matters of difference arising between them involving the rights, obligations, or interests of either in relation to the other or to the inhabitants of the other, along the common frontier between the United States and the Dominion of Canada, shall be referred from time to time to the International Joint Commission for examination and report, whenever either the Government of the United States or the Government of the Dominion of Canada shall request that such questions or matters of difference be so referred.

The International Joint Commission is authorized in each case so referred to examine into and report upon the facts and circumstances of the particular questions and matters referred, together with such conclusions and recommendations as may be appropriate, subject, however, to any restrictions or exceptions which may be imposed with respect thereto by the terms of the reference.

Such reports of the Commission shall not be regarded as decisions of the questions or matters so submitted either on the facts or the law, and shall in no way have the character of an arbitral award.

The Commission shall make a joint report to both Governments in all cases in which all or a majority of the Commissioners agree, and in case of disagreement the minority may make a joint report to both Governments, or separate reports to their respective Governments.

In case the Commission is evenly divided upon any question or matter referred to it for report, separate reports shall be made by the Commissioners on each side to their own Government.

U.S.-Canada Boundary Waters Treaty, *supra* note 134, art. IX.

136. Memorandum from Lauren McKinsey, The 49th Parallel Institute for Canadian/American Relations, to the Flathead Basin Commission 2 (Nov. 9, 1984) [hereinafter McKinsey Memo]; *see also* Letter from James M. Medas, Deputy Assistant Secretary of State for Canada, to David LaRoche, Secretary, U.S. Section, U.S.-Canada International Joint Commission (Dec. 19, 1984) (requesting the IJC "to examine and report upon . . . the transboundary water quality and quantity implications of the proposed coal mine development on Cabin Creek").

137. McKinsey Memo, *supra* note 136, at 2.

138. One innovative element of the study will be the preparation of two different case studies, one assuming that mining will meet design specifications and not experience technical failures, and the other assuming that there will be failure, such as the collapse of holding ponds. Flathead Int'l Study Bd. Directive, *supra* note 103, at 1; Second Progress Report, *supra* note 103, at 6-9. Technical work done under the auspices of the Treaty's International Joint Commission has developed a reputation for being nonpartisan and technically expert. L. BLOOMFIELD & G. FITZGERALD, BOUNDARY WATER PROBLEMS OF CANADA AND THE UNITED STATES 60-64 (1958); *see also* Bilder, *Controlling Great Lakes Pollution: A Study in United States-Canadian Environmental Cooperation,* 70 MICH. L. REV. 469, 518-20 (1972).

139. MONT. CODE ANN. § 75-7-308 (1985). The Act encourages close cooperation among the various governmental entities, but the Commission's powers are entirely recommendatory. *Id.* § 75-7-305.

140. Among the restrictions imposed by the State Lands Department are noise muffling, aesthetic design specifications, and timing restrictions to protect area wildlife. MONTANA DEP'T OF STATE LANDS, PRELIMINARY ENVIRONMENTAL REVIEW: PROPOSED OIL AND GAS EXPLORATION, CENEX WELL #13-11, COAL CREEK STATE FOREST, FLATHEAD COUNTY, MONTANA 75 (1984) [hereinafter CENEX PRELIMINARY ENVIRONMENTAL REVIEW]; *see also* Letter from Robert Haraden, Superintendent, Glacier National Park, to Don Artley, State Division of Forestry, Missoula, Montana (Nov. 21, 1984) (identical letter to James Gragg, Dep't of State Lands, Montana, *reprinted in* MONTANA DEP'T OF STATE LANDS, SUPPLEMENTAL INFORMATION TO OCT. 25, 1985 PRELIMINARY ENVIRONMENTAL REVIEW: PROPOSED OIL AND GAS EXPLORATION, CENEX WELL #13-11, COAL CREEK STATE FOREST, FLATHEAD COUNTY, MONTANA (Jan. 23, 1985) [hereinafter SUPPLEMENTAL CENEX PRELIMINARY ENVIRONMENTAL REVIEW].

141. This area is called Badger-Two Medicine, and the site of the most controversial recent oil drilling proposal is known as Hall Creek, just a few miles from the park border. We were told that the entire region is a "world class wildlife area." Though physically also a prime area for wilderness designation--which would bar mineral develop-

ment--the Forest Service has not proposed such a designation because of opposition from the Blackfeet Tribe, which claims treaty rights of access. *See* Blackfeet Treaty, *supra* note 22; *see generally,* K. Pitt, The Ceded Strip: Blackfeet Treaty Rights in the 1980's, at 37-40, 63 (1986) (unpublished manuscript) (concluding that the Blackfeet retain unrestricted access rights to this area). On the wilderness issue, *see* 2 LEWIS & CLARK PLAN EIS, *supra* note 16, at app. C-15; FOREST SERV., U.S. DEP'T OF AGRIC., LEWIS & CLARK NATIONAL FOREST PLAN: SUPPLEMENT TO THE DRAFT ENVIRONMENTAL IMPACT STATEMENT 2-9, 3-3, 3-4 (1984); LEWIS & CLARK FOREST PLAN, *supra* note 16, at 4-6. *See also* FOREST SERV., DEP'T OF AGRIC., LEWIS & CLARK NATIONAL FOREST PLAN: RECORD OF DECISION 10 (1986) (decision by James C. Overbay, Regional Forester) [hereinafter LEWIS & CLARK RECORD OF DECISION] ("Because of the oil and gas potential and my belief that exploration should take place to determine the extent of the reserve, I recommend only limited acreage of currently leased land for wilderness."); *cf.* proposed Montana Wilderness Act of 1986, S. 2790, 99th Cong., 2d Sess., 132 CONG. REC. S11,974 (daily ed. Aug. 15, 1986) (reserving existing Blackfeet rights).

142. The Forest Service's position is that buffer zones or transition zones between the national parks or wilderness and the forests are not permitted. *See infra* note 176. The Forest Supervisor told us:

> We do a professional analysis of the proposal, and if the law permits the activity and any adverse environmental effects can be mitigated, then we have no basis to say no to it. . . . We don't advocate for oil and gas, or for wilderness. We rely upon scientific data to decide whether to authorize the activity.

143. We were told, "The local public is split over the issue of oil and gas development. . . . The economy here is more dependent on the oil industry than it is [in the Flathead Basin]."

144. Glacier Two-Medicine Alliance, 88 Interior Bd. Land App. 133, 134, 143 (1985).

145. *See* letter from Robert Haraden, Superintendent, Glacier National Park, to Lloyd Swanger, District Ranger, Lewis & Clark National Forest (May 10, 1984); *see also* ROCKY MOUNTAIN RANGER DIST., LEWIS & CLARK NAT'L FOREST, U.S. DEP'T OF AGRIC. & GREAT FALLS RESOURCES AREA, U.S. DEP'T OF THE INTERIOR, ENVIRONMENTAL ASSESSMENT: HALL CREEK APD, AMERICAN PETROFINE CO. OF TEXAS, FEDERAL SOUTH GLACIER 1-26, Lease No. M53323, at 131, 141-142 (1985) [hereinafter 1985 HALL CREEK ENVIRONMENTAL ASSESSMENT].

146. *Id.* at app. C3-1 (FWS Jeopardy Opinion, June 26, 1984).

147. *Id.* at app. C3-11 (FWS Opinion, Jan. 14, 1985).

148. A federal court of appeals opinion held that FWS biological opinions do *not* have to be based on ironclad data to stand up. North Slope Borough v. Andrus, 642 F. 2d 589, 609-10 (D.C. Cir. 1980).

149. In fact, a BLM executive told us that:

> [T]he Fish and Wildlife Service was concerned [about the Hall Creek project]. I don't know what pressure they got from upstairs. I won't say we don't work in a political environment. . . . I'm just a peon. I don't make decisions in a vacuum. I don't always do what I personally want.

150. Glacier-Two Medicine Alliance, 88 Interior Bd. Land App. 133 (1985).

151. *Id.* at 154.

152. On one issue--controlling access and poaching by the Blackfeet--the requirements will not easily be met. The Blackfeet, under an 1896 Treaty, *supra* note 22, claim a right of access both to parts of the forest and Glacier National Park for hunting, timbering, and fishing. The Blackfeet claim they can ignore closures on an existing road when they wish to exercise their claimed treaty rights. *See* United States v. Kipp,

369 F. Supp. 774 (D. Mont. 1974). *But cf.* United States v. Dion, 106 S.Ct. 2216 (1986) (holding that the Eagle Protection Act abrogated tribal treaty rights and thereby precluded a treaty- based defense to an Endangered Species Act charge).

153. Bob Marshall Alliance v. Watt, 16 ENVTL. L. REP. (Envtl. L. Inst.) 20,759 (D. Mont. 1986), *appeal filed*, No. 86-4019 (9th Cir. July 22, 1986).

154. *See* Park County Resource Council v. United States Dep't of Agriculture, 613 F. Supp. 1182, 1185 (D. Wyo. 1985), *aff'd*, 817 F.2d 609 (10th Cir. 1987). But, though the 10th Circuit affirmed the district court's decision authorizing leasing based on an environmental assessment, it rejected the district court's holding barring NEPA challenges to already issued leases.

155. There is no evidence Lewis & Clark officials have been diverted at all from their agenda of promoting oil and gas development. The park knows this, and, when pressed, officials will admit it. One top official said, "Though our people will be on their planning team . . . I don't think for a minute they [Lewis & Clark] invited us for any reason but to sell us a bill of goods about how good their process is." Another told us:

> Right now the park is helpless to stop oil and gas drilling [on the Lewis & Clark]. Talking to Dale [Gorman, the Forest Supervisor] and Lloyd [Swanger, the District Ranger] and their staffs, I know they don't have the preservation ethic, and their public is in Great Falls. They get away with things that couldn't happen on the Flathead. . . . The next step is to drill more wells. . . . They will drill. I'm convinced of that.

156. O'Neill Letter, *supra* note 99.

157. *See supra* notes 150-151 and accompanying text.

158. Early in the Hall Creek case, BLM sensed that there was no consensus among the affected agencies, and BLM therefore did not want to proceed until each involved federal agency agreed to the plan. However, because the tradition has been to follow the recommendation of the Forest Service as the surface management agency, we were told that the State Director of the BLM ordered "that the Forest Service has the right to decide what they want and you [local BLM officials] should march along with the tune played by them."

159. *See supra* notes 148-149 and accompanying text.

160. This project presents potential impacts to the wildlife corridor similar to those posed by Hall Creek. *See supra* note 141; LEWIS & CLARK FOREST PLAN, *supra* note 16, at 3-32 to - 33, 4-4, app. K-1.

161. FOREST SERV., U.S. DEP'T OF AGRIC. & BUREAU OF LAND MANAGEMENT, U.S. DEP'T OF THE INTERIOR, STUDY PLAN FOR RUNNING OWL FED 1-35 APD, CHEVRON, USA, INC. 14 (1986) [hereinafter RUNNING OWL STUDY PLAN] (The Running Owl well is now known as Badger Creek well). An additional sign of change is the intention of Glacier officials to participate in the study process, rather than wait until the work is done and then comment, as they did at Hall Creek. Letter from Alan O'Neill, Acting Superintendent, Glacier National Park, to John Dale Gorman, Supervisor, Lewis & Clark National Forest (Apr. 8, 1986).

162. FOREST SERV., U.S. DEP'T OF AGRIC. & BUREAU OF LAND MANAGEMENT, U.S. DEP'T OF THE INTERIOR, CONTENT ANALYSIS ON SCOPING PERIOD FOR CHEVRON EIS 23 (July 22, 1986) (answering comments received on the Running Owl well) (released with RUNNING OWL STUDY PLAN, *supra* note 161).

163. *Id.* at 19, 24-25.

164. LEWIS & CLARK FOREST PLAN, *supra* note 16, at 4-5, 4-6, 6- 24.

165. *Id.* at 1-13. But overall the *Forest Plan* appears dramatically to increase the total timber harves over the 50-year life of the *Plan*. *See id.* at A-16; 1 LEWIS & CLARK PLAN EIS, *supra* note 16, at 2-68, 2-69, 4-43, 4-45.

166. LEWIS & CLARK PLAN EIS, *supra* note 16, at 1-13. The *Lewis & Clark Record of Decision* for the *Plan* explicitly cites concern for Glacier as a principal reason for the shift in timber planning, *supra* note 141, at 23, and the forest's *Environmental Impact Statement* makes reference to the 1983 GLACIER RESOURCES MANAGEMENT PLAN, *supra* note 15, as a reason for minimizing visual impacts from logging activity near the forest-park boundary. 1 LEWIS & CLARK PLAN EIS, *supra* note 16, at 4-59.

167. See *supra* notes 77-78 and accompanying text.

168. LEWIS & CLARK FOREST PLAN, *supra* note 16, at app. K-1, K-3.

169. Such rhetoric *is* still mouthed at congressional hearings where park protection legislation is proposed. *See, e.g., 1982 Public Land Management Hearings, supra* note 10, at 923 (Letter from Atlantic Richfield Co.) ("The language . . . is so far reaching that economic activity adjacent to (or related to) the [national park] system could be paralyzed.").

170. "To ask [a developmental agency] to take another mandate seriously is easy only if it impacts their primary objectives marginally. . . . There are very few incentives that can be offered to agencies to persuade them to move away from traditional . . . modes of action." S.L. YAFFEE, PROHIBITIVE POLICY: IMPLEMENTATION OF THE ENDANGERED SPECIES ACT 97 (1982).

171. "[T]he Selway Mountains in eastern Washington, the north Cascades in western Washington, and the Selway Bitterroot region in Idaho, have had only sporadic grizzly sightings during the past decade. The Cabinet-Yaak ecosystem in northwestern Montana is under considerable development pressure . . . and bear numbers . . . are at a precariously low level." Keith Aune Affidavit, *supra* note 60, *reprinted in Onshore Leasing Hearing, supra* note 4, at 181-82.

172. See MONTANA FINAL PROGRAMMATIC EIS, *supra* note 29, at 26 (1986) ("Public perception, on a local as well as a national level, of grizzly bear population status and of the management abilities of responsible agencies greatly influence management programs.").

173. A well-connected local person said, "[T]here is a chance of stopping them [the oil companies]. An oil man said to me, 'We're going back to Wyoming. Every time you try to do something in Montana, someone sues you.'"

174. Listing of Biosphere Reserves in the United States (June 9, 1986) (provided by the National Park Service). These include: Big Bend, Big Thicket, Redwood, Cumberland Island, Cape Lookout, Channel Islands, Denali, Everglades, Glacier Bay, Glacier, Great Smoky Mountains, Haleakala, Hawaii Volcanoes, Isle Royale, Death Valley, Joshua Tree, Gates of the Arctic, Noatak, Olympic, Organ Pipe Cactus, Rocky Mountain, Sequioa-Kings Canyon, Congaree Swamp, Virgin Islands, Yellowstone.

175. One park superintendent told us he sometimes can't get officials at a nearby military base even to notify him when they take actions affecting the park; and if they do advise him, it may be after the fact. Interview with William Ehorn, Superintendent, Channel Islands National Park, California, in Ventura, Cal. (Apr. 24, 1986). Other park officials have spoken out on:

> the military's disregard of natural areas. As a national park ranger, I have been 'strafed' by a Navy jet in a rain forest and surrounded by attack helicopters . . . . More serious, 20 uniformed soldiers marched through Olympic National Park last fall, leaving campfire scars in subalpine meadows and all their garbage behind.

Letter from Galen Hunt, National Park Ranger, to Editor, *reprinted in Members Forum,* 171 NAT'L GEOGRAPHIC n.p. (May 1987).

176. The very word "buffer" is still poison in legislative and some administrative circles. *See Yellowstone Ecosystem Hearing, supra* note 4, at 94, 115, 132. "We had excellent relations with the Flathead, but you can't talk about buffer zones with them," a former park executive said. "No buffer zones", a Lewis & Clark executive told us.

As for Forest Service policy on 'Buffer Zones'. . . we . . . are directed not
to maintain 'undeveloped wildland' as buffers to Wilderness. I believe this
direction has been used as a reason not to consider 'buffers' on National
Forest System Lands adjacent to National Park Systems Lands. However,
direction is clear that we need to consider effects of actions on these adjacent lands, and coordinate management decisions. The term 'Buffer Zone'.
. . appears to be the problem.

Letter from F. Carl Pence, Forest Planner, Bridger-Teton National Forest, to Robert B.
Keiter (July 30, 1986) (ref. 1650); *see also 1983-1984 Public Land Management Hearings, supra* note 10, at 433-34 (Letter from the Minerals Exploration Coalition) ("The intent of the legislation . . . seems to be the creation of additional 'buffer zones'
around the National Parks."); *1982 Public Land Management Hearings, supra* note 10, at
918 (Letter from Wester Timber Association) ("The bill, in effect, creates an unspecified
buffer strip around each unit of the National Park System.") Buffer zones were one goal
of proposed park protection legislation which has not yet been enacted. National Park
System Resources Act of 1986, S. 2092, 99th Cong., 2d Sess., 132 CONG. REC. S1561 (daily
ed. Feb. 25, 1986) ("The Secretary [of the Interior] may designate . . . park resource
protection areas within the . . . boundaries of contiguous federally managed areas.").
However, it is noteworthy that the *Plan* for the Bridger-Teton National Forest recommends against oil and gas leasing within a half-mile of Grand Teton National Park. *Forest
Officials Say New Plan Not an "About-Face,"* Daily Boomerang (Laramie, Wyo.), Aug.
23, 1986, at 10.

Apparently, there was a Forest Service document ordering forest officials to work
cooperatively with park managers, but it is not current policy and we cannot get anyone
to supply us with a copy. "I finally found out that the Memorandum of Understanding I had seen regarding interagency cooperation on buffer zones around National Parks
was a draft prepared by the Washington Office . . . [I]t has not been released in final .
. . ." Letter from Nancy J. Cotner, Area Manager, BLM, Great Falls, Mont., to
Robert B. Keiter (July 18, 1986).

177. Letter from Robert Haraden, Superintendent, Glacier National Park, to Don Artley,
Chief, Planning Bureau, State Division of Forestry, Montana Department of State Lands
(Nov. 21, 1984) ("We do not agree with [your] conclusion . . . that 'approval of the Plan
will not jeopardize the environmental quality of adjacent lands, including . . . Glacier
National Park' . . . ."); *see also* CENEX PRELIMINARY ENVIRONMENTAL REVIEW, *supra* note
140, app. B (three previous letters from Glacier indicating potential environmental
problems); SUPPLEMENTAL CENEX PRELIMINARY ENVIRONMENTAL REVIEW, *supra* note
140 (further Glacier comments). The proposed Cenex well is located approximately
one mile beyond the park's western border, just outside the riparian zone of the
North Fork.

178. Among the restrictions imposed by the State Lands Department are noise muffling
requirements, aesthetic design specifications, and timing restrictions to protect area wildlife.
CENEX PRELIMINARY ENVIRONMENTAL REVIEW, *supra* note 140, at 74-75.

Yet, even the Cenex well proposal--an important precedent as the first instance
of drilling in the North Fork region--would have gone through had not environmental organizations persisted in their opposition. Environmentalists filed a lawsuit against
the project alleging that the state's environmental review process violated the Montana
Environmental Protection Act, MONT. CODE ANN. §§ 75-1-101, -201 (1985). North
Fork Preservation Ass'n v. Dep't of State Lands, No. DV-85-131B (Dist. Ct. Mont. filed
Feb. 20, 1985). The project, as well as the lawsuit, is currently stalled by a title defect,
and we were told Cenex has had trouble raising exploration money as the site is not considered attractive by knowledgeable investors.

179. Memorandum from Robert Haraden, Superintendent, Glacier National Park, to Bureau
of Indian Affairs Area Director (Aug. 6, 1985) (Ref. No. L2423); Letter from Robert
Haraden to Blackfeet Tribal Chief Old Person (May 31, 1985); *see also* Letter from
Robert Haraden to Mike Fairbanks, Superintendent, Blackfeet Indian Agency, Bureau of

Indian Affairs (Sept. 1, 1982). We were told that the Reservation is economically quite hard-pressed with very high unemployment, and the park is reluctant to be perceived as an opponent of economic development.

180. Lewis & Clark officials told us, for example, that the park had not opposed drilling on Blackfeet lands located near the forest's proposed Hall Creek well. Why, they asked, is one well thought troublesome when the other is not? *See supra* text following note 144.

181. *See supra* notes 141, 152; *see also* Glacier-Two Medicine Alliance, 88 Interior Bd. Land App. 133, 154 (1985) ("No analysis of the effect of not being able to deny access to the members of the Blackfeet Tribe of Indians has been made a part of the EA, and a question remains as to the ability to deny this access.").

182. Furthermore, at this writing both NEPA injunctions are under appeal to the Ninth Circuit. *See* Conner v. Burford, 605 F. Supp. 107 (D. Mt. 1985), *appeal filed,* No. 85-3929 (9th Cir. June 17, 1985); Bob Marshall Alliance v. Watt, 16 ENVTL. L. REP. (Envtl. L. Inst.) 20,759 (D. Mont. 1986), *appeal filed,* No. 86-4019 (9th Cir. July 22, 1986).

183. *See supra* note 29 and accompanying text.

184. 1 FLATHEAD PLAN EIS, *supra* note 16, at III-36, IV-66; LEWIS & CLARK FOREST PLAN, *supra* note 16, at 6-22 to 6-24. BLM policy is to lease all legally leasable land. *See Yellowstone Ecosystem Hearing, supra* note 4, at 124; *see also* Bureau of Land Management, U.S. Dep't of the Interior, Instruction Memorandum No. 84-254 (Feb. 2, 1984).

185. When we asked a Glacier official with lengthy tenure at the park about Glacier's role, if any, in the RARE II wilderness process, he was quite vague and finally said, "[W]e must have played a low profile on that." A former high official said, "[W]e played no role in forest service wilderness, nor did the Park Service anywhere in the country to my knowledge."

186. According to a 1980 Solicitor's Opinion from the Denver Region, U.S. Dep't of the Interior, "No precedent exists for denial of an application for a permit to drill under an onshore oil and gas lease based on environmental protection considerations . . . such denial would have constitutional implications concerning the taking of property rights and the payment of just compensation . . . ." *Quoted in Onshore Leasing Hearing, supra* note 4, at 519 (testimony of Edward R. Madej, Consultant, Sierra Club); *see also Onshore Leasing Hearing, supra* note 4, at 350, 353 (statement of Norman J. Mullen) (describing the Forest Service's indication of its helplessness to prevent wildlife damage in the Grand Mesa National Forest on land that had once been leased). In fact, the Department of the Interior has no record of a denial of any application for a permit to drill in the Yellowstone region. *See Yellowstone Ecosystem Hearing, supra* note 4, at 26.

187. The stipulations are reprinted in FLATHEAD FOREST PLAN, *supra* note 16, at app. O-1 to O-16.

188. J. SAX, DEFENDING THE ENVIRONMENT 51 (1970).

189. Other conference sponsors included the World Health Organization, the International Biological Program, and the International Union for the Conservation of Nature. Among the 13 project areas identified at the conference, Project No. 8, "Conservation of the Natural Areas and of the Genetic Material They Contain," dealt with development of a worldwide network of areas, or biosphere reserves. Trosper & Cooper, *An Overview of the Management Situation with Respect to Glacier National Park,* in TOWARDS THE BIOSPHERE RESERVE: EXPLORING RELATIONSHIPS BETWEEN PARKS AND ADJACENT LANDS 36, 36 (R.C. Scace & C.J. Martinka eds. 1983) [hereinafter TOWARD THE BIOSPHERE RESERVE].

190. There are presently 41 biosphere reserves in the United States. *See* PROCEEDINGS OF THE CONFERENCE ON THE MANAGEMENT OF BIOSPHERE RESERVES 192 (J.P. Peine ed. 1984) [hereinafter BIOSPHERE CONFERENCE].

238   *OUR COMMON LANDS*

191. *See* PROGRAMME ON MAN AND THE BIOSPHERE, UNITED NATIONS, UNESCO MAB REPORT SERIES NO. 12, CONSERVATION OF NATURAL AREAS AND OF THE GENETIC MATERIAL THEY CONTAIN 10-14, 16, 17 (1973). For a general explanation of the program see Franklin, *The Biosphere Reserve Program in the United States,* 195 SCIENCE 262 (1977).

192. PROGRAMME ON MAN AND THE BIOSPHERE, UNITED NATIONS, UNESCO MAB REPORT SERIES NO. 22, TASK FORCE ON: CRITERIA AND GUIDELINES FOR THE CHOICE AND ESTABLISHMENT OF BIOSPHERE RESERVES 11-12, 15-20 (1974); *see also* MAN AND THE BIOSPHERE PROGRAM, U.S. DEP'T OF STATE, REPORT NO. 1, GUIDELINES FOR IDENTIFICATION, EVALUATION AND SELECTION OF BIOSPHERE RESERVES IN THE UNITED STATES (1st rev. 1983). The program also includes provision of areas for environmental research and for education and training.

193. *See* Kellert, *Enhancing Public Appreciation of the Role of Biospheres Reserves,* in TOWARD THE BIOSPHERE RESERVE, *supra* note 189, at 123, 125.

194. "Preserv[ing] biological diversity" is already a congressional policy in the Foreign Assistance Act. *See* 22 U.S.C. § 2151q (Supp. III 1985); *see also supra* note 43.

195. Sadler, *Nature Conservation in the Canadian Rockies--Man and Biosphere in Regional Context,* in TOWARD THE BIOSPHERE RESERVE, *supra* note 189, at 83, 84 (citation omitted).

196. *Id.* at 83 (citation omitted).

197. *Id.* at 86.

198. Generally, national park managers have been slow to see the biosphere reserve concept as a basic idea on which to build.

> In general the managers that came to the conference did not necessarily relate to the biosphere program. . . . Strong testament to this was the running joke . . . about Man and the Biosphere dedication plaques. . . . Some managers didn't even know where their plaques were. Others indicated that the plaque was the only visible sign of the program.

Peine & Morehead, *Synopsis of the Conference on the Management of Biosphere Reserves,* in TOWARD THE BIOSPHERE RESERVE, *supra* note 189, at 1, 1.

199. It is important to distinguish this scientific goal--protecting biological integrity--from the use of the park as a scientific laboratory (e.g., catching, collaring, and studying bears), a policy that, we were told, Glacier generally opposes.

200. *See* S.K. FAIRFAX, COMING OF AGE IN THE BUREAU OF LAND MANAGEMENT 51 (1981), *cited in* Bradley & Ingram, *Science vs. the Grass Roots: Representation in the Bureau of Land Management,* 26 NAT. RESOURCES J. 493, 513 (1986).

201. The concept is beginning to receive some popular attention, however. *See, e.g.,* Eckholm, *New Tactics Transform Wildlife Conservation,* N.Y. Times, Nov. 18, 1986, at 17, at 22, col. 2 (midwest ed.).

Senator Chaffee's National Park System Resources Act of 1986, S. 2092, 99th Cong., 2d Sess., 132 CONG. REC. S1561 (daily ed. Feb. 25, 1986), included provisions that gave more formal status to biosphere reserves. Section 110 of the bill provided that the Secretary of the Interior shall provide Congress with recommendations for needed adjustments in biosphere reserve boundaries to include contiguous federal lands, and shall offer proposals to assure that such contiguous lands will be managed to protect the core area.

The biosphere reserve designation must be distinguished from World Heritage Site designation, which Glacier seeks (unsuccessfully so far), and which does carry some legal obligations. World Heritage sites are governed by an international convention in which each member nation agrees to "endeavor, in so far as possible, and as appropriate for each country . . . to take the appropriate legal, scientific, technical, administrative and financial measures necessary for . . . identification, protection, conservation, presentation and rehabilitation . . . ." Protection of World Cultural and Heritage Convention, *done* Nov. 23, 1972, art. 5(d), 27 U.S.T. 37, 41, T.I.A.S. NO. 8226, at 5, 1037 U.N.T.S. 151, 154 (entered into force Dec. 17, 1975); *see* 16 U.S.C. § 470a-1 (1982); 36 C.F.R. §§ 73.1-.17

(1986); *see also* Memorandum from Associate Solicitor, Conservation and Wildlife, to Assistant Secretary for Fish and Wildlife and Parks, U.S. Dep't of the Interior (Jan. 21, 1981) (unpublished opinion on Implementation of World Heritage Convention and P.L. 96-515) (arguing thaf the implementing federal statute does create domestic legal obligations); J.H. Jackson, The Application of International Conventions in Domestic Law of the United States (Sept. 1986) (unpublished paper presented to the 1986 Colloquium of the United Kingdom Committee of Comparative Law). *But see* Australia v. Tasmania, 46 A.L.R. 625, 663 (1983) (Australian High Court held that "[T]he obligations imposed by the [World Heritage] Convention are political or moral, but not legally binding.").

While Glacier has been nominated, along with its companion Waterton Lakes National Park in Canada, as a World Heritage site, it has not attained that designation. We were told that the Canadian government has withdrawn its support at the request of the British Columbia government. A Glacier official told us, "We sort of hoped it would slip through, but they stopped it." The fear is that Heritage Site designation would have legal "teeth," and could tie the hands of the British Columbia government in settling the Cabin Creek controversy. *See also* Memorandum from Chief, International Park Affairs Division, to Assistant Solicitor, Parks and Recreation (June 12, 1986) (Subject: International Joint Commission Studies; Glacier National Park; World Heritage Implications, Ref. No. L66(773)) (discussing the current status of the Glacier nomination to the World Heritage List).

202. *See supra* note 46; *see also* Haraden, *Development of Nonrenewable Resources and Glacier National Park Biosphere Reserve,* in TOWARD THE BIOSPHERE RESERVE, *supra* note 189, at 114.

203. *See supra* note 201.

204. "The approach is still being tested and must be regarded as evolving rather than developed." Sadler, *supra* note 195, at 86.

205. Memorandum from Assistant Superintendent to Superintendent, Glacier National Park (Mar. 14, 1985) (Re: 1985 MAB Program, ref. N22).

206. *See, e.g.,* R. NASH, WILDERNESS AND THE AMERICAN MIND 156-59, 165-66 (3d ed. 1982); A. RUNTE, NATIONAL PARKS: THE AMERICAN EXPERIENCE 26 (1979).

207.

Glacier National Park . . . is largely appreciated for its spectacular scenery, its symbolic association with the American West, and the opportunities it presents for viewing visible, abundant, and large wildlife. The general public's recognition of it as a national park appears to have little relation to its ecological or scientific value.

Kellert, *supra* note 193, at 124.

208. This suggests a way in which the park's short-term strategy might be integrated with its long-term goals: By developing top quality scientific briefing papers on all issues of peripheral development affecting the park, park officials could increase their prestige, credibility, and influence. There is presently a great unfilled need for such technically reliable studies.

209. S. Ponce, Executive Briefing: Status of Water Rights for Glacier National Park (May 1, 1986) (Water Rights Branch, Nat'l Park Serv.); *see also supra note 58.*

210. A formal version of this approach was developed for the management of wilderness in the national forests. *See G.* STANKEY, D. COLE, R. LUCAS, M. PETERSON & S. FRISSELL, THE LIMITS OF ACCEPTABLE CHANGE (LAC) SYSTEM FOR WILDERNESS PLANNING (USDA Forest Serv. Research Paper No. INT-176, 1985). We were told that the idea has been picked up by park officials. *See also* National Park Serv., U.S. Dep't of the Interior, Report on Impact of Special Designation 11 (Mar. 25, 1986) (prepared by Glacier officials for the International Joint Commission International Study Board) ("[The Limits of Acceptable Change] process is being used to assure that the unique qualities of the North Fork ecosystem will not be eroded and lost through time.").

211. A tribal member conveyed some sense of the distance between the park and the Blackfeet by telling us that "the park treats the Blackfeet like a third world nation. It says we must stay undeveloped to protect the park."

212. We were told by a Glacier official that most of the cattle do not belong to the Blackfeet because grazing is by lease on reservation land. He added that a similar trophy hunting plan succeeded with the Apaches.

213. For example, Congress responded with explicit prohibitory legislation when it appeared that geothermal development on Yellowstone's borders might imperil that park's geysers. 30 U.S.C.A. § 1005 (West Supp. 1987).

214. Great Falls Resource Area Office, Bureau of Land Management, U.S. Dep't of the Interior, Decision Notice and Finding of No Significant Impact (Apr. 13, 1987).

215. *See supra* notes 144-56 and accompanying text.

216. Telephone Interview with Gary Slagel, Acting Area Manager, Bureau of Land Management, U.S. Dep't of the Interior (May 18, 1987).

PART III

Protecting Specific Park Resources

Clean Water Act

Endangered Species Act

Water Rights

Historic Preservation Act

Clean Air Act

Wild and Scenic Rivers Act

Chapter 8

THE CLEAN WATER ACT: STILL VITAL TO THE PARKS

James T. Banks[*]

I. INTRODUCTION

The federal Clean Water Act[1] (CWA) is recognized widely as one of the nation's most mature and effective statutory tools for environmental protection. Among its ambitious goals are the attainment of "fishable and swimmable" water quality and the elimination of pollutant discharges into the country's lakes, rivers, streams, and wetlands. The Act provides for stringent federal standards, detailed federal and state permit programs, and federal grant funds to assist states and municipalities in their efforts to abate sewage discharges.

Over the past fifteen years, the nation has seen tremendous progress in restoring what once were drastically polluted surface waters. Industrial and municipal discharges are being controlled through sophisticated, often expensive treatment technologies mandated by the Act. Recent surveys demonstrate that water quality has improved or at least stabilized nationwide despite steady population and industrial growth pressures. The worst of our pollution problems are being addressed; what remains in doubt is whether the Act and its programs are being utilized effectively to maintain the high-quality, ecologically valuable waters in and around natural areas. The absolute protection of these waters has not been emphasized by the Environmental Protection Agency (EPA) or state agencies in any systematic way, but the statutory tools are available.

A little-used provision of EPA's regulations under the Act holds tremendous potential for protecting the waters and adjacent land areas in and around national parks and other federal and state

243

protected areas. The provision establishes a virtual non-degrada-
tion standard for so-called "Outstanding National Resource Waters"
(ONRWs). Its effect could be to curtail, perhaps even preclude,
development of all sorts on these waterways and in upstream watersheds. This probably explains why the special provision for ONRWs
has never been utilized fully, and why without focused citizen involvement in state standard setting under the CWA, it will remain
unused for years to come. This chapter explores the framework of
the Act and describes the potential for developing a comprehensive system under EPA's regulatory provision for protecting ONRWs.

II. THE STATUTORY FRAMEWORK

Congress created in the Clean Water Act an intricate partner-
ship among EPA, the states, and citizens across the country aimed
at restoring and maintaining the quality of lakes, rivers,
streams, and wetlands that for decades had suffered horribly. First
enacted in its comprehensive form in 1972 and revised extensively in 1977, the Act contains regulatory policies, standards, and enforcement mechanisms to address virtually all types of pollutant
discharges into surface waters. By and large, the standard-setting task for controlling pollutant effluents was left to EPA.[2] The
job of issuing and enforcing permits to implement those standards,
however, has been delegated gradually to the states.[3] The job of
establishing ambient water quality standards--of deciding "how
clean is clean"--has belonged to the states from the beginning.[4]
Congress has never been able to decide which type of regulatory
standard should be relied upon as the principal control mechanism
to safeguard surface water quality. For this reason, the CWA contains nearly every conceivable type of standard, and the most stringent control will apply in every instance. For example, a particular
discharge effluent could be subject to all of the following: (1) a
health-based standard (concentration limit) established without
regard to cost;[5] (2) a technology-based standard (mass limitation) limited by costs and established without regard to health
or environmental effects;[6] (3) a water quality standard (ambient
concentration limit) based on health and environmental considerations, water uses, cumulative impacts by all sources, and, to some
extent, economics;[7] and (4) an antidegradation standard based
on how polluted the waterway already has become.[8] Whichever of

these standards produces the most stringent limits in a discharge permit is the one that controls, and for that reason they are all useful to some extent in protecting the valuable, often fragile, aquatic ecosystems in protected areas. In addition, the Act provides that states may devise any type of standard and apply that standard if it is more stringent than federal requirements.[9]

The provision for ONRWs is especially useful, however, because it is purposely directed toward waters in national parks and other protected areas, and because it contains a virtual nondegradation requirement that, almost by definition, will be more stringent that any other standard. The provision is part of the Act's water quality standards program. In order to fully comprehend its utility, that program must be understood in some detail.

III. WATER QUALITY STANDARDS AND THE SPECIAL PROVISION FOR PROTECTING ONRWs

The water quality standards program under the CWA consists of three interrelated components: use designations, water quality criteria, and the antidegradation policy. The first two work together; the third applies independently wherever it is relevant.

Each state is required to designate all of its surface waters for a particular use or combination of uses.[10] Typical use designations include drinking water supplies, aquatic life protection or propagation, sport fishery, and aquatic recreation (contact or noncontact). The Act authorizes designations for other uses as well, including withdrawal for agricultural and industrial uses.[11] The theory is that levels of protection will vary depending on the water quality actually needed for each of these uses.

The states establish their uses and must submit them for EPA's approval. In the early 1970s, most states decided that nearly all of their surface waters should be protected for aquatic life and recreation, in keeping with the Act's overall policy of achieving "fishable-swimmable" water quality throughout the nation. Now that uses are established, the important issue of environmental advocates becomes any proposals to change these uses. These proposed changes must be submitted by the states for EPA's approval. The Agency has established by regulation a number of "tests" that a state must pass if it wishes to downgrade a waterway to a less-protected use.[12] The regulations also require states to upgrade their use designations in certain circumstances.[13]

States may propose changes in their designated uses at any time. However, the Act requires them to review their standards every three years and, if necessary, to revise their designated uses according to the rules laid down in EPA's regulations.[14] This mandatory, triennial review/revision process affords the opportunity for citizens to propose changes, including protections for ONRWs as described below, and to insist that state agencies either adopt these proposals or adequately explain and justify their reasons for rejecting them. Indeed, this process affords the National Park Service an opportunity to propose changes in state standards and to make recommendations for ONRW designations--an effective and aggressive means of using existing law to further protect the resources managed by the Service.

The second component of the program is EPA's water quality criteria. These are concentration numbers for specific pollutants that EPA believes are adequate to preserve the various use designations. For example, EPA may decide that a stream designated for fish propagation should have at least 5 mg/l of dissolved oxygen. Thus far, EPA has issued criteria for many dozens of pollutants, including the sixty-five so-called priority toxic pollutants commonly regulated under the Act. It has not issued criteria covering every conceivable use (e.g., industrial use), but has fairly thoroughly covered human consumption, contact recreation, and both freshwater and saltwater aquatic life protection.

In adopting concentration numbers to protect their designated uses, states might simply incorporate EPA's criteria. In the alternative, they may devise their own numbers, either starting from scratch or by modifying EPA's numbers depending on site-specific considerations or other factors peculiar to the state. In either case, the state must convince EPA that its concentration numbers are sufficiently stringent to protect the designated uses.[15] This approval process occurs within the triennial review or more frequently if needed.

With this background as a framework, the special provision for ONRWs comes into focus. The third component of the water quality standards program is the anti-degradation policy. The policy is articulated in EPA's regulations,[16] but its foundation was laid by Congress in 1972 when it established the objective of the Act "to restore and *maintain* the chemical, physical, and biological integrity of the Nation's waters," and the national policy that "fishable-swimmable" water quality will be achieved, wherever attainable, by 1983.[17] The Act's emphasis on maintenance of water quality led EPA to establish an enforceable policy that limits the amount of permissible degradation, irrespective of designated uses or criteria, in several important circumstances. This, in broad form, is called the anti-degradation policy.

The policy has three parts. The first simply requires that instream, existing uses and the level of water quality necessary to sustain them shall be maintained and protected.[18] Thus, if actual uses (e.g., fish propagation is occurring) are superior to designated uses (e.g., industrial water supply), the state must set its standards at levels stringent enough to protect them, even if the state, for whatever reason, would prefer to protect only the inferior designated use. States must maintain the streams as they find them, which often involves serious debates about what was found when a biological survey was performed. Frequently, the critical question will be why the state has not even performed a recent survey.

The second element is a requirement for maintaining extremely high quality waters. With some editorial changes for clarity, it reads as follows:

"where the quality of . . . waters exceeds the levels necessary to support [fishable-swimmable water quality] that quality shall be maintained and protected unless the State finds [after full involvement of concerned citizens] that [allowing degradation] is *necessary to accommodate important economic or social development* in the [affected area].[19]

Obviously, this avenue for degradation of pristine waters is very limited. Degradation must be "necessary" for development to occur, not merely helpful, and the development causing the degradation must be "important," not merely desirable. Moreover, where degradation of pristine waters is allowed by this process, the policy limits it by requiring that existing instream uses still be fully protected and by insisting that all point source and nonpoint source discharges to the waterway by subjected to the Act's most stringent otherwise applicable requirements.

This second element of the antidegradation policy is important to preserving the waters and watersheds in national parks and other protected areas. But it is relevant only where the quality of those waters already exceeds the fishable-swimmable level, a factor that may not be present in many ecologically valuable areas, such as swamps, where dissolved oxygen levels are naturally low, or in areas where human-induced degradation already has been felt. It was for this reason that EPA included in the policy a third component for the ONRWs.

The third element provides that:

> Where high quality waters constitute an outstanding National resource, such as waters of National and State parks and wildlife refuges and waters of exceptional recreational or ecological significance, that water quality shall be maintained and protected.[20]

In the author's judgment, this provision offers a tremendous opportunity to obtain *very stringent* protection for ONRWs. Notice several things about the provision. First, while the waters to be protected must be of "high quality," they need not exceed water quality levels necessary to support fishable-swimmable uses. That is, unlike the case under the second element of the policy, the existing water quality need not exceed EPA's or the state's criteria numbers to be considered "high quality." As used in this context, the phrase obviously relates to the purposes for which an area has been protected; if the quality is satisfactory to serve those purposes, it should be eligible for protection.

Second, there is no escape valve from the nondegradation principle of this requirement. Unlike in the second component, states cannot decide to lower water quality in ONRWs based on the "necessity" of "important economic or social development." Existing water quality simply must be "maintained and protected."

Finally, while the provision for ONRWs applies to designated areas (e.g., national parks, state parks, wildlife refuges), the area need not have been formally set aside or otherwise designated for protection. The provision applies to both designated areas "*and* waters of exceptional recreational or ecological significance," whether or not designated. This is a factual determination that, in the author's view, can and should be made *within the Act's water quality standards program*, even if other governmental programs have not produced such findings.

In sum, this provision of EPA's regulations offers stringent, perhaps absolute, protection against any degradation of the waters that merit such attention. Indeed, it is due to this absolute protection that no state has thus far designated ONRWs under the federal regulation. Many states have concocted similar designations under state laws, but routinely stop short of the nondegradation principle discussed above. In order to appreciate fully how this provision can be enforced, at least three other features of the water quality standards program must be reviewed. First, under the Act and EPA's regulations, a state must ensure that its standards are established at a level that will provide for attainment or maintenance of the standards for downstream waters--even if the downstream waters are in another state.[21] Thus, if ONRW protection can be secured, regulated activities in upstream states can be affected to the extent that their discharges would result in degradation of the ONRW. For this reason, obtaining ONRW designations may be especially attractive in areas near the border of an upstream state.

Second, EPA's regulations require much more than mere adoption of the anti-degradation policy by the states. They require that each state adopt "methods for implementing" the policy as part of the state's program.[22] In the context of ONRWs, it is the author's view that these methods must, of necessity, include mechanisms for: (1) identifying "waters of exceptional recreational or ecological significance"; (2) establishing, through field surveys, the existing (or baseline) water quality in each of those waters; (3) revising, if necessary, the state's standards (uses and/or criteria) so that no degradation of the baseline will occur; (4) advising upstream states of the need for their standards to be set at correspondingly protective levels; and (5) instituting a review procedure that flags every permit application for discharges (new or existing) that might degrade the baseline quality so that necessary discharge limitations can be incorporated into permits and enforced.

Finally, the Act provides that if EPA disapproves state water quality standards (or changes in those standards), the Agency must promulgate and enforce federal standards in their place.[23] EPA's regulations list the antidegradation policy (and implementing methods) as among the elements that must be submitted to the Agency in the triennial review.[24] If the measures necessary to protect ONRWs are not submitted, it is the author's belief that a state submission is plainly inadequate, triggering EPA's duty to act. This conclusion is even stronger where citizens have placed in front of the state, through its triennial review, the information, data, and proposed mechanisms (listed above) that would fulfill these requirements.

How can concerned citizens and organizations use this process to secure protection for ONRWs? The discussion below recommends a framework for action that, if applied with enough technical and legal resources, can begin to produce results.

IV. A BLUEPRINT FOR ACTION

A strategy can be developed on either a national or state level to secure protection for ONRWs. The discussion that follows describes a state-level model for action.

1. **Understand the state review/revision process.** Find out where the state stands in its triennial review (each state is on a different schedule and many are years overdue). Find out how the state process works (notice, comment, etc.), and thoroughly understand what rights of public participation, guaranteed by the federal CWA, are available in that state (e.g., formal or informal hearings, opportunities to petition the state for action).

2. **Develop your own baseline of designated areas.** Determine what waters and wetlands lie within national parks, state parks, wildlife refuges, and any other federal or state designated areas that are protected for their recreational or ecological value (e.g., sanctuaries, national trails, wilderness areas, national forests, wild and scenic rivers, etc.). Be able to describe precisely the physical bounds of these waters. Obtain any data or other information from the state or university research programs on the existing water quality, biological activity, and scientific or recreational uses being made of these waters.

3. **Develop a case for other important waters.** From the scientific literature or other sources (e.g., fisheries management agencies), decide what nondesignated waters within the state can be justified as having "exceptional recreational or ecological significance." Develop your own thoughtful definition of this phrase and screen candidate water bodies to ensure that whatever proposals you develop are internally consistent. Wherever possible, develop the same baseline information, described above, for designated waters.

4. **Produce recommendations on "implementing methods."** Review both the state's water quality standards program and its permit program to determine whether the necessary coordination

and review mechanisms are in place to implement protections for ONRWs in the permit process. If the system lacks these essential tools, develop specific recommendations for amendments to the state programs.

5. **Submit a petition or similar document.** Prepare for extensive participation in the state's review process. Place your specific recommendations and data before the state agency in a manner that builds a clear record, requires a decision, and positions you to make the same case to EPA when the state's submission is reviewed for federal approval.

6. **Follow through.** The entire process will require extensive discussions and negotiations with state agency personnel, water quality experts, biologists, and federal EPA officials. The mechanisms are in place at each level of government to guarantee your right to be heard and to ensure that defensible, documented decisions are made by responsible officials. The right to judicial review, if necessary, is available.

V. CONCLUSION

The Clean Water Act contains an excellent, albeit unused, mechanism for preserving the quality of ecologically valuable waters within and near National Park System units. EPA has followed the tough policy stance laid down by Congress in promulgating a regulatory provision that can halt degradation of ONRWs by point-source pollutant discharges. Many years of experience demonstrate that this provision will not be implemented fully without the insistence and professional advocacy of concerned citizens and others, such as the Park Service, with a responsibility for stewardship of the nation's natural areas. The necessary legal mechanisms are in place. What is needed now are the energetic and sophisticated efforts of those who wish to see ONRWs protected as Congress and EPA have prescribed.

NOTES

*Director of Environmental Affairs, Waste Management, Inc., Washington, D.C.

1. 33 U.S.C. § 1251.
2. *See, e.g.*, 33 U.S.C. §§ 1311, 1312, 1316, 1317.
3. 33 U.S.C. § 1342.
4. 33 U.S.C. § 1313.
5. 33 U.S.C. § 1317(a).
6. 33 U.S.C. § 1311(b).
7. 33 U.S.C. § 1313.
8. 40 CFR § 131.12.
9. 33 U.S.C. § 1370.
10. 33 U.S.C. § 1313(a)(3)(A).
11. 33 U.S.C. § 1313(c)(2).
12. 40 C.F.R. § 131.10(g).
13. 40 C.F.R. § 131.10(i).
14. 33 U.S.C. § 1313(c)(1).
15. 40 C.F.R. § 131.11.
16. 40 C.F.R. § 131.12.
17. 33 U.S.C. § 1251(a). (Emphasis added.)
18. 40 C.F.R. § 131.12(a)(1).
19. 40 C.F.R. § 131.12(a)(2). (Emphasis added.)
20. 40 C.F.R. § 131.12(A)(3).
21. 40 C.F.R. § 131.10(b).
22. 40 C.F.R. § 131.12(a).
23. 33 U.S.C. § 1313(b)(1).
24. 40 C.F.R. § 131.6.

Chapter 9

THE ENDANGERED SPECIES ACT: PROTECTING THE LIVING RESOURCES OF THE PARKS

Michael J. Bean[*]

I. INTRODUCTION

Not long after its establishment as the first national park, Yellowstone became the last refuge for the American bison. Having numbered in the millions only a few decades earlier, by the turn of the century the bison had been reduced to a tiny herd of twenty-one animals in Yellowstone National Park.[1] Everywhere else in the United States it had completely vanished from the wild.

From the nucleus of that remnant park population and a few captive animals scattered in zoos and private collections around the country, the bison has since been restored to a secure status, safe from the once-imminent threat of extinction. Today, other species similarly imperiled find in the National Park System refuge from the myriad threats that beleaguer them elsewhere. From the snail kite and Florida panther of the Everglades and Big Cypress to the elusive forest birds of Hawaii, hopes for the future recovery of many endangered species hinge on populations now largely confined to national parks. The large contiguous tracts of forest found in eastern parks, for example, represent some of the best habitat still available for many species of migratory songbirds that are significantly declining due to the fragmentation of forests elsewhere.[2]

This chapter examines the relationship of the federal endangered species program and the Endangered Species Act[3] that it implements to the National Park System. In particular, it examines the potential of each to reinforce and supplement the purposes of the other. As the Yellowstone example makes clear, long before Congress passed the Endangered Species Act in 1973, the National Park System was already serving its goals of preventing the avoidable extinction of species and of making possible their eventual recovery. This was no mere coincidence, for the preservation of native wildlife has been an integral mission of the National Park System since its establishment. Indeed, the 1916 National Park Service Act, the organic legislation that serves as the legal foundation for the National Park System, declares that the "fundamental purpose" of the Park System is "to conserve the scenery and the natural and historic objects and the wild life therein and to provide for the enjoyment of the same in such manner and by such means as will leave them unimpaired for the enjoyment of future generations."[4]

The lofty prose of the 1916 Act, however, has not always mirrored the actual experience within the Park System. In the 1950s, for example, then-routine fish poisoning carried out in preparation for the introduction of trout resulted in the elimination of the Great Smoky Mountain National Park population of the smoky madtom, a rare catfish then known to exist only in that park. Its rediscovery elsewhere in 1980 prevented this species from achieving the dubious distinction of having been deliberately made extinct in the course of National Park System management operations.[5] Introduction of nonnative fish for recreational angling in other parks has had similar, though perhaps less dramatic, adverse effects on native fish.[6] Other species losses have apparently occurred within national parks as a result of the insularization of park habitats from similar habitats outside park boundaries.[7]

Today, Park Service operations are subject to the requirements of the Endangered Species Act. So too are federal agency actions occurring outside park boundaries that may affect endangered or threatened species within a park. Together, these duties can serve both to restrain management options of the National Park Service and expand its influence over threats arising outside park boundaries. To examine how these various duties operate, it is necessary first to consider the basic elements of the Endangered Species Act.

II. THE ACT CONSIDERED

The Endangered Species Act protects plants and animals that have been formally listed as "endangered" or "threatened." The former category consists of species that have been determined to be in danger of extinction throughout all or a significant portion of their range;[8] the latter is a less imperiled category that includes species not now endangered, but likely to become so within the foreseeable future.[9] The "species" that may be so listed include not only full species, but subspecies and (in the case of vertebrate animals) distinct geographic populations as well.[10]

Responsibility for listing species as threatened or endangered is vested in the Secretary of the Interior and (in the case of most marine animals) the Secretary of Commerce. The Secretary of the Interior carries out this duty through the U.S. Fish and Wildlife Service, a sister agency of the National Park Service. When a species is formally proposed for listing by publication in the *Federal Register*, it receives a limited form of protection from the actions of federal agencies. Once a species is actually listed, a formidable battery of protections apply to it. If the species is listed as endangered, no person may "take" it (a term defined to include not only capturing and killing, but also harassing and harming);[11] import or export it; sell, ship, or receive it in interstate or foreign commerce; or possess it if it has been unlawfully taken.[12] For species listed as threatened, none of these prohibitions apply automatically; however, the either Secretary may make any or all of them applicable by regulation if necessary for the conservation of the species.[13] Exceptions from these prohibitions can be granted by permit for scientific research and for activities intended to enhance the propagation and survival of listed species.[14]

The penalties for violating these prohibitions can be quite substantial. Criminal penalties of up to $20,000 in fines and up to a year in prison may be imposed against certain violators, as well as civil penalties of up to $10,000 and forfeiture of guns, vehicles, or other equipment used to aid the violation.[15] Because of the severity of these penalties, the Endangered Species Act often serves as a more effective enforcement tool against persons killing endangered or threatened wildlife in national parks than do more general provisions prohibiting the taking of wildlife in national parks.

While the Endangered Species Act's prohibitions relating to taking and trade are important, arguably more so are its provisions imposing special duties on federal agencies. When Congress passed the Act in 1973, it recognized that for many species the federal government itself has often been the vehicle of destruction of species and their habitats (as with the smoky madtom). Section 7 of the Act specifies duties that were intended to prevent the federal government from ever again causing the extinction of any species. The most significant of these requires *each* federal agency to "insure that any action authorized, funded, or carried out by [it] is not likely to jeopardize the continued existence of any" listed species "or result in the destruction or adverse modification of" its critical habitat.[16]

Whenever a federal agency plans any action that may affect a listed species, it must consult with the Fish and Wildlife Service (or the National Marine Fisheries Service of the Commerce Department) to determine whether the planned action is consistent with the obligation to protect listed species. At the end of the consultation process, the Service provides the action agency with its "biological opinion" on the consequences of the proposed action. If that opinion concludes that the proposed action is likely to result in jeopardy to the species or adverse modification of its critical habitat, the agency must abandon the action or modify it to eliminate that result, or proceed ahead at the risk of being enjoined by a citizen lawsuit. Since the Service's biological opinions have been given considerable deference by the courts,[17] they are in practice major tools for beneficially influencing the activities of federal agencies.

For the National Park System, Section 7 of the Endangered Species Act represents both a restraint on Park Service management and a tool that can be used to protect living park resources. The National Park Service, for purposes of Section 7, is treated like any other federal agency. The actions it authorizes or carries out, including road and facilities building, trail maintenance, fishing regulation, snowmobile authorization, and so forth, must be the subject of consultation with the Fish and Wildlife Service or the National Marine Fisheries Service if the actions could affect any endangered or threatened species. The biological opinions of those agencies do not merely "rubber stamp" the proposals of the Park Service, as the current controversy over new visitor facilities development in Yellowstone National Park demonstrates.[18] Section 7 can serve as an effective brake on proposals to intensify use or otherwise manage the parks in a manner detrimental to the survival of endangered species. It also provides an additional source of legal authority to give special protection to particular park areas, such as crocodile sanctuaries in Everglades National Park, where stringent boating restrictions have been imposed.

Section 7 also offers a means of protecting park resources not just from questionable park management practices, but from the far larger threat arising from activities outside park boundaries. To the extent these activities have a federal agency connection, such as through a federal license or permit, and have the potential to affect endangered or threatened species within or outside the parks, they too are subject to Section 7. The National Park Service, and conservation organizations with an active interest in living park resources, should therefore carefully monitor external development activities that may effect protected species. Where effects are likely, the Park Service and park advocates should play an active role by encouraging rigorous review by the Fish and Wildlife Service, including careful scientific scrutiny of potential impacts on habitat, food chains, mating habits, and other crucial factors.

III. FUTURE COMMITMENT TO ENDANGERED SPECIES

The fundamental goal of the Endangered Species Act is to bring about the recovery of threatened and endangered species to a point at which they no longer are in peril of extinction. "Recovery plans," which the Fish and Wildlife Service and experts from other state and federal agencies prepare to guide efforts aimed at bringing about the recovery of listed species, can and should include measures to be undertaken within national parks. Where such species have been extirpated from a park, restoration of the species there should be carefully examined so as to not only aid the recovery of the species, but also to restore to the park part of its original complement of living resources. For example, a proposal is now under serious consideration to reintroduce the gray wolf into Yellowstone National Park.

The realization of the goals of both the National Park Service Organic Act and the Endangered Species Act will depend upon timely action to identify and protect the unique living resources of the nation. Currently, more than eight hundred species of plants and animals in the United States receive the protection of the Endangered Species Act. Nearly four times that number, however, are believed to warrant the Act's protection. These candidates for future listing, many of which occur within the National Park System, receive no formal protection under the Endangered Species Act and will continue to receive none until they are formally listed. Greater legislative protection for these unlisted candidate species would be highly desirable. In the absence of such remedial legislation, however, the National Park Service should make it a high priority to gather the data needed to determine whether these candidates are in fact deserving of the Act's protection and, while their status remains undecided, to monitor and protect these species so as to ensure no further erosion of their conservation status.

The Park Service's National Natural Landmarks program (NNL) could also play a key role in protecting these candidate species. The NNL program was established in 1962 by the Secretary of the Interior to encourage preservation of the best remaining examples of the major biotic communities and geologic features in the continental United States, Puerto Rico, the Virgin Islands, Hawaii, Guam, American Samoa, and other Pacific islands. The program seeks to encourage the preservation of natural diversity, which comprises species, biotic communities, and their associated habitats. It is the only natural areas program of national scope to identify and recognize best examples of both biological and geological features without regard to site ownership or management. The program's mandate falls well within the preservation mandate of the Park Service.

The program, however, is not faring well. It continues to "suffer from the lack of supporting legislation that would confer a stronger mandate, a more secure annual appropriation, various preservation incentives, and a formal connection with state natural areas programs."[19] Its contribution to a national endangered species protection strategy could be expanded.

Finally, because the Endangered Species Act and the National Park System are complementary efforts that can serve the common goal of preserving biological diversity, National Park Service employees should receive special training in the operation of that law and in the opportunities it provides for cooperative advancement of mutual goals. Conversely, appropriate Fish and Wildlife Service personnel should be specially trained to be better aware of the needs of the Park System and of the opportunities for meshing that system's operations with the objectives of the endangered species program.

NOTES

*Chairman, Wildlife Program, Environmental Defense Fund, Washington, D.C.

1. J. TREFETHEN, CRUSADE FOR WILDLIFE 92 (1961).

2. R. F. Whitcomb, *Birds and the Beltway*, ATLANTIC NATURALIST, vol. 36 (1986).

3. 16 U.S.C. § 1531.

4. 16 U.S.C. § 1.

5. U.S. FISH AND WILDLIFE SERVICE, ENDANGERED SPECIES TECHNICAL BULLETIN, vol. IX, no. 4 at 4 (Nov. 1984).

6. P. Shullery, *A Reasonable Illusion*, ROD & REEL..

7. W.D. NEWMARK, MAMMALIAN RICHNESS, COLONIZATION, AND EXTINCTION IN WESTERN NORTH AMERICAN NATIONAL PARKS (University of Michigan, Ph.D. thesis, 1986).

8. 16 U.S.C. § 1532(6).

9. 16 U.S.C. § 1532(20).

10. 16 U.S.C. § 1532(16). Illustrative of the flexibility this affords is the bald eagle, which is listed as an endangered species in forty-three states and a threatened species in five others, and is neither threatened nor endangered in Alaska (it does not occur in Hawaii).

11. 16 U.S.C. § 1532(19).

12. 16 U.S.C. § 1538(a).

13. 16 U.S.C. § 1533(d).

14. 16 U.S.C. § 1539(a)(1)(A).

15. 16 U.S.C. § 1540.

16. 16 U.S.C. § 1536(a)(2).

17. *See, e.g.*, Tennessee Valley Authority v. Hill, 437 U.S. 153 (1978), National Wildlife Federation v. Coleman, 529 F.2d. 359 (5th Cir. 1976), and Roosevelt Campobello International Park Commission v. EPA, 684 F.2d 1041 (1st Cir. 1982).

18. One aspect of controversy over visitor facilities revolves around two developments: the Fishing Bridge campground and trailer park, and the Grant Village complex. Over the past twenty years, the Park Service has become increasingly aware of the importance of restoring Fishing Bridge to natural conditions in order to protect environmental values and critical grizzly bear habitat. During Section 7 consultations, the U.S. Fish and Wildlife Service approved construction of the new facilities at Grant provided the Park Service agreed to remove the Fishing Bridge campground by 1985, and the recreational vehicle park by 1986. *See* U.S. DEPARTMENT OF INTERIOR, NATIONAL PARK SERVICE, FISHING BRIDGE AND THE YELLOWSTONE ECOSYSTEM: A REPORT TO THE DIRECTOR (1984) at 144-46. The Park Service agreed to this arrangement, but in 1985 political pressure from the Wyoming congressional delegation forced postponement of the agreement and the development of a new environmental impact statement on the campground closure. Section 7 consultations between the two agencies were reopened. When a draft environmental impact statement on the action was released in October 1987, the Park Service preferred alternative called for only a partial removal of the Fishing Bridge facilities and the completion of Grant Village. *See generally*, NATIONAL PARK SERVICE, DRAFT ENVIRONMENTAL IMPACT STATEMENT/DEVELOPMENT CONCEPT PLAN, FISHING BRIDGE DEVELOPED AREA (1987). This issue is still pending final resolution.

19. *See* U.S. Department of Interior, National Park Service, Memorandum to Acting Chief, Interagency Resources Division, from Acting Unit Chief, Natural Landmarks Unit, April 11, 1986.

Chapter 10

WATER RIGHTS AND THE DUTIES OF THE NATIONAL PARK SERVICE: A CALL FOR ACTION AT A CRITICAL JUNCTURE

Charles F. Wilkinson[*]

I. INTRODUCTION

Water and water rights cut across virtually every facet of the management of the National Park System. Water is critical to the maintenance of fish and wildlife habitat. It enhances recreational opportunities and contributes to the public's visual and sensory appreciation of our nation's scenic, historic, and biotic treasures. In many parks, water plays a continuous carving and flushing role in forming and maintaining the character of canyons. Finally, water is necessary to support the National Park Service visitor centers and Park Service personnel, allowing them to fulfill their obligations as trustees of the national parks and national monuments.

The Park Service is entering a critical phase concerning its management of water resources within the National Park System. The Park Service and the Interior Department Solicitor's Office have identified no fewer than 105 pending water rights cases in which Park Service rights are at issue; all of these cases are expected to be litigated within the next five to seven years, and an estimated twenty-five to thirty cases will have been tried by the end of 1987.[1] Beyond the matters already in litigation, the pressure on water supplies is extremely heavy in most regions of the American West, and it is imperative that the Park Service act promptly and effectively to protect the integrity of the lands it is called upon to manage. A national park is no longer a park if its streams are drawn low and warm.

This chapter sets out the legal principles that establish expansive water rights for the National Park System. It also recommends that the Park Service adopt a three-pronged approach regarding water resources: (1) its should aggressively document, justify, and quantify federal reserved water rights throughout the National Park Service System, and should assert those rights in pending state court water ajudication actions wherever necessary to protect park waters; (2) wherever possible, the Park Service should act quickly to assert these rights in federal court in order to avert adjudication in state forums; and (3) the Park Service should begin a program of rulemaking to designate site-specific appropriations of unappropriated water, exercising its congressionally delegated management authority over natural resources within the parks and monuments. A more specific discussion follows.

II. THE SCOPE OF CONGRESSIONALLY RESERVED WATER RIGHTS IN THE NATIONAL PARK SYSTEM

The Park Service derives its authority over water on federal lands from two principal sources: the *Winters* doctrine and congressionally established authority. This section discusses the scope of federal agency authority under both sets of circumstances.

A. The Reserved Rights Doctrine

The Supreme Court first explicitly recognized the doctrine of federal reserved water rights in the famous *Winters* decision in 1908.[2] In *Winters*, the Court interpreted an agreement between the United States and Indian tribes residing on the Fort Belknap Indian Reservation and ruled that Congress had impliedly reserved (or set aside) sufficient water, as a matter of federal law, to fulfill the purposes of the reservation, which were to provide for irrigation and generally to make the reservation habitable. In 1963, the Supreme Court expressly stated that the reserved rights doctrine applies to federal as well as Indian lands.[3] Then, in *Cappaert v. United States*,[4] the Supreme Court unanimously upheld federal reserved water rights in Devil's Hole in Death Valley National Monument, a unit of the National Park System. In *Cappaert*, the Court set out what is still the leading formulation of the reserved rights doctrine:

This Court has long held that when the Federal Government withdraws its land from the public domain and reserves it for a federal purpose, the Government, by implication, reserves appurtenant water then unappropriated to the extent needed to accomplish the purpose of the reservation. In so doing the United States acquires a reserved right in unappropriated water which vests on the date of the reservation and is superior to the rights of future appropriators. Reservation of water rights is imposed by the Commerce Clause, Art. IV, section 3, which permits federal regulation of federal lands. The doctrine applies to Indian reservations and other federal enclaves, encompassing water rights in navigable and nonnavigable streams.

* * *

In determining whether there is a federally reserved water right implicit in a federal reservation of public land, the issue is whether the Government intended to reserve unappropriated and thus available water. Intent is inferred if the previously unappropriated waters are necessary to accomplish the purposes for which the reservation was created.

* * *

The implied reservation of water doctrine, however, reserves only that amount of water necessary to fulfill the purpose of the reservation, no more.[5]

Thus the reserved rights, or *Winters*, doctrine is applicable wherever the federal government withdraws portions of the public land from other uses or dispositions and dedicates it to a particular purpose, for example, creating Grand Teton National Park. The government is held to have impliedly reserved unappropriated water on the reserved lands to the extent necessary to accomplish the purposes of the reservation.

In effect, the *Winters* doctrine superimposes and implies federal water rights on top of the state systems of allocation. Under the prior appropriation, or "first in time, first in right," doctrine in force in the western states, a water user obtains vested water rights superior to all future users by diverting water from a stream and applying it to a beneficial use such as irrigation or mining.

Federal reserved water rights, on the other hand, are not limited by state definitions of "diversion" or "beneficial use." These federal rights may include inchoate rights such as minimum instream flows and water for ecosystem maintenance. Reserved water rights, which are constitutionally authorized under the federal government's sweeping powers over commerce and federal property, vest in the federal government as of the date of a reservation and are superior to the rights of later appropriators under state law.

The precise contours of the reserved rights doctrine remain indefinite but the following general principles can be gleaned: (1) reserved water rights can be created by express language, as well as by implication; (2) absent express reservation, intent to reserve water is inferred if the water is necessary to accomplish the purpose of the reservation; (3) the doctrine encompasses rights in both navigable and non-navigable waters, and in both surface and groundwater; (4) the right extends to the quantity of water needed to fulfill the primary purposes of the reservation, and includes existing as well as future water requirements; and (5) the priority date of the federal right is the date of the original reservation, with all subsequent rights obtained under state law being junior in priority.

B. Reserved Water Rights in National Parks

The existence of reserved water rights in the national parks is beyond question; indeed, the National Park Service Act of 1916 is one of the strongest congressional statements of purposes that would protect streams and lakes. Nevertheless, there is uncertainty as the precise scope of these rights.

Examination of the 1916 Organic Act, and succeeding executive and judicial opinions, suggests that reserved rights in national parks are extraordinarily broad. The 1916 Organic Act sets forth an uncompromising and enduring statement of purpose:

> The service thus established shall promote and regulate the use of . . . national parks, monuments and reservations hereinafter specified . . . by such means and measures as conform to the fundamental purpose of the said parks, monuments and reservations, which purpose is to conserve the scenery and the natural and historic objects and the wild life therein and to provide for

the enjoyment of the same in such manner and by such means as will leave them unimpaired for the enjoyment of future generations.[6]

This "fundamental purpose," looking both to recreation and preservation, echoes the vision and words of Stephen Mather, the driving force behind the creation of the National Park Service. In his 1919 report on water impoundments within the national parks, Mather eloquently expressed this philosophy:

> Is there not some place in this great nation of ours where lakes can be preserved in their natural state; where we and all generations to follow can enjoy the beauty and the charm of mountain waters in the midst of primeval forests? The country is large enough to spare a few such lakes and beauty spots. The nation has wisely set apart a few national parks where a state of nature is to be preserved.[7]

Supreme Court decisions support a vigorous reserved rights doctrine in the national parks. As noted, the 1976 *Cappaert* decision stands for expansive reserved water rights in the parks. Similarly, in *United States v. New Mexico*,[8] the Court implied a broad view of the water rights reserved for national parks, although it narrowly construed reserved water rights in the national forests. In addressing the issue of whether Congress had impliedly reserved water for minimum instream flows within the Gila National Forest, the Court stated that the more expansive purposes of the National Park Service Organic Act offered an "instructive comparison" to the language in the Forest Service Organic Act of 1897. The opinion strongly implied that the relevant purposes of national parks reservations included aesthetic, recreation, and preservation purposes: "National forests were not to be reserved for aesthetics, environmental, recreational, or wildlife-preservation purposes . . . They are not parks set aside for nonuse, but have been established for economic reasons."[9]

The only other judicial statement on water rights in the parks is by the Colorado Supreme Court. A Colorado water court had awarded an absolute decree establishing water rights for all existing diversions and off-stream uses and conditional decrees for future diversions and for minimum instream flows and lake levels in Rocky Mountain National Park. The Colorado Supreme Court, in *United States v. City and County of Denver*,[10] affirmed these decrees in 1982 with a few modifications. Noting that the National Park Service Organic Act provided for permit and lease agreements and that the concession system had been congressionally sanctioned, the court extended reserved water rights to concession uses.

Perhaps the most thorough analysis of these issues is in a 1979 opinion issued by the Solicitor of the Department of the Interior.[11] In a significant and far-reaching opinion, the Solicitor addressed reserved water rights on all federal land administered by the Department of the Interior. The opinion concluded that the "fundamental purpose" provision of the Organic Act encompassed water within the national parks for (1) scenic, natural, and historic conservation (including minimum stream flows and lake levels); (2) wildlife conservation; (3) sustained public enjoyment of park resources (including water for concession uses and recreational boating); and (4) Park Service personnel uses.[12]

C. Reserved Rights in National Monuments

The starting point for analysis of national monuments is the Antiquities Act of 1906, which empowers the President to proclaim national monuments and to reserve federal land containing "historic landmarks, historic and prehistoric structures, and other objects of historic or scientific interest . . ."[13] The 1906 Act thus provided the President with power to reserve certain lands. With the passage of the comprehensive Park Service Organic Act of 1916, however, the purposes for which national monuments were reserved were significantly expanded: "The fundamental purpose of the said parks [and] monuments . . . is to conserve the scenery and the natural and historic objects and the wild life therein and to provide for the enjoyment of the same."[14]

A critical issue, therefore, is whether water rights for national monuments should be implied from the purposes of the Antiquities Act, from the purposes recited in a monument's enabling proclamation or legislation, or from the Organic Act. That issue may be particularly important where the establishing proclamation is very general or very brief. In view of the comprehensive purposes established by the Organic Act, the most logical analysis is to look to the umbrella provisions of that Act for a definition of the purposes for which water was reserved for the national monuments. The Supreme Court has twice followed such an approach in analogous situations. In *United States v. New Mexico*, the presidential authority to withdraw national forests was established by the Creative Act of 1891, but the Court looked to the Forest Service Organic Act of 1897 to determine the purposes of the national forests. In *Cappaert v. United States*, the Supreme Court held that President Truman had impliedly reserved a sufficient quantity of water to allow the desert pupfish to spawn within the Devil's Hole, Death Valley National Monument, when Truman dedicated the pool under the Antiquities Act. While the Court neatly tailored the amount of water reserved to be consistent with the intention expressed in the presidential proclamation, the existence of instream rights was based in part upon the language of the National Park Service Organic Act.[15]

National monuments, in other words, possess the same expansive water rights as national parks. This is consistent with Congress's aim in 1916 to consolidate all Park Service installations in one system. As the Department of the Interior Solicitor has put it, "pre-1916 national monuments receive the reserved rights discussed above in the national park context, carrying a priority date of the date of the establishing presidential proclamation."[16]

The one dissenting voice is that of the Colorado courts. In *United States v. City and County of Denver*, the Colorado Supreme Court concluded that reserved rights in national monuments exist only to the extent necessary to fulfill the purposes of the proclamation establishing the particular monument, as authorized by the Antiquities Act.[17] In light of this conclusion, the court refused to recognize instream flows for recreational boating within Dinosaur National Monument, and asked the district court to reconsider its finding that instream flows were reserved for fish preservation purposes. The district court, on that remand, construed the presidential proclamation narrowly, stating that the biological, aesthetic, scenic, and recreational features of Dinosaur were secondary purposes, and denied instream flows for fish preservation.[18] For the reasons discussed above, however, national monuments seem to have more generous purposes than those currently acknowledged in Colorado.

D. Reserved Rights in Wilderness Areas and in the Wild and Scenic Rivers System

The National Park Service also has an obligation to assert reserved rights in wilderness areas and in wild and scenic rivers under its management. Both of these preservation systems were established for recreational, scenic, conservation, and historic purposes, and speak, respectively, to the primacy of maintaining a wilderness areas's "primeval character" and a wild river's "free-flowing condition."[19] In the only judicial opinion directly address-ing reserved water rights in either of these preservation sys-tems, the district court in *Sierra Club v. Block*[20] stated that be-cause wilderness areas were withdrawn and reserved for a par-ticular purpose, water rights were impliedly reserved. Similarly, the Solicitor has concluded that reserved water rights exist to fulfill recreation, scientific, conservation, and aesthetic purposes in these two preservation systems.[21] While these water rights will be quite extensive, they often will have little impact on down-stream users, because wilderness areas and wild and scenic rivers tend to be at high elevations and because their water uses are nonconsump-tive.

III. ADJUDICATION OF RESERVED WATER RIGHTS

Reserved water rights are products of federal law. Their exist-ence and scope does not turn on questions of state law. Neverthe-less, with the passage of the McCarran Amendment in 1952,[22] the United States consented to joinder for determination of its rights in general stream adjudications in state courts. Federal water rights, therefore, present one of the rare instances in which state courts rather than federal courts have jurisdiction over the United States as a defendant. Furthermore, even where cases are initiated in federal courts, those courts must defer to ongoing state water court proceedings, so as to conserve judicial resour-ces and avoid piecemeal adjudication.[23]

The existence of state court jurisdiction does not eliminate all federal court jurisdiction. Importantly, the McCarran Amend-ment applies only to general stream adjudications--suits joining all potential water rights claimants in a watershed in proceedings to determine their relative rights in a water source. Thus, in order to assert jurisdiction, states must institute comprehensive proceedings rather than singling out federal entities. In those instances where the state has not brought a general stream adjudication, federal court actions may proceed. Indeed, the Supreme Court has expressly recognized a broad federal reach, stating that federal courts have a "virtually unflagging obligation . . . to exercise the jurisdiction given them."[24]

United States v. Adair[25] is one example in which the priority of federal proceedings has been sustained. The Ninth Circuit Court of Appeals reviewed the district court's exercise of jurisdiction to determine whether water rights had been reserved by the Klamath Indian Tribe, and if so, what priorities should be assigned to these rights. After asserting jurisdiction, the district court decided the case upon the merits in favor of the Klamath Indians, although it left actual quantification of the water rights to a state court proceeding. In upholding the district court's exercise of federal jurisdiction, the Ninth Circuit looked to considerations relied on earlier by the United States Supreme Court:[26] (1) the district court had carefully tailored its jurisdiction to consider only federal law claims; (2) since the federal district court had already reached a decision on the merits, wise judicial administration and conservation of judicial resources cut against vacating the lower court opinion; and (3) although ongoing, the Oregon state proceeding was essentially nascent, and for all practical purposes, stayed.

The National Park Service, as trustee of the national parks and monuments, has a duty expeditiously to identify, establish, and quantify reserved water rights so as to leave the national parks and monuments "unimpaired for the enjoyment of future generations." After *Adair*, it is clear that a carefully tailored assertion of federal reserved rights by the Park Service can sometimes be brought before a federal court. One need only read the Dinosaur National Monument opinions by the Colorado courts to appreciate the need for the Park Service to act swiftly in order to procure federal court determinations of federal reserved water rights.

The Park Service also has the responsibility, whether in state or federal court, of preparing water rights cases to the teeth. These are exceedingly complex pieces of litigation and only painstaking preparation can afford waters of the national parks the protection they deserve.

IV. APPROPRIATION OF WATER UNDER CONGRESSIONALLY DELEGATED AUTHORITY

The reserved rights doctrine is one source of federal protection for water rights on reserved federal lands, including national parks. Congress' implied reservation of water preempts state laws of allocation to the extent that certain quantities of water are necessary to achieve the purposes of the reservations. A different approach is taken where Congress legislatively delegates the authority to protect the purposes for which land is administered by federal agencies. Thus, the Park Service may be held to have the power to designate certain waters or flows as essential to fulfillment or protection of those statutory purposes. (Congressionally delegated authority over water has sometimes been described-- unhelpfully, it seems to me--as the creation of "nonreserved rights.")

Congress has the power both to control water use on the public lands without deferring to state law[27] and to delegate such power to federal land management agencies.[28] The inquiry is whether Congress in fact has made such a delegation to the Park Service as part of its organic authority, either through the National Park Service Organic Act and its amendments, or through specific park establishment legislation. Park Service authority of this kind finds support in both Solicitor Krulitz's 1979 opinion,[29] and, more generally, in a 1981 opinion issued by the Department of Justice:

> Federal water rights may be asserted without regard to state law [through] specific Congressional directives that override inconsistent state law, and the establishment of primary purposes for the management of federal lands . . . that would be frustrated by the application of state law.[30]

The Park Service has sweeping authority to administer the parks and monuments under the 1916 Organic Act: "[The Park Service] shall promote and regulate the use of the . . . national parks [and] monuments . . . to provide for the enjoyment of the same in such manner and by such means as will leave them unimpaired for the enjoyment of future generations."[31] In 1978, Congress amended the Organic Act to reaffirm this basic principle, stating that "the promotion and regulation of the various areas of the National Park System . . . shall be consistent with" the fundamental purpose for which the national parks and monuments were dedicated.[32] In other words, as a Senate Committee has put it, the Park Service "has an absolute duty, which is not to be compromised, to fulfill the mandate of the 1916 Act to take whatever actions and seek whatever relief as will safeguard the units of the National Park System."[33]

I have concluded in another article that the Forest Service possesses delegated authority to establish minimum stream flows in the

WATER RIGHTS 271

national forests,[34] and, although the issue is not free from doubt, the same result should obtain with respect to the Park Service.

The Park Service should assert water rights under delegated authority in order to address a real and immediate threat to the integrity of the National Park System. Only a handful of park-related water rights cases have been adjudicated. While the Park Service prepares to litigate reserved rights for the remaining parks and monuments, it should also assert administratively established water rights under delegated authority. Unlike congressionally reserved rights, such minimum flows would not carry a priority date of the establishment of the park or monument in question. Thus, the right to such flows would be prospective only, becoming effective as of the date established, and those rights may often confront significant claims of preexisting rights by prior appropriators. Nevertheless, the Park Service should proceed by rule making, on a site-specific basis, to set minimum flows administratively. This action would supplement the congressionally reserved rights to be established in state court stream adjudication or other federal litigation by providing a further basis for protection of waters in those parks where reserved rights may be found inadequate.

V. CONCLUSION

Water issues in the western states are debated in an intensely emotional and political atmosphere. The Park Service, however, should develop and implement an aggressive water rights program in order to fulfill its obligation to protect the watercourses within the national parks. It should fully prepare the factual, scientific, and legal basis for reserved water rights to flows or levels needed to maintain the purposes or qualities of each park unit, and it should assert those rights in every appropriate legal forum.

Where necessary or desirable, the Park Service should utilize state procedures to establish water rights for the parks and monuments. But state law is often inadequate, especially in the area of instream flows. The Park Service ought to be a national leader in articulating and defending the view that noncompetitive uses of water deserves equal dignity with the consumptive uses that water development interests have succeeded in promoting through state laws. There is nothing inappropriate in furthering federal interests through federal water laws, just as federal interests in land are furthered through federal land laws.

The Park Service should be diligent and innovative in proving the congressionally reserved rights of the parks and monuments in pending litigation. Where necessary, the Park Service should institute litigation in federal courts to establish reserved rights. It should also institute its own program to set instream flows administratively. Inevitably, there will be instances where the law is unclear. There ought to be no doubt of the Park Service's allegiance in such circumstances, however: it ought to be aggressive in resolving such ambiguities in favor of federal rights--in favor, ultimately, of the streams and lakes of the parks and monuments.

WATER RIGHTS
273

NOTES

*Professor of Law, University of Oregon School of Law. I extend my thanks to Jeremy Firestone, a 1986 graduate of the University of Michigan Law School, for his fine assistance in preparing this chapter.

1. Memorandum re Water Rights Litigation, from National Park Service Associate Director, Natural Resources, Nov. 10, 1985.

2. Winters v. United States, 207 U.S. 564 (1908).

3. Arizona v. California, 373 U.S. 546, 599-601 (1963).

4. Cappaert v. United States, 426 U.S. 128 (1976).

5. 426 U.S. at 138-41 (quoted with approval in United States v. New Mexico, 428 U.S. 969 (1978)).

6. 16 U.S.C. § 1.

7. U.S. DEPARTMENT OF THE INTERIOR, THIRD ANNUAL REPORT OF THE DIRECTOR OF THE NATIONAL PARK SERVICE TO THE SECRETARY OF THE INTERIOR OF THE FISCAL YEAR ENDED JUNE 30, 1919 at 49.

8. United States v. New Mexico, 438 U.S. 696 (1978).

9. *Id.* at 708, quoting 30 CONG. REC. 966 (1897) (Cong. McRae). The Court did, however, disclaim any intent to express a conclusion about park water rights. *Id.* at 696, n. 20.

10. United States v. City and County of Denver, 656 P.2d 1 (1982).

11. 86 Interior Dec. 553 (1979).

12. *Id.* at 594-99.

13. 16 U.S.C. § 431.

14. *Id.* at § 1.

15. The Antiquities Act came into play, not to define the purposes of the reservation, but only to define the outer limits of the President's authority. 426 U.S. 128, 142 (1976).

16. 86 Interior Dec. 553, 600 (1979).

17. 656 P.2d 1, 28 (1982).

18. District Court, Water Division No. 6, Colorado, Case No. W-85 (In the Matter of the Application for Waters Rights of the United States of America in Dinosaur National Monument in Moffat County, Colorado).

19. *See* 16 U.S.C. §§ 1131(c), 1271.

20. 622 F. Supp. 842 (D. Col. 1985). The court held that establishment of a Forest Service wilderness gave rise to reserved water rights that the Forest Service had a general duty to preserve and protect.

21. 86 Interior Dec. 553, 607-10 (1979).

22. 43 U.S.C. § 666.

23. Colorado River Water Conservation District v. United States, 424 U.S. 800, 819 (1976).

24. *Id.* at 817-18.

25. 723 F.2d 1394 (9th Cir. 1983) *cert. denied*, ___ S. Ct. ___ (___).

26. *Supra* n. 23 at 820 and n. 26, and Arizona v. San Carlos Apache Tribe, 463 U.S. 545 (1983).

27. Justice Rehnquist stated in *United States v. New Mexico:* "The question posed in this--what quantity of water, if any, the United States reserved out of the Rio Mimbres when it set aside the Gila National Forest in 1899--is a question of implied intent and not power." 438 U.S. at 698.

28. The courts have long recognized the power of Congress in public land law as in other fields to delegate authority to administrative agencies "to fill up the details." *See, e.g.,* United States v. Grimaud, 220 U.S. 506 (1911).

29. 86 Interior Dec. at 574-75. A supplemental opinion, by Solicitor Martz, limited the scope of this power under the Federal Land Policy and Management Act of 1976 but not under the National Park Service Organic Act. 88 Interior Dec. 253 (1981). The new Reagan administration Interior Solicitor Coldiron then issued an opinion, which disclaimed the existence of these rights. 88 Interior Dec. 1055 (1981).

30. U.S. Department of Justice, Office of Legal Counsel, Federal "Non-Reserved" Water Rights (June 16, 1982).

31. 16 U.S.C. § 1.

32. 16 U.S.C. § 1a-1.

33. s. REP. NO. 95-528, 95th Cong., 1st Sess., 9 (Oct. 21, 1977).

34. *See* Wilkinson & Anderson, *Land and Resource Planning in the National Forests,* 64 OR. L. REV. 1, 230-35 (1985). For additional commentary on the issue, *see* Shurts, *FLPMA, Fish and Wildlife, and Federal Water Rights,* 15 ENVTL. L. 115 (1985); Trelease, *Uneasy Federalism--State Water Laws and National Water Uses,* 55 WASH. L. REV. 751 (1980); Note, *Federal Acquisition of Non-Reserved Water Rights After New Mexico,* 31 STAN. L. REV. 885 (1979).

Chapter 11

PARK PLANNING, HISTORIC RESOURCES, AND THE NATIONAL HISTORIC PRESERVATION ACT

*Thomas F. King**

I. INTRODUCTION: THE NATIONAL HISTORIC PRESERVATION ACT AND THE NATIONAL PARK SERVICE

The National Historic Preservation Act of 1966 (NHPA), as amended,[1] assigns two quite different sets of responsibilities to the National Park Service. First, the Department of the Interior is charged with a variety of leadership and coordination functions in historic preservation, such as maintaining the National Register of Historic Places and providing grants-in-aid to the State Historic Preservation Officers (SHPOs). These responsibilities are delegated to the Park Service, and referred to as the "external programs." Second, and more germane to Park System planning, all federal agencies are given a series of responsibilities designed to ensure the administration of their historic properties "in a spirit of stewardship for the inspiration and benefit of present and future generations," and the fostering of conditions "under which our modern society and our prehistoric and historic resources can exist in productive harmony and fulfill the social, economic, and other requirements of present and future generations."[2] These responsibilities include:

- Establishing programs to identify historic properties under their jurisdiction or control;[3]

- Using historic properties for agency purposes, in a manner consistent with their preservation, in preference to the construction or use of nonhistoric properties;[4]

275

■ Leasing historic properties or exchanging them for other properties, where the lease or exchange will insure their preservation;[5]

■ Considering the effects of Park Service undertakings, such as project planning, on historic properties, and affording the Advisory Council on Historic Preservation the opportunity to comment on such undertakings;[6]

■ Documenting historic properties that must be destroyed;[7]

■ Generally, carrying out programs and projects in ways that will further the purposes of the NHPA.[8]

While these requirements can form the basis for a comprehensive program of historic properties management, the Park Service has not implemented the Act's requirements in a thorough, consistent, or imaginative fashion. As a result, the Park Service has lost substantial respect within the historic preservation community. Indicative of the concern felt by preservationists about Park Service performance is the response to a questionnaire distributed in 1985 to all State Historic Preservation Officers[9] by the House of Representatives Subcommittee on Public Lands. The questionnaire asked, among other things, which federal agencies were doing particularly good or bad jobs in carrying out their NHPA responsibilities. Although most states identified such agencies as the Corps of Engineers, the Office of Surface Mining, and others involved in major construction or land-disturbing activities as prime offenders, almost 20 percent of the respondants identified the Park Service as doing a bad job. Only 10 percent categorized the Park Service as doing a good job.[10] In July 1986 the the National Conference of State Historic Preservation Officers[11] formally criticized the Park Service for failing to carry out its responsibilities under the NHPA, noting that this failure has resulted in the loss of significant historic properties in the national parks, and called upon the Park Service to revise and clarify its preservation policies.[13]

In my own experience, the allegations of the State Historic Preservation Officers are well founded. In some cases, the Park Service has carried out its NHPA responsibilities magnificently, and in many, perhaps most, cases it does no worse than other land management agencies such as the Bureau of Land Management. But the Park Service by no means has the model historic preservation program that it likes to think it has, or that the leadership role assigned to it by the NHPA would suggest it should have. Its management of historic properties is typically unimaginative, inconsistent among regions and units, and ponderously bureaucratic. The Park Service frequently violates its internal historic preservation guidelines, if not the requirements of the NHPA itself, resulting in damage to or destruction of historic properties.[13]

II. PROBLEMS IN IMPLEMENTING PARK SERVICE RESPONSIBILITIES

The following factors contribute to the less than stellar recordof the Park Service in historic preservation:

1. Confusion of roles

As noted above, NHPA assigns two different kinds of historic preservation responsibilities. As a federal land management agency, the Park Service is given responsibilities that essentially undergird the mandates embodied in its Organic Act to protect and enhance historic properties in its care. At the same time, NHPA gives it the responsibility for administering a wide range of external programs of assistance to State Historic Preservation Officers, local governments, federal agencies, and the public. The Park Service is responsible for providing grants to and reviewing the performance of SHPOs, for overseeing the certification of local government historic preservation programs, for maintaining a comprehensive National Register of Historic Places, for carrying out archaeological salvage work, for providing historic preservation guidelines to federal agencies, and for reviewing the rehabilitation of historic buildings to determine whether their owners should qualify for investement tax credits.

The Park Service's "in-house" and external roles are not necessarily compatible. As manager of some of America's most treasured places, the Park Service can and should be highly protective of the historic properties under its stewardship. Although it has to grapple with problems of balancing preservation against other aspects of land use, notably visitor access, safety, and provision of services, the Park Service is not faced with the kinds of absolute conflicts that characterize programs like those of the Corps of Engineers or the Forest Service, where preservation must be

balanced against the needs of timber production, water supply, surface mining, or highway construction. As a result, park-based
models of management can be more heavily oriented toward preservation than is realistic for nonpark programs. Conversely, what
makes for a balanced preservation program in the Corps of Engineers provides far less protection to historic properties than
the National Park Service should provide in national park system units. Thus, a Park Service professional responsible for
both in-park and external programs must have something of a split
personality, applying differing sets of models and values in each
context.

The Park Service insists on assigning to virtually all its profes-
sionals--whether in Washington, in the regional offices, and
even in the parks--both in-house and external functions. There is
no evidence that the Park Service has ever thought through the
conflicts that this engenders; on the contrary, management typically denies that any such conflicts exist. The fact is, however,
that these conflicts lead many Park Service professionals to perform neither their in-park nor their external duties very well.

2. Conflict of values

Park Service involvement in historic preservation predates
the NHPA by many years. Preservation is one of the central missions assigned the Park Service in its organic legislation. This mission was more explicitly outlined in 1935 with the passage of
the Historic Sites Act,[14] which provided the basis for what was,
at the time, the closest thing the nation had to a comprehensive
historic preservation program, the National Historic Landmarks
Program, under which the Park Service identified properties of
"national significance" and designated them as National Historic
Landmarks. According to Park Service historians, the Park Service
initially intended to acquire such landmarks and protect them, but
this quickly proved infeasible; as a result, the program has remained
largely preoccupied with assigning landmark designations to properties that remain under the control of others. To ensure that designations were made in a thoughtful way, the Park Service undertook, and still carries on, a program of "theme studies," in
which major themes in national history are set forth and documented. Properties particularly representative of specific themes
are then designated National Historic Landmarks. Recently, for example, the Park Service has been involved in a "War in the Pacific"

theme dealing with World War II, and a "Man in Space" theme that has resulted in landmark designations for various spacecraft launch sites and research facilities.

The NHPA assigned the Park Service wider responsibilities with respect to a broader range of historic properties. The National Register of Historic Places is explicitly designed to include properties of national, state, and local significance,[15] and the NHPA never mentions "themes." Efforts to integrate the landmarks program with the National Register have created another set of conflicts within the National Park Service. On the one hand, the National Register seeks to be responsive to the broad mandate given it by the Act, to include properties of all kinds, at all levels of significance; on the other hand, it is driven by the philosophy of the landmarks program to give greater weight to properties of national significance and to organize its evaluations of properties with reference to "themes." The landmarks program is also oriented essentially toward public interpretation; landmarks are those properties that have the potential for use in commemorating and interpreting themes. The National Register, on the other hand, is supposed to embrace not only properties of interpretive value, but properties of value in research, properties associated with local historical people and events but not necessarily useful for commemorating or interpreting them, and properties that by virtue of their history or architectural qualities simply contribute to the ambience and character of communities.

This conflict of values is another source of confusion for in-park preservation. Imagine, for example, that a given National Park System unit has been created for the purpose of preserving and interpreting certain prehistoric ruins that exemplify a particular theme. Besides the ruins in question, suppose the unit contains a number of historic ranches and a decaying mining town. Clearly, the Park Service is responsible for preserving and interpreting the ruins, but what about the other properties? NHPA requires that they be managed too, if they are eligible for inclusion in the National Register. The two responsibilities may be in direct conflict: money spent stabilizing the mining town, for example, is money not spent on interpreting the ruins, and vice versa. Similarly, if the buildings on one of the ranches intrude on some of the ruins, there may be a strong impetus to tear them down in order to investigate and interpret what lies beneath them.

Such conflicts are inevitable and are not necessarily difficult to resolve. Reasonable people may agree, for example, that in the interests of efficient management and effective interpretation, the mining town should be leased to someone willing to maintain it at no cost to the government, left to decay, or even documented and burned down, or that ranch buildings, however historically valuable, should be documented and removed. There is no particular difference between making such a decision and deciding that in the public interest, certain historic properties should be destroyed in order to make way for a highway or a reservoir. Such decisions do have to be made, and NHPA in no way says that they should not be made; it merely requires that they be made on the basis of full information, in consultation with all interested parties, and with provisions for appropriate mitigating actions.

Such conflicts become intractable in the Park Service because both the interpretation mission and the protection of the properties that impede the mission are defined as historic preservation. Seeking to accomodate both responsibilities within a single frame of reference, the Park Service tends to evaluate all historic properties under its care with primary reference to landmark themes and the legislated purposes of National Park System units.[16] This automatically downgrades the significance of properties that do not contribute to such themes and purposes, and to greater or lesser extents defines them out of existence. It also brings the Park Service into conflict with its broader NHPA responsibilities, the State Historic Preservation Officers, and the Advisory Council on Historic Preservation, whose duty it is to promote adherence to NHPA purposes by federal agencies.

3. Decentralization and convulsive reorganization

Historic preservation in the Park Service, as in many other agencies, is complicated by decentralized management. A frequent complaint among preservationists outside the Park Service is that decentralization creates inconsistency and failures of accountability.[17] Preservation professionals in the parks report to their superintendents; those in the regional offices report to their regional directors, and those in Washington, theoretically responsible for policy direction, can communicate officially with the field only through the Director, down to the regions and on to the individual parks.

There are many good reasons for decentralization, but neither the Park Service nor, in my experience, any other agency has quite worked out an ideal balance that takes advantage of its benefits without being thwarted by its complications. In the Park Service, as in most other agencies, there are strongly held and strongly conflicting beliefs about centralized versus decentralized management; typically, Washington-based preservation professionals want more centralization, except when they want to avoid responsibility by blaming the field, while those in the regional offices and parks want "WASO" off their backs, except when they need help contending with distasteful direction from the regional director or park superintendent. These conflicting beliefs lead to failures of communication and to frequent convulsions of reorganization, now toward centralization, now toward decentralization, now toward schemes that seek variously defined middle grounds. The cumulative result is that considerable difficulty exists in figuring out who is responsible for what and how to get anything done.

4. Anti-preservation bias

Many preservationists believe that there are pervasive biases among Park Service managers against the preservation of historic properties. With backrounds primarily in visitor management and protection, recreation, or natural resource management, most park superintendents and regional directors are perceived to have little knowledge of, and little patience for, preserving old buildings and archaeological sites. A vignette that rather sums up the problem is a statement made by a highly placed Park Service official at the end of a meeting concerning the disposition of the historic Crater Lake Lodge. As we were exchanging pleasantries, the official announced that he "thinks there is value in these historic places," as though this were a revelation shared with me in some confidence, and as though Congress had not found and declared such value repeatedly and had not assigned its protection explicitly to the Park Service.

There is no malice in the Park Service's orientation toward things other than historic properties; I doubt if there are any, regional directors or superintendents who burn with the desire to knock down historic buildings or bulldoze archaeological sites. Rather, it is a matter of thoughtlessness--historic preservation is not considered, or at least not given high priority, when management decisions are made. Natural resources and recreation needs usually dominate the agenda. There is nothing necessarily wrong with giving low priority to historic preservation vis-a-vis other public interests, as long as this is the outcome of a rational, objective weighing and balancing of all interests. Park Service decision making, however, although encumbered by a vast array of planning processes and procedures, is unfortunately not demonstrably characterized by such objectivity. Too often, historic preservation is simply not part of the equation; it is considered, if at all, only as a possible impediment to realizing the management objectives selected.

5. Unclear guidance

The Park Service organizes its in-park compliance with the NHPA and several other historic preservation statutes of less global scope with reference to a manual called "NPS-28."[18] This manual emphasizes the systematic consideration of historic properties at each phase of park planning as an integrated part of the overall planning effort. This is a proper and positive emphasis, but NPS-28 contains many flaws that tend to defeat its purpose. It canonizes the confusion noted above about evaluation of properties, directing that evaluation be done in the context of landmark themes and park purposes, though at the insistence of the State Historic Preservation Officers and the Advisory Council, it also gives passing approval to coordination with state historic preservation plans and use of the National Register's evaluation criteria. The product of a committee, NPS-28 is ponderous and convoluted. The product of compromise between professional preservationists and managers, its guidance is often unclear, indirect, and hedged with caveats. As a result, it is widely ignored.

Consider, for example, the case of Fort Union, an historic trading post site in North Dakota. Fort Union's buildings long ago disappeared; only their buried, archaeological vestiges remain. Over the years, a good deal of local interest has developed in reconstructing the post, apparently based on the assumption that a reconstructed Fort Union, flags flying bravely over the pallisade, would attract tourists. Local interest was translated into congressional pressure on the Park Service to reconstruct the fort.

The NPS-28 manual is unusually unambiguous about reconstruction: "The Service does not endorse, support, or encourage the reconstruction of historic structures." Acknowledging that there are "limited circumstances when reconstruction will be considered,"

NPS-28 goes on to outline the standards that must be met before the Park Service will reconstruct a site. Reconstruction can occur only where "surface or subsurface (historical or archaeological) remains will not be destroyed." It can occur only if it "is essential for public understanding." Reconstruction is permissible only if "all prudent and feasible alternatives to reconstruction" have been considered, leading to the conclusion that reconstruction is "the only alternative permitting appreciation of the historical or cultural association for which the park was established." Furthermore, "archaeological, historical, and architectural data must be sufficient to permit accurate reproduction of both . . . mass and detail."[19]

NPS-28 accurately reflects widely accepted preservation principles and longstanding Park Service policy on reconstruction. In 1936, what is now the National Park System Advisory Board adopted an internationally recognized maxim on the subject: "Better preserve than repair, better repair than restore, better restore than reconstruct." Park Service policy is based on the recognition that "[n]o matter how well conceived and executed, a restoration will be an artificial modern interpretation of the past rather than an authentic survival from it."[20]

NPS-28 notwithstanding, however, as of this chapter's writing the Park Service is undertaking the reconstruction of Fort Union. The project, whose funding and scheduling are open ended, is likely to end up costing the taxpayers several million dollars. It will certainly destroy the archaeological vestiges of the actual trading post. Information on which to base the reconstruction is so sketchy that archaeological excavations are needed to determine such basic matters as how foundations and chimneys were constructed. The results of these excavations, however, were so scheduled that their results would not be available until after physical reconstruction began. Alternative ways to interpret the site are certainly available: a modern visitor center with models and other exhibits, stabilized archaeological excavations, and self-guided tours through the site are all possibilities. None of these well-established alternatives, and certainly not the standards imposed by NPS-28, have prevented the Park Service from bowing to the pressure to reconstruct.

Fort Union is not an isolated example. Another major reconstruction project is under consideration at Pecos Pueblo, despite the fact that according to NPS-28, "[t]he Service . . . does not permit reconstruction . . . of prehistoric structures."[21] Archaeological excavations have been carried out at Custer Battlefield National Historic Site with little or no attention to NPS-28 directives that give preference to *in situ* preservation and conducting excavations only on the basis of careful planning.[22] The list could be expanded considerably, if space permitted.

6. Ineffective planning

The centerpiece of Park Service planning is supposed to be the "General Management Plan" (GMP), which spells out each unit's priorities and how they will be achieved over a period of years. Ideally, the Park Service can identify in the GMP the historic properties or property types it has to manage within the unit, and establish strategies for dealing with them. Based on this ideal and on the proposition that, with its large cadre of preservation professionals, the Park Service did not need intensive second guessing by the Advisory Council or the SHPOs, a "Programatic Memorandum of Agreement" (PMOA) was developed to satisfy NPS responsibilities under Section 106 of the NHPA. Under the PMOA, the Advisory Council and the SHPOs are involved in the development of the GMPs and similar planning documents. Once a GMP has been developed, activities carried out in compliance with the GMP do not require review by the Council and the states.[23]

Unfortunately, the promise of the GMPs has not been realized. GMPs are often based on seriously flawed data about historic properties or fail to make effective use of the data available. In the hypothetical example discussed above (which pitted archaeological preservation against the management of other historic properties), the GMP would in all probability devote extensive discussion to the ruins while paying little attention to the ranches and mining town, thus failing to highlight the major sources of conflict between preservation and the park's mission. This problem is exacerbated when a unit's historic properties have not been thoroughly identified and inventoried, a particularly common problem in large units, recently created units, and units whose primary missions arc natural resource protection and recreation. Many GMPs--for example, virtually every GMP prepared for the new Alaskan parks--deal with historic preservation in a nonsubstantive manner, providing background on the unit's history and prehistory, perhaps discussing its known historic properties, and then simply concluding that these properties will be managed in accordance with NPS-28.

Even if NPS-28 were the best historic preservation manual in existence, its programmatic application would be no substitute for dealing specifically with a unit's resources and management needs. Often, the unit's management needs are not thoroughly delineated and are even less well justified. Where a unit's major mission is natural resource protection and interpretation, the need to demolish an historic structure that intrudes upon a natural setting may be taken for granted with slight consideration given to its preservation and adaptive use. Again, demolition may in fact be the correct action in the public interest, but the decision to demolish should be based on a clearly stated recognition of a management conflict and thorough consideration of resolution alternatives. GMPs do not consistently provide the context in which such issues are identified and addressed; they should, in order to qualify as useful planning documents.

NPS-28 also requires each unit to develop a "cultural component" for its "Resource Management Plan" (RMP), which is integrated with the GMP.[24] The RMP could provide another context for the thorough consideration of a unit's preservation problems and the development of solutions. However, RMPs have evolved into budget planning documents designed to establish how much money is required to carry out resource management activities that the unit wishes to pursue, rather than establishing actual plans for addressing the unit's long-term resource management needs. As budget documents, the RMPs can be useful and important, but they seldom function as comprehensive plans to guide decision making about a park's historic resources.

Finally, in my experience, Park Service planning tends to focus on individual park units in isolation from their surroundings, ignoring historic preservation activities in the vicinity that may be under the jurisdiction of other federal agencies, the SHPOs, or local governments. Even where a state is extensively involved in the interpretation of historic properties in the vicinity of a park, arranging interagency coordination is difficult. It is usually the state that must take the initiative in seeking such coordination. Similarly, when considering historic properties that may be subject to disturbance in connection with a park's major mission, it is not uncommon for Park Service planning to ascribe values to the properties or establish management policies with little or no consideration for the evaluation systems and management directions used by the SHPO, despite the fact that the SHPO is implementing directions provided by Park Service external programs. Three unfortunate effects may result from such inconsistencies. First, they tend to complicate communication about the significance and proper treatment of resources in the park. Second, bad feelings can arise within the ranks of the SHPOs, who naturally look to the Park Service for consistency. Finally, inconsistency impedes park participation in preservation planning in areas not under Park Service jurisdiction, where threats to park resources may occur.

In a nutshell, general planning throughout the national park system, which should provide the ideal context for identifying and resolving conflicts between historic preservation and other Park Service responsibilities, and for identifying and taking advantage of preservation opportunities, is seldom used creatively for these purposes. One often gets the impression that plans are developed only because they are required by Park Service policy, rather than being developed for use as tools in integrating and implementing the Park Service's diverse mandates for preservation, conservation, interpretation, and recreation.

III. SOLUTIONS

The solution most commonly proposed for the problems facing historic preservation in the national parks is to involve the Advisory Council and the SHPOs more thoroughly in National Park Service decision making by invalidating the existing PMOA and soliciting the comments of the Council and the SHPOs on each action that might affect a historic property.[25] I have personally resisted this proposal because I feel that however ineffective Park Service management of its historic properties may be, the Park Service, by the nature of its mission, does much less damage to historic properties than do agencies like the Department of Housing and Urban Development or the Office of Surface Mining, and that it is to the more destructive agencies that we should devote the most attention. With its clear mandate to protect historic properties, and its large cadre of professionals, the Park Service should be able to do the job right; it seems a fundamental misallocation of priorities to have the Advisory Council and SHPOs, with their limited resources, spend time second guessing Park Service decisions. Another avenue to improvement should be found.

Much of the problem could be solved if preservation planning in each park were transformed from the rote exercise it has often become into an activity that results in clear direction to management. NPS-28 could be revised and simplified, and management and preservation professionals alike could be unequivocally directed to use it. One goal should be for each park to implement an historic preservation plan, either as part of its GMP or as a separate document cross-referenced with the GMP. Each plan should accomplish the following:

- Identify the park's known historic properties and, where the park may contain undiscovered historic properties, predict their distributions and nature based on reliable background data and establish procedures for testing such predictions.

- Distinguish between historic properties or property types that relate to the park's interpretive purposes and those that do not, recognizing that while the Park Service may wish to develop and use only the former, it has stewardship responsibilities for the latter as well.

- Establish priorities for the development and use of those historic properties that relate to the park's interpretive purposes and specify how such development and use will be undertaken in a way that minimizes damage to the historic, archaeological, cultural, and architectural values of the properties.

- Consider alternatives for the protection and wise use of historic properties that do not relate to the park's primary purposes and select approaches appropriate to the significance and nature of the properties, balanced against other management needs.

- Establish a system to ensure that whenever construction, issuance of permits, or changes in land use, may affect historic properties of any kind, or may affect areas where such resources may occur but have not yet been discovered, appropriate steps are taken to identify, evaluate, and protect such properties from damage, or if damage cannot be avoided, to take actions to mitigate it.

Each plan should provide unambiguous direction for park management, comprehendible to all concerned. Each plan should be prepared in consultation with the SHPO, federal and state agencies that manage lands near the park, affected local governments and Indian tribes, and the interested public. The Park Service should strive for a creative, mutually supportive relationship with any preservation plans maintained by these affected parties. Such consultation and coordination should continue as the park's plan is implemented. Actions that are not consistent with the plan and failures in implementation should be subject to more intensive oversight, with review by the Director of the National Park Service and the Advisory Council.

Arguably, such procedures are supposed to be developed now as the result of NPS-28 and the Park Service's general planning processes. The fact is, however, that it does not happen with any consistency and is not likely to happen until NPS-28 is made more useable, Washington provides clear direction, and Park Service plans come to be regarded as directions to be followed rather than documents to be shelved.

Improving Park Service planning would not require changes in the National Historic Preservation Act or other legislation; rather, it would require action by the Director to reorient the regions, service centers, and parks in their thinking about planning and implementation.

The Park Service should also consider the complementary action of divesting itself of its external historic preservation programs. As long as Park Service professionals must wear two hats, trying to serve the differing and seldom complementary needs of the parks on one hand and the external programs on the other, they will have difficulty doing either well. The proper business of the Park Service is the administration of park system units; the external programs would be better managed by an agency without the conflicting requirements caused by park administration. The Park Service could concentrate on its central mission if that mission were not continually confused with the needs and priorities of its external programs.

This change would naturally be resisted by the preservation establishment within the Park Service; it would mean a loss of turf. The shift could be effected without legislation, but only if the external programs were retained within the Department of the Interior through a redelegation of the Secretary of the Interior's historic preservation authorities. This result would probably not be desirable; the conflicts that exist within the Park Service would persist if the programs were assigned to another bureau, but if the programs were broken out to stand as a bureau on its own, it would be subject to domination by the larger land and resource management agencies whose functions are more central to Interior's traditional mission. Reassigning the external programs to an agency outside the Department of the Interior would require leigislative action.[26]

IV. CONCLUSIONS

The national park system can and should be an historic property "bank," where places of enduring significance--not only to the nation but to its regions and localities--are kept in safety throughout the years. Because the system must also conserve other resources, provide for interpretation and recreation, and be managed in an environment of finite financial and personnel resources, preservation of historic places must be balanced against other priorities by sensible planning and management. Parks are not hermetically sealed enclaves impervious to influences from lands and resources around them, nor are they shielded from influencing those same resources. Planning and cooperation must be done in concert with the entire spectrum of affected interests.

The State Historic Preservation Officers and other preservationists are willing and ready to work with the Park Service in managing the parks and addressing threats, whether threats arise from within or outside the parks. It is a source of continuing frustration that even while Park Service respresentatives view their agency as the standard bearer for the national historic preservation program, the Park Service has such difficulty attending to its preservation housekeeping. The National Park Service badly needs to reconsider its national priorities, eliminate excess baggage in its external programs, and address itself to the real planning and management challenges involved in doing right by the historic resources of the National Park System.

NOTES

*Director, Office of Cultural Resource Preservation, Advisory Council on Historic Preservation. The Council is an independent federal agency whose primary function is to review federal projects and programs that affect historic properties. This chapter, written in 1986, reflects the author's personal views, not necessarily the official position of the Advisory Council.

1. 16 U.S.C. § 470.

2. 16 U.S.C. §§ 470-1(1) and (3).

3. 16 U.S.C. § 470h-2(a)(2).

4. 16 U.S.C. § 470-2(a)(1).

5. 16 U.S.C. § 470h-3.

6. 16 U.S.C. § 470f, commonly refered to as "Section 106" after its statutory designation.

7. 16 U.S.C. § 470h-2(b).

8. 16 U.S.C. § 470h-2(d).

9. State Historic Preservation Officers, or SHPOs, are the state officials who coordinate NHPA activities in each state and territory. 16 U.S.C. § 470a.

10. For a summary of responses, *see* CULTURAL RESOURCES: RESULTS OF QUESTIONNAIRE ON STATE HISTORIC PRESERVATION ACTIVITIES, U.S. General Accounting Office, GAO/RCED-86-60FS (Dec. 1985).

11. The national membership organization representing SHPOs in national affairs. Board members are elected by, and answer to, the SHPOs.

12. Resolution passed by the Board of Directors, National Conference of State Historic Preservation Officers, July 1, 1986, Boston, Massachusetts.

13. Recent examples include: a decision to reconstruct Fort Union National Historic Site, with the consequent destruction of the archaeological remains of the original historic trading post, against the advice of both the Advisory Council and the SHPOs, and in contravention of standing Park Service policy; a decision to demolish the historic Crater Lake Lodge, now in abeyance after a great public outcry; the issuance of a permit allowing a national Boy Scout camp to be constucted, with the consequent disturbance of the landscape, on an archaeologically sensitive portion of Valley Forge National Historical Park, Pennsylvania, contravening the Valley Forge General Management Plan and specific assurances given by the Park Service to the Advisory Council; and refusal by the Park Service to accept responsibility for the historic Buffalo River Bridge in the Buffalo National River, leading to its demolition despite an acknowledged need for a river crossing point as part of the park's trail system. Other less current examples, and less verifiable allegations by SHPOs and others, abound.

14. 16 U.S.C §§ 461-467.

15. *Cf.* REPORT OF THE COMMITTEE ON INTERIOR AND INSULAR AFFAIRS ON THE NATIONAL HISTORIC PRESERVATION ACT AMENDMENTS OF 1980, H.R. REP. NO. 96-1457, 96th Cong., 1st Sess., at 25: "Subsection 101(a)(1) reauthorizes the Secretary of the Interior's responsibility to expand and maintain the National Register of Historic Places which, as under the 1966 Act, is intended to include properties of State and local, as well as national, historic significance."

16. For example, NPS-28 provides for maintenance of a "Regional Cultural Resource Analysis System" as "a tool for identifying a Region's foremost cultural resources protection and preservation needs." This system is to be based on "a statistical profile which identifies the historic themes associated with each park (*e.g.*, Native Villages and Communities or the Civil War) and then evaluates the resources in the park on the basis of their overall significance." Based on this theme-driven evaluation system, the regional

director is to establish the region's historic preservation priorities. CULTURAL RESOURCES MANAGEMENT GUIDELINES, NPS-28, 1985, at 7.

17. For example, in "A Consolidated National Council on Historic Preservation," a paper distributed to the members of the National Conference of State Historic Preservation Officers in 1986, Massachusetts SHPO Valerie Talmadge characterized relations between National Park Service regional offices and the Washington office, and between divisions within the Washington office, as "segmented and fractured . . . where paranoia and agency politics rule over common sense and cooperation." In a 1985 letter to Congressman John Seiberling of Ohio, the President of the National Conference, South Carolina SHPO Charles Lee, complained that the Park Service's organization was such that it was often impossible to find anyone with the authority and responsibility to make a decision.

18. *See generally*, NPS-28, *supra* n. 15.

19. *See supra* n. 15 at 9-10.

20. U.S. Department of the Interior, National Park Service, MANAGEMENT POLICIES (1978) at V-15.

21. NPS-28, *supra* at 8.

22. NPS-28, *supra* at 11.

23. Programmatic Memorandum of Agreement Between the National Park Service, the Advisory Council on Historic Preservation, and the National Conference of State Historic Preservation Officers, December 19, 1979, mimeograph copy. Comprehensive amendments ratified Sept. 11, 1981.

24. NPS-28, *supra* at 8-9.

25. This solution has been suggested frequently to me by congressional staff, and is periodically suggested by representatives of the National Conference of State Historic Preservation Officers and the National Trust for Historic Preservation.

26. This and other legislative options are currently under consideration by the National Conference of State Historic Preservation Officers.

Chapter 12

THE CLEAN AIR ACT: NEW HORIZONS FOR THE NATIONAL PARKS

Elizabeth A. Fayad[*]

I. INTRODUCTION

Before 1977, the Clean Air Act did not contain any protections specific to the national parks. The Environmental Protection Agency (EPA) used its general authorities to develop a program to prevent the deterioration of air quality in clean air areas, including parks.[1] In 1977, however, specific language outlining a program of protections for air quality-related values in the national park system was included with the enactment of Part C--Prevention of Significant Deterioration of Air Quality in the Clean Air Act amendments. Upon signing the amendments into law on August 7, 1977, President Jimmy Carter stated, "With this legislation, we can continue to protect our national parks and our major national wilderness areas and national monuments from the degradation of air pollution."[2]

One of the purposes of Part C of the Clean Air Act (CAA or Act) is "to preserve, protect, and enhance the air quality in national parks, national wilderness areas, national monuments, national seashores, and other areas of special national or regional natural, recreational, scenic, or historic value."[3] The "enhance" language in the purpose section is particularly important because it clarifies that the mandate of this part of the Clean Air Act is not only to prevent decreases in but to improve the air quality in these special areas.

Part C is divided into two subparts. The first is primarily concerned with air quality, that is, concentrations of pollutants, and is referred to as the prevention of significant deterioration of air quality provisions. The second part provides specific

293

visibility protections for certain units of the national park system. The two subparts are interrelated and overlap, as the Environmental Protection Agency regulations implementing them demonstrate. These amendments were signed into law over ten years ago. The goals set forth in them have not been realized and citizens have cause for concern about air quality in the national park system. Recently, the National Park Service stated in response to congressional questions that "(m)onitoring data shows that no park unit in the lower forty-eight United States is 'pristine' with respect to air quality . . . (A)ir pollution causes some visibility impairment at all monitoring locations in the lower 48 states virtually all the time." [4] The Service has just begun monitoring in Hawaii and Alaska.

Poor visibility is not the only effect of air pollution documented in the parks. Hearings before the Subcommittee on National Parks and Recreation of the Committee on Interior and Insular Affairs revealed detailed examples of air pollution damage to aquatic resources, vegetation and forests, and cultural and material resources in the national park system. [5] In some parks, the air quality is so poor that there is concern for the health of the visitors. [6] A recent study by the National Parks and Conservation Association contains detailed references to the harm to many units of the system from acid rain, which is caused by emission of sulfur dioxide and nitrogen oxides--the pollutants responsible for much of the visibility impairment in the parks. [7] Air pollution decreases the visitor's ability to enjoy the parks since the ability to see beautiful vistas and breathe clean air are important values. Air pollution is also harming many of the natural and cultural resources of the parks.

This chapter describes how the two aspects of Part C, the prevention of significant deterioration of air quality (PSD) and the visibility provisions, apply and how they can be used to protect park air quality resources. The Clean Air Act provides several opportunites for citizen involvement in the processes that determine the protections afforded the parks from the adverse effects of air pollution. A discussion of the shortcomings of the PSD and visibility provisions and suggestions on how the Clean Air Act should be amended to improve the program are also included.

A note of caution at the outset: The Clean Air Act is a complicated statute not readily given to simplification. The words of Judge Irving R. Kaufman at the beginning of a decision involving the PSD provisions illustrate this:

> These challenges to a final ruling of the Environmental Protection Agency call upon us to steer a course through the labyrinth that is the Clean Air Act. Few statutes present more complex problems for the nation's courts than this 120-page treatise designed to safeguard our precious air resources. And, fewer are more important.[8]

II. THE PREVENTION OF SIGNIFICANT DETERIORATION OF AIR QUALITY

Two levels of overall air quality standards exist in the Clean Air Act. The primary national ambient air quality standards (NAAQS) are air quality standards that the Environmental Protection Agency has determined are necessary to protect public health.[9] The secondary NAAQS are designed to protect public welfare, which "includes, but is not limited to, effects on soils, water, crops, vegetation, man-made materials, animals, wildlife, weather, visibility, and climate, damage to and deterioration of property, and hazards to transportation, as well as effects on economic values and on personal comfort and well-being."[10] The prevention of significant deterioration provisions go beyond the NAAQS to protect public health and welfare.[11]

The PSD provisions contained in Subpart 1 of Part C apply to certain parks and wilderness areas and those air quality regions that meet, or are better than, the national ambient air quality standards--the "clean air areas." In addition to certain public lands and clean air areas, the PSD provisions also apply to air quality regions that cannot be classified as either attainment (meeting the NAAQS) or nonattainment (failing to meet the NAAQS).[12] They do not apply in nonattainment areas.

The PSD provisions divide lands into different "classes" for defining the levels of protection provided for existing air quality. Only specified increases (increments) over baseline concentrations of sulfur dioxide and particulate matter are permitted.[13] The

Act contemplates that the PSD provisions would apply to other pollutants, specifically hydrocarbons, carbon monoxide, photochemical oxidants, nitrogen oxides, and any other pollutant for which a national ambient air quality standard has been promulgated[14] and Congress directed EPA to establish a program to prevent the significant deterioration of air quality by these specified pollutants. EPA, however, has not done so. This failure to act, specifically on the nitrogen oxide increments, has limited the effectiveness of the PSD program as a park protection measure (and generally as a program to keep clean air areas clean). Nitrogen oxides are a precursor of acid rain and a factor in the regional haze that obscures the visibility in many national parks. As a result of a lawsuit by the Sierra Club Legal Defense Fund, EPA has been ordered to promulgate regulations for a PSD program for nitrogen oxides by October 1988.[15] The centerpiece of the PSD program is a permitting requirement for new or modified sources. The PSD provisions require consideration of the diverse resources within an air quality region or a specified unit, that is, a national park or wilderness area, and whether a proposed new source will have an effect on them.[16] EPA has authority to prevent or correct a violation of the increments, but the states manage the consumption of allowable increases.[17] This assumes that the state has been delegated PSD authority because its state implementation plan (SIP) contains adequate measures to prevent the significant deterioration of air quality in its clean air areas. If the state has not been granted the PSD authority, EPA regulations are incorporated by reference into the plans and EPA administers the PSD program for that state.[18] A permit may not be granted if the NAAQS would be exceeded in the clean air areas.[19]

The Clean Air Act is based on the notion of "cooperative federalism." Congress intended that states take the lead in preventing the potential deterioration of air quality in their clean air areas while permitting industrial growth.[20] Section 161 requires that the SIPs contain emission limits and such other measures as necessary to keep these areas relatively clean.[21] States have flexibility in selecting measures, in addition to the permitting requirement, to prevent deterioration of air quality, since other sources and factors could be responsible for adverse impacts on park air quality or a violation of the PSD standards.[22]

This chapter describes the PSD program as federal statutes and regulations govern it and how federal courts have interpreted it. It is essential, however, for park activists to be familiar with their own state's implementation plan when the state has been delegated PSD authority, as most states have. PSD regulations in most states are similar to the EPA regulations but the implementation plans describe in detail the state's strategy for preventing the significant deterioration of air quality in its clean air areas. The failure of a state to follow its approved plan would give rise to a cause of action against the state to comply with the CAA.[23] Further, the SIP process is on-going: states are required to reevaluate their PSD programs.[24] Park defenders who participate in a state's development of its SIP can facilitate the development of SIPs that favor the protection and enhancement of park air quality resources.

A. Designation of Class and the Redesignation Process

Not all units of the national park system are treated the same under the Clean Air Act. The 1977 amendments provide more specific protections for Class I areas--larger natural area parks and park wilderness areas--than for other classes. There are currently forty-eight Class I areas in the national park system.[25] The additional protections stem not only from the fact that smaller amounts of additional pollution from certain new stationary sources are allowed under the PSD increments but also from the mandated role of the federal land manager (FLM) in the permitting process. The visibility protections under section 169A of the Clean Air Act apply only to mandatory Class I areas.[26]

All international parks, units of the National Wilderness System larger than five thousand acres, national memorial parks larger than five thousand acres, and national parks larger than six thousand acres that were in existence on August 7, 1977, were designated Class I areas. These Class I areas cannot be redesignated to a lower class and are referred to as "mandatory" Class I areas. Other areas designated as Class I before August 7, 1977, were to remain Class I but they could be redesignated by the states. All other lands in attainment areas were to be designated Class II.[27]

The statute specifies the additional increases of pollutants that could be permitted as long as the NAAQS are not exceeded.[28] The increases are smallest for Class I and become progressively larger, allowing for more development, through Class II and Class III. For example, the 24-hour maximum allowable increase for particulate matter in Class II areas (37 micrograms per cubic meter) is almost four times greater than the allowable increase for Class I areas (10 micrograms per cubic meter). The Class III increment (75 micrograms per cubic meter) is almost eight times the Class I increment.[29]

States were given the authority to redesignate lands except for the mandatory Class I lands and some lands controlled by Indian tribes. Certain areas of the national park system that exceed ten thousand acres may be redesignated only to Class I or Class II. Other areas may be redesignated to Class III.[30]

All redesignations require notice and public hearing in the areas proposed for redesignation and in areas that may be affected by it. The health, environmental, economic, social, and energy effects of the redesignation must be analyzed and considered by the decision maker.[31] Before a public hearing on redesignation, the EPA Administrator is required to make available any specific plans for new or modified major emitting facilities that may be permitted if a redesignation to Class III is approved.[32] A Class III redesignation also requires the approval of the governor of the state, as well as consultation with various state governmental units. Redesignations may not affect maximum allowable concentrations of air pollutants in other areas.[33]

If the area proposed for redesignation includes federal lands, the state must provide written notice to the appropriate federal land manager, that is, the secretary of the department managing the area,[34] who must be given the opportunity to confer with the state and submit written comments and recommendations.[35] States are not bound by the recommendations of the FLM, but if a state chooses to ignore these recommendations, it must provide an explanation of its failure to follow the FLM's advice concerning redesignation.[36]

Indian governing bodies have authority to redesignate tribal lands[37] and to date the only redesignations to Class I of any lands have been accomplished by them. Under both the redesignation and permitting processes, if the state disagrees with an Indian tribe's determination or if the tribe disagrees with a state determination, the decision may be appealed to the EPA Administrator. The Administrator's resolution then becomes part of the applicable plan.[38]

The 1977 Amendments to the Clean Air Act directed the federal land manager to review all national monuments, primitive areas, and national preserves and recommend for redesignation as

Class I areas where air quality-related values (AQRVs) are important to the purposes of the area.[39] For redesignation recommendations, the Secretary of the Interior defined "air quality-related values" as "all those values possessed by an area except those that are not affected by changes in air quality and include all those assets of an area whose vitality, significance, or integrity is dependent in some way upon the air environment. These values include visibility and those scenic, cultural, biological, and recreational resources of an area that are affected by air quality."[40] To assess whether the air quality-related values were important attributes of the area, the Secretary used the following standard: "Important attributes of an area are those values or assets that make an area significant as a national monument, preserve, or primitive area. They are the assets that are to be preserved if the area is to achieve the purposes for which it was set aside." [41]

The Secretary of the Interior reviewed eighty-two national monuments and two national preserves in the National Park System and the eleven primitive areas administered by the Bureau of Land Management in 1980. After reviewing the ninety-five study areas, the Secretary found that forty-four possessed air quality related values as important attributes and recommended that they be designated to Class I.[42] The areas that generated the most opposition from those who feared redesignation to Class I would hamper development were Scotts Bluff National Monument, Chaco Canyon National Monument,[43] and Congaree Swamp National Monument, none of which was ultimately recommended for redesignation.[44] Of the forty-four areas that were recommended for redesignation by the Secretary, none has been redesignated to Class I by the states.

The National Clean Air Coalition, a coalition of national environmental, health, and religious groups and unions, has been urging Congress to take action on the recommended redesignations because these areas are nationally significant and deserving of the highest degree of protection. Congress has declined to take action. The National Clean Air Coalition also supports the redesignation to Class I of several parks created after 1977 and several parts of parks that were added to Class I parks after 1977.[45] Lands added to parks do not automatically become Class I even if the park they were added to may have been Class I. Further, national monuments containing Class I areas should be designated Class I in their entireties. The relatively small number of parks classified as Class I, the fact that there is only one Class I park in Alaska (the part of Denali National Park and Preserve that was previously Mount McKinley National Park), and the situation that allows different lands in the same park to be classified differently limits the effectiveness of the PSD program as a park protection measure.

Since states have authority to redesignate lands to Class I and Congress has failed to act, park activists should consider petitioning their state governments to improve protections for park air quality resources by redesignating park lands to a higher class. As is described later in more detail, redesignation to Class I does not prevent development in an area; it limits the amount of additional pollution permitted and requires new stationary sources to use the best available technology to control pollution. Park activists should also be vigilant and participate in proceedings that may seek to redesignate lands to a lower class. The federal land manager has a limited, advisory role in the redesignation process, but the principal defenders of the air quality of park units continue to be local park activists.

B. The PSD Permitting Process

The PSD permitting provisions are triggered when an individual or corporation requests a permit to construct a "major emitting facility"[46] in a clean air area.[47] "Major emitting facility" is defined in some detail in the CAA.[48] It includes particularly dirty stationary sources that emit at least one hundred tons of air pollutants per year and any sources that have the potential to emit two hundred fifty tons per year of any pollutant.[49] "Any pollutant" is not limited to sulfur dioxide or particulate matter; it can even include pollutants that are not otherwise regulated by the CAA.[50]

In determining whether a source will emit or have the potential to emit the specified tonnage of pollutants, EPA must consider the effects of the facility's pollution control devices. "The potential to emit" refers to the plant's operating at full capacity with designed controls; it is not the potential to emit if pollution controls were not in the design.[51]

The term "source" includes any building, structure, facility, or installation that emits or may emit any air pollutant.[52] In its original regulations governing PSD permits, EPA had included in its definition of "source" "equipment, operation, or combination thereof." Industry argued that this interpretation was too expansive and would subject too many industrial activities to PSD review. The court in *Alabama Power Co. v. Costle* found that the definition should be consistent with the definition of stationary source found in the new-source performance standards of the CAA and should not include the disputed terms.[53]

"Construction" is broadly defined in the CAA to include modifications.[54] "Modification" means "any physical change in, or change in the method of operation of, a stationary source which increases the amount of any air pollutant emitted by such source or which results in the emission of any air pollutant not previously emitted."[55]

States have the power to exempt new or modified facilities of nonprofit health or educational institutions.[56] This exemption reflects Congress' desire to save these entities whatever costs are associated with a PSD review.[57] Generally, however, economic considerations, such as cost to the applicant, are not relevant in deciding whether a PSD permit is required.[58]

At the time the first permit is filed, the baseline concentration of each pollutant in the area is determined.[59] This is based on air quality data from EPA, the state air pollution board, and monitoring required of the applicant.[60] Maximum allowable increases of sulfur oxide and particulate matter are figured from this baseline. The Act contemplates that only certain specified amounts of pollutants be permitted over the established baseline; the baseline does not change once it has been established. Thus, if a state has approved a number of PSD permits, the entire increment could be exhausted and additional PSD permit requests would have to be denied. This is particularly important as far as parks are concerned since a fairly large number of permits in areas of Class I parks have already been approved.

It is important that the baseline area defined by the state be as large as possible and the baseline be set as early as possible. This is necessary to prevent "air pollution creep," which occurs as minor sources increase in numbers. EPA proposed that the baseline be the air quality as it existed on August 7, 1977, (the date of enactment of the CAA Amendments) for all the areas where the PSD provisions apply. The court in *Alabama Power* found that approach inconsistent with the statute and required EPA to adopt rules for setting the baselines as the permits are requested.[61] States are free, however, to set different baselines. While states may not adopt standards more lenient than those specified in the Clean Air Act, they may generally adopt measures that are stricter than federal requirements.[62]

Section 165 of the Act outlines the information necessary for a permit for a major emitting facility.[63] Generally the applicant must demonstrate that the facility will not cause or contribute to air pollution in excess of the NAAQS in any region, the PSD increments more than once a year, or any other applicable standard under the CAA.

The facility must be subject to the best available control technology (BACT) for each pollutant regulated under the CAA.[64] BACT is determined on a case-by-case basis by the permitting authority (either the state or EPA). Just because a certain technology is considered BACT for one source does not mean it will be BACT for another similar source.[65] The decision maker must weigh the energy, environmental, and economic impacts before reaching a decision on the appropriate technology for controlling emissions of pollutants from the source. The potential for adverse impacts on a national park can be a compelling argument for stringent BACT. BACT must be at least as effective in reducing pollutants as any standards promulgated for new stationary sources or hazardous air pollutants under the Clean Air Act.[66]

The permit application for each major new source must contain preconstruction monitoring data for one year unless complete and adequate analysis is possible in a shorter time frame (not less than four months).[67] Once the application is complete, Section 165 mandates that it be acted upon within one year.[68]

Each state with authority to administer its PSD program must notify the EPA Administrator of each application filed for a permit under the PSD provisions and keep the Administrator informed of every action related to the application.[69] If the proposed facility might affect Class I areas under federal management, the Administrator must notify the federal land manager and the federal official with direct responsibility for management of the area (in situations involving parks, the superintendent).[70] The statute does not mandate a role for the federal land manager and the superintendent in the permitting process if the lands involved are designated Class II or III. Section 165(d)(2)(B) charges the federal land manager and the superintendent with an affirmative responsibility to protect the air quality-related values (AQRVs)--specifically including visibility--of the Class I lands.[71] Congress intended that the AQRVs include all the fundamental purposes for which such lands were established and preserved.[72] When considering a PSD permit request, the Department of the Interior considers air quality-related values to include visibility, odor, flora, fauna, and geological, archeological, historical, and other cultural resources, and soils and water quality resources.[73]

C. The Adverse Impact Test

The CAA requires the FLM and the superintendent to determine, in consultation with the Administrator, whether the proposed facility will have an adverse impact on the AQRVs of the Class I area.[74] This is perhaps the key park protection provision in the PSD provisions for Class I areas. The federal land manager considers an adverse impact to be one that:

- Diminishes the national significance of the area

- Impairs the structure and functioning of ecosystems or

- Impairs the quality of visitor experience[75]

The Department of the Interior has further determined that an analysis of the "projected frequency, magnitude, duration, location and reversibility"[76] of the effects must be made before determining if they are adverse. This is accomplished by answering the following questions:

1. Will the effects last long enough and/or occur frequently enough to impair the structure and functioning of ecosystems in the park, impair visitor experience or diminish the national significance of the area?

2. Will the effects occur on a scale large enough to impair the structure and functioning of the ecosystems in the park, impair visitor experience or diminish the national significance of the area?

3. Are the effects reversible if the stress causing them is removed?[77]

After the air quality-related values have been identified and an analysis made of the effect on them of the additional pollution, there are three tests specified to determine if the permit affecting a Class I area will be granted:

1. If the FLM, the superintendent, the Administrator, or the governor of an adjacent state containing the Class I area determines the facility *may* cause or contribute to a change in the air quality and identifies the potential adverse impact of the change, the permit will not be granted unless the owners demonstrate that emissions of particulate matter and sulfur dioxide will not cause or contribute to concentrations that exceed the maximum allowable increases for a Class I area.[78]

2. If the FLM determines that the facility *will* have an adverse impact on the AQRVs and the state or EPA agrees, the permit may not be approved even if the emissions will not exceed the Class I increments.[79]

3. If the FLM certifies that the emissions *will not* have an adverse impact on the AQRVs, even if the emissions will cause or contribute to concentrations that exceed the maximum allowable increases for a Class I area, the state or EPA may issue a permit.[80] In this case, the Act specifies increases which may not be exceeded in any event.[81] This test will become more important as PSD permits are approved and more of the maximum allowable increases are used.

If the FLM declines to certify that the AQRVs will not be adversely affected by the proposed new source, the applicant may appeal to the governor. If after notice and public hearing, the governor finds that the facility cannot be constructed without violating the twenty-four-hour or three-hour sulfur dioxide standards and that a variance from the standards will not adversely affect AQRVs, a permit may be granted if the FLM concurs.[82] If the FLM does not agree with the governor, the final decision is made by the President and it is not reviewable in any court.[83] The variances under this section from the normal PSD increments are limited and may not occur more than eighteen days per year.[84]

The Department of the Interior has promulgated internal procedures for determination of the adverse impact test under sections 165(d)(2)(C)(ii) and (iii), situations where the FLM has found adverse impacts and where the increments would be exceeded and the FLM has been requested by the applicants to certify that there will not be an adverse impact.[85] These procedures are designed to provide a checklist for the bureaus within the department and to provide for public participation in some adverse impact determinations. Public participation is accomplished by submitting a notice of preliminary determination in the Federal Register and allowing a thirty-day public comment period.[86]

Approximately two hundred applications for PSD permits have been submitted for review to the National Park Service, which handles the applications that may affect lands managed by the Fish and Wildlife Service as well as those managed by the Park Service. The federal land manager has never found that there will be an adverse impact on the AQRVs of a Class I area in a PSD permitting review.

D. Case Study: Certification of No Adverse Impact at Theodore Roosevelt National Park

The most controversial of the PSD permit requests involving Class I lands managed by the National Park Service involved Theodore Roosevelt National Park and Lostwood National Wildlife Refuge in North Dakota. This request was problematic because the applicants requested a certification of no adverse impact. Six PSD permit applications (for two power plants, three natural gas processing plants, and one coal-to-methanol plant) were submitted in 1982 to North Dakota, which had been delegated PSD authority. Regional scale modeling performed by the state showed that sulfur dioxide concentrations in Theodore Roosevelt Park would be as high as 3.8 times the twenty-four hour increment and 1.6 times the three-hour increment.[87] Since the increments would be exceeded, five of the six applicants elected to proceed under section 165(d)(2)(C)(iii) by requesting certification from the FLM that the proposed sources would have no adverse impact on the resources in the park.

Review by the Department of the Interior revealed that the increased concentrations of sulfur dioxide would not have any effects on most plant and animal species in the park. The increased pollution could, however, affect two species of lichens. Analysis also showed that there would be some effects on visibility but it was found to be a 2 percent decrease in the standard visual range, which is believed to be below the threshold limit for human observation.[88] The federal land manager determined that the increased pollution would have very little impact, and no adverse impact, on either the park or the wildlife refuge.[89]

Several groups, including the National Parks and Conservation Association, the Environmental Defense Fund, and the Sierra Club, challenged the department's findings on both procedural and substantive grounds. On procedural grounds, commentators argued that the action of the FLM in certifying no adverse impact required an Environmental Impact Statement or an Environmental Assessment under the National Environmental Policy Act (NEPA). The department responded that the action was not a "major Federal action significantly affecting the environment," which is a necessary finding before NEPA applies, and even if it were, it would be exempted from NEPA requirements by the Energy Supply and Environmental Coordination Act of 1974.[90]

Commentators also requested an adjudicatory hearing on the adverse impact determination by the department. This was denied because the Clean Air Act requires the state to have the public hearing with notice and an opportunity to be heard. If the FLM also had a hearing it would be duplicative and would slow the process.[91]

In the technical review prepared for the initial finding of no adverse impact, the FLM described the applicants' proposed BACT and made comments regarding its sufficiency.[92] When commentators questioned BACT discussions, the FLM responded that BACT did not enter into his determination of no adverse impact. The department's recommendations on BACT would be submitted to the state, but the state has responsibility to determine BACT requirements after weighing all energy, economic, and environmental concerns.[93]

A commentator argued that the standard should be that "an adverse impact on air quality related values must include any changes in the physical, chemical, or biological environment (other than changes in air quality) which measurably or predictably modify the natural environment of the park."[94] The department rejected this argument because any changes that do not diminish the national significance of the area, impair the functioning of the ecosystem, or impair the quality of the visitor experience are minor and acceptable. The department found that the changes in the environment that would result from the sources in question were based upon a "worst case analysis" with ample margins of safety for park protection and may not occur at all. Arguments that any changes in visibility should be considered adverse were rejected on the basis of EPA visibility regulations which define an adverse impact on visibility as one that occurs to such an extent or with such intensity, duration, or frequency as to interfere with the preservation of the area or with the visitor's visual enjoyment of the area.[95]

NPCA argued that reversibility was an inappropriate factor to consider, because every visitor to the park was entitled to enjoy it without experiencing degradation of park values. A diminution in values that could be reversed in twenty years should be considered an adverse impact. The FLM responded that "reversibility" was one of the factors considered by the FLM in determining the magnitude and scope of potential effects but it is not one of the three criteria for adverse impact determinations (diminish the national significance, impair the functioning of the ecosystem, impair the quality of visitor experience).[96]

Several commentators questioned the vegetation effects methodology. The FLM responded that this was not a case of elimination of an entire lichen species (which the notice implies would be an adverse impact presumably under the standard that it would impair the functioning of the ecosystem) but rather the potential for the temporary disappearance of a few individual lichens. Again, the FLM relied on its analysis that the projected effects may not even occur because the department used worst case assumptions, and that even if they did occur, they would be minimal, extremely limited in scope and magnitude, temporary, and reversible.[97]

Commentators also questioned the FLM's methodology for determining visibility impairment and the standard the department was applying. In analyzing whether a visibility impairment is an adverse impact, the FLM takes into account the magnitude, duration, and frequency of the occurrence of perceptible visibility impairment as it may affect the scenic features of the area that are important to either the national significance or the visitor's enjoyment of the area. The fact that there is a perceptible impairment does not necessarily mean that an adverse impact will be found.[98]

The groups opposed to the department's findings did not pursue a court challenge to the decision to certify that there would be no adverse impact on the air quality-related values at Theodore Roosevelt National Park from the proposed major stationary sources. The case is interesting because it illustrates the process that the department will apply in reviewing PSD permit requests and the kinds of arguments that park activists must be prepared to make if they wish to challenge a PSD permit request.

Several points raised in the proceedings merit consideration beyond the facts in the Theodore Roosevelt National Park PSD decision. The Organic Act of the National Park Service finds that the primary purpose for the establishment of the Service "is to conserve the scenery and the natural and historic objects and the wild life therein and to provide for the enjoyment of the same in such manner and by such means as will leave them unimpaired for the enjoyment of future generations."[99] The Organic Act suggests that any change in the ecosystem of the park at issue that might be caused by the additional pollution of the permit applicant should be considered an adverse impact. The standard used by the Park Service now--that the effects last long enough, occur often enough, and are large enough to impair the structure and functioning of the ecosystem--is not consistent with its mandate to preserve the areas. The science of how an ecosystem functions is not exact enough for a determination that a change in the ecosystem is not large enough to be considered adverse. A change should be considered adverse if it does not leave the park unimpaired for future generations. Parks have become increasingly important as biological monitoring stations, and to serve in this function they must be afforded protection from adverse environmental changes.

The department's certification of no adverse impact was based on the two findings that the changes would probably occur even if the permit requests were not granted and that the applicants would contribute little additional pollution. The intent of the Clean Air Act is to draw the line on additional pollution in Class I areas. If the applicant will contribute additional pollution, even small amounts of additional pollution, and an adverse impact on park AQRVs may occur, it is not permissible for the FLM to certify that there will be no adverse impact on the grounds that existing sources do most of the damage, and damage would occur in any event.

Another problem with the FLM's approach to determining adverse impact is that the FLM has not inventoried all the resources of every park. Unless one knonws what exists in the park, it is difficult to make a determination of possible effects of additional pollution. To carry out their responsibilities under the Clean Air

Act, the FLMs should seek adequate funding levels so that a careful inventory of all the resources in the different park units and other areas subject to the Act can be accomplished.

III. SECTION 169A OF THE CLEAN AIR ACT: VISIBILITY PROTECTIONS

The 1977 Amendments to the Clean Air Act also included Section 169A, which addresses poor visibility caused by air pollution in mandatory Class I areas. Congress declared "the prevention of any future, and the remedying of any existing, impairment of visibility" by man-made air pollution in these areas to be a national goal.[100] Congress deemed this section necessary because other safeguards--the NAAQS and the PSD increments--were not sufficient to protect Class I areas from visibility deterioration. Testimony presented at congressional hearings suggested that even limited additional pollution in Class I areas could result in significant reductions in visual range. For example, EPA found that "particulate levels meeting the secondary standards would decrease visibility in areas like the Grand Canyon to only 12.5 miles. Visibility would be reduced further to 3-4 miles during high humidity, even when the ambient standards are met."[101] Further, the PSD provisions cover only new stationary sources located in clean air areas. Congress realized that existing sources and new sources located in nonattainment areas also caused poor visibility in many Class I areas. The visibility section was designed to fill these gaps with special protections to preserve the views in Class I areas.

Congress directed the Secretary of the Interior to review all Class I areas and identify those where visibility constituted an important value. The EPA Administrator was directed to promulgate the final listing of areas where the visibility protections would apply.[102] The Secretary evaluated the 158 Class I areas in 1978. He considered whether the area was established because it had scenic value, whether the scenic values contributed to visitor enjoyment, whether the views were in the foreground or the backround, if natural sources of haze affected visibility, and, if so, whether the scenic values still required protection from man-made pollution.[103] Ultimately, EPA listed 156 areas as having visibility as an important value.[104]

Section 169A requires the Administrator to promulgate regulations to provide guidance to the states on methods of identifying and measuring visibility impairment in the relevant areas, modeling techniques to determine the cause of the impairment, and methods to prevent and remedy visibility impairment.[105] These regulations must not require the use of buffer zones.[106]

States are required to amend their implementation plans to contain emission limits, schedules of compliance, and other measures necessary to meet the visibility regulations.[107] Congress specified that the new plans contain two elements. First, states are directed to include a requirement that major stationary sources, in existence in 1977 but not yet fifteen years old, whose emissions may reasonably be expected to affect visibility in a protected area install the best available retrofit technology (BART) to control their emissions.[108] Second, the plan must include a strategy for making reasonable progress toward achieving the national visibility goal within ten or fifteen years.[109] In determining "reasonable progress" such factors as "the costs of compliance, the time necessary for compliance, the energy and nonair quality environmental impacts of compliance, and the remaining useful life of any existing source subject to such requirements" must be considered.[110] Section 169A requires that the FLM be consulted on the plan revisions and that the FLM's conclusions and recommendations be summarized in the required notice to the public.[111]

The definition of "stationary source" was similar to the definition in the PSD provisions in terms of the industrial activities covered.[112] However, the term in the visibility section applies to those named sources that emit or have the potential to emit 250 tons of any pollutant rather than the 100-ton threshold in the PSD provisions. The definition does not include language covering any other sources that emit large amounts of pollutants except for those specified.

Best available retrofit technology determinations are made on a case-by-case basis, taking into consideration such factors as "the costs of compliance, the energy and nonair quality environmental impacts of compliance, any existing pollution control technology in use at the source, the remaining useful life of the source, and the degree of improvement in visibility which may reasonably be anticipated to result from the use of such technology."[113] States are required to apply BART to newer sources (less than fifteen years old in 1977) within the specified categories but they are also free to apply it to older existing sources if they choose to do so.[114]

The EPA Administrator was required to establish emission guidelines for fossil-fuel fired generating power plants with a total generating capacity in excess of 750 megawatts.[115] Additionally, the Administrator was given rule-making authority to exempt any major stationary source (except the covered power plants) from the BART requirements if the source demonstrates that it would not emit any pollutants that alone or in combination with any other pollutants would significantly impair visibility in the protected areas.[116] In the case of the covered power plants, they could be exempted if they showed that they were far enough away from the protected areas that their emission of pollutants would not alone, or in combination with other pollutants, significantly impair visibility in the protected areas.[117] Any exemption from BART proposed by the Administrator requires the concurrence of the FLM and the state.[118]

Section 169A could be an important tool for conservationists to use in protecting park visibility. Its usefulness has been curtailed, however, by EPA's slow progress in implementing its provisions. While there are some regulations in place, ten years after the Clean Air Act was amended to include specific visibility protections no source has ever been required to install BART, and the complex problem of regional haze has yet to be addressed by the agency. EPA has done little to remedy exising pollution obscuring the views from and in many of the nation's magnificent national parks.

A. EPA's Visibility Program--The 1980 Rulemaking

In 1980 EPA announced a "phased approach" to meeting the national visibility goal. Phase I required control of visibility impairment traceable to a single existing source or group of sources. To prevent future impairment, new sources would be permitted and limitations on their emissions imposed. States were also required to develop long-term strategies for making reasonable progress toward the national visibility goal. Future phases, to be developed when monitoring techniques improved, would contain regulations to address regional haze and urban plumes, the more complicated problems associated with visibility.[119] In the meantime, however, states could begin to address regional haze under their long-term strategies.[120]

The regulations cover the thirty-six states that contain mandatory Class I aread.[121] EPA did not list any state because emissions from its sources could affect a Class I area in another state. This is an erroneous decision if EPA is serious about controlling regional haze. However, to date, EPA has not proposed any regulations addressing this issue. Several states, particularly in the Midwest, suspected of allowing the pollution that causes regional haze are not covered by existing EPA visibility regulations. When and if EPA addresses the regional haze problem, all fifty states should be covered by the regulations.

In the 1980 rulemaking, EPA invited federal land managers to identify "integral vistas."[122] An "integral vista" is "a view perceived from within the mandatory Class I Federal area of a specific landmark or panorama located outside the boundary of the mandatory Class I Federal area."[123] These identifications would be forwarded to the states for incorporation into their visibility SIPs.

EPA required the thirty-six states containing Class I areas to amend their state implementation plans within nine months and ordered that the amendments assure reasonable progress toward achieving the national visibility goal. The states were also directed to determine which sources would be required to install BART and to add measures to assure that new sources would not have an adverse impact on visibility.[124]

For purposes of the new-source review, an "adverse impact" on visibility is defined as "visibility impairment which interferes with the management, protection, preservation, or enjoyment of the visitor's visual experience of the Federal Class I area. This determination must be made on a case-by-case basis taking into account the geographic extent, intensity, duration, frequency and time of the visibility impairments, and how these factors correlate with (1) times of visitor use of the Federal Class I area, and (2) the frequency and timing of natural conditions that reduce visibility."[125] This definition is troublesome in several respects. First, it specifically excludes adverse impacts on the ability to see and enjoy integral vistas important to many parks.[120] It is too subjective; the definition emphasizes the number of people who see the impairment, as if it were acceptable for some number to be subjected to poor visibility because of the time they visited the Class I area. Further, the definition is biased toward visitor perceptions. Visitors are often not the best judge of impairment because they do not have the opportunity to visit the particular park many times.

For this reason, they may have no reference point or perspective in judging incremental degradation over time. For example, a visitor seeing the Grand Canyon for the first time may be dazzled by it even on a day with poor visibility. However, it remains to be seen how EPA or the states will apply the adverse impact concept.

In the 1980 rulemaking EPA also outlined the steps necessary before a source could be required to install best available retrofit technology because its emissions were affecting visibility in a Class I area. EPA required the following procedures:[127]

- The state or the FLM determines if there is a visibility impairment. "Impairment" is defined as "any humanly perceptible change in visibility (visual range, contrast, coloration) from that which would exist under natural conditions."[128]

- The state identifies the source causing the impairment.

- The state performs a BART analysis. Most BART determinations would involve technologies designed to control particulate matter and nitrogen oxides. These two pollutants are responsible for much of the visibility impairment addressed by these regulations.[129] If even the most stringent controls will not improve visibility, the state does not have to require the source to install BART. BART would be expressed as an emission limitation for the source. The source would then have to operate enough controls to meet the limitation.[130]

- States must reanalyze BART if it is shown that pollutants other than the ones controlled by previous BART determinations are causing visibility impairment in a Class I area.

- The source may apply to EPA for an exemption if it shows that it does not significantly contribute to visibility impairment. "The frequency, extent, time, intensity and duration" of the impairment are considered and the federal land manager and the state must agree to the exemption.[131]

EPA also required the states to develop long-term strategies. In order to remedy existing impairment, states were to consider existing land use plans and air pollution control plans, additional emission limits on sources not covered by BART, and the retirement of existing sources.[132] EPA also required that the SIPs be reviewed by the state and the FLM every three years to determine progress made toward the national visibility goal.[133] This periodic review requirement provides an excellent opportunity for citizen involvement in the SIP process.

In order to prevent future impairment of visibility, under the authority of Section 169A EPA extended requirements for review of new sources. Permits would be required for all new sources meeting the threshold limits even if located in nonattainment areas if emissions from it might affect a Class I area. The regulations also covered new sources regardless of location that might affect an identified integral vista. However, unlike the PSD review for new sources affecting visibility in a Class I area, states could consider costs in determining the level of protection for integral vistas. There is a different standard for intergral vistas because they are protected under the long-term strategy for making reasonable progress toward the national visibility goal. Section 169A requires that costs be considered when fashioning strategies to meet the national visibility goal. The requirement for new-source permitting closes a loophole caused by the *Alabama Power Co.* ruling that the PSD program may not cover sources that will be located in nonattainment areas.

The regulations also specified that the state must notify the FLM in a timely manner of any permit requests. If the FLM advises the state within thirty days of receiving notification that the proposed source may have an impact on visibility in a Class I area, the state must provide an explanation of its failure to agree with the FLM's determination.[134] This implies that the state must have a reasonable basis for its failure to adopt the recommendations of the FLM.

B. Actions Following the 1980 Rulemaking

Protection of visibility values in Class I areas has not progressed in the manner contemplated by the 1980 EPA rulemaking. Federal land managers evaluated the Class I areas to determine if there were integral vistas associated with them that should be protected. The primary considerations for making these determinations were the legislation establishing the unit and whether the view contributed to the visitor's enjoyment of the area. In a preliminary listing, the National Park Service identified approximately 170 vistas associated with 43 of the 48 Park Service mandatory Class I areas.[135] The list was never finalized. In 1985, Secretary of the Interior Donald Hodel announced that "designation of integral vistas would not be good for the parks."[136] Heavy pressure from development groups and Western governors and senators opposed to listing of integral vistas may have played a role in the Secretary's finding that "most states already have discretion to identify and protect vistas. That means that States can achieve the goal of visibility protection without additional regulations by the Department of the Interior . . . Issuing final integral vistas regulations would only serve to create a confrontational atmosphere for the public and private interests involved. State resentment and objection would likely lead to prolonged litigation during which time our entire protection effort would be in doubt."[137]

The protection of integral vistas remains a high priority for environmental groups. A unit of the National Park System is established for all Americans and for future generations, not only for the residents of the particular state where it is located. Further, there are many instances in the legislative histories establishing various units of the system where congressional intent to protect the views from and around the area was the primary reason for establishing it as a national park.[138] The federal government should protect the stunning views from our great national treasures.

In any event, the Secretary's view misconstrues the role of the FLM. Under current law and EPA regulations, it is clearly appropriate for federal land managers to identify integral vistas and to describe the benefits of protecting them. This would be useful to industry so that siting and planning decisions for new sources could take them into consideration. But the listing of integral vistas would not require the states to adopt any particular level of protection for them. The state would have to consider protecting the vistas, but it could decide that other factors, such as the need for economic development, outweighed the benefit of protecting the vista. For example, Roosevelt Campobello International Park, a mandatory Class I area, has four integral vistas identified for Clean Air Act purposes by its FLM, the chairman of the Roosevelt Campobello International Park Commission.[139] In approving the final identification of the vistas, EPA reassured the state of Maine that "if the FLM ever objected to discharges from existing fish processing plants on the ground that they caused impairment of visibility, the State of Maine could override the objection based on the economic needs of the community."[140]

Persons interested in assuring the highest levels of protection for the important views from the parks should be involved with the implementation plan process in their states. EPA regulations require a public hearing before visibility requirements are adopted under the SIP process,[141] and the state's strategy meeting the national visibility goal must be reexamined at least every three years.[142] States are free to designate integral vistas and provide protections for them, and citizens should press them to do so. Alaska and Washington have already designated integral vistas in their approved SIPs. Utah and Maine are in the process of identifying integral vistas and the level of protection they will be given.

Even though EPA's 1980 rulemaking specified that SIPs be revised within nine months of the regulation's effective date (which would have been September 1981),[143] EPA took no action to enforce the regulations or to move forward with the other phases of its visibility program. By 1982 only one state (Alaska) had submitted a SIP that contained a visibility protection plan.[144] That same year, the National Parks and Conservation Association and the Environmental Defense Fund sued EPA for its failure to take action on the states' failure to propose visibility protection plans.[145] EPA had no defense and the case was settled. The agency agreed to specific deadlines for completion of its review of the SIPs.[146]

C. The 1985 Rulemaking--New-Source Reviews and Monitoring

In the first phase of the settlement agreement, EPA promulgated federal rules for visibility new-source reviews and monitoring for those states that had failed to revise their SIPs in accordance with EPA's 1980 requirements.[147] The agency made it clear that it was doing so under protest. EPA is most anxious to delegate responsibility to the states for the visibility protection program at the earliest possible moment.[148]

EPA's monitoring network is a cooperative effort between EPA and the FLMs. The monitoring is designed to establish both background visibility in the protected areas and reasonably attributable visibility impairment caused by a source or group of sources. The monitoring must be "sufficient for use in determining the potential effects of a new stationary source on visibility in the area, the stationary source or sources that are causing any visibility impairment, and progress toward remedying that impairment."[149] The plans for monitoring in each area and the monitoring data are available for public inspection,[150] and each year the monitoring plans are to be reviewed by the Administrator. Any person at any time may request a change in the monitoring plan. These requests are to be acted upon within one year.[151] Additionally, applicants for permits could be required to monitor air quality in the Class I areas near the proposed site for development.[152]

The 1985 rulemaking amended EPA's PSD regulations to include a new-source review regardless of where the source proposed to locate. EPA outlined three separate approaches depending on whether the state had permitting authority and where the source proposed to locate. Separate programs were established for states where the state or EPA administered the PSD program through delegation of the federal program, for states with approved state PSD programs, and for states with nonattainment areas.[153]

The rulemaking clarified that in evaluating a proposed new source's impact on visibility the permitting authority must consider both existing sources and permitted but not constructed sources as part of the existing background. The permitting authority must address the cumulative impacts of the sources and their impacts on visibility.[154]

EPA also made clear that the FLMs do not have sole authority to determine "adverse impact." The responsibility is shared between the FLM and the permitting authority but the final decision rests with the permitting authority. A permitting authority may reject the determination of the FLM but there must be a rational basis for the rejection. The FLM's expertise is to be given some deference.[155]

D. 1987 Proposed Rulemaking--BART and Long-Term Plans

As required by its 1982 settlement agreement, on March 12, 1987, EPA issued a notice of proposed rulemaking. This action of the agency, if finalized in its present form, would disapprove the SIPs of thirty-two states for failing to comply with EPA visibility regulations regarding impairment that may be traced to a specific source and for failure to develop a long-term plan to improve visibility. EPA proposes to incorporate federal requirements into those states' SIPs.[156]

EPA began the process of determining if its plan for an individual state would require the application of BART by requesting the FLMs to identify visibility impairment in the class I protected areas and associated integral vistas. The Department of the Interior responded that "scenic views are affected by uniform haze at all NPS monitoring locations within the lower 48 States. Furthermore, the DOI identified nine Class I areas where impairment in the park may be traceable to specific sources."[157]

EPA's proposed regulations seem to require a "smoking stack." The requirements for finding a visibility impairment are stringent --the frequency, duration, time of day or year of the impairment, the type of impairment, the location of the observer, the observed impairment, and the weather must be documented. In some cases, it may be necessary to characterize the aerosols, to perform modeling, and to photograph from the air or land. Additionally, EPA requires information on the frequency and severity of the episodes so that the anticipated improvement from application of BART may be estimated.[158] If there are a large number of major, minor, and urban sources, it is unlikely that EPA that will determine any one of them contributes significantly to the poor visibility.[159] If the impairment is attributable to minor stationary sources or prescription burning, improvement should be addressed as part of the long-term strategy rather than BART.[160]

EPA did not find the Interior Department's information adequate to determine that BART should be applied. In some cases, EPA found that the impairment was occurring in an integral vista and not within the boundary of the park. Since the department never finalized its list of integral vistas, EPA did not have to consider protecting them. In other cases, there were several sources that could have been causing the impairment. Poor visibility caused by regional haze is not addressed by existing regulations. In the four areas[161] where the FLM certified there was impairment, EPA deferred action until August, 1988 because there was not sufficient information to make a determination about the source causing the poor visibility. For five of the Class I areas,[162] EPA found that there was insufficient documentation that the impairment was within the park's boundaries. In two areas, Brigantine Wilderness, New Jersey, and Cape Romain Wilderness, South Carolina, EPA found that there were several sources that could be causing the impairment, including several urban areas. BART would not be required by EPA to remedy the visibility problems in Tuxedni Wilderness in Alaska because Alaska has an approved visibility SIP. EPA agreed to forward the information to Alaska for consideration by the state when it next reevaluated its visibility plan.[163]

EPA also proposed to disapprove the SIPs of thirty-two states for failure to develop a long-term strategy to make reasonable progress toward achieving the national visibility goal. The strategy must address any impairment to the visibility of a Class I area or an integral vista properly identified and certified by the FLM at least six months before the plan is submitted to EPA for approval. EPA specifies six measures that must be considered before a SIP could be approved:

1. Emission reductions due to ongoing air pollution control programs

2. Additional emission limitations and schedules for compliance

3. Measures to mitigate the impact of construction activities

4. Source retirement and replacement schedules

5. Smoke management techniques for agricultural and forestry management purposes, including such plans as currently exist within the state for these purposes, and

6. Enforcement of emission limitations and control measures.[164]

For the federal long-term program that EPA will establish for states without an approved SIP, EPA relies on prevention of future impairment through the new-source review procedures.[165] EPA considers smoke to be a cause of poor visibility in some protected areas. Through the National Wildfire Coordinating Group and a working group of the Forest Service, Interior, and EPA, EPA is attempting to develop a national program to improve smoke management.[166] Since EPA is deferring action on existing impairments, the federal program will not consider additional emission limitations, source retirement, construction activities, and enforceability of emission limitations.[167] The states, however, are free to utilize these steps in formulating their SIPs.

EPA believes that this long-term strategy is sufficient to address the certifications of impairment made by the FLMs before June 1, 1986. EPA notes, however, that the FLM may certify impairment at any time.[168] If additional certifications are made, EPA or the state, if it has an approved visibility SIP, may have to reconsider requirements for BART or other control methods.[169]

In the March 12, 1987, notice of proposed rulemaking, EPA discussed integral vistas. Two states (Alaska and Washington) have identified and protected integral vistas, and their SIPs have been approved by EPA. The only integral vistas identified by a FLM (because the FLM is not the Secretary of the Interior or Agriculture) are the ones associated with Roosevelt Campobello International Park. These vistas look out over the state of Maine and EPA is proposing to disapprove Maine's SIP for failure to consider protection for the vistas. EPA also is proposing new regulations to govern consideration of a new-source or major modification that may have an adverse effect on visibility in an integral vista when the state does not have an approved SIP. The regulations require coordination with the FLM. If the permitting authority agrees with a determination by the FLM that the source will affect visibility in an integral vista, the permitting authority may issue permits to those sources whose emissions are consistent with the national visibility goal, but economic costs may be considered.[170]

IV. SUMMARY AND RECOMMENDATIONS

Air quality is deteriorating in many of our irreplacable parks. Conservationists must be vigilant, both to protect against new sources of pollution that could affect park air quality and to press for action on existing sources of pollution. Legislation is also needed to improve existing law.

At this time, the most important forum for conservationists to address park air quality issues, including visibility, is the SIP development process for their states. The federal agencies with the most authority to respond to the poor and in many cases deteriorating air quality in the parks are the Environmental Protection Agency and the Department of the Interior. These agencies have demonstrated their reluctance to use their authorities aggressively and have continually expressed their desire to have the states handle the requirements of the Clean Air Act to the greatest extent possible.

It is essential for the conservation community to be familar with the individual state agency responsible for the state's air quality. Get on the mailing list and be familar with the SIP and its status, for example, whether it has an approved visibility section and when it will be reevaluated. Be aware of the politics involved--who heads the agency and how that person was appointed.

Citizens should press for the redesignation of more units of the system to Class I. This could be accomplished either by requesting the states to take action or by federal legislation. There are more than forty-eight areas in the national park system that are worthy of the highest degree of protections from potentially devastating air pollution. The protections for Class II lands are inadequate--the levels of additional pollution permitted are too high and there is no mandatory role in the permitting process for the federal land manager. The Clean Air Act should be amended to require an adverse impact determination when a source seeks to locate near Class II units of the system.

The regulatory process is at a critical point with respect to certain aspects of the visibility program. EPA is under court order to complete the program within specific time frames. There are proposed rules, as discussed above, for requiring BART when visibility impairment has been certified by the FLM and for developing a long-term strategy to reach the national visibility goal. It is apparent that the FLMs are not moving quickly to certify impairments, and EPA is extremely reluctant to require the application of BART. It is essential that the environmental community continue to participate in the rule-making proceedings in order that the strongest possible rules be promulgated.

Citizens should press for agency action on the regional haze and urban plume problems that are responsible for so much of the visibility deterioration in our National Park System. Clearly, great progress has been made in the technology necessary to perform precise monitoring and modeling.[171] EPA can no longer rely on the absense, or inadequacy, of such technology to continue delaying action on these issues. However, given the apparent reluctance or inability by EPA to address these problems, congressional action may be necessary before further EPA rulemakings addressing these problems are forthcoming.

States have the authority under the CAA to develop SIPs that identify integral vistas and require their protection from visibility deterioraton. States could mandate the installation of BART. Further, states have the authority to do more to remedy visibility impairment than EPA requires.

The Clean Air Act and its complications make the going rough for citizen involvement, but the stakes are high. We must preserve and improve the air quality in our national parks for ourselves and for future generations.

GLOSSARY OF CLEAN AIR ACT TERMS USED IN THIS CHAPTER

Administrator: The Administrator of the Environmental Protection Agency.

Agency: The Environmental Protection Agency.

AQRVs: Air quality-related values.

BACT: Best available control technology defined in the PSD provisions.

BART: Best available retrofit technology as defined in the visibility section, (§ 169A).

CAA: Clean Air Act.

FLM: Federal land manager.

PSD: Prevention of significant deterioration of air quality.

NAAQS: National ambient air quality standards--standards that apply throughout the country. Primary NAAQS are the standards necessary to protect the public health. Secondary NAAQS protect the public welfare.

Nonattainment Areas: Areas that do not meet the NAAQS.

SIP: State Implementation Plan; the state's strategy for meeting the requirements of the Clean Air Act.

NOTES

*Staff Attorney and Park Threats Coordinator, National Parks and Conservation Association, Washington, D.C.

1. For a thorough description of the genesis of the prevention of significant deterioration (PSD) of air quality provisions and the litigation that led to their enactment, *see* Alabama Power Co. v. Costle, 636 F.2d 323, 346-351 (D.C. Cir. 1979). *Alabama Power Co.* was a massive case brought by a variety of plaintiffs dissatisfied with EPA's final regulations implementing the PSD program. The rules were challenged by energy companies and mining concerns, among others, as being too stringent and by conservation groups as being too lenient. The court affirmed some of the rules and remanded others to EPA for reconsideration.

2. 42 U.S.C. § 7470-7479 (1983).

3. Statement by the President upon signing H.R. 6161 into law, 13 Presidential Documents 1214 (1977).

4. 42 U.S.C. § 7470 (2) (1983).

5. National Park Service Response to Senate Budget Committee, March 1987.

6. *Impacts Of Air Pollution On National Park Units: Hearings Before The Subcomm. On National Parks And Recreation Of The House Comm. On Interior And Insular Affairs*, 99th Cong., 1st Sess. (1985).

7. For example, in February 1987, EPA announced that Acadia National Park (Maine) did not attain the health-based standard for levels of ozone based on 1983-1985 data.

8. S. BUFFONE AND C. FULCO, ACID RAIN INVADES OUR NATIONAL PARKS (1987).

9. Connecticut v. E.P.A., 696 F.2d 147, 150-151 (2d. Cir. 1982).

10. 42 U.S.C.§ 7409 (1983).

11. 42 U.S.C.§ 7602(h) (1983).

12. 42 U.S.C. § 7470(1) (1983).

13. 42 U.S.C. § 7472 (1983); *Alabama Power Co.* 636 F. 2d at 349.

14. 42 U.S.C. § 7473 (1983).

15. 42 U.S.C. § 7476 (1983).

16. Sierra Club v. Thomas, No. C-86-0971-WWS (N.D. Cal., April 9, 1987). EPA has proposed regulations, including increments, for the prevention of significant deterioration of air quality due to emissions of nitrogen oxides. 53 Fed. Reg. 3698 (1988).

17. 42 U.S.C. § 7475 (1983).

18. *Alabama Power Co..* 636 F. 2d at 361.

19. 40 C.F.R. § 52.02 (1986). For a discussion of how the delegation has worked, *see* U.S. GENERAL ACCOUNTING OFFICE, GAO/RCED-85-73, EPA'S DELEGATION OF RESPONSIBILITIES TO PREVENT SIGNIFICANT DETERIORATION OF AIR QUALITY: HOW IS IT WORKING? (1985).

20. H.R. REP NO. 95-294, 95th Cong., 1st Sess. 7 (1977).

21. 42 U.S.C. § 7471 (1983).

22. Alabama Power Co. v. Costle, 636 F. 2d 323, 361-364 (D.C. Cir. 1979). The court speculated that "[s]ignificant deterioration may occur due to increased emissions from unregulated minor sources and major emitting facilities grandfathered out of the permit process, due to the use of different models to calculate increment consumption, due to the discovery through monitoring that limitations have inadvertently been exceeded, due to redesignation of an area to a more restrictive class, or due to allocation through administrative error of too many permits." *Id.* at 362.

23. 42 U.S.C. § 7604 (1983).

24. 40 C.F.R. 51.6 (1986).

25. The forty-eight areas are: Acadia National Park, Arches National Park, Badlands National Monument (wilderness area), Bandelier National Monument (wilderness area), Big Bend National Park, Black Canyon of the Gunnison National Monument (wilderness area), Bryce Canyon National Park, Canyonlands National Park, Carlsbad Caverns National Park, Capitol Reef National Park, Chiricahua National Monument (wilderness area), Crater Lake National Park, Craters of the Moon National Monument (wilderness area), Denali National Park and Preserve, Everglades National Park, Glacier National Park, Grand Canyon National Park, Grand Teton National Park, Great Smoky Mountains National Park, Great Sand Dunes National Monument (wilderness area), Guadalupe Mountains National Park, Haleakala National Park, Hawaii Volcanoes National Park, Isle Royale National Park, Joshua Tree National Monument (wilderness area), Kings Canyon National Park, Lassen Volcanic National Park, Lava Beds National Monument (wilderness area), Mammoth Cave National Park, Mesa Verde National Park, Mount Ranier National Park, North Cascades National Park, Sequoia National Park, Olympic National Park, Petrified Forest National Park, Pinnacles National Monument (wilderness area), Point Reyes National Seashore, Redwood National Park, Rocky Mountain National Park, Saguaro National Monument (wilderness area), Shenandoah National Park, Theodore Roosevelt National Park, Virgin Islands National Park, Voyageurs National Park, Wind Cave National Park, Yellowstone National Park, Yosemite National Park, and Zion National Park.

26. *See* Part III, *supra.*

27. 42 U.S.C. § 7472 (1983).

28. *Id.* at § 7473.

29. 42 U.S.C. § 7473(b) (1983); Citizens Against Refinery's Effects v. E.P.A., 643 F.2d 178, 180 (4th Cir. 1981).

30. 42 U.S.C. § 7474(a)(1983).

31. *Id.* § 7474(b)(1)(A).

32. *Id.* § 7474(b)(1)(C).

33. *Id.* § 7474(a).

34. *Id.* § 302(i).

35. 42 U.S.C. § 7474(b)(1)(B).

36. "Congress intended redesignation to be a cooperative effort between the state and the federal government with final authority in the state." Kerr-McGee Chemical Corp. v. United States Department of the Interior, 709 F.2d 597, 601 (9th Cir. 1983).

37. 42 U.S.C. § 7474(c) (1983).

38. *Id.* § 7474(e).

39. 42 U.S.C. § 7474(d)(1983).

40. 45 Fed. Reg. 43,002, 43,003 (1980).

41. *Id.*

42. The 44 areas recommended for redesignation are: Glacier Bay National Monument (now National Park), Katmai National Monument (now National Preserve), Canyon de Chelly National Monument, Chiricahua National Monument, Organ Pipe Cactus National Monument, Saguaro National Monument, Sunset Crater National Monument, Wupatki National Monument, Channel Islands National Monument (now National Park), Death Valley National Monument, Joshua Tree National Monument, Lava Beds National Monument, Muir Woods National Monument, Pinnacles National Monument, Black Canyon of the Gunnison National Monument, Colorado National Monument, Dinosaur National Monument, Great Sand Dunes National Monument, Big Cyprus National Preserve, Biscayne National Monument (now National Park), Fort Jefferson National Monument,

Craters of the Moon National Monument, Bandelier National Monument, Capulin Mountain National Monument, El Morro National Monument, Gila Cliff Dwellings National Monument, White Sands National Monument, John Day Fossil Beds National Monument, Badlands National Monument, Cedar Breaks National Monument, Natural Bridges National Monument, Buck Island Reef National Monument, Devils Tower National Monument, Fossil Butte Natioanl Monument, Paiute Primitive Area, Paria Canyon Primitive Area, Chemise Mountain Primitive Area, Powder Horn Primitive Area, Beartrap Canyon Primitive Area, Centennial Primitive Area, Humbug Spires Primitive Area, Dark Canyon Primitive Area, Grand Gulch Primitive Area, and Scab Creek Primitive Area.

43. Chaco Canyon National Monument was redesignated in December 1980 as Chaco Culture National Historical Park.

44. 45 Fed. Reg. 43,002 (1980).

45. The National Clean Air Coalition supports the redesignation to Class I of the following parks: Denali (part of the park is already Class I), Gates of the Artic, Glacier Bay, Katmai, Kenai Fjords, Kobuk Valley, Lake Clark, Wrangell-St. Elias, Great Basin, Channel Islands, Redwood (part of the park is already Class I), Sequoia (part of the park is already Class I), Chaco Canyon, Crater Lake (part of the park is already Class I), Big Bend (part of the park is already Class I) and Biscayne. Additionally, the Coalition supports the redesignation to Class I of the following National Preserves: Aniakchak, Bering Land Bridge, Denali, Gates of the Artic, Glacier Bay, Katmai, Lake Clark, Noatak, Wrangell-St. Elias, and Yukon Charley Rivers.

46. *Alabama Power Co.*, 636 F.2d at 374-376; Connecticut v. E.P.A., 696 F.2d 147, 166-167 (2d Cir. 1982).

47. *Alabama Power Co.*, 636 F.2d at 364-368. EPA argued that PSD permits should be required whether the source was going to be located in an attainment or nonattainment area if the emissions from the source affected the air quality in a clean air area. The court found that the language of the statute was specific that location of the source in an attainment area was the "key determinant of the applicability of the PSD review requirements." The court found other authority in the Clean Air Act, such as sections 110 (implementation plans) and 126 (interstate pollution abatement) for EPA to use in combatting the problem of interstate pollution and its effect on attainment areas. EPA has not accepted the court's invitation and has failed to address the problem of interstate pollution in any meaningful way. This failure illustrates the importance of an aggressive, committed, and well-funded EPA to the achievement of the goals of the Clean Air Act.

48. 42 U.S.C. § 7479(1) (1983).

49. Fugitive emissions (as opposed to emissions from industrial point sources like stacks) could be included in the threshold amounts but the EPA must do so by rule. *Alabama Power Co.*, 636 F.2d at 368-370. Whether fugitive emissions of surface coal mines, whose operations can affect the air quality, especially visibility, of nearby parks, should be included in the determination of threshold amounts still has not been decided by EPA.

50. "Air pollutant" is defined by Section 302(g), 42 U.S.C. § 7602(g)(1983).

51. *Alabama Power Co.*, 636 F.2d at 352-55.

52. 40 C.F.R. § 52.21(b)(5)-(6) (1986).

53. *Alabama Power Co.*, 636 F.2d at 395-96.

54. 42 U.S.C. § 7479(2)(C) (1983).

55. 42 U.S.C. § 7411(1983).

56. 42 U.S.C. § 7479(1). "In determining whether a facility qualifies as nonprofit for PSD exemption, then, the EPA Administrator should look primarily at the disposition of the

profits, if any, of the facility and secondly, at its purposes." Town of Brookline v. Gorsuch, 667 F.2d 215, 221 (1st Cir. 1981).

57. *Id.* at 220-221.

58. Hawaiian Electric Co. v. E.P.A., 723 F.2d 1440, 1448 (2d Cir. 1984).

59. 42 U.S.C. § 7479(4), Connecticut v. E.P.A., 696 F.2d 147 (2d Cir. 1982).

60. 42 U.S.C. § 7479(4) (1983).

61. *Alabama Power Co.*, 636 F.2d at 374-76.

62. 42 U.S.C. § 7416 (1983).

63. *Id.* § 7475.

64. *Id.* 7475(a)(4).

65. "While baghouse control systems in general may be presumed to constitute BACT for particulate matter, the EPA is nevertheless obligated to consider certain factors that would arise from the use of baghouses in the particular facility immediately involved. Thus, EPA might decide for a given facility baghouses are inappropriate for economic, energy or environmental reasons." Northern Plains Resource Council v. E.P.A., 645 F.2d 1349, 1359 (9th Cir. 1981).

66. 42 U.S.C. § 7479 (3).

67. 40 C.F.R. § 52.21(m) (1986).

68. 42 U.S.C. § 7475(c) (1983).

69. 42 U.S.C. § 7475(d)(1) (1983).

70. *Id.* § 7475(d)(2)(A). The CAA specifies in several instances that both the Federal Land Manager and the federal official with direct responsibility for management of Class I lands (presumably the superintendent) have roles in the PSD process. The Department of the Interior, however, requires that both be given notice but that only the FLM (the Assistant Secretary for Fish, Wildlife and Parks) has any role in deciding adverse impact on AQRVs. A situation where a superintendent publicly disagrees with the FLM has not occurred yet.

71. *Id.* § 7475(d)(2)(B).

72. s. REP. NO. 717, 94th Cong., 2d Sess. 27 (1976).

73. NATIONAL PARK SERVICE, NATURAL RESOURCES PROGRAMS, REPORT SERIES 85-2, PERMIT APPLICATION GUIDANCE FOR NEW AIR POLLUTION SOURCES 3 (1985).

74. 42 U.S.C. § 7475(d)(2)(B) (1983).

75. 47 Fed. Reg. 30,222, 30,223 (1982).

76. *Id.*

77. *Id.*

78. 42 U.S.C. § 7475(d)(2)(C)(i).

79. *Id.* § 7475(d)(2)(C)(ii).

80. *Id.* § 7475(d)(2)(C)(iii).

81. *Id.* § 7475(d)(2)(C)(iv). Except for the three-hour maximum allowable increase for sulfur dioxide, the standards are the same as for Class II.

82. *Id.* § 7475(d)(2)(D)(i).

83. *Id.* § 7475(d)(2)(D)(ii).

84. *Id.* § 7475(a)(2)(D)(iii).

85. 47 Fed. Reg. 30,226 (1982).

86. *Id.* at 30,227.

87. NATIONAL PARK SERVICE, AIR QUALITY DIVISION, TECHNICAL REVIEW OF SIX PSD PER-
MIT APPLICATIONS POTENTIALLY AFFECTING THEODORE ROOSEVELT NATIONAL PARK AND
LOSTWOOD NATIONAL WILDLIFE REFUGE 1 (July 1982).

88. *Id.* at 12-16.

89. 47 Fed. Reg. 30,222 (1982).

90. 47 Fed. Reg. 41,480, 41,481 (1982).

91. *Id.*

92. NATIONAL PARK SERVICE, *supra* note 87 at 2-4.

93. 47 Fed. Reg. 41,480, 41,481 (1982).

94. *Id.*

95. *Id.* at 41,481-82.

96. *Id.* at 41,482.

97. *Id.*

98. *Id.*

99. 16 U.S.C. § 1.

100. 42 U.S.C. § 7491(a)(1) (1983).

101. H.R. REP. 95-294, 95th Cong., 1st Sess. 204-205 (1977).

102. 42 U.S.C. § 7491(a)(2) (1983).

103. 44 Fed. Reg. 69,122 (1979).

104. The two areas not listed were Rainbow Lake, Wisconsin, and Bradwell Bay, Florida.
The list is codified at 40 C.F.R. § 81.400 (1986).

105. 42 U.S.C. § 7491(a)(4) (1983).

106. *Id.* § (e).

107. *Id.* § (b)(2).

108. *Id.* § (b)(2)(A).

109. *Id.* § (b)(2)(B).

110. *Id.* § (g)(1).

111. *Id.* § (d).

112. *Id.* § (g)(7).

113. *Id.* § (g)(2).

114. H.R REP. 95-294 at 206.

115. 42 U.S.C. § 7491(b) (1983).

116. *Id.* § (c)(1). "The purposes of this authority are to permit exemption for smaller,
isolated sources which make an insignificant contribution to visibility impairment."
H.R. CONF. REP. 95-564 at 154.

117. 42 U.S.C. § 7491(c)(2).

118. 42 U.S.C. § 7491(c)(3).

119. 45 Fed. Reg. 80,084 (1980).

120. "The long-term strategy can, however, begin to address the more complex problems
such as regional haze. For example, although visibility impairment resulting from multi-
source situations may not be reasonably attributable to any specific source, other programs
for control of such sources should consider the impact, to the degree possible, of control decisions on visibility." 45 Fed. Reg. 34,762, 34,777 (1980).

121. *Id.* at 80,086. The list is codified in 40 C.F.R. § 51.300(b).

122. 45 Fed. Reg. 80,086 (1980).

123. 40 C.F.R. § 51.301(n) (1986).

124. 45 Fed. Reg. 80,086 (1980).

125. 40 C.F.R. § 51.301(a).

126. *Id.*

127. *Id.* at 80,086-87.

128. *Id.* at 80,086; 40 C.F.R. § 51.301(x).

129. *Id.* Phase II would cover requirements for sulfur dioxides, which are a primary cause of regional haze.

130. *Id.* at 80,087.

131. *Id.* at 80,087; 40 C.F.R. § 51.303.

132. 45 Fed. Reg. at 80,087; 40 C.F.R. § 51.306.

133. 45 Fed. Reg. at 80,088; 40 C.F.R. § 51.307.

134. 45 Fed. Reg. at 80,088; 40 C.F.R. § 51.307 (a).

135. 46 Fed. Reg. 3,646 (1981).

136. Department of the Interior news release, October 25, 1985.

137. *Id.*

138. *See, e.g.,* Statement of T. Destry Jarvis, National Parks and Conservation Association, to E.P.A. Docket No. A-79-40 on Visibility Protection for Federal Class I Areas (August 21, 1980). The statement refers to the legislative history establishing several units of the National Park System.

139. 40 C.F. R. § 51.301(g).

140. 46 Fed. Reg. 22,707, 22,708 (1981).

141. 40 C.F.R. § 51.302(a) (1986).

142. *Id.* at § 51.306(c).

143. 45 Fed. Reg. 80,084, 80,086 (1980).

144. Alaska's SIP revisions were approved in 1983. 48 Fed. Reg. 30,623 (1983).

145. Congress made clear that the Administrator was not required to meet the long-range goal by any specific date. 42 U.S.C. § 7491(f). However, when EPA finalized regulations concerning the visibility program in the last months of the Carter Administration, the Agency became bound to follow through on them.

146. The original settlement agreement is described at 49 Fed. Reg. 20,647 (1984). It has been amended to give EPA more time to complete its actions.

147. 50 Fed. Reg. 28,544 (1985).

148. *Id.*

149. 40 C.F.R. § 52.26(c)(2) (1986).

150. *Id.* (c)(4)-(5).

151. *Id.* (d).

152. *Id.* § 52.27(f),§ 52.28(h).

153. 50 Fed. Reg. at 28,547.

154. *Id.* at 28,548.

155. *Id.* at 28,549.

156. 52 Fed. Reg. 7,802 (1987); 52 Fed. Reg. 45,132 (1987).

157. 52 Fed. Reg. at 7,804 (1987).

158. *Id.*

159. *Id.* at 7,805.

160. *Id.* at 7,804.

161. Moosehead Wilderness and Roosevelt Campobello International Park in Maine, Saguaro Wilderness and Petrified Forest National Park in Arizona, Grand Canyon National Park in Arizona and Canyonlands National Park in Utah, and Voyageurs National Park in Minnesota.

162. Bryce Canyon, Carlsbad Caverns, Isle Royale, Pinnacles, and Mesa Verde National Parks.

163. *Id.* at 7,805-06.

164. *Id.* at 7,807.

165. *Id.*

166. *Id.* at 7,808.

167. *Id.*

168. 40 C.F.R. § 51.302(c)(i).

169. 52 Fed. Reg. at 7,808.

170. *Id.* at 7,808-9; 52 Fed. Reg. 45,132, 45,136 (1987).

171. *See, e.g.,* Letter from Martin Smith, Deputy Assistant Secretary/Director, Office of Policy Analysis, Department of the Interior, to EPA Central Docket Section (LE-131A), dated July 30,1987. The letter describes National Park Service modeling.

Chapter 13

NO HOLIER TEMPLES: PROTECTING THE NATIONAL PARKS THROUGH WILD AND SCENIC RIVER DESIGNATION

Brian E. Gray[*]

I. INTRODUCTION

Among the various federal laws that govern the national parks, the National Wild and Scenic Rivers Act[1] (the "Act") is more like a tiny rivulet than a stream or river. Few rivers within the parks have been designated as components of the national wild and scenic rivers system, and the management authority embodied in the Act is more limited than that granted by other statures, such as the National Park Service Organic Act[2] and the National Parks and Recreation Act of 1978.[3] Nonetheless, the Wild and Scenic Rivers Act is potentially as significant to the water resources of the parks as the Wilderness Act[4] is to their land resources. For the Wild and Scenic Rivers Act is a strong congressional directive that river areas designated pursuant to its authority be preserved in their natural, or at least existing, condition. Under the Act, the National Park Service must manage component rivers for the overriding purpose of preservation, rather than for the myriad uses that we have come to associate with the national parks, such as promotion of tourism, the construction of housing accommodations, and the provision of amenities. Moreover, because an adequate supply of water obviously is necessary to accomplish the purpose of preserving the free-flowing condition of designated rivers, the Act stands as the clearest expression yet of Congress' intent to assert a federal right to water. The Act thus augments the authority of the Park Service to claim federal reserved water rights for the national parks.[5]

To date, it does not appear that the Wild and Scenic Rivers Act has been invoked specifically to protect water resources within the national parks. Where rivers that flow through parks have been designated pursuant to the Act, the purpose generally has been to preserve the river itself rather than to expand the Park Service's authority to manage the water resources and surrounding lands within the park as a whole. The protection of our remaining wild rivers is a laudable goal, and designation of a river as part of the national rivers system is the best means of ensuring its preservation. The objective of this chapter, however, is to suggest that the Wild and Scenic Rivers Act can serve the additional purpose of enhancing the statutory protections for the water resources--rivers, streams, aquatic life, water sheds, and riparian habitat--of the national parks themselves. Following a description of the Act and the regulations adopted by the Park Service to implement its directives, I will explore some of the ways in which the legislation may be used to complement the existing statutes that govern the national parks and recommend a few legislative revisions of the Act that would make it an even more effective source of protection for the parks.

II. AN OVERVIEW OF THE NATIONAL WILD AND SCENIC RIVERS ACT

In enacting the National Wild and Scenic Rivers Act of 1968, Congress declared it to be

> the policy of the United States that certain rivers of the Nation which, with their immediate environments possess outstandingly remarkable scenic, recreational, geologic, fish and wildlife, historic cultural, or other similar values, shall be preserved in free-flowing condition, and that they and their immediate environments shall be protected for the benefit and enjoyment of present and future generations.[6]

The purpose of the Act was to complement "the established national policy of dam and other construction at appropriate sections of the rivers of the United States" with "a policy that would preserve other selected rivers or sections thereof in their free-flowing condition to protect the water quality of such rivers and to fulfill other vital national conservation purposes."[7]

Thus, in establishing the national wild and scenic rivers system, Congress' purposes were decidedly preservationist. According to the Act, the lands and water resources that comprise the system must be managed essentially as wilderness.[8] The Act vests primary management authority over designated rivers in the federal agency or department with jurisdiction over the lands through which the rivers flow.[9] Thus, rivers that pass through the national parks are administered by the Secretary of the Interior, and the Park Service as the Secretary's delegate.[10] The Act grants the Service broad, but focused, authority. It directs that "[e]ach component of the national wild and scenic rivers system shall be managed in such a manner as to enhance the values which causes it to be included in said system without, insofar as is consistent therewith, limiting other uses that do not substantially interfere with public use and enjoyment of these values."[11] The Act also states that each federal agency with jurisdiction over land that includes or adjoins a component river shall take action "as may be necessary to protect such rivers in accordance with the purposes of [the statute]."[12]

To protect and to enhance the values for which the national wild and scenic rivers system was established, Congress prohibited certain activities in and along designated rivers. The most important proscription is the directive that "[t]he Federal Energy Regulatory Commission shall not license the construction of any dam, water conduit, reservoir, powerhouse, transmission line or other project works . . . on or directly affecting any river that is designated . . . as component of the national wild and scenic rivers system."[13] The Act also states that "no department or agency of the United States shall assist by loan, grant, license or otherwise in the construction of any water resources project that would have a direct and adverse effect on the values for which such river was established."[14] Finally, the Act regulates, but does not necessarily prohibit, mineral development along designated rivers. Congress chose generally to allow mining to continue, but subject to regulatory restrictions to ensure that the adverse effects of the mining on the river area are minimized.[15] In the case of rivers that are classified as "wild,"[16], however, Congress directed that, "subject to valid existing rights," all minerals located in federal lands in and along the river be withdrawn from appropriation.[17]

Thus, the Act prohibits all federal agencies and departments from taking any action, either along a designated river or upstream or downstream of the protected segment, that would be inconsistent with Congress' primary objective of preserving the free-flowing, wilderness character of the river. The consequences of these provisions of the Act for both the Park Service and other agencies that have jurisdiction over designated rivers or their adjacent lands will be discussed below in parts IIIA and IIIB.

In addition to these management directives, Congress also expressly claimed unappropriated water in amounts and flow levels necessary to fulfill the purposes of the Wild and Scenic Rivers Act. Congress' assertion of a federal water right has passed with little notice or criticism.[18] Yet, the Act represents the only instance, to my knowledge, in which Congress explicitly has claimed a right to water based on federal, rather than state, law.[19] Unfortunately, however, Congress did so in a confusing, perhaps even elliptical, manner.

On one hand, the Act disclaims any effects on state water resources laws. According to Section 13(b), nothing in the Act should be read as "an express or implied claim or denial on the part of the Federal Government as to exemption from State water laws."[20] On the other hand, Section 13(c) provides:

> Designation of any stream or portion thereof as a national wild, scenic or recreational river area shall not be construed as a reservation of the waters of such streams for purposes other than those specified in this [Act], or in quantities greater than necessary to accomplish these purposes.[21]

In addition, Section 13(d) states that the jurisdiction of the states over designated rivers shall be unaffected by their inclusion in the national rivers system, but only "to the extent that such jurisdiction may be exercised without impairing the purposes of [the Act] or its administration."[22]

Making sense of these seemingly contradictory provisions is no easy task.[23] My own view is that Congress intended to accomplish two not incompatible goals. First, as it has done throughout the nation's history,[24] Congress deferred generally to state water law. This is the purpose of Section 13(b). Second, Congress also sought to ensure that there would remain enough water flowing in the rivers designated as components of the wild and scenic rivers system to fulfill the purposes of the Act and to protect the values for which the rivers were included in the system. This is the meaning of Sections 13(c) and 13(d). Congress proposed to reconcile these policies by creating a federal right to water to serve the enumerated purposes of the Wild and Scenic Rivers Act and by limiting the scope of the federal right to only that quantity necessary to accomplish the statutory purposes.[25] The significance of this federal water right for those wild and scenic rivers that flow through the national parks is the subject of part IIIC.

To date, seventy-three rivers have been designated as components of the national wild and scenic rivers system. The original 1968 legislation included ten rivers.[26] Since then, Congress has designated an additional fifty-four rivers.[27] The other nine were included in the national rivers system by the Secretary of the Interior at the behest of the Governors of the state through which the rivers flow.[28]

Of the seventy-three component rivers only seventeen flow through national parks or other lands under the jurisdiction of the Park Service, and thirteen of these twenty-two are in Alaska.[29] Thus, as stated at the outset of this chapter, the Wild and Scenic Rivers Act has been used sparingly to protect the water resources, and their adjacent lands, of the national parks. Indeed, even in the Alaska National Interest Lands Conservation Act of 1980,[30] which designated as wild and scenic seventeen rivers within the newly established Alaska national parks, there is no indication that Congress included the rivers in the national system for the specific purpose of augmenting the Park Service's management authority over the parks as a whole.[31]

Congress' neglect notwithstanding, the National Wild and Scenic Rivers Act is potentially of great significance to the national parks. For designation of rivers that flow through the parks as components of the national rivers system is an excellent means of protecting the water resources of the parks from activities, both within and without park boundaries, that threaten the integrity of the parks themselves. The balance of this chapter will explore the potential uses of the Act to enhance both the Park Service's and the public's authority over the rivers and riparian lands within the national parks.

III. THE SIGNIFICANCE OF THE NATIONAL WILD AND SCENIC RIVERS ACT FOR THE NATIONAL PARKS

This evaluation of the possible applications of the Wild and Scenic Rivers Act to the national parks will address four basic questions: First, what are the purposes of the Act and what values does it direct the Park Service to promote? Second, what uses of the parks, and adjacent land within the watersheds of designated rivers, are consistent with the policies and management directives of the Act? Third, to what extent does the Act empower the Park Service to claim water to fulfill the purpose of the designation of rivers within the national parks? Fourth, what rights does the public have under the Act?

In considering each of these questions, it is important to remember that there have been but a handful of judicial opinions that have interpreted the Act.[32] Thus, the Wild and Scenic Rivers Act is something of a rarity among federal statutes. For the most part, the Act means precisely what it says; as yet, the words of the statute have not been embellished by judicial interpretation. What follows, then, is an analysis, not necessarily of how the Act has been construed, but of how the statute should be interpreted to serve the purposes of the national park system.

A. The Purposes and Values of the Act

As mentioned in Part II,[33] the Wild and Scenic Rivers Act provides that each component river "shall be administered in such a manner as to protect and enhance the values which causes it to be included in [the national rivers] system without, insofar as is consistent therewith, limiting other uses that do not substantially interfere with public use and enjoyment of these values."[34] This directive is significant for two reasons. First, it makes clear Congress' intention that rivers within the national system be used only in accordance with the various purposes and values set forth in the statute. Although Congress could have articulated more clearly its objective, the purposes of the Act appear to include:

1. Protection of fish and wildlife.

2. Preservation of geologic, historic, and cultural values.

3. Maintenance of scenic views and aesthetic values.

4. Promotion of recreational uses, such as fishing and whitewater boating and rafting.

5. Protection of water quality.

6. Preservation of the free-flowing character of the rivers for the benefit of present and future generations.[35]

Second, the directive also indicates that Congress did not propose to limit the uses of designated rivers to those purposes articulated in the statute. Rather, Congress intended that other, non-enumerated uses be permitted if, and to the extent that, such uses do not "substantially interfere" with the express purposes and values of the Act recited above.

According to well-established principles of administrative law, the decision whether to allow, and how to regulate, a particular use of a wild and scenic river rests almost exclusively with the Park Service. As the Supreme Court stated recently in a different context, the administration of a congressionally created program "'necessarily requires the formulation of policy and the making of rules to fill any gap left, implicitly or explicitly, by Congress.'" [36] In reviewing policy decisions made by an executive department, the courts must give "considerable weight" to the "department's construction of a statutory scheme it is entrusted to administer."[37] If the department's decision "'represents a reasonable accommodation of conflicting policies that were committed to the agency's care by the statute,'" the courts will uphold the decision "unless it appears from the statute or its legislative history that the accommodation is not one that Congress would have sanctioned.'"[38] Congress' use of the terms "substantially interfere" suggests that it intended to vest in the Park Service substantial discretion to determine which nonenumerated uses of wild and scenic rivers within the parks would be compatible with the express values of the Act and which would not. Members of the public aggrieved by a particular policy decision could not successfully challenge the Park Service's action unless the agency's judgment was clearly inconsistent with the words or purposes of the statute.[39] Consequently, the important question is: What uses of wild and scenic rivers are consistent with the express purposes of the Wild and Scenic Rivers Act, and what uses substantially interfere, and there-

fore are inconsistent, with those purposes of the Wild and
Scenic Rivers Act, and what uses substantially interfere, and therefore are inconsistent, with those purposes?

**B. Permissible and Impermissible Uses of Wild and Scenic Rivers
Within and Without the National Parks**

The list of possible uses of wild and scenic rivers within
the national parks may be divided into two categories: (1) uses that
occur along the designated portion of the river within the park,
which are under the direct regulatory jurisdiction of the Park Service; and (2) uses that take place outside the parks, which are subject only to the indirect authority of the Park Service.

1. Uses Within the Parks

As discussed in part II, the inclusion of a river in the national wild and scenic rivers system means that the Park Service must
manage the river essentially as a wilderness waterway.[40] While the
Park Service may permit activities that are compatible with preservation of the natural, wild condition of the river, it may not sanction uses that significantly detract from the public's enjoyment of
the wilderness character of the streamcourse. For the most part,
the Park Service's management guidelines for wild and scenic rivers[41]
are consistent with this principle.

The general management guideline provides:

> Each component [river] will be managed to protect
> and enhance the values for which the river was desig-
> nated, while providing for public recreation and resour-
> ces uses which do not adversely impact or degrade those
> values. Specific management strategies will vary accord-
> ing to classification but will always be designed to protect
> and enhance the values of the river area.[42]

The guidelines then focus on three interrelated topics: resource
management, land management, and people management.

The guidelines state that the Park Service's "[r]esource management practices will be limited to those which are necessary for
protection, rehabilitation or enhancement of the river area resources."[43] Timber harvesting, perhaps the greatest potential threat
to the scenic beauty and aesthetics of designated rivers, must
"be conducted so as to avoid adverse impacts on the river area
values."[44] Because commercial timber cutting is prohibited in
the national parks,[45] however, it is unlikely that there will be sig-

nificant conflicts over this provision of the guidelines. The Act itself forbids hunting along a component river that flows through a national park,[46] but the guidelines do not address the subject specifically. The Park Service generally permits recreational fishing in designated rivers. In rivers in which the native fish population is unstable--such as the mainstream of the Middle Fork of the Salmon River in Idaho--fishing is limited to "catch-and-release."[47]

In general, the land management provisions of the guidelines also are consistent with the purposes of the Wild and Scenic Rivers Act. The Park Service has stated that it will not construct "[m]ajor public use facilities such as developed campgrounds, major visitor centers and administrative headquarters" along a designated river corridor.[48] The limitation of this guideline to "major" facilities is somewhat problematic. Preservation of a wild river area in its primitive state, or maintenance of the "largely primitive" and "largely undeveloped" shorelines of scenic river areas,[49] would seem to preclude the construction of any structures for the convenience of visitors, because such facilities would detract from the natural, wilderness character of the river. It appears that in implementing the guideline, however, the Park Service has limited the erection of new structures to things such as toilets and refuse containers, which are necessary to minimize the cumulative effects of virtually continuous human use.[50] In any event, the designation of a park river as wild and scenic certainly would prevent the Park Service from authorizing the construction of campgrounds, cabins, grocery stores, or fast-food facilities along, or within view of, the river. Indeed, if the Merced River had been protected by a statute like the Wild and Scenic Rivers Act since the early days of its inclusion in Yosemite National Park, the tragedy of Yosemite Valley[51] could not have occurred.

Although the Wild and Scenic Rivers Act authorizes the Secretary of the Interior "to acquire lands and interest in land" within the boundaries of a designated river area,[52] the guidelines state that provided they remain consistent with the purposes of the Act.[53] Arguably, this decision to sanction and generally to preserve private in-holdings is inconsistent with Congress' directive that wild river areas have shorelines that are "essentially primitive" and that scenic river areas be "largely primitive" with shorelines "largely undeveloped."[54] Such an argument ignores, however, two competing policy considerations. First, the Park Service has limited resources, which in this era of high federal deficits and efforts at budget-balancing are likely to be reduced for the foreseeable future.[55] Under these circumstances, it is not unreasonable, and therefore should not be unlawful, for the Park Service to spend its available funds on projects such as maintenance of existing facilities and resources, rather than the relatively expensive acquisition of private in-holdings. Second, the private ownership and use of some land---indeed, perhaps most such land along rivers that were sufficiently pristine to have been included in the national rivers system--is compatible with the "esthetic, scenic, historic, archeologic, and scientific" values which led to the designation of the river in the first place.[56] For many, the experience of traveling on a wild and scenic river may be enhanced by the view of a traveling on a wild and scenic river may be enhanced by the view of a few cattle ranches, small gold mining sites, and rustic private homes scattered along the shore.[57]

The guidelines regulate human uses of wild and scenic river areas principally through a permit system, which limits the number of persons and boats using the rivers at any one time.[58] This system appears to be an effective means of dispersing rafters and other boaters along the river, which enhances each group's enjoyment of the scenery and solitude of the river.

Unfortunately, however, the benefits of limiting the number of persons who may use a wild and scenic river area at any given time are substantially undermined by the guideline that regulates what uses may take place. This guideline provides that "[m]otorized travel on land or water is generally permitted in wild, scenic and recreational river areas, but will be restricted or prohibited where necessary to protect the values for which the river area was designated."[59] As a result, companies that run motorized rafts and, even worse, jet boats that are capable of navigating upstream at 20 knots or so[60] may be permitted to use the wild and scenic rivers. Such uses are wholly inconsistent with the Wild and Scenic Rivers Act. As discussed above,[61] the principal purpose of the Act was to preserve rivers in their natural, free-flowing condition as "vestiges of primitive America"[62] and to protect the scenic, recreational, fish and wildlife, aesthetic, and other related values of such rivers.[63] Human-powered craft can run the wild and scenic rivers without interfering with or detracting from these values. An oar or paddle dipping into the current is silent and unobtrusive. In contrast, motorized boats pollute the air and water with their exhaust, disturb the stillness of the river canyon with their noise, and generally detract from the aesthetics of the wilderness river environment.[64]

With this one exception, the Park Service's guidelines for the management of the wild and scenic rivers under its jurisdiction conform to the policies and directives of the Wild and Scenic Rivers Act. One may quibble with a particular Park Service decision --such as to permit private in-holdings within the river corridor- -but it must be remembered that the Park Service has substantial managerial discretion over designated river areas, limited only by the specific directives of the statute and the mandate that a particular use "not substantially interfere with public use and enjoyment" of the values of wild and scenic rivers. Only the decision to permit the use of motorized boats on component rivers clearly violates this stricture. The remaining guidelines fall within the administrative prerogatives granted by the Act.

2. *Uses Outside the Parks*

While the Wild and Scenic Rivers Act establishes rather broad regulatory policies for the Park Service's management of designated rivers inside the parks, it defines much more precisely the restrictions that it places on the activities of other agencies outside the parks. In this respect, the Act offers substantial protections for the parks against external threats to their land and water resources.

As noted in part II,[65] the strongest management directive contained in the Act is Section 7(a), which prohibits the Federal Energy Regulatory Commission from licensing any water resources project "on or directly affecting" a national wild and scenic river and forbids all other federal agencies from providing any form of assistance to a water resource project that would adversely affect a component river.[66] This provision is of vital importance to the national parks, because it prevents the construction of any water supply, flood control, or hydroelectric project that could be harmful to designated rivers within the parks.

The Federal Power Act prohibits the licensing or authorization of any "dams, conduits, reservoirs, power houses, transmission lines, or other works for storage or carriage of water, or for the development, transmission, or utilization of power, within . . . any national park or national monument . . . without specific authority of Congress."[67] But nothing in that statute or in the other laws that govern the national parks prevents the construction or operation of a water project located upstream of the boundaries of the park that diminishes the flow of water below the level needed to fulfill the purposes of the park.[68] Nor do these laws prohibit the construction of a project located downstream of the park that threatens to inundate the river valley within the park. Thus, designation of park rivers as components of the national wild and scenic rivers system is the best, and in some instances the only, means of ensuring that water projects located outside the parks do not degrade the resources of the park itself.[69]

Apart from Section 7(a), perhaps the most important provision of the Wild and Scenic Rivers Act for the parks is the directive that all federal agencies with jurisdiction over lands that adjoin a designated river "shall take such action respecting management policies, regulations, contracts, plans, affecting such lands . . . as may be necessary to protect such rivers in accordance with the purposes of [the Act]."[70] In this regard, Congress specified that "[p]articular attention shall be given to scheduled timber harvesting, road construction, and similar activities that might be contrary to the purposes of [the Act].[71]

One of the most substantial external threats to some parks is the siltation and pollution of their rivers and streams from logging, mining, and agricultural activities in the watershed upstream of the park boundaries. The debris from timber harvesting generally is carried by rainfall and surface runoff into the rivers of the watershed, and logging activities such as clear-cutting can leave the hillside unprotected against soil erosion, which then causes siltation of the streams and increases the turbidity of the water. Placer mining washes large amounts of earth and rock into adjacent rivers, and the tailings from hardrock mining can pollute neighboring waters. Herbicides and pesticides used in agriculture also contribute to the pollution of streams and rivers.[72]

These activities, to the extent that they pollute a designated river downstream, are flatly inconsistent with the Wild and Scenic Rivers Act. One of the statutory definitions of a wild river area is one in which the waters are unpolluted.[73] Congress mandated that the waters of wild rivers remain free of pollution and that contaminants in less pristine component rivers be eliminated or at least diminished.[74] Moreover, the siltation and chemical degradation of wild and scenic rivers is contrary to the policies of preserving the scenic views and aesthetic values of the rivers and of promoting recreational use.[75] A river that contains mill tailings, sediment and logging debris, or whose waters are undrinkable because of pollution, is neither aesthetically enjoyable nor suited for wilderness recreational use. And, perhaps most importantly, siltation and pollution are deleterious to the fish and wildlife that inhabit the river.[76] Activities that degrade the aquatic and riparian habitat are inconsistent with the protections afforded by the Act for fish and wildlife, not to mention recreational fishing.[77]

Thus, the Wild and Scenic Rivers Act stands as a clear congressional mandate to the Park Service and other federal agencies not to sanction any forestry, mining, or agricultural activities that "might be contrary" to the purposes of the Act.[78] To the extent that these activities occur on federal land, the Act affords the parks substantial protections. Unfortunately, however, not all external threats to the parks take place on federal land or are subject to the jurisdiction of federal land management agencies. As with the other statutes that govern the parks, the Wild and Scenic Rivers Act does not expressly regulate private activities on nonfederal land that are inconsistent with the purposes of the statute. It is for this reason that Professor Joseph Sax has characterized the national parks as "helpless giants," vulnerable to a variety of activities outside their boundaries because "Congress has given [the Park Service] very little explicit authority to regulate private lands."[79]

The solution to the external threats dilemma is complex. To a certain extent, the federal water right created by the Act[80] addresses the problem. Among other things, this water right grants to the Park Service the authority to demand from upstream water users and landowners water in sufficient quantity and of adequate quality to accomplish the purposes of the Wild and Scenic Rivers Act.[81] But the federal water right is only a partial solution. For, as discussed in the following section, the water right for wild and scenic rivers does not confer on the Park Service any direct authority to regulate external threats that arise outside the water rights system.[82] Accordingly, full protection for the wild and scenic rivers areas of the parks will require the amendment of the Wild and Scenic Rivers Act to provide the Park Service with express jurisdiction over private land use that is inconsistent with the purposes and directives of the Act. The nature of this additional legislation is the subject of part IV.

C. A Federal Water Right for the Wild and Scenic Rivers

As discussed in part II, the Wild and Scenic Rivers Act expressly--albeit obliquely--creates a federal right to enough water to accomplish the various purposes of the Act.[83] This federal water right is not yet well-understood. There has been very little scholarly discussion of the subject and, to my knowledge, the right has been recognized and quantified for only one of the nation's seventy-three wild and scenic rivers.[84] As water users become better acquainted with the federal water right for wild and scenic rivers however, and as the right is quantified for for additional rivers, it is likely to become extremely controversial. For the federal right can be asserted to preempt consumptive uses of water that are junior in time to the designation of the river to the extent that such uses interfere with the instream flows needed to fulfill the purposes of the Wild and Scenic Rivers Act.

Before examining the significance of the federal water right for the wild and scenic rivers within the parks, five preliminary questions must be answered. First, what are the water rights of the national parks independent of the Wild and Scenic River Act? Second, what kind of water right does the Act create? Third, what quantity of water has Congress claimed pursuant to the Act? Fourth, what is the priority date of the water right? Fifth, does the federal right preempt state-created water rights that are senior-in-time?

The Wild and Scenic Rivers Act aside, the national parks are entitled to water under the federal reserved rights doctrine. In a nutshell, the doctrine holds that

> when the Federal Government withdraws its land from the public domain and reserved it for a federal purpose, the Government, by implication, reserves appurtenant water then unappropriated to the extent needed to accomplish the purpose of the reservation. In so doing the United States acquires a reserved right in unappropriated water which vests on the date of the reservation and is superior to the rights of future appropriators.[85]

To date, the United States Supreme Court has applied the federal reserved rights doctrine to Indian reservations, national recreation areas, national wildlife refuges, national monuments, and national forests.[86]

Drawing on these decisions, Professor Charles Wilkinson argues in his chapter (in this volume) on federal reserved water rights that the doctrine establishes a federal claim to water for a broad spectrum of uses of the national parks, including maintenance of instream flows, ecosystem management, protection of fish and wildlife, recreation, consumptive uses at Park Service facilities, and preservation of the natural and historic treasures of the parks.[87] Professor Wilkinson makes a convincing case that the Park Service should be awarded federal reserved rights to water in quantities sufficient to fulfill all of these purposes, and the courts ought to follow his suggestions. There are indications, however, that the Supreme Court may not construe the purposes of the national parks, and thus the scope of the reserved water rights for the parks, quite so broadly.

The Court has made clear in its most recent opinion on the subject that it will construe the reserved rights doctrine narrow-ly to minimize conflicts between federal water rights and state law. In *United States v. New Mexico*,[88] the Court held that the reserved rights doctrine is applicable to the national forests. It emphasized, however, that the doctrine is a judicially created exception to Con-gress' historical deference to state water law.[89] The Court also ob-served that "[i]n the arid parts of the West . . . claims to water for use on federal reservations inescapably vie with other public and private claims for the limited quantities to be found in the rivers and streams."[90] From these facts, the Court reasoned that when Congress withdraws land from the public domain to create a national forest--or a national park, for that matter-- and does not state whether it also claims water for such land, Con-gress probably intended to reserve only that amount of water neces-sary to serve the primary purposes of the reservation.[91]

The Court identified two "primary purposes" for which the na-tional forests were established: preserving timber and "secur[ing] favorable water flows for private and public uses under state law."[92] It recognized that the forests have long been administered to per-mit uses other than these two statutory purposes, such as for recrea-tion and protection of fish and wildlife. Indeed, the Multiple-Use Sustained-Yield Act of 1960[93] expressly directed the forest service to manage the forests for these additional purposes. The Court characterized recreation and fish and wildlife protection, however as merely "secondary uses"[94] or "secondary purposes"[95] of the forests.

Without legislative history to the contrary, the court held, it must conclude that Congress did not intend to reserve water for these secondary uses.[96]

In the course of its opinion, the Court contrasted the two primary purposes of the national forests with the broader purpose of the national parks. Quoting from section 1 of the National Park Service Organic Act, the Court defined the purposes of the parks as being "to conserve the scenery and the natural and historic objects and the wild life therein and provide for the enjoyment of the same . . . unimpaired for the enjoyment of future generations.'"[97] This reference, together with the long history of the reserved rights doctrine,[98] strongly indicates that the Court would hold that there exists a federal reserved water right for the national parks. The harder question, though, is: what purposes or uses of the parks are entitled to receive water pursuant to this reserved right?

Two aspects of the Court's opinion in *New Mexico* render it highly questionable whether it would broadly apply to reserved rights doctrine to serve the panoply of uses recommended by Professor Wilkinson. First, the Court was unwilling to confer reserved water rights for any uses other than the purposes of the national forests explicitly set forth in the Forest Service Act.[99] If the Court were to follow this approach in assigning water rights to the national parks, it would apply the reserved rights doctrine only to those purposes set forth in the National Park Service Organic Act, rather than to the broader purposes identified by Professor Wilkinson. Indeed, notably absent from the Supreme Court's recitation in *New Mexico* of the purposes of the national parks were uses such as ecosystem management, recreation, and provision of Park Service facilities, not to mention an explicit directive to maintain instream flows in park rivers, all of which Professor Wilkinson identified as entitled water under the federal reserved right. Second, the Court emphasized throughout its opinion that it was bound to interpret the scope of the reserved rights doctrine narrowly, because the doctrine is "built in implication and is an exception to Congress' explicit deference to state water law in other areas."[100] Moreover, the Court stressed that, when a river is fully appropriated, the assertion of federal reserved water rights "will frequently require a gallon-for-gallon reduction in the amount of water available for water-needy state and private appropriators."[101] Consumptive uses of water at Park Service facilities will reduce, to some extent, the water available to users downstream of the parks. Although maintenance of instream flows and ecosystem management do not consume water, and therefore do not take water away from downstream users, they do create demands for water, which can limit the rights of junior consumptive users upstream of the parks.[102] In view of these potential conflicts between the reserved rights doctrine and the rights of state water users, and the Court's professed discomfort with the doctrine, it is unlikely that the Supreme Court would adopt the broad definition of reserved water rights for the national parks advocated by Professor Wilkinson.

I may well be overly pessimistic in my assessment of how the Supreme Court will define the scope of the reserved rights doctrine for the parks.[103] Indeed, my own views on the subject, both as a lawyer and as a citizen interested in the national parks, are virtually identical to those of Professor Wilkinson. As stated earlier, I hope that the courts will follow his lead and use the reserved rights doctrine to grant the Park Service enough water to serve the myriad uses that he describes. If so, the federal water right established by the Wild and Scenic Rivers Act would be less significant for the parks, because the purposes for which the parks would receive water under the reserved rights doctrine would be largely coextensive with the purposes of the Wild and Scenic Rivers Act. If the courts are not so forthcoming, however, then designation of park rivers as wild and scenic would become very important. Under these circumstances, the federal water right established by the Wild and Scenic Rivers would be the only means by which the United States could ensure that sufficient water remains available to fulfill the purposes of the Act that do not receive water under the reserved rights doctrine.

Before turning to the analysis of the wild and scenic rivers water right, though, we must first determine what kind of right the Act creates. Probably because the Act characterizes the designation of wild and scenic river areas as "a reservation of the waters of such streams,"[104] the water right typically is referred to as a "federal reserved water right."[105] This definition is not quite accurate, however, and could lead to an unduly circumscribed judicial interpretation of the scope of the water right.

As discussed above,[106] the reserved right is premised on the withdrawal or reservation of land from the public domain. When Congress or the Executive withdraws public land, the courts have reasoned, the United States must have intended implicitly to claim enough unappropriated water to serve that land and to fulfill the purposes of the reservation.[107] In contrast, the water right for wild and scenic rivers has little to do with the withdrawal or reservation of land. Rather, when the United States designates a river as a component of the national rivers system, it claims water primarily to benefit the river itself--to preserve its wild and free-flowing character; to maintain its fisheries and wildlife habitat; to protect its historic, archeologic, and scientific features; and to facilitate recreational uses of the river. While most of the nation's wild and scenic rivers flow through federal lands, and of course benefit the public's enjoyment and aesthetic appreciation of those lands, a few designated rivers do not serve federal land in any way. The Lower American River in California, for example, flows entirely through state and privately owned lands. Yet, the Wild and Scenic Rivers Act creates a federal water right for the Lower American just as it does for the component rivers that flow across the federal lands.

If the water right established by the Act is not a reserved right, then, what is it? Following the current fashion, it might be termed a "federal non-reserved water right."[108] I have always found this title rather awkward, however. Therefore, I prefer to call the water right for wild and scenic rivers simply a "federal water right"--one that is based on Congress' express assertion of its powers under the commerce and supremacy clauses of the Constitution.[109] Thus defined, it is analogous to, and rests on the same foundations as, the federal water right held by the Secretary of the Interior in the waters of the Lower Colorado River, which the Supreme Court recognized in *Arizona v. California*.[110]

One might wonder why it is necessary to classify the federal water right for wild and scenic rivers separately from the various federal reserved water rights, such as the one for the national parks. In my view, it is important clearly to distinguish between the two, because of the history and doctrinal underpinnings of the reserved right. Unlike the reserved right, the water right for wild and scenic rivers is express. Congress stated in the Act itself-- albeit in a back-handed manner[111]--that it was reserving the water of component rivers for the purposes specified in the statute.[112] The difference between such an express claim to water and the implied claim that forms the basis of the reserved rights doctrine may not seem overly significant at first blush. Recall, however, that in *New Mexico* the supreme Court declared itself bound to construe narrowly the scope of the federal reserved water right, because the doctrine is "built on implication and is an exception to Congress' explicit deference to state water law in other areas."[113] It was for this reason that the Court distinguished between Congress' "primary purposes" for the reservation and the "secondary uses" or "secondary purposes" of the reservation, and held that only the former were entitled to receive water under the reserved rights doctrine.[114]

The water right created by the Wild and Scenic Rivers Act is every bit as much of an exception to Congress' traditional deference to state water law as is the federal reserved right. But it is an explicit exception, rather than an implicit one. Unlike in the reserved rights cases, the courts should have no misgivings about whether they are correctly inferring a congressional intent of reserve water independent of state water law. Nor would the courts be justified in distinguishing between primary purposes and secondary uses or purposes of the national wild and scenic rivers system. The Act itself defines the purposes of the system and provides that, for each component river, the United States reserves for itself enough water to fulfill all such statutory purposes.

Having identified the nature of the federal water right for wild and scenic rivers, the definition of the scope of the right is relatively simple. The Act requires the United States to claim water in sufficient quantities to accomplish the various purposes of the statute. As discussed in part IIIA, these purposes include protection of fish and wildlife; preservation of the geologic, historic, and cultural values of the river area; maintenance of scenic views and aesthetic values; promotion of recreational uses such as fishing and whitewater boating; protection of water quality; and preservation of the natural (or at least the existing) free-flowing character of the river for the benefit of present and future generations.[115] Inasmuch as these express statutory purposes are considerably broader than the explicit purposes of the National Park Service Organic Act,[116] the quantity of water withdrawn from appropriation under state law by the Wild and Scenic Rivers Act is potentially far greater than that reserved implicitly by National Park Service Act. This is especially true for the statutory purposes that require the greatest amounts of water, such as maintaining instream flows for fish and wildlife, recreational boating and fishing, dilution of pollutants, and scenic and aesthetic values.

Other than to identify the purposes of wild and scenic rivers for which the United States may claim water, the scope of the federal water right cannot be defined in the abstract. Quantification of the right for individual rivers will depend on a host of considerations peculiar to river in question, such as the average annual and monthly natural water supply, the flow under peak runoff and drought conditions, the availability of releases from upstream impoundment facilities to augment the natural flow, and the variety of expected uses of the designated segment of the river. Depending on the river these uses could demand great quantities of water. Most wild and scenic rivers are enjoyed by whitewater rafters, kayakers, and other boaters. Because recreation is an explicit purpose of the Act, the federal water right includes sufficient quantities to enable such craft to navigate and to enjoy the river. A certain river may contain a scenic waterfall. Inasmuch as the Act specifies that scenic and aesthetic values are among its purposes, the water right ensures that water will be available to maintain the flow over the falls. In addition, a particular river may provide the spawning grounds for salmon and other anadromous fish. Since protection of fish and wildlife, as well as recreational fishing, are express statutory purposes, the federal water right requires the provision of minimum stream flows to maintain the water temperature of the river and the release of spring flood runoff to flush sand and silt from gravel bars to allow the fish to spawn.

The Act provides that it does not reserve from appropriation under state law water "in greater quantities than is necessary to accomplish" the statutory purposes.[117] Thus, as the Solicitor of the Interior has observed, " river designation does not automatically reserve the entire flow of the river."[118] But the Act also states that it does reserve whatever quantities are required to fulfill its purposes. Substantial amounts of water could well be needed to accomplish purposes such as providing instream flows for fish and wildlife, recreational uses of the river, and preservation of scenic views and aesthetic values. The reservation of such flows would have no adverse effects on--indeed, it could only benefit --downstream users, who would be able to appropriate the water for their own consumptive uses outside the designated river segment. The federal water right for wild and scenic rivers could have significant consequences for upstream users, however, because the right empowers the Park Service to demand that such users allow enough water to flow downriver to supply the instream needs and other authorized uses of the designated segment. The exact contours of the relationship between the federal water right and the rights of state water users necessarily depend on the priority date of the federal water right and the effect of the Wild and Scenic Rivers Act on state users that are senior-in-time to the federal right.

In establishing a federal water right for the national wild and scenic rivers, Congress failed to specify a priority date for the right. As a consequence, the courts will be forced to fill the statutory void. To date, only one court has been asked to do so. In *New Mexico ex rel. Reynolds v. Molycorp*,[119] pursuant to a stipulation among the parties, the district court ruled that the priority date for the wild and scenic rivers water right is the date on which the Congress included the river in the national rivers system.[120] This holding follows the recommendation of the Solicitor of the Interior[121] and is consistent with the logic of the prior appropriation system.[122]

The primary function of the priority date is to provide notice to prospective users that there is a preexisting claim to the water of the stream that, by virtue of the prior appropriation doctrine, is legally superior to the proposed use. This notice serves to warn the new claimants that there might not be enough water left in the river following the senior appropriations to satisfy their proposed uses. The date on which the river was included in the national wild and scenic rivers system is the appropriate priority date of the federal water right, because the designation places other potential water users on notice that, pursuant to its powers over interstate commerce, the United States has claimed as much water of the river as is necessary to fulfill the purposes of the Wild and Scenic Rivers Act.[123]

The question then becomes whether the Act establishes a federal claim limited to water that is unappropriated at the time of the designation of the river or instead requires the United States to assert the right to all water needed to accomplish the statutory purposes, even if this means interfering with preexisting water rights. Although the Act states that it reserves "the waters of [component] streams,"[124] the legislative history indicates that Congress intended only to reserve unappropriated water. As Senator Gaylord Nelson reported to the full Senate following the passage of the Act out of the Conference Committee, "Enactment of the bill would reserve to the United States sufficient unappropriated water flowing through Federal lands involved to accomplish the purposes of the legislation."[125] Yet, in its only discussion of existing water rights, the Act provides that "any taking by the United States of any water right which is vested under either State or Federal law at the time [a] river is included in the national wild and scenic rivers system shall entitle the owner thereof to just compensation."[126] This provision clearly grants legal recognition to water rights that predate the designation of the river. It also demonstrates, however, Congress' expectation that it might be necessary in some instances for the United States to purchase or to condemn existing water rights in order to ensure that there is enough water available to accomplish the purposes of the designation.

How can Congress' intention to claim only unappropriated water be resolved with its provision for acquisition of vested water rights? As I read these directives, Congress overriding purpose was to ensure that the United States would be able to administer "[e]ach component of the national wild and scenic rivers system . . . in such manner as to protect and enhance the values which caused it to be included in said system."[127] If there is enough unappropriated water available in the river at the time of the designation, then there would be no need to interfere with vested water rights. If there was not, however, Congress appears to have directed the Park Service to purchase or to condemn existing water rights to the extent necessary to provide the required water. Thus, the federal water right extends only to unappropriated water. Congress "claimed" or "reserved" only that water not already appropriated by someone else at the time of the designation. If the federal water right proved incapable of providing sufficient water to accomplish the purposes of the wild or scenic river area, then government would have to acquire the balance independently of the federal water right.

With this understanding of the meaning and and scope of the federal water right in mind, we now may discuss the significance of the right for wild and scenic rivers within the national parks. The most obvious application of the federal water right would be to prevent upstream junior users from diminishing the flow of the river below the level needed to supply the various purposes for which the river was included in the national rivers system. Thus, consistent with traditional prior appropriation law, the federal water right empowers the Park Service to place a call on the river to demand from junior users sufficient water to supply its senior rights. Moreover, the water right grants the Park Service the legal authority to defeat proposals for new diversion projects upstream of the parks that threaten the values of the wild or scenic river area. In this case, the federal water right complements the explicit prohibition in the Act against the federal licensing of or assistance to any water or power project that "would have direct and adverse effect" on a designated river.[128]

The federal water right also may be used to ensure that the quality of the water flowing in park rivers is sufficient to fulfill the purposes of the Wild and Scenic Rivers Act. It is well-established that a water right confers on the holder not just a certain quantity of water, but also water of adequate quality to fulfill its demands.[129] Thus, if a junior upstream water user unreasonably diminishes the quality of water available to a senior downstream user--for example, by increasing the salinity of the river from irrigation run-off--the senior appropriator has the right to require the junior to alter its practices to enhance the quality of the return-flow. This right is important for the national parks, because it enables the Park Service to protect park rivers from the upstream uses of water that threaten to impair the fish habitat, aesthetics, or recreational uses of the rivers by diminishing water quality. In so doing, the federal water right provides a means of enforcing Congress' directive in the Wild and Scenic Rivers Act to eliminate or to diminish the pollution of waters of component rivers.[130]

The water right embodied in the Act thus helps to redress one of the inadequacies in the regulatory provisions of the statute that I mentioned previously--Congress' failure expressly to regulate private activities on nonfederal land that are inconsistent with the purposes of the Act.[131] When the private activity is the diversion of water by a junior appropriator to the detriment of the wild or scenic river area downstream, the Park Service may assert the federal water right to enjoin the diversion. This is true despite the Park Service's lack of direct regulatory jurisdiction over the upstream water user.

A related but more problematic application of the federal water right would be to control private uses of land that adversely affect the wild and scenic rivers of the parks. A variety of land use practices can threaten the integrity of a park river. As discussed above, the most significant are timber harvesting and mining upstream of the park boundaries. These activities deposit debris and sediment in the river, which increase the turbidity of the river and can harm its fisheries and aquatic habitat.[132]

Just as the Wild and Scenic Rivers Act itself does not expressly regulate these uses of private land,[133] neither does the federal water right created by the Act apply directly to such activities. A water right confers on the holder the legal authority to enjoin the exercise of junior water rights that unreasonably injure the senior user. The right does not grant the power, however, to enjoin the use of private land that affects water quality, but which is not undertaken pursuant to water right permit. In other words, while timber cutting and mining upstream of the national parks can severely degrade the water quality of park rivers, and thereby infringe upon the federal water right embodied in the Wild and Scenic Rivers Act, that right does not confer on the Park Service the direct authority to enjoin or otherwise to complain about such practices.

Of course, the federal water right does create certain legal rights against upstream users of private land, but they are not rights that can be asserted in a water rights adjudication. The Park Service might be able, for example, to bring a nuisance action against timber cutting or mining that is harmful to park rivers. The use of nuisance law to protect the parks against external threats has been the subject of several recent articles,[134] and therefore I will not venture a complete analysis here. There at least two problems, however, in relying on the common law of nuisance to regulate upstream activities that pollute wild and scenic rivers that flow through the parks.

First, it is not clear whether federal or state law would govern the nuisance action. Professor Sax has recommended that Congress authorize the Park Service to enact regulations to govern external activities that threaten the the parks and to bring federal common law "nuisance-type" claims to enjoin any other such private activities that cannot be anticipated in the regulations.[135] But Congress has not yet done so, and the Supreme Court's opinion in *City of Milwaukee v. Illinois*,[136] suggests that, in the absence of such enabling legislation, the courts might be reluctant to create a federal common law nuisance claim to redress external threats to the water resources of the parks.[137] If the courts were to hold that they are precluded from applying federal common law, then the only source of "nuisance-type" protection for park rivers would be state law.

This would not necessarily be a bad thing, were it not for the content of most state nuisance doctrines. For the second problem with relying on nuisance law to protect park rivers is that the hallmark of nuisance adjudication is to balance the competing property rights and interests involved in the case.[138] This does not provide much security for the wild and scenic rivers water right and the values that it serves. A state court, or federal judge applying state law, could well find that the economic benefits to the region of continued mining or timber cutting upriver of a national park would outweigh the environmental or aesthetic harm that it caused. The court then would be justified in denying the Park Service's nuisance claim despite the undeniable degradation of the wild and scenic river water right. Such a result would be inconsistent with what the Supreme Court has told us about the nature of federal water rights--that they are not to be balanced against competing interests.[139] Yet, because the water right is enforceable against private land practices only indirectly through the doctrine of nuisance, the values served and protected by the right would be balanced against those private activities. This is a very poor means of guarding the wild and scenic rivers of the parks against degradation from external threats.

Thus, the federal water right created by the Wild and Scenic Rivers Act affords mixed protections for the national parks. It can be used effectively to prevent the construction or operation of upstream water diversion facilities that threaten to diminish the quantity of the water flowing to the parks. And it may be applied to protect the parks against upstream uses *of water* that impair the quality of the water that does make its way downstream to the parks. But, because the right does not operate directly against uses of private land that are not undertaken pursuant to a water permit, such as mining or timber harvesting, it is inadequate to the task of providing complete protection to the parks against external threats to their water resources. As will be discussed in the last part of this chapter, the use of the Wild and Scenic Rivers Act to regulate comprehensively the myriad private activities that potentially diminish the values protected by the Act will require further congressional action.

IV. IMPROVING THE WILD AND SCENIC RIVERS ACT: SUGGESTED LEGISLATIVE REFORMS

As the discussion in part III indicates, the Wild and Scenic Rivers Act is a powerful but incomplete tool for the protection of rivers that flow through the national parks. In its present form, the Act is fundamentally sound; there is no need to repeal or to amend any of its existing provisions. To enable the Park Service and the public, to fulfill the various purposes of the Act, however further congressional action is needed to supplement the regulatory and enforcement authority that the statute presently provides.

The Act could be reformed with only three amendments. First, Congress should grant the Park Service the direct authority to regulate, and if necessary to prohibit, private activities that threaten to harm the values protected by wild and scenic designation. Second, Congress should expressly direct the Park Service to take whatever action is necessary to fulfill the purposes of the statute, including the issuance of regulations, the commencement of litigation, and the assertion of the federal water right embodied in the Act. Third, Congress ought to augment the enforcement powers of the Park Service and the Department of Justice by including an express private right of action in the statute.

A. Regulation of Private Activities That Threaten the Integrity of Park Rivers

The greatest inadequacy of the Wild and Scenic Rivers Act is its failure directly to regulate private activities on nonfederal land that diminish or degrade the water flowing into component rivers.[140] As discussed in the previous section, the federal water right created by the Act partially redresses this omission.[141] Because the water right may be asserted directly only against other water users, however, it too is inadequate to the task of adequately controlling several of the more significant external threats to the parks, especially upstream mining and timber cutting.[142]

To fill this gap, Congress should amend the Act to authorize the Park Service to regulate, and if necessary, to prohibit, any use of land or water by public agencies or private individuals that threatens to interfere with the accomplishment of any of the purposes of the statute.[143] This amendment, which undoubtedly would be controversial, would extend the Park Service's existing jurisdiction over private activities that take place on federal land to activities that occur on nonfederal land. For example, the Act presently requires all federal land management agencies to regulate mining, timber cutting, and all other private uses of the federal lands "as may be necessary to protect" the wild and scenic rivers in accordance with the purposes of the Act.[144] It also forbids the Federal Energy Regulatory Commission, the Army Corps of Engineers, and all other federal agencies with jurisdiction over the use of watercourses from licensing or assisting any water project that would have "a direct and adverse effect" on the values and purposes of a designated river area.[145] The proposed amendment would direct the Park Service to apply these same restrictions to private uses of land and water that presently fall just beyond the purview of the statute because they take place on private land and do not require a federal permit or federal assistance.[146]

If this amendment were enacted, the Park Service would be able directly to regulate all of the private uses of land and water that threaten the wild and scenic rivers of the national parks. For example, it could promulgate regulations that forbid mining or timber cutting in a manner that allows tailings or sediment to be deposited in the river. The regulations also might prohibit the clear-cutting of timber on state or private forest land along certain slopes, where the practice might cause soil erosion and siltation of the river. Moreover, the Park Service could regulate directly various uses of water that it presently can control only through the water rights system. For example, it could declare unlawful upstream diversions by senior appropriators that reduced the flow in the river below that needed to serve the purposes of the Act. The Park Service also could regulate agricultural runoff and return flow or municipal discharges of effluent that threaten water quality of component rivers.

Under the proposed amendment, the Park Service's authority over these private activities would not be unbridled. First, it would have jurisdiction only over those uses of land and water outside the parks that threaten to harm one or more of the values for which the wild or scenic river was established.[147] Absent a finding that a particular use of land or water endangers one or more uses of the river area and is inconsistent with a specific purpose of the statute, the Park Service could not apply its regulations. Second, the Park Service's authority would not extend to private activities that take place on federal land managed by some other department, such as the Forest Service, or that are directly regulated by another federal agency, such as the Federal Energy Regulatory Commission. The Act currently requires these agencies to exercise their regulatory and management authority in accordance with the statutory purposes.[148] Accordingly, it is not necessary to expand the Park Service's jurisdiction to include private activities that are already subject to federal regulation under the Wild and Scenic Rivers Act.[149] Third, any action taken by the Park Service to guard its rivers against external threats would be subject to the takings clause of the fifth amendment.[150] If, in a particular case, the protection of the river required that a conflicting land or water use be terminated or severely restricted, and the regulation infringed upon vested property rights, then the regulated party would have the right to sue the United States for taking its property and for payment of just compensation.[151]

If enacted, the proposed amendment would provide the Park Service with all of the statutory authority it needs to regulate external activities that threaten the integrity of the wild and scenic river areas within the parks. Federal agencies do not always see fit to exercise the powers granted to them by Congress, however, and the Park Service is no exception.[152] What is needed in addition to regulatory authority broad enough to fulfill the purposes and goals of the Wild and Scenic Rivers Act is a clear congressional directive to the Park Service to protect park rivers and some means of ensuring that it acts on its statutory duties.

B. A Clear Statutory Directive to Protect Park Rivers

The Wild and Scenic Rivers Act, as presently written, is not without expressions of Congress' intentions about how the Park Service and other federal agencies are to accomplish the purposes of the Statute. For example, Section 10 provides that

> [e]ach component of the national wild and scenic rivers system shall be administered in such a manner as to protect and enhance the values which caused it to be included in said system without, insofar as is consistent therewith, limiting other uses that do not substantially interfere with public use and enjoyment of these values.[153]

In addition, Section 12 states that the Department of the Interior, the Department of Agriculture, and also other federal agencies with jurisdiction over designated river areas or adjacent lands "shall take such action respecting management policies, regulations, contracts, [and] plans affecting such lands . . . as may be necessary to protect such rivers in accordance with the purposes of [the Act]."[154]

As discussed previously,[155] although these provisions direct the Park Service and other federal departments to protect wild and scenic rivers within or affected by their jurisdiction, the methods and extent of protection are left largely to the judgment and discretion of the agency. In general, judicial deference to administrative decisionmaking is sound judicial policy. Federal agencies such as the Park Service, which have developed unparalleled expertise over their regulatory subject area and are accountable to Congress and to the public for their policy decisions, are far better suited than the courts to the task of managing federal resources. The scope of this administrative discretion, however is limited by the legislation that defines the agencies' jurisdiction and responsibilities. As the Supreme Court has stated recently, an executive agency or department "may not act contrary to the will of Congress when exercised within the bounds of the Constitution. If Congress has directly spoken to the precise issue in question, if the intent of Congress is clear, that is the end of the matter."[156] Thus, it is appropriate for the courts to intervene in the administrative process to ensure that federal agencies act in accordance with Congress' statutory directives.

In an effort to accommodate this responsibility with the general principle of deference to administrative policymaking, the courts have decided not to compel an executive agency to perform a specific action within its statutory jurisdiction unless Congress clearly and expressly has directed the agency to do so.[157] Indeed, in several well-known decisions involving the Park Service's and Forest Service's duty to protect parks, wilderness areas, and other lands within their jurisdiction, the courts have expressed great reluctance to choose for the agency how best to accomplish that duty and accordingly have refused to compel specific agency action.

The two most recent of these cases provide the best examples of the courts' reluctance to order the Park Service or the Forest Service to take specific steps to protect its land and water resources.[158] In *Sierra Club v. Andrus*,[159] the Sierra Club alleged that the Secretary of the Interior, the Park Service, and the Bureau of Land Management had a statutory duty to determine, to assert, and to defend the federal reserved water rights for

Grand Canyon National Park, Glen Canyon National Recreation Area, and various BLM land in southern Utah and northern Arizona.[160] The United States moved to dismiss the complaint on the ground that, while Congress had required the Secretary "'to take whatever actions and seek whatever relief as will safeguard the units of the National Park System'" and BLM land under his jurisdiction, Congress had not specified that the Secretary pursue any particular course of action, such as asserting federal reserved water rights.[161] The court agreed and dismissed the complaint. It observed that there were no present threats to the various water resources at issue in the case and noted that the Department of the Interior was participating in an interagency task force established by presidential order to formulate principles and standards for theidentification and quantification of federal reserved water rights. The court concluded that the Secretary had broad discretion to determine how best to accomplish his statutory responsibilities and ruled that the task force was an acceptable means of protecting the lands and water resources in question.[162]

Sierra Club v. Block[163] makes this point even more forcefully. The Sierra Club sued the Secretary of Agriculture and the Forest Service, alleging that the defendants violated the Administrative Procedure Act[164] by failing to claim federal reserved water rights for the wilderness areas in Colorado under their jurisdiction. In an important and controversial opinion, the district court held that the reserved rights doctrine applies to wilderness areas.[165] The court refused, however, to direct the defendants to claim or to exercise their reserved water rights. According to the court, there was no question that the Wilderness Act "impose[d] a duty on the administering agencies to protect and preserve all wilderness resources, including water."[166] It noted, however, that Congress created "no specific *statutory* duty to claim reserved water rights in the wilderness areas even though Congress impliedly reserved such rights in order to effectuate the purposes of the [Wilderness] Act."[167] In the absence of such a congressional directive, the court concluded, it could not "say that federal defendants unlawfully withheld agency action under § 706(1) of the Administrative Procedure Act]."[168]

The significance of this holding is underscored by the fact that the district court was overtly disturbed by the Forest Service's failure to claim reserved water rights for wilderness areas in Colorado and frustrated by its inability to remedy the situation. The court stated that it was

> dismayed by federal defendants' benign neglect of this issue of federal reserved water rights in wilderness areas as well as their failure to take any kind of action to determine whether they existed. To the extent that this benign neglect may have fostered as improper understanding of the law, federal defendants have not acted with the degree of responsibility rightfully to be expected of them. Just as clearly as judges should not inject themselves into the prerogatives of the Executive, that same Executive should not ignore or disregard the intent and policy established by Congress.[169]

Nevertheless, the court held that, without an express congressional directive, it had no authority to command the Forest Service to claim reserved water rights.[170]

Cases like *Andrus* and *Block* illustrate the desirability of authorizing and encouraging suits by interested private parties to ensure that the Park Service and other federal resource management agencies fulfill their statutory responsibilities. These cases also highlight, however, the fundamental flaw with such litigation. In the absence of an explicit directive from Congress, the courts will not intervene in what they regard as a discretionary executive decision to decide how best to manage wild and scenic river areas to accomplish the various purposes of the Wild and Scenic Rivers Act. The effect of such judicial deference is to allow succeeding administrations to flout the will of the various Congresses and prior administrations that have placed rivers in the national wild and scenic rivers system by simply failing to take certain actions that are necessary to protect such rivers.[171] According to the cases just considered, as long as the Park Service can demonstrate that there are several ways to fulfill the mandates of the Act--such as acquiring upstream water rights instead of asserting the federal water right for wild and scenic rivers[172]--the courts will not compel the Service to undertake any other specific action, even if it would much more effectively accomplish the purposes of the statute.[173]

As suggested at the outset of this subsection, in general the Park Service is far better able than the courts to decide how best to manage the national parks and the wild and scenic river areas within its jurisdiction.[174] But by the same token, Congress is much better suited to determine which of the purposes of the Wild and Scenic Rivers Act are sufficiently important that they ought to be protected and promoted under all circumstances and in a particular manner. Congress therefore ought to amend the Act expressly to direct the Park Service to take certain specific actions necessary to fulfill the purposes of the statute.

Based on the previous discussion of the existing failings of the Act, two such directives come to mind. First, Congress should require the Park Service, through the Department of Justice, to assert and to have quantified federal water rights for all wild and scenic rivers for which there exists the possibility of upstream water claims. This directive would be applicable to those designated rivers that originate in or pass through nonfederal land on which water development projects are permitted.[175] The proposed amendment would benefit the national interest by ensuring that the Park Service employs the most effective tool available to it to guard the rivers within its jurisdiction against upstream developments that could reduce the instream flow of water below the level needed to serve the uses protected by the Wild and Scenic Rivers Act. For if the Park Service failed to follow Congress' directive, the courts would be authorized to compel the United States to institute litigation in accordance with the clear terms of the statute.[176] The amendment also would be in the interests of the states--and private water users under their authority--because it would require the United States to quantify its federal water rights. This would benefit all water users by providing notice of the existence of the federal water right for wild and scenic rivers and by informing all prospective junior users of the precise seasonal minimum flows that the United States would be claiming to serve the purposes of the Act. The proposed amendment thus would help to eliminate the uncertainty commonly associated with federal water rights.[177] Moreover, by directing the Park Service to claim federal water rights only for those rivers on which there is the possibility of upstream development, the amendment would avoid unnecessary litigation. Federal water rights for wild and scenic rivers that have their headwaters wholly within the park or other Federal lands in which water development projects are prohibited need not be adjudicated, because there is no possibility of impairment of the instream flows for such rivers.

Second, Congress should amend the Wild and Scenic Rivers Act to require the Park Service to promulgate regulations governing all uses of nonfederal land outside the parks that potentially diminish the quantity or degrade the quality of the water that flows into component rivers. The purpose of this directive would be to ensure that the Park Service implemented the amendment proposed in the preceding section, which would empower the Service to regulate the external threats to the parks that currently fall outside its jurisdiction.[178] To provide guidance to the courts, which inevitably would be asked to review the agency's compliance with this directive, Congress should specify which activities are to be covered by the regulations. At a minimum, this noninclusive list should include:

1. Rules governing mining, timber-cutting, and agricultural practices within the water shed of any designated river.

2. A permit requirement for the discharge of any mill tailings, timber, herbicides, pesticides, fungicides, or debris into any component river, including its upstream nondesignated segments and tributaries, whether from point or nonpoint sources.[179]

3. A permit requirement for any activities, such as clearcutting, that might cause erosion of hillsides within the watershed of component rivers and sedimentation of the rivers themselves.

4. Civil enforcement authority, including civil penalties for permit violations and damages and injunctive relief to redress noncompliance with the regulations.

To a large extent, this statutory directive could be modeled after the provisions of the Clean Water Act that establish the National Pollutant discharge elimination system and "dredge and fill" permit systems,[180] as well as the enforcement provisions of that statute.[181] Unlike the Clean Water Act, however, because the object of the wild and scenic river regulations--the national parks --is of paramount federal interest, enforcement authority ought to be vested principally in the United States.

With the amendments discussed in this and the preceding section in place, the Wild and Scenic Rivers Act would contain both
adequate regulatory authority to permit the Park Service to control all external activities that have threatened the water resources
of the national parks and a means of ensuring that the Park Service exercises that authority. The final piece in the puzzle is
the creation of a private right of action, which would augment the
Park Service's enforcement powers by granting interested
private parties to the right to take direct legal steps to protect the
parks from external threats.

C. A Private Right of Action

In general, decisions by the Park Service and other federal
agencies that affect the national parks, or the failure of such agencies to take action to protect the parks, are subject to legal challenge by private parties and are reviewable by the courts under
the Administrative Procedure Act.[182] Members of the public
may not sue to remedy actions taken by private parties that violate the various laws that protect the parks, however, unless the
relevant statutes create a private right of action. The Wild and
Scenic Rivers Act does not contain an express private right of action, and it is unlikely that the courts would hold that the Act
creates such a right by implication.[183] Thus, unlike most of the
major environmental statutes enacted during the 1970s,[184] the Wild
and Scenic Rivers Act does not provide any means for private
litigants to assist the Park Service and the Department of Justice in enforcing the regulatory provisions of the Act.

The addition of an express private right of action to the Wild
and Scenic Rivers Act would be desirable for several reasons. First,
it would enable interested private litigants to supplement the enforcement authority of the Park Service, which may be limited by
budget constraints.[185] The benefits of this "private attorneys general"
concept have long been recognized by the courts[186] and by Congress.[187] Second, a private right of action would allow interested
citizens to ask the courts to redress violations of the Act by regulated private parties when the Park Service or the Department
of Justice fails to exercise its enforcement authority in accordance
with Congress' stated objectives.[188] Third, the inclusion of such a
private right in the Act could help to enhance the public's aware-

ness of the national wild and scenic rivers system and of their responsibilities to protect and preserve the resources within the system.[189] The private right of action for the Wild and Scenic Rivers Act should be modeled after the "citizen suits" provisions of the Clean Air Act,[190] the Clean Water Act,[191] and the Resource Conservation and Recovery Act.[192] In general, these acts confer standing and a cause of action on persons or entities that have an interest that may be adversely affected by the challenged action to sue the United States and parties regulated by the statutes to enforce the defendants legal obligations. The wild and scenic rivers private right of action would grant to such interested plaintiffs the right to sue to enjoin private activities that violate the statute, the regulations described above in part IVB,[193] or the terms of any permit issued by the Park Service to regulate external activities that threaten the wild and scenic river areas of the parks.[194] The private right of action also should permit the plaintiffs to seek civil penalties and damages from the defendants for injuries to the wild and scenic river areas caused by their illegal conduct.[195] All such awards would be payable to the Park Service, which would be required to use the funds to repair the damage to the parks caused by the defendants' illegal activities.[196]

V. CONCLUSION

The Wild and Scenic Rivers Act offers attractive legal possibilities for those interested in protecting and enhancing the aesthetic beauty and ecological integrity of our national parks, for designation of park rivers as components of the national rivers system would both clarify and significantly augment the Park Service's authority to regulate the array of activities that presently threaten the resources of the parks. According to the directives of the Act, the Park Service must manage component rivers, and their surrounding lands, essentially as wilderness.[197] Thus, the Park Service must regulate human uses of wild and scenic river areas--which include mining, motorized transportation, boating, fishing, camping, and hiking--so as to enhance the values which caused the areas to be included in the national wild and scenic rivers system.[198] Because the values protected by the Act are dominantly and comprehensively preservationist,[199] the designation of additional park rivers would greatly improve upon the existing statutes and regulation that permit the Park Service to manage the national parks for a much broader set of purposes, including the promotion of tourism and the provision of amenities.[200]

Of perhaps even more importance to advocates or park preservation is the protection afforded by the Wild and Scenic Rivers Act against external threats to the resources of the parks. The strongest directive contained in the Act is that the Federal Energy Regulatory Commission, and other federal agencies that fund or have jurisdiction over water development and hydroelectric projects, take no action that would impair the values for which a river was placed in the national rivers system.[201] This directive effectively prohibits the construction or operation of upstream projects that would diminish the quantity or quality of water needed to serve the values of wild and scenic river areas within the parks and of downstream projects that, by their impoundments of water, threaten to inundate the watershed within the park.[202] In addition, the Act requires all federal agencies with jurisdiction over land that is adjacent to designated rivers to manage their land "as may be necessary to protect such rivers in accordance with the purposes of [the Act]."[203] This mandates strict regulation of activities such as timber harvesting and mining that potentially impair the scenic beauty of the watershed surrounding wild and scenic river areas or pollute the water that flows into designated rivers.[204]

Although the Wild and Scenic Rivers Act does not directly regulate private activities that take place on nonfederal land and are neither licensed nor assisted by the United States, the federal water right created by the Act does grant the Park Service indirect authority over such activities. Through the water rights system, the Park Service can compel junior appropriators to release water needed downstream to fulfill the purposes of the Act and to curtail uses of water that unreasonably diminish water quality.[205]

Together, these direct and indirect controls over external threats offer substantial benefits for the national parks. For they empower and direct the Park Service and other federal agencies to manage the lands and other resources within their jurisdiction so as to promote the broad preservationist purposes of the Wild and Scenic Rivers Act. In this way, designation of park rivers as components of the national rivers system extends the statutory protections for the parks beyond their borders, creating a buffer zone along vital river corridors to stand between the parks and at least some of the external threats to their continued well-being.

Unfortunately, these extraterritorial protections currently are available to but a handful of the national parks in the lower forty-eight states.[206] To readdress this problem, Congress should direct the Park Service to study and to report on those parks that may be adversely affected by activities beyond their borders and therefore could benefit from the inclusion of one or more of their rivers in the national wild and scenic rivers system. Moreover, to ensure that the Park Service and the public have adequate authority effectively to regulate the myriad uses of land and water that threaten the resources of the parks, Congress also should amend the Wild and Scenic Rivers Act as recommended in part IV of this chapter.

I began this essay with the observation that, for the national parks, the Wild and Scenic Rivers Act is more rivulet than a stream or river. This is true in part because few rivers within the parks have been included in the national rivers system and because the Act is considerably narrower than other statutes that govern the parks. Yet, it is also the case that the full powers and implications of the Act have not been comprehended, let alone implemented in the service of park protection. When this is achieved, the Wild and Scenic Rivers Act may be more aptly described as a collection of rivulets, with each rill representing a value enshrined in the Act, a source of authority for the Park Service to protect the water resources of the parks, or a private right to enjoy and to preserve the wild and scenic river areas within the parks.

As anyone who has spent time in the Southwest knows, far downstream the waters of these tiny rivulets join, and together they become the Green, the Paria, or the Virgin, capable of sculpting the great wonders of the Canyonlands, Bryce Canyon, and Zion. Ultimately, these same waters combine to form the Colorado. There, they may give us the Grand Canyon, or they may become Lake Mead, the Coachella Canal, and Laguna Salada.

The time has passed to save the lower reaches of the Virgin and Grand Canyons or to restore the jaguar and green lagoons of the Colorado River Delta.[207] But it is not too late to preserve our greatest of wonders--the national parks. As with our other water resources, the many rivulets of the Wild and Scenic

Rivers Act may be used for alternative purposes. We can have Glen Canyon, or we can have Lake Powell. May we choose wisely, and learn from our past mistakes.

NOTES

*Associate Professor of Law, University of California, Hastings College of the Law. B.A. 1976, Pomona College; J.D. 1979, University of California at Berkeley.

1. 16 U.S.C. §§ 1271-1287 (1982 & Supp. II 1984).

2. 16 U.S.C. §§ 1-18f (1982 & Supp. II 1984).

3. Pub. L. No. 95-250, 92 Stat. 163 (1978) (codified as amended in scattered sections of 16 U.S.C.).

4. 16 U.S.C. §§ 1131-1136 (1982 & Supp. II 1984).

5. *See* Tarlock, *Protection of Water Flows for National Parks,* 22 LAND & WATER L. REV. 29 (1987); Wilkinson, *Water Rights and the Duties of the National Park Service: A Call For Action at a Critical Juncture, infra,* Chapter 10.

6. 16 U.S.C. § 1271 (1982). For a thorough overview of the Act and its legislative history, written shortly after enactment, *see* Tarlock and Tippy, *The Wild and Scenic Rivers Act of 1968,* 55 CORNELL L. REV. 707 (1970).

7. 16 U.S.C. § 1271 (1982). The Act defines three classes of rivers:

1. "Wild river areas" are those "rivers or sections of rivers that are free of impoundments and generally inaccessible except by rail, with watersheds and shorelines essentially primitive and waters unpolluted." *Id.* § 1273(b)(1).

2. "Scenic river areas," a less restrictive classification, denominates those rivers or sections that "are free of impoundments, with shorelines or watersheds still largely primitive and shorelines largely undeveloped, but accessible in places by roads." *Id.* § 1273(b)(2).

3. "Recreational river areas," the least restrictive category, includes "[t]hose rivers or sections of rivers that are readily accessible by road or railroad, that may have some development along their shorelines, and that may have undergone some impoundment or diversion in the past. *Id.* § 1273(b)(3).

By using the phrase "sections of rivers," Congress made clear that portions of rivers or river systems may be included in the national rivers system. Indeed, Congress defined the term "river" very broadly. As used in the statue, "river" refers to "any flowing body of water or estuary or a section, portion, or tributary thereof, including rivers, streams, creeks, runs, kills, rills, and small lakes." *Id.* § 1286(a). Thus, designation of an entire watershed or river system neither is required by the Act nor is typical of the rivers that have been placed in the system to date.

8. *Compare* Section 11 of the Wild and Scenic Rivers Act, 16 U.S.C. § 1281(a) (1982) (administration of rivers shall emphasize protection of "esthetic, scenic, historic, archeologic, and scientific features") *with* Section 4(b) of the Wilderness Act, 16 U.S.C. § 1133(b) (1982) (wilderness areas shall be managed so as to preserve "wilderness character" and "shall be devoted to the public purposes of recreational, scenic, scientific, educational, conservation, and historic use").

9. *See* 16 U.S.C. § 1247(a) (1982).

10. *See, e.g., id.* § 1247(a)(56) (Cache La Poudre River). In general, rivers that flow through the national forests are managed by the Secretary of Agriculture, acting through the Forest Service. *See, e.g., id.* An exception is for rivers that are included in the National Wild and Scenic Rivers System by the Secretary of the Interior pursuant to section 2(a)(ii) of the Act. *See infra* note 28. Although the Act requires the state to "permanently administer[]. . ." these rivers "without expense to the United States other than for the administration and management of federally owned lands," 16 U.S.C. § 1273(a), they are under the general jurisdiction of the Secretary of the Interior. *See* Swanson Mining Corp. v. FERC, 790 F.2d 96 (D.C. Cir. 1986).

11. 16 U.S.C. § 1281(a) (1982).

12. *Id.* § 1283(a). Congress recognized that some component rivers may flow through federal reservations that also must be managed primarily for preservationist and compatible purposes. Thus, in cases of conflict between the Wild and Scenic Rivers Act and the other land management statute--for example, the Wilderness Act or the National Park Service Act--Congress specified that "the more restrictive provisions shall apply." *Id.* § 1281(b) & (c).

13. *Id.* § 1278(a). In China Flat Co., 27 F.E.R.C. 61,024 (1984), the Comission ruled that the Act vests in the Secretary with responsibility for managing the designated river the authority to determine whether a proposed project either is on or directly affects the river. The Secretary's determination is binding on the Commission. *See* Swanson Mining Co. v. FERC, 790 F.2d 96, 103-05 (D.C. Cir. 1986).

14. 16 U.S.C. § 1278(a) (1982). In this case, the Act expressly delegates to the Secretary charged with administering the river the determination of whether the project would impair the uses protected by the statute. *Id.* In Swanson Mining Co. v. FERC, 790 F.2d 96 (D.C. Cir. 1986), the court of appeals held that the prohibition against FERC licensing of a hydroelectric project "on or affecting" a component river, *see supra* text accompanying note 13, is more restrictive than the general limitation of federal assistance discussed in the text. Thus, FERC may not license a project that is located on or which would directly affect a designated river, even if the project would not adversely affect the values for which the river was included in the wild and scenic system. *See* 790 F.2d at 102-03.

15. *Id.* § 1280(a)(i) (1982). The regulations apply only to mining claims that are not perfected as of the date on which the river was included in the national system. Mining activities pursuant to perfected claims are subject only to the general federal mining and mineral leasing laws. *Id.*

16. *See supra* note 7.

17. 16 U.S.C. § 1280(a)(iii) (1982). The phrase "subject to valid existing rights" is ambiguous. The Department of the Interior has interpreted it to mean that existing mining activities are allowed to continue, provided that they are "conducted in a manner that minimizes surface disturbance, sedimentation and pollution, and visual impairment." U.S. DEPT. OF THE INTERIOR, HERITAGE CONSERVATION AND RECREATION SERVICE, FINAL ENVIRONMENTAL IMPACT STATEMENT, PROPOSED DESIGNATION OF FIVE CALIFORNIA RIVERS IN THE NATIONAL WILD AND SCENIC RIVERS SYSTEM, APP. D-13 (1980). On the other hand, the subsection could well be construed as a congressional directive that all mining activities be halted in wild river areas, subject to the constitutional reequirement that just compensation be paid for the taking of vested mineral rights.

18. *Cf.* Tarlock & Tippy, *supra* note 6, at 733-39 (discussing "federal rights to protect the flow of the river and control pollution").

19. Of course, the courts have held, time and again, that in creating various federal reservations Congress *implicitly* claimed unappropriated water necessary to fulfill the purposes of the reservation. *See, e.g.,* United States v. New Mexico, 438 U.S. 696 (1978) (national forests); Cappaert v. United States, 426 U.S. 128 (1976) (national monuments); Arizona v. California, 373 U.S. 546, 595-601 (1963) (Indian reservations, national recreation areas, and national wildlife refuges), *decree entered,* 376 U.S. 340, 343-46 (1964); Winters v. United States, 207 U.S. 564 (1908) (Indian reservations); Sierra Club v. Block, 622 F. Supp. 842 (D. Colo. 1985) (wilderness areas), *appeal dismissed sub nom.* Sierra Club v. Lyng, Nos. 86-1153, 86-1154 & 86-1155 (10th Cir. Oct 8, 1986), *on remand,* Sierra Club v. Lyng, 661 F. Supp. 1490 (D. Colo. 1987); United States v. City and County of Denver, 656 P.2d 1 (Colo. 1982) (national parks). When Congress has addressed expressly the subject of water rights, it generally has deferred to state law. *See, e.g.,* Reclamation Act of 1902, 43 U.S.C. § 383 (1982); Forest Service Organic Act of 1897, 16 U.S.C. § 481 (1982); Desert Land Act of 1877, 43 U.S.C. § 321 (1982); Act of July 9, 1870, 43 U.S.C. § 661 (1982); Mining Act of 1866, *id.* The leading judicial interpretations of these statutes are California v. United States, 438 U.S. 645 (1978);

United States v. New Mexico, 438 U.S. 696 (1978); California Oregon Power Co. v. Beaver Portland Cement Co., 295 U.S. 142 (1935); and United States v. Rio Grande Dam & Irrigation Co., 174 U.S. 690 (1899). On a few more recent occasions, Congress has discussed the relationship between federal water rights and state law, but only to state that the enactment of a particular land management statue shall not be construed as either "an express or implied claim or denial on the part of the Federal Government as to exemption from State water laws." Wilderness Act of 1964, 16 U.S.C. § 1133(d)(6) (1982); *see* Federal Land Policy and Management Act of 1976, Pub. L. No. 94-579, § 701 (g)(2), 90 Stat. 2743, 2786 (1976).

20. 16 U.S.C. § 1284(b) (1982).

21. *Id.* § 1284(c).

22. *Id.* § 1284(d).

23. I am not the first to express frustration over this statutory confusion. In his unjustly infamous opinion on federal water rithts under the jurisdiction of the Department of the Interior, former Solicitor of the Interior Leo Krulitz called Section 13(b) "a *non sequitor* roughly designed to preserve the *status quo* of federal-state relations in water law under establised 'principles of law,' including the reserved water rights doctrine." Federal Water Rights of the National Park Serv., Fish and Wildlife Serv., Bureau of Reclamation and the Bureau of Land Management, 86 Int. Dec. 553, 607-08 n.99 (1979) ("Krulitz Opinion").

24. *See supra* note 19.

25. This reading of section 13(d) is consistent with the district court's interpretation in Sierra Club v. Lyng, 661 F. Supp. 1490 (D. Colo. 1987) of identical language contained in section 4(d)(7) of the Wilderness Act. 16 U.S.C. § 1133(d)(6) (1982). There, the court held that these statutory terms are "simply a disclaimer." 661 F. Supp. at 1493. It noted that "[c]ourts often bear the responsibility of adjudicating the interaction between newly created congressional programs and pre-existing state law." *Id.* (footnote omitted). The court held that, in enacting section 4(d)(7) of the Wilderness Act,

> Congress sanctioned this completely normal process by expressly disclaiming any decisional responsibility in this regard. . . . By its own terms, § 4(d)(7) does not purport to work any substantive change in the rights parties may acquire under the various doctrines of water law, including the [federal] reserved rights doctrine. Any decisions in that regard are properly left to case-by-case adjudication.

Id. at 1493-94.

26. These rivers are listed at 16 U.S.C. § 1274(a)(1)-(10) (1982). In the 1968 Act and in subsequent legislation, Congress also has identified ninety rivers as candidates for inclusion in the national rivers system. *Id.* § 1276(a). For each of these "study rivers," Congress idrected the secretary of the Interior--or, in the case of rivers flowing through national forest lands, the Secretary of Agriculture--to "study and submit to the President reports on the suitability or nonsuitability for addition to the national wild and scenic rivers system." *Id.* § 1275(a); *see id.* § 1276(b). The Act requires the Secretary to conduct the studies "in as close cooperation with apporpriate agencies of the affected State and its political subdivisions as possible." *Id.* § 1276(c). Congress has included a few of the study rivers in the national rivers system. For the most part, however, it has declined to designate rivers from the study list.

27. *See id.* § 1274(a)(11)-(61); Pub. L. No. 100-149, 101 Stat. 879 (1987) (Merced River); Pub. L. No. 100-174, 101 Stat. 924 (1987) (Kern River).

28. Section 2(a)(ii) of the Wild and Scenic Rivers Act, 16 U.S.C. § 1273(a)(ii) (1982), authorizes the Secretary of the Interior, upon the request of the Governor, to place into the national system rivers that "are designated as wild, scenic or recreational rivers by the legislature of the State or States through which they flow." Before he may designate

a river under Section 2(a)(ii), the Secretary must determine that (1) the river "meet[s] the criteria established in [the Act] and such other criteria supplementary thereto as he may prescribe"; and (2) the state will be able permanently to administer the river "without expense to the United States other than for administration and management of federally owned lands." *Id.*

The nine rivers that have been included in the national system pursuant to Section 2(a)(ii) are: the Upper and Lower Little Miami River and the Little Beaver Creek in Ohio; the Lower St. Croix River in Minnesota and Wisconsin; the New River in North Carolina; and the Smith, Klamath, Eel, Trinity, and Lower American Rivers in California.

For a critical discussion of the controversial designation of the five California rivers by former Secretary Cecil D. Andrus in January 1981, *see* Fairfax, Andrews & Buchsbaum, *Federalism and the National Wild and Scenic Rivers Act*, 59 WASH. L. REV. 417 (1984). The United States Court of Appeals for the Ninth Circuit upheld the designation in all respects in County of Del Norte v. United States, 732 F.2d 1462 (9th Cir. 1984), *cert. denied*, 469 U.S. 1189 (1985).

29. The national wild and scenic rivers that are at least partly within a park are:

River	State	Park, Monument, Preserve, or Recreation Area
Alagnak	Alaska	Katmai NPR
Alatna	Alaska	Gates of the Arctic NP
Aniakchak	Alaska	Aniakchak NM & NRP
Charley	Alaska	Yukon-Charley Rivers NPR
Chilikadrotna	Alaska	Lake Clark NP & PR
Flathead, S.Fork	Montana	Glacier NP
Flathead, N.Fork	Montana	Glacier NP
John	Alaska	Gates of the Arctic NP
Klamath	California	Redwood NP
Kobuk	Alaska	Gates of the Arctic NP
Koyukuk, N.Fork	Alaska	Gates of the Arctic NP
Mulchatna	Alaska	Lake Clark NP & PR
Noatak	Alaska	Gates of the Arctic NP and Noatak NPR
Rio Grande	Texas	Big Bend NP
Salmon	Alaska	Kobuk Valley NP
Tinayguk	Alaska	Gates of the Arctic NP
Tuolumne	California	Yosemite NP

This list does not include the Skagit River, which flows through the North Cascades National Park in Washington, because the rivr corridor throught the park is managed by the Forest Service as a National Recreation Area easement. It does include the Klamath River in California, however, even though it only flows through one river mile of Redwood National Park.

30. 16 U.S.C. §§ 3101-3233 (1982).

31. At least the legislative history does not reveal that Congress had such a purpose. *See* S. REP. NO. 96-413, 96th Cong., 2d Sess. 137-72, 215-16, *reprinted in* [1980] U.S. CODE CONG. & AD. NEWS 5070, 5080-5116, 5159-60.

32. With one exception, the few cases that have construed the Act have addressed matters that are peripheral to the subject of this chapter. *See, e.g.,* Sierra Club v. FERC, 754 F.2d 1506 (9th Cir. 1985) (Congress intended to exempt tributaries of Tuolumne

River from proscriptions of section 7(a) of the Act); County of Del Norte v. United States, 732 U.S. 1462 (9th Cir. 1984) (Secretary did not violate NEPA regulations or act arbitrarily or capriciously in designating rivers pursuant to Section 2(a)(ii) of Act), *cert. denied*, 469 U.S. 1189 (1985); United States v. Hells Canyon Guide Service, 660 F.2d 735 (9th Cir. 1981) (Forest Service's permit system for boating on Snake River is a valid exercise of discretion under statute); Kiernat v. County of Chicago, 564 F. Supp. 1089 (D. Minn. 1983) (Act does not generally preempt local land use laws). The exception is Swanson Mining Co. v. FERC, 790 F.2d 96 (D.C. Cir. 1986). *See supra* note 14.

33. *See supra* text at note 11.

34. 16 U.S.C. § 1281(a) (1982).

35. *See id.* §§ 1271, 1273(b), 1282(a) & 1283(c).

36. Chevron, U.S.A. v. Natural Resources Defense Council, 467 U.S. 837, 843 (1984) (Morton v. Ruiz, 415 U.S. 199, 231 (1974)).

37. *Id.* at 844 (footnote omitted).

38. *Id.* at 845 (quoting United States v. Shimer, 367 U.S. 374, 383 (1961)).

39. *See id.*; Chemical Manufacturers Assoc. V. Natural Resources Defense Council, 105 S. Ct. 1102, 1108 (1985).

40. *See supra* text at note 8.

41. Department of the Interior & Department of Agriculture, National Wild and Scenic Rivers System: Final Revised Guidelines for Eligibility, Classification and Management of River Areas, 47 Fed. Reg. 39,454 (1982).

42. *Id.* at 39,458-59.

43. *Id.* at 39,459.

44. *Id.*

45. The National Park Service Organic Act authorizes the Park Service to sell or dispose of timber only where "the cutting of such timber is required in order to control the attacks of insects or diseases or otherwise conserve the scenery or historic objects in [the] park." 16 U.S.C. § 3 (1982).

46. 16 U.S.C. § 1284(a).

47. The guidelines do not address the subject of mining in wild and scenic river areas. As discussed in note 17 *supra*, however, the Department of the Interior has set forth in other documents general principles to regulate mining. In wild river areas, existing mining may continue so long as it is "conducted in a manner that minimizes surface disturbance, sedimentation and pollution, and visual impairment." 1 U.S. DEPARTMENT OF THE INTERIOR, HERITAGE CONSERVATION AND RECREATION SERV., *supra* note 17, at App. D-13. New mining claims are prohibited, however, within one-quarter mile of wild rivers. *Id.* In scenic and recreational river areas, new and existing mining may take place subject to the same conduct requirements as for mining in wild river areas. *Id.* at App. D-15 & D-17.

48. 47 Fed. Reg. 39,459 (1982).

49. *See* 16 U.S.C. §§ 1273(b)(1)-(2) (1982).

50. Indeed, the guidelines state that park and river managers "may provide basic facilities to absorb user impacts on the resource." 47 Fed. Reg. 39,459 (1982). The guidelines specify that

> [w]ild river areas will contain only the basic minimum facilities in keeping with the "essentially primitive" nature of the area. If facilities such as toilets and refuse containers are necessary, they will generally be located at access points or at a sufficient distance from the river bank to minimize their intruseive impact. In scenic and recreational river areas, simple comfort and convenience facilities such as toilets, shelters, fireplaces, picnic tables and

refuse containers are appropriate. These, when placed within the river area, will be judiciously located to protect the values of popular areas from the impacts of public use.

Id.

51. Congressional hearings in 1974 revealed that Yosemite Valley contained 1498 lodging units, with sleeping accomodations for 4668 persons, and the following concession facilities:

3 restaurants; 2 cafeterias; 1 hotel dining room; 4 sandwich centers; 1 seven-lift garage; 2 service stations with a total of 15 pumps; 7 gift shops; 4 grocery stores; 1 delicatessen; 1 bank; 1 skating rink; 3 swimming pools; 1 pitch-and-putt golf course; 2 tennis courts; 33 kennels; 114 horse and mule stalls; 1 barber shop; 1 beauty shop; and 13 facilities for the sale of liquor.

National Park Service Planning and Concession Operations: Joint Hearings Before Certain Subcommittees of the Committee on Government Operations and the Permanent Select Subcommittee on Small Business, 93rd Cong., 2d Sess. 120 (1974). For those who have visited Yosemite Valley, the effects of this development, and its attendant congestion, need not be described. For those who have not, *see* SAX, MOUNTAINS WITHOUT HANDRAILS: REFLECTIONS ON THE NATIONAL PARKS 12-13 (1980).

52. 16 U.S.C. § 1277(a) (1982). The Act limits the Secretary's land acquisition authority, however, in several important ways. First, it provides that the Secretary "shall not acquire fee title to an average of more than 100 acres per mile on both sides of the river." *Id.* Second, it prohibits the acquisition of state-owned land except by donation. *Id.* Third, if fifty percent (50%) or more of the acreage of a wild and scenic river area is owned by the United States or a state or local government, the Act provides that the Secretary may not acquire by condemnation any additional land within the designated river area. *Id.* § 1277(b). Fourth, the Act states that the Secretary may not condemn any lands that "are located within an incorporated city, village, or borough which has in force and applicable to such lands a duly adopted, valid zoning ordinance that conforms with the purposes of [the Act]." *Id.* § 1277(c).

These restrictions limit the Park Service's ability to use land acquisition as a means of managing wild and scenic river areas within its jursidiction. The purpose of the first limitation apparently was to protect existing private in- holdings. While this goal is understandable, and perhaps even salutory, *see infra* notes 55-57 and accompanying text, it is difficult to understand why an absolute prohibition on federal acquisition of a fee interest in such lands is necessary or desirable. For example, as the statute is now written, it would be unlawful for the United States to accept a donation in fee simple or private land located within a wild and scenic river area in which the federal government previously had purchased or condemned 100 acres per river mile.

The express purpose of the remaining three restrictions was to prohibit the exercise of the power of eminent domain over certain categories of lands. Although condemnation is a harsh, and sometimes unfair, method of acquiring property, it often is the only means available to the United States to secure title to land needed for federal purposes. As will be discussed in the following section, the exisiting Wild and Scenic Rivers Act grants the Park Service inadequate regulatory authority over activities that may adversely affect the nation's wild and scenic rivers, but which take place on nonfederal land. *See infra* notes 72-82 and accompanying text. As a consequence, the acquistion of such land for inclusion in a wild and scenic river area may be the only means of protecting the area from the offending activities. Yet, if the conditions set forth in any of the three limitations on federal condemnation authority apply, the Park Service would be prevented from using its power of eminent domain to bring the land within its regulatory jurisdiction.

The Park Service's management guidelines, which favor the retention of private inholdings as long as the private ownership and use is consistent with the purposes of the Wild and Scenic Rivers Act, *see infra* note 53 and accompanying text, promote the same purposes as the statutory restrictions, but allow the Park Service sufficient freedom to resort to the power of eminent domain in the presumptively rare circumstances in which it offers the only effective means of protecting the wild and scenic river area.

The current situation at Rio Grande Wild and Scenic River, Texas, is illustrative of the drawbacks of park management under such conditions. When Congress designated the river in 1978, *see* 16 U.S.C. § 1274(a) (17) (1982), it included over 100 miles of the Rio Grande that flow through Big Bend National Park and state-owned lands such as the Black Gap Wildlife Management Area. The combined federal and state lands constitute more than fifty percent of the wild and scenic river area. As a consequence, section 1277(b) of the Act prohibits the Park Service from acquiring fee title to any additional land. The Park Service is authorized to acquire by condemnation, *see id.* § 1277(b), but the Act provides that scenic easements "shall not affect, without the owner's consent, any regular use exercised prior to the acquisition of the easement." *Id.* § 1286(c). Thus the Park Service has no means of acquiring either fee interests or easements in land for the purpose of protecting the river area from existing activities on private land within the watershed that threaten the designated portion of the Rio Grande itself.

This problem is compounded by the boundary of the Rio Grande Wild and Scenic River Area adopted by the Park Service in 1981. Notwithstanding Congress' directive that the management plan for the Rio Grande shall establish a "detailed boundary which shall include an average of not more than 160 acres per mile," *id.* § 1274(a) (17), the Park Service defined the wild river area as including only the Rio Grande itself, from the international border in the middle of the river to the bank of the river on the United States side. In other words, the Park Service included no land within the boundaries of the river area. *See* NATIONAL PARK SERVICE, FINAL LAND ACQUISITION PLAN, RIO GRANDE WILD AND SCENIC RIVER (1981). Having declined even the limited powers conferred by Congress over private lands within the Rio Grande watershed, the Park Service is bereft of the land management authority needed to protect the river in accordance with the purposes of the Act.

53. 47 Fed. Reg. 39,459 (1982).

54. 16 U.S.C. §§ 1273(b)(1)-(2) (1982).

55. *See U.S. Parks Chief Warns of Funds Cutback Impact,* N.Y. Times, June 17, 1986, at 11, col. 1 (nat'l ed.) ("some big parks might have to close by 1988 if funds are cut from the park system to help balance the national budget").

56. *See* 16 U.S.C. § 1281(a) (1982).

57. Professor Joseph Sax has had similar thoughts about the value of preserving some communities within the newer national parks, such as the Buffalo National River in Arkansas. Sax, *Do Communities Have Rights? The National Parks as a Laboratory of New Ideas,* 45 U. PITT. L. REV. 499 (1984). In his usual fashion, Professor Sax eloquently summarizes the reasons to maintain certain in-holdings:

> Diversity is a good thing, in human settlements as well as nature. Or, to put it another way, eclecticism is not a bad thing. There is a strong inclination, in parks as elsewhere, to be intolerant of things and practices that do not conform to some preconceived plan. . . . There is nothing incongruous about having a few human settlements remain within newer parks such as the Buffalo River, even though the parks are principally devoted to maintaining natural systems. . . . The reason diversity is interesting is precisely because it reveals differences, variety and the range of the human spirit.

Id. at 509.

58. 47 Fed. Reg. at 39,459 (1982). The Forest Service's authority to regulate the use of designated rivers through a permit system was upheld in United States v. Hells Canyon Guide Service, 550 F.2d 735 (9th Cir. 1981).

59. 47 Fed. Reg. 39,459.

60. Several years ago, while paddling the scenic portion of the Rogue River in Oregon, I had the unpleasant experince of being nearly swamped by the wake of these boats. This experience, along with having to endure the noise of their motors for several miles in each direction, convinced me that such boats are absolutely incompatible with the scenic, aesthetic, and wilderness values of the Wild and Scenic Rivers Act.

61. *See supra* note 7 and accompanying text.

62. 16 U.S.C. § 1273(b)(1) (1982).

63. *See id.* §§ 1271 & 1281(a).

64. The Park Service's decision to allow motorized travel on land should not be too significant. The off-road use of vehicles generally is prohibited in the national parks, 36 C.F.R. § 4.19 (1986), and wild river areas are, by definition, inaccessible by roads. 16 U.S.C. § 1273(b)(1) (1982). While scenic and recreational river areas may contain some roads, *see id.* §§ 1273(b)(2)-(3), neither the Act nor the guidelines would permit the construction of new roads along such rivers. While the Act does not expressly prohibit the building of new roads, such construction would be contrary to Congress' directive that the esthetic, scenic, historic, and other values of component rivers be protected *and* enhanced. *Id.* § 1281(a). It also would be inconsistent with the "nondegradation and enhancement policy for all designated river areas" set forth in the guidelines. 47 Fed. Reg. 39,458 (1982). The use of existing roads by motorized vehicles of course would be consistent with the original designation of the river as "scenic" or "recreational." *See Id.* at 39,459.

65. *See supra* notes 13-14 and accompanying text.

66. 16 U.S.C. § 1278(a) (1982).

67. *Id.* § 797a (1982).

68. The use of the federal reserved water rights doctrine to protect the parks from upstream uses of water that threaten the instream flows and other needs of the parks is discussed in detail in part IIIC *infra*.

69. It is for this reason that various environmental groups interested in protecting the lower Yosemite Valley in Yosemite National Park sought to have Congress designate the Merced River as wild and scenic. Congress included the Merced River in the national rivers system in 1987. *See* Pub. L. No. 100-49, 101 Stat. 879 (1987).

70. *Id.* § 1283(a) (1982).

71. *Id.* Congress augmented these provisions by directing the manager of each component river to "cooperate with the Administrator, Environmental Protection Agency and with appropriate State water pollution control agencies for the purpose of eliminating or diminishing pollution of waters of the river." *Id.* § 1283(c).

72. *See generally* 1 U.S. DEPT. OF THE INTERIOR, HERITAGE CONSERVATION & RECREATION SERV., *supra* note 17, at III-34 to III-49.

73. 16 U.S.C. § 1273(b)(1) (1982).

74. *Id.* § 1283(c).

75. *See id.* §§ 1271 & 1281(a).

76. *See* 1 U.S. DEPT. OF THE INTERIOR, HERITAGE CONSERVATION & RECREATION SERV., *supra* note 17, at III-37 to III-51.

77. *See* 16 U.S.C. §§ 1271 & 1284(a) (1982).

78. *Id.* § 1283(a).

79. Sax, *Helpless Giants: The National Parks and the Regulation of Private Lands,* 75 MICH. L. REV. 239, 241 (1976).

80. 16 U.S.C. § 1284(c); *see supra* notes 18-25 and accompanying text.

81. *See supra* note 25 and accompanying text.

82. *See infra* notes 133-34 and accompanying text.

83. 16 U.S.C. § 1284(c) (1982); *see supra* notes 18-25 and accompanying text.

84. *See* New Mexico *ex rel.* Reynolds v. Molycorp, Civ. No. 9780-JB (D.N.M. Mar. 2, 1984) (order approving stipulation filed Feb. 23, 1984) (Red River).

85. Cappaert v. United States, 426 U.S. 128, 138 (1976).

86. See *supra* note 19 and cases cited therein.

87. Wilkinson, *supra* note 5. In defining broadly the scope of the reserved water right applicable to the national parks, Professor Wilkinson finds himself in substantial agreement with the conclusions of former Solicitor Krulitz. *See* Krulitz Opinion, *supra* note 23, at 596-97.

88. 438 U.S. 696 (1978).

89. *Id.* at 702 (footnote omitted): "Where Congress has expressly addressly the question of whether federal entities must abide by state water law, it has almost invariable defered to the state law."

90. *Id.* at 699.

91. *Id.* at 702. The Court explained that

> [w]here water is necessary to fulfill the very purposes for which a federal reservation was created, it is reasonable to conclude, even in the face of Congress' express deference to state water law in other areas, that the United States intended to reserve the necessary water. Where water is only valuable for a secondary use of the reservation, however, there arises a contrary inference that Congress intended, consistent with its other views, that the United States would acquire water in the same manner as any other appropriator.

Id.

92. *Id.* at 718.

93. 16 U.S.C. § 528-531 (1982).

94. 438 U.S. at 702.

95. *Id.* at 715.

96. *Id.*

97. *Id.* at 709 (quoting 16 U.S.C. § 1 (1982)).

98. *See supra* note 19.

99. Indeed, the Court refused even to apply the reserved rights doctrine to express purpose of "improv[ing] and protect[ing] the forest" set forth in the Forest Service Organic Act, 16 U.S.C. § 475 (1982), or to the explicit purposes of the Multiple-Use Sustained-Yield Act of 1960, which include "outdoor recreation, range, timber, watershed, and wildlife and fish." *Id.* § 528. The Court dismissed the latter by characterizing them as "secondary purposes" of the forests. United States. v. New Mexico, 438 U.S. at 713-15. And, in an impressive legerdemain, the Court held that the former was subsumed within the other two purposes of the Organic Act of "securing favorable conditions of water flows" and "furnish[ing] a continuous supply of timber." *Id.* at 706-08

100. 438 U.S. at 715.

101. *Id.* at 705.

102. For most parks, there can be no conflict with upstream water users, because the parks are located at the top of their respective watersheds. But this is not true for all parks, some of which are located downriver of significant state-regulated water use. Examples include Big Bend National Park in Texas, Everglades National Park in Florida,

Grand Canyon National Park in Arizona, Grand Teton Nation Park in Wyoming, Redwood National Park in California, and Zion National Park in Utah. *See* Tarlock, *supra* note 5, at 34-37, 45-46.

103. In fact, the only case that actually has applied the reserved rights doctrine to the national parks tends to support Professor Wilkinson's analysis. In United States v. City and County of Denver, 656 P.2d 1 (Colo. 1982), the Colorado Supreme Court held that Rocky Mountain National Park is entitled to water under the reserved rights doctrine, but remanded the case to the water court for quantification of the right without discussing the purposes or uses of the park entitled to receive water. *Id.* at 30-31. In the course of its analysis of reserved rights for Dinosaur National Monument, however, the court discussed briefly the subject of instream flows in the national parks. It rejected the United States' claim to reserved rights to water flows for recreational boating through the national monument. The government had argued that the National Park Service Organic Act, which governs both national parks and monuments, has as one of its purposes the public enjoyment of the scenery andd natural objects of the parks and monuments. *See* 16 U.S.C. § 1 (1982). Reasoning that public enjoyment included recreational use, that recreational uses included boating, and that boating required water, the government contended that the Act implicitly reserved water for adequate instream flows for recreational boating through the monument. *See* 656 P.2d at 27-28. The court stated that it could not

> accept the federal government's assertion that the National Park Service Act expands the purposes for which national monuments are granted reservations of water. Acceptance of this argument would mean that Congress has, *sub silentio*, eliminated all basic distinctions between national monuments and national parks. We are, in effect, asked to treat monuments as having the same recreational and aesthetic purposes as national parks. Our review of the statutory and legislative record convinces us that Congress intended national monuments to be more limited in scope and purpose than national parks.

Id. at 28.

Although the court did not come right out and say it, it certainly implied that one of the broader purposes for which Congress established the national parks was recreational boating. Thus, *Denver* could well be read as standing for the principle that the federal reserved right for the national parks includes water to provide adequate instream flows for boating and rafting. All this from a court that has been at the vanguqrd of states' rights to their natural resources!

104. 16 U.S.C. § 1284(c) (1982).

105. *See* New Mexico ex rel. Reynolds v. Molycorp, Civ. No. 9780- JB (D.N.M. filed Feb. 23, 1984) (stipulation), at 8-9; Krulitz Opinion, *supra* note 23, at 607-09; Tarlock & Tippy, *supra* note 6, at 733-39.

106. *See supra* note 85 and accompanying text.

107. *See supra* note 19.

108. *See* U.S. Dept. of Justice, Office of Legal Counsel, Memorandum For Carol E. Dinkins, Asst. Atty. Gen., Land and Nat. Resources Div., Federal "Non-Reserved Water" Rights (1982); Krulitz Opinion, *supra* note 23, at 611-17; Comment, *Federal Nonreserved Water Rights*, 48 U. CHI. L. REV. 758 (1981).

109. U.S. CONST. art. I, § 8, cl. 3 & art. VI, cl. 2.

110. 373 U.S. 546 (1963). The Court held that, in the Boulder Canyon Project Act of 1928, 43 U.S.C. § 617-617t (1982), Congress apportioned the water of the Lower Colorado among Arizona, California, and Nevada and vested in the Secretary of the Interior the sole authority to allocate water to the various contracting parties within each state. 373 U.S. at 575-90. Whether this authority is characterized as a federal water right or simply as federal power over the water is immaterial. For all practical purposes

the two are the same. Rather, what is important for the present analysis is the Court's conclusion that the Secretar is not bound by state law in contracting for the sale of Colorado River water. For like the Boulder Canyon Project Act, the Wild and Scenic Rivers Act is an express congressional claim to the use of water for specific federal purposes, notwithstanding any state laws to the contrary.

111. *See supra* notes 18-25 and accompanying text.

112. 16 U.S.C. § 1284(c) (1982).

113. 438 U.S. at 715.

114. *See id.* at 702, 715.

115. *See supra* note 35 and accompanying text; *see generally* 16 U.S.C. §§ 1271, 1273(b), 1281(a) & 1283(c) (1982).

116. 16 U.S.C. § 1 (1982); *see supra* note 97 and accompanying text.

117. 16 U.S.C. § 1284(c) (1982); *see supra* notes 20-22 and accompanying text.

118. Krulitz Opinion, *supra* note 23, at 609.

119. Civ. No. 9780-JB (D.N.M. filed Feb. 23, 1984) (stipulation).

120. *Id.* at 9.

121. Krulitz Opinion, *supra* note 23, at 608-609.

122. For the uninitiated, a concise description of the prior appropriation doctrine may be found in J. SAX & R. ABRAMS, LEGAL CONTROL OF WATER RESOURCES 278-79 (1986).

123. It is arguable that the priority date of the federal water right should be the date on which the United States first published notice in the Federal Register that it was considering the addition of the river to the national rivers system, *see e.g.*, Heritage Conservation and Recreation Serv., Intent to Prepare Environmental Impact Statement, 45 Fed. Reg. 52,459 (1980), or in the case of a river that is designated from the list of study rivers, 16 U.S.C. § 1276 (1982), the date on which Congress placed the river on the study list. *See* Tarlock & Tippy, *supra* note 6, at 738. Both acts certainly put subsequent appropriators on notice that the United States might be claiming the water of the stream for use in the wild and scenic rivers system. Indeed, the relation back doctrine of prior appropriation law--which holds that the priority date of water diversion projects is the date on which the permit for the project was issued, rather than the date on which the water was actually appropriate--provides some support for using the date of initiation of the study of the river as the priority date. In view of the Act's prohibition of the licensing of any water diversion project "on or directly affecting" a study river, 16 U.S.C. § 1278(b) (1982), however, it is unlikely that the earlier priority date would be of any real significance.

124. 16 U.S.C. § 1284(c) (1982).

125. 114 CONG. REC. 28,313 (1968); *see* Krulitz Opinion, *supra* note 23, at 608-09.

126. 16 U.S.C. § 1284(b) (1982).

127. *Id.* § 1278(a).

128. *Id.* § 1278(a); *see supra* notes 13-14 and accompanying text.

129. *See* C. MEYERS & A.D. TARLOCK, WATER RESOURCE MANAGEMENT 314-22 (3d ed. 1988). In resolving disputes between competing users over water quality, the courts usually apply the ubiquitous reasonable use test. *Id.* at 319.

130. 16 U.S.C. § 1283(c) (1982).

131. *See supra* note 79 and accompanying text.

132. *See supra* notes 71-72 and accompanying text.

133. *See supra* note 79 and accompanying text.

134. *See e.g.*, Sax, *supra* note 79, at 267-69; Note, *Protecting National Parks from Developments Beyond Their Borders*, 132 U. PA. L. REV. 1189, 1191-97 (1984); Squillace, *Com-*

mon Law Protection for Our National Parks, supra, Chapter 3 in this volume; *cf.* Keiter, *On Protecting the National Parks From the External Threats Dilemma,* 20 LAND & WATER L. REV. 355, 391-93 (1985) (state zoning and land use statutes).

135. Sax, *supra* note 79, at 267-69.

136. 451 U.S. 304 (1981).

137. In *Milwaukee,* the Courth held that the Federal Water Pollution Control Act Amendments of 1972, 33 U.S.C. §§ 1251-1376 (1982), comprehensively regulate the field of water pollution and therefore preempt the federal common law remedy that the Court previously had recognized in Illinois v. City of Milwaukee, 406 U.S. 91, 103 (1972). *Milwaukee,* 451 U.S. at 317-26. Based on this conclusion, and the judicial assumption that "it is for Congress, not the federal courts, to articulate the appropriate standards to be applied as a matter of federal law," *id.* at 317 (footnote omitted), it is certainly possible that the courts would hold that the Wild and Scenic Rivers Act comprehensively addresses the subject of wild river protection and therefore preempts the judicial creation of a supplementary federal common law nuisance claim. For contrary speculation about the preclusive effects of *City of Milwaukee, see* Note, *supra* note 134, at 1195-97.

138. *See* R. CUNNINGHAM, W. STOEBUCK & D. WHITMAN, THE LAW OF PROPERTY 413-17 (1984); J. DUKEMINIER & J. KRIER, PROPERTY 917-958 (1981).

139. Cappaert v. United States, 426 U.S. 128, 138-39 (1976). Of course, *Cappaert* involved a federal reserved right rather than a federal water right created by statute, *see supra* notes 104-109 and accompanying text, but this should not make a difference. The federal water right embodied in the Wild and Scenic Rivers Act should be at least as protective of federal interests vis-a-vis state law as is the judicially created reserved water right.

140. *See supra* notes 78-82 and accompanying text.

141. *See supra* notes 128-131 and accompanying text.

142. *See supra* notes 132-133 and accompanying text.

143. In the case of river areas managed by the Secretary of Agriculture, Congress should grant the Forest Service equivalent regulatory authority.

144. 16 U.S.C. § 1283(a) (1982). Indeed, the Act requires that "[p]articular attention be given to schedule timber harvesting, road construction, and similar activities which might be contrary to the purposes of [the Act]." *Id.* The Act also directs all federal land management agencies to issue mining regulations that "among other things, provide safeguards against pollution of the river involved and unnecessary impairment fo the secenery within the component in question." *Id.* § 1280(a).

145. *Id.* § 1278(a).

146. Any lingering doubts about the constitutionality of this kind of extraterritorial regulation should have been put to rest a decade ago by Professor Sax's persuasive and influential analysis of the issue. Sax, *supra* note 79, at 250-258; *see* Minnesota v. Block, 660 F.2d 1240 (8th Cir. 1981) (Congress may regulate use of snowmobiles and motorboats on nonfederal lands and waters in order to protect the Boundary Waters Canoe Area), *cert. denied,* 455 U.S. 1007 (1982); *see also* Garci v. San Antonio Metropolitan Transit Authority, 469 U.S. 528 (1985).

147. As with the Park Service's authority to manage the designated river areas themselves, I would expect that the decision whether to regulate a particular external activity would be left to the broad administrative expertise of the agency. *See supra* notes 36-39 and accompanying text.

148. 16 U.S.C. §§ 1278(a) & 1283(a) (1982).

149. While it certainly would be possible to devise a management system that vested plenary authority in the Park Service to regulate private activities over which other federal

agencies also have jurisdiction, the potential for inter-agency conflicts and turf fights probably outweighs the benefits of placing integrated, but overlapping, management authority in one agency.

150. U.S. CONST. amend. V.

151. Injured parties may sue the United States under the Tucker Act. 28 U.S.C. § 1491 (1982). For a collection of the most important Supreme Court cases on the takings clause, *see* J. Dukeminier & J Krier, *supra* note 138, at 1093-1211.

152. *See, e.g.,* Hudson, *Sierra Club v. Department of Interior: The Fight to Preserve the Redwood National Park,* 7 ECOLOGY L.Q. 781 (1978).

153. 16 U.S.C. § 1281(a) (1982).

154. *Id.* § 1283(a).

155. *See supra* notes 36-39 and accompanying text.

156. *Japan Whaling Assoc. v. American Cetacean Soc.,* 106 S. Ct. 2860, 2867 (1986).

157. The Supreme Court reaffirmed this doctrine last Term in Japan Whaling Association v. American Cetacean Society, 106 S. Ct. 2860 (1986). The facts of the case are complex. In the Packwood Amendment to the Magnuson Fishery and Conservation Act, enacted to enforce the International Convention for the Regulation of Whaling ("International Whaling Convention" or "IWC"), Congress directed the Secretary of Commerce to monitor and to investigate whether "nationals of a foreign country, directly or indirectly, are conducting fishing operations or engaging in trade or taking which diminishes the effectiveness of the International Convention." 16 U.S.C. § 1821(e)(2)(A)(i) (1982). If the Secretary concludes that such activities are taking place, he may certify his findings to the President. Congress then provided that, on the basis of the certification, the Secretary of State must reduce, by at least fifty percent, the offending nation's quota for the exportation of fish to the United States. *Id.* § 1821(e)(2)(B).

In 1984, the Secretary of Commerce determined that Japan was in violation of the International Whaling Convention, but decided to negotiate with the Japanese rather than to certify the violation to the President, which would have triggered the mandatory quota reduction. The agreement between the United States and Japan provided that, between 1984 and 1988, Japan would adhere to certain whaling restrictions and would cease commercial whaling by 1988. 106 S. Ct. at 2864-65. In return, the Secretary of Commerce Agreed not to certify Japan to the resident under the Packwood Amendment. *Id.* at 2865. Several days before the consummation of the agreement, however, a coalition of wildlife protection groups filed suit seeking a writ of mandamus to compel the Secretary to certify Japan. The district court granted summary judgment in favor of the plaintiffs and issued the writ. On appeal, the court of appeals affirmed, but the Supreme Court reversed.

The Court observed that, while the Packwood Amendment clearly directs the Secretary of State to reduce the import quota of a country certified by the Secretary of Commerce to be in violation of the fishing restrictions, the law does not require the Secretary of Commerce to issue the certificate. Rather, Congress mandated only that the Secretary monitor and investigate foreign whaling practices and reach a decision with respect to the investigation. *Id.* at 2864 (citing 22 U.S.C. § 1978(a)(3)(A)-(C) (1982)). Nothing in the statute or its legislative history, according to the Court, takes the next logical step of expressly directing the Secretary to certify a foreign country's violation of the International Whaling Convention. *Id.* at 2867- 68. The court acknowledged that the language of the Packwood Amendment might reasonably be construed to mandate issuance of the certificate. In the absence of a clear congressional directive requiring the Secretary to do so, however, the Court held that it must defer to the Secretary's interpretation of the statute as allowing him to withhold certification despite his finding that Japan had disobeyed the IWC. *Id.*

The Court concluded its opinion by emphasizing that when a statute directs an executive agency to pursue a particular policy, but is silent as to the specific means of accomplishing the task, the agency has broad discretion to choose among the various methods of fulfilling the statutory purposes. According to the Court, Congress' primary goal in enacting the Packwood Amendment was

> to protect and conserve whales and other endangered species. The Secretary furthered this objective by entering into the agreement with Japan. . . . Given the lack of any express direction to the Secretary that he must certify a nation whose whale harvest exceeds an IWC quota, the Secretary reasonably could conclude, as he has, that, "a cessation of all Japanese commercial whaling activities would contribute more to the effectiveness of the IWC and its conservation program than any other single development."

Id. at 2871-72 (quoting Affidavit of Secretary of Commerce Malcolm Baldrige).

158. The third case, Sierra Club v. Department of the Interior, 376 F. Supp. 90 (N.D. Cal, 1974) (order denying defendants' motion to dismiss), 398 F. Supp. 284 (N.D. Cal. 1975) (order directing defendants to comply with statutory duties to protect Redwood National Park), 424 F. Supp. 172 (N.D. Cal. 1976) (order expunging previous directive), is commonly viewed as the strongest authority yet for judicial intervention into the areea of national park administration. *See* Wilkinson, *The Public Trust Doctrine in Public Land Law,* 14 U.C. DAVIS L. REV. 269, 284-90 (1980). In that litigation, the Sierra Club asked the court to order the Park Service to use its statutory powers to protect Redwood National Park from the adverse effects of logging upstream along Redwood Creek. 376 F. Supp. at 92-93. The district court ruled in its first opinion that the National Park Service Organic Act, 16 U.S.C. § 1 (1982), and the Redwood National Park Act of 1968, *Id.* §§ 79a-79j, imposed on the Park Service a duty to protect the resources of the park, which was subject to judicial review under the Administrative Procedure Act, 5 U.S.C. § 706(1) (1982). 376 F. Supp. at 95-96. In its second opinion, the court held that the Park Service had not fulfilled that duty and ordered the defendants to "take reasonable steps within a reasonable time to exercise the posers vested in them by law . . . in order to afford as full protection as is reasonably possible to the timber, soil, and streams within the boundaries of the Redwood National Park." 398 F. Supp. at 294. The court directed the Park Service, "if reasonably necessary," to acquire interests in land upstream of the park, to enter into land use agreements with upstream landowners, to modify the boundaries of the park, and to seek from Congress additional funding for the park. *Id.*

Up to this point, the *Redwood* litigation established strong precedent for active judicial enforcement of the Park Service's statutory responsibilities over the parks. The court even directed the Park Service to take specific actions to protect Redwood National Park that were not expressly set forth in the statutes. In its third opinion, however, the court eviscerated its prior rulings. The court held that the defendants had discharged their obligations under the previous order by submitting a report to Congress, which set forth five alternatives for the protection of the park. Based on the Department of the Interior's representations that it was without funds to undertake any of the five options, the court excused the defendants from acting on their own reecommendations. 424 F. Supp. at 173. The court also ruled that its previous directive that the Department seek additional funding for the park from Congress was not "mandated by existing law." *Id.* at 175 n.2. In concluding its opinion, the court emphasized the limits of the authority of the courts--at least in the absence of a specific directive from Congress--to compel executive departments to take specific actions within their jurisdiction. According to the court, it was Congress, rather than the Executive or the Judiciary, that had primary responsibility for the protection of Redwood National Park:

> To a lesser extent--some responsibility rests upon the Executive, acting through the President's Office of Management and Budget, to decide whether and to what extent it will make recommendations to the Congress for such new new legislation and/or additional funds; also it is up to the

Executive to decide whether litigation should be commenced . . . against the timber owners. Such recommendations are obviously desirable--but they are not mandated by existing law.

* * * * *

It is beyond the province of this court to say whether and, if so, to what extent the Congress or the Executive should act--much less to order such action.

Id. at 175.

Thus, in the end, the most activist judicial enforcement of the Park Service's statutory duties amounted only to a requirement that the Service submit a list of alternatives to Congress. Beyond that, a very well-intentioned court found itself powerless to act.

For a thorough analysis of the Redwood National Park litigation and its subsequent history, *see* Hudson, *supra* note 152.

159. 487 F. Supp. 443 (D.D.C. 1980), *aff'd on other grounds sub nom.* Sierra Club v. Watt, 659 F.2d 203 (D.C. Cir. 1981).

160. *Id.* at 445.

161. *Id.* at 448.

162. *Id.* at 451-52.

163. 622 F. Supp. 842 (D. Colo. 1985), *appeal dismissed sub nom,* Sierra Club v. Lyng, Nos. 86-1153, 86-1154 & 86-1155 (10th Cir. Oct 8, 1986), *on remand,* Sierra Club v. Lyng, 661 F. Supp. 1490 (D. Colo. 1987).

164. 5 U.S.C. §§ 706(1) & 706(2)(A) (1982).

165. *Block,* 622 F. Supp. at 862.

166. *Id.* at 864.

167. *Id.* (emphasis in original).

168. *Id.*

169. *Id.* at 865.

170. *Id.* The court did order the defendants, however, to submit a memorandum that explains tht specific alternatives to asserting federal reserved water rights that they plan to pursue in order "to comply with their staturoty obligations regarding protection and preservation of wilderness water resources." *Id.* The "Report on Methods for Protecting Wilderness Water Resources on Lands Administered by the Forest Service, United States Department of Agriculture," is reprinted as an attachment to Sierra Club v. Lyng, 661 F. Supp. 1490, 1502 (D. Colo. 1987). In it the Forest Service declared that "[b]ecause the assertion of federal reserved rights claims in ongoing litigation is within the plenary discretion of the Attorney General of the United States, the Forest Service can only recommend that any claims for such rights be asserted." *Id.* at 1503. The Forest Service concluded, however, that because there exist no "identified present threats to wilderness water resources, it is unnecessary . . . to make any recommendation at this time." *Id.* It also stated that "claiming wilderness reserved rights is at best, only a marginally effective means of protecting national forest wilderness water resources in Colorado." *Id.* Thus, the Forest Service instead proposed six alternative means of preserving adequate stream flows in Colorado wilderness areas. These ranged from the regulation of the uses of Forest Service land "outside of, but in a position to affect, water resources in any designated wilderness area," *id.* at 1503-04, to the acquisition of land or water rights where necessary to eliminate any threat of adverse effect upon wilderness water resources." *Id.* at 1504.

As in its previous opinion, the district court vented its frustration with the Forest Service, characterizing the Report as "glib," "facile," "grossly inadequate," and "completely deficient in the kind of detail necessary for the court to conduct a review of agency action." *Id.* at 1499. 1501, 1502. The court also reiterated its view that prompt assertion of federal reserved water rights would be the best means of protecting the water resources of the wilderness areas and of removing what it terms the "Damoclean uncertainty concerning the allocation of water rights among the interest groups involved in this litigation." *Id.* at 1500. "'Nevertheless, despite the promising nature of such a course of action," the court held, "I am without power to order the Attorney General to instigate litigation.'" *Id.* (quoting *Block,* 622 F. Supp. at 864). It concluded that the "[c]reation of any such duty lies with the Congress." *Id.* Thus, instead of directing the Forest Service to claim federal reserved rights, the court simply ordered the Service to revise its Report to address in detail the consequences and relative benefits of the six alternatives noted therein as compared to the assertion of federal reserved rights or other alternatives such as "the possibility of using non-reserved federal water rights." *Id.* at 1502.

171. *See Administration Is Assailed On Rivers,* N.Y. Times, Feb. 10, 1985, § 1 at 26, col 1.

172. *See Andrus,* 487 F. Supp. at 448.

173. *See Block,* 622 F. Supp. at 865.

174. *See supra* notes 155-156 and accompanying text.

175. *See, e.g.,* 16 U.S.C. § 946 (1982).

176. The proposed amendment thus would overcome the district court's apprehension in *Block* that, in the absence of a "specific legal duty on the part of federal defendants to claim reserved water rights," it could not "order the Attorney General to instigate litigation to claim these rights." 622 F. Supp. at 864.

177. *See* Riley, *The Water Wars,* NAT'L L.J., Feb. 18, 1985, at 1.

178. *See supra* part IVA.

179. For a discussion of the differences between point and nonpoint sources under the Clean Water Act, *see* F. ANDERSON, D. MANDELKER & A.D. TARLOCK, ENVIRONMENTAL PROTECTION: LAW AND POLICY 356-62. (1984); 2 W. RODGERS, ENVIRONMENTAL LAW: AIR AND WATER §§ 4.9, 4.10, 124-62 (1986).

180. 33 U.S.C. §§ 1311, 1341-1345 (1982).

181. *Id.* §§ 1319 & 1365.

182. 5 U.S.C. §§ 701-706 (1982). The Act provides for judicial review of agency action unless the relevant statutes preclude such review or the action is committed to agency discretion by law. *Id.* § 701(a); *see* Heckler v. Chaney, 470 U.S. 821 (1985). The Supreme Court has held that the latter exception to judicial review is not applicable unless there is "no law to apply." *Id.* at 830; Citizens to Preserve Overton Park v. Volpe, 401 U.S. 402, 410 (1971).

183. After struggling for several years over the appropriate standard for determining whether to recognize an implied private right of action in statutes that, by their terms, are silent on the subject, *see* Frankel, *Implied Rights of Action,* 67 VA. L. REV. 553, 559-70 (1981), the Supreme Court appears to have concluded not to do so unless it appears from the text of the statute or its legislative history that Congress intended to create a private cause of action even though it did not do so explicitly. *See* Middlesex County Sewerage Auth. v. National Sea Clammers Ass'n, 453 U.S. 1, 13 (1981); Universities Research Ass'n v. Coutu, 450 U.S. 754, 770 (1981); Transamerica Mortgage Advisors, Inc. v. Lewis, 444 U.S. 11, 15 (1979). There is nothing in either the text or the legislative history of the Wild and Scenic Rivers Act that evinces such an intention. Even if the courts applied the more liberal test for ascertaining the existence of an implied right of action announced in Cort v. Ash, 422 U.S. 66, 78 (1975), it is unlikely that they would find such an implied right in the Wild and Scenic RIvers Act For, like the Rivers and Harbors Act of 1899, 33 U.S.C. §§ 401-416 (1982), the Wild and Scenic Rivers Act is a general regulatory measure rather than a statute enacted "for the especial benefit of a particular class." California v. Sierra Club, 451 U.S. 287, 294 (1981).

184. *See* Clean Air Act, Section 304, 42 U.S.C. § 7604 (1982); Clean Water Act, Section 505, 33 U.S.C. § 1365 (1982); Resource Conservation and Recovery Act, Section 7002, 42 U.S.C. § 6972 (1982).

185. As Professors Richard Stewart and Cass Sunstein have pointed out, private enforcement also will be limited by budgetary considerations. Thus, private litigants will "enforce a statute beyond the level permitted by an agency's limited budget only if they believe that the benefits of additional enforcement outweigh its costs." Stewart & Sunstein, *Public Programs and Private Rights*, 95 HARV. L. REV. 1193, 1289-90 (1982). This method of enforcement is desirable, they conclude, because "private litigants--who are often closer to local controversies than are public officials--may know more about the costs and benefits of particular enforcement initiatives." *Id.* (footnote ommitted).

186. *See, e.g.*, Scenic Hudson Preservation Conference v. Federal Power Comm'n, 354 F.2d 608 (2d Cir. 1965), *cert. denied*, 384 U.S. 941 (1966).

187. *See infra* note 188.

188. This was a primary reason for Congress' inclusion of the "citizen suits" provisions in the major environmental statutes of the 1970's. *See supra* note 184. As authors of the House Committee Report on the Federal Water Pollution Control Act Amendments of 1972 commented:

> There can be little question based on the increasing number of public works projects which are being litigated that individual citizens and environmental groups have turned and are continuing to turn to legal action as a remedy for what they consider to be errors on the part of the Government. They are no longer willing to rely on the administrative process to work but instead have taken the initiative in having the forum for decision-making be in the court room.

H.R. REP. NO. 911, 92nd Cong., 2d Sess. 132 (1972).

189. As stated in the House Committee Report on the Federal Water Pollution Control Act Amendments of 1972: "The Committee was impressed during the hearings with the intensity of feeling generated by the apparent growing reliance on legal actions as a means of controlling pollution and environmental problems. . . . The Committee appreciates the growing citizen awareness of their rights to utilize the courts." *Id.; see generally* J. SAX, DEFENDING THE ENVIRONMENT: A STRATEGY FOR CITIZEN ACTION (1971), which remains the classic study of the benefits of direct public participation in legal decisions that affect the environment.

190. 42 U.S.C. § 7604 (1982).

191. 33 U.S.C. § 1365 (1982).

192. 42 U.S.C. § 6972 (1982).

193. *See supra* notes 178-181 and accompanying text.

194. *Id.* As discussed previously, the Administrative Procedure Act presently authorizes private litigants to seek judicial review of actions taken by the Park Service and other federal agencies with respect to the national parks and the national rivers system. Thus, there would be no need to amend the Wild and Scenic Rivers Act to include a private right of action against the United States.

195. The citizen suits provisions of the existing environmental statutes do not authorize private litigants to claim damages. Nor do they permit citizen plaintiffs to sue for civil penalties "for wholly past" violations of the statutes. Gwaltney of Smithfield v. Chesapeake Bay Foundation, Inc., 108 S. Ct. 376, 384 (1987). Rather, a private litigant must establish that the defendant's violations of the statute are on-going. *Id.* The Clean Water Act and the Resource Conservation and Recovery Act do provide, however, that private litigants may seek to compel the Environmental Protection Agnecy to impose civil penalties against the defendants. 33 U.S.C. § 1365(a) (1982); 42 U.S.C. § 6972(a) (1982). The Supreme Court has held that EPA has authority under its enforcement powers

to obtain civil penalities for past, as well as continuing violations. *Swaltney,* 108 S. Ct. at 381–82. All three statutes preserve whatever rights the plaintiffs also possess under any other state or federal statute and under the common law. Clean Air Act, § 304(e), 42 U.S.C. § 7604(e) (1982); Clean Water Act, § 505(e), 33 U.S.C. § 1365(e) (1982); Resource Conservation and Recovery Act, § 7002(f), 42 U.S.C. § 6972(f) (1982).

196. In recent years both Congress and the courts have recognized "damages for injury to, destruction of, or loss of natural resources." Comprehensive Environmental Response, Compensation, and Liability Act, § 107(a)(4)(C), 42 U.S.C. § 9607(a)(4)(C) (1982); *see* Puerto Rico v. SS Zoe Colocotroni, 628 F.2d 652 (1st Cir. 1980), *cert. denied,* 450 U.S. 912 (1981).

197. *See supra* notes 6–12 and accompanying text.

198. 16 U.S.C. § 1281(a) (1982).

199. *See supra* note 35 and accompanying text.

200. *See generally* J. Sax, *supra* note 51, at 11–15.

201. 16 U.S.C. § 1278(a) (1982); *see supra* notes 11–12 and 65– 69 and accompanying text.

202. *See supra* note 12 and accompanying text.

203. 16 U.S.C. § 1283(a) (1982).

204. *See supra* notes 70–77 and accompanying text.

205. *See supra* notes 128–131 and accompanying text.

206. *See supra* note 29 and accompanying text.

207. *See* A. LEOPOLD, A SAND COUNTY ALMANAC WITH OTHER ESSAYS ON CONSERVATION FROM ROUND RIVER 141–48 (1966).

PART IV

Regulating Development in and Around
National Parks

Oil and Gas Leasing

Mining in the Parks Act

Geothermal Steam Act

Hydopower, Dams, and FERC

Surface Mining Control and Reclamation Act

Chapter 14

OIL, GAS, AND PARKS

*Philip M. Hocker**

I. INTRODUCTION

Many types of resource development crowd our national parks and infringe on their natural systems. Exploration for and development of oil and gas are the most aggressive, the best-financed, the most powerful, and the most dangerous threats to many parks. Although national parks themselves are not legally available for oil and gas leasing or development, energy development near parks may have a severe impact on park values.

Oil and gas development is the gravest single threat to the wild ecosystem that embraces and sustains Yellowstone National Park.[1] It endangers the values of Glacier, Everglades, and several other crown jewels of the National Park System. The pitch of the conflict between the oil industry and park advocates has intensified in recent years, and today the conservation movement is pressing for greater protection of parks and wildlands from oil and gas impacts on several fronts: administrative, litigative, and legislative.

The leasing laws that govern administration of federal oil and gas need major reform to ensure that America's enduring national park heritage is not damaged for short-term energy development profits. This chapter reviews some of the history, both administrative and litigative, of oil and gas management on sensitive federal lands, with emphasis on the Yellowstone National Park area, and discusses the needs and prospects for change.

389

II. THE TROUBLE WITH OIL AND GAS

The challenge and the frustration of national park protection today is knowing that the values for which our parks have been set aside are not divisible from the quality of nature beyond their bounds. In the past, many parks were buffered from nearby urbanization and industrialization by remoteness and large federal land holdings around the parks' borders. Near Yellowstone, Glacier, Grand Teton, Yosemite, and other parks, the adjacent lands have been set aside as national forests. On those forests adjacent to national parks, as throughout the National Forest System, the public lands' oil and gas are available for leasing and development, except in congressionally-designated wilderness areas. Exploration for oil and gas, whether successful or not, brings an accumulation of impacts that can seriously impair many of the values and resources of the parks.

Energy developers like to assert that the actual acreage of ground directly disturbed by a well is small. The implication that the impact on a wild area is only a few acres is rudely false. As Chief Forester Watts of the United States Forest Service (USFS) pointed out in 1946, "The effect on the wilderness and on big game [from oil or gas exploration or development] would extend far beyond the actual area under lease." [2]

The impacts begin with simple human presence in areas where man-shy wildlife will move miles out of their normal range to avoid intrusion. Seismic exploration, the next step, requires frequent helicopter flights and the detonation of hundreds of small explosive charges, spread over miles of countryside. If seismic indications are positive, exploration drilling will follow: construction of miles of pioneer road through pristine country and operation of one or a series of drill rigs for months at a time will occur. Road traffic to remote wells can disrupt wildlife migration or calving routes. Freshly-bulldozed earth erodes more quickly than natural slopes, increasing soil erosion into free-running streams, and stream pollution can also result from accidental spills of drilling material.

When exploration is unsuccessful, the roads and drill sites can sometimes be reclaimed to a near-natural condition. Often, though, oil prospecting roads are retained by the Forest Service to permit timber sales and other development activity in remote areas where the timber values themselves would not justify road construction.

If exploration succeeds, the impacts quickly become those of a dozen or more wells, the general minimum for a commercially viable field.[3] The drill pads for each well demand more grading, and they must be linked together with pipelines for collection and shipment of the product, each line buried in steep slopes. Electrical power must be brought in to power the permanent well field equipment, another utility ribbon across the ridges. Often, small processing buildings are needed at each wellhead to precondition the gas or oil before it can be piped. All this is accompanied by a steady stream of maintenance and support workers. Original agency intentions to minimize impacts of the project on wildlife and other values fade naturally over time, while the impetus that began the process persists.

Each of these facilities must be serviced regularly, so a year-round steady stream of small-truck traffic to and fro is required in what had been roadless mountainside. And because the road is there, other human activity inevitably follows. Some of the activity may be deliberate: timber sales on the national forests have often been planned to follow the new easy access an oil exploration road provided. But some of the activity is individual: hunters use the new oil roads to shorten the time needed to intercept migrating elk herds. One analysis of a drilling proposal found that "Rapid decline in the elk herds in the area would occur unless the State were to develop special management procedures."[4]

The energy industry is well financed and aggressive. Mountains and roadless expanses that would naturally protect a region from small-scale resource development are not a barrier to helicopters and heavy equipment if the corporate budget is large. A typical wildcat test well today may cost $15 million; the road costs alone to reach an unusually remote and rugged location may be budgeted at as much as $800,000.[5] Preliminary seismic exploration prior to test-drilling may cost more than a million dollars. These large expenditures are financed because the potential returns from a successful discovery and field development are much larger than the exploration risks. The financial scale of an oil and gas operation makes it possible to press human activity far into previously pristine areas where difficult terrain has traditionally been a strong defense against less profitable exploitation.

Impacts from energy development can affect a national park both directly and indirectly. Watersheds upstream of a park may be silted or polluted by development activity. Wildlife herds that are an important part of a park ecosystem may be disrupted. Grizzly bear habitat may be so disturbed that the bears simply abandon an area altogether.[6] National park roadways may be used for truck access to a drilling area, interfering with regular park traffic.

Recognition of the potential harm to wild areas from oil field development is not new. In 1946 the Director of the National Park Service recommended that elk migration routes south of Yellowstone not be leased, due to the disruption of the elk herd that would result from oil field development. With a clear vision of the Service's responsibility beyond park boundaries, Director Newton Drury wrote, "the National Park Service is interested in the maintenance of the elk herd in, *and adjacent to,* park areas."[7] The precedent is well established, but the process of expanding that concern and making it consistently effective is unfinished.

Despite the awareness of danger, most of the legally available land near Yellowstone, Grand Teton, Glacier, and other national parks has been leased by the Bureau of Land Management (BLM) based on favorable recommendations of the U.S. Forest Service. On the six national forests around Yellowstone, over 175 oil/gas wells have been drilled. Fortunately, the only discoveries on the six forests have been at the southern end of the Wyoming Range, remote from the parks, but this has been a result of luck and geology, not sound public policy.

For example, in 1985 Marathon Oil received approval for a controversial well on a lease in grizzly bear Situation I habitat near the east entrance highway to Yellowstone National Park; they drilled promptly, despite unsuccessful court challenges. A few months later, a BLM state official told me the BLM had "breathed a sigh of relief when that hole was dry." Yet the BLM and USFS had issued the lease, approved the well without objection, and rejected appeals and protests from conservation and citizen groups. Similarly, the Park Service failed to contest the decision despite its potential impact on the park and the bears. Luck, not government policy, has prevented the loss of key lands needed by the Yellowstone grizzly to oil field development.

In another recent instance, in December 1986 Exxon drilled a wildcat well on a ridgetop overlooking the east entrance to Grand Teton National Park. Field development there, if exploration is successful, would threaten both an important scenic vista and a key elk migration corridor. Exxon's attorneys are also fighting to keep a lease near that well site, improperly issued by BLM despite Forest Service protest, that straddles prime riverine moose habitat and the park's east entrance highway. Control over the future of this area, its scenic splendor, and its important wildlife habitat has been handed over to Exxon and fate, not protected as Congress intended.

Exploration pressure has risen steadily over the past decade. In the future, "[d]emand for access to National Forest System lands for the purpose of mineral exploration and development is expected to continue to increase." [8] Our national parks deserve, and desparately need, more than luck for protection.

III. THE LEASING SYSTEM

Federally-owned onshore oil and gas are administered under the Mineral Leasing Act of 1920.[9] Intended as a reform, for certain minerals the leasing system reserves much more authority and control over mineral activity to the federal government than the 1872 Mining Act.[10] Nationwide, about 120 million acres of the public domain are covered by onshore oil and gas leases. The leases lie primarily on BLM and national forest lands. National parks and monuments are specifically excluded from lease issuance under the Act.[11] National recreation areas (NRAs) are not excluded from leasing; by the mid-1970s Glen Canyon NRA was extensively leased and seven test wells had been drilled on Park Service lands.[12]

Leases for oil and gas convey a right to explore for and produce those minerals on the leased area. The specific rights of the lessee may be limited by special terms attached to the lease agreement, usually in the form of "stipulations." Most leases are issued through a "simultaneous lottery" drawing, cover up to 2,560 acres each, and have a term of ten years. A seventy-five dollar filing fee is required to participate in the lottery, and a rental fee of one dollar per acre per year is charged. This rises to three dollars per acre per year in the final five years of the lease term (though the rise to three dollars has been suspended by the Secretary of the Interior at this writing). On areas of "known geologic structures," that is, those with high probable oil or gas value, leases are issued through competitive bid for five-year terms and a rental of two dollars per acre per year. Previously unleased tracts or those that stimulate insufficient interest for a lottery may be leased "over-the-counter" to the first applicant for a seventy-five dollar filing fee and one dollar per acre per year rent for ten years. In all cases, the royalty interest that is collected on oil or gas production is of far higher value than the nominal rentals on unproductive acreage.

The decision to issue a lease is discretionary, and is ultimately the responsibility of the Secretary of the Interior. Under the Mineral Lands Leasing Act, "Lands . . . *may* be leased by the Secretary."[13] The Secretary's role is delegated to the Bureau of Land Management for day-to-day administration. In the rare cases where a lease application has been denied, the oil industry has litigated to attempt to compel issuance. The issue of the Secretary's discretionary authority has been tested repeatedly, and found to include the power to deny, as well as approve, lease issuance.

In addition to other public interests, wildlife and environmental values may form a legitimate basis for a secretarial decision to decline to issue a lease. Concern for protecting the surface values of the Kenai National Moose Range led Secretary Stewart Udall to disapprove leasing there; his action was ultimately upheld by the D.C. Circuit in 1965.[14] In recent years, industry has claimed that lease issuance is obligatory, based primarily on two legal theories derived from provisions of the Wilderness Act of 1964[15] and the Federal Land Policy and Management Act of 1976 (FLPMA).[16]

The Wilderness Act, after years of delay in Congressman Wayne Aspinall's Interior Committee, was passed in 1964 with a twenty-year window during which mineral prospecting in wilderness areas would be permitted. During this window, which closed on December 31, 1983, the mineral leasing laws extended to wilderness areas "to the same extent as applicable prior to the effective date of this Act."[17] By 1981 no Secretary had approved leasing of a wilderness area.

As the cut-off deadline approached, lease applicants James R. Learned and others filed suit, claiming that leasing was compelled by an alleged congressional intent that the wilderness areas be explored during the twenty-year period.[18] The specific wilderness named was the Teton, immediately south of Yellowstone National Park, in an area that had been protected from leasing under a long-standing policy directive originally promulgated by the Secretary of the Interior in 1947. The Sierra Club, National Parks and Conservation Association, and other groups intervened in defense of the government's right to deny lease issuance. The U.S. District Court for the District of Wyoming held for the government, finding that the secretarial policy was "an exercise of the Secretary's discretionary power and authority and is valid."[19]

A more successful attack has been based on Section 204 of FLPMA.[20] This section imposes procedural requirements, including reports to Congress, on all "withdrawals" of the public domain. "Withdrawal" is specifically defined to mean "withholding an area of Federal land from settlement, sale, location, or entry, under some or all of the general land laws."[21] From that definition, the oil and gas industry argues that a policy or practice of refusing to lease constitutes a "withdrawal" and the government agency must fulfill the various procedural and reporting requirements.

However, because leasing is not mentioned in the definition, a strong argument can be made that the "withdrawal" language of FLPMA does not apply to leasing decisions in any manner. Yet, the cases have turned on other points.

The agencies have made themselves vulnerable to challenge. A common agency practice when faced with lease applications in potential wilderness areas had been to either decline leasing pending final wilderness decisions, or simply shelve the applications without deciding for or against lease issuance. These practices were challenged by Mountain States Legal Foundation in a September 1978 lawsuit against then-Secretary Cecil Andrus, charging that the failure to make leasing decisions on two RARE II national forest roadless areas[22] amounted to a *de facto* withdrawal. The plaintiffs argued that the Secretary should be compelled to report the "withdrawal" to Congress and comply with other requirements for withdrawals, or else issue the leases. The court agreed with the plaintiffs and held that the failure to make a decision on lease applications amounted to a "withdrawal" under FLPMA. The court ordered the Secretary either to report a withdrawal to Congress, or to "cease withholding said lands from oil and gas leasing . . . for the purposes of preserving the wilderness characteristics of the lands."[23]

This case had a deep impact on USFS and BLM field personnel in local offices throughout the West. It was widely discussed, and was reported to them by oil industry attorneys and land agents as meaning that the agencies were compelled to issue oil and gas leases generally. However, the court had specifically circumscribed its ruling to contradict that interpretation:

> We cannot allow the Defendants to accomplish by inaction what they could not do by formal administrative

order. By our decision herein, we do not purport to require the Secretary of the Interior to accept, reject, or even take action on the outstanding oil and gas leases. We merely hold that the action taken by the Secretary of the Interior, in concert with the Secretary of Agriculture, in failing to act on the outstanding lease applications falls within the definition of withdrawal under 43 U.S.C. § 1702(j) and the Secretary of the Interior is required to notify Congress of such withdrawal or institute action on the applications.[24]

At the same time, however, the court also questioned the propriety of the agencies' efforts to protect large tracts for RARE II designations, reasoning that the Secretary's discretion to deny leases could be exercised only on considerations pertinent to individual leases.[25]

The distinction between the *Mountain States* case and *Learned*, decided a year later in the same court, is enlightening. In *Learned*, the Secretary had studied leasing in the Teton wilderness personally, and had issued a formal policy memorandum[26] exercising his personal discretion to bar leasing for protection of specific scenic land in the area of Jackson Hole, Wyoming. This was upheld as a legitimate exercise of discretion,[27] whereas inaction alone was rejected in *Mountain States*.

Inaction has been attacked again in *Mountain States Legal Foundation v. Hodel*, filed in January 1986 in U.S. District Court for the District of Wyoming.[28] The case has not been decided, but the central complaint is that the government has failed to take action on a group of lease applications on the Shoshone National Forest, which abuts Yellowstone National Park on the east. The plaintiffs may have a strong case for forcing action, but it must be emphasized that this is not the same as a legal case for forcing lease issuance. However, the Forest Service and BLM staff have denied extremely few lease applications, and BLM operates under a policy favoring lease issuance. Thus a lawsuit forcing action is practically equivalent to one forcing issuance in agency eyes.

The Secretary of the Interior's authority over mineral leasing applies equally to national forest lands, even though the surface resources of these lands are managed by the Department of Agriculture.[29] On "acquired lands" held by the Forest Service or other agencies, the secretary of the appropriate department must consent to lease issuance;[30] this provision gives the USFS nominal control in some cases, mostly on Eastern forests. On public domain national forests, the Forest Service role in leasing is purely advisory except to the extent that its authority in land planning and management may override Department of the Interior leasing authority.[31]

Nonetheless, by interagency agreement and an unwritten gentleman's code, the USFS role is crucial.[32] BLM Director Burford has testified that "the Forest Service has a veto [on leasing], and they are the ones that say whether or not we can lease on lands which have been made national forests out of the public domain." [33] Forest Service personnel in the field, however, feel constrained to make recommendations with which they know the local BLM staff will be comfortable. Under the present administration, that has meant virtually always recommending issuance of leases.

BLM policy since 1984 has been that "the only areas that are not open to some form of oil and gas leasing should be those closed by legislation or regulation, or those included in or considered eligible for a formal withdrawal."[34] Where the limiting of a lease right by stipulation is found to be necessary for protection of environmental values, the Bureau's policy is that the stipulation is always subject to waiver.[35] In January 1987, the Bureau drafted new policies defining its goal to be to "act as a minerals advocate in its coordination with other agencies and seek to reduce regulatory burdens . . . regardless of which agency or governmental level" has imposed them.[36] While this policy statement was not officially adopted, it nonetheless was considered an accurate reflection of the BLM's world view.

Since Forest Service responsibility for the protection of surface environmental resources of their lands (and for impacts on adjacent national parks) is constrained, in leasing issues, to advising the BLM, and since BLM policy is forthrightly in favor of leasing and development with little advance regard for consequences, it is almost impossible for Forest Service staff to oppose lease issuance, for social if not legal reasons.

IV. THE AGENCIES AND DRILLING AND DEVELOPMENT

The underlying philosophy of the leasing system is one of federal passivity. Action is in the hands of private companies. The federal agencies' role is one of overseeing and adjusting, not of taking independent aggressive action, for example, to protect park values. To the Forest Service, offering leases and patiently awaiting industry interest is totally opposite to timber management, in which USFS personnel can literally mark the fall of each tree identified for sale.

The system has much to be said for it: it has stimulated the expenditure of vast sums of private capital on oil and gas exploration across the nation and a continuing improvement in the efficiency of prospecting and development technology. In the process, however, other nonenergy public values have been denied their due standard of protection. The passive approach of the agencies has become habitual, even when circumstances call for an active posture. There is a sense of operating by "remote control" in the agencies' methods. BLM and USFS officials may be standing at the wheel of a large ship, but even turning the wheel may not change the course; winds and currents may carry the vessel on unintended paths.

Conflicting incentives affect lease administration. Issuance of leases is primarily intended to promote industry action to explore and develop oil and gas. However, it also brings immediate revenues to the federal treasury from lease filing fees, rentals, and royalties. Decisions to issue leases are motivated by three forces: the intent to encourage development, response to political pressures from industry, and the desire to collect rents.

Many leases, perhaps 90 percent, reach the end of their ten-year life and expire with no drilling activity having taken place. The BLM and USFS have often issued leases in sensitive areas with the hope that by approving leases they could have it both ways: avoid industry pressures and simultaneously collect rents, without having to deal with drilling proposals or development. The issue, though, is one of protecting the public welfare--which means the welfare of wildlife habitat, scenic values, pristine watersheds, and nearby parks. By issuing leases, federal officials have been relinquishing control to industry. The tradition of passivity has been translated into specific management decisions.

A bitter "Catch-22" scenario has been played repeatedly over these cases: when conservationists have opposed plans to lease sensitive areas, the government has claimed that leasing itself has no environmental consequences (being merely a paper transaction) and that there was no cause for alarm. Later, when test drilling is proposed, the federal agency position is that it cannot deny permission, because a right has been conveyed under the lease. Theoretically, this situation could be resolved in either of two ways: (1) leases could be issued that were conditional and that conveyed no final right to drill or develop, or (2) the agencies could prepare thorough studies of development impacts in advance of lease issuance, and issue only those leases where development could take place without unacceptable impacts.

The Forest Service and BLM have resisted studying the environmental impacts of development of proposed leases before discovery wells are drilled. They object to developing "speculative" scenarios of field development, due to the uncertainty involved. Instead, they prefer to perform environmental assessments once a specific drilling or development proposal has been submitted, even though, at that stage, the government's control has largely been surrendered with the lease.

The difficulty with the agencies' approach is that leasing ordinarily involves a legal commitment to allow exploratory drilling, with full field development to follow if adequate quantities of oil and gas are discovered. Yet the National Environmental Policy Act (NEPA) requires that any such commitment of federal resources must be based upon full study of the potential environmental impacts.[37] The agencies were ignoring the law and eventually were bound to be challenged.

Leasing on the Palisades Roadless Area, south of Grand Teton National Park, provided a test case for the "lease now, study later" approach. The Forest Service proposed to issue leases on over 140,000 acres without first preparing an environmental impact statement (EIS). The Sierra Club filed suit, and the Court of Appeals for the D.C. Circuit rendered a landmark decision, *Sierra Club v. Peterson,* applying NEPA logic to leasing decisions. The court found that:

> [T]he agency has taken a foreshortened view of the impacts which could result from the act of *leasing.* The agency has essentially assumed that leasing is a discrete transaction which will not result in any "physical or biological impacts . . . The conclusion that no significant impact will occur is improperly based on a prophecy that exploration activity on these lands will be insignificant and generally fruitless . . . [T]he decision to allow surface disturbance activities has been made at the

leasing stage and, under NEPA, this is the point at which the environmental impacts of such activities must be evaluated.[38]

After the Court of Appeals decision was rendered, the immediate issue was resolved through the USFS/BLM issuance of the disputed leases with "no surface occupancy" (NSO) stipulations. The NSO leases grant a right to explore and extract oil, but under conditions that decline to make any legal commitment of a right to disturb the environment of the leased lands. In effect, the applicants were required either to slant drill from the external boundaries of the NSO lands, or to seek a waiver of the NSO stipulations for a specific drilling site--presumably after the proper NEPA impact analysis.

Recently, the Tenth Circuit Court of Appeals has held, in another case arising from Wyoming's Shoshone National Forest, that leasing decisions could be made on the basis of an environmental analysis and accompanying "FONSI" (finding of no significant impact).[39] The court emphasized that full EIS analysis of applications to drill on the leased lands would be required where merited by the probable impacts. But the opinion apparently assumed that the permit could be denied where EIS review projected significant environmental impacts, though it evaded any direct consideration of that issue.

NSO stipulations are not reliable protection for sensitive areas, however. The agency inclination is to remove the barrier of an NSO upon request. Once the lease is issued, the government feels strong pressure to make the leased area available to the lessee. The original intent of the NSO stipulation was to prevent disturbance of specific small areas, such as developed campground sites or ranger stations, within a lease tract. Since slant drilling from nearby drill pads makes oil and gas accessible without disturbing the NSO area, the mineral was still available to the lessee on reasonable terms. However, leasing large expanses with NSO stipulations has been a comfortable tool for the Forest Service to avoid confronting the environment/energy tradeoff directly.

The legality of leasing large, unbroken areas with NSO restrictions, where the leased mineral is not practically accessible under the terms of the lease, had been in some doubt prior to the *Peterson* decision. A stipulation similar in intent to the NSO, called the "Wilderness Protection Stipulation," had been in use by the Department of the Interior from 1978 to 1980 to prevent surface disturbance in BLM Wilderness Study Areas (WSAs). These stipulations were challenged by the Rocky Mountain Oil and Gas Association, and the challenge was supported by the Wyoming District Court, which wrote:

> With one hand the government refuses to permit drilling and exploration and at the same time extends the other hand to collect lease rentals. Such a position cannot be condoned by this court . . . A lease without development rights is a mockery of the term "lease."
>
> * * * * *
>
> Such a system of issuing 'shell' leases with no development rights is clearly an unconstitutional taking and is blatantly unfair to the lessees.[40]

The District Court decision was reversed, but the specific issue of secretarial authority to issue leases with limited or no development rights is obviously not resolved. The *Sierra Club v. Peterson* decision gave strong implicit support to the legality of NSOs, but did not directly address the seeming contradiction between leasing a resource and barring access to it. There will be more litigation on this point, brought by lessees holding NSO-limited leases. If these anticipated cases are lost, the environmental safeguards represented by the NSOs will be voided, and large wild areas that have been leased subject to NSO stipulations will be more vulnerable to drilling and development that the government may not be able to control.

Even if courts sustain a "caveat lessor" doctrine, that is, that the terms of a lease that are accepted by the lessor are binding even if apparently contradictory to the lease itself, agency personnel at the local level may be reluctant to enforce it. They typically yield to a plea on fairness grounds by leaseholders and approve permits.

"This court must therefore consider the reasonableness of leasing lands which have an NSO stipulation covering the entire area of the lease," the U.S. District Court for the District of Montana decreed in *Conner v. Burford*.[41] Extending the principle of *Sierra Club v. Peterson* that environmental consequences must be evaluated prior to lease issuance, the Montana court found that

To use the NSO stipulation as a mechanism to avoid an EIS when issuing numerous leases on potential wilderness areas circumvents the spirit of NEPA . . . Obviously, a comprehensive analysis of cumulative impacts of several oil and gas development activities must be done before any single activity can proceed. Otherwise, a piecemeal invasion of the forests would occur, followed by the realization of a significant and irreversible impact.[42]

The decision applied similar logic to Endangered Species Act[43] considerations of cumulative effects on the grizzly bear, listed as a "threatened" species under the Act. The *Conner* decision, though presently under appeal in the Ninth Circuit Court of Appeals, is based on an accurate assessment of the reality underlying Forest Service and BLM use of NSO stipulations over large areas: the goal is to evade NEPA requirements for a comprehensive look at the impacts of lease issuance, and to fragment the decision-making process.

In a similar case, *Bob Marshall Alliance v. Watt,* the same court found that, in attempting to issue leases without an environmental impact statement, "[t]he defendants have initiated a pattern of procrastination, not examination, of environmental concerns." [44] The court elaborated: "Later site specific analysis and protective stipulations simply do not comply with NEPA's comprehensive mandate to make early informed decisions and research cumulative effects of major proposed actions."[45]

V. NATIONAL FOREST MANAGEMENT ACT CONSIDERATIONS

The Forest Service is most comfortable when cutting trees. As an agency, the USFS has consistently declined to develop management plans for minerals, including oil and gas. The omission becomes glaring when contrasted with the painstakingly detailed plans the USFS develops for timber harvesting on the national forests.[46] In most National Forest Management Act plans prepared to date, oil and gas management is given even less direction than such other important nontimber values as wildlife, watershed protection, or natural diversity. This failure applies to forest lands adjacent to national parks just as seriously as to other areas.

The National Forest Management Act of 1976 (NFMA) amended the Forest and Rangeland Renewable Resources Planning Act of 1974[47] (RPA) to require the preparation of plans for units of the National Forest System. These plans must "form one integrated plan for each unit of the . . . System" and shall reflect "proposed and possible actions."[48] The amended RPA requires that plans be directed by regulations specifying guidelines that "require the identification of the suitability of lands for resource management" and "provide for methods to identify special conditions or situations involving hazards to the various resources and their relationship to alternative activities."[49]

Where leaseable mineral activity is likely to exert environmental effects on a national forest, it must be dealt with thoroughly to comply with NFMA direction. The Shoshone Plan Final Environmental Impact Statement (FEIS), for example, concedes that in flood plains and wetlands, mineral "development and production to the degree existing east of the Forest would be unmitigable,"[50] which clearly poses a "hazard to the various resources" of the forest demanding planning and control under NFMA.

Furthermore, RPA Section 6(i) requires that "resource plans and permits, contracts, and other instruments for the use and occupancy of National Forest System lands shall be consistent with the land management plans." [51] This is an inclusive requirement, subject to valid existing rights. Leases clearly fall within the requirement that they must "be consistent with the land management plans." Therefore, the land management plans must specify leasing actions in sufficient detail so the "consistency" can be judged. A subsequent leasing decision, even by the Secretary of the Interior, must conform to the forest plan.

The amended RPA also requires that "any road constructed . . . in connection with a . . . *lease* shall be designed with the goal of reestablishing vegetative cover on the roadway and areas where the vegetative cover had been disturbed."[52] The regulations for National Forest System Land and Resource Management Planning expand the need to consider "the relationship of nonrenewable resources, such as minerals, to renewable resources" in forest planning, and detail the need for considering mineral exploration and development in the planning area.[53]

Unfortunately, no forest management plan yet drafted or completed responds adequately to the need to plan for integrated management of minerals and leasing alongside other forest resources. Conservation groups, particularly the Sierra Club and National Wildlife Federation, have raised the issues of mineral planning inadequacy in administrative appeals on specific forests, and litigation appears likely.

It is clear that the tone of passivity that underlies federal agencies' approach to leasing management is being maintained by the Forest Service in its planning process, and must be affirmatively changed. Can litigation alone change the fundamental agency attitudes involved? The goal, after all, is not elegant cases and decisions, but improved management in the field by the responsible agencies.

VI. IMPROVING THE LAW: LEGISLATIVE PROPOSALS

Though conservationists feel that existing law requires much more than the agencies are now doing in considering impacts of leasing and coordinating lease planning with other resources before leases are issued, many of us involved with this issue believe that lawsuits based on current law will not suffice.

Several proposals for amendments to the Mineral Leasing Act of 1920 were introduced in the Ninety-ninth Congress. Conservation motives were not the only ones present in Congress; there has been growing unhappiness with the current system of awarding leases. Beginning with a scandal at Fort Chaffee, Arkansas, in which leases with high potential for natural gas were awarded for low fees over-the-counter, Senator Dale Bumpers has pressed for adoption of an all-competitive system of lease issuance.[54]

Senator Bumpers's persistence and a series of subsequent scandals over apparently fraudulent lease awards have converted many members of Congress to the view that an all-competitive system, or a "tiered" system[55] in which leases are first offered by competitive bid and are later available by other methods if bidding interest is weak, is preferable to the simultaneous lottery and over-the-counter approach.

A competitive leasing system will benefit conservation interests directly. As Wyoming Governor Herschler has stated, our need is for "leasing for production, not leasing for speculation."[56] A focus on leasing for oil and gas where production is intended will frame the necessary tradeoff decisions between energy and environmental values more clearly. While conservationists will not win all those decisions, the honesty of the situation will be fairer to all parties than the present "Russian Roulette" approach.

Several bills considered in the Ninety-ninth Congress included important provisions for improving the prelease planning and public participation process. H.R. 4741, introduced by Congressmen Seiberling, Miller, and others was the most far-sighted.[57] If passed, it would have required integration of lease planning with plans for other resources, consideration of impacts of full-field development, and public notice and participation. The use of no surface occupancy stipulations would have been restricted to areas where recovery of oil or gas would be feasible without surface occupancy.

Hearings in the Ninety-ninth and earlier Congresses have established the widespread problems with the current system and the difficulty of reforming it through litigation. While no bill was passed, the stage has been set for a strong push for favorable action in the One-Hundredth Congress.

VII. TOWARD THE FUTURE

The process of bringing consideration of park values and environmental concerns into the leasing program has been cumulative. From the adverse decisions of *Mountain States Legal Foundation v. Andrus* and *Rocky Mountain Oil and Gas Association v. Andrus* in 1980, a procession of cases has built favorable case law. This has been translated into improved agency decision making, though to a frustratingly small extent.

Conner v. Burford is under appeal in the Ninth Circuit. Briefing and argument are completed, and a decision is expected during 1987. If the district court's decision is upheld, the entire Forest Service "lease now, study the impacts later" policy will be voided, as it deserves. If this happens, however, top USFS officials have stated that they will seek relief from Congress.[58]

If they do, conservationists will face a direct attempt to rewrite NEPA and the Endangered Species Act to exclude oil and gas exploration and development impacts. I am impressed with the Service's obduracy, but not with their judgment; assaults on NEPA, which they may attempt, will not succeed.

On the affirmative side, conservationists will continue to press the application of NEPA and similar protective law to oil and gas at the preleasing stage. On national forests, we should demand full

application of the planning goals of the National Forest Management Act to minerals leasing, through administrative appeals
and, if necessary, litigation. However, the agencies' determination to interpret each court decision as only applying to its specific
locale means that step-by-step litigation cannot bring system-wide
reform within a reasonable time. To really achieve the level of
protection that national parks need from indiscriminate leasing,
fresh protective legislation is imperative.

The National Parks Protection Act (NPPA) would be a
major step toward improving the level of concern federal agencies
would be required to show for the impacts of their actions on nearby national parks. As introduced by Senator Chafee in 1986,[59] this
Act would require that before leasing or sanctioning other federally funded activities on federal lands adjacent to the parks, the
Secretary of the Interior must determine that the activities "will
not degrade or destroy the natural or cultural resources . . . of the
National Park System."[60] This provision would provide a possible basis for addressing some of the abuses caused by indiscriminate lease issuance today. However, specific legislation in addition to the NPPA, specifically directed at the federal oil and gas
management process, is essential to produce a generally responsible
leasing system.

The need for leasing reform has been highlighted by the Interior Department's promotion in late 1986 of blanket leasing of
the coastal plain of the Arctic National Wildlife Refuge in Alaska. Congress must respond to the Department's recommendation,
and the debates over protection of the critical range for the Por-
cupine caribou herd will spill over into a general debate on leasing impacts.

The legislative reform of the leasing system should cover certain fundamental areas. It should:

- Establish a system of competitive bidding as the
  sole mean of issuing oil and gas leases;

- Mandate the preparation of a leasing plan, with a study
  by the responsible agency of the full impacts of
  exercising development rights under the lease, prior to
  lease issuance. This study should be integrated with
  other resource plans, such as Forest Plans (USFS) or
  Resource Management Plans (BLM) for the lands in
  question, and should consider off-site impacts;

- Require coordination of leasing plans with National Park System Resource Management Plans and General Management Plans, to prevent conflicts with park values and objectives;

- Give the Secretary of Agriculture direct responsibility for, and approval/disapproval authority over lease decisions on all national forest lands, acquired as well as public domain;

- Provide for complete public notification of leasing decisions, and opportunities for comment and appeal.

It will be a tough fight. The oil and gas lobby is strongly opposed to such legislation. In my view the planning steps are required under current laws, and the proposed legislation will simplify an otherwise protracted litigative process to get the agencies to comply. The provision for Secretary of Agriculture approval authority will simplify the present dual-responsibly arrangement between the USFS and BLM, and lead to improved accountability and management.

Leasing system reform legislation will be a process bill. Process bills have some advantages; they cover a wide range of territory and a variety of actions--many not easy to foresee in advance. However, by their very breadth they are threatening to a wide range of prodevelopment interests at once, and they depend for their effect on sometimes subtle interpretation and on continued dedication by the executing agencies. We should consider a broader range of legislative approaches. The major site-specific legislative approach to protecting the federal land environs of national parks from adverse development in recent years has been wilderness designation. It is a powerful tool, the more so since December 31, 1983, when oil and gas leasing became illegal in wilderness areas, but a broader spectrum of site-specific legislative tools is needed.

Specific legislative withdrawals of areas from oil and gas leasing, where nearby national park or other values would be endangered if a producing field were to be developed, should be sought by national park advocates. There are areas (such as the Mount Leidy Highlands east of Grand Teton National Park) where wilderness designation is inappropriate, but mineral development threats should be prevented.

Legislation cannot remove the need for steady watchfulness by park protectors and by the Park Service itself over potential threats from adjacent mineral development. Even passage of the most favorable leasing system reforms will only begin a long process. Where the National Park Service has been willing to take a strong stand on nearby leasing, it has had a strong effect on decisions. In the Yellowstone area there are both good and bad recent examples: in 1985 Grand Teton National Park officials expressed strong concern over nearby leasing proposals[61] and succeeded, along with other forces, in halting lease issuance on sensitive wildlife areas. However, when in 1982 the Forest Service considered issuing oil and gas leases within the Washakie Wilderness on the east border of Yellowstone National Park, the National Park Service made no statements of opposition.[62]

On a variety of fronts, park protection advocates will persist. Our knowledge of the complexity of protecting national parks has grown alongside our knowledge of the complexity of the parks themselves. That they are constantly teaching us the lesson of their own complexity, largely unknown when they were established, is a proof of the parks' enduring importance to us all.

POSTSCRIPT

Due to publication delays, a year has passed since the foregoing chapter was written. There have been a number of significant developments in that year; they are summarized below.

Legislation:

In December 1987, Congress passed the Federal Onshore Oil and Gas Leasing Reform Act of 1987 as a Subtitle of the omnibus budget reconciliation package. The content of the Reform Act had been the subject of intense lobbying, and was a hard-negotiated compromise between House and Senate versions. The final legislation mandates a lease-issuance system based on competitive bidding, but retains a lottery backup for leases on which minimum bids are not received. Under the new law, the Forest Service will hold statutory authority to determine whether leases will be issued on national forest lands (as opposed to its previous role as a mere advisor to the Bureau of Land Management), and the Forest Service "shall regulate all surface-disturbing activities conducted pursuant to any lease."

Important provisions in the House version of the leasing reform, that would have clarified the requirement for study, before a lease is issued, of the environmental consequences of prospecting and development of oil or gas on the lease, were dropped at the insistence of the Senate and the Reagan administraion. This bitter blow was sweetened only slightly by a commitment to hold further Congressional hearings on the problem from oil leasing, and to conduct a joint General Accounting Office/National Academy of Sciences study of oil development impacts and lease planning. That process is underway.

Both the Forest Service and the Bureau of Land Management are writing their administrative regulations for the implementation of this act in the Spring of 1988; the content of those regulations will be crucial to bringing real change on the ground. The Forest Service's new statutory authority may be reflected in a new vitality within the Service's minerals management staff, and a new willingness to assert that minerals issues are important components of national forest planning and management. One can hope.

During the congressional deliberations on leasing reform, several members of Congress asserted that requirements for pre-lease planning were properly addressed as part of the land management statutes rather than in amendments to the Leasing Act. The House Forestry Subcommittee held a brief hearing on December 8, 1987, to review the pre-lease planning question in terms of the National Forest Management Act. This approach will see more debate.

Litigation:

The 1985 Montana District Court ruling in *Conner v. Burford* (main text footnote 41) was substantially upheld by the Ninth Circuit Court of Appeals on January 13, 1988. The Ninth Circuit relied heavily on *Sierra Club v. Peterson* (see discussion above) in its opinion. The Circuit did not support the District's rejection of No-Surface-Occupancy stipulations, however, and held that they could not be used to defer evaluation of lease-development impacts. While consistent with the letter of the law, this ruling ignores the field reality: no oil company has been denied permission to drill based on lease stipulations, according to the Director of Minerals and Geology for the Forest Service (personal communication, 31 March 1988). Issuing leases with scanty evaluation of the impacts of their development is folly, no matter what stipulations are used to retain theoretical discretion. The government has not yet applied the Ninth Circuit ruling to its administration, and has stated that it is relying on the less-demanding Tenth Circuit decision in *Park County* (see main text) within that jurisdiction.

Mountain States Legal Foundation v. Hodel (main text footnote 28), alleging that failure to issue leases on the Shoshone National Forest amounted to a FLPMA withdrawal, was mooted by the Forest Service rushing to issue all of the contested leases. However, plaintiffs amended their complaint to include the Bridger-Teton National Forest, and have obtained a favorable ruling (filed August 19, 1987). The Forest Service, more as a result of pressure than court instruction, attempted to bypass its forest planning process and issue leases covering 964,000 acres of the Bridger-Teton National Forest directly from a cursory environmental assessment. The final decision on issuance (or preparation of a full environmental impact statement) is pending at this writing; legal challenge is likely in either case.

Further attempts by oil interests to compel lease issuance under Section 204 of FLPMA may be affected, on Forest Service lands, by the Leasing Reform Act. The Act's grant of power to "object" to lease issuance does not appear to be constrained by withdrawal concerns, so the FLPMA argument may not be applicable.

Administration:

Beyond the legislative and legal tug-of-war, federal agencies continue to grant the oil industry first claim on public land assets, even where there are serious conflicts and the agencies retain decision-making discretion. In March 1988, an oil well was succesfully drilled in the middle of the Anasazi towers of Hovenweep National Monument (the Bureau of Land Management administers the area, except for small monument designations around the actual structures, and had leased it all). In April 1988, the Bridger-Teton National Forest approved exploratory drilling in Sohare Creek, in key elk and and grizzly bear habitat, despite opposition from nearly Grand Teton National Park. On the Beartooth Plateau, northeast of Yellowstone National Park, the Forest Service is moving steadily toward approval of a wildcat well at Line Creek; traffic to the rig would drive twelve miles over alpine tundra, through prime bighorn sheep and mountain goat range.

Our national fixation with finding more oil, rather than making the most of what we have, is epitomized by the current debate over opening the Arctic National Wildlife Refuge (ANWR) in Alaska. A one-and-a-half mile per gallon improvement in the fuel efficiency of new automobiles would provide as much fuel for the United States as is forecast to lie within ANWR. We have a long fight ahead of us. Persevere.

NOTES

*President, Mineral Policy Center, Alexandria, VA. Mr. Hocker is a licensed architect, conservationist, and a former resident of Jackson Hole, Wyoming, who has advocated protection of the Greater Yellowstone area since 1972, and has held offices at the local, state, and national levels in the Sierra Club. Thanks are due to Karin P. Sheldon, Esq., and William S. Curtiss, Esq., of Sierra Club Legal Defense Fund, Inc., for their work on several of the cited lawsuits. The opinions expressed in this article are solely those of the author.

1. Oil and gas leases have been issued on the Shoshone National Forest up to the East Entrance to Yellowstone National Park. Leases are in place within four miles of the Yellowstone northern boundary.

2. Letter, Lyle G. Watts, Chief Forester, U.S. Forest Service, to Director, National Park Service, May 24, 1946. Archive RG 79, Box 2252, File 609-01-1. (References to the "Archive" are to materials preserved in U.S. National Archives, Washington, D.C.).

3. Memorandum from Rick Robitaille, Petroleum Association of Wyoming, to Teton Country Oil and Gas Committee (Dec. 11, 1986) (giving average developed field statistics for seven counties in western Wyoming).

4. U.S. DEPARTMENT OF THE INTERIOR, U.S. GEOLOGICAL SURVEY, AND U.S. DEPARTMENT OF AGRICULTURE, U.S. FOREST SERVICE, DRAFT CACHE CREEK-BEAR THRUST ENVIRONMENTAL IMPACT STATEMENT, DES 81-33, at V-24 (1981).

5. *Id.* at IV-18.

6. U.S. DEPARTMENT OF AGRICULTURE, U.S. FOREST SERVICE, OIL AND GAS EXPLORATION AND LEASING WITHIN THE WASHAKIE WILDERNESS, DRAFT ENVIRONMENTAL IMPACT STATEMENT, 02-00-81-09, at E-4 to E-11 (1981).

7. Memorandum from Director, National Park Service (Newton B. Drury), to Chairman, Coordination Committee, Nov. 26, 1946. Archive RG 79, Box 2252, File 609-01-02. (Emphasis added.)

8. U.S. DEPARTMENT OF AGRICULTURE, FOREST SERVICE, FINAL ENVIRONMENTAL IMPACT STATEMENT FOR THE SHOSHONE NATIONAL FOREST LAND AND RESOURCE MANAGMENT PLAN, 02-14-85-01, at IV-69 (1986).

9. Mineral Lands Leasing Act of Feb. 25, 1920, 30 U.S.C. § 181.

10. General Mining Law of 1872, Act of May 10, 1872, 30 U.S.C. § 21.

11. 30 U.S.C. § 181.

12. U.S. DEPARTMENT OF THE INTERIOR, NATIONAL PARK SERVICE, DRAFT GENERAL MANAGEMENT PLAN, GLEN CANYON RECREATION AREA, DES 77-28, at 46 (1977).

13. 30 U.S.C. § 226(a). (Emphasis added.)

14. Duesing v. Udall, 350 F.2d 748, 752 (D.C. Cir. 1965). *See also* Udall v. Tallman, 380 U.S. 1, 23 .

15. The Wilderness Act, 16 U.S.C. §§ 1131-1136 (1964).

16. Federal Land Policy and Management Act of 1976, 43 U.S.C. §§ 1701-1782.

17. The Wilderness Act, *supra*, § 1133(d)(3).

18. I discussed this history personally with Wayne Aspinall on Dec. 21, 1981, while *Learned* was awaiting judgment. Aspinall, who had chaired the House Interior Committee when the Wilderness Act was debated and adopted, stated that in his judgment the intent of Congress had been to extend secretarial leasing discretion to wilderness, not to compel issuance.

19. Learned v. Watt, 528 F. Supp. 980, at 982 (D. Wyo. 1981).

20. 43 U.S.C. § 1714.

21. 43 U.S.C. § 1702(j).

22. The Palisades area on the Idaho-Wyoming border just south of Grand Teton National Park, and the Bear-Marshall-Scapegoat-Swan roadless area in Montana.

23. Mountain States Legal Foundation v. Andrus, 499 F. Supp. 383, 397 (D. Wyo. 1980).

24. *Id.* at 397.

25. 499 F. Supp. at 392.

26. Krug Memorandum, 12 Fed. Reg. 5859 (1947).

27. Learned v. Watt, 528 F. Supp. at 981-82.

28. Mountain States Legal Foundation v. Hodel, No. 86-22, (D. Wyo. filed Jan. 15, 1986).

29. 30 U.S.C. §§ 181, 226(a).

30. 30 U.S.C. § 352.

31. *See* Part V., *infra.*

32. The roles of the Bureau of Land Management and the Forest Service in oil and gas leasing are delineated in *Interagency Agreement Between the Bureau of Land Management and the Forest Service for Mineral Leasing,* approved June 19, 1984, *distributed in* BLM Instruction Memorandum 84-585 (July 9, 1984). This agreement is subject to periodic revision.

33. *Oversight Hearings on the Greater Yellowstone Ecosystem Before the Subcommittee on Public Lands and the Subcommittee on National Parks and Recreation of the House Committee on Interior and Insular Affairs,* 99th Cong., 1st Sess., H.R. Doc. 99-18, at 25-26 (1985) (statement of Robert Burford).

34. Instruction Memorandum No. 84-254, from Director, Bureau of Land Management, to All State Directors (1984). *See also* Change 1 (June 26, 1984) and Change 2 (Nov. 13, 1984) to the original Memorandum 84-254.

35. Instruction Memorandum No. 84-415, from Director, Bureau of Land Management, to All State Directors (1984).

36. *BLM's Proposed Mineral Policy Receives Criticism,* Casper Star-Tribune, Jan. 28, 1987, at A-1.

37. National Environmental Policy Act, 42 U.S.C. § 4321.

38. Sierra Club v. Peterson, 717 F.2d 1409 (D.C. Cir. 1983), *rev'g* U.S. District Court for the District of Columbia (Case No. 81-123). (Emphasis in original.)

39. Park County Resource Council v. United States Department of Agriculture No. 85-2000 (10th Cir.)

40. Rocky Mountain Oil and Gas Ass'n v. Andrus, 500 F. Supp. 1338, at 1345 (D.Wyo. 1980), *rev'd on appeal* as Rocky Mountain Oil and Gas Ass'n v. Watt, 696 F.2d 734 (10th Cir., 1982).

41. 605 F. Supp. 107, 108 (D. Mont. 1985), *appeal docketed,* No. 85-3929 (9th Cir. 1986).

42. 605 F. Supp. at 109.

43. Endangered Species Act, 16 U.S.C. § 1536.

44. Bob Marshall Alliance v. Watt, 16 ENVTL. L. REP. 20759, at 20763 (D. Mont. 1986), *appeal docketed,* No. 86-4014 (9th Cir. July 22, 1986).

45. *Id.* at 20762, col 1.

46. For an interesting discussion of the Forest Service's institutional predisposition to favor forestry over minerals management, and of alleged underlying economic factors reinforcing that disposition, *see* D. Leal, G. Black, and J. Baden, Oil and Gas Exploration and Development in the Greater Yellowstone Ecosystem (unpublished manuscript,

to be issued in a primer on the Greater Yellowstone Ecosystem by the Political Economy Research Center, Bozeman, Montana).

47. 16 U.S.C. § 1600, amended by Pub. L. No. 94-588, 90 Stat. 2949 (Oct. 22, 1976).

48. 16 U.S.C. §§ 1604(f)(1) and (2).

49. 16 U.S.C. §§ 1604(g)(2)(a) and (c).

50. SHOSHONE NFMA PLAN FEIS, *supra*, at IV-75.

51. 16 U.S.C. § 1604(i).

52. 16 U.S.C. § 1607(b). (Emphasis added.)

53. 30 C.F.R. §§ 219.1(b)(2) and 219.22.

54. For the details of the Fort Chaffee story, *see Hearing on Oil and Gas Leasing Policy and Certain Oil and Gas Leases Issued on Lands Within Fort Chaffee, Arkansas, before the Subcomm. on Energy Resources and Materials Production of the Senate Comm. on Energy and Natural Resources*, S. Doc. 96-62, 96th Cong., 1st Sess. (1979). *See also,* 127 CONG. REC. S626 (Jan. 27, 1981).

55. The "tiered" approach was first suggested by Governor Herschler of Wyoming in a letter to Secretary of the Interior William Clark, dated Jan. 15, 1985. The concept has been widely accepted.

56. *Oversight Hearing on the Department of the Interior's Federal Onshore Oil and Gas Leasing Program before the Subcomm. on Mining and Natural Resources of the House Comm. on Interior and Insular Affairs* (1985). (Testimony submitted on behalf of Governor Herschler.)

57. H.R. 4741, 99th Cong., 2nd Sess. (1986), *The Federal Oil and Gas Leasing Amendments Act of 1986, see* 132 CONG. REC. E1490, E1493, (May 1, 1986).

58. Personal meeting with Chief Forester R. Max Peterson and Associate Chief Forester Dale Robertson, et al., Washington, D.C., July 17, 1986. Robertson made statements to the same effect in testimony before the Subcommittee on Mining and Natural Resources of the Committee on Interior and Insular Affairs, U.S. House of Representatives, on July 16, 1986.

59. National Park System Resources Act of 1986, S. 2092, 99th Cong., 2d Sess. (1986).

60. *Id.* at § 103(a)(1).

61. Letter from Jack E. Stark, Superintendent, Grand Teton National Park, to Reid Jackson, Forest Supervisor, Bridger-Teton National Forest (Apr. 8, 1985).

62. OIL AND GAS EXPLORATION AND LEASING WITHIN THE WASHAKIE WILDERNESS, *supra.*

Chapter 15

THE MINING IN THE PARKS ACT: THEORY AND PRACTICE

Philip S. Barnett[*]

I. INTRODUCTION

Ordinarily, if not universally, the creation of a park is made subject to "valid existing rights." This is a good thing for the creation of parks, for if condemnation and purchase of mining claims and other inholdings were a prerequisite to the creation of parks, the establishment of a park would be more difficult and expensive than it is. At the same time, however, the saving clause can be a bad thing for the management of the parks. Inevitably, when a park is created with valid existing mineral rights, conflicts will arise between the public's interest in the preservation of the park and the mineral claimants' interests in mineral development.

With the passage of the Mining in the Parks Act[1] in 1976, Congress hoped to reconcile these clashing preservationist and developmental interests. Unfortunately, ten years later, this reconciliation has yet to occur. Although the Act and its implementing regulations contain generally adequate provisions for the regulation of mining operations, and indeed should be commended for several of their requirements, they are deficient in key respects pertaining to mineral patents and claim validity. Moreover, regardless of the theoretical virtues and defects of the Act and the regulations, the objectives of both have been thwarted by the Park Service's failure to enforce their provisions in the field.

415

II. THE ORIGIN OF MINING CLAIMS IN THE PARKS

It may come as a surprise to many to learn that there are mining claims in national parks. After all, as Congress noted in passing the Mining in the Parks Act, "[r]ecognition of an area as a national park or national monument is generally considered to be the highest form of protection which the Congress can give an area of Federal land." [2] One does not normally associate national parks with bulldozers, blasting equipment, and the other paraphernalia of active mines.

Nevertheless, there are such claims in the parks--literally thousands of them. Indeed, a 1985 Park Service report found precisely 3,307 claims in 24 different parks.[3] Over two-thirds of the claims are in nine parks in Alaska, with most of the other claims occurring in other Western states.[4]

Typically, claims in the parks were staked prior to the creation of the park. At that time, the lands were usually unreserved public lands subject to the century-old Mining Law of 1872.[5] In brief, the Mining Law allows any citizen to prospect for hardrock minerals (such as gold, silver, lead, and copper) on public lands; to obtain an unpatented mining claim conveying ownership of the minerals upon making a "discovery" (which requires the finding of a commercially viable deposit); and to convert the unpatented claim to a patented one conveying full fee ownership of the minerals and the surface.

With patented or unpatented mining claims already located, what creates the mineral inholdings in the park is the very law that creates the park. Normally, the statute will include a savings provision that withdraws the park lands from further entry and location under the mining law subject to "valid existing rights," namely the previously located mining claims.[6] Thus, at the very moment that the park is born, so is the potential for the mineral conflicts that the Mining in the Parks Act and its implementing regulations seek to avoid.

III. THE MINING IN THE PARKS ACT AND ITS IMPLEMENTING REGULATIONS IN THEORY

Until 1976, mines on valid claims in the parks could operate essentially without regulation by the National Park Service. Incredibly, the Park Service had no mechanism other than informal jawboning for regulating the mines. This state of affairs was inconsistent with the National Park Service Organic Act of 1916, which "speaks of but a single purpose, namely conservation."[7] It also posed serious environmental problems for certain parks. For instance in Death Valley National Monument during the early 1970s, nearly a dozen mines spewed tons of spoil and waste rock onto the desert floor, causing Congress to remark that "the very character of Death Valley is now threatened with serious alteration." [8]

Thus, in response to these and related impulses, Congress passed the Mining in the Parks Act.[9] As the first section of the Act explains, its purposes are broad and general: "The Congress finds and declares that . . . all mining operations in areas of the National Park System should be conducted so as to prevent or minimize damage to the environment and other resource values."[10]

Unfortunately for the regulation drafters at the Park Service, the operative provisions of the Act are equally broad and general. In fact, the language of the Act is remarkable principally for its generality. In its key provision, the statute directs that "all activities resulting from the exercise of valid existing mineral rights on patented or unpatented mining claims within any area of the National Park System shall be subject to such regulation prescribed by the Secretary of the Interior as he deems necessary or desirable for the preservation and management of those areas."[11] Of necessity, therefore, one must look to the implementing regulations, which were promulgated in 1978, to understand the modern regulatory framework applicable to mining in the parks.[12]

A. The Modern Regulatory Framework Applicable to Mining in the Parks

In their central provisions, the Park Service mining regulations rely on "plans of operations" to regulate mining in the parks. Specifically, an operator wishing to mine in a park must submit a detailed description of its operations to the Park Service, called a plan of operations.[13] Among other things, the description must set forth the proposed operations, the estimated timetable of the operations, a reclamation plan, the steps to be taken to meet federal and state environmental standards, and an environmental report analyzing the likely impacts of the mine.[14]

Upon receipt of the plan, the Park Service prepares its own "environmental analysis."[15] The environmental analysis is, for practical purposes, the same as an "environmental assessment" under the National Environmental Policy Act.[16] The purpose of the analysis is to determine whether the mine will "adversely affect or significantly injure the ecological or cultural resources of the unit."[17] If the plan will not adversely affect or significantly injure park resources, it can be approved, but not otherwise.

Following approval, the Park Service requires the operator to post a bond to cover the costs of reclamation.[18] The general reclamation standard for unpatented claims requires that the operator "return . . . the area to a condition equivalent to its pristine beauty."[19] The bond provides insurance that the reclamation will be achieved, for it is conditioned "upon faithful compliance with the applicable regulations, the terms and conditions of the permit . . . and the plan of operations."[20]

Finally, upon completion of the operations and a determination by the Park Service that the operator followed the plan of operations and completed the required reclamation, the bond is released, and the regulatory procedures end.[21]

B. Evaluation of the Act and the Regulations

The parks are of course the country's most treasured lands; they have received the "highest form" of protection possible.[22] Thus, one would expect the regulatory scheme sketched above to afford parks the highest degree of protection possible. In some respects this is true, but surprisingly, in others it is not.

Initially, the Act and the Park Service regulations should be praised for their broad scope. The Bureau of Land Management (BLM) uses plans of operations to regulate mining on the public lands,[23] as does the Forest Service to regulate mining in the national forests.[24] Yet BLM exempts from the plan requirements mines that disturb fewer than five acres annually,[25] while the Forest Service exempts mines that will not cause a significant disturbance of surface resources.[26] Only the Park Service requires plans of operations for all mines.[27] In addition, whereas operations on patented lands are exempted from the BLM and Forest Service regulations,[28] they are subject to the Park Service regulations.[29] There is, however, one anomalous exception to this rule. In Alaska, but not elsewhere, operations on patented claims are not subject to the Park Service plan regulations if access is not across federally owned lands.[30]

Even more important, the Park Service regulations have particularly good reclamation and bonding provisions. As previously noted, under the Park Service regulations, mining operators are required to reclaim their lands (when the claims are unpatented) to a condition equivalent to the land's pristine beauty;[31] they are also required to post a performance bond sufficient to cover the cost of completing the required reclamation.[32] In the BLM and Forest Service regulations, the reclamation standards are significantly weaker[33] and the bonding is discretionary.[34]

Although the Park Service regulations are in these respects the stringent regulations that they should be, there are equally important respects in which the regulations are weaker than necessary. In the first place, the Park Service regulations provide for automatic approval of a mining plan if the Park Service fails to act on the plan within sixty days.[35] No similar provision exists in the BLM or Forest Service regulations, and none should exist in the Park Service regulations. The possibility of automatic approval improperly puts the risk of excessive agency delay on the park lands.[36] This case is discussed further in Part IV.

The most important deficiencies in the Act and the regulations, however, pertain to mineral patents and validity determinations. Certain public land laws prevent mineral claimants from converting unpatented claims to patented ones conveying fee title if the claim is located on lands with a protected status. For instance, the National Wild and Scenic Rivers Act provides that for claims in the national wild and scenic river system, "issuance of a patent to any mining claim . . . shall . . . convey a right . . . only to the mineral deposits and such rights only to use the surface and surface resources as are reasonably required to carrying on prospecting or mining operations." [37] This sort of restriction is highly salutary, for it prevents mineral claimants from going to patent, obtaining fee title, and then using the claims for such nonmineral uses as vacation resorts or housing subdivisions. Yet for no good reason, the restriction does not apply to park lands.

Thus, until Congress acts to amend the law, each of the over three thousand mining claims in the parks is a potentially permanent inholding subject to any number of objectionable nonmineral uses.

A related deficiency would be even simpler to correct, for it could be corrected by regulation. BLM has recently promulgated a regulation requiring that agency to determine the validity of mining claims located in wilderness areas before approving operations on them.[38] The Park Service should promulgate a similar regulation. Until the Park Service commits to determining claim validity before approval, there always is a substantial possibility that the agency will approve operations for claims that are actually invalid, due for instance to the claimant's failure to make a discovery prior to the withdrawal date. Indeed, whenever the Park Service has inquired into validity, it has found the vast majority of the claims in the parks to be invalid.[39]

Without doubt, the Mining in the Parks Act and its implementing regulations are a vast improvement over the status quo ante, which allowed for essentially unregulated mining. In some areas, such as reclamation and bonding, the Act and the regulations should be particularly commended. Nevertheless, important deficiencies need to be corrected. Specifically, the automatic approval provision needs to be eliminated; legislation needs to be enacted that prohibits mineral claimants from taking unpatented claims to patent; and the Park Service needs to promulgate a regulation requiring validity determinations before approval of operations on unpatented claims.

IV. THE PARK SERVICE'S IMPLEMENTATION OF THE ACT AND THE REGULATIONS IN PRACTICE

It is a truism that whatever the merits of the Mining in the Parks Act and its implementing regulations in theory, the Act and the regulations will be useless in practice unless they are enforced in the field. It may be equally true that one would not expect enforcement to be a problem, given the protected status of the parks and the Parks Service's obligation to manage them "to conserve the scenery and the natural and historic objects and wild life therein."[40] The unfortunate fact, however, is that enforcement is a serious problem. Simply put, the Park Service ignores the requirements of the Act and the regulations and allows mines to operate essentially without regulation, just as the mines did before 1976. At least this is the case in Alaska, where over two-thirds of all mining claims in the parks are located, and in the Lake Mead National Recreation Area adjacent to the Grand Canyon.

In Alaska, the failure of the Park Service to follow its regulations has been a massive one. From 1978, when the Park Service regulations were first adopted, through 1985, the Park Service annually approved thirty to fifty plans of operations for mines in

eight national parks in Alaska. Yet despite the regulatory requirement that each approval be preceded by an environmental analysis,[41]
the Park Service did not perform a single environmental
analysis for a single one of the mining operations it approved.[42]
In other words, it approved hundreds of mines in the country's
most protected lands without considering the impacts they might
have. An equally widespread failure to implement the regulatory
requirements characterized the Park Service's reclamation and bonding efforts. Although the Park Service has a mandatory obligation
to obtain performance bonds,[43] it never once required one from
an operator in Alaska prior to the filing of the *Northern Alaska
Environmental Center* lawsuit in May 1985.[44]

The environmental consequences of this failure to comply with
the regulations were disastrous, naturally enough. In Denali National Park and Preserve, for instance, a dozen or more mines polluted over 150 miles of the park's most important streams; etched
over seventy-five miles of illegal access routes across fragile tundra;
and neglected over $10 million worth of mandatory reclamation
work.[45] In more general terms, the federal district court described
the situation this way:

> There are currently approximately 40 mining opera-
> tions underway in the national parks in Alaska. A num-
> ber of these . . . are causing extensive environmental
> damage to the parks . . . Specifically, [Park Service docu-
> ments] report that waste-water discharges grossly exceeded
> water quality standards at all operations tested, . . . that
> the mining has major adverse effects on fish habitat and
> water quality, . . . that mining will cause a decline in
> animal populations, . . . and that it would degrade the
> mining areas' scenic value.[46]

In the face of these facts, the court invalidated all past approvals
and required that thorough-going environmental reviews precede
future approvals.[47]

More or less the same situation could be found in the Lake
Mead National Recreation Area adjacent to the Grand Canyon National Park. The act creating the park provided for the leasing of
hardrock minerals within the boundaries of the park.[48] Yet until
the filing of an environmentalist lawsuit in 1983, the Park Service
regularly leased the minerals without consideration of the environmental impacts of mining, threatening serious damage to the park.[49]

The *Northern Alaska Environmental Center* and *Dickenson* cases teach an important lesson: the enactment of the Mining in the Parks Act and the promulgation of implementing regulations are not necessarily enough to protect the parks from the adverse impacts of mining. The parks also need administration of the Act and the regulations by an agency that will enforce their requirements.

Fulfillment of the purposes of the Mining in the Parks Act requires that the Act and the regulations be strengthened as described in Part III.B. But this objective also requires that the Park Service faithfully implement the requirements that are already on the books--something that it has been all too reluctant to do in the past.

NOTES

*Staff Attorney, Sierra Club Legal Defense Fund, Inc., Juneau, Alaska. Mr. Barnett is counsel of record for the plaintiffs in Northern Alaska Environmental Center v. Hodel, 15 ENVTL. L. REP. 21048 (D. Alaska), *preliminary injunction expanded,* 16 ENVTL. L. REP. 20244, (D. Alaska 1985), *aff'd,* F.2d 466 (9th Cir. 1986), the first reported case to be decided under the Mining in the Parks Act. The views expressed in this article are those of the author; they are not necessarily shared by the plaintiffs in the *Northern Alaska Environmental Center* litigation or any of the other clients of the Sierra Club Legal Defense Fund, Inc.

1. 16 U.S.C. § 1901.

2. H.R. REP. NO. 1428, 94th Cong., 2d Sess. 3-4, *reprinted in* [1976] U.S. CODE CONG. & ADMIN. NEWS 2487, 2488.

3. TEMPLE, BARKER & SLOANE, INC., MINERAL OWNERSHIP AND DEVELOPMENT ACTIVITY IN AND AROUND THE NATIONAL PARKS III-6 (Feb. 22, 1985).

4. *Id.* at III-5, 6.

5. 30 U.S.C. § 21.

6. *See, e.g.,* Alaska National Interest Lands Conservation Act, Pub. L. No. 96-487, § 206, 94 Stat. 2371, 2384 (1980).

7. National Rifle Ass'n v. Potter, 628 F. Supp. 903, 909 (D.D.C. 1986). Specifically, the Organic Act requires that the Park Service manage the parks, "which purpose is to conserve the scenery and the natural and historic objects and wild life therein and to provide for the enjoyment of the same in such manner and by such means as will leave them unimpaired for the enjoyment of future generations." 16 U.S.C. § 1.

8. H.R. REP. NO. 1428, *supra* note 2, at 4.

9. *See generally* Novak, *Mining in the National Parks,* 2 J. ENERGY L. POL'Y 165 (1982).

10. 16 U.S.C. § 1901(b).

11. 16 U.S.C. § 1902.

12. *See* 36 C.F.R. pt. 9.

13. 36 C.F.R. § 9.9(a).

14. *Id.* § 9.9(b).

15. *Id.* § 9.10(b).

16. *Compare id.* § 9.10(b), (d) *with* 40 C.F.R. §§ 1501.4(b), 1508.9.

17. 36 C.F.R. § 9.10(a)(2). Actually, this standard applies to mines on unpatented claims; slightly more lenient standards apply when the claim being worked is a patented one and hence in private ownership. *See id.* § 9.10(a)(1).

18. *Id.* § 9.13.

19. *Id.* § 9.11(b). As is the case regarding the substantive standards for approval, slightly more lenient standards apply when the claim being worked is a patented one. *See id.* § 9.11(a)(1).

20. *Id.* § 9.13(a).

21. *Id.* § 9.13(f).

22. H.R. REP. NO. 1428, *supra* note 2, at 3-4.

23. *See* 43 C.F.R. §§ 3809.1-4 to -6.

24. *See* 36 C.F.R. §§ 228.4-.5.

25. 43 C.F.R. § 3809.1-3.

26. 36 C.F.R. § 228.4(a).

27. *See* 36 C.F.R. § 9.2(b).

28. *See* 43 C.F.R. § 3809.0-5(d); 36 C.F.R. § 228.2(d).

29. *See* 36 C.F.R. § 9.2(k).

30. *See* 36 C.F.R. § 13.15(d)(1).

31. *Id.* § 9.11(b).

32. *Id.* § 9.13.

33. *See* 43 C.F.R. § 3829.0-5(j). (BLM regulations require as reclamation "reasonable measures as will prevent unnecessary undue degradation of the Federal lands"); 36 C.F.R. § 228.(g). (Forest Service regulations require as reclamation "practicable [measures to] reclaim the surface disturbed in operations . . . as will prevent or control onsite and off-site damage to the environment and forest surface resources.")

34. *See* 43 C.F.R. §§ 3809.1-9; 36 C.F.R. § 228.13.

35. 36 C.F.R. § 9.10(c).

36. The federal District Court for the District of Alaska has invalidated the automatic approval provision to the extent that it provides for approval of plans of operations before the Park Service completes its environmental analysis of the plan. Northern Alaska Environmental Center v. Hodel, 15 ENVTL. L. REP. 21048, 21050 n. 7 (D. Alaska 1985), *aff'd*, 803 F.2d 466 (9th Cir. 1986).

37. 16 U.S.C. § 1280(a)(ii).

38. 43 C.F.R. §§ 8560.4-6 (promulgated Apr. 29, 1986).

39. *See, e.g.*, Novak, *supra* note 9, at 172 (99.9 percent of claims located in Death Valley National Monument were found to be invalid after Park Service investigation). The Park Service does assert that as a matter of informal policy it makes validity determinations for claims in the continental United States, *see* 44 Fed. Reg. 11068 (1979); it does not make such determinations for claims in Alaska, however, where most of the claims in the parks are located. *Id.*

40. 16. U.S.C. § 1.

41. *See supra* text accompanying notes 15-17.

42. *See* Northern Alaska Environmental Center, 15 ENVTL. L. REP. 21048 (D. Alaska 1985), *aff'd*, 803 F.2d 466 (9th Cir. 1986).

43. *See supra* text accompanying notes 18-20.

44. *See* Northern Alaska Environmental Center, 15 ENVTL. L. REP. at 21049 n. 3.

45. *See generally* NATIONAL PARK SERVICE, FINAL ENVIRONMENTAL IMPACT STATEMENT: KANTISHNA HILLS/DUNKLE MINE STUDY REPORT (1985).

46. Northern Alaska Environmental Center, 15 ENVTL. L. REP. at 21049. (Emphasis added.)

47. *Id., preliminary injunction expanded*, 16 ENVTL. L. REP. 20244 (D. Alaska 1985).

48. 16 U.S.C. § 460n-3(b)(3).

49. *See* Sierra Club v. Dickenson, No. 83-1657 (D. Ariz.) (dismissed pursuant to settlement Aug. 25, 1986). The lawsuit also resulted in a 90 percent reduction of the acreage subject to leasing. *Id.*

Chapter 16

THE GEOTHERMAL STEAM ACT: UNLOCKING ITS PROTECTIVE PROVISIONS

Elizabeth M. Dodd[*]

I. INTRODUCTION: THE THREAT TO NATIONAL PARKS

Yellowstone National Park is the world's oldest national park. It was established in 1872, shortly after an official expedition confirmed what many had regarded as incredible accounts of the area's bubbling mud pots, steaming pools, and soaring geysers. Today, the park's significance is better understood. Covering 2.2 million acres, the park contains some two hundred geysers and more than three thousand other thermal features.[1] The Yellowstone ecosystem, which includes an area greater than the park itself, contains three hundred geysers and ten thousand other thermal features.[2] The number of geysers in the park is higher than that found in all other geyser basins in the world combined, making it first among the ten major geyser fields around the globe.[3] The Old Faithful Geyser alone draws about three thousand visitors per eruption (every sixty-eight minutes) in the busiest summer weeks. Ninety percent of all park visitors stop to see Old Faithful.[4]

The park is also the world's oldest wildlife preserve. It shelters grizzly bears, bison, endangered bald eagles and peregrine falcons, trumpeter swans, and many other kinds of waterfowl. The continent's largest herds of elk and bighorn sheep congregate in the greater Yellowstone ecosystem.[5] Many of the geothermal features of the park are critical to the survival of park animals in the winter.[6] The heated water and steam melt heavy snows that otherwise cover forage for elk and bison, and the warmed rivers provide ice-free flows for Canada geese and trumpeter swans. In recognition of the park's unique thermal and biological characteristics, the

United Nations has designated the park a World Heritage Site and also an International Biosphere Reserve.[7]

But the millions of tourists and naturalists who travel to the park each year are not the only ones intrigued by the geysers of Yellowstone. The energy industry is also interested, because the presence of the geysers indicates the availability of thermal energy and the possibility of commercial exploitation.

The development of geothermal energy consists of harnessing the natural heat of the earth's core and converting that heat to electricity. In several places around the world, steam and water traveling through porous or fractured rock has brought this heat relatively near the surface.[8] In simplified terms, geothermal energy development entails drilling wells to reach the super-heated water or steam, bringing that heat source to the surface, and transporting it short distances (not over one mile) through pipes to a power plant for conversion to electricity.

A fully developed geothermal steam field is a highly industrialized site consisting of drilling rigs, above-ground pipeline, overhead wires, cooling towers, and power plants. Because the power plant must be close to the source of the water or steam, which loses too much heat if transported any great distance, development of a steam field cannot be concentrated in a single location.[9] At the Geysers in Northern California, for example, there are over two hundred operating wells that feed no fewer than nineteen power generating plants in an area of fifty square miles.[10]

Industrialization at the borders of Yellowstone is not the only problem represented by geothermal development in the area. Another perhaps less obvious problem is the potential for degrading the park's own geothermal features. There is plenty of historical precedent. Of the ten major geyser areas in the world, seven have been destroyed or seriously damaged by exploration or development. For example, the Beowawe Geysers in Nevada, once the second most active geyser field in North America, stopped flowing altogether in 1961 after about a decade of exploration work. In New Zealand's Geyser Thermal Valley, once the world's fifth largest geyser field, the valley's major geyser stopped erupting three years after a nearby power plant became operational. After eleven more years of production, all geysers in the valley became inactive. There is also evidence from New Zealand that exploratory drilling can adversely affect thermal reservoirs some nine to twelve miles distant. Other geyser fields in Iceland, Italy, and Nevada have also suffered from energy exploration and development.[11]

Until 1984, the federal government actively encouraged development next to Yellowstone. It designated almost half a million acres of land on the western and southern borders of the park as the Island Park Geothermal Area (IPGA),[12] and directed the preparation of an environmental impact statement on the effects of geothermal energy development in the area.[13] The environmental impact statement conditionally recommended leasing the lands to energy developers, except for a two-mile buffer strip next to the park,[14] and as of January 1986, 107 lease applications covering 175,000 acres had been received.[15] Although the federal government has not yet issued leases, owing in part to a special congressional ban enacted in 1984 and 1985, the states and private landowners have leased almost 25,000 acres within the IPGA to the energy industry.[16]

Eight thermal springs in Yellowstone National Park are within five miles of the IPGA border; one spring actually straddles the dividing line between the park and the IPGA. Six more thermal springs are within ten miles of the western boundary of the park, and Old Faithful and other major geyser basins are within thirteen miles of the border.[17] A significant proportion of the state and private land already leased to geothermal developers is located within twelve miles of the park boundary.[18]

Yellowstone is not the only national park whose thermal features are threatened by geothermal development at its borders. At Lassen Volcanic National Park in northern California, thirty-eight lease applications are pending within fifteen miles of the park's southern boundary, covering some 61,000 acres. At Crater Lake National Park in Oregon, leases have been issued on national forest land surrounding the park, and the lessee has already drilled exploratory wells within a hundred yards of the park boundary. At Hawaii Volcanoes National Park, geothermal development had begun on private land adjacent to the park, and full field development was staved off only by a complicated land exchange including the Department of the Interior, Hawaii, and the private landowner.[19]

This chapter will examine the federal Geothermal Steam Act of 1970, which authorizes leasing of federal lands for geothermal energy development. After a brief summary of the Act (Part II), the chapter will explore provisions of the originally enacted statute that might be useful in controlling adverse effects of geothermal development near our park lands (Part III), and will explain the important park protection amendments added in 1986 (Part IV). The chapter will discuss the National Environmental Policy Act's role in controlling geothermal development (Part V), and will conclude with some general observations about the effectiveness of current legislation and case law for protecting park lands (Part VI).

II. THE GEOTHERMAL STEAM ACT--AN OVERVIEW

The Geothermal Steam Act of 1970[20] (GSA) authorizes the Secretary of the Interior to issue leases on certain federal lands for development of geothermal steam and related geothermal resources.[21] Through the passage of the Act, Congress intended to "provide the statutory framework needed to encourage private enterprise to invest in and develop this new resource."[22] The report of the Interior and Insular Affairs Committee of the House of Representatives stated that

> [t]he hearings on the present bill and the extensive record developed in connection with the earlier [legislative proposals] demonstrate quite clearly that the geothermal resources underlying the public lands in the Western States represent a vast reservoir of untapped energy with a potential for relatively pollution free, economical production of electric power to help overcome the increasingly critical power shortage confronting the Nation.[23]

The Geothermal Steam Act of 1970 is now the exclusive means of obtaining rights to geothermal resources under federal lands.[24]

Under the GSA, the Secretary of the Interior is responsible for issuing all geothermal leases and otherwise administering the leasing system.[25] With certain exceptions, all lands administered by the Department of the Interior and the Department of Agriculture through the Forest Service are available for leasing under the Act.[26] National parks and other lands administered by the National Park Service, national recreation areas, wildlife refuges, Indian trust or restricted lands, and other specific categories of lands are exempted.[27]

The Secretary of the Interior determines which lands available for leasing under the Act are within a "known geothermal resources area" (KGRA).[28] Prospective lessees must competitively bid for these leases, and the lease goes to the "highest responsible qualified bidder."[29] All lands outside a KGRA are leased without competitive bidding to the first qualified applicant.[30]

Geothermal leases have a primary term of ten years. They expire after that period unless one of two things occurs. First, if the lessee produces steam in commercial quantities during the ten-year period, an additional forty-year term is available.[31] Second, even if no commercial quantities of steam are produced in ten years, the lease can be extended five years if the lessee is diligently prosecuting drilling operations. If the lessee produces commercial quantities of steam during those five years, the lease can then be extended an additional thirty-five years.[32] At the end of the forty-year term, the lessee can renew any commercially productive leases for a second forty-year term if the Secretary determines that the lands are not needed for other purposes.[33] Leases that have ceased producing commercially viable steam may be extended up to five years for production of valuable byproducts.[34]

In return for the lease, lessees pay a royalty of 10 to 15 percent of the amount or value of the steam and an annual rental based on the acreage of the leasehold.[35] The statute limits the number of acres that an individual, corporation, or other entity can lease within a single state.[36] However, lessees who join together to operate under a corporative or unit plan of development are exempted from the acreage limitations, as are lessees who contract with outside entities for development of the leasehold.[37]

III. ENVIRONMENTAL PROVISIONS OF THE ORIGINAL ACT

The Geothermal Steam Act has not been used extensively in efforts to protect public lands or other natural resources against damage from geothermal industrial development. This is undoubtedly because the Act--at least prior to the 1986 amendment--did not contain language that was clearly helpful in such an effort. The Act on the whole deals with the mechanisms for issuing and administering leases, not with the mechanisms for protecting federal lands and other natural resources from the adverse effects of such leasing. The following section will analyze the provisions of the Act prior to the 1986 amendment that addresses environmental concerns.

A. Terms and Conditions

Section 1014(a) provides that leases on Interior Department lands may be issued "only under such terms and conditions as the Secretary may prescribe to insure adequate utilization of the lands for the purposes for which they were withdrawn or acquired." Section 1014(b) similarly provides that leases on Forest Service lands may be issued "only with the consent of, and subject to such terms and conditions as may be prescribed by, the head of that Department [of Agriculture] to insure adequate utilization of the lands for the purpose for which they were withdrawn or acquired." There is similar language authorizing terms and conditions for lands subject to the authority of the Department of Energy.

These provisions clearly grant the secretaries administering the leased lands broad authority to impose protective terms and conditions on leases. The provisions do not require any particular terms or conditions, but broadly authorize conditions related to protecting the purposes for which the lands were set aside. Since passage of the Federal Land Policy and Management Act in 1976, most lands administered by the Bureau of Land Management (BLM) are subject to multiple-use principles that include conservation and preservation.[38] The national forests also have multiple-use purposes that can serve as the basis for protective conditions.[39]

The Act itself indicates that the terms and conditions may address protection of the surface of leased lands. Section 1007(c), related to readjustment of lease terms, provides that when the Secretary adjusts lease terms "as to use, protection, or restoration of the surface" for lands not administered by the Department of the Interior, the Secretary must notify and obtain the approval of the Secretary administering the lands.

While the Act provides for readjustment of the lease terms and conditions, Section 1007(a) provides that the Secretary may not readjust the terms until ten years after the date geothermal steam is produced, and then only at ten-year intervals. This provision shows the importance of imposing adequate protective conditions at the time the lease is issued.

B. Rules and regulations

The Act provides that

> [t]he Secretary shall prescribe such rules and regulations as he may deem appropriate to carry out the

provisions of this chapter. Such regulations may include, without limitation, provisions for . . . (b) development and conservation of geothermal and other natural resources, (c) the protection of the public interest . . . (f) the filing of surety bonds . . . to protect surface use and resources . . . (g) use of the surface by a lessee of the lands embraced in his lease . . . (i) protection of water quality and other environmental qualities.

This section requires the Secretary of the Interior to promulgate rules and regulations to implement the Act. The suggested subjects include environmental protection, as outlined above.

Although the Secretary does not appear to be required by the statute to address any of the suggested topics ("[s]uch regulations *may* include"), including environmental protection, the legislative history of the Geothermal Steam Act suggests otherwise. The report of the House Committee on Interior and Insular Affairs states that certain sections of the Act "provide that the Secretary of Interior, in carrying out the provisions of the Act, prescribed *[sic]* rules and regulations which include, among other items, prevention of waste, conservation of geothermal and other natural resources, and protection of the public interest."[40] The report later states that the "environmental control factors *to be provided in the rules and regulations* will minimize any adverse effects," and that "[a]ny use of geothermal steam and associated geothermal resources would be undertaken only after careful study and the development of the rules and regulations essential to protect the environment."[41]

The Secretary has promulgated regulations pursuant to this section. These regulations, currently found in Title 43 of the *Code of Federal Regulations*, Parts 3200-3280, address some but not all of the types of environmental protections envisioned by Congress and discussed in the House report.[42]

C. Ability to Terminate Leases

The Secretary may terminate any lease "for *any* violation of the regulations or lease terms" unless the lessee corrects the problem or diligently pursues corrective action within a certain time period.[43] This provision gives the Secretary ample power to enforce the protective terms and conditions placed on leases at their issuance (see Section 1014), and to enforce regulations for the protection of the public lands and natural resources (see Section

1023). This section underscores the importance of imposing specific protective terms in leases at the outset.

D. Control Following Relinquishment

Although a lessee may voluntarily relinquish all rights under a lease, the lessee will not be relieved of "liability for breach of any obligation of the lease, other than an obligation to drill, accrued at the rate of relinquishment, or from the continued obligation, in accordance with the applicable lease terms and regulations . . . (3) to protect or restore substantially the surface and surface resources."[44] Although this provision is applicable only where a lessee decides to relinquish a lease prior to expiration of the lease term, it ensures that the lessee has continuing responsibility for protecting and restoring the surface and shows Congress' concerns for protection of surface resources. It also ensures that the lessee will not be relieved from breach of any lease term related to protection of the environment or natural resources in effect prior to the date of relinquishment.

E. Surface Protections

As noted above, surface protections are expressly mentioned in connection with adjusting lease terms and conditions and as a limitation on the lessee's right of relinquishment.[45]

In addition, Section 1013 provides that the lessee "shall be entitled to use so much of the surface of the land covered by his geothermal lease as may be found by the Secretary to be necessary for the production, utilization, and conservation of geothermal resources." This section limits the the lessee's use of the surface to those lands that are deemed "necessary" for operations. As the House report provides, "[p]lantsite selection will be restricted to the immediate location of the resource so that the impact will be generally limited to that local environment."[46]

F. Suspension of Lease Operations

Section 1010 authorizes the Secretary to permit the lessee to suspend operations and production "on a producing lease" on application by the lessee. More important, the Secretary may "on his own motion, in the interest of conservation suspend operations on any lease." While there is no explanation of the meaning of "in the interest of conservation" in the statute or the legislative history, this section on its face confers broad authority on the Secretary to halt lease activity when environmental values are at risk.[47]

G. Waiver of Requirement to Produce Byproducts

Normally, if production of geothermal steam "is susceptible of producing a valuable byproduct," the Secretary will require "substantial beneficial production or use" of the byproduct.[48] (Byproducts include most minerals in solution or associated with geothermal steam that for economic reasons would not be developed by themselves or that have a value of less than 75 pecent of the value of the steam. Included is dimineralized water.)[49] However, the Secretary also has the authority to waive this production requirement "in the interest of conservation of natural resources." [50]

H. Multiple-use Principles of Land Use

Section 1016 provides that administration of the Act "shall be under the principles of multiple use of lands and resources." Accordingly, geothermal leases "insofar as feasible" shall allow for other leases on the same property "and for other uses of the areas covered by them." Operations under geothermal leases must not unreasonably interfere with or endanger leases or permits issued pursuant to other acts of Congress. However, Section 1016 also provides that other leases and land uses shall not "unreasonably interfere with or endanger operations" connected with any geothermal lease. As a practical matter, the provisions of Section 1016 cancel each other out, and no particular use appears to be favored over another.

I. Effectiveness of the Provisions for Protecting Parks

All of the provisions of the Geothermal Steam Act as originally enacted that address environmental protections suffer from the same weakness: they do not require the Department of the Interior to take affirmative steps to protect lands and natural resources from the adverse effects of geothermal development. The most that can be said about these provisions is that they confer broad authority upon the Secretary to provide environmental protections. Thus, a Secretary who is interested in ensuring environmentally sound geothermal development could use the Act for this purpose; a Secretary who has no such interest could not be compelled by the terms of the Act to control such development.

A Secretary interested in using the Act to protect national park resources, including geothermal features and other park values, could undoubtedly take the following actions. First, the Secretary has clear authority to restrict development on lands near

parks under Section 1023, which authorizes regulations to implement the Act. That section provides that the Secretary can issue
regulations for "conservation . . . of natural resources," "protection
of the public interest," and "protection of . . . environmental
qualities." Thus the Secretary could issue regulations protecting the
parks from noise, adverse air and water quality impacts, adverse
effects on park wildlife, and other impacts associated with geothermal development. Such regulations would undoubtedly be
upheld under the Secretary's clear authority to protect the
public interest and environmental qualities in administering the
geothermal program.

Second, the Secretary could impose lease terms and conditions
under Section 1014 that emphasize the conservation and preservation purposes of leased lands located near park lands. While these
purposes are among many authorized uses of "multiple-use" lands,
the Secretary could determine that these uses were paramount in
lands adjacent to or near parks, and thereby justify restrictive lease
terms.

These two steps--issuance of regulations and lease terms to
protect park values from development on nearby lands--are particularly strong measures since the Secretary is authorized to terminate leases for any violation of the regulations or lease terms
under Section 1101.

Third, the Secretary could suspend lease operations that
were adversely affecting park values under Section 1010. That section provides for the suspension of operations by the Secretary "in
the interest of conservation." Thus, even in the absence of protective regulations or lease terms, the Secretary could halt activity
harmful to park resources pursuant to this section.

IV. THE PARK PROTECTION AMENDMENT OF 1986

In October 1986, Congress adopted an amendment to the
Geothermal Steam Act as a rider to a continuing resolution for annual appropriations.[51] The amendment was signed into law on October 30, 1986. The initial impetus for amendments came from
leaseholders whose leases would have expired on December 31,
1986 without a legislative extension of their primary terms. The
quid pro quo for these extensions, won by the National Parks and

Conservation Association, was unprecedented park protection language.[52]

A. What the Leaseholders Got

Under the GSA, the primary term of any geothermal lease is ten years. If during that time the leaseholder does not produce or utilize steam "in commercial quantities," the lease expires. If the leaseholder does produce commercial quantities of steam within the ten-year period, the lease is continued for forty additional years.[53]

The first geothermal leases were issued in 1974.[54] Many of these original leaseholders obtained a two-year extension of their primary lease terms to December 31, 1986. However, many still were unable to produce steam in commercial quantities during 1986, and as the end of their extended primary terms drew near, they sought another extension. The leaseholders cited an unfavorable economic climate and governmental delays as reasons for their failure to produce steam in commercial quantities.[55]

The 1986 amendment to the Geothermal Steam Act extends the primary term of any geothermal lease in effect on July 24, 1984 to December 31, 1988, if the Secretary of the Interior makes three findings. First, the Secretary must find either that the failure to complete a bona fide sale of the geothermal resource was "due to administrative delays by government entities, beyond the control of the lessee" or that such a sale would be "uneconomic."[56] Second, the Secretary must find that substantial investment has already been made "in development of" the lease or "for the benefit of the lease." [57] Third, the Secretary must find that the lease would otherwise expire prior to December 31, 1988.[58]

B. What the National Parks Got

The amendment gives unprecedented protection to thermal features in certain units of the National Park System. It does this is four major ways:

1. *Identification of Significant Thermal Features*

The amendment directs the Secretary to compile a list of "significant thermal features" located in certain units of the National Park System, including national parks, national preserves, a national recreation area, a national monument, and a memorial parkway.[59] To do this, the Secretary must publish a proposed list in the *Federal Register* and invite public comment. The Secretary must spell out the basis for including each feature in the list, and must consider certain criteria in determining its significance. These criteria include the size, extent, and uniqueness of the thermal feature, its scientific and geologic significance, the extent to which the feature is in a natural, undisturbed condition, and the significance of the geothermal feature to "the authorized purposes of which the National Park System unit was created." [60]

After receiving public comments on the proposed list, the Secretary may add or delete features. Then, within sixty days of publishing the proposed list, the Secretary must send the list, together with all public comments, to the Senate Committee on Energy and Natural Resources and the House Committee on Interior and Insular Affairs. The Secretary must inform these committees of any deletions or additions to the list as originally proposed, provide a statement of reasons for the changes, and explain the basis for including each significant feature. Until the Secretary has complied with these requirements, no geothermal leases may be issued.[61]

2. Monitoring

The amendment provides, without elaboration, that the Secretary "shall maintain a monitoring program" for significant thermal features included on the list.[62]

3. Withdrawls of Lands from Leasing

Once the list is in place, the Secretary must make certain determinations with respect to possible threats to thermal features every time a lease application is received. Specifically, the Secretary must determine for each application whether exploration, development, or utilization of any lands covered by the application "is reasonably likely to result in a significant adverse effect" on any listed feature. This determination must be made on the basis of scientific evidence, and is subject to public notice and comment.[63]

If the Secretary finds that any of these activities--exploration, development, or utilization--is reasonably likely to result in a significant adverse effect on a listed feature, the Secretary cannot issue the lease in question. Furthermore, the Secretary must withdraw the sensitive lands from any further leasing.[64]

4. Protective Stipulations

Even where the Secretary does not find a likelihood of *significant* adverse effects on listed features, he must include lease stipulations necessary to protect listed features whenever exploration, development, or utilization is "reasonably likely to adversely affect these features." [65] The determination that any lease activity is "reasonably likely to adversely affect" listed features must be based on scientific evidence. The mandatory lease stipulations include, but are not limited to, requiring reinjection of geothermal fluids, requiring annual reports from the lessee, requiring continuous monitoring by the lessee, and requiring temporary or permanent suspension of lease activity if the Secretary determines that "ongoing exploration, development, or utilization activities are having a significant adverse effect on [listed features] until such time as the significant adverse effect is eliminated."[66]

5. Other Provisions

The remaining sections of the amendment can be stated briefly. Subsection (e) provides that the Secretary of Agriculture "shall consider the effects" on listed features in determining whether to consent to leasing on lands administered by the Department of Agriculture. Subsection (f) states that the amendment does not affect the existing ban on leasing within the Island Park Known Geothermal Resources Area. Subsection (g) provides that the amendment has no effect on the Secretary's authorities or responsibilities under the Geothermal Steam Act or any other law, and subsection (h) states that the amendment shall remain in effect until Congress determines otherwise.

C. The Amendment Considered

In summary, the amendment sets out a four-part protection scheme. Using specified criteria, the Secretary must identify significant thermal features within twenty-two units of the National Park System. Once these features are listed, the Secretary must review all lease applications for potential effects on these features. If significant adverse effects are likely to occur, the Secretary must deny the application and close the lands to leasing. If adverse effects are likely, the Secretary must impose protective stipulations on the leases. Finally, the Secretary must establish a monitoring program for the listed features.

While the amendment, in contrast to the original Act, expressly directs the Secretary to take certain protective actions, agency discretion still plays an important role. The criteria for determining the significance of thermal features, for example, are general
and the amendment gives little guidance as to how the criteria
should be applied. The kind or amount of scientific evidence needed
to support agency determinations respecting the effects of leasing is also unspecified. The amendment provides no particulars
regarding the scope of the required monitoring program. Thus, the
effectiveness of the legislation for protecting park lands will
turn in no small measure on the agency's interpretation of the language of the amendment.

V. THE NATIONAL ENVIRONMENTAL POLICY ACT: A TRADITIONAL TOOL FOR CONTROLLING GEOTHERMAL DEVELOPMENT

Since passage of the Geothermal Steam Act, environmentalists have used the National Environmental Policy Act (NEPA)[67]
in attempts to control geothermal development on sensitive federal
lands. NEPA requires that federal agencies study the environmental effects of prospective federal actions and prepare a comprehensive "environmental impact statement" (EIS) for any "major federal
action significantly affecting the quality of the human environment."[68] The federal agencies that issue or oversee geothermal
leases--specifically, the Bureau of Land Management and the Forest
Service--are no exception.

The NEPA issue here, as with other kinds of federal leasing
decisions, is whether issuing a geothermal lease is by itself a major
federal action significantly affecting the environment, thus requiring preparation of an EIS. Environmentalists contend that because
lease issuance by itself may irrevocably convey the right to develop
the leasehold,[69] the leasing agency must prepare a prelease EIS on
full-field development or, in the alternative, reserve in the lease
the government's right to preclude all development on the leasehold
if subsequent environmental studies show that unacceptable impacts
would result. The energy developers contend that an EIS makes no
sense at the leasing stage because field development is purely a
matter of speculation at that point. They also contend that the
Bureau of Land Management and the Forest Service retain authority

to impose conditions and require mitigation measures sufficient to protect the environment, even if full-field development occurs.

The only court case that has addressed the EIS issue in the context of geothermal leasing is Sierra Club v. Hathaway.[70] In that case, the Sierra Club tried to stop the Secretary of the Interior from issuing geothermal leases in the Alvord Desert in Oregon without first preparing an EIS. In upholding the trial court's denial of a motion for a preliminary injunction, the Ninth Circuit adopted the developers' position noted above, finding that lease issuance only authorized very limited, "casual" use of the leasehold, and that the federal agencies would review future development activities if and when they were proposed. The court concluded that "[t]he lease provisions coupled with the regulations establish continuing federal control with required specific consideration of the environmental aspects of the leasing program."[71] Unfortunately, the court never directly addressed the issue of whether lease issuance by itself conveys some irrevocable right to develop a leasehold, nor did it expressly state whether the federal agencies retain the right to preclude--as opposed to condition--development if unacceptable impacts are discovered.

In 1983, an important decision by the D.C. Circuit Court of Appeals respecting federal oil and gas leases seemed to contradict Sierra Club v. Hathaway.[72] By holding that NEPA requires preparation of an EIS prior to issuing oil and gas leases, the court in Sierra Club v. Peterson reasoned that the Bureau of Land Management in an ordinary leasing situation does not retain the right after lease issuance to preclude surface-disturbing activities, even if environmentally unacceptable. Under a normal lease, all BLM can do post-leasing is require mitigation of adverse impacts; it cannot withhold consent for surface-disturbing activities. Thus, the decision to allow potentially significant surface-disturbing activities is made at the leasing stage, and an EIS must precede this decision.[73]

In Sierra Club v. Peterson, the D.C. Circuit provided an alternative to preparation of an EIS prior to leasing. The following excerpt from the opinion explains the staged leasing concept:

> To comply with NEPA, the Department [of the Interior] must either prepare an EIS prior to leasing or retain the authority to preclude surface disturbing activities until an appropriate environmental analysis is completed. If the Department retains the authority to preclude all surface disturbing activities pending submission of a lessee's

site-specific proposal as well as the authority to refuse to approve proposed activities which it determines will have unacceptable environmental impacts, then the Department can defer its environmental evaluation until such site-specific proposals are submitted. If however, it is unable to *preclude* activities which might have unacceptable environmental consequences, then the Department cannot issue leases sanctioning such activities without first preparing an EIS.[74]

The *Sierra Club v. Peterson* court also exempted lands protected by a bona fide "no surface occupancy" stipulation from the EIS requirement, since an effective "no surface occupancy" stipulation reserves authority to the federal government to preclude all surface-disturbing activities if unacceptable environmental damage will occur.[75]

In the last few years, the Interior Board of Land Appeals (IBLA), which hears administrative appeals of Department of the Interior decisions, has relied heavily on the *Peterson* case in reviewing appeals of Bureau of Land Management decisions to issue geothermal leases without EISs. Two cases in particular stand out. The first case involved challenges to geothermal leases on BLM-managed lands adjacent to Mono Lake on the east side of the Sierra Nevada in California.[76] In that case, the IBLA determined that BLM either had to prepare an EIS prior to leasing or had to adopt a staged leasing approach in which BLM unequivocally retained the right to deny development at subsequent stages if unacceptable impacts would result.[77]

The second IBLA decision concerned geothermal leases in the Deschutes National Forest on the eastern slope of the Cascades in Oregon.[78] IBLA again relied on *Sierra Club v. Peterson* and its own Mono Lake decision to require that BLM either prepare a prelease EIS or adopt staged leasing by including a stipulation in each lease specifying that no surface disturbance would be permitted unless a later site-specific and activity-specific review showed no unacceptable impacts.

This favorable trend in IBLA opinions may have already indirectly benefited national parklands. At Lassen Volcanic National Park in northern California, famous for its hot springs, fumaroles, and other thermal features, environmentalists have long been concerned about lease applications on national forest lands adjacent to the park. From 1979 to 1981, the Forest Service produced a string of inadequate environmental assessments on the leasing proposals and refused to prepare an EIS. In 1981, it adopted an environmental assessment that recommended leasing right up to the park boundaries and did not discuss the possible effects of drilling on park geothermal resources. Park defenders appealed. Before any final decision was issued, however, the Forest Service and BLM, perhaps seeing the handwriting on the wall, decided on their own to prepare an EIS. The draft EIS, issued in May 1986, included a determination by the United States Geological Survey that some geothermal resources inside and outside the park were in fact connected, and that drilling outside the park would almost certainly damage the park's unique geothermal features.[79] In a significant victory for the park, the Forest Service and BLM recommended withdrawing from leasing all sensitive lands surrounding the park.[80]

VI. CONCLUSION

How much park protection can we count on, given the current state of legislation and the established case law?

As discussed in Part III, the Geothermal Steam Act as originally enacted gives substantial authority to the Secretary to provide environmental protections. While the Act does not require any particular protective measures, it gives effective tools to any Secretary interested in controlling the adverse effects of development near park lands. Specifically, the Secretary is empowered to promulgate protective regulations, set lease terms and conditions, terminate leases for violations of these regulations or lease terms, and suspend operations on any leasehold "in the interest of conservation."

The park protection amendment to the Geothermal Steam Act, while still untested, promises important safeguards for the geysers, bubbling mud pots, and hot springs of some of our most treasured national parks. The Secretary must identify significant thermal features within parks, and must review all lease applications that might adversely affect these features. If the Secretary determines on the basis of scientific evidence that lease activity is reasonably likely to have significant adverse effects on the thermal features, the application must be denied and those lands closed to leasing. If nonsignificant adverse effects are likely, the Secretary must impose stringent lease stipulations to protect the features. Important here is the fact that the Secretary does not have unbridled discretion in making these determinations.

While the language of the amendment is strong, it is not as comprehensive as conservationists would like. First, the amendment does not protect significant features in all National Park System units, being limited only to the features and units described on the final list. It has been suggested that other park units, such as Death Valley National Monument, contain thermal features equally deserving of protection.[81]

Second, and more important, the amendment contains no protections whatsoever for park resources other than thermal features. It does not address the potentially serious impacts of geothermal development near park lands on wildlife, scenic resources, and other park values. However, other provisions of the Geothermal Steam Act might be used by a conservation-minded Secretary to protect those park values. In particular, a strong Secretary could promulgate regulations and impose lease terms and conditions specifically geared to protecting the entire range of park resources. NEPA also might be used to protect other park values. The recent IBLA decisions requiring BLM either to prepare an EIS prior to lease issuance or to retain the right to preclude development at a subsequent stage are encouraging. The only remaining step is to tie these cases to park protection. BLM must be required either to consider the effects of geothermal development on all nearby park resources or, where staged leasing is adopted, to reserve the right to preclude lease development if unacceptable impacts on park resources are discovered.

Third, the amendment fails to protect park resources, including park thermal features, from development on state-owned and privately-owned lands either within or close to park boundaries. Other provisions of the GSA and NEPA are of questionable help in this regard. Nor is this a mere hypothetical problem. Hawaii Volcanoes National Park, Lassen Volcanic National Park, and Yellowstone National Park have all been threatened by development projects on state or private lands near or inside their boundaries. Acquisition solved the potentially disastrous problems in Hawaii and at Lassen; development near Yellowstone has never been economically feasible without supplementing the small state and private acreages with federal leases, now partially banned by legislation.

One general problem with park protection and geothermal development is implicit in the division of agency responsibility. The National Park Service is responsible for administering and protecting parks and all of their resources, yet BLM is the agency exclusively responsible for issuing and administering geothermal leases on federal lands. While both agencies are part of the Department of the Interior, they are essentially separate, independent organizations with widely differing goals and responsibilities.[82] BLM is not expressly required in either the Geothermal Steam Act as enacted or the recent amendment to consult the Park Service regarding issuance of geothermal leases near park lands. In fact, communication and cooperation among the interested agencies has not been good. The 1986 amendment to the GSA may improve this situation somewhat, at least with regard to leases potentially affecting the thermal features of certain parks.

Another general problem for park protection is the fact that agency discretion plays such a major role in the leasing scheme. Other than meeting the minimum requirements of pollution control laws such as the Federal Water Pollution Control Act[83] and the Clean Air Act,[84] there is extremely little in the way of substantive environmental protection that the Secretary of the Interior *must* provide with regard to geothermal leasing. Whether analyzing the environmental effects of leasing in an environmental assessment or an EIS, setting lease terms or conditions, or determining if lease activity will significantly adversely affect thermal features in a park, the Secretary retains substantial leeway. For the interested public, and also for such affected agencies such as the National Park Service, this means constant vigilance.

NOTES

*Shute, Mihaly & Weinberger, San Francisco, CA. Former Staff Attorney, Sierra Club Legal Defense Fund, San Francisco, CA.

1. B. Hamilton, *Geothermal Energy: Trouble Brews for the National Parks*, SIERRA, July, 1983, at 21.

2. R. Anderson, *Yellowstone Unbound*, NATIONAL PARKS, Nov./Dec. 1985, at 10.

3. U.S. DEPARTMENT OF AGRICULTURE, U.S. FOREST SERVICE, FINAL ENVIRONMENTAL IMPACT STATEMENT OF THE ISLAND PARK GEOTHERMAL AREA: IDAHO, MONTANA, WYOMING, Jan. 15, 1980 at 111 (hereinafter cited as ISLAND PARK FEIS).

4. A. Thuermer, Jr., *Breaking Faith with Old Faithful*, High Country News, June 24, 1983 at 11.

5. Anderson, *Yellowstone Unbound, supra* at 10.

6. ISLAND PARK FEIS, *supra* at 112.

7. *Id.* at 66.

8. *See* U.S. DEPARTMENT OF THE INTERIOR, GEOLOGICAL SURVEY CIRCULAR 647, CLASSIFICATION OF PUBLIC LANDS VALUABLE FOR GEOTHERMAL STEAM AND ASSOCIATED GEOTHERMAL RESOURCES, at 6 (1971).

9. *Geothermal Energy: Legal Problems of Resource Development*, STANFORD ENVIRONMENTAL LAW SOCIETY, May, 1975 at 23-24.

10. Allyn Stone and Bill Wallace, *A Hot Idea Losing Steam: Geothermal Decline Hits Lake Country*, San Francisco Chron., Jan. 12, 1987 at 4.

11. ISLAND PARK FEIS, *supra* at 111-12.

12. *Id.* at 1. Federal lands within the Island Park Geothermal Area (hereinafter cited as the IPGA) consist of 477,346 acres administered by the U.S. Forest Service, and 10,685 acres administered by the Bureau of Land Management (BLM). Included among the acres administered by BLM are some private lands with mineral rights reserved to the federal government. *Id.* There are also approximately 25,000 acres of private and state lands within the IPGA. *Id.* at 166-67.

13. *Id.*

14. *Id.* at i.

15. Energy, Mining and Minerals Division, National Park Service, "Geothermal and Oil and Gas Activities Adjacent to Yellowstone National Park," revised Jan. 5, 1986 (table).

16. ISLAND PARK FEIS, *supra* at 166-67. In 1984, Congress baned issuance of federal leases in the Island Park Known Geothermal Resource Area. Pub. L. No: 98-473, 98 Stat. 1874 (1984). This consists of about 53,760 acres within the IPGA that the Secretary of the Interior has determined are likely to contain commercially viable resources. *See* Part II. In 1985, the ban was continued "until Congress determines otherwise." Pub. L. No. 99-190, 99 Stat. 1267 (1985).

17. Thuermer, *Breaking Faith with Old Faithful, supra* at 1.

18. ISLAND PARK FEIS, *supra* at 166-67.

19. *Proposed Amendments To The Geothermal Steam Act: Hearing On S. 1322 Before The Subcommittee On Natural Resources Development And Production Of The Senate Committee On Energy And Natural Resources*, 99th Cong., 2d Sess. (1986) (statement of T. Destry Jarvis). (Hereinafter cited as *Senate Hearing.*)

20. 30 U.S.C. §§ 1001-1025.

21. Prior to the Act, the Secretary had no explicit authority to issue leases for geothermal resources, and attempts to obtain rights to this energy source through existing leasing laws, such as the Mineral Leasing Act of 1920, proved unworkable. The Act defines geothermal steam and associated geothermal resources as "(i) all products of geothermal processes, embracing indigenous steam, hot water and hot brines; (ii) steam and other gases, hot water and hot brines resulting from water, gas, or other fluids artificially introduced into geothermal formations; (iii) heat or other associated energy found in geothermal formations; and (iv) any byproduct derived from them." Section 1001(c).

22. H.R. REP. NO. 1544, 91st Cong., 2nd Sess. (1970), *reprinted in* [1970] U.S. CODE CONG. & ADMIN. NEWS 5113, 5115-16.

23. *Id.* at 5114.

24. 30 U.S.C. § 1022(b).

25. *Id.* § 1002.

26. *Id.* §§ 1002, 1014.

27. *Id.* § 1014.

28. *Id.* §§ 1001, 1020. A "known geothermal resources area" is defined in the Act as an area in which the "geology, nearby discoveries, competitive interests, or other indicia would, in the opinion of the Secretary, engender a belief in men who are experienced in the subject matter that the prospects for extraction of geothermal steam or associated geothermal resources are good enough to warrant expenditures of money for that purpose." *Id.* § 1001(e). By mid-1986, the Department of the Interior estimated that 1.6 million acres of federal lands were classified as "known geothermal resources areas." Geothermal Steam Act Amendments of 1985, *supra* note 19, Appendix A at 82.

29. 30 U.S.C. § 1003. In mid-1986, there were 267 outstanding competitive leases covering 438,509 acres. Geothermal Steam Act Amendments of 1985, *supra* note 19.

30. 30 U.S.C. § 1003. In mid-1986, there were 981 noncompetitive leases outstanding, covering some 1,685,101 acres. Geothermal Steam Act Amendments of 1985, *supra* note 19, Appendix A at 95.

31. 30 U.S.C. § 1005(a). Production of geothermal steam in commercial quantities means completing at least one well capable of producing steam and making a bona fide sale of the steam. *Id.* 1005(d).

32. *Id.* § 1005(c).

33. *Id.* § 1005(b).

34. *Id.* § 1005(a).

35. *Id.* § 1004.

36. *Id.* § 1006.

37. *Id.* § 1017. For a more detailed discussion of the major provisions of the Act, *see* Special Study, *supra* note 9, at 55-64.

38. *See, e.g.,* 43 U.S.C. § 1701(a).

39. *See* Multiple-Use Sustained Yield Act of 1960, 16 U.S.C. §§ 528-531.

40. H.R. REP. NO. 1544, *supra* note 22 at 5129.

41. *Id.* at 5129 (emphasis added), 5131.

42. *See, e.g.,* 43 C.F.R. § 3261.3(a). The Department of the Interior has also promulgated standard Geothermal Resource Operating Orders, or GRO orders, which establish lease performance standards for lessees and provide some degree of environmental protection. The effectiveness of the regulatory scheme and the GRO orders for purposes of environmental protection is discussed in Sierra Club, 79 IBLA 240 (1984) and Sierra Club, 7 IBLA 1 (1985).

43. 30 U.S.C. § 1011. (Emphasis added.)

44. *Id.* at § 1009.

45. *Id.* §§ 1007(c), 1009.

46. H.R. REP NO. 1544, *supra* note 22, at 5129.

47. Courts have interpreted broadly the Secretary's suspension powers exercised "in the interest of conservation" under the Mineral Leasing Act of 1920 and the Outer Continental Shelf Lands Act. *See, e.g.,* Copper Valley Machine Works, Inc. v. Andrus, 653 F.2d 595, 600 (D.C. Cir. 1981). *See also* Getty Oil Corp. v. Clark, 614 F. Supp. 904, 915 (D. Wyo. 1985) (Mineral Leasing Act of 1920); Gulf Oil Corp. v. Morton, 493 F.2d 141, 144-46 (9th Cir. 1973) (Outer Continental Shelf Lands Act). The Geothermal Steam Act also provides that the Secretary may waive, suspend, or reduce the rental or royalty on any lease "in the interests of conservation and to encourage the greatest ultimate recovery of geothermal resources," if certain determinations are made. 30 U.S.C. § 1012.

48. *Id.* § 1008.

49. *Id.* § 1001.

50. *Id.* § 1008.

51. Department of the Interior and Related Agencies Appropriations Act for 1987, Pub. L. No. 99-591, 115 (1986). (Hereinafter cited as Geothermal Steam Act Amendment).

52. The National Parks and Conservation Association, the Sierra Club, and other conservation organizations had lobbied for park protection amendments to the Geothermal Steam Act for ten years. Until 1986, however, the energy industry was successful in blocking these amendments. Additional amendments are being considered in the 100th Congress.

53. 30 U.S.C. § 1005(a), (b).

54. *Senate Hearings, supra* note 19 at 12. (Statement of Robert H. Lawton, Deputy Assistant Director, Energy and Mineral Resources, Bureau of Land Management.)

55. *See, e.g., id.* at 33-35 (statement of Domenic J. Falcone, Executive Vice President, Geothermal Resources International, Inc.) and at 41 (statement of Kenneth Press Nemzer, Chairman of the Geothermal Resources Association).

56. Geothermal Steam Act Amendment, *supra* note 51, § (1)(a).

57. *Id.* § (1)(b).

58. *Id.* § (1)(c).

59. *Id.* § (2)(a). The twenty-two units specifically included in the amendment are: Mount Ranier National Park, Lassen Volcanic National Park, Yellowstone National Park, Bering Land Bridge National Preserve, Gates of the Arctic National Park and Preserve, Yukon-Charley Rivers National Preserve, Katmai National Park, Aniakchak National Monument and Preserve, Wrangell-St. Elias National Park and Preserve, Glacier Bay National Park and Preserve, Denali National Park and Preserve, Lake Clark National Park and Preserve, Hot Springs National Park, Sequoia National Park, Hawaii Volcanoes National Park, Lake Mead National Recreation Area, Big Bend National Park, Olympic National Park, Grand Teton National Park, John D. Rockefeller Memorial Parkway, Haleakala National Park, and Crater Lake National Park.

60. *Id.*

61. *Id.* The Secretary published a proposed list of significant geothermal features on Feb. 13, 1987. 52 Fed. Reg. 4,700 (1987). The list identified significant thermal features in seventeen of the twenty-two units listed in the 1986 amendment. Numerous individuals, organizations, and federal agencies then submitted comments, which were widely divergent in viewpoint. The Bureau of Land Management, for example, criticized the National Park Service's approach to determinting "significance" as well as their definition of

"thermal feature," and argued strenuously for drastically reducing the list. *See* U.S. Department of the Interior memorandum to Director, National Park Service, from State Director, Bureau of Land Management, California, regarding Comments on the NPS Federal Register Notice of Proposed Significant Thermal Features in 22 National Park Units, dated Mar. 16, 1987. The final listing, transmitted to Congress on June 30, 1987, identified significant thermal features in thirteen units of the National Park System. 52 Fed. Reg. 28,790 (1987).

62. Geothermal Steam Act Amendment, *supra* note 51, § (2)(b).

63. *Id.* at § (2)(c).

64. *Id.*

65. *Id.* at § (2)(d).

66. *Id.*

67. 42 U.S.C. § 4321. (hereinafter cited as NEPA).

68. 42 U.S.C. § 4332(2)(c).

69. For example, courts have held that a lease is a contract between the government and the lessee that vests property rights enforceable against the government. *See*, Sun Oil v. United States, 572 F.2d 786, 793 (Ct. Cl. 1978), which involved a disputed oil and gas lease. Further, a lessee's rights under a lease can be limited only by his knowing consent to explicit lease stipulations that restrict or prohibit him from the beneficial enjoyment of his leasehold. *See* Chevron Oil Co., 24 IBLA 159, 165 (1976). In the context of offshore oil and gas leasing, it has been held that without an express reservation in a lease of the right to prohibit occupancy of the leasehold, the Secretary of the Interior may not disapprove all development activities. Union Oil Co. v. Morton, 512 F.2d 743 (9th Cir. 1975).

70. Sierra Club v. Hathaway, 579 F.2d 1162 (9th Cir. 1978).

71. *Id.* at 1168.

72. Sierra Club v. Peterson, 717 F.2d 1409 (D.C. Cir. 1983).

73. *Id.* at 1414-15.

74. *Id.* at 1415. (Emphasis in original.)

75. *Id.* at 1412.

76. Sierra Club, 79 IBLA 240 (1984).

77. Later, on reconsideration, IBLA determined that BLM had in fact adopted a staged leasing approach, and permitted the leasing to proceed on that basis. Sierra Club (On Reconsideration), 84 IBLA 175 (1984). However, the area was shortly thereafter designated part of the Mono Basin National Forest Scenic Area and closed to all geothermal leasing.

78. Sierra Club, 87 IBLA 1 (1985).

79. *See*, U.S. DEPARTMENT OF AGRICULTURE AND U.S. DEPARTMENT OF THE INTERIOR, DRAFT ENVIRONMENTAL IMPACT STATEMENT: LEASING GEOTHERMAL RESOURCES, LASSEN NATIONAL FOREST, May 1986, Chapter 4 at 1-5, 39-40.

80. *Id.*, Chapter 2 at 7. As this book went to press, no final EIS or decision regarding leasing around Lassen Volcanic National Park had been issued.

81. *See*, National Park Service internal memorandum to Environmental Protection Specialist Energy, Mining, and Minerals, Washington) from Acting Chief, Water Resources Division Ft. Collins) regarding Proposed Listing of Significant Geothermal Features Within Units f the National Park System, dated Mar. 16, 1987. This memorandum recommends listing Devil's Hole in Death Valley National Monument as a significant thermal feature. *See also* Geothermal Summary Report for National Park Service Units, External Impacts, ated Apr. 21, 1986, listing forty-six National Park System units with geothermal and ssociated volcanic activity.

82. The difference in the agencies' philosophies is reflected in the current controversy over listing significaat thermal features. The Park Service has proposed a fairly comprehensive list of features, while the BLM argued for a drastically reduced list. *See supra* note 61.

83. 33 U.S.C. § 1251.

84. 42 U.S.C. § 7401. *See also,* Geothermal Resource Operating Order No. 4, providing that "[a]dverse environmental impacts from geothermal-related activity shall be prevented or mitigated through enforcement of applicable Federal, State, and local standards." Geothermal Resource Operating Orders are binding on lessees. 43 C.F.R. § 3262.1(a).

Chapter 17

HYDROPOWER, DAMS, AND THE NATIONAL PARKS

F. Lorraine Bodi[*]

I. INTRODUCTION

Although it may seem surprising, our national parks are not completely protected from dams and hydroelectric development. There are, at present, over one hundred dams located in national parks, over two hundred dams located in other components of the park system, and many other dams that threaten park resources from outside their boundaries. Some of these dams--such as Glines Canyon Dam in the Olympic National Park, O'Shaugnessy Dam in Yosemite National Park, and the Boise Cascade dams in Voyageurs National Park--are already producing hydropower. Others--Sherburne Dam near Glacier National Park, Jackson Lake Dam near Grand Teton National Park, and numerous small dams---are now slated for new hydropower development.

Dams and hydroelectric projects can seriously diminish the cultural, recreational, and environmental resources of the park system. The construction and operation of dams and hydroelectric projects can lower water quality by increasing sedimentation and can alter such important river characteristics as velocity, flow, and temperature. Dams and hydroelectric projects can also inundate cultural and archeological sites, degrade or destroy riparian and gravel habitats, block human recreation and animal migration, and kill fish by forcing them to pass through power-generating turbines. For large dams and hydroelectric projects, mitigative conditions and siting alternatives are often resisted because they reduce project revenues. As a consequence, environmentally sound hydropower has been the exception rather than the norm.

Until the 1980s, most of the nation's water resource development affecting the park system took the form of relatively large
reservoir storage projects developed by the Army Corps of Engineers, the Bureau of Reclamation, or utility companies.
During the perceived energy shortages of the 1970s, however, that
picture changed. With tax and regulatory incentives provided by
the Public Utilities Regulatory Policies Act of 1978,[1] the Energy Security Act of 1980,[2] and the Crude Oil Windfall Profit
Tax Act of 1980,[3] many small hydroelectric projects, primarily
"run-of-the-river" projects backed by private investors and industry, have been proposed in the vicinity of the parks. In
some areas, such as the Ross Lake National Recreation Area,
cumulative impacts from multiple projects have become a concern.
Ironically, the cascade of new projects has come at a time when
projected energy deficits have metamorphosed into energy surpluses
around the country.

Who decides how to regulate all of these new and existing dams
and hydroelectric projects? The answer is complicated, often uncertain, and is of utmost importance to the future integrity of the
National Park System.

II. THE COMPLICATED LEGAL FRAMEWORK FOR DAMS IN AND NEAR THE PARK SYSTEM

As a general rule, the National Park Service oversees and
manages activities within the boundaries of the National Park System. The Park Service must administer these areas "in light of the
high public value and integrity of the National Park System," and
may not act "in derogation of the values and purposes for
which the various areas have been established, except as may have
been or shall be directly and specifically provided by Congress."[4]
Nevertheless, when it comes to dams and hydroelectric projects,
neither the Park Service nor park values are the final arbiter of
what is or is not acceptable in the parks. Depending on the location and particular circumstances surrounding a project, federal
agencies other than the Park Service may actually make the ultimate regulatory decisions. And, in some situations, it is not entirely clear which federal agency does have authority to make the
ultimate decisions.

This section describes the complicated legal framework for dams
and hydroelectric projects in and near the park system. It sum-

marizes the respective, but interrelated, authorities of the Park Service, the Federal Energy Regulatory Commission (FERC), the federal water resource development agencies, the Bureau of Reclamation, and the Army Corps of Engineers.

A. The National Park Service

As mentioned previously, the Park Service must administer all lands and waters within the park system in a manner that protects park values and resources. However, Park Service jurisdiction does not extend to activities such as hydroelectric development on lands and waters outside the park system, even if these activities may impair or disturb values and resources within the parks. For activities outside the park system, the Park Service may present recommendations to federal dam operators and regulators, but has no authority to force implementation: it is considered simply another advisory agency when advocating its position on the many new hydroelectric projects proposed on rivers above and below the parks.

Even within the boundaries of the park system, Park Service jurisdiction over dams and hydroelectric development is far from absolute. Under the terms of the 1921 Federal Power Act (FPA) amendments, which governs hydroelectric licensing, new hydroelectric projects are prohibited in national parks and monuments:

> [n]o permit, license, lease, or authorization for dams, conduits, reservoirs, powerhouses, transmission lines . . . within the limits, as constituted, March 3, 1921, of any national park or national monument shall be granted or made without specific authority of Congress.[5]

Several questions remain, however, regarding the application of this prohibition to the National Park System. First, there is the question of whether park system components added after 1921 are included in the prohibition. This is not as serious a concern as it might seem at first glance, because the FPA provides no authority for licensing projects in national parks or monuments regardless of when constituted, as will be discussed in Part III.B.

More serious is the question of the application of the prohibition to park system components--such as national recreation areas and national rivers--that are not, strictly speaking, national parks or monuments. Because these components of the park system have evolved since 1921, the law does not expressly provide for them. One view, apparently the Park Service view, is that the prohibition was extended to the entire park system through the General Authorities Act of 1970, which states that "the various authorities relating to the administration and protection of areas under the administration of . . . the National Park Service . . . shall be applicable to all areas within the National Park Service."[6] The narrower view, that the prohibition does not apply outside of national parks and monuments, had been adopted by FERC, the federal dam licensing agency under the FPA. Based on this interpretation, FERC has issued hydroelectric approvals for projects located within the boundaries of national recreation areas, including a project proposed for the Glen Canyon National Recreation Area. Hydro proposals within the boundaries of the Ross Lake National Recreation Area and near New River Gorge National River raise the same potential issues.

Another major uncertainty regarding Park Service jurisdiction arises in connection with existing dams and hydroelectric projects within park boundaries that either predate the park or were specifically authorized by Congress. One example is the Glines Canyon Dam, located on the Elwha River in Olympic National Park, and originally licensed by the FPC, now FERC. Since the license expired in 1986 and since relicensing under the FPA requires examination of a project on a clean slate, under "then-existing" laws and regulations, the Park Service has asserted that it, not FERC, has regulatory authority over the project. FERC, on the other hand, is treating relicensing the same as for any other project. Many enviromental groups and agencies have become involved in the Glines Canyon dispute, and it will most likely be several years before the jurisdictional issues are untangled. Of course, even under Park Service jurisdiction, it is not at all clear how hydroelectric projects such as Glines Canyon would be regulated. Nor is it clear what standards and procedures the Park Service would apply, whether permits would be issued, whether dam removal would be required, and so forth.

In sum, while the Park Service administers the National Park System, its authority over dams and hydroelectric projects in and near the parks is far from complete. There are active and substantial uncertainties about the Park Service's role vis-a-vis new projects in areas that are not national parks and monuments, as well as about existing projects within national parks and monuments.

Depending on how the uncertainty is resolved, the Park Service may have a greater or a lesser role in the development, operation, and modification of hydroelectric projects.

B. The Federal Energy Regulatory Commission

With very limited exceptions, construction and operation of nonfederal hydroelectric development is regulated by FERC. In theory, the legal framework governing FERC hydroelectric approvals is quite protective of natural resources and recreational values. In practice, FERC has generally encouraged hydroelectric power production at their expense. The result has been frequent litigation against FERC and court rulings that reinforce the importance of natural resource protection in the statutory scheme.

The centerpiece of FERC's regulatory authority is the FPA,[7] a statute that dates back to the beginning of this century. Under the FPA, FERC is authorized to issue hydroelectric licenses "for the development, transmission, and utilization of power across, along, from, or in any of the streams or other bodies of water over which Congress has jurisdiction . . . or upon any part of the public lands and reservations of the United States."[8] Public lands and reservations subject to FERC licensing authority include national forests and Indian reservations, but do not include "national parks or national monuments."[9]

FERC interprets this limitation narrowly and its licensing authority broadly. Accordingly, the agency has chosen to exercise jurisdiction over new hydroelectric projects in national recreation areas as well as new hydroelectric projects at existing federal dams within national parks. FERC could also be expected to claim jurisdiction over projects in private inholdings within national parks and monuments, since these are not expressly excluded under the FPA.

Section 10(a) has been called the "backbone" of the FPA. It directs FERC to find that a licensed project is "best adapted to a comprehensive plan for improving or developing a waterway or waterways" for hydroelectric generation and "for other beneficial water uses, including recreational purposes."[10] Section 10(a) has been interpreted by the courts to require--before license issuance--evaluation and resolution of needs for power, energy alternatives, impacts to fish and wildlife and other natural resources, the preservation of wild rivers and wilderness areas, the maintenance of

natural beauty, and the preservation of historic sites.[11] Pursuant to
Section 10(a), FERC is authorized to condition or deny hydropower
licenses to accommodate environmental concerns, which could certainly include park values and resources. In actual practice, FERC's
failure to condition or deny licesnses for projects with significant
adverse impacts has led to a steady stream of litigation for the past
twenty years. FERC has only once denied a license on environmental grounds, and that denial occurred over three decades ago.[12]
Because of FERC's failure to take its environmental obligations
seriously, the Electric Consumers Protection Act of 1986, discussed
in Part VI.D below, reinforced the requirements of Section
10(a) and other provisions of the FPA, though this new
authority has yet to be tested.

In addition to requirements under the FPA, FERC's
authority to approve nonfederal hydroelectric projects is tempered
by its obligations under other environmental laws. FERC decisions
must also satisfy laws such as NEPA,[13] the Fish and Wildlife Coordination Act (FWCA),[14] the Endangered Species Act,[15] the Wild
and Scenic Rivers Act,[16] and the Pacific Northwest Electric Power
Planning and Conservation Act (Northwest Power Act).[17] As in the
case of the FPA, FERC's enthusiasm for promoting hydropower
has often outweighed its enthusiasm for protecting environmental and other natural resource values under these statutes.

Once FERC issues a license, requests for license amendment
may be initiated by FERC, the licensee, or an interested party
under the terms of standard "reopener" clauses inserted in all licenses.[18] However, license amendments are subject to notice and opportunity for hearing and, under Section 6 of the FPA, may be
not so extensive as to constitute a change in license conditions
without mutual agreement.[19] As a practical matter, license modification proceedings can extend for many years without resolution.[20]

Finally, if past experience holds true, any party or agency, including the Park Service, faces an uphill battle to have its
views considered by FERC. In order to influence FERC decisions
and to have its views made a part of the decision making record,
an interested party or agency, including the Park Service, must
formally intervene in FERC proceedings by filing a motion or petition for intervention. Intervention is particularly important because,
under FERC regulations, only an intervenor can appeal a decision
to which it objects.[21]

Intervenors in FERC proceedings need not be represented by attorneys. Nevertheless, because FERC generally follows a strict interpretation of its procedures and deadlines, many of which are shorter than thirty days, intervenors concerned about park issues should be familiar with FERC regulations and administrative practice to avoid dismissal of their concerns based on procedural technicalities.

C. The Federal Dam Operators

Under various laws and congressional authorizations, the Department of the Interior, Bureau of Reclamation, and the Department of the Army, Corps of Engineers, both construct and operate multiple-purpose dams and reservoirs. In some instances, existing Bureau and Corps projects located in and near units of the National Park System actually create reservoirs or release discharges within park boundaries. For example, just upstream of the New River Gorge National River in West Virginia, the Corps of Engineers operates Bluestone Dam, which discharges into the national river. Not only do Corps-controlled water releases regularly affect recreational use of the river, the Corps is also considering the addition of peaking hydropower capacity at the dam--with unknown consequences for the National River. Downstream of Bandelier National Monument, the Corps' Cochiti Dam has inundated several hundred acres of the monument, including bald eagle nesting habitat and numerous archaeological sites. Dams regulated by the International Joint Commission (between the U.S. and Canada) release water into Voyageurs National Park in vacillating patterns that have damaged critical park waterfowl habitat.

The extent of Park Service control over the operation of these projects varies depending on each project's specific authorizing legislation, local circumstances, and the effectiveness of interagency cooperation. As a general rule, however, the Park Service has only limited influence in many situations in which park resources are affected or at risk.

In some remarkable cases, even literal protective legislative language has failed to protect park resources from federal dams. For instance, the Colorado River Storage Project Act of 1956 expressly stated that "no dam or reservoir constructed under the authorization of this chapter shall be within any national park or monument."[22] Furthermore, the Act specifically provided protection for Rainbow Bridge National Monument from waters that would approach it as a result of the construction of the Glen Canyon Dam, directing the Secretary of the Interior to "take adequate protective measures to preclude impairment of the . . . Monument."[23]

Despite these clear legislative provisions, when the gates of Glen Canyon Dam were finally closed by the Bureau, the rising waters inundated portions of the monument. In a suit brought against the Secretary of the Interior, *Friends of the Earth v. Armstrong*,[24] the court refused to direct the Secretary to take protective measures, reasoning that the protective provisions of the Act had been implicitly repealed by later congressional appropriation acts, which specifically deleted, then later failed to fund the protection of Rainbow Bridge National Monument. Today, the tepid waters of Lake Powell lap at the bottom of Rainbow Bridge arch, and most visitors to the monument arrive by boat.

FERC may also play a role in nonfederal hydropower development at Bureau and Corps dams. For example, FERC has been willing to consider hydroelectric applications at federal water projects within national parks. Based on an application by the Town of Jackson, Wyoming, to study the hydropower potential at the Bureau's Jackson Lake Dam in Grand Teton National Park, FERC determined that it had jurisdiction to issue a permit for the project despite the FPA's explicit prohibition of new hydro projects in parks. FERC concluded that the Bureau's project was not, strictly speaking, part of the park, and therefore was subject to FERC licensing.[25]

Pending and additional hydropower proposals at federal dams in and near units of the National Park System will continue to raise jurisdictional questions involving the Bureau, the Corps, and FERC. The only constant seems to be the Park Service's lack of jurisdiction over such projects.

IV. RECENT ISSUES AND CASES

The legal framework governing hydroelectric projects in and near units of the National Park System, particularly the FERC process, has been undergoing review and challenge by environmental groups, federal and state agencies, Indian tribes, and Congress. In several recent cases, challenges by coalitions of such groups have been successful and FERC actions have been invalidated. The issues raised in these cases, while not directly involving the National Park System, are issues with relevance for the National Park Service as it deals with the issues of dams and hydroelectric development. Other issues in the hydroelectric regulatory process have been resolved by the Electric Consumers Protection Act of 1986.

A. The Relicensing of Rock Island Dam: *Confederated Tribes v. FERC*[26]

Rock Island Dam, the first dam to span the Columbia River, was built in 1933 and was substantially rebuilt and upgraded in the mid-1970s. For the last ten years, federal and state fish and wildlife agencies have been unsuccessfully requesting state-of-the-art juvenile fishway measures to reduce turbine mortalities. In 1981, despite these outstanding requests, FERC decided to issue a new forty-year license for Rock Island Dam without any specific fish and wildlife conditions, relying exclusively on a standard condition reserving FERC's right to impose "reasonable modifications" after license issuance. FERC disregarded the unanimous requests of intervenor agencies, Indian tribes with treaty fishing rights, and the National Wildlife Federation for license conditions requiring juvenile fishways and spills to divert fish around rather than through the turbines, saying that these issues would be addressed in a separate proceeding. FERC also did not require the project operator to submit the fish and wildlife report required under its own regulations, and did not prepare an environmental assessment (EA) or environmental impact statement (EIS) to support its decision.

The National Marine Fisheries Service, the state of Washington, the Yakima Indian Nation, and the National Wildlife Federation appealed FERC's decision. The Ninth Circuit Court of Appeals ruled in the plaintiffs' favor on all points, finding that FERC was obliged to fully evaluate fishery issues before licensing and could not defer them to a later separate proceeding. The court explained that this obligation of FERC's was "well-defined" and was not a new principle of law. The court also found that FERC should have prepared an EIS to consider alternative project operations.

In light of the Rock Island decision, the Park Service and parties to FERC proceedings have firm grounds to insist that impacts on park values and available alternatives be fully considered and resolved prior to licensing.

B. The Winchester Dam Exemption: *Steamboaters v. FERC*[27]

The Winchester Dam is a small hydro project at an existing dam on the North Umpqua River in Oregon. The project is located across a major anadromous fish migration route, which makes it difficult for the project to meet statutory requirements to ensure protection of fish and wildlife. FERC initially issued a small hydro exemption for Winchester Dam subject to mandatory conditions set by the Oregon Department of Fish and Wildlife, the U.S. Fish and Wildlife Service, and the National Marine Fisheries Service (NMFS). On appeal, however, FERC agreed with the applicant, Elektra Power Company, that it could waive the most stringent of these conditions, those set by the NMFS, as a matter of statutory interpretation. FERC reached this conclusion despite years of interpreting FPA to require adherence to mandatory conditions set by NMFS. FERC also disregarded requests by NMFA and the Steamboaters (a fishing group) for preparation of an EA or EIS, claiming, based on the conditions set by the state fishery agency and the U.S. Fish and Wildlife Service, that these documents were unnecessary.

NMFS and the Steamboaters both appealed issuance of the exemption to the Court of Appeals. The court agreed with FERC that it could waive NMFS' conditions but disagreed that FERC could entirely disregard these conditions. The court invalidated the exemption because of FERC's failure to prepare the necessary environmental review documents and independently assess project impacts. It ruled that FERC must take an independent, hard look at the adequacy and enforceability of all mitigative conditions, and must respond to NMFS' conditions before approving a project such as Winchester Dam.

The Winchester Dam decision strengthens the precedent of the Rock Island case. The National Park Service and others can rely on the case to ensure that FERC, the Bureau of Reclamation, and the Corps of Engineers fully evaluate the adequacy and enforceability of conditions to mitigate adverse impacts on park values and resources as part of their NEPA responsibilities. As an agency guided by a preservation mandate, the Park Service is also frequently placed in the position of seeking stricter development controls relative to other concerned parties, somewhat like the position of the NMFS in this proceeding. *Steamboaters* will certainly bear on similar situations directly involving the Park Service.

C. Multiple Hydro Proposals in the Salmon and Snohomish River Basins: *National Wildlife Federation v. FERC* **and** *Washington Department of Fisheries v. FERC* [28]

Two cases involving FERC's use of project-specific hydroelectric approvals in the Salmon and Snohomish River basins, where numerous projects have been proposed, were recently decided by the Ninth Circuit Court of Appeals. The Salmon River in Idaho, one of the most significant remaining spawning areas for spring and summer chinook salmon in the Columbia Basin, supports fish runs that are depressed to the point of near extinction--a result of existing hydro development. The Snohomish River in Washington contains few existing hydroelectric projects, but is a highly productive area for natural runs of salmon and steelhead.

In the Salmon and Snohomish Basins, state and federal fish and wildlife agencies and Indian tribes with treaty fishing rights have asked that FERC develop "comprehensive plans" under Section 10(a) of the FPA to identify appropriate and inappropriate sites for hydrolectric development, taking into account fish and wildlife needs. As part of this process, these parties have also requested the imposition of uniform study guidelines for applicants and consideration of the cumulative impacts of projects pending before FERC. Despite the clear language of Section 10(a), FERC does not develop comprehensive plans for river basins. Of course, in the past, FERC never faced the numbers of river basin hydroelectric projects that it faces today.

In response to appeals by the National Wildlife Federation, the Nez Perce Tribe, the Washington Department of Fisheries, and the Tulalip Tribe, the Court of Appeals found that FERC's piecemeal approach was "not based on any evidence at all, let alone substantial evidence." The court confirmed that FERC must develop all necessary information to support licensing, evaluate cumulative impacts of multiple hydro projects, and prepare a comprehensive plan for each basin before licensing new projects.

The Salmon and Snohomish decisions have a dual relevance for the National Park System. First, the National Park Service and parties to FERC proceedings concerned about specific and cumulative impacts can draw support from the decisions. Second, the decisions may be applicable to the Park Service itself as it develops and considers comprehensive plans for lands and waters under its administration and lands that comprise larger ecosystems around National Park System units.

D. The Electric Consumers Protection Act of 1986

In October 1986, Congress passed the Electric Consumers Protection Act of 1986 (ECPA), the first major overhaul of the FPA in over fifty years. Although the ECPA does not make dramatic changes in the FPA as it has been interpreted by the courts, it does underscore the need for the FERC to improve its consideration of environmental and recreational values, including values served by the park system.

Two provisions of the ECPA are directly relevant to National Park Service authorities. First, the Act amends Section 4(e) of the FPA to require that FERC accord "equal consideration to the purpose of energy conservation, the protection, mitigation of damage to, and enhancement of, fish and wildlife (including related spawning grounds and habitat), the protection of recreational opportunities, and the preservation of other aspects of environmental quality." Each of these four new purposes should play a role in hydro development affecting any national park component. The legislative history of the ECPA explains that equal consideration is a substantive as well as a procedural standard for FERC licensing.[29] The ECPA also amends Section 10(a) of the FPA to expressly require "the adequate protection, mitigation, and enhancement of fish and wildlife" and to insert the "other purposes referred to in Section 4(e)" amendments.

Second, in order to satisfy the comprehensive planning requirement of the ECPA, the Act specifies that FERC must, at a minimum, consider plans developed by states, and by any agency established pursuant to federal law with authority to prepare a plan. This should include deference to plans established by the Park Service and othere federal land management agencies. FERC must also consider the recommendations of Indian tribes and federal and state agencies exercising jurisdiction over recreation, cultural, and other resources, including the Park Service. Both of these amendments are binding on hydroelectric approvals beginning in October 1986.

V. RECOMMENDATIONS AND SOLUTIONS

Hydroelectric development is often controversial, particularly when it occurs in or near national parks and threatens natural resources preserved by parks. Yet, there are no uniform standards or regulatory procedures that apply to hydroelectric development in and near the parks. Under current law, the facts surrounding a particular hydroelectric project must be carefully evaluated before one can ascertain which agency has regulatory authority and which substantive standards must be met. In some cases, even a careful evaluation leaves unanswered questions.

As this chapter has shown, the greatest gaps and uncertainties lie in the following areas:

- The role of the National Park Service in regulating federal and nonfederal dams and hydroelectric projects outside the parks, where the projects disturb park resources,

- The role of the Park Service in regulating existing federal and nonfederal dams and hydroelectric projects within parks,

- FERC's authority to license new hydroelectric projects in park system commponents such as national recreation areas,

- FERC's authority to license new hydroelectric projects on private lands and federal dams within park boundaries.

Effective resolution and clarification of these issues will require new legislative initiatives. H.R. 4089, a proposed bill that emerged in the second session of the Ninety-ninth Congress, is a significant step in that direction, but suffers from limitations.

H.R. 4089 would reinforce the FPA's prohibition against new or expanded dams located on national park or monument lands; it would also go further to prohibit new or expanded dams outside parks that inundate national park or monument lands. As with the current language of the FPA, however, the bill overlooks express protection for units of the park system that are not formally designated national parks or monuments, an issue of continuing controversy.

H.R. 4089 contains innovative proposals for existing dams and hydroelectric projects located in and near the park system. (As in the case of new and expanded facilities, the bill's provisions for existing projects fail to expressly address components that are not national parks or monuments.) For all existing federal and nonfederal dams that either inundate or are located on park or monument lands, the bill would require a permit from the Park Service, subject to terms and conditions "necessary to protect the resources for which the park or monument was established." The Park Service permit requirement would become effective five years after enactment for dams not subject to FERC licensing or at the expiration of a FERC license where one applies.

H.R. 4089 raises many questions that warrant further attention regarding a Park Service permit program. First, it is unclear whether the new permit program would supplement or supplant FERC's licensing authority under the FPA. Second, the bill does not explain whether the Park Service would have authority to deny a permit and direct dam breaching or removal, both of which FERC is authorized to do under the FPA. Third, there is some question why Park Service permits should be delayed until expiration of FERC licenses, which can run for a period of up to fifty years.

The one issue that H.R. 4089 does not address in any way is enhancement of the National Park Service's role in regulating dams and hydroelectric projects that are outside the parks and that impair park resources without inundating park lands. At a minimum, Park Service views regarding such projects, whether new or existing, should be given great weight by FERC and other licensing agencies. This is a particularly important matter in areas where multiple hydro projects have been proposed above and/or below park boundaries.

Absent H.R. 4089 or similar legislation, hydropower and the national parks will continue to be a confused and contentious matter. Without legislative clarification, many proposed and existing hydroelectric projects affecting the park system will undoubtedly end up before the courts for resolution.

NOTES

˙Attorney, Seattle, Washington. J.D. 1976, George Washington University; B.A. 1972; M.S. 1972, University of Pennsylvania. Parts of this article have been adapted from F. Lorraine Bodi and E. Erdheim, *Swimming Upstream: FERC's Failure to Protect Anadromous Fish*, 13 ECOLOGY L.Q. 7 (1986).

1. Pub. L. No. 95-617, 92 Stat. 3117, codified as amended at 16 U.S.C. §§ 823(a)-825(s), 2601-2645, 2701-2708 (1982).

2. 16 U.S.C. §§ 2705(d), 2708(b) (1982).

3. 26 U.S.C. § 48( )(13) (1982).

4. 16 U.S.C. § 1a.

5. 16 U.S.C. § 797a.

6. 16 U.S.C. § 1a.

7. 16 U.S.C. §§ 791a-825r (1982).

8. *Id.*, § 797(e).

9. *Id.*, § 796(2). Federal agencies responsible for Indian reservations can specify binding license conditions for projects located on reservation lands. *Id.*, § 797(e). *See* Escondido Mutual Water District v. La Jolla Band of Mission Indians, 466 U.S. ___, 104 S. Ct. 3562 (1984). Ironically, the Park Service does not have this authority for projects within parks or monuments, since these are not defined as reservations.

10. 16 U.S.C. § 803(a).

11. 16 U.S.C. § 803(a). Udall v. FPC, 387 U.S. 428, 450 (1967); Scenic Hudson Preservation Conference v. FPC, 354 F.2d 608, 620 (2d Cir. 1965) *cert. denied*, 384 U.S. 941 (1966); Confederated Tribes and Bands of the Yakima Indian Nation v. FERC, 746 F.2d 466, 471 (9th Cir. 1984), *cert. denied*, 105 S. Ct 2358 (1985). It should be noted that land management and fishery agencies retain the right to specify mandatory license conditions under some circumstances. *See, e.g.*, 16 U.S.C. §§ 797(e), 811, 823.

12. Namekagon Hydro v. FPC, 216 F.2d 509 (7th Cir. 1954). For a detailed discussion of FERC's failure to adequately consider environmental issues, *see* Blumm and Kloos, *Small Scale Hydropower and Anadromous Fish: Lessons and Questions from the Winchester Dam Controversy*, 16 ENVTL. L.J. 585 (1986).

13. 42 U.S.C. §§ 4321-4370 (1982).

14. 16 U.S.C. §§ 661-667 (1982).

15. 16 U.S.C. § 1536(a) (1982).

16. *Id.*, § 1278(a).

17. *Id.*, § 839b.

18. The condition reserves FERC's right to make "reasonable modifications" in order to protect fish and wildlife. *Standardized Conditions for Inclusion in Preliminary Permits and Licenses. See, e.g.*, 14 FERC p. 62,187 (1981).

19. 16 U.S.C. § 799 (1982).

20. For a discussion of such a proceeding, *see* Bodi, *FERC's Mid-Columbia Proceeding: Ten Years and Still Counting*, 16 ENVTL. L.J. 566 (1986).

21. 18 C.F.R. § 385.713.

22. 43 U.S.C. § 620.

23. *Id.*

24. Friends of the Earth v. Armstrong, 485 F.2d 1 (10th Cir. 1973), *cert. denied*, 94 S. Ct. 933 (1974).

25. Town of Jackson, Wyoming, ___ FERC ___ (1985).

26. 746 F.2d 466 (9th Cir. 1984), *cert. denied*, 105 S. Ct. 2358 (1985).

27. 759 F.2d 1382 (9th Cir. 1985); 777 F.2d 1384 (9th Cir. 1985). For detailed discussion of this case, *see* Blumm and Kloos, note 14, *supra*.

28. No. 84-7325 (9th Cir., Sept. 30, 1986).

29. H.R. REP. NO. 99-834, 99th Cong., 2d Sess. (1986).

Chapter 18

THE SURFACE MINING CONTROL AND RECLAMATION ACT OF 1977: TEN YEARS OF PROMISE AND PROBLEMS FOR THE NATIONAL PARKS

*Patrick McGinley**

I. INTRODUCTION

The National Park System contains precious cultural and natural resources that are symbols of the strength and character of our nation: Instilled in American school children is an appreciation for the epic struggle of early Americans to survive in a vast and pristine wilderness. Woven as a common thread though successive generations of Americans is a recognition that at the very core of the American experience is the relationship of its men and women to the land and its natural resources.

The early explorers were lured from relatively crowded Europe to North America by the promise of precious metals, furs, and vast open areas of fertile farm land; gold and silver enticed settlers to the Rockies and California, while the fertile valleys and lush forests of the Pacific Northwest were the goal of yet another wave of pioneers. Abundant wildlife, virgin forests, and clean air and water nurtured native Americans and those who followed them. It was in recognition of this heritage that the National Park System was created. National parks serve as important symbolic, yet tangible links among past, present, and future generations of Americans.

The legislative mandate of the National Park Service is to protect, preserve, and conserve park resources in perpetuity. The ability of the Park Service to comply with this mandate is challenged by a multitude of internal and external threats to park integrity. Most of the units of the National Park System were pristine areas once surrounded by vast wilderness. These "buffer zones," which isolated and protected the parks from all forms of development, have been substantially depleted by various forms of development. A recent National Park Service report found that:

> no parks of the system are immune to external and in- ternal threats, and . . . these are causing significant and demonstrable damage. There is no question but that these threats will continue to degrade and destroy irreplaceable park resources until such time as mitigation measures are implemented. In many cases this degradation or loss is irreversible.[1]

Among these threats to the National Park System are those posed by the mining of coal and other minerals in and adjacent to parklands. Park Service information reveals that the United States Geological Survey has identified twenty-five units where coal definitely underlies all or part of the park. Located within these twenty-five units are more than 950,000 acres of privately owned coal reserves that might be minable under existing law.[2]

The Surface Mining Control and Reclamation Act of 1977[3] (SMCRA) is a federal statute that addresses the environmental impacts caused by the surface and underground mining of coal, and to some extent, the mining of other minerals. The following discussion focuses on the extent to which the Act protects the land and associated valued attendant National Park System units.

II. LEGISLATIVE HISTORY

SMCRA was enacted by Congress after a long and bitter fight. That battle involved, on one side, conservation groups, some state governments that had already enacted similar legislation, and responsible elements of the coal industry; on the opposing side were powerful elements of the coal industry and its supporters in coal state legislatures and in Congress who argued forcefully against the need for a federal presence in the area of coal mining and reclamation.

The supporters of federal legislation were aware of or had experienced first hand the severe environmental degradation and economic decline that accompany unregulated or underregulated

surface and underground coal mining. The sorry tale of coal mining that devastated large areas of the eastern coal-producing states
is well documented in the legislative history of SMCRA:

> Acid mine drainage which has ruined an estimated 11,000
> miles of streams; loss of prime hardwood forest and the
> destruction of wildlife habitat by strip mining; the degrad-
> ing of productive farmland; recurrent landslides; siltation
> and sedimentation of the river systems; . . . and per-
> petually burning waste dumps--these constitute a per-
> vasive and far-reaching ambiance.[4]

The havoc spawned by coal mining in the east was not limited
solely to environmental harm. Congress also noted the adverse
economic impact of such practices:

> Tragically, coal mining in America has left its crippling
> mark upon the very communities which labored most to
> produce the energy which once impelled the Nation's in-
> dustrial plant and now generates much of its electrical
> power . . . In some small watersheds, other indirect
> economic and social problems can be related to the over-
> all adverse consequences of mining.[5]

It was obvious to all who objectively analyzed the problem that
the adverse impacts of coal mining had occurred because of an almost total failure of state law to deal adequately with the problem.
In enacting SMCRA, Congress agreed with this perspective:

> despite claims from some quarters that the state reclama-
> tion laws have improved so significantly that federal min-
> ing standards are no longer needed, the hearing record
> abounds with evidence that this is simply not the case.
> For a variety of reasons, including the reluctance of the
> States to impose stringent controls on its own in-
> dustry, serious abuses continue.[6]

Thus, proponents of SMCRA believed that the only way to
bring the situation under control was to enact a program of nationally applicable minimun mining and reclamation standards that
would be enforced either by the federal government or by the
states with rigorous federal oversight.

While opponents of federal strip mine legislation did succeed
for a time in delaying the inevitable by procuring Presidential
vetoes, in the end their's was a phyrric victory. In the view of

many, the final version of the legislation signed in 1977 by President Carter placed a much greater regulatory burden on coal operators than the two earlier vetoed bills. Obviously, a substantial segment of the coal industry failed to understand that the public had completely lost its patience with strip mine ravages that had occurred for decades across the eastern and western coal fields.

While many of the strip and undergound coal mining abuses that triggered the demand for federal legislation were primarily characteristic of the eastern coal regions, Congress appreciated the great potential for harm that under-regulated coal mining posed for the immense area of federal land located in the Great Plains, Rocky Mountains, Southwest, and other areas west of the Mississippi. Thus, while many of the provisions of SMCRA focus on the impact of mining practices in the largely private land holdings in the eastern United States, the Act also is directed, in significant measure, toward the impacts of coal mining and reclamation practices on federal lands, including units of the National Park System, espcecially those west of the Mississippi:

> In the Western States and the Northern Great Plains region the discovery of vast reserves of lignite and subbituminous coal has inspired plans for the expansion of coal surface mining on a very large scale, thus major adverse impacts to the region's land and people lie ahead. Since the climate is arid and water therefore in short supply, the removal of thick coal seams and the consequent disruprtion of stream and river channels forming part of the hydrologic regime of the area will pose difficult and in some cases insurmountable reclamation problems.[7]

Strong enforcement provisions of the Act allow the appropriate federal or state regulatory agency to seek injunctive relief, civil penalties, criminal fines and imprisonment, and permit suspension or revocation where surface mining law or regulation is violated by a coal operator. Cessation of operation orders and notices of violation are among the administrative remedies available to the regulatory agency.[8] SMCRA also requires that federal, state, and local land use plans be considered by coal operators and coal mine permitting agencies.[9]

III. EFFECTIVE ENFORCEMENT OF SMCRA REQUIRES
FEDERAL AND STATE COOPERATION

SMCRA is one of a number of federal environmental regulatory statutes enacted in the 1970s in which Congress created a framework and expressed a preference for delegation of enforcement responsibility to the states.[10]

Each of these statutes sets uniform, minimum federal standards that preempt less stringent state laws, but allow for voluntary state implementation and enforcment. For example, under SMCRA, if a state can show (1) that its laws and regulations promulgated thereunder are as stringent as SMCRA requires and (2) that it has adequate staff and funding, it may be granted "primary jurisdiction" by the Secretary of the Interior to enforce SMCRA.[11]

As an incentive to encourage states to assume this responsibility, these statutes typically provide for substantial federal funding of certain costs of the state regulatory program. If a state chooses not to assume primacy under SMCRA, the Department of the Interior initiates a federal regulatory program for the state. In practice, every state that contains substantial coal reserves has opted to take primacy jurisdiction under SMCRA.[12] These types of federal environmental statutes are commonly referred to as examples of "cooperative federalism."[13]

Congress created a new federal agency, the Office of Surface Mining Reclamation and Enforcement (OSMRE) in the Department of the Interior to oversee this cooperative federalism venture. The cooperative federalism nature of SMCRA is relevant to a consideration of the Act as it relates to the National Park System; SMCRA allows states to assume primacy jurisdiction to enforce its mandate in instances of private (nonfederal) ownership of real property interests within and near park system units.

IV. LAX STATE ENFORCEMENT THREATENS PARK UNITS

Several situations in particular illustrate how the protection of a park system unit from coal mining activities rests in substantial measure on the effectiveness of state enforcement. The case of the New River Gorge National River is an excellent example. In 1978, Congress designated this National River, a 62,000-acre scenic corridor that includes a fifty-two mile portion of the New River and its narrow gorge in southern West Virginia.[14] The low-sulfur coal deposits in the gorge once supported a booming coal industry, but the forest has reclaimed much of the past disturbance.

At this writing, less than 10 percent of the land within the authorized boundary is federally owned or otherwise under federal protection. The majority of the nonfederal land is held in large tracts by individuals and corporations that look to those properties for future timbering and coal production. Much of this private land is steep sloped and extremely vulnerable to the harmful effects of coal mining.

The West Virginia Department of Energy has assumed primary jurisdiction for enforcing SMCRA on private landholdings within the park's boundaries and on lands adjacent to the park. However, state supervision has had a negative impact on the Park Service's ability to deal with coal mining activities that pose threats to park values. A very real concern is that the state has returned to its past practices of lax enforcement and slavish concern for the welfare of local coal operators rather than vigorously enforcing the environmental protection provisions of SMCRA and giving special consideration to the park.

This negative impact results from the lessened control the National Park Service has when the state has primary responsibility for SMCRA permitting, inspections, and enforcement. The Park Service also has been unable to develop a quality inventory of mining sites outside the boundaries that affect the park watershed; thus it relies for the most part on the state for such monitoring. This reliance has created a negative incentive which deters the Park Service from devoting more time and resources to minerals management.

Although there are currently no permitted surface coal mines currently active within the boundaries of the National River, inadequately reclaimed mine sites continue to release acid mine drainage into the New River and its tributaries. Active mines located outside the park boundary can also adversely affect the unit where state regulatory authority fails to ensure coal operator compliance with the West Virginia Surface Mining and Reclamation Act.[15]

Surface coal mining activities have been allowed on private lands within the New River corridor by the West Virginia Department of Energy (DOE) under the guise of "prospecting" and "exploration" activities. Coal prospecting is exempted from the rigorous permitting and public participation requirements of the Act and its West Virginia counterpart.[16] In West Virginia, when an operator desires to remove and sell more than 250 tons of coal during prospecting, it must obtain the written approval of the regulatory authority. In neighboring states, including Ohio, Pennsylvania, and Maryland, removal of more than 250 tons during prospecting is prohibited.

The West Virginia Department of Energy has, in numerous cases, approved prospecting activities where the operator has proposed the extraction and sale of five thousand to twenty thousand tons of coal. The DOE has approved a number of these dubious excess tonnage prospect permits in the New River corridor.[17] Critics of West Virginia DOE have cogently argued that these "excess tonnage" prospect permits have been used by the state as a subterfuge to allow unpermitted mining operations.[18] At a minimum, the continued approval of prospecting permits within the National River perpetuates a regulatory climate that slights the national significance of the only predominantly natural area in the state protected in the National Park System, and may actually encourage operators to feel comfortable applying for full-scale surface mining permits within the park. This regulatory loophole is one that the OSMRE should immediately correct at the federal level, so that state programs deal uniformly with the issue of prospecting in National Park System units.

The Park Service's dependence on the West Virginia DOE provides an excellent example of facts that lend urgency to the concern that states readily become captives of the local coal industry. The DOE was established by the West Virginia Legislature in 1985.[19] The agency was created to implement and enforce all state laws dealing with oil and gas development, coal mining and reclamation, and coal mine safety. The very first Commissioner of Energy was a strip mine operator who was also a principal stockholder in a company that performed abandoned mine reclamation work for the state.[20] This Commissioner refused to divest his holdings in his coal company or his reclamation company.[21] During his first year in office, he authorized the approval of a strip mine permit for his own company, and his reclamation firm received state contracts totaling more than $2 million.[22]

The West Virginia DOE has referred to itself not as a regulatory agency but rather as a "service agency for the coal industry."[23] On pain of dismissal from employment, DOE strip mine inspectors no longer can file enforcement actions before state magistrates without the approval of the Commissioner of Energy.[24] Investigations by the United States General Accounting Office found serious problems with the adequacy of coal mine reclamation bonding in West Virginia,[25] and found further that the DOE was failing to cite two-thirds of the violations of reclamation law and regulations during state inspections of active mine sites.[26]

Concerns about the intentions and effectiveness of state agencies that have acquired primary jurdisdiction under SMCRA is not limited to West Virginia or to a small number of Appalachian states.[27] Rather, such concern is found in both the eastern and western coal fields. In Oklahoma, enforcement by the state regulatory authority was so ineffective that a coal company in the state filed a citizen complaint against a competitor because of the latter's flagrant violation of state reclamation law. When a federal inspector finally visited the strip mine, he found no less than 141 violations of Oklahoma law and regulations.[28]

In Pennsylvania, more than 15,000 acres of mined land have been abandoned without reclamation since the enactment of SMCRA.[29] Most of that land has not been reclaimed because the Pennsylvania Department of Environmental Resources (DER), faced with intense lobbying from coal trade associations and political pressure from powerful legislators, refused to comply with the SMCRA requirement that coal operators post reclamation bonds in amounts sufficient to allow the state to reclaim when a mine is abandoned without reclamation. Because of its unwillingness to require adequate bonds, the DER now has a reclamation bond revenue shortfall of approximately $100 million. The abandoned and unreclaimed mine sites lay as open sores across the Pennsylvania topography, sources of landslides, acid mine drainage, soil erosion, and stream sedimentation. Under a plan initiated by DER in 1986, Pennsylvania taxpayers will pick up the tab for reclaiming these abandoned sites.

In Kentucky, the state regulatory authority allowed coal operators to string groups of "two-acre" mines together in such a way as to allow the operators to avoid the permitting requirements and environmental protection standards of SMCRA.[30] Thousands of acres of Kentucky's mountains were marred by unregulated two-acre mines before citizen outrage and court action forced the state to curtail the practice.[31]

These are but a few examples of state agencies that seem to be returning to their pre-SMCRA norm in the absence of vigorous OSMRE oversight of their activities. If OSMRE continues to condone lax or nonexistent state enforcement of SMCRA, unregulated and underregulated coal mining on private lands within and near park system units will continue to pose threats to the park values and to the physical integrity of parkland. The SMCRA cooperative federalism framework vests great discretionary power in the hands of state officials whose interests are not limited to the protection of national parklands; it seems clear that without oversight, many state regulatory programs will favor and protect the local coal industry while giving short shrift to park and environmental concerns.

As with other environmental protection laws, the viability of SMCRA depends in large measure on the commitment and integrity of those charged with implementing and enforcing it; they must appreciate the fact that Congress, having created a national park system that is to survive in perpetuity, enacted SMCRA to provide a tool to be used fairly yet forcefully to protect land and water resources including the national treasures contained with the park system.

Although ineffective and lax state and federal enforcement of SMCRA has been commonplace, there is no doubt that SMCRA was intended by Congress to be used aggressively by federal and state regulatory agencies to ensure that available mining and reclamation techiques be used to put an end to the environmentally devastating coal mining practices of the past. SMCRA contains provisions that allow federal and state regulatory authorities to protect "environmental resources" in the broadest sense; agencies are given the authority, indeed the responsibility, to affirmatively use the Act as a means not only to protect land, air, and water resources, but also to advance aesthetic, historic, cultural, and land use planning interests. Public parkland generally, and national park system areas specifically, were intended to be beneficiaries of the emphatic congressional directives found in SMCRA.

V. SMCRA AND THE NATIONAL PARK SYSTEM

The legislation enacted in 1977 contained a variety of provisions with direct implications for the management and protection of national park system units.

A. Protection of Sensitive Lands Under Section 522(3)

1. Application to National Park System Units

The most important provisions of SMCRA that relate to the national park system are found in Section 522.[32] Section 522 provides for the designation of lands as unsuitable for some or all types of surface coal mining operations, and totally prohibits mining in certain sensitive areas. While the scope of that section is not limited to national park system lands, it is the only provision of the Act that specifically mentions those lands. Section 522(e)(1) explicitly prohibits surface coal mining[33] within boundaries of park system units with certain narrow exceptions.

In addition to prohibiting mining on parklands, subsection (c)(3) also prohibits mining "which adversely affects any publically owned parks." Other subsections of Section 522 contain provisions that grant federal and state regulatory agencies discretionary powers with regard to the designations of unsuitability, but with regard to park system lands where mining in areas near such parkland "will adversely affect" the lands, no such discretion is granted.[34]

Limitation on mining in or adversely affecting national park system lands is subject to a caveat that will be discussed in more depth below. Basically, that caveat makes all regulatory decisions under Section 522(e) subject to "valid existing rights."

But, as a general proposition, Section 522(e) is an absolute bar to surface or underground coal mining operations within the boundaries of park system units. However at least one very important caveat must be placed on this broad general proposition.

2. Valid Existing Rights

The Section 522(e) prohibition is made "subject to valid existing rights."[35] The meaning of that language has not yet been resolved after extended rulemaking and litigation spanning almost a decade since the enactment of SMCRA.

The legislative concern behind the valid existing rights (VER) prohibition is that SMCRA prohibition of all or certain types of coal mining might be considered an unconsitutional "taking" of private property without payment of just compensation, in violation of the fifth amendment to the United States Constitution.

In promulgating VER regulations under SMCRA, OSM stated: "the legislative history of the Act indicates that Congress wanted to avoid any taking in the implementation of Section 522(e) . . . OSM has endeavored to determine the point at which payment would be required because a taking has occurred.[36]

Congressional concern about possible unconstitutional taking was triggered by the Supreme Court's holding in a 1922 case, *Pennsylvania Coal Co. v. Mahon.*[37] In *Mahon*, the Supreme Court reviewed a Pennsylvania statute that prohibited underground coal mining beneath homes and other structures as a means of preventing destructive subsidence.[38] The court held that the state law caused unconsitutional taking of coal company property. Justice Holmes wrote: "What makes the right to mine coal valuable is that it can be exercised with profit. To make it commercially impractical to mine certain coal has very nearly the same effect for constitutional purposes as appropriating it or destroying it."[39]

Obviously the holding of *Mahon* could not be ignored by legislators who sought to prohibit coal mining where it could damage public interests including protection of the National Park System. The valid existing rights concept was intended to provide a statutory escape hatch that would assist SMCRA regulators in avoiding situations where an unsuitability designation under Section 522 of SMCRA would constitute an unconstitutional taking.

The first version of OSM regulations interepreted VER to mean that a coal operator must have had the right under deed or lease to conduct mining operations and have acquired all necessary permits incident to such operations prior to the effective date of the Act in order to be judged to possess VER.[40] Given the broad remedial nature of SMCRA, this interpretation seems most consistent with legislative intent and is most protective of park system values.

Subsequently, a court challenge by the coal industry resulted in a minor judicially imposed modification of the regulation; thenceforth, in order to establish VER an operator needed to show only that a good faith attempt to apply for all permits by August 1, 1977, (the effective date of SMCRA) had been accomplished.[41]

Under the Reagan Administration, OSM undertook massive "regulatory reform" efforts.[42] Included in that effort was an attempt by the agency to substantially modify the definition of VER in a manner applauded by the coal industry and attacked by conservation organizations. The new proposed OSM definition reflected the agency's concern with the *Mahon* holding and the case's import with regard to the constitutionality of Section 522 designations:

> a person possesses valid existing rights for an area . . . if the application of any of the prohibitions [of Section 522(e)] . . . to the property interest that existed on [August 3, 1977] . . . would effect a taking of the person's property which would entitle the person to just compensation under the Fifth and Fourteenth Amendments to the Constitution of the United States.[43]

The Reagan Administration's proposed rule was rejected by the United States District Court and remanded to OSM because of procedural defects without reaching the merits.[44] At the time of publication the precise scope of VER definition has not yet been determined.[45]

However, an important intervening occurence has diminished concerns that a Section 522 designation might be considered a taking under the rationale of *Pennsylvania Coal v. Mahon*. The Supreme Court, in *Keystone Bituminous Coal Assn. v. DeBenedictis*,[46] severely limited the circumstances in which regulation of coal mining to protect public interests will be considered a taking.

Where coal mining activities may harm important public interests in the manner of a public nuisance, states may prohibit such activities:

> The special status of this type of state action can also be understood on the simple theory that since no individual has a right to use his property so as to create a nuisance or otherwise harm others, the state has not "taken" anything when it asserts its power to enjoin the nuisance-like activity.[47]

The Court rejected any notion that the *Mahon* holding requires payment to coal operators whose mining operations harm others:

> Courts have consistently held that a state need not provide compensation when it diminishes or destroys the value

of property by stopping illegal activity or abating a public nuisance. It is hard to imagine a different rule that would be consistent with the maxim "Sic utere two ut alienum non laedas." [Use your own property in such a manner as not to injure that of another.[48]]

Even in the absence of nuisance-like effects of coal mining, the *Keystone* court suggests that state regulation in furtherance of public interests will not work a taking:

It is well settled that a "taking" may be more readily found when the interference with property can be characterized as a physical invasion by government, than when interference arises from some public program adjusting the benefits and burdens of economic life to promote the common good . . . the Court has repeatedly upheld regulations that destroy or adversely affect real property interests.[49]

Chief Justice Rehnquist's dissenting opinion in *Keystone* suggests the breadth of the majority's holding and the extent to which *Mahon* has been limited:

A broad exception to the operation of the First Compensation Clause based on the exercise of multifaceted health, welfare, and safety regulations would surely allow government much greater authority than we have recognized to impose societal burdens on individual landowners, for nearly every action government takes it intended to secure for the public an extra measure of "health, safety, and welfare."[50]

OSM's proposed regulation, which limits VER to cases where no taking has occurred, appears in a quite different light after *Keystone*. Cases where a Section 522 prohibition "would effect a taking of the person's property which would entitle the person to just compensation" will be difficult to establish if the rationale of *Keystone* is followed. Nevertheless, uncertainty about the future course of judicial review of this issue necessitates concern about the willingness of SMCRA regulatory authorities to implement the unsuitability provisions of the Act vigorously. Thus, the importance of the VER definition cannot be overstated.

Notwithstanding *Keystone*, should the courts hold that Congress intended a coal operator's burden to establish VER to be minimal, the strong protection afforded parkland under Section 522(e) will be virtually gutted. The impact of such a judicial interpretation would be extremely significant because of the vast amount of private inholdings within National Park System units and equally large privately held coal tracts located adjacent to units of the park system where the coal was owned or leased prior to enactment of SMCRA.[51] Should this narrow interpretation of VER be judicially recognized, no coal mining operations would be limited by the prohibitions contained in Section 522(e). A narrow interpretation of VER would therefore emasculate one of the most important SMCRA provisions for parks.

Such an outcome of VER litigation appears unlikely, however, given rules of statutory construction usually afforded remedial statutes like SMCRA. The legislative history of SMCRA, and Section 522(e) in particular, indicates that its protective sweep was intended by Congress to be broad:

> the decision to bar surface mining in certain circumstances is better made by Congress itself. Thus section 522 (e) provides that, subject to valid existing rights, no surface coal mining operation except those in existence on the date of enactment, shall be permitted on lands within the boundaries of units of certain Federal systems such as the national park system . . . or in other special circumstances.[52]

Obviously, Congress intended to limit substantially mining that could adversely affect park system lands; only those mining operations "in existence on the date of enactment shall be permitted" does not suggest that Congress intended the valid existing rights caveat to be interpreted to allow mere ownership of coal rather than an "active mining operation" to trigger exemption from Section 522(e) protection.

It should be noted that in the preamble to its recently proposed VER regulation changes, OSM suggested that it had the option of buying land by exercising the power of eminent domain as an alternative to allowing mining in a park. In some situations condemnation could, indeed, be an attractive option. Unfortunately, the Reagan Administration has taken a negative attitude toward such land acquisitions. Such a position flies in the face of OSM's suggestion that condemnation is a realistic option to forestall adverse affects to parks. In order to make this condemnation option a viable one, the Land and Water Conservation Fund should be reinvigorated, so that the federal estate can be completed and potential land use conflicts eliminated.[53]

3. "Continually Created" Valid Existing Rights

Litigation also continues over what has been referred to as "continually created VER." OSM has promulgated a regulation that changed its original VER definition by adding a subsection that attempts to address situations where "an area comes under the protection of Section 522(e),"[54] *after* August 3, 1977.

Such a situation would arise where a park unit is expanded to embrace a contested surface mining area. In 1983 OSM added a paragraph (d) to the existing VER definition to provide for "continually created VER." Again, the ostensible OSM purpose in so doing was "to avoid unconstitutional taking" of property interests under the *Pennsylvania Coal Co. v. Mahon* rationale. The proposed "continually created VER" regulation stated that for areas entering the national park system after SMCRA's date of enactment

> valid existing rights shall be found if--(1) On the date the protection comes into existence, a validly authorized surface coal mining operation exists on that area; or (2) the prohibition caused by Section 522(e) of the Act, if applied to the property interest that exists on the date the protection comes into existence, would effect a taking of the person's property which would entitle the person to just compensation under the Fifth and Fourteenth Amendments to the United States Constitution.[55]

Like the other Reagan Administration proposals, the VER regulation was remanded for OSM reconsideration. The United States District Court remanded subsection (2) for further notice and comment because of procedural irregularities in its promulgation. However, the court indicated that subsection (1) of the regulation may not necessarily have been inconsistent with SMCRA.[56]

While an inconsistency may not exist, this opinion was prior to *Keystone Bituminous Coal Assn. v. DeBenedictis,* and OSM's fear of working a taking by regulation has now lost most if not all of its vitality. Indeed, after *Keystone,* such a substantial limitation on

Section 522 designations may well be *inconsistent* with Congressional intent. Certainly if mining activities create nuisance conditions,[57] the ruling in *Keystone* would negate any claim that an unconstitutional taking has occured.

4. Application of Section 522(e) to Private Inholdings

Another aspect of the regulatory definition of VER also remains in litigation. Citizens groups and environmental organizations have challenged 30 C.F.R. Section 761.11(h), promulgated by OSM in 1983. Section 761.11(h) prohibited "surface coal mining, permitting, licensing or exploration of Federal lands in the National Park System, National Wildlife Refuge System, National System of Trails, National Wilderness Preservation System, Wild and Scenic Rivers System, or National Recreation Areas, designated by Act of Congress.[58]

This challenge was based on the view that, in adopting that regulation, the Secretary of the Interior acted arbitrarily and capriciously in failing to protect against mining on privately owned inholdings within the protected areas. The District Court also remanded this regulation because its promulgation was not preceded by notice and comment required by the Administrative Procedures Act.[59]

5. Right of States to Make VER Decisions Regarding Private Lands

Also in limbo is the Reagan Administration's regulation authorizing state determinations of VER on private inholdings within section 522(e) areas. The court read the environmental groups' challenge as arguing that SMCRA required the Secretary of the Interior, rather than the states, to make the regulatory decision in all cases involving a VER determination on private inholdings within protected lands.[60] The court recognized that the Secretary could make decisions under the program for protection of federal lands provided by Section 523(c) of the Act. But it held that the Secretary's authority does not extend to private inholdings, because Section 503(a) of the Act permits states to assume exclusive jurisdiction over surface mining operations conducted on nonfederal lands.[61] Thus, the court rejected this challenge to the OSM regulations. This issue is still being litigated.

A very real concern with the interpretation of the Act as expressed above, if the regulation is ultimately upheld, is that state regulatory agencies will follow their traditional tendency to favor local coal operations rather than protect the values of park system units.

B. Section 522(a)(2): Mandatory Designations Where Reclamation is Not Feasible

The scope of Section 522 is not limited strictly to National Park System lands. The section also contains other mandatory and discretionary provisions that limit coal mining near or adjacent to a park system unit.

For example, if the Secretary of the Interior finds that "reclamation pursuant to the requirements of this chapter is not technologically and economically feasible," the Secretary "shall designate an area as unsuitable for all or certain types of surface coal mining operations."[62] Implementation of that provision, however, requires either success in a petition process administered by the Secretary of the Interior through OSM,[63] or, where federal lands are involved, a decision by the Secretary to independently declare the lands unsuitable for all or certain types of coal mining activity.[64]

Any person who has an interest that is or may be adversely affected by coal mining operations has the right to file an unsuitability petition with the regulatory agency. Petitioners must demonstrate how they meet an "injury in fact" test by describing the injury and by showing the nature of the injury. Federal and state regulations set forth specific requirements that petitioners must follow.[65]

C. Section 522(a)(3): Discretionary Designations

In addition to the mandatory designation requirements of section 522(a)(2), the Act also grants discretion to the Secretary and to state regulatory authorities, where appropriate, to make unsuitability designations in certain speciific situations. Section 522(a)(3) provides, in part, that

> a surface area may be designated unsuitable for certain types of surface coal mining operations if such operations will--

(A) be incompatible with existing State or local land use plans or programs; or

(B) affect fragile or historic lands in which such operations could result in significant damage to important historic, cultural, scientific, and esthetic values and natural systems; or

(C) affect renewable resource lands in which such operations could result in a substantial loss or reduction of long-range productivity of water supply or of food or fiber products, and such lands to include aquifers and aquifer recharge areas; or

(D) affect natural hazard lands in which such operations could substantially endanger life and property, such lands to include areas subject to frequent flooding and areas of unstable geology.[66]

Decisions of unsuitability under these criteria may be made on the basis of a petition by "any person having an interest which is or may be adversely affected.[67] In addition, Section 522(b) requires the Secretary of the Interior to apply these criteria in a mandated review of all federal lands.

D. The Bryce Canyon National Park Unsuitability Decision: Future Promise and Problems

Only one case has been litigated thus far that has dealt with an actual application of Section 522 in the context of National Park System lands. *Utah International v. Department of the Interior*[68] dealt with a petition filed by various conservation and environmental groups, pursuant to Section 522(c) of SMCRA,[69] to have an area (the Alton coal field) adjacent to Bryce Canyon National Park declared unsuitable for surface mining because of potential adverse effects such mining would have on the park. The Bryce Canyon case provides an excellent vehicle for reviewing the unsuitability designation/petition mechanism of SMCRA.

The unsuitability petition was submitted to OSM. The area addressed by the petition included approximately 325,000 acres, or more than 500 square miles, at the southern and eastern boundaries of the park. About 203,900 acres were owned by the federal government, 16,300 acres by Utah, and 68,000 acres privately owned. The petition applied only to federal lands. Only a portion of the 203,900 acres of federal land covered by the petition was ultimately designated as unsuitable for mining.[70]

Two corporations, Utah International (UII) and Nevada Electric Investment Company (NEICO), had obtained coal leases for areas located within the designated areas and claimed to have spent substantial amounts in their development. However, the companies had not yet applied for permits, which were necessary prerequisites to the initiation of mining operations.

The original petition suggested several reasons why the area should be designated as unsuitable for surface mining. The petitioners contended that the land could not be reclaimed following surface mining, that mining would adversely affect Bryce Canyon National Park and the experience of park visitors, that mining would adversely affect water resources and renewable resource lands,[71] and that alternative energy sources were available.

The Secretary of the Interior rejected all but one of the petitioners' arguments, the contention that related to adverse impacts on the National Park and its visitors. The Secretary focused on Section 522(a)(3)(B) as a basis for making a finding of unsuitability. As noted above, that subsection provides that an area may be designated unsuitable if coal mining would affect fragile or historic lands in a manner that could cause significant damage to important historic, cultural, scientific, and aesthetic values and natural systems.

UII and NEICO challenged the Secretary's unsuitability designation, seeking reversal of the decision on a number of procedural and factual grounds. Utah joined in the suit with the companies, fearing that the decision might deny the state the economic benefit of lands it owned within the designated area.[72] The original petitioners also challenged the Secretary's decision, contending that a larger area should have been designated unsuitable for mining.

1. The Petition Process: Nature of Hearing Required

The corporate plaintiffs first argued that OSM's nonadjudicatory process, which lead up to the Secretary's decision, did not afford them a fair opportunity to protect their rights. The companies contended that the hearings held by the Department of the Interior should have been adjudicatory (that is, like judicial trials), rather than patterned after legislative hearings. The court rejected this contention with the observation that

> There can be little doubt in reading SMCRA and its legislative history that the focus of the petition designation process is land use planning. This involves the weighing of certain competing policy and value considerations that affect several parties. Decisions of this nature are best arrived at through legislative rather than adjudicatory hearings.[73]

The court noted that the fact that the unsuitability designation prohibited mining by only one or two parties did not make it an adjudication. Rather, the court observed that the decision affected the national interest in Bryce Canyon National Park and each individual who might visit the park.

2. Secretary has Discretion in Designation Procedures

It is important to note, however, that in the future the Secretary has the discretion to modify the unsuitability designation procedures to allow adversary, adjudicatory-type hearings, including cross-examination of witnesses.[74]

The court in *Utah International* observed that agencies, as a general proposition, may do this because "of their familiarity with the interests which they regulate. Because of this familiarity they are in a better position to determine what procedures will best protect the interests of the parties and at the same time facilitate the tasks of the agency involved."[75]

The district court noted that the Supreme Court has held that "administrative agencies should be free to fashion their own rules."[76] Specifically with regard to Section 522 of SMCRA, the district court found that the Department of the Interior's own regulations suggested that the Secretary could have imposed more rigorous procedures in the case.[77]

Whether additional adjudicatory procedures would be more or less protective of National Park System values is not clear. Trial-type procedures might be abused by well-financed corporate interests that could better afford an extended and expensive trial process. On the other hand, more rigorous procedures, including cross-examination, enable conservationists to challenge vague assurances and unsupported conclusions often relied upon by unsympathetic administrators.

Similar uncertainties arise regarding other procedural issues. For example, placement of the burden of going forward and the burdens of persuasion and proof in a trial-type setting also raise issues not easily resolved. Moreover, the political/philosophical coloration of the Department of the Interior could have a tremendous impact on unsuitability decisions. Would the fact that a Secretary in the mold of a James Watt or a Cecil Andrus suggest that a legislative or adjudicatory process would best protect national park values?

In the case of Bryce Canyon, there is little doubt that Secretary Watt would not have excercised the discretion granted in Section 522 to make an unsuitability designation as Secretary Andrus did. In similar situations where coal industry-oriented state regulatory agencies have passed on unsuitability petitions under state permanent programs, environmental values have been given short shrift or ignored altogether.[78] In other cases, some state regulatory agencies have designated areas as unsuitable after a fair and thorough legislative fact-finding process.[79]

In the case of a Secretary who is not sensitive to protecting National Park System values, would it be better to utilize adjudicatory processes? There is no simple answer to such inquiries. One thing is clear, however: in the case of the Bryce Canyon petition, the legislative-type designation procedure did work with a measure of effectiveness to protect park values. For future reference it is important to point out that the court in *Utah International* found that the language of SMCRA offers some important features of adjudicatory process, including factual allegations, "supporting evidence," "intervention" by interested parties, and a "written decision" with a "statement of reasons."[80] But the District Court emphasized:

> Congress stopped short of requiring an adjudicatory hearing apparently in recognition of the fact that such procedures could be used to frustrate the accomplishment of SMCRA's objectives . . . The factual determinations made by the Secretary related to matters of public policy and value choices: the effect of general phenomena upon the national park, the experience of park visitors, or upon the condition of public properties. This court is convinced

that the Alton decision was a rulemaking proceeding for which additional procedures were not required under the Constitution.[81]

As it stands today, SMCRA designation procedures affecting National Park System units can at least be said to provide an opportunity for park protection. The Bryce Canyon decision is evidence of that potential; whether this potential can be fulfilled in other cases would seem to depend in large measure upon positions taken by the Secretary. In any event, the refusal of the Secretary to designate an area adjacent to a National Park System unit as unsuitable would be one very difficult to challenge in the courts. The judicial deference given agency judgments and the narrow scope of judicial review applied in such cases would not offer much hope to the disappointed Section 522(c) petitioner whose petition is denied by the Secretary.

3. Designation of Lands Outside Park System Units

Another important aspect of the Bryce Canyon case was the argument of the coal companies that Section 522(1)(3)(B) does not authorize the Secretary to designate lands outside the boundaries of a national park. The companies contended that "the thrust of section 522 and the Act itself is to prohibit coal mining only where significant and irreparable damage result."[82]

They admitted, however, that areas outside of national parks could be designated as unsuitable if mining would have an adverse impact on a park. The district court found no merit in the companies' challenge. On the contrary, the court held that "there is nothing in either the code or the regulations that require a finding of irreparable harm in order to designate an area as unsuitable . . . [section 522(a)(3)(B)] requires only that damage to the interest enumerated therein be significant. It is not required that it be irreparable or permanent.[83]

The court's determination clarified the authority of the Secretary to designate as unsuitable areas outside of national park system units. This interpretation of SMCRA is consistent with congressional intent and recognizes explicitly that coal mining simply cannot be tolerated in certain instances involving precious, finite, and fragile resources of national importance.

E. Secretary's Duty to Review and Designate Lands

In addition to the designation of areas as unsuitable through the vehicle of the Section 522(c) petition process, SMCRA contains another equally important unsuitability designation process. That process is outlined in Section 522(b), which mandates that the Secretary conduct a review of all federal lands to determine whether there are areas that are unsuitable for all or certain types of coal mining. The criteria the Secretary is obligated to use are the same as those utilized in the unsuitability petition process.[84]

F. Federal-State Cooperative Agreements

Section 523 relates to coal mining on federal lands generally; it allows the Secretary to enter into a "cooperative agreement" with a state regulatory authority that would allow the state to enforce the permitting and enforcement requirements of the Act on federal lands. However, notwithstanding the existence of such a cooperative agreement, Section 523(c) makes clear that the Secretary may not delegate the duty to designate certain federal lands as unsuitable under Section 522.

G. Right of Citizens to Petition for Unsuitability

In litigation challenging OSM's permanent program regulations,[85] the court also was forced to decide issues relating to the unsuitability designation process. In that case, the coal industry petitioners challenged OSM's regulation that allowed citizens to petition for designation of federal lands as unsuitable.

The industry argued that since SMCRA expressly provided for a petition process only for state lands, but did not mention such a procedure for federal lands, OSM regulations allowing petitions relating to federal lands were unlawful. In essence, the industry attacked the federal lands petition process used successfully in the Bryce Canyon case.

The court rejected the industry arguments, holding that the legislative history of the Act supports the view that the Secretary is required under SMCRA to promulgate a federal petition process. The court also found support for its position in Section 523(a) which mandated that the Secretary implement a federal lands program that "incorporate[s] all of the requirements of this chapter." The court observed: "Because one of the requirements of 'this chapter' is the petition process, the Secretary is required to implement one under the Act."[86]

H. Protection of Park Air Quality Under SMCRA

Degradation of air quality is not generally considered when one examines the adverse effects of coal mining operations. Air pollution from coal mining, however, is often a substantial and serious problem. Yet units of the National Park System are currently unprotected from threats to park air quality that might arise from such activities.

Uncontrolled fugitive emissions occur at all surface coal mining operations. The most serious air quality impacts occur in the arid and semi-arid coal regions of the west and midwest. There, many large mining operations regularly exceed the Environmental Protection Agency's twenty-four-hour and annual average ambient air quality standards for particulates. Most of these emissions are generated by the handling of coal and spoil and by large truck and machinery traffic on haul roads.[87] Fugitive dust from mine sites varies in size from large particles that may settle to the ground rapidly to smaller particles that can remain suspended over a long period of time. The smaller particles can be transported by air currents up to twenty kilometers from the mine site.[88]

The Department of the Interior has found that small particulates are a threat to the health of people living near or frequenting areas around coal mining operations.[89] Twenty-seven to forty-two percent of total emissions from a coal mine site are in the small-particle size range that can lead to respiratory and other health problems.[90]

Fugitive emissions can also cause serious adverse environmental impacts. Of particular concern are unique natural areas and other lands protected by the Clean Air Act as Class I and Class II air quality areas.[91] Unregulated particulates can substantially impair visibility in these often pristine areas. The greatest source of fugitive dust from coal surface mines is roads and vehicular traffic.[92] Coal industry consultants concur with this assessment: "The distribution of emissions . . . indicated that the majority of all TSP (total suspended particulates) at all of the mines is emitted from haul truck travel (coal and overburden) and light and medium duty vehicle travel. If overburden removal by draglines is added as a source category, then [these sources of emissions] account for over 70% of all TSP emissions at each of the mines."[93]

Notwithstanding this widely accepted potential for adverse impacts on air quality and the recognition that many of the most dramatic natural area parks are located in vulnerable western lands, government agencies have failed to effectively regulate surface coal mines in this regard. In 1984, EPA proposed to require that fugitive emissions from new and modified surface coal mines be included in determining whether such mines are "major emitting facilities." Under the provisions of the Prevention of Significant Deterioration (PSD) program of the Clean Air Act, such "facilities" are required to obtain permits for construction or modification.[94] In conjunction with this rulemaking, EPA requested the Department of the Interior's opinion on the use of SMCRA as a means to protect air quality and related values of the National Park System from adverse impacts of surface coal mining operations.

In response to EPA, the Department of Interior concluded that "DOI has sufficient authority to protect Class I and mandatory Class II areas from the adverse impact on their air quality related values."[95] The Department of the Interior has thus argued that EPA action under the Clean Air Act is not needed to protect park system lands. Given the record of the Department of the Interior in recent years, it is not surprising that when actually called upon to use SMCRA as a tool to protect park air quality, the agency has taken a contradictory and extremely narrow view of OSM's authority to regulate fugitive dust.[96]

The Department of the Interior claims that SMCRA protects National Park System units from impacts on air quality and related values in five different ways.[97] However, while Section 522(e)(3) requires the regulatory authority to consider the views of the National Park Service in determining whether a "mining activity will adversely affect any publicly owned park,"[98] the authority need only *consider* National Park Service opinions. The Park Service has no authority under SMCRA to enforce its recommendations. Not surprisingly, the designation procedure related to Section 522(e)(3) has never been used by the Secretary of the Interior to designate an area as unsuitable because of potential adverse impacts on air quality in parks. Under Section 522(b), the Secretary also has the authority to designate federal lands as unsuitable for mining. As yet, the Secretary also has not exercised this provision

on the basis of air quality considerations.[99] Section 515(b)(4) of
SMCRA also authorizes the Secretary to "effectively control erosion
and attendant air and water pollution."[100] The Secretary has refused,
however, to regulate anything but air emissions attendant soil
erosion.[101]

In spite of the narrow interpretation of Section 515(b)(4) in it
regulations, the Department of the Interior has admitted that
the true breadth of the section is much greater than concerns merely limited to soil erosion:

> It is now recognized that a substantial portion of the air
> pollution at surface coal mines results from erosion. EPA
> has indicated that a major source of emissions from sur-
> face mines is the road dust generated by vehicles travell-
> ing on mine roads. The full extent of the Secretary's
> authority to regulate air pollution attendant erosion
> has not yet been tested, but it is likely to include the
> regulation of road dust.[102]

Section 515(b)(17) of SMCRA also gives OSM authority to regulate the impacts of coal mine haulage roads. As noted above, all
interested parties agree that the major percentage of fugitive emissions generated by surface coal mining operations occurs as a result
of traffic on haul roads. In spite of this fact, OSM has not promulgated substantive performance standards to control fugitive emissions from haulage road traffic.

It is clear that SMCRA does provide some authority for the
Department of the Interior to regulate air quality impacts of
coal mines and reinforce the thrust of the Clean Air Act. To date,
that authority has been ignored, thus blocking attainment of
SMCRA's goals relating to air quality protection of National Park
System units.

VI. CONCLUSION

Decades of struggle by citizens finally culminated in the passage of SMCRA. With the stripped and ravaged mountains of Ap-
palachia as testimony to state and federal failure to protect the
people and the natural environment of the coal regions, those who
struggled so long thought that their battle had been won. Ten years
after enactment of SMCRA, it is clear that the promise of the Act
has not yet been fulfilled. That promise will remain hollow unless
the Department of the Interior ceases its attempts to gut effective

implementation and enforcement and industry-captive state regulatory agencies express greater sensitivity to the unique role of National Park system units in our national conciousness and our hard-pressed environment. If properly implemented and enforced, SMCRA could be a much more invigorated mechanism for protecting the national parks. Park defenders will undoubtably be forced to show increased, persistent vigilance in the pursuit of that goal.

NOTES

*Professor of Law, West Virginia University College of Law, Morgantown, WV.

1. U.S. Department of the Interior, National Park Service, STATE OF THE PARKS--1980: A REPORT TO CONGRESS, at ix (1980).

2. S. Metzger and M. Mantell, *Federal Mining Laws and the National Park System*, (1986). When considering these figures, one should bear in mind that coal may not be found under all of the privately held land, and even where coal exists, it might not be economically feasible to mine some or all of it.

3. 30 U.S.C. § 1201-1328.

4. [1977] U.S. CODE CONG. & ADMIN. NEWS, at 596.

5. *Id.* at 596-597.

6. *Id.* at 596.

7. *Id.* at 597.

8. *See* 30 U.S.C. §§ 1268, 1271.

9. *See* 30 U.S.C. §§ 1201(k), 1258(a)(3)(8). Included would be National Park Service Resource Management Plans and Land Protection Plans.

10. *See, e.g.*, Clean Air Act, 42 U.S.C. §§ 7401-7642; Federal Water Pollution Control Act, as amended, by the Clean Water Act of 1977, 33 U.S.C. §§ 1251-1376; Resource Conservation and Recovery Act of 1976 (RCRA), 42 U.S.C. §§ 6901-6987; Safe Drinking Water Act, 42 U.S.C. §§ 300(f)-(j).

11. *See* 30 U.S.C. § 1253. When a state is granted primary jurisdiction (or "primacy"), it enforces its own state law rather than SMCRA. In each case where a state has been granted primacy, the state's legislature has enacted new laws and/or amended the old ones to ensure that they are no less stringent than the standards set forth in SMCRA and its implementing regulations. Thus, for example, when a coal operator violates a state surface mining permit condition, a state inspector may issue a cessation order appealable to the state regulatory agency and thence to state court. When a state regulatory authority seeks injunctive relief against an operator, a complaint and motion for an injunction is filed in state court.

12. If a state regulatory program fails to implement, enforce, or maintain its federally approved primacy program, the Department of the Interior is required to establish a federal regulatory program for the state. *See* 30 U.S.C. § 1254(a)(3), (b) and § 1271(b). On at least three such occasions since the enactment of SMCRA, the Department of the Interior has displaced the state regulatory authority by establishing its own enforcement program. The state programs involved were West Virginia, Tennessee, and Oklahoma.

13. *See* P. McGinley, *Federalism Lives! Reflections on the Vitality of the Federal System in the Context of Natural Resource Regulation,* 32 KAN. L. REV. 147, 149-151 (1983); Squillace, *Cooperative Federalism Under the Surface Mining Control and Reclamation Act: Is This Any Way To Run A Government?,* 87 W. VA. L. REV. 687 (1985).

14. Title XI of the National Parks and Recreation Act of 1978, Pub. L. No. 95-625, 92 Stat. 3544 (1978).

15. W. Va. Code § 22A-3-1. West Virginia sought and obtained primary jurisdiction to enforce SMCRA. Thus, the West Virginia statute and the regulations promulgated thereunder are examples of state legislative response to the cooperative federalism mechanism of SMCRA.

16. *See* 30 U.S.C. § 1262 and W. Va. Code § 22A-3-7.

17. ENV'T REP. 2085-2086 (1987).

18. In April 1987, the federal Office of Surface Mining Issued cessation orders to two West Virginia excess tonnage prospect operations. Confirming the view of DOE critics, OSM shut down the "prospecting" operations because they conducted full scale mining operations without a permit. Charleston Gazette, April, 1987 at .

19. W. Va. Code § 22A-3-7.

20. *Charleston Gazette*, August 22, 1985.

21. Eventually, OSMRE ruled that a conflict of interest did exist and ordered the Commissioner to divest his coal company interests.

22. Charleston Gazette, August 3, 1985; Charleston Daily Mail, August 2, 1985.

23. Charleston Gazette, August 27, 1985.

24. Memorandum from West Virginia Energy Commissioner Kenneth R. Faerber to Department of Energy inspectors, October 6, 1986.

25. U.S. GENERAL ACCOUNTING OFFICE, REPORT TO THE CHAIRMAN, SUBCOMMITTEE ON ENVIRONMENT, ENERGY, AND NATURAL RESOURCES, COMMITTEE ON GOVERNMENT OPERATIONS, U.S. HOUSE OF REPRESENTATIVES GAO-RCED-86-221 (Sept. 1986).

26. U.S. GENERAL ACCOUNTING OFFICE, REPORT TO THE CHAIRMAN, SUBCOMMITTE ON ENVIRONMENT, ENERGY, AND NATURAL RESOURCES, COMMITTEE ON GOVERNMENT OPERATIONS, U.S. HOUSE OF REPRESENTATIVES GAO-RCED-87-40 (Dec1986). A more recent study found that "DOE cites one violation per 26 complete inspections while OSM observed one uncited violation per two complete inspections." OSM visited 351 West Virginia mine sites in arriving at these figures. OSM Fiscal Year 1986 Annual Evaluations Report for the Regulatory and Abandoned Mine Land Reclamation Programs under SMCRA in the State of West Virginia. (Draft, March 1987).

27. GAO found that "while conducting most of the required inspections, state inspectors missed many violations, according to OSMRE [Office of Surface Mining Reclamation and Enforcement] inspectors who accompanied [GAO] on our mine visits. During approximately a one-year period prior to our site visits, state inspectors had cited a total of 118 violations at the 82 randomly selected mine sites we visited in the four states (West Virginia, Pennsylvania, Ohio, and Montana). During our visits with OSMRE inspectors, which on average, followed the latest complete state inspections by 7-16 days to minimize chances for mine site conditions to change, 129 violations were observed, 78 (60 percent) of which OSMRE inspectors judged to be present but uncited by the state inspector at the time of the last complete state inspection. OSMRE inspectors concluded that 44 of the 78 violations had the potential to cause off-site environmental damage, such as water pollution, soil erosion, or property damage." *Id.* at 18-19.

28. *See* Squillace, *supra* note 13.

29. Pittsburgh Press (March 22, 1985) citing an unpublished report of the Pennsylvania Department of Environmental Resources dated January 1984.

30. When enacted, SMCRA provided a loophole that exempted coal mines of fewer than two acres from the permitting requirements of the Act. Unscrupulous coal operators seized on this statutory language as a vehicle for avoiding the restrictive provisions of SMCRA. Thus, an operator who wished to mine a 200-acre tract would seek multiple two-acre exemptions for the tract. In Kentucky, the state agency interpreted this narrow two-acre exemption so broadly that, figuratively speaking, thousands of loaded coal trucks passed through the loophole. Recently, Donald P. Hodel, Secretary of the Interior, testified in favor of an amendment to SMCRA that would repeal the two-acre exemption:

> not unexpectedly, some coal operators, particularly in Appalachia, instituted
> a variety of practices to take advantage of the two-acre limitation. In some
> instances, an operator would mine a number of sites along a coal seam, skip-
> ping 50 to 100 feet between pits. Each site would then be claimed as a
> separate mine under the two-acre exemption, creating what has been
> dubbed a "string of pearls." While deeding coal haul roads to local govern-

ments is beneficial to communities, in the case of some two-acre operators, the practice has been abused. This mechanism has been used in an attempt to decrease surface areas affected by the mines to less than two acres. Many more sites were improperly claimed under the exemption using this practice. Some companies contracted with small, independent operators, each of whom claimed the exemption. The companies thereby retained control of the mining process but disavowed any reclamation responsibility because of the exemption. Another technique has been to creat "shell" corporations under which a number of separate companies were formed, sharing common equipment, employees, officers, and stockholders. These "separate" companies then mined under the guise of the two-acre exemption while actually affecting much larger areas.

Testimony of Donald P. Hodel, Secretary of the Interiord, before the Committee on Interior and Insular Affairs. Congress, in fact, repealed the two-acre exemption in SMCRA in the 100th Cong., 2d Sess., 1987.

31. *See* HEARING BEFORE THE SUBCOMMITTEE ON ENVIRONMENT, ENERGY, AND NATURAL RESOURCES, COMMITTEE ON GOVERNMENT OPERATIONS, 99th Cong., 2d Sess., at 11-12.

32. 30 U.S.C. § 1272.

33. "Surface coal mining operations" is defined in 30 U.S.C. § 1291 (28) to include the surface impacts incident to an underground coal mine.

34. SMCRA § 522(e) provides:

After August 3, 1977, and subject to valid existing rights, no surface coal mining operations except those which exist on August 3, 1977, shall be be permitted . . . (1) on any lands within the boundaries of units of the National Park System, National Wildlife Refuge System, National System of Trails, National Wilderness Preservation System, Wild and Scenic Rivers System, or National Recreation Areas designated by Act of Congress; (2) on any Federal lands within the boundaries of any national forest.

It has been observed that:

Section 522(e) of the Act may be termed "designation by Act of Congress." [Its] designations do not require initiation by citizen petition, but instead prohibit surface mining by force of law in certain protected areas. These areas include national parks and certain federal forest lands. Mining operations that will adversely affect any public park or place listed on the National Register of Historic Sites are also proscribed under section 522(e) unless special permission is obtained. Finally, the Act prohibits surface mining within specified distances of any occupied dwelling, public road, public building, public park or cemetery.

McGinely and Barrett, Pennsylvania Coal Company v. Mahon *Revisited: Is the Federal Surface Mining Act a Valid Exercise of the Police Power or an Unconstitutional Taking?,* 16 TULSA L.J. 418, 422 (1981).

35. SMCRA § 522, 30 U.S.C. 1272.

36. 44 Fed. Reg. 14992 (1979).

37. 260 U.S. 393 (1922). In reviewing SMCRA after its enactment, its principal sponsor in the House of Representatives, Morris K. Udall, has stated: "I admit some discomfort undertaking to write such a law with the admonitions of *Pennsylvania Coal v. Mahon* echoing in my ears. The balancing of private economic interests and the public good in this exercise is tricky and constitutional questions abound." Udall, *The Enactment of the Surface Mining Control and Reclamation Act of 1977 in Retrospect,* 81 W. VA. L. REV. 553, 557 (1979).

38. Coal mine subsidence is the lowering of strata overlying a coal mine, including the surface land, caused by the extraction of underground coal. Subsidence often causes substantial damage to foundation walls and frequently causes sinkholes or troughs that that make the land difficult or impossible to develop. *See* Blazy and Strain, *Deep Mine Subsidence, State Law and Federal Response*, 1 E. MIN. L. INST. § 1.01 at 1-5 (1980).

39. 260 U.S.C. 393, 414-415 (1922).

40. 30 C.F.R. § 761.5(a), 44 Fed. Reg. 15342 (1979).

41. *In Re:* Permanent Surface Mining Litigation, I,__F. Supp.__, (D.D.C. Feb. 26, 1980). For a review of the administrative history of the "valid existing rights" definition, *see* 51 Fed. Reg. 41952 (1986).

42. *See* Harris and Close, *Redefining the State Regulatory Role*, 12 ENVTL. L. 921 (1982).

43. *See* 40 Fed. Reg. 41349 (1983); 30 C.F.R. 8761.5 (1984). One commentator has pinpointed the problems with such a vague definition of VER: "The fundamental problem with the final valid existing rights definition is that it required each [federal or state] regulatory authority to interpret judicial [taking] opinions to determine rights . . . [I]t is doubtful that Congress intended the regulatory authority to have that role in this context." Beck, *Coal Law Update*, 6 E. MICH. L. INST. at 10.04 [1], (1985).

44. *In Re:* Permanent Surface Mining Regulation Litigation, 21 ENV'T REP CAS. 1557, 1559 (D.D.C. 1985).

45. *See* 51 Fed. Reg. at 41954 (1986). OSM has promised a revised definition of VER by June, 1988.

46. __480 U.S.__, 55 U.S.L.W. 4326 (Mar. 1987).

47. *Id.* at 4332, note 20, *citing* Sax, *Takings, Private Property and Public Rights*, 81 YALE L. J. 149, 155-161 (1971); Michaelman, *Property, Utility, and Fairness: Comments on the Ethical Foundations of "Just Compensation Law*," 80 HARV. L. REV. 1165, 1235-1237 (1967).

48. *Id.* at 4332, n. 22 (citations omitted).

49. *Id.* at 4331, n. 18 (citations omitted).

50. *Id.* at 4338.

51. *See generally* Temple, Barker, and Sloane, MINERAL OWNERSHIP AND DEVELOPMENT ACTIVITY IN AND AROUND THE NATIONAL PARKS (1985).

52. [1977] U.S. CODE CONG. & ADMIN. NEWS, at 631; H.R. REP NO. 95-218, 95th Cong., 1st Sess. at 95 (1977).

53. The twenty-five year authorization of the Land and Water Conservation Fund Act expires in 1989. Congress is currently exploring alternatives for its reauthorization and future. *See,* LWCF Coalition Supports Sen. Chafee's New Bill, NATIONAL PARKS (Sep./Oct. 1987) at 37.

54. *See* 47 Fed. Reg. 25281 (1981) and 30 C.F.R. § 761.5(d).

55. 30 C.F.R. § 761.5(d) (1984); 48 Fed. Reg. 41315 (1983).

56. *In Re:* Permanent Surface Mining Litigation, 22 ENV'T REP. CAS. 1557, 1564-65 (D.D.C. 1985). *See* 51 Fed. Reg. 41955-41956 (1986).

57. A public nuisance exists where private acts create a substantial and unreasonable interference with rights common to the public. *See* Restatement of Torts, § 2 (1984).

58. 30 C.F.R. § 761.11(h) (1984).

59. 5 U.S.C. § 553. *See* comments of the court at 22 ENV'T REP. CAS. 1565. The court also held that there appeared to be no rational basis for distinguishing between Federal and nonfederal lands in this context since the Section 522(e)(1) prohibition is made subject to VER, and exempts surface coal mining operations existing on August 3, 1977, on any lands within the statutorily protected areas.

60. *In Re:* Permanent Surface Mining Regulations Litigation, 21 ENV'T REP. CAS. 1557 (D.D.C. 1985).

61. *Id.*

62. 30 U.S.C. § 1272(a)(2). *See also* Section 523 of SMCRA which makes clear that even where a state regulatory program is developed, the Secretary retains responsibility to designate federal lands as unsuitable for mining in accordance with Section 522(b) of the Act.

63. SMCRA §§ 522(a)(2) and (3); 30 U.S.C. § 1272(a)(2) and (3).

64. SMCRA § 522(b); 30 U.S.C. § 1272(b).

65. *See* 30 C.F.R. § 764.13.

66. 30 U.S.C. § 1272(a)(3).

67. 30 U.S.C. § 1272(c).

68. 553 F. Supp. 872 (D. Utah 1982).

69. 30 U.S.C. § 1272(c). Section 522(c) provides:

> Any person having an interest which is or may be adversely affected shall have the right to petition the regulatory authority to have an area designated as unsuitable for surface coal mining operations, or to have such a designation terminated. Such a petition shall contain allegations of facts with supporting evidence which would tend to establish the allegations. Within ten months after receipt of the petition, the regulatory authority shall hold a public hearing in the locality of the affected area, after appropriate notice and publication of the date, time, and location of such a hearing. After a person having an interest which is or may be adversely affected has filed a petition and before the hearing, as required by this subsection, any person may intervene by filing allegations of facts with supporting evidence which tends to establish the allegations. Within sixty days after such hearing, the regulatory authority shall issue and furnish to the petitioner and any other party to the hearing, a written decision regarding the petition, and the reasons therefore. In the event that all the petitioners stipulate agreement prior to the requested hearing, and withdraw their request, such hearing need not be held. 30 U.S.C § 1272(c).

70. This area is known as the Alton Coal Field; lying generally northeast of these coal fields is Bryce Canyon National Park.

71. *I.e.*, lands used or useable for grazing and agricultural purposes.

72. Although the decision pertained only to federal land, there were approximately 12,400 acres of state-owned school trust lands contained within the geographical boundaries of the designated area.

73. Utah International, Inc. v. Dept. of the Interior, 553 F. Supp. at 880.

74. *Id. See, In Re:* Permanent Surface Mining Regulation Litigation, 620 F. Supp. at 1554 (D.D.C. 1985).

75. *Id.* at 880.

76. Vermont Yankee Nuclear Power Corp. v. Natural Resources Defense Council, Inc., 435 U.S. 519 (1977).

77. 553 F. Supp. at 879. The court relied on 30 C.F.R. § 769.1 (1980), which stated that tho prooodures oet forth therein were only minimum procedures

78. In West Virginia, the state regulatory authority has denied the two petitions it has reviewed.

79. In Pennsylvania, the Department of Environmental Resources has granted unsuitability petitions in order to protect public water supplies and pristine, high-quality watersheds.

80. 553 F. Supp. at 881.

81. *Id. See also, In Re:* Permanent Surface Mining Regulation Litigation I, slip op. at 24-25 (D.D.C. 1980), *and In Re:* Permanent Surface Mining Litigation, 620 F. Supp. at 1544 (D.D.C. 1985).

82. *Id.* at 882.

83. *Id.* at 882.

84. Section 522(a)(2) and (3), 30 U.S.C. § 1272(a)(2) and (3).

85. *In Re:* Permanent Surface Mining Litigation, 620 F. Supp. at 1544 (D.D.C. 1985).

86. *Id.* at 1540.

87. U.S. Department of the Interior, Office of Surface Mining, *Final Environmental Impact Statement*, OSM-EIS-1 at BIII-5 (January 1979). (Hereinafter cited as OSM-EIS-1).

88. *Id.*

89. *Id.* at BIII-6.

90. *Id.*

91. 42 U.S.C. § 7470.

92. *See* Office of Surface Mining Permanent Program Regulations, 44 Fed. Reg. 15221 (1979).

93. TRC Environmental Consultants, *Modeled Air Quality Impacts of Four Hypothetical Surface Coal Mines*, at 15 (May 15, 1986).

94. 49 Fed. Reg. 43211 (Oct. 26, 1984). *See* Clean Air Act, 42 U.S.C. § 7475(a).

95. Department of the Interior, letter from Asst. Secretaries Horn and Griles to Craig Potter, Asst. Administrator, Office of Air and Radiation, Environmental Protection Agency (May 29, 1986). *See also,* Memorandum from Department of the Interior, Associate Solicitor, Division of Energy and Resources, to Asst. Secretary, Fish, Wildlife and Parks and Asst. Secretary, Land and Minerals Management (May 15, 1986). (Hereinafter cited as DOI Memo.)

96. *See* Brief of the Secretary of the Interior in *In Re:* Permanent Surface Mining Regulation Litigation II, No. 84-5743 (D.C. Cir. 1986).

97. DOI Memo at 4, *supra* note 95. The memo identifies the following five provisions of SMCRA:

> Section 522(e), 30 U.S.C. § 1272(e), explicitly provides for the protection of parks; section 522(c), 30 U.S.C. § 1272(c), establishes an unsuitability petition process; section 515(b)(41), 30 U.S.C. § 1265(b)(4), contains an operator performance standard to control air pollution attendant soil erosion; section 515(b)(17), 30 U.S.C. § 1265(b)(17), requires that the construction, maintenance and post-mining conditions of roads will control or prevent erosion and damage to public property; and section 508(a)(9), 30 U.S.C. § 1258(a)(9), requires proof of operating compliance, at the permitting stage, with the Clean Air Act and any other applicable air quality-related laws and regulations.

98. 30 U.S.C. § 1272(e)(3). *See also* 30 C.F.R. § 773.13(a)(3)(ii) and § 773.15.

99. A recent Secretarial Issue Document on coal leasing failed to include either impacts on the parks or on air quality-related values as criteria for a finding of unsuitability. *Secretarial Issue Document--Federal Coal Management Program*, Office of the Secretary of the Interior (Jan. 1986). However, the Bureau of Land Management, which oversees the federal coal leasing program, has proposed revisions to the unsuitability criteria that are intended to further protect national parks. *See* 52 Fed. Reg. 18404 (1987).

100. 30 U.S.C. § 1265(b)(4).

101. 30 C.F.R. §§ 816.95, 817.95. *See* 30 C.F.R. §§ 780.15, 784.26 relating to mine operations submission of air pollution control plans as part of SMCRA permit applications.

102. DOI Memo at 7. Of course, the reason why "the full extent of the Secretary's authority to regulate air pollution" has not been tested is because the Secretary has chosen to ignore air pollution and has read his authority narrowly in spite of the above recognition of the broad scope of SMCRA section 515(b)(4).

PART V

APPENDICES

National Park Service Environmental Impact Statements

National Parks and BLM Wilderness Study Areas

A Primer on Legal Research

Selected References

Appendix A

FINAL ENVIRONMENTAL IMPACT STATEMENTS PREPARED BY THE NATIONAL PARK SERVICE (1970-1986)

This list was compiled by J. William Futrell and the staff of the Environmental Law Institute, Washington, D.C. EISs are listed chronologically in order of their issuance.

1970

George Washington Memorial Parkway, Dyke Marsh, Virginia

1972

Lake Mead National Recreation Area, Salmonid Fish Hatchery, Arizona/Nevada

1973

Great Smoky Mountains National Park, Special Use Permit, Gatlinburg Aerial Tramway, Tennessee

Haleakala National Park, Wilderness, Hawaii

John D. Rockefeller Memorial Parkway, Wyoming

Bandelier National Monument, Pollution Abatement, New Mexico

Grant-Kohrs Ranch National Historic Site, Montana

Fossil Butte National Monument, Wyoming

Great Sand Dunes National Monument, Wilderness, Colorado

Yosemite National Park, Wilderness, California

Badlands National Park, Wilderness, South Dakota

Carlsbad Caverns National Park, Wilderness, New Mexico

Grand Teton National Park, Trois Teton Wilderness, Wyoming

Carlsbad National Park, Pollution Abatement, New Mexico

Cumberland Gap National Historical Park, Wilderness Proposal, Kentucky/Tennessee/Virginia

Black Canyon of the Gunnison National Monument, Wilderness, Colorado

Canyonlands National Park, Squaw Flat Confluence Overlook Road, Utah

Colorado National Monument, Wilderness Proposal, Colorado

Amistad National Recreation Area, Diablo East Development Site, Texas

Joshua Tree National Monument, Wilderness Proposal, California

John Day Fossil Beds National Monument, Oregon

Grand Canyon Complex, Wilderness Proposal, Arizona

1974

Bryce Canyon National Park, Wilderness Proposal, Utah

Moores Creek National Military Park, Boundary Change, North Carolina

Grand Teton National Park, Jackson Hole Airport Actions, Wyoming

Glacier National Park, Many Glacier Sewage System Plan, Montana

Glacier National Park, Lake McDonald Master Sewage Plan, Montana

501

Bighorn Canyon National Recreation Area, Transpark Road, Montana/Wyoming
Point Reyes National Seashore, Wilderness Proposal, California
Guilford Courthouse National Military Park Development Concept Plan, North Carolina
Mesa Verde National Park, Wilderness Proposal, Colorado
Padre Island National Seashore, Master Plan, Texas
Hawaii Volcanoes National Park, Natural Resources Management Plan, Hawaii
Ross Lake National Recreation Area, Diablo Lake Resort, Development Concept Plan, Washington
Yellowstone National Park, Master Plan, Wyoming
Glacier National Park, Wilderness Proposal, Montana
Crater Lake National Park, Wilderness Proposal, Oregon
Zion National Park, Wilderness Proposal, Utah
Katmai National Park, Wilderness Proposal, Alaska
Rocky Mountain National Park, Wilderness Proposal, Colorado
Fort Sumter/Fort Moultrie National Monument, Master Plan and Development Concept Plan, South Carolina
Olympic National Park, Wilderness Proposal, Washington
Carlsbad Caverns, National Park, Master Plan, New Mexico
Klondike Gold Rush National Historical Park, Master Plan, Alaska

<u>1975</u>

Big Bend National Park, Wilderness Proposal, Texas
Mount Ranier National Park, Wilderness Proposal, Washington
Big Cypress National Preserve, Florida
Saguaro National Monument, Wilderness Proposal, Arizona
Lincoln Home National Historic Site, Master Plan, Illinois
Indiana Dunes National Lakeshore, West Beach Unit, Comprehensive Design, Indiana
Cowpens National Battlefield, Master/Development Concept Plans, South Carolina
Hawaii Volcanoes National Park, Wilderness Proposal, Hawaii
Dinosaur National Monument, Wilderness Proposal, Utah/Colorado
Lower St. Croix National Scenic Riverway, Master Plan, Minnesota/Wisconsin
Organ Pipe Cactus National Monument, Wilderness Proposal, Arizona
Rocky Mountain National Park, Master Plan, Colorado
Buffalo National River, Master Plan, Arkansas
Pecos National Monument, Master/Development Plan, New Mexico
Hawaii Volcanoes National Park, Master Plan, Hawaii
National Capital Parks, Rehabilitation of the National Mall, Washington, D.C.
Grand Teton National Park, Master Plan, Wyoming
City of Refuge National Historical Park, Master Plan, Hawaii
White Sands National Monument, Master Plan, New Mexico
Grand Canyon National Park, Master Plan (Grand Canyon Complex), Arizona
Pinnacles National Monument, Master Plan, California

<u>1976</u>

Franklin Delano Roosevelt National Historic Site, Master Plan, New York

Mount Ranier National Park, Master Plan, Washington

Grand Canyon National Park, Development Concept Plan (Grand Canyon Village), Arizona

Independence National Historical Park, Pennsylvania

Bandelier National Monument, Master Plan, New Mexico

Glen Canyon National Recreation Area, Special Use Permit, Underground Transmission Line, Greenhaven Development, Arizona

Gaudalupe Mountains National Park, Master Plan, Texas

Olympic National Park, Master Plan, Washington

St. Croix National Scenic Riverway, Master Plan, Minnesota/Wisconsin

Black Canyon of the Gunnison National Monument, Wilderness, Colorado

Zion National Park, Master Plan, Utah

Big Thicket National Preserve, Texas

Knife River Indian Villages National Historic Site, South Dakota

Mount McKinley National Park, Electric Distribution Line, Alaska

1977

Wilson's Creek National Battlefield, Master Plan, Missouri

Olympic National Park, Master Plan, Washington

Cedar Breaks National Monument, Wilderness Proposal, Utah

Fire Island National Seashore, Master Plan, New York

1978

Tuskegee Institute National Historic Site, General Management Plan, Alabama

Everglades National Park, Wilderness Proposal, Florida

Natchez Trace Parkway, Additional Construction, Tennesee/Alabama/Mississippi

Pine Creek State and National Scenic River, Pennsylvania

Gulf Islands National Seashore, General Management Plan/Development Plans, Mississippi/Florida

Youghiogheny State and National Wild and Scenic River, Maryland/Pennsylvania

Obed National Wild and Scenic River, Tennessee

Biscayne National Monument, General Management Plan, Florida

Buffalo National River, Wilderness Proposal, Arkansas

1979

Cumberland Gap National Historical Park, Master Plan, Kentucky/Tennessee/Virginia

Glen Canyon National Recreation Area, General Management Plan/ Wilderness Proposal, Arizona/Utah

Everglades National Park, Master Plan, Florida

Grand Canyon National Park, Colorado River Management Plan, Arizona

Big Bend National Park, Master Plan, Texas

Gateway National Recreation Area, General Management Plan, New Jersey

Gunnison Wild and Scenic River, Colorado

Owyhee National Wild and Scenic River, Idaho/Oregon

Sequoia-Kings Canyon National Parks, Development Concept Plan, California

1980

Voyageurs National Park, Master Plan, Minnesota

Grand Canyon National Park, Ferral Burro Management and Ecosystem Restoration Plan, Arizona

Stones River National Battlefield and Cemetery, General Management/Development Concept Plans, Tennessee

Chickasaw National Recreation Area, General Management Plan, Oklahoma

Redwood National Park, General Management Plan, California

Yosemite National Park, General Management Plan, California

1981

Lassen Volcanic National Park, General Management Plan, California

Cumberland Island National Seashore, General Management/ Wilderness Plans, Georgia

Blue Ridge Parkway, 765-kV Transmission Line, Virginia

Shiloh National Military Park, General Management/Development Concept Plans, Tennessee

Big Horn Canyon National Recreation Area, General Management/Development Concept Plans/Wilderness Proposal, Wyoming

Lowell National Historical Park, General Management Plan, Massachusetts

Lincoln Boyhood National Monument, Master Plan, Indiana

Everglades Jetport, Florida (with FAA)

1982

Great Smoky Mountains National Park, General Management Plan, Tennessee/North Carolina

Badlands National Park, Master Plan, South Dakota

Santa Monica Mountains National Recreation Area, General Management Plan, California

Delaware Water Gap National Recreation Area, Management of U.S. 209, Pennsylvania

Death Valley National Monument, Natural/Cultural Resources Management Plans, California/Nevada

1983

Cape Lookout National Seashore, General Management/Development Concept Plans/Wilderness Study, North Carolina

Yellowstone National Park, Grizzly Bear Management Plan, Wyoming/Montana/Idaho

West Potomac Park and Franklin Delano Roosevelt Memorial, Washington, D.C.

Colorado and Lower Delores Wild and Scenic Rivers, Colorado/Utah

Green and Yampa Wild and Scenic Rivers Study, Colorado/Utah

1984

Redwood National Park, U.S. 101 Bypass, California

Snake Wild and Scenic River, Oregon/Washington

Loxahatchee Wild and Scenic River Study, Florida

1985

Denali National Park, Kantishna Hills/Dunkle Mine Study, Alaska

1986

George Washington Memorial Parkway Improvements, Virginia

Lake Mead National Recreation Area, General Management Plan, Arizona/Nevada

Appendix B

BLM Wilderness Study Areas Adjacent to National Park System Units

The following information was compiled from BLM Wilderness Status Maps for ten western states: Arizona, California, Colorado, Idaho, Montana, Nevada, New Mexico, Oregon, Utah, and Wyoming. The notation (202) following the identification number denotes WSAs considered for special management status under Section 202 of the Federal Land Policy and Management Act (FLPMA) (see text, Chapter 5, for explanation).

NPS Unit	Adjacent WSA	WSA Name	Acreage
Arches NP	UT-060-131B	Lost Spg. Canyon	3,880
	UT-060-138	Negro Bill Canyon	7,620
Bighorn Canyon NRA	MT-067-206 (202)	Pryn Mt.	16,927
	MT-067-207	Big Horn Tackon	4,550
Black Canyon NM	CO-030-388	Gunnison Gorge	20,712
Canyonlands NP	UT-060-045	Horseshoe Canyon	20,500
	UT-060-164	Indian Creek	6,870
	UT-060-167	Bridger Jack Mesa	5,290
	UT-060-169	Butler Wash	24,350
	UT-ISA-002	Dark Canyon	62,040
Capitol Reef NP	UT-050-221 (202)	Fremont Gorge	2,540
	UT-050-248	Mt. Pennell	74,300
Carlsbad Caverns NP	NM-060-819A	Mudgetts	2,941
Colorado NM	CO-070-113	Black Ridge Canyons	18,150
Craters of the Moon NM	ID-33-1	Great Rift	355,850
Death Valley NM	CDCA-117	Saline Valley	389,215
	CDCA-117A	Lower Saline	6,400
	CDCA-119	Little Sand Spg.	32,236
	CDCA-123	Hunter Mt.	23,284
	CDCA-127	Panamint Dunes	87,852
	CDCA-134	Wildrose Canyon	34,549
	CDCA-136	Suprise Canyon	52,356
	CDCA-137	Manly Peak	33,110
	CDCA-137A	Middle Peak Canyon	8,482
	CDCA-142	Slate Range	88,108
	CDCA-143	Funeral Mts.	56,900
	CDCA-147	Greenwater Range	145,624
	CDCA-148	Greenwater Valley	57,400

507

	CDCA-149	Ibex Hills	40,272
	CDCA-156	Owlshead Mt.	123,000
	CDCA-219	Saddle Peak Mts.	9,120
	CDCA-220	S. Saddle Peak Mts.	6,375
	CDCA-221	Avawatz	100,180
	NV-050-355	Bonnie Clair Flat	66,800
Dinosaur NM	CO-010-214	Diamond Breaks	36,015
	CO-010-224 (202)	Ant Hills	4,354
	CO-010-224A (202)	Chew Winter Camp	1,320
	CO-010-226	Peterson Draw	5,160
	CO-010-228	Tepee Draw	5,490
	CO-010-229D (202)	Vale of Tears	7,420
	UT-80-414	Daniels Canyon	2,475
Fort Bowie NHS	AZ-040-66	Bowie Mountain	6,156
Glen Canyon NRA	UT-040-079	Burning Hills	61,550
	UT-040-080	Fifty Mile Mt.	148,162
	UT-040-082	Scorpion	35,884
	UT-050-236B	French Spring	25,000
	UT-050-237	Horseshoe Canyon	38,800
	UT-050-241	Fiddler Butte	73,100
	UT-050-247	Little Rockies	38,700
	UT-060-175	Middle Point	5,990
	UT-060-181	Mancos Mesa	51,440
	UT-ISA-001	Grand Gulch	105,520
	UT-ISA-003	Escalante Canyons	360
	UT-ISA-004	Escalante Canyons	119,300
	UT-ISA-005	The Gulch	760
Great Sand Dunes NM	CO-050-135	Sand Castle	1,644
Joshua Tree NM	CDCA-328	Coxcomb Mts.	68,604
	CDCA-334	Eagle Mts.	60,056
	CDCA-335	Pinto Mts.	24,710
Lake Mead NRA	AZ-020-01A	Mt. Wilson	24,821
	AZ-020-007	Van Deeman	1,550
	AZ-020-008	Mocking Bird	5,750
	AZ-020-009	Black Mt. North	20,398
	AZ-020-010	Burns Spring	29,961
	AZ-020-014	Grapevine Wash	2,200
	NV-050-229	Muddy Mts.	96,170
	NV-050-231	Lime Canyon	30,74?
	NV-050-235	Garret Buttes	111,000
	NV-050-236	Jumbo Spring	3,811
	NV-050-338	Silver Peak	33,62?
	NV-050-423	El Dorado	11,06?
	NV-050-438	Ireteba Peaks	13,37?
Mesa Verde NP	CO-030-252	Weber Mt.	6,30?
Natural Bridges NM	UT-060-191	Cheesebox Canyon	15,41?

	UT-060-201	Road Canyon	52,420
	UT-060-204	Fish Creek Canyon	46,440
Pinnacles NM	CA-040-303 (202)	Pinnacles	5,838
Sequoia-Kings Canyon NP	CA-010-022	Sheep Ridge	4,905
	CA-010-023A	Milk Ranch	6,382
Zion NP	UT-040-143	Canaan Mt.	47,810
	UT-040-145 (202)	Orderville Canyon	1,750
	UT-040-146 (202)	Deep Creek	3,320
	UT-040-147 (202)	Red Butte	804
	UT-040-148 (202)	Spring Canyon	4,433
	UT-040-159 (202)	The Watchman	600
	UT-040-150 (202)	N. Fork Virgin River	1,040
	UT-040-153 (202)	LaVerkin Creek	567
	UT-040-154 (202)	Taylor Creek Canyon	35
	UT-040-176 (202)	Goose Creek Canyon	89
	UT-040-177 (202)	Beartrap Canyon	40
	UT-040-230	Parunuweap Canyon	30,800

TOTALS:

21 NPS units affected   92 WSAs   3,620,380 acres

Appendix C

A BASIC PRIMER ON LEGAL SOURCE MATERIALS FOR NONLAWYERS

This book is intended to aid citizen activists, as well as lawyers, in understanding the law governing protection of our national parks. But since our authors are necessarily lawyers (or experienced with legal materials), many of the concepts and legal source materials on which they rely may be unfamiliar to nonlawyers.

To assist diligent activists who may want to use or review some of the legal sources cited by our authors, we have included the following basic explanation of legal source materials designed for nonlawyers and beginning law students. Nolo Press, of Berkeley, California, has kindly permitted NPCA to excerpt and publish the following introduction to legal materials authored by attorney Stephen Elias. The excerpts are taken from a more comprehensive explanation titled *Legal Research: How to Find and Understand the Law* (2nd Ed., 1986, available from Nolo Press, 950 Parker St., Berkeley, CA). The portions of that book we borrow here have been edited and reorganized to concentrate on materials pertinent to park protection law discussed in the book.

--ed.

I. AN OVERVIEW OF THE LAW

When someone new to the law, whether law student, paralegal, or citizen interested in her own case, thinks of "going to court" for the first time, she often imagines movie-type scenes with argumentative attorneys, stern judges and courtrooms filled with spectators and the press. The sheer complexity of all this can seem to be too much to learn to deal with. As one judge puts it:

> The lay litigant enters a temple of mysteries whose ceremonies are dark, complex and unfathomable. Pretrial procedures are the cabalistic rituals of the lawyers and judges who serve as priests and high priests. The layman knows nothing of their tactical significance. He knows only that his case remains in limbo while the priests and high priests chant their lengthy and arcane pretrial rites. (Quoted from Daley v. County of Butte, 227 Cal. App. 2d 380, 392 (1964).)

In fact, the great majority of court matters are handled in a quite straightforward manner, without fanfare, argument, or stress. Typical of these cases are guardianships, conservatorships, adoptions, name changes, probating of simple estates, uncontested divorces, and the sealing of criminal records. On the other hand, any case can get messy when a real dispute exists or lawyers have a financial incentive to string the matter out, as can often be the case in complicated business disputes for which attorneys can bill by the hour.

Whether the case is disputed or undisputed, filing and prosecuting a case in court always involves carefully following a number of technical court rules. The trick in getting a case into and successfully through the courts is knowing these procedural rules in minute detail. Among the highest of compliments a lawyer can be paid is, "she sure knows her way around the courthouse"--that is, she has mastered the rules of the game.

511

While researching these rules is beyond the scope of this first discussion, understanding the stages of judicial procedure and related terminology can help to de-mystify the process.

A. How a Court house Works: Steps in Litigation

All cases in the state and federal courts are handled by procedures and rules which are substantially similar. This is true even though the details of different state rules vary and similar procedures are often referred to by different names. For example, an eviction action in California is called "unlawful detainer" and in Massachusetts, "summary process." Yet, both types of proceedings are basically quite similar. Let's look at how a typical case develops and proceeds through the courts.

1. **The Plantiff's Complaint:** A case begins when a "complaint" is filed by the plaintiff (the party who sues). This document tells what happened and what the plaintiff wants done about it (i.e., money damages, injunctive relief, etc.).

2. **The Defendant's Response:** After the defendant (the party who is sued) is actually provided (served) with a copy of the complaint, she is given a certain time period to respond in writing (usually 30 days). If no response is made, a "default" judgment may be obtained by the plaintiff, which means the plaintiff wins without having to fully prove his case.

3. **The Defendant's Response:** There are a variety of ways the defendant may respond. Most commonly, the defendant files an "answer," a written statement setting out which allegations in the complaint it wishes to contest. Another common response is to file a written request, called a motion, to the court for some type of action. The most common motion is a "motion to dismiss" (or demurrer, as it's still called in some states). Together, the plaintiff's charging papers and the defendant's responsive papers are referred to as the "pleadings" in the case.

   a. The Answer: This is the defendant's main court paper. Here she admits or denies each charge or allegation in the complaint. Under the procedural rules of most states, the defendant's answer can also contain affirmative defenses (i.e., factual statements of the reasons or excuses for why the defendant did what he did) and counterclaims (i.e., claims that the plaintiff in fact owes the defendant money). The defendant can also state that she doesn't have enough information about the allegations and therefore denies the complaint on that basis.

   b. Motion to Dismiss: Here the defendant, instead of answering the complaint, asks the court to dismiss the suit. Usually, the basis for this request boils down to this: even if the facts in the plaintiff's complaint are true, so what? Or to put the same thing a little more formally, the defendant is saying that the plaintiff has no legal theory (given the facts as the plaintiff has alleged them) upon which to properly base a lawsuit. The defendant is requesting the court to stop the plaintiff from wasting everyone's time and to end the matter then and there.

   The court does not decide any facts as part of a hearing on a motion to dismiss. Strictly for the purpose of deciding the motion, the judge assumes that the factual allegations in the complaint are true and then decides whether the law supports the claim for relief. If the judge denies the motion to dismiss, the defendant must either file an answer or appeal the denial. If the judge grants the motion, the case is ended unless the plaintiff successfully appeals the decision.

4. **Summary Judgment:** Once the pleadings are on file, either side may seek a judgment without trial if she can show the absence of a dispute about any importan facts in the case (called "triable issues of material fact"). This showing is made in th

form of written statements under oath, termed "declarations" or "affidavits." If they show a lack of basic factual disagreement between the parties, as is often the case, the judge will then proceed to apply the law to the facts and decide the case.

5. **Discovery:** From the time that the pleadings in a case are filed (and occasionally before), each party has the right to engage in an activity termed "discovery." This is the general name for a number of specific procedures by which the parties seek information from each other both to bolster their case and prevent Perry Mason types of surprises at trial. The discovery stage of a case often adds considerably to the delays and expense associated with litigation. Why? Because each side usually attempts as best it can to avoid giving up information to the other. Disputes are constantly arising between parties to a lawsuit over what information must be turned over to the other sides and what can be kept from disclosure. These disputes are resolved by the trial court in "discovery motion" proceedings. If a party does not like the result, it is sometimes possible to take the matter to a higher court before the underlying case proceeds further. Accordingly, discovery often results in cases going into a "holding pattern."

Normally, discovery consists of the following devices:

- **Depositions:** Witnesses are required to go to the office of one of the attorneys and answer questions, under oath, about their knowledge of the dispute in the presence of a stenographer who records the testimony. Usually the attorney for the side of the case on which the witness will testify is also present.

- **Interrogatories:** Written questions are sent by one party to another to be answered under oath within a specified period of time. Interrogatories are also used to request identification of documents.

- **Admissions of Fact:** Factual statements are set out which the other side must admit or deny. If the other side does nothing, the statement is taken as being admitted.

- **Production of Documents:** Requests are made by one party to another for the production of specified documents. In a complicated case, one side may ask the other for file cabinets full of material. There are often arguments (motions heard by a judge) about how much fishing one side can do in the other's records.

6. **Motions:** At any time after the pleadings but before the trial, the plaintiff or defendant may ask the court to order the other side to do something or to refrain from doing something. Sometimes these requests (called "motions") are used to preserve the status quo until the case can come to trial on the merits. For example, if the circumstances are truly urgent, the court can issue a "temporary restraining order" (TRO) or "preliminary injunction" stopping the defendant from taking some action pending trial on the underlying case. Motions may also be filed to enforce discovery (i.e., to require a party to answer questions or produce documents when appropriate), to protect a party against abusive discovery (e.g., requiring attendance at a week-long deposition), or to request other court actions.

7. **Getting the Trial Set:** In many court systems, a case is never set for trial unless one of the parties requests it. Accordingly, when a party feels adequately prepared, he can file a document with the court requesting a trial. These documents are called by a wide variety of names, including "memorandum to set," "at-issue memorandum," and "motion to set for trial." Whatever their names, these requests to have a case set for trial may either be opposed by the other party, for a variety of reasons, or agreed to. Usually, once a case is set for trial, the judge schedules a pre-trial conference between the parties, their lawyers, and the judge.

8. **Pre-Trial Conference:** At the pre-trial conference, the judge makes sure that everyone understands what the remaining issues are in the case and gets an idea of how long the trial will take. Many judges use these conferences--often quite successfully--to pressure the parties to settle the case. If, however, no settlement is reached, the trial date is fixed.

9. **Trial:** A trial can occur before a judge and jury or only a judge, depending on the state, the type of case, and the wishes of the parties. Fortunately for the taxpayer and most civil litigants, few civil cases actually go to trial. Most are settled somewhere along the way or dismissed for lack of follow through (termed "lack of prosecution").

10. **Appeal:** When a judge issues a final judgment or order in a case, the party adversely affected is usually entitled to file an appeal to a higher court.

B. An Overview: Some Questions and Answers Concerning Case Law

1. What is a Case?

"Cases" begin as civil disputes or criminal charges that end up in court for resolution by a judge or jury. As the word is used in the legal profession, however, a case is also an "opinion," written by one or more judges, that applies principles of law to a set of facts presented in a dispute. When we speak of looking up a case, or checking the case law, it is the opinion of a judge or judges deciding a dispute that we are talking about. In the great majority of instances in state court, "cases" record opinions of appeal courts, not trial courts. However, in federal court, trial court judges also commonly write opinions that are published.

2. What is a Trial Court?

The court in which a dispute or charge is first presented for resolution is called the "trial court," even though decisions in that court may be rendered on motions rather than after a trial.

3. What Happens in Trial Courts?

Assuming a case goes to trial (the vast majority of lawsuits are settled and never reach a trial), disputed facts in the case are resolved by the judge, or by the jury if a jury trial is held. A trial is solely for finding facts; when, as in many instances, there is no real dispute about the facts, the trial judge may issue a "summary judgment" without holding a trial. The trial judge alone decides which laws should be applied to the facts. Where trial is conducted before a jury, however, the judge issues "instructions" about the applicable law to the jury, which then determines the facts as the basis for applying the law. (In limited instances, even in jury cases, the judge may be required to determine matters of fact as well as law.)

4. Do State Trial Courts Write Opinions?

Judges in state trial courts generally don't write formal opinions discussing the law they apply to the cases before them. In many cases, however, they do issue jury instructions. And when trying cases without a jury, they prepare a document termed "Findings of Fact and Conclusions of Law." In it the judge explains the verdict she then reached on the basis of the facts. Courts also often issue "orders" (usually very brief) informing the parties (the plaintiff and the defendant) what they have decided and why. None of these documents are published; they are not considered "case law" in the sense that we use that term when we speak of looking up a case or checking the case law, since they are not intended as guidance for other courts.

5. Do Federal Trial Courts Write Opinions?

There is at least one federal trial court, called United States District Court, in each state. Occasionally, district court judges issue opinions explaining their decisions when significant issues of the law are involved. These opinions are called "district court cases" and are published in a series of books (available in most law libraries) known as the *Federal Supplement* (abbreviated as F. Supp.). By no means are all federal district court cases reported; in fact, most are not.

6. *When and Where Can You Appeal From a Decision by a State Trial Court?*

When a party doesn't agree with the decision by the judge or jury in the state trial court, he can usually appeal to an "intermediate appellate court." Intermediate appellate courts occupy a position between the trial court and the state's highest court. They have different titles depending on the state, but usually contain at least the word "appellate" or "appeals," such as "North Carolina Court of Appeals." In a few states, such as Vermont and Minnesota, there are no intermediate appellate courts; appeals go directly to the state's highest court (termed the state Supreme Court). In New York (and Texas for criminal cases) the state's highest court is called the Court of Appeals rather than the Supreme Court.

7. *When and Where Can You Appeal from a Decision by the U.S. District Court?*

The intermediate appellate courts of the United States are called Courts of Appeals, and are organized by geography into eleven judicial "circuits" (plus the Washington D.C. Circuit and the Federal Circuit). Appeals from a U.S. District Court go to the appeals court for the circuit in which the district court is located. For example, cases from District Courts in New York go to the U.S. Court of Appeals for the Second Circuit. Similarly, Texas is in the Fifth Circuit and federal appeals originating in that state are all heard in the Fifth Circuit. The states in each circuit are shown on a map in the front of the volumes of the *Federal Reporter* (2nd series) in which the opinions of the Courts of Appeals are reproduced.

8. *What Do Intermediate Appellate Courts Do?*

Appellate courts on both the federal and state levels analyze the proceedings in the trial courts for legal errors by reviewing the trial court record and lawyers' arguments (ironically called "briefs"). They can then approve or disapprove of the trial court decisions. Appellate courts are primarily concerned with whether the "law" was interpreted correctly and seldom reverse the lower court determination of the facts of a case, unless they conclude that there was clear error. Federal circuit courts usually hear appeals in three-judge panels. There are several panels of judges in each circuit.

9. *Do Intermediate Appellate Courts Issue Opinions?*

Yes. The opinions of intermediate appellate courts, as well as opinions of the state and federal Supreme Courts, are usually published in bound volumes called reports (discussed below).

10. *What Effect do State Appellate Court Cases Have on Other Courts in the State?*

Published appellate court cases provide guidance to other appellate and lower courts in that state (and occasionally to courts in other states). This guidance, broadly called "precedent" or "persuasive authority" is subject to its own varying rules with regard to the extent of its authoritativeness. If a case is not published, as sometimes happens when the case does not possess any issue of interest in the legal community, its status as precedent is uncertain, but it will seldom be cited for obvious reasons.

11. *What Effect do U.S. Courts of Appeal Cases Have on Other Cases?*

Published U.S. Courts of Appeal cases serve as guidance (precedent and authority) for U.S. District Courts that are located within their circuits, and for state courts in these circuits in respect to federal law issues. They are also given substantial though varying degrees of deference, particularly by other federal courts, outside of their circuits.

12. *How do You Take a Case to the Supreme Court?*

If you don't agree with the outcome of an appeal in an intermediate appellate court, you can attempt to "take your case all the way to the Supreme Court." There are fifty state supreme courts [including those of New York (oddly, New York uses the term "Supreme Court" to refer to its primary trial court and calls its highest court the Court of Appeals) and Texas which go by different names] and the United States Supreme Court. Some state supreme courts and the U.S. Supreme Court have discretion in deciding whether to consider most types of cases (though limited categories of cases may involve mandatory review). To have a case considered, you must usually file a "Petition for Writ of Certiorari," or, as it is usually called, "Petition for Cert." If the Supreme Court (state or federal) grants cert, it will consider the case. If it denies cert, then it won't. In some states, you have the right to appeal directly to the state Supreme Court.

13. Do Supreme Courts Grant Cert in Most Cases?

No. The U.S. Supreme Court in particular only grants "cert" in a very small percentage of cases presented. Typically, the cases chosen present interesting or important questions of law or an issue that two or more intermediate appellate courts have disagreed on. For example, if the Court of Appeals for the 6th Circuit decides that the military registration system is unconstitutional because it doesn't include women, and the Court of Appeals for the 7th Circuit decides that the system is constitutional, the U.S. Supreme Court might grant "cert" in these cases and resolve the conflict.

14. What Decisions do Supreme Courts Review?

The U.S. Supreme Court considers cases from the U.S. Circuit Courts of Appeal, from state supreme courts (where the state courts have decided questions of federal law) and occasionally, directly from the U.S. District Courts. Direct appeals from the District Courts are limited to certain types of cases, usually involving important constitutional issues. State supreme courts consider cases from state intermediate appellate courts and, infrequently, directly from state trial courts.

15. Are Cases Ever Filed Directly in Appellate or Supreme Courts?

Yes. Occasionally cases can be brought directly in the intermediate appellate courts or supreme courts, but only when the cases present highly specialized issues of law of a type specifically assigned to the appellate court by statute or constitutional provision, and involve little factual dispute. Thus, under the federal and state constitutions, the Supreme Courts are given "original jurisdiction" (as opposed to their usual appellate jurisdiction) in certain types of cases. For example, if one state sues another, the suit can be brought in the U.S. Supreme Court.

16. Do Supreme Courts Issue Opinions?

Yes. When the U.S. Supreme Court or a state supreme court decides a case, it almost always issues an opinion. (One significant exception: in certain types of cases that come to the U.S. Supreme Court as a matter of right rather than by "cert," the Court may summarily "affirm.") U.S. Supreme Court cases serve as precedent and binding authority for all courts on questions of federal law, and state supreme court cases serve as precedent and authority for all courts within the state. They are important sources of law.

C. A Closer Look at How Opinions are Structured

Normally, every case opinion contains four basic elements:

(1) a detailed statement of the facts which are accepted by the court as true. These facts are taken from the lower court's determination of the facts, unless the lower court's determinations were clearly in error.

(2) a formulation of the legal issue or issues presented to the appellate court for resolution.

(3) a statement of the actual decision of the court (i.e., the holding) and the legal basis for it. The appellate court always takes some specific action. If the appellate court agrees with the lower court, the lower court decision is "affirmed." If the lower court decision is "reversed," the appellate court has disagreed with it and struck it down.

Sometimes lower court decisions are affirmed in part and reversed in part. If the appellate court agrees substantially with the lower court, but disagrees with some particular point, it may modify or amend the decision. If the lower court has written and published a decision, the appellate court may order that decision vacated, occasionally even "depublished" (taken out of the official reporter). Sometimes, in the case of a complete or partial reversal, the case is sent back to the lower court to take further action consistent with the appellate court's opinion. This is called a remand.

(4) a discussion of why the holding was made--the court's reasoning or "rationale."

Many opinions present these four components in just this order. Others do not. For instance, one common format used by the courts is a summary of the issue and the decision in the first couple of paragraphs followed by a statement of the facts and the reasoning.

Fast Track: How to Read a Case

- Read the one paragraph synopsis at the beginning of the case.

- Skim the headnotes of the case.

- If you find one or more that look relevant, jump to the place in the text that contains the headnote number in brackets.

- Skim the following text.

- If the opinion appears to be relevant, locate the place in the opinion where the facts are described.

- After you read the facts, locate the court's statement of the issue that is relevant to your search.

- Once you understand what issue the court is addressing, find the court's decision on the issue.

- Once you know what the decision is, read the court's rationale for the decision.

D. Some Legal Nomenclature

- The U.S. and State Constitutions and cases which interpret them produce *Constitutional Law*

- Congress passes laws called statutes which constitute *federal statutory law*

- Federal courts decide cases and write opinions which constitute *federal case law*

- Federal administrative agencies created by Congress and agencies in the executive branch issue regulations and decide cases which constitute *federal administrative law* of those agencies

- Federal courts apply procedural requirements drawn from statutes, regulations, and case precedents governing administrative agencies, which constitute the law of *federal administrative procedure* (or, also, "administrative law")

- Sovereign Indian tribes have their own courts and laws which constitute *tribal law*

- State legislatures pass statutes which constitute *state statutory law*

- State courts decide state cases and write opinions which constitute *state case law*

- State administrative agencies created by state legislatures and staffed by governors write regulations and decide cases which constitute *state administrative law*

- Local governments pass *ordinances* which become police codes, building codes, planning codes, health codes, etc.

II. BACKGROUND LEGAL RESOURCES

A. Why Use Background Resources?

Rather than plunging directly into the primary sources of the law (statutes, cases, and regulations), it often makes great sense to start with the many broader introductory materials available in most law libraries. This is especially true if a researcher is unfamiliar with the broad legal category. Fortunately, nearly every major area of the law has been discussed and summarized by experts in many different resources and formats.

Getting a general understanding of an area before looking for the specific answer to a narrow question is particularly important when it comes to doing legal research. Why? Because the answers to almost all specific legal questions depend on a number of variables. Legal background materials, which will help you gain this overview of your problem, are usually directed at one of three audiences: non-lawyers, law students, or lawyers. However, many books, articles, and increasingly, computer programs and data bases can be of immense help to all users.

B. Legal Textbooks and Treatises As Background Resources

In many situations books that have been published specifically as textbooks for law students offer an excellent point of departure for legal research. Years ago, most of these textbooks were published by West Publishing Company and were referred to by that publisher as its "hornbook" series. Now there are several competing sets of law school texts (such as the University Textbook Series), and the name "hornbook" isn't used quite as much as it used to be.

Whoever the publisher and whatever you call the books, these resources are intended for use in law school. As law student readers will well know, most law schools use the case method of teaching law. This involves reading actual decisions by courts and then discussing the cases in class. To help the student put these cases in a proper perspective, textbooks have been written by experts in each field (often the professors themselves).

These books, which are conceptual in nature, are excellent resources for gaining a comprehensive understanding of the variables in any specific area of concern. They can be found in most libraries, particularly those associated with law schools. Key subject areas in which texts, casebooks, or hornbooks may be found include administrative law, energy law, environmental law, public land law, natural resources law, and water law.

When a book attempts to cover an entire area of law, it is called a treatise. Typically, law treatises have titles like *Prosser on Torts, Powell on Real Property,* and *Corbin on Contracts.* When a book covers just a small portion of a general legal field, or introduces a new concept into the legal realm, it is called a monograph. Whatever they are called, however, thousands of these books can be found in the "stacks" of the normal law library, and can often be very helpful in providing an overview of the problem being searched.

There is a big difference between these resources and the textbooks discussed above. While textbooks cover entire legal topics with the intent to teach, treatises and monographs cover their topics with the intent to provide in-depth reference materials. As such, these resources generally delve much deeper into an area than you would usually care to go. They also become dated more quickly despite occasional supplementation. However, if you really want to amass expertise on a topic and have the patience to put up with the ultimate in hairsplitting, give these resources a try.

C. Law Reviews and Other Legal Periodicals

Because the law is always developing and changing, a continuing discussion and analysis is maintained among legal professionals. Much of this analysis of new legislation, current legal theories and viewpoints, and the interpretation of important cases is found in law journals published by law schools, commercial publishers, and professional legal societies such as bar associations. The articles are written by students, practicing attorneys and law professors, and sometimes present a whole new view of an area of the law. In short, law reviews tend to focus on where the law is going as opposed to legal encyclopedias, which concentrate on where it has been.

While these articles are usually more academic, many are also practical, containing valuable descriptions of the state of the law in the specific area being discussed, and can provide you with leads for your specific research task. Because they often explore the development of new legal concepts or new administrative programs, law review articles can provide helpful suggestions for new approaches to legal problems. Law reviews are published in paperback pamphlets usually on a variety of schedules--monthly, quarterly, semi-annual, annual, and sporadic. Most law libraries contain the more influential of these journals and law reviews, and some libraries (especially in large law schools) have virtually a complete set.

Articles are normally located by using either of two printed indexes, the *Index to Legal Periodicals* or *Current Law Index*. Both are organized by subject matter and author and contain the title of the article, the law review or journal where it is located (in abbreviated form), and the volume and page number. Both indexes contain numerous volumes which are organized according to the years in which the contents were published. The example below is an excerpt from the *Index to Legal Periodicals* that lists the article titled "Open Meetings under the Arkansas Freedom of Information Act," which appears in the *Arkansas Law Review*.

Freedom of information

The Freedom of Information Act privacy exemption: who does it really protect? K. Maxwell, R. Reinsch. 7 *Com. & L.* 45-59 Ap '85

Open Meetings Under the Arkansas Freedom of Information Act. J.J. Watkins. 38 *Ark. L. Rev.* 268-358 '84

The "Ark" refers to Arkansas, the "L" means Law, and the "Rev" is an abbreviation for *Review*. The numbers following these letters indicate that the article is in Volume 38 of the *Arkansas Law Review* at pages 268-358, and that Volume 38 was published in 1984.

If you look at some of the other listings, you will see strange abbreviations for law reviews, like *Com & L* and *Ad. L. Rev.* You are not expected to magically guess what these abbreviations mean. Lawyers don't carry this information around with them. Rather, when you become mystified by an entry, simply consult the table of abbreviations at the front of the volume.

Note: A computer-based index to a broad range of legal periodicals and other law-related publications is now available in some of the larger law libraries. Called the *Legal*

Resource Index, and published by the Information Access Corporation (the same company that publishes the *Current Law Index*) this resource provides a cumulative listing and is thus easier to use than the printed indexes, which are organized by date.

D. Specialized Loose-Leaf Materials

Particularly helpful in fields related to environmental, public lands, and natural resources law are the specialized loose-leaf materials that maintain up-to-date references to current developments. Most practicing lawyers and many others who work in the legal system find it necessary to specialize. This is due primarily to the volume of information generated by the courts and legislatures in each field of law. Specialization typically means not only mastering a particular body of knowledge--e.g., tax, zoning, bankruptcy, or personal injury--but maniacally keeping on top of it. Several publications cater to this need by offering an exhaustive loose-leaf compilation of the recent developments in the area and weekly or monthly loose-leaf supplements. These materials provide information about new laws, regulations, and judicial and administrative decisions that might have an impact on the field of law covered by the publication.

For anyone who must maintain an up-to-the-minute grasp on what's going on in a particular legal area, these services can prove invaluable. However, they may be too specialized for your purposes unless your research topic falls squarely within one of these special categories. If it does, locate the appropriate service, read the instructions on how to use it at the front of the first volume, check the index, and you may solve your problem almost immediately. Particularly helpful in fields relating to national park issues are the Environmental Law Institute's (ELI) *Environmental Law Reporter* and the Bureau of National Affairs' (BNA) *Environment Reporter*.

E. Basic or Traditional Background Resources Used By Lawyers

1. Legal Encyclopedias

Legal encyclopedias contain detailed discussions of virtually every area of the law. These encyclopedias are organized alphabetically by subject matter in the same way as regular encyclopedias, but with broader main topics and a lot more sub-headings. In addition, they contain thorough indexes at the end of the entire set of volumes and detailed tables of contents at the beginning of each subject area discussion. The discussions are footnoted with references to cases and statutes that provide the primary-law foundation for the statements in the text. Keep in mind that legal encyclopedia articles discuss and describe the law--they aren't part of the law.

a. National Legal Encyclopedias

Two encyclopedias, *American Jurisprudence* and *Corpus Juris*, provide a national overview of American law. The entries in these encyclopedias contain footnote references to court decisions from many different states (and from federal courts where relevant). *American Jurisprudence*, which is published by Bancroft-Whitney/Lawyers Coop, is almost always abbreviated as *Am. Jur. Corpus Juris* is published by the West Publishing Company and commonly abbreviated as *C.J.* It's important to note that both of these publications, originally prepared many years ago, are now being distributed in a second (updated) series (*Am. Jur. 2d* and *C.J.S.*)

In the legal field, hardbound books are normally updated on an annual basis by "pocket parts" which slip inside the back or front cover of the volume. However, there always comes a time when the hardcover volumes (either individually or as an entire set) become so seriously out of date that pocket parts become too cumbersome. When this occurs, the publisher puts out either a brand new hardcover book or a new series, as happened with both sets of legal encyclopedias. Thus, *Am. Jur. 2d* is the same publication as *Am. Jur.*, but updated. The same is true for *C.J.S.* (*Corpus Juris Secundum*). You should always use the most recent series unless you are specifically looking for something that you believe was carried in the earlier series but dropped in the latter.

Because they cover the entire range of American law, these encyclopedias provide an excellent resource for beginning your research, especially if you have not been able to confidently classify your problem (and thus start with a more specific resource). Each entry provides a solid treatment of the particular topic, gives you a good idea of the all-important variables associated with your issue, and refers you to specific statutes and cases (the stuff the law is made of).

Which encyclopedia should you use if your law library has both? Many favor *Am. Jur. 2d* over *Corpus Juris Secundum (CJS)* because they feel that *CJS* tends to have too much unnecessary information.

2. American Law Reports

This Bancroft-Whitney/Lawyers Coop publication has two titles--The *American Law Reports* (abbreviated *A.L.R.*) and *American Law Reports, Federal* (abbreviated *A.L.R. Fed.*). *A.L.R.* covers issues primarily arising under state statutes and in state cases, as well as federally-oriented issues that arose before 1969, the year *A.L.R. Fed.* was first published. *A.L.R. Fed.* covers issues that arise primarily under federal statutes or in federal cases. Depending on the problem being researched, each of these titles is an excellent place to begin when you have analyzed your problem as falling within the state/civil/substantive or federal/civil/substantive areas.

Both publications are multi-volume sets of discussions of narrow issues that have been suggested by newly-decided court cases. Each discussion first comments on the case itself and then discusses other cases that have considered the same or similar issues.

As legal research tools, *A.L.R.* and *A.L.R. Federal* are different than encyclopedias in that they don't attempt to cover every subject. This, of course, means some bad news and some good. You may not find what you're looking for, but if you do you'll be well rewarded. Fortunately, *A.L.R.* has an excellent index attached to it that allows you to very quickly find out whether the news is good or bad for you.

A.L.R. comes in four series (*A.L.R., A.L.R. 2d, A.L.R. 3d and A.L.R. 4th*) according to the date of the articles. Unlike the legal encyclopedias, the newest series does not replace the previous one. *A.L.R. 4th* may contain an almost entirely new set of topics not covered in *A.L.R. 3d*, for example. The older series are kept up to date with pocket parts and hardbound volumes called the *Later Case Service*. You should always check the index of the newest series first, but if you don't find what you're looking for, go to the previous set. *A.L.R. Federal* is still in the first series.

Because *A.L.R.* is published by Bancroft-Whitney/Lawyers Coop, an article of interest will give you cross-references to other Bancroft-Whitney/Lawyers Coop publications on the same issue and be of great assistance. In this connection, Bancroft-Whitney/Lawyers Coop publishes a book called *The Living Law* that gives you detailed instructions on how to use *A.L.R.*

III. STATUTES AND REGULATIONS

When someone makes a reference to "the law," she is usually talking about the written laws that are passed by legislators and administrators at the federal, state, and local levels. Statutory law is by no means the only source of law--but it's a very big one. Certainly you normally cannot research a legal question without checking one or more state or federal statutes, administrative regulations, or local ordinances. In this context, then, to know what the "law" is, you need to first find out whether a statute, regulation, or ordinance applies to your situation.

Let's take a closer look at what "statutory" laws are called and where they come from:

- Federal statutes are laws made by Congress. State statutes are laws made by state legislatures.

■ Rules and regulations are laws promulgated by administrative agencies under the authority of federal or state statutes.

■ Ordinances, local codes, and regulations are laws made by city councils, county boards or supervisors, and special districts.

How to locate and interpret each type of statutory law is discussed later in this chapter. Fortunately, state and federal statutes and federal regulations are usually organized in such a way as to make them readily accessible. State regulations and local laws can also usually be located, albeit with somewhat more effort.

A. Some Basics About Statutes and How They Are Labeled

Although statutes are very accessible, there are two potentially confusing aspects to researching them. The first is that statutes often come in groups and you have to read the entire collection of statutes to understand any specific one. The second is that the numbers and titles statutes are commonly known by are often completely different than the numbers and titles they are found under in the books that contain them. For instance, many people have heard of Title I, the statute that earmarks federal funds for low-income children. However, if you went to find this statute, you need to know the entirely different label under which it appears in the *United States Code*. The rest of this section discusses each of these potentially sticky points in a little more detail.

Efficiency Note: Although the information in this section will ultimately prove useful and even indispensible if you engage in any serious statutory research, you may currently wish only to locate a particular statute to which you already have the appropriate reference (citation) or description. If so, turn to Section B for federal statutes and Section C for state statutes. You can then return to this section for a more in-depth understanding of how statutes are made and organized.

1. Statutory Schemes

The word "statute" refers to an individual piece of legislation. When legislatures focus on a particular area of the law, they usually produce a number of statutes regulating many different facets of the subject. For example, when legislatures turn their attention to regulating relationships between mobile home park owners and tenants, they may pass four or five statutes that cover eviction, two statutes that refer to security deposits, another as to when landlords may enter a rented mobile home, and so on.

Statutes with a common subject matter form "statutory schemes." This point has important implications for doing statutory research. Why? Because, if your research takes you to a particular statute that forms part of a statutory scheme, you will generally need to read at least some of the other related statutes to gain a full understanding of the single statute you are most interested in.

To help you better understand the concept of statutory schemes, let's look at the Civil Rights Act of 1964 which contains a large number of individual statutes dealing with discrimination in such matters as housing, public accomodations, and employment. Some of the statutes specifically prohibit discriminatory acts on the basis of race, creed, national origin, color, or sex. Other statutes provide remedies for violations--that is, penalties for discrimination and procedures for enforcement of the law.

The basic Civil Rights Act, of which these various statutes form a part, was originally passed by Congress in 1964. Both the original statutes, and some added later, have been amended from time to time during the past twenty-plus years. Thus, while the statutes together constitute a statutory scheme, the scheme in its present form involves a number of different statutes passed by a number of different sessions of Congress.

The part of the Civil Rights Act of 1964 that deals with employment discrimination is commonly known as Title VII. Thus you may hear it said that someone has filed a Title VII complaint about a discriminatory employment practice.

For instance, many Title VII complaints have been filed by women protesting employment discrimination based on sex. In fact, Title VII is itself a collection of statutes and can be termed a statutory scheme in its own right. If you file a Title VII complaint you will necessarily deal with separate statutes for such matters as (1) what must be alleged in the complaint, (2) what defenses are available to the employer, (3) what kinds of remedies the court is authorized to grant, (4) whether attorneys fees should be paid, and so on. Commonly, all related parts of such a statutory scheme will be compiled as a sequence of separate sections under numerical headings typically used to organize the entire collection of statutes enacted by a single jurisdiction (state or federal).

2. Statutes Labeled According To Internal Structure

As we will see later in this chapter, all federal statutes are organized by subject matter, indexed, and published under a specific title number in a series of books called the *United States Code.* If you want to read a federal statute you always locate it in this code (see Section B). Unfortunately, in some instances when you hear about a statute, the label that is used may not correspond to the *U.S. Code* citation numbers.

Take, for example, Title VII of the Civil Rights Act (mentioned above). If you wanted to find the Title VII statutory scheme and read it for yourself, you would run into an immediate problem. You would not find an entry for Title VII in the index to the *United States Code.* Why not? Because in this case, the "Title VII" is the numerical designation used by Congress to identify the employment discrimination portions of its original civil rights statutory scheme, and not the *United States Code* designation. In fact the Civil Rights Act is located in Title 42 of the *United States Code.*

Does this mean that when you are referred to a statutory scheme by a title number that this number will always or usually be different from the one used by the *United States Code*? No. Usually they will be the same, but its important to realize that this isn't always true because sometimes "Title" is used to refer to a specific portion of a general statutory scheme, while other times it refers to the general *U.S. Code* numerical heading under which the entire scheme has been compiled.

Does all this appear a bit confusing? It really needn't be if you will carefully read the following material.

Let's first address the question of why a statutory scheme labeled Title VII ended up in Title 42 of the *United States Code.* The basic answer is that each title more or less comprises a general subject matter, and Title 42 contains all civil rights legislation. If you want to research bankruptcy laws, you can consult Title 11. If your question involves patent law, Title 37 is for you.

Where did the "Title VII" come from, then? When statutes are written, they are assigned internal organizing labels for legislative purposes that have nothing to do with the ultimate need of legal researchers. Thus, when the employment discrimination part of the Civil Rights Act was assigned the internal structural label of "Title VII," there was no thought given as to how the statute if passed would ultimately be accessed by researchers. Why should there have been? When the statutory scheme was drafted it had obviously not yet even been passed.

What happened in the instance of the Civil Rights Act, while not routine, is fairly common. Because antidiscrimination laws are important, there was a lot of media interest and the statutory scheme got to be known by its internal label, Title VII. Title I, which deals with education, is another example. Even after it was passed and assigned a place in the *United States Code* under a particular title, it was still referred to by its original label.

In other situations, important pending legislation is referred to by the media and others under the name of its author, as was the case with the Landrum-Griffin and Taft-Hartley labor relations bills. Even after these bills became law and were codified (put in the code) many people continue to call them by their authors' names. Simply put, re-labeling a statute with a number in the *United States Code* does not necessarily cause its name to be changed in the public mind.

3. Statutes Labeled According To Public Law or Chapter Numbers

Another popular way of referring to statutes is by their public law or chapter labels. What is a public law or chapter number and how does a statute come to have one? Answering this question requires a brief journey into the process by which legislation becomes law.

Federal statutes start out as "bills" introduced in a particular legislative session. They are assigned labels and numbers depending on which side of the legislature they originate in. For example, a bill introduced in the U.S. Senate might be referred to as Senate Bill 2 (S. 2), whereas a bill which originated in the U.S. House of Representatives might be known as House of Representatives Bill 250 (H.R. 250).

Of the many bills introduced in Congress, few become law. To do so they have to be passed by both houses and signed by the President, or passed over her veto. Once a bill becomes law (officially called a statute), however, it is assigned a new label and given a new number. The basic label is Public Law (P.L.). Following the P.L., the statute will have one number that corresponds with the number of the Congress (e.g. 94th) that passed it followed by a second number which is simply the number assigned to that specific law by the Congress. Thus, P.L. 94-586 refers to Public Law 586 passed by the 94th Congress.

Bills passed by state legislatures are usually labeled in pretty much the same way. Each bill that is passed by the state legislature and signed by the governor is assigned a chapter number, usually in the order the bill becomes law. Thus, even though any particular state statute is ultimately put in a state code under a particular title number or code designation (e.g. penal code, civil code), it also has a chapter number which is usually unrelated to its code designation.

Knowing what these labels mean is crucial for three basic legal research tasks:

1) finding a recently enacted statute;

2) finding a statute's legislative history; and

3) locating the original wording of a specific statute that has been subject to amendments.

Each of these items is covered later in this chapter. Let's turn to how federal statutes can best be researched under normal circumstances.

B. Finding Federal Statutes

1. Overview of Annotated United States Code

As mentioned, all federal statutes are collected and organized by subject matter into a set of books called the *United States Code*. To help the researcher understand the statutes, two publishers (West and Bancroft-Whitney/Lawyer's Coop) have produced annotated versions of the *United States Code* (abbreviated as *U.S.C.A.*) and the Bancroft-Whitney/Lawyer's Coop version is called *United States Code Service, Lawyer's Edition* (commonly abbreviated as *U.S.C.S.*).

These extremely useful sets of books set out all the federal laws, and, in addition, contain information pertaining to each statute in the form of "annotation." The annotations include:

■ one-sentence summaries of court cases that have interpreted the statute,

■ notes about the statute's history (amendments, etc.),

■ cross references to other relevant statutes,

- citations to administrative regulations that may be helpful in interpreting the statute (see Section J below),

- citations to the legislative history of the statute (see Section H below for more on legislative history),

- research guides (i.e. references to other relevant materials by the same publisher.

Because of all this helpful information, these annotated codes are almost always used in place of the bare *U.S. Code* when doing research on federal statutes. Throughout this book, when we refer to "the federal code" or to the *U.S.C. (United States Code)*, we are actually refering to these annotated editions (*U.S.C.A.* or *U.S.C.S.*).

2. Using Annotated Federal Code Indexes to Find a Federal Statute

Although we suggested earlier that each *United States Code* title contains statutes with a similar subject matter, this is not always true. Some titles contain statutory schemes that are different than the main subject matter covered by the title. For instance, Title 42 contains statutory schemes relating to water resources, water planning, voting rights, civil rights, and the National Science Foundation, in addition to its general topic of public health and welfare. Each of the annotated codes provides a separate index for each title and a general index for the entire collection of statutes. Accordingly, if you don't know what title covers your subject matter, you should turn to the general index for the entire code and find out.

For example, suppose you are interested in federal statutory restrictions on the use of federal education funds by state schools. If you happen to know that such restriction are found in Title 20, you can use the index to that title. If you didn't happen to know in advance that Title 20 contains the education statutes, however, you would use the general index at the end of the entire code.

Note: If you are using the *U.S.C.S.* and don't find what you are looking for in its index, try the *U.S.C.A.* index, or vice versa. Since you're looking for a specific federal statute, either code's index will do fine.

3. Using Popular Name Indexes to Find a Federal Statute

As noted above, in some instances you may hear a federal statute referred to by its popular name, e.g., the Civil Rights Act, the Taft-Hartley Act, the Marine Mammals Protection Act, and so on. You can find these statutes by either using the "popular names index" volume published by the *U.S.C.A.* or by consulting the *Shepard's Acts and Cases By Popular Names*. This latter publication is particularly useful for finding both state and federal statutes and cases through their popular names. Not all libraries carry it, however.

The *U.S.C.A.* popular names index is usually included as part of the general index to that publication and located directly following it on the shelves. This index refers you to the correct title and section (e.g., Title 20 § 607) for the named statute.

4. Understanding Federal Statutory Citations

The reference to any primary law source (e.g., cases, statutes, or regulations) is termed a "citation." The citation, which is always written in a standard form, tells you precisely where the law is located. In the case of federal statutes, the citation contains the title of the code where the statute is found and the section number of the title. For example, the citation for the Civil Rights Act of 1964 is: 42 U.S.C.A. § 2000a-h.

Library Note: Finding this statute in the law library is easy. Locate the set of books labeled *U.S.C.A.* (maroon) or *U.S.C.S.* (black and blue). Look at the spine of the volumes marked 42 to find the one that includes Sec. 2000a-h.

Caution: Unfortunately, it is usually insufficient to just locate one statute when an answer to a legal question is being sought. As we saw in Section A, statutes that cover an entire subject area tend to come in bunches (statutory schemes) and it might be necessary to read five or six separate statutes before you would fully understand what the law is on the subject.

When you use an index, you will notice that statutes are often referred to with an "et seq." at the end of a single statutory reference: 42 U.S.C.A. § 601 *et seq.* (West 1983). "Et seq." means "and following," and lets you know that more than one statute is involved. Fortunately, in such a case, the statutes are all located together so it's only a question of reading from one to another through the entire statutory scheme. Even if, however, the index only refers to a statute without an accompanying *et seq.*, it is important for you to read the statutes directly preceding or directly following it to see if they pertain to the same subject.

Fast Track: How to Find a Federal Statute More Than One Year Old

- If you know the citation, select either *U.S.C.A.* or *U.S.C.S.*, find the appropriate title, and turn to the indicated section in the hardcover version. Regardless of what you find, check the pocket part for amendments, repeals, etc. (see the discussion of pocket parts in #6, below).

- If you know the common or popular name of the statute but don't have the citation, consult the *Shepard's* or *U.S.C.A. Popular Names Index.*

- If you don't know the citation and don't know what the statute is called, but you are able to figure out from the subject matter which title the statute will be found in, consult the subject index for the specific title (found in the last volume of the title).

- If you don't find what you're looking for in the specific title index, or you don't know what title to start with, consult the general subject index at the end of the entire series.

5. Statutes At Large

As mentioned, the usual way to find federal statutes is to look in one of the federal codes. However, you should also know that federal statutes are bound in volumes called *Statutes at Large* and can always be found by their public law number instead of through the codes. This can be especially useful if you are looking for a specific statute that has been amended or deleted and no longer appears in the *United States Code.*

For example, suppose a significant income tax reform bill wins passage in 1987 and is signed by the President. If a new volume of the *United States Code* is published in 1988, the laws for the tax years prior to passage of the tax reform measure will no longer appear in the code. This is because the annotated codes provide you with the statutes as they currently stand rather than with a history of the statute which, for most purposes, will be irrelevant.

If, however, the IRS decides to audit you in 1988 and a dispute arises over your tax return for 1986, you may want to locate the law in effect for that tax year even though it no longer currently applies. The *Statutes at Large* permit you to do this.

The volumes for this publication are stored in numerical order according to the number of the Congress passing the bill. Thus, if you were looking for Pub. L. No. 87-879, you would find the volumes that contain the statutes for the 87th Congress, turn to where Public Law 879 appears in the numerical order within the volume, and *voila,* you have your statute. We explain how to find the public law number of a statute in the following section.

6. Updating of Federal Statutes

Federal statutes often are amended or replaced by subsequent sessions of Congress. Indeed, many laws are totally changed by amendment and deletion in just a few years. This continuous change has required a method for keeping the hard-cover federal annotated codes up to date. This method, in virtually universal use for all collections of annotated statutes, both state and federal, is called the "pocket part system."

a. Pocket Parts

"Pocket parts" are paper supplements that fit inside each hardcover volume, usually at the back. They are published once a year to account for any statutory changes occuring in the interim. When the pocket parts get too bulky because of legislative changes, either a new hardcover volume that incorporates all of the changes since the last hardcover volume was published is published, or a separate paperback volume that sits on the shelf next to the hardcover book is published.

Caution: If the book you are using does not have a pocket part or a separate paperback pamphlet next to the hardcover volume on the bookshelf, and the book was not published in the year you are doing your research, inform the law librarian and ask if there is a current pocket part available. Never rely on out-of-date codes when doing statutory research unless you know that the statute being sought has not been amended since the publication of the book.

The pocket parts for *U.S.C.A.* reprint the sections of any statutes in the hardcover version that have been changed (amended). Sections of the statute that have not been amended are not reproduced in the pocket part; instead, you are referred to the hardcover volume for the text.

Pocket Part Note: When you know the approximate date a statute was passed, you should first check the publication date of the hardcover volume. If this date is prior to your statute, then go right to the pocket part. In fact, many researchers prefer to start with the pocket part and then work backwards to the hardcover. Either way is fine so long as you never, ever, forget to check the pocket part. If you do, you may find that the statute you thought you discovered in the hardcover volume has long since been amended or deleted.

b. Advance Legislative Services

Because pocket parts to the federal code only appear once a year (usually in April or May), there are often times when a newly passed statute or amendment that you may be interested in is not yet included. For instance, if a new statute becomes effective in October of 1986, it may not show up in the pocket part until April or May of 1987.

Fortunately, each federal code has a monthly advance legislative service that prints statutes a month or two after they have been passed by Congress. The one for *U.S.C.A.* is called the *U.S.C.A. Quarterly Supplement* while the one for *U.S.C.S.* is known as the *U.S.C.S. Advance Legislative Service.*

New statutes are also printed in a publication known as the *U.S. Code and Administrative News.* This publication is found near the *U.S.C.A.* in most libraries. The volumes are very thick and are organized by legislative session (e.g., 93rd Congress, 94th Congress, etc.). Some volumes contain the verbatim text of statutes, and the others contain the legislative history of the statutes; they are labeled accordingly. See Section H in this chapter for a discussion of how to research legislative history.

These advance services are, in one sense, a pocket part to the pocket part and make it possible to find a federal statute shortly after it becomes law. The new or newly-amended statutes are organized in these services by Public Law Number. As we have seen, this is the number the statute carries when it emerges from Congress. If you don't know the Public Law Number, you can use the subject matter index in either of the supplements. Also, if you know the *U.S.C.A.* or *U.S.C.S.* citation for the new or amended statute, you can utilize a table in the legislative service that converts or cross-references the citation to the Public Law Number.

Fast Track: How to Find a Federal Statute or Amendment Passed Within the Past Year

- If the proper citation is known, check the pocket part of *U.S.C.A.* or *U.S.C.S.*

- If the new statute or amendment is not in the pocket part, go to the most recent legislative service update and check the index of new statutes. If you don't find what you're looking for, work backwards through the indexes of prior paperback volumes published subsequent to the statute's date.

- If the citation is not known, check the subject index for the most recent legislative service update volume.

- If you find no reference, work backwards through the subject index of the prior volume.

- If you still find no reference, check the pocket part for the general index to the *U.S.C.A.* or *U.S.C.S.* under the appropriate subject headings.

7. Finding Bills Currently Before Congress

Instead of looking for changes to a statute that have already been passed by Congress, you may want to examine legislation currently being considered. Perhaps a piece of environmental protection legislation particulary interests you and you want to be sure it says what you have been told it does.

At the outset, here's a short-cut: call the office of your elected representative (Senator or Representative) and request that a copy of the bill and other relevant documents (official "comments" explaining the bill, for example) be sent to you. This works most of the time. However, if you want to do the research youself, follow these steps:

- Locate the *Congressional Index* (published by Commerce Clearing House).

- If you don't know the bill number, use the *Congressional Index* subject matter index to find it.

- If you already know the bill number, use the status table to find out the bill's current status.

- Review the bill's contents in the *Congressional Index* digest section.

- If you wish to see legislative history for a specific pending statute, use a publication called *Congressional Information Service/Index (CIS)*.

- Consult a publication called *Digest of Public General Bills and Resolutions* for lengthy descriptions of pending legislation.

- If you wish to see an actual copy of the current bill, you will usually have to obtain this through your elected representative, though many federal depository libraries receive current copies on microfiche.

C. State Statutes

Many of the principles that apply to researching federal statutes can be used when dealing with state statutes. However, there are some differences in federal and state legislative processes and in the resources that you use to find and interpret statutes.

D. How to Find Judicial Interpretations of Statutes

It would be nice if research into the meaning of statutes began and ended with your reading of the statutes themselves. Unfortunately, statutes are subject to varying interpretations no matter how clearly they are worded or how closely they are studied. Lawyers are paid large sums of money to argue that the word "may" really means "shall," and vice versa. The ability of lawyers to interpret the meanings of common words in new (and often absurd) ways is sometimes breathtaking and often bizarre.

There are two primary ways to find out what courts have had to say about a particular statute:

- annotations that accompany the statutes in annotated codes; and

- *Shepard's Statutory Citations.*

1. Annotations

By now you should understand that the letter "A," or "Ann.," when it appears as the last abbreviation in a citation to a code, almost always stands for "annotated." Directly following each statute in an annotated publication is information about the history of the statute--when it was first passed, when different sections have been added, and in the case of federal statutes, where the legislative history can be found.

Judicial interpretations are identified by one sentence summaries of case-law interpretations of the statutes directly following the notes on the statute's history. In fact, some statutes have been interpreted by the courts so many times that the publisher includes a little index to the case summaries, which are organized by issues raised by the statute.

It is often difficult to tell whether a case summarized in one sentence in an annotation is in fact relevant to the particular problem you are researching. In this context, remember that the editor who has been assigned to write these blurbs may not have had her second cup of coffee when she wrote the one you're interested in. Thus, the summaries also contain a case citation that allows you to look up the case and read it for yourself. Concisely put, it is essential that you read the case itself and not just rely on what it says in the annotation.

2. Shepard's Citations for Statutes

There are several different research tools provided by a service known generically as *Shepard's.* Sometimes they are in different parts of the same volume and sometimes in volumes of their own. Here we are just discussing *Shepard's* as it applies to statutes. Later, we'll discuss *Shepard's* as it applies to cases.

Shepard's Citations for Statutes provides you with a complete listing of each time a particular statute, regulation, or constitutional provision has been referred to and perhaps interpreted by a published decision of a federal or state court. This invaluable tool is one you will definitely want to master.

First, however, you will need to know some basics about *Shepard's.*

- *Shepard's Citations for Statutes* are dark red, thick, hard-cover volumes with gold and brighter red update paperbound volumes.

- A separate *Shepard's Citations for Statutes* exists for each state and for federal statutes.

- The relevant *Shepard's Citations for Statutes* (e.g., the one applicable to New York state if you are dealing with a New York statute) usually comes in several volumes, according to the date of the included references which are marked on the spine. Thus, typically, one volume might list all references to the statute that were made prior to 1970, another volume might have all references made between 1970 and 1978, and a third might have all references made between 1978 and the present.

■ Within each *Shepard's* volume the references are organized in the same way as the statutes being referred to are labeled in the codes of each state (and the federal government). Thus, if you want to know whether a particular New York criminal statute has been interpreted by a court, you would first locate the place in the *New York Shepard's* that covers the New York criminal laws, and then look for the specific statute by number. In the case of other states, where the statutes are not grouped by topic but only by sequential number, you would only need to find the statute by its number.

■ What you find, for each separate statutory section, is a list of citations to all reported judicial opinions that cite the statute for any reason.

Sanity Note: Don't freak out at all the numbers you encounter on a *Shepard's* page. Relax! Almost everyone says "Yuk" when they see a *Shepard's* page for the first time.

Remember: You must repeat the process with each volume that may contain later case references to the statute.

There may be a few things still bothering you. For example, how can you ever memorize what all the letters in the citations mean? The answer is simple. You don't need to. At the front of each *Shepard's* there is a table of abbreviations for easy reference.

Another question you might have is how do you know whether the case listed in *Shepard's* says anything meaningful about the statute? You don't. *Shepard's* lists all cases that mention a particular statute. It's up to you to find out if the case is important to your particular question. This means that you have to skim the portion of each case where the statute is mentioned. However, because some statutes are organized into numerous subsections, *Shepard's* will tell you which precise subsections of a statute are discussed in the case. This will help to focus your search and allow you to eliminate cases that deal with irrelevant subsections.

Fast Track: How to Shepardize Federal Statutes

■ Note the date the statute you wish to shepardize was passed.

■ Locate *Shepard's United States Citations for Statutes.*

■ Select the volumes covering the time since the statute was passed.

■ Find the title number of the citation as it appears in boldface at the top of the page (e.g., Title 25 U.S.C.).

■ Under the appropriate title number, find the section number of the statute (e.g., Title 25 U.S.C. Section 863).

■ Look up the cases cited under the section number. The citations refer to the exact page of the cases where the statute is referred to.

■ Follow this procedure for all volumes and pamphlets up to the most recent.

Fast Track: How to Shepardize State Statutes

■ Note the date the statute you wish to shepardize was passed.

■ Locate the *Shepard's* volume for your state's statutes.

■ Select the volumes covering the time since the statute was passed.

- If your state statutes are organized into codes, find the title of the code in the upper margin in boldface (e.g., *Penal Code*). If your state goes by a Title system, find the Title number at the top of the page. If your state's statutes are consecutively numbered without reference to a code or title, find the place in *Shepard's* where the number appears in boldface.

- If you are dealing with a code or title, find the section number of the statute (e.g., Title 19 Section 863).

- Note the citations under the section number. These citations are to the pages in the cases where the statute is referred to.

- Follow this process for all volumes and pamphlets up to the most recent.

E. Using *Words and Phrases* to Interpret Statutes

In the Land of the Law judges are master. Thus, to properly interpret a statute you usually need to know how courts have previously interpreted one or more of the specialized words and phrases (i.e., jargon) it contains. One tool to help you do this is *Words and Phrases* (West Publishing Co.), a multi-volume set of one-sentence interpretations of common words and phrases that are commonly pulled from cases and organized alphabetically according to words and phrases that are found in statutory and case law. In essence, this publication allows you to find out whether courts have interpreted or used any particular word or phrase you are interested in, and if so, how. In a real sense, *Words and Phrases* is a kind of dictionary that offers contextual definitions instead of abstract and disconnected entries found in most law dictionaries.

F. Using Attorney General Opinions to Interpret Statutes

As the highest legal officers in state and federal governments, attorneys general are often asked by government agencies to interpret statutes. When they do, it is often in the form of a written opinion. While these attorney general opinions are not binding on the courts, they have influence, especially when there is no precedent to the contrary. More importantly, they can be very helpful in deciphering an otherwise hopelessly complicated statute.

Attorney general opinions are collected in publications usually called something like *Opinions of the Attorney General of the State of. . .* A separate set exists for each state and for the federal government. If a statute is the subject of an attorney general's opinion, the citation to the opinion citing the statute will often appear after the case citations in *Shepard's Citations for Statutes.*

G. Using Legislative History to Interpret Statutes

You will often be uncertain about the meaning of a statute no matter how much you study it. For instance, many statutes provide that certain government employees are entitled to an administrative hearing if they lose their jobs. What such statutes often don't say is whether the hearing must be provided before the discharge or after it.

Clearly, the answer to such questions can be vitally important to all concerned. Assuming you are unable to find a court decision on the question, how should you proceed? One common way (and in many cases the only way) is to find out what the legislators intended at the time they passed the statute. Their intent can be inferred from legislative committee reports and hearings and floor debates--what is called the statute's legislative history. Because those documents and exchanges may clarify broad objectives, and occasionally reflect legislators' more specific assumptions or understanding about the effect of particular portions of a statute, they are used by the courts (along with other techniques of statutory interpretation) to try to divine what the legislature intended.

Legislative Intent Note: Before you investigate legislative history, you should keep a couple of points firmly in mind. The first is that the courts ordinarily prefer to determine legislative intent from the "plain words" of the statute itself. Thus, if a judge believes the words of a statute are reasonably clear, she may be reluctant to consider further inquiry into the legislative history.

The second point is a bit more cosmic. "Legislative intent" can be seen as a kind of mass delusion that the judicial community buys into when it doesn't know how to interpret a statute any other way. Why a delusion? Because most of the time "legislative intent" doesn't really exist. Typically, a few legislators know what's intended by the words of any particular statute, while the great majority who haven't even read it vote for or against the bill for reasons unrelated to how it's worded.

1. Finding Federal Legislative History

Conducting a full investigation of legislative history for a federal statute can be an exhausting and often inconclusive task. You will be probably glad to know that most of the time it is also unnecessary. Normally, locating the more important federal committee reports is all the legislative history research you need to do. (For more detailed guidance, consult Goehlert, *Congress and Law Making: Researching the Legislative Process,* Clio Books, 1979.)

Most statutes in the annotated federal codes are followed by a citation of the specific public laws that enacted and amended the provision and the date of enactment, and may also include a reference to the *U.S. Code Congressional and Administrative News,* which contains federal legislative history. If the federal statute you are looking for does not have a citation to its legislative history, you can check the subject matter index, popular names table, and statutory reference in the volume of the *U.S. Code Congressional and Administrative News* for the year of enactment. There is one major limitation to the value of these indexes and tables, however. They are not cumulative. In other words, they only index materials from the legislative session covered by that volume.

Suppose, for example, that you are dealing with a statute passed in 1984 but don't know its Public Law Number or its *U.S. Code* citation. You can use the subject matter index for the *U.S. Code Congressional and Administrative News* for that year to find the legislative history. If, however, you already have the Public Law Number of a statute, find the volume containing the Public Laws for the Ccongress indicated in the Public Law Number. For instance, if the number is 94-584, find the volume containing material for the 94th Congress. Then, use the statutory reference table to locate the committee reports. If you don't know the Public Law Number, the *U.S. Code* citation, or the approximate year the statute was passed, you will have difficulty finding the appropriate committee reports. Then your best bet is to search for the *U.S. Code* citation.

It is important to remember that the typical statute is amended many times over its lifespan. Each amendment has its own committee reports. When we refer to the legislative history of a "statute", therefore, we generally are referring to a collection of legislative histories. Each of these legislative histories must be separately accessed, because any given volume of the *U.S. Code Congressional and Administrative News* only contains the committee reports for the section covered by that volume.

Finally, it may occassionally be important to recognize that the *U.S. Code Congressional and Administrative News* does not necessarily compile all of the committee reports relevant to a particular bill. Nor does it reproduce the hearings on the bill or floor debates in Congress. Relevant hearings, though usually less authoritative, may be cited in the committee reports, or can be traced through a separate index to government documents (Ask your librarian.) Floor debates can be traced by bill number through the index to the *Congressional Record* for each Congress.

2. Finding State Legislative History

State legislative history is usually more difficult to uncover than federal legislative history. Many state legislatures do not work on the "committee report" system, and most states don't have a publication that is as handy as the *U.S. Code Congressional and Administrative News*. However, many states have legislative analysts whose comments on legislation are considered by the state legislators in the same way as the committee reports are considered by Congress. These comments are sometimes published in the advance legislative update services as an introduction to the new statute, or are available at the analysts' office.

Statutes (and accompanying comments) that are printed in these advance legislative services are later bound and retained in volumes called Session Laws, according to the year they were passed. Thus it is sometimes possible to discover the "legislative history" of an older statute by finding these legislative analyst comments with the statute in the bound Session Laws. To find a statute in the Session Laws, you need the chapter number assigned it by the legislature. That number appears directly after the text of the statute as printed in a code.

It is also common for individual legislative committees to have their own staff counsel draft memoranda to guide them in their deliberations. These memoranda are normally not available in law libraries but may be kept on file with the legislature. The best course for a researcher is probably to ask a law librarian what kinds of legislative history are available in that state. (For more detailed information about state legislative history, see Fisher, *Guide to State Legislative Materials,* American Association of Law Libraries Publication No. 15, 1979. If you are interested in California materials, see Henke, *California Law Guide,* Parker and Son, 1982.)

Caution: Remember, don't get too carried away researching legislative history. It is often possible and usually preferable to determine the meaning of a statute without resorting to the legislative history. Many statutory provisions have been interpreted by courts, and courts tend to not use legislative history unless an ambiguity really exists.

H. Regulations and How to Find Them

Legislatures often pass laws which need active enforcement. For example, Congress has passed a complex series of statutes that provide for the collection of the federal income tax. However, the federal government obviously wouldn't be solvent very long if it relied on everyone to voluntarily line up and empty their pockets. Accordingly, Congress created the Internal Revenue Service (IRS) to implement its programs. State legislatures have created a similar alphabet soup of bureaucratic agencies to carry out their programs.

Legislatures give such agencies the power to make rules and guidelines to carry out the specific legislative intent underlying the creation of the agency and programs over which it has authority. These rules and guidelines are collectively termed "regulations." Some are directed at the general public, some at business entities, and some at the agency itself. If they are consistent with the parent legislation, they often have the force and effect of law. This is a fancy way of saying that, depending on the extent of authority conferred on the agency, regulations may be just as binding and enforceable as statutes. Therefore, when regulations are at issue in a dispute, it is often crucial to first determine whether they are valid and thus have the force and effect of law.

Note: In order to write valid regulations, admininistrative agencies must correctly interpret the authorizing statute. An agency's interpretation of a given statute is often given great deference by a court called on to interpret the statute, because of expertise supposedly possessed by the agency. However, courts are willing to overturn agency regulations when they conclude that the agency misinterpreted the law or issued a regulation when it didn't have the authority to do so.

1. How to Read and Understand Regulations

The same general rules of statutory interpretation apply to interpreting regulations:

- Read at least three times;

- Watch out for "ands" and "ors";

- Understand the statute being carried out by the regulation, and any specific requirements of that statute relate to the regulation. (The statute implemented is usually listed at the beginning or end of a group of regulations.)

- Reconcile regulations with other regulations issued by the same agency;

- Interpret regulations that can result in criminal punishment strictly;

- Interpret regulations that are passed for the general welfare liberally;

- Don't interpret a regulation contrary to what common sense dictates under the circumstances;

- Account for all cross-references.

There are some additional factors to consider in the interpretation of regulation. The most important of these include:

- Agency interpretations of a regulation should either be followed or argued against, and not ignored. Because regulations are often written to implement a general statutory scheme, they have tended to be both wordy and hard to understand, even more so than statutes. Increasingly, however, regulations are being written so that they can be more clearly understood.

- Regulations should be interpreted in a way that best fulfills the intent of the authorizing statute.

2. Finding Federal Regulations in the Code of Federal Regulations

Most federal regulations are published in the *Code of Federal Regulations (C.F.R.)*, a multi-volume and well-indexed paperbound set organized by subject matter. The *C.F.R* is organized into 50 separate titles. Each title covers a general subject matter. For instance, Title 36 includes National Park Service and Forest Service regulations, Title 43 contains Bureau of Land Management regulations, Title 10 contains energy regulations, and so on. *C.F.R.* titles often, but not always, correspond to the *U.S.C.* titles in terms of their subject matter. Thus, Title 43 of the *United States Code* also includes the Bureau of Land Management's organic legislation, the Federal Land Policy and Managment Act; but 42 *U.S.C.* contains statutes on the Medicaid program while the regulations are found in Title 45 of the *C.F.R.* Along with each regulation the *C.F.R.* provides a reference to the statute that authorizes it and a reference to where (and when) the regulation was published in the *Federal Register*. As we'll see below, in order to be valid all regulations are supposed to be published first in the *Federal Register*.

There are two ways to find a federal regulation published in *C.F.R.* if you don't already have the correct citation. There is a general subject matter index. And, at the end of this index, there is a detailed table of contents for each *C.F.R.* title. A new edition of the *C.F.R.* is published each year on a staggered quarterly basis. Titles 1-16 are published as of January 1, Titles 17-27 are published on April 1, Titles 28-41 are published on July 1, and Titles 42-50 are published on October 1. Each year the *C.F.R* covers change colors.

Note: Updating is important. When the new annual edition is published, the regulations contained in it are current as of that date. What, however, if the *C.F.R.* volume that contains the regulation you are interested in was published January 1, 1987 and you are doing your research in July 1987? How can you make sure you are up-to-date? Simple. First, consult the latest monthly pamphlet called *C.F.R.-L.S.A.* ("List of *C.F.R.* Sections Affected"). Find the title and section number for the regulation you are interested in. Then see if there have been any changes between the last published volume and the date of the pamphlet.

Fast Track: How to Find Federal Regulations

- Consult either the general subject matter index to the *Code of Federal Regulations* or the *Index to the Code of Federal Regulations* (commercially published by C.I.S.).

- After the pertinent regulation is found, read the latest monthly issue of the *C.F.R. List of Sections Affected* to see whether changes in the regulation have been made since the *C.F.R.* was published.

- Finally, consult the *C.F.R. List of Sections Affected* in the latest daily issue of the *Federal Register* for the most current status of a regulation.

- For regulations that have been newly issued since the latest *C.F.R.* volume was published, consult the cumulative index to the *Federal Register* under the appropriate agency.

3. Using the Federal Register

Federal law generally requires the publication of all new federal regulations in the *Federal Register*. The *Federal Register* also contains proposed regulations, schedules of government agency meetings, Presidential documents, and lists of bills that have been enacted.

The *Federal Register* can be hard to use as it contains many pages of very small type on newsprint. It is published daily, and a cumulative monthly index is available to help you find the regulation you're after. However, this index is generally organized according to the agency that initiated the action, so unless you know which agency you're dealing with, it's of little help.

If you have a *C.F.R.* citation to the new regulation, or you want to bring your *C.F.R.* search completely up-to-date, you can consult the list of *C.F.R.* sections affected in the latest issue of the *Federal Register*. This will give you a listing of all *C.F.R.* sections that have been affected for the current month.

4. Finding State Regulations

State regulations are usually more difficult to locate than federal regulations. While at least thirty states have an administrative code containing a portion of the state's regulations, a common practice is for each agency's regulations to be separately maintained in looseleaf manuals published by the individual agency. This means that it is often necessary to know which state agency is responsible for writing a particular regulation before you can find it. Some larger law libraries carry all or most of the regulations for their state, but more often it is necessary to visit the agency itself and obtain the relevant regulations.

Regulations are constantly being changed by the agencies that issue them, and it s important to always check to make sure that the regulation that you've found is up o date. This can be done by checking with the agency.

IV. FINDING COURT CASES OR "CASE LAW"

Since we have previously covered the basics about cases, lets discuss how cases are published and the devices that can help you read and understand the ones that cast light on your problem. Here are two points central to this subject:

(1) Most published cases are located in volumes called "case reports," "reports," or "reporters."

(2) the precise location of any published case can be determined by the use of references called "case citation." Case citations are the organizing tool by which judicial opinions can be identified. The search for relevant cases and citations utilizes many of the research tools already described (see Part II-"Backround Legal Resources.") In addition, compilations of brief summaries or "digests" of cases, and regularly published listings or "tables of cases" also provide access to case citations (see Part IV).

A. Case Reports

If you are in a law library as you read this, locate the reports containing all published U.S. District Court cases (the *Federal Supplement*). You will see over 700 hardcover volumes; more than twenty volumes a year are added to the collection. If you look around, you will see that some sets of volumes reporting the cases of the other court systems are even larger. All told, there are many thousands of books containing court cases-- courts have been cranking out opinions for a long, long time.

There are many separate reports for different courts and for geographical areas; an opinion may be published in more than one. Regional reporters collect the cases of several courts in a specific area of the country into one series of volumes. The big question, of course, is how can you find a case when there are so many volumes and so many different reports? The answer is simple: citations.

B. Case Citations

Every reported (published) case has a unique citation. The case citation consists of four or five items:

- the volume number(s) of the reporter(s) where the case is published,

- the name of the reporter(s) where the case is published,

- the page number(s) of the reporter(s) where the case begins,

- the year the case was decided,

- for federal court of appeal cases, a designation of the circuit, and

- for federal district court cases, a designation of the state and specific district (where there is more than one federal judicial district within a state).

Let's take a closer look at each of these.

1. Volume Number

The volumes of each separate reporter are numbered consecutively. The reporter containing U.S. District Court cases (*Federal Supplement*) is numbered in a single series. More often, however, reports have been published in two or more series. For example, the reports containing U.S. Court of Appeal cases (the *Federal Reporter*) are published in two series. The first series goes up to volume 300 and includes cases published through 1925. The second series started over at one and is currently close to 800; it contains cases from 1926 to the present. Some reports are even up to three series. The first element a case citation provides is the volume number of the reporter in which the case is located. A case citation will tell you whether your case is in volume two, volume 379, etc. It also tells you the name and series (2d, 3d, etc.) of the reporter, which are discussed in the next section.

2. Name of Reporter

Obviously a citation wouldn't be much help without the name of the reporter (usually in abbreviated form) and its series. Consider the following example:

509 F. Supp. 825 (E.D. Penn. 1981)

We now know that the first number is the volume number. The "F. Supp." is the abbreviated form of the report known as the *Federal Supplement*. The *Federal Supplement* (F. Supp.) is the report that contains many of the published U.S. District Court cases. Federal district court cases that deal with federal rules of civil procedure are published in a series called *Federal Rules Decisions* (F.R.D.). Examples of other abbreviations for reports are "A." (*Atlantic Reporter*), "P." (*Pacific Reporter*), and "U.S." (*United States Reports*). When a reference is made to a second or third series of a report, it looks like this: A.2d (*Atlantic Reporter*, Second Series).

3. The Page Number

We've seen that all citations contain a volume number and an abbreviation of the reporter name. You have undoubtedly already figured out what the third item is for. It provides the page number the case starts on. In the example above, you know that the case is found in volume 509 of the *Federal Supplement* beginning on page 825.

4. The Year of Decision

Citations also carry the year the case was decided. Thus 509 F. Supp. 825 usually would contain a (1981). This information can be helpful because the old law tends to be bad law, and when you're doing research you usually want to first check the most recent cases relating to your problem.

5. The Circuit or District

Citations to cases decided by the federal courts of appeal usually designate the circuit of the particular court deciding the case. Thus, a case decided by the Court of Appeals for the Third District would appear as 654 F.2d 925 (3rd Cir. 1984). A U.S. District Court citation should indicate the judicial district of the case; in the example above, "E.D. Penn." means that the case is from the Eastern District of Pennsylvania.

Note: Citations often take many slightly different forms. For example, it is not uncommon to see the date first or different abbreviations that designate the report. A nationwide system of citations contained in a book titled *A Uniform System of Citation,* 13th ed. (colloquially called the "Harvard Blue Book") has been developed primarily for law school use. We follow it here.

C. Case Names

In addition to its citation, every case has a name. *Sierra Club v. Department of the Interior* is a case name. Most case names usually have certain elements in common. The first of these is that there are usually two names, one on either side of a "v." that stands for versus. This format reflects the adversary aspect of our justice system.

Sometimes, however, cases only have one name with some Latin attached. For example, *In re Gault* is the name of a juvenile case (the "in re" means "in the matter of"). These types of case names normally appear where the proceeding is brought by the state or the individual's "best interest," or where the proceeding is being conducted on a no-fault basis, and is thus not considered to be an adversary proceeding such as would warrant the "v."

When a case starts out in the trial court, the first name is the plaintiff's and the name in back is the defendant's. However, when an appeal is brought, the name of the party initiating the appeal (the "appellant") will appear first. Thus, where the defendant loses and appeals, the defendant's name will usually appear first on the appeal. Since most cases are opinions issued by appellate courts, a case name may in fact consist of the defendant's name in front and the plaintiff's name in back. This fact gives rise to an extremely important rule of legal research: If you can't find a case under one name, reverse the names and try again. It works more often than you think.

D. Summary of Basic Citation Format

You now know that cases have names [e.g., *Staffin v. Greenberg*] and citations, which consist of volume numbers [509], abbreviations of the report name [509 F. Supp.], page numbers [509 F. Supp. 825], district or circuit (for federal cases) [509 F. Supp. 825 E.D. Penn.], and dates [509 F. Supp. 825 (E.D. Penn. 1981)]. The full citation for this example is: *Staffin v. Greenberg,* 509 F. Supp. 825 (E.D. Penn. 1981). If *Staffin v. Greenberg* were a federal court of appeals case decided by the 8th Circuit Court of Appeals, it would look something like this: *Staffin v. Greenberg,* 650 F.2d 678 (8th Cir. 1981).

E. Parallel Citations

Cases are often found in more than one report. For example, U.S. Supreme Court cases can be found in three separate reports put out by three separate publishers. When you see a Supreme Court case referred to (i.e., "cited"), you will often see three citations following the case name. For example: *Haring v. Prosise,* 462 U.S. 306, 76 L. Ed. 2d 595, 103 S. Ct. 2368 (1983). The first citation refers to the United States Reporter, the second to the Lawyer's Edition, 2d Series, and the third to the Supreme Court Reporter. These three citations are known as *parallel citations* because they refer to the same case.

It often happens that you are provided one citation to a particular case and when you get to the library you discover that the library only subscribes to the other publication for which you don't have the cite. You can translate one citation into another using *Shepard's Case Citations,* which under each citation lists first the parallel citations.

F. Advance Sheets

A significant lag time usually exists between the date a particular case is decided and publication of a new hardcover report. To provide you with access to new cases during the interim, the publishers of the report provide you with weekly update pamphlets called "advance sheets." The chances are great that if a case has been decided within the past six months of when you are doing your research, it will be found in an advance sheet rather than in the latest hardcover volumes.

Advance sheets are numbered and paginated in accord with the rest of the report and thus serve as the report until a new hardcover report is produced. Later, when the hardcover report is published, the citation will not change.

G. *Law Week* and Other Loose-Leaf Publications

A weekly loose-leaf publication called *United States Law Week* contains the full text of U.S. Supreme Court decisions often within a week or two of their release. *Law Week* also publishes key extracts from opinions from other courts around the country that its editors deem to be of general interest. The weekly pamphlets are collected in a large loose-leaf binder and indexed both by subject matter and case name.

Note:If you are looking for a recent case involving a topic that is covered by one of the loose-leaf services (e.g. family law, environmental law, media law), you might find the case in one of these publications, often well in advance of the reporter advance sheet. In particular *Environmental Reporter* regularly publishes all new court cases of significance in fields related to parks and public lands, as well as environmental compliance.

H. How to Find State Court Cases

Most states arrange for their appellate court cases to be published in official state reports. Especially in the larger states there are usually two official reports--one for the supreme court cases and another for the intermediate appellate court cases. Ask your law librarian where the official state report is shelved. In addition, the cases of each state (of all types) are published in a series of reports called "regional reporters," which form the bulk of the *National Reporter System* published by West. West has divided the country into seven regions, and the cases produced by the courts of each state in a particular region are published together. For example, cases from Alabama, Florida, Louisiana, and Mississippi are all published in the *Southern Reporter*.

I. Other Services Provided by Case Reports

In addition to judicial opinions, the publishers of case reports also provide many helpful tools to assist you in understanding an opinion, finding other opinions that are similar, and finding an opinion in the report even if you don't have a citation. These tools include the following:

1. Headnotes

Every judicial opinion contained in a report by definition deals with one or more legal issues. The publisher's editorial staff analyzes the issues discussed in each opinion and summarizes them in numerically organized "headnotes" which are placed directly ahead of the opinion itself. The headnotes are numbered in the order in which the legal issues they summarize appear in the opinion. The part of the opinion covered by each headnote is marked off in the opinion with a number in brackets.

Headnotes can be very useful in several ways. They serve as a "table of contents" to the opinion, so that if you are only interested in one of the many issues raised in a case, you can skim the headnotes, find the relevant issue, and then turn to the corresponding bracketed number in the opinion. Headnotes also allow discussions of legal issues in one case to be cross-indexed to similar discussions in other cases by the use of "digests," and are helpful when you are "shepardizing" a case (see Parts V–VI below).

Warning: Remember that headnotes are not part of the case as such and cannot be absolutely relied on to state the principle of law as it appears in the opinion. Never quote a headnote in any argument you submit to a court.

2. Table of Cases

Each report has a "table of cases" usually at the front (but sometimes at the back) of the volume. This table contains a listing of all cases in that particular volume of the report and their page references. This is a very valuable tool when you have been given the wrong page number citation for a case.

3. Table of Statutes

Each volume of the report has a "table of statutes" that have been subject to interpretation by the cases reported in that particular volume. This can be helpful if you know that a statute has been interpreted in some case within a specific period of time. If the statute you are interested in was interpreted by a case, the table of statutes will tell you precisely which one and provides its citation.

4. Subject Index

Each report also has a "subject index" of the cases reported. Thus, you could find what you were looking for by using the subject index instead of the table of statutes. For example, you might look under "national parks," or "public lands" and the index would refer you to the proper case.

V. USING *SHEPARD'S CASE CITATIONS*

In Part III we encountered *Shepard's Statutory Citations*. Now it is time to look at *Shepard's Case Citations*, possibly the single most powerful tool in the law library. *Shepard's Case Citations* can take you from a single, marginally relevant case that you've found to any number of other cases that bear directly on your issue. It is also essential to the crucial task of finding out just what's happening to a particular case so you know whether it can still be considered as precedent or persuasive authority.

A. Using *Shepard's* to Update Cases

As we have noted, the law is constantly changing. New fact situations call for different decisions in order to reach a just result. New social or technological developments give rise to entirely new legal theories and cause massive changes in existing legal doctrine. This means that a case you may find in the course of your research may or may not represent the way current courts would decide the same issue. Accordingly, each time you find a case that appears relevant, you must find out whether it is still "good law." *Shepard's* helps you do this by giving you the citations to every reported case that has ever mentioned that case.

Thus, in addition to helping you track the principles discussed in any particular case, *Shepard's* will alert you to rulings by a higher court on the case itself. For example, you may uncover a state supreme court case that is very helpful to a point of law you are seeking to establish, only to find out by using *Shepard's* that the U.S. Supreme Court reversed the decision or "distinguished" it (implying a more limited scope for the original ruling).

Sometimes a case is of such marginal importance that it is never used by another court. An important case may be referred to by thousands of other cases for a variety of reasons. For example, the 1954 case that struck down school segregation, *Brown v. Board of Education,* has been referred to by virtually every subsequent desegregation case. *Sierra Club v. Dept. of the Interior* is assuming a similar place in public land law affecting the national parks. *Shepard's* keeps track of these references and catalogs them under the case citation for the *Brown* or *Sierra Club* cases. Then, if you want to know which cases have referred to the *Brown* case, you have only to locate the *Brown* citation in *Shepard's;* under it is a list of citations to cases citing *Brown.*

As we've seen, there are two ways that *Shepard's* keeps you up to date. One way is to tell you whether a particular case has been appealed and if so what happened--the subsequent history of the case. The other way is to inform you when any particular case has been referred to by another subsequent case. We will refer to this as the case's subsequent utilization.

1. Subsequent History

Suppose you read a case called *Jones v. Smith* which is located at 500 F. Supp. 325. Since the case is published in the *Federal Supplement,* we know it was decided by a U.S. District Court. The District Court may not have had the last word, however; the case quite possibly was appealed to a higher court (typically, a Circuit Court of Appeals, but in rare instances the U.S. Supreme Court).

Once a case has been appealed, the published opinion of the lower or intermediate appellate court may or may not continue to be a valid expression of the law. This of course depends on whether the underlying case is affirmed, reversed, or modified on appeal. Thus, before relying on the U.S. District Court case, you must check for any changes that might have resulted from an appeal. *Shepard's* allows you to do this.

2. Subsequent Utilization

As mentioned, *Shepard's Citations for Cases* also provides information on *how* a cited case has been used by subsequent citing cases. Sometimes a cited case is used in the citing case as binding precedent. Other times, a cited case is discussed but distinguished (i.e., differentiated) on the basis of different facts. Still other times a cited case may be disapproved of or overruled by the citing court. Only the court that decided the cited case, or a higher court, can overrule a previous case--that is, can decide that the case is no longer "good law."

3. What Shepard's Citations for Cases Looks Like

Shepard's Citations for Cases are imposing dark red hardcover books and a series of paperback update pamphlets that are red, yellow, or white, the same as *Shepard's Citations for Statutes* look. Just remember that here we're covering the *Shepard's* publication that helps you analyze the status of cases. The outside of the volume tells whether it covers statutes, or cases, or both. For example, the *Shepard's Mississippi Citations* has the following on its outside cover: Cases, Constitutions, Statutes, Codes, Laws, Etc.

This *Shepard's* volume obviously has everything. *Minnesota Shepard's,* on the other hand, has the case citations in one volume and everything else in another. The main point is simple: When you want to "shepardize" a case, make sure you're using the volume that covers cases (you'll know right away if you're using the wrong volume because you'll encounter statute citations instead of case citations).

Fast Track: How to Shepardize State Court Cases

- Select one of the parallel citations of the case you wish to shepardize. This will probably be either the citation to the official reporter or a *West Regional Reporter.*

- Note the date the case you are shepardizing was decided.

- Find the *Shepard's* volumes that cover the *Reporter* in the citation you have selected. If you chose the *Northwestern Reporter* citation, for example, select the *Shepard's* for the *Northwestern Reporter.*

- Select the volume or volumes that contain citations for cases decided *after* the case you are shepardizing (obviously--to find subsequent cases).

- If the *Shepard's* volume contains citations for more than one reporter, find the part that covers citations for the reporter named in the citation you have selected. For instance, if your citation is for the *Northwestern Reporter,* locate the pages that cover this series rather than the pages that pertain to your state's official reports.

- In *Shepard's,* find the volume number (in boldface) that corresponds to the volume number of the case being shepardized.

- Under this volume number, find the page number of the citation for the *cited case.*

- Under this page number, review the citations given for the *citing cases.*

- Use the letters to the left of the citation to decide whether the case is worth reviewing.

- Use the numbers to the right of the citation to decide whether the citing case is referring to the cited case for issues you might be interested in.

- After you write down all potentially useful citations, go on to more recent *Shepard's* volumes and update pamphlets and repeat these steps.

4. Shepard's Notations and Abbreviations

Shepard's has a system of abbreviations that indicate just how the citing case has treated the cited case (e.g., agreed with it, disagreed with it, etc.). These abbreviations appear just before each citation listed under the cited case. For example, when higher appellate court reverses a published decision of a lower court, it usually vacates the lower court's opinion. This means that the opinion is not to be considered as law for any purpose. When this occurs, *Shepard's* places a "v" just before the citation of the case that has vacated the lower court opinion.

Most of the information provided by *Shepard's*, however, is about how different cases have treated the cited case, not just what happened to the case on appeal. For example, an "f" in front of the citing case indicates that it explicitly followed the reasoning and/or decision of the cited case. The various abbreviations and their meanings are listed on an introductory page of each *Shepard's* volume.

Most cases involve multiple legal issues. However, later cases commonly refer to only one (sometimes several) of the issues. For example, if a case touches on twenty different legal issues, a citing case may only refer to it for three of these. *Shepard's* thus includes, with the citation of the citing case, the number of the headnote in the cited case that most closely corresponds to the concept the cited case is being used for, generally set off to the right of the citing case reporter citations (and before the citing case page number), like a footnote. *Shepard's* does this for all cases that have headnotes, regardless of the publisher of the report in which the cases appear. Thus, if you look up 231 NE 2d 112 in *Shepard's*, the citing cases listed for volume 231, under page 112, will include citations that look like: 474 N.E. 2d^6 785 and 474 N.E. 2d^7 785. The little numbers (6 and 7) between the N.E. 2d and the page numbers (785) are numbers of the headnotes in the cited case which best describe the issues for which the case is being cited in the citing case.

By telling you why the citing case referred to the cited case, *Shepard's* permits you to review only those cases that deal with the particular issue of interest. When a cited case treats fifteen or twenty separate legal issues, as is common, it would clearly be a waste of time to read every citing case, when only a small portion of such cases deal with the issue you want to research. On the other hand, *Shepard's* can be fallible and may overlook or misstate issues discussed in the citing case. So instinct can also be important.

Fast Track: How to *Shepardize* U.S. Supreme Court Cases

- Select one of the three parallel U.S. Supreme Court citations for the case you wish to shepardize.

- Note the date the case you are sheparzizing was decided.

- Find the *Shepard's* volume labeled *United States Case Citations.*

- Select the volume or volumes that contain citations for cases decided after the date of the case you are shepardizing.

- Select the part of the *Shepard's* volume that pertains to the citation you are using for the case being shepardized. For instance, if your citation is for the *U.S. Supreme Court Reporter,* locate the pages that cover this report rather than the pages that pertain to the *United States Reports* or the *Supreme Court Reports, Lawyer's Edition.*

- In *Shepard's,* find the boldface volume number that corresponds to the volume number of the case being shepardized.

- Under this volume number, find the page number carried in the citation for the cited case.

- Under the page number, review the citations given for the citing cases.

- Use the letters to the left of the citation to decide whether the case is worth reviewing.

- Use the numbers to the right of the citation to decide whether the citing case is referring to the cited case for issues you might be interested in.

- After you write down all potentially useful citations, go on to more recent *Shepard's* volumes and update pamphlets and repeat these steps.

Essentially the same approach applies to shepardizing all types of citations.

B. Using *Shepard's* to Find Similar Cases

Shepard's was designed primarily as an updating tool. However, as we've pointed out, it can be used for much more than updating. Once you've found a case that's relevant, *Shepard's* can be used to find other cases dealing with the same issue. Every citing case is potentially relevant; thus, if you start out with one cited case, you may find any number of useful cases that have referred to it. Then, each of these citing cases can be shepardized.

Suppose, for example, *Shepard's* lists five cases that have referred to your initial case. Then you shepardize each of these five cases and find an additional two citing cases for each one. In very little time, you have a list of ten cases that may be relevant to your situation.

Of course, as with the updating task, you can use the headnote numbers to filter out irrelevant cases so that you don't case down every citation listed under the cited case. Still, once you find one case, *Shepard's* often serves as a reliable map to other cases that may be of even greater help.

C. Using *Shepard's* to Find Parallel Citations

Above, we raised the possibility that you will be given a single citation to a case and then discover that the library you are using doesn't subscribe to the report in the citation. In that event, you will need to translate your citation into a parallel citation that matches the report that the library does carry. The easiest way to do this is to use *Shepard's*. Simply find the earliest *Shepard's* volume that shows your initial citation and look at the top citation under this. It should be in parentheses. This is the parallel citation.

VI. THE WEST DIGEST AND KEY NUMBERING SYSTEM

When researching case law you're looking for cases with facts and issues that are as close to your problem as possible. The closer the facts, the more authority a case will provide for your position. Obviously, the more cases you examine that have taken up the same legal issue, the better the chance of finding a case with the facts or issues like yours.

In the preceeding discussions we saw how *Shepard's* can be used to go from a single relevant case to a cornucopia of helpful judicial authority. Digests are another tool that provide invaluable assistance in finding similar cases. Digests are often used as a primary way to access cases. For example, you may not have the name of a relevant case when you begin your research, but you will know the general subject matter area. Thus, if you want to know what kinds of potential impacts may constitute a "major federal action significantly affecting the environment" under the environmental impact statement requirements of the National Environmental Policy Act, you may want to use the digests, which contain tables of contents and subject matter indexes, as a basic tool in finding relevant case law. To find cases under the above topic, for example, you would look at the Ninth Decennial Digest heading for "Health and Environment" and subhead 25.10(3) or "environmental impact statement"--"major action with significant effect."

A. Digest Defined

Digests are collections of headnotes (remember these are the one-sentence summaries of how a particular case decided specific legal issues) that are taken from cases as reported in case reports. The digests group these headnotes from different cases together by topic, with accompanying case citations. Because most of the common digests are published by West Publishing Co., the following description applies to West's digests. But similar systems are used by other specialized digests, such as the Pike and Fisher *Administrative Law Service.*

B. The *West Key* Numbering System

The most important point to understand about the *West Key* numbering system is that West Publishing Co. reports virtually all published cases that emerge from the state and federal courts. This means that West has been able to create a uniform and comprehensive classification scheme for all legal issues raised in these cases.

West's Digests are organized according to this system. Accordingly, any given headnote from one case anywhere in the United States can be grouped with the headnotes from all other cases that deal with that same issue. For example, a particular issue dealing with water rights can be assigned a subtopic number and grouped with the other headnotes from other state and/or federal courts that carry this same topic and subtopic number. All together, West classifies its materials according to 414 topics and a vast number of subtopics.

West calls this classification scheme the "key number system." The topic label and subtopic number together constitute the "key" to finding other cases in the digest that have discussed the same or similar issue.

There are a number of different *West Digests.* There is an overall digest that groups all headnote entries from all parts of the country and from all courts. This is made up of two sub-digests--the *Decennials* (compiled over ten year periods) and a *General Digest* (yearly since the last comprehensive *Decennial*). West has then broken this overall digest into digests that are more restrictive in their scope. Thus:

- the U.S. Supreme Court Digest is specific to one court,

- the *Federal Practice Digest* is specific to all federal courts (including the U.S. Supreme Court),

- the state digests are specific to each state, (e.g. *Illinois Digest*), and

- the regional digests are specific to one region (e.g., the *Southwestern Digest* covers Arkansas, Kentucky, Missouri, Tennessee, and Texas.)

As you probably gathered, some of these digests overlap. For instance, both the *U.S. Supreme Court Digest* and the *Federal Practice Digest* cover U.S. Supreme Court cases. And both the *Southwestern Regional Digest* and the *Texas Digest* cover Texas cases. All of these digests duplicate entries in the comprehensive *Decennial* and *General Digests.* Because all West digests utilize exactly the same classification system (the key number system) an entry in the *Texas Digest* (for example) will also be found in the *Southwestern Digest* under the same key topic and subtopic number.

In the event of an overlap, which digest should you start with? Generally, it pays to start with the specific and move to the more general if the specific doesn't statisfy your research needs. Thus, assume you are looking for a Texas case on a specific point. You would want to start with the *Texas Digest*. Then, if you are not satisfied with what you find, you can consult the *Southwestern Digest* for cases decided by the other courts in the region. You won't find any additional Texas cases under your key topic and number, however, since they would have been contained in the *Texas Digest*.

C. Using a Digest Table of Cases to Locate Citations

It is common to hear cases referred to by their names only. Thus, a couple of divorce lawyers might talk about the *Marvin v. Marvin* palimony case, or a politician might rant and rave about the harm that the *Miranda* case is doing the country. It often happens in legal research that you know the name of a case but not its citation.

When this occurs, the *West Digest System* is extremely helpful. Just about every reported case is listed by case name in one of the West digests. Each digest comes with a table of cases that lists the cases covered by that digest. Thus, the table of cases that is published as part of the *West Federal Practice Digest, Third Series,* lists every federal case reported between 1975 and the present, alphabetically by case name. The *West Federal Digest, Second Series* lists cases reported between 1961 and 1975. For pre-1961 cases, the Table of Cases for the *West Modern Federal Practice Digest* should be consulted. Also, for earlier federal cases, *Moore's Federal Practice Digest* Table of Cases can also be used.

Alternatively, a comprehensive listing of *all* reported cases is found in the *Decennial Digests* and current *General Digests*--though you may have to hunt a bit in the Table of Cases for volumes in the general time frame in which the case was reported. (Remember, that case reports may come out significantly after a case was decided.)

Fast Track: How to Find Federal Cases When Citation is Unknown

- Locate the Table of Cases for *West's Federal Practice Digest (Third Series* for cases reported between 1975 and present, *Second Series* for cases between 1961-1975, and *Modern Federal Practice Digests* for earlier cases).

- Find the case name in the hardcover volume or pocket part and note the citation.

- If there is more than one entry for the case name, determine from notes which case is the correct one. If cases involve the same topic, note both citations and read both cases.

- If you don't find an entry for the case name, reverse the names and look in the Defendant-Plaintiff Table of Cases.

Appendix D

Selected References

The National Park System in Law Reviews and Law Journals

Andreason, Cynthia Thorley, *Indian Worship v. Government Development: A New Breed of Religion Cases,* 2 UTAH L. REV. 313 (1984).

Andrews, Barbara T., and Buchsbaum, Andrew P., *Federalism and the Wild and Scenic Rivers Act: Now You See It, Now You Don't,* 59 WASH. L. REV. 417 (1984).

Beaver, Clinton D., *Wyoming School Trust Lands Trapped Inside Grand Teton National Park--Alternative Solutions for the Commissioner of Public Lands,* 20 LAND & WATER REV. 207 (1985).

Becker, Ralph E., Jr., *Land-Use Implications of the Clean Air Act for the Mountain West: The Utah Example,* 5 J. CONTEMP. L. 127 (1978).

Bennett, G.J., and Brand, C.M., *Conservation, Control and Heritage: Public Law and Portable Antiquities,* 12 ANGLO-AMER. L. REV. 141 (1983).

Bryan, Julie A., *The National Park Service Organic Act Prohibits Turning the Doorstep of Canyonlands National Park Into a Nuclear Wasteland,* 7 J. ENERGY L. & POLC'Y 95 (1986).

Cocks, K.D., *A Systematic Method of Public Use Zoning of the Great Barrier Reef Marine Park, Australia,* 12 COASTAL ZONE MNGT. J. 359 (1984).

Coggins, George Cameron, *Protecting the Wildlife Resources of the National Parks from External Threats,* 22 LAND & WATER REV. 1 (1987).

Coggins, George Cameron, and Glicksman, Robert L., *Federal Recreational Land Policy: The Rise and Decline of the Land and Water Conservation Fund,* 9 COLUMBIA J. ENV. L. 125 (1984).

Coggins, George Cameron, and McCloskey, Michael, *New Directions for the National Park System: The Proposed Tallgrass Prairie National Park,* 25 KAN. L. REV. 477 (1977).

Coggins, George C.,*The Law of Wildlife Management on the Federal Public Lands,* 60 OREGON L. REV. 59 (1981).

Cohen, Russell A., *The National Natural Landmark Program: A Natural Areas Protection Technique for the 1980s and Beyond,* 3 UCLA J. ENV. L. & POLC'Y 119 (1982).

Davis, John S., *The National Trail System Act and the Use of Protective Federal Zoning,* 10 HARV. ENV. L. REV. 189 (1986).

Draper, John B., *The Rainbow Bridge Case and Reclamation Projects in Reserved Areas,* 14 NAT. RES. J. 431 (1974).

Edwards, Gregory W., *Keeping Wilderness Areas Wild: Legal Tools for Management,* 6 VA. J. NAT. RES. L. 101 (1986).

Fish, Jerry R., *Preservation and Strategic Mineral Development in Alaska: Congress Writes a New Equation,* 12 ENVIRON. L. 137 (1981).

Fisher, Todd A., *The Winters of Our Discontent: Federal Reserved Water Rights in the Western States,* 69 CORNELL L. REV. 1077 (1984).

Frank, Ronald F., and Eckhardt, John H., *Power of Congress Under the Property Clause to Give Extraterritorial Effect to Federal Lands Law: Will 'Respecting Property' Go the Way of 'Affecting Commerce'?* 15 NAT. RES. LAWY'R 663 (1983).

548   *OUR COMMON LANDS*

Futrell, J. William, *Parks to the People: New Directions for the National Parks System*, 25 EMORY L. J. 255 (1976).

Getches, David H., *The Future of Western Water Law*, 6 RES. L. NOTES 1 (1985). (University of Colorado)

Greenbaum, Roger A., *New Jersey's Pinelands Plan and the 'Taking' Question*, 7 COLUMBIA J. ENV. L. 227.

Havlick, Scott, *Mountain Bicycles on Federal Lands: Over the River and Through Which Woods?* 7 J. ENERGY L. & POLC'Y 123 (1986).

Hiscock, John W., *Protecting National Park Buffer Zones: Existing, Proposed and Suggested Authority*, 7 J. ENERGY L. & POLC'Y 35 (1986).

Holt, H. Barry, *Can Indians Hunt in National Parks? Determinable Treaty Rights and United States v. Hicks*, 16 ENVIRON. L. 207 (1986).

Hopkins, Regina Marie, *The Alaskan Monuments of 1978: Another Chapter in the Great Alaskan Land War*, 8 BOST. COLL. ENV. AFF. L. REV. 59 (1979).

Jarvetz, Steve M., *The Public Trust Totem in Public Land Law: Ineffective--and Undesirable--Judicial Intervention*, 10 ECOL. L. Q. 455 (1982).Keiter, Robert B., *On Protecting the National Parks from the External Threats Dilemma*, 20 LAND & WATER REV. 355 (1985).

Keller, James R., *State Ownership in the Marginal Sea Around the Channel Islands National Monument*, 18 URBAN L. ANN. 313 (1980).

Lambert, John F., *Private Landholdings in the National Parks: Examples from Yosemite National Park and the Indiana Dunes National Lakeshore*, 6 HARV. ENV. L. REV. 35 (1982).

Law Related Issues for Park and Recreation Managers, 21 TRENDS 1 (1983).

Lemons, John and Stout, Dean, *A Reinterpretation of National Park Legislation*, 15 ENVIRON. L. 41 (1984).

McNally, Kendra Shawne, *The Grand Canyon National Park Enlargement Act: Perspectives on Protection of a National Resource*, 18 ARIZ. L. REV. 232 (1976).

Madden, Janet L., *Tax Incentives for Land Conservation: The Charitable Contribution Deduction for Gifts of Conservation Easements*, 11 BOST. COLL. ENV. AFF. L. REV. 105 (1983).

Mastbaum, David, *No Park is an Island: A Simple Solution to a Thorny Problem*, 9 RES. L. NOTES 7 (1986). (University of Colorado, Natural Resources Law Clinic)

Maynard, Robert, *The Clean Air Act Amendments of 1977 and the National Parklands*, 11 U. MICH. J. L. REF. 290 (1978).

Mead, Katherine Lamere, *Wyoming's Experience with Federal Non-Indian Reserved Rights: The Bighorn Adjudication*, 21 LAND & WATER REV. 433 (1986).

Meyers, Charles J., *Federal Groundwater Rights: A Note on Cappaert v. United States*, 13 LAND & WATER L. REV. 377 (1978).

Meyers, Gary D., and Meschke, Jean, *Proposed Federal Land Use of the Columbia River Gorge*, 15 ENVIRON. L. 71 (1984).

Meyerson, Frederick A.B., *A Comparative Analysis of Land Preservation Incentives: Brazil and the United States*, 22 COLUMBIA J. TRANSNAT. L. 389 (1984).

Miller, Jody, *Taming the Rapids: Negotiations of Federal Reserved Water Rights in Montana*, 6 PUB. LAND L. REV. 167 (1985).

Nation, Rosemary E., *The Acquisition of National Parkland: A Challenge for the Future*, 7 DALHOUSIE L. J. 260 (1983).

Newell, Evelyn B., *Model Free Exercise Challenges For Religious Landmarks*, 34 CASE WEST. RES. L. REV. 144 (1983).

Novak, Eva, *Mining and National Park System*, 2 J. ENERGY L. & POLC'Y 165 (1982).

Note, *Protecting the National Parks from Developments Beyond Their Borders*, 132 U. PA. L. REV. 1189 (1984).

Ostrov, Jerome, *Visibility Protection Under the Clean Air Act: Preserving Scenic and Parkland Areas in the Southwest*, 10 ECOL. L. Q. 397 (1982).

O'Sullivan, Lisa L., and Thomas, Marjorie, *The Metamorphisis of the Federal Non-Reserved Water Rights Theory*, 4 PUB. LAND L. REV. 114 (1983).

Pitt, Kenneth P., *Eagles and Indians: The Law and the Survival of a Species*, 5 PUB. LAND L. REV. 100 (1984).

Putney, James B., *Clark v. Community for Creative Non-Violence: First Amendment Safeguards--Their Sum is Less Than Their Parts*, 39 U. MIAMI L. REV. 997 (1985).

Randle, Ellen M., *The National Reserve System and Transferable Development Rights: Is the New Jersey Pinelands Plan an Unconstitutional 'Taking'?*, 10 BOST. COLL. ENV. AFF. L. REV. 183 (1982).

Reeves, Simon, *The Whys and Wherefores of Historic Places Legislation*, NEW ZEALAND L. J. 172 (June 1983).

Roe, Charles E., *The Second Battle of Gettysburg: Conflict of Public and Private Interests in Land Use Policies*, 4 ENVIRON. AFF. 16 (1975).

Rosenberg, David M., *The Concept of National Preserves In Senate Bill 49: A Dangerous Precedent*, 21 HARV. J. LEGIS. 549 (1984).

Rothman, Hal, *Second-Class Sites: National Monuments and the Growth of the National Park System*, 2 ENVIRON. REV. 45 (Spring 1986).

Rounthwaite, Ian H., *The National Parks of Canada: An Endangered Species?* 46 SASKATCHEWAN L. REV. 43 (1981-82).

Samuelson, Kirk S., *Water Rights for Expanded Uses on Federal Reservations*, 61 DENVER L. J. 67 (1983).

Sax, Joseph L., *The Almost Tragic Tale of Boxley Valley: A Case History in the Management of National Parks*, 29 LAW QUAD. NOTES 30 (1985). (University of Michigan)

Sax, Joseph L., *Buying Scenery: Land Acquisitions for the National Park Service*, 4 DUKE L. J. 709 (1980).

Sax, Joseph L., *Do Communities Have Rights? The National Parks As A Laboratory Of New Ideas*, 45 U. PITT. L. REV. 499 (1984).

Sax, Joseph L., *Fashioning a Recreation Policy for Our National Parklands: The Philosophy of Choice and the Choice of Philosophy*, 12 CREIGHTON L. REV. 973 (1978-79).

Sax, Joseph L., *Helpless Giants: The National Parks and the Regulation of Private Lands*, MICH. L. REV. 239 (1976).

Sax, Joseph L., *The Legitimacy of Collective Values: The Case of the Public Lands*, 56 COLORADO L. REV. 537 (1985).

Sax, Joseph L., *The Rights of Communities: A Blank Space in American Law*, OCCASIONAL PAPER SERIES (1984). (University of Colorado, Natural Resources Law Center)

Sax, Joseph L., *Why We Will Not (Should Not) Sell the Public Lands: Changing Conceptions of Private Property*, UTAH L. REV. 313 (1983).

Sayre, C. Franklin, *Cultural Property Laws in India and Japan*, 33 UCLA L. REV. 851 (1986).

Schneebeck, Richard, *State Participation in Federal Policy Making for the Yellowstone Ecosystem: A Meaningful Solution or Business as Usual?* 21 LAND & WATER REV. 397 (1986).

Schulze, William D., et al., *The Economic Benefits of Preserving Visibility in the National Parklands of the Southwest*, 23 NAT. RES. J. 149 (1983).

Shepard, Blake, *The Scope of Congress' Constitutional Power Under the Propery Clause: Regulating Non-Federal Property to Further the Purpose of the National Parks and Wilderness Areas*, 11 BOST. COLL ENV. AFF. L. REV. 479 (1984).

Suniville, Gerald H., *The National Park Idea: A Perspective on Use and Preservation,* 6 J. CONTEMP. L. 75 (1979).

Svoboda, Paul A., *Protecting Visitors to National Recreation Areas Under the Federal Tort Claims Act,* 84 COLUMBIA L. REV. 1792 (1984).

Symposium on Transboundary Problems in Natural Resources Law, KAN. L. REV. (1983).

Szypszak, Charles A., *The Protection, Salvage, and Preservation of Underwater Cultural Resources in the Chesapeake Bay,* 4 VA J. NAT. RES. L. 373 (1985).

Tarlock, A. Dan, *For Whom the National Parks,* 34 STAN. L. REV. 255 (1981).

Tarlock, A. Dan, *Protecting of Water Flows for National Parks,* 22 LAND & WATER REV. (1987).

Thomas, Charlotte E., *The Cape Cod National Seashore: A Case Study of Federal Administrative Control Over Traditionally Local Land Use Decisions,* 12 BOST. COLL. ENV. AFF. L. REV. 225 (1985).

Tinianow, Jerome C., *In Defense of Federal Parks Near Urban Areas,* 14 NAT. RES. LAWY'R 567 (1982).

Van Sader, William P., *Current Tax Trends Affecting Historic Rehabilitation: Catalyst or Obstacle to the Preservation of Our Nation's History?* 13 FORDHAM URBAN L. J. 231 (1984-85).

Viramontes, Daniel, *Status of Mining Claims Within National Rivers of the United States,* 24 NAT. RES. J. 221 (1984).

Watts, James F., *The Criminal Law Enforcement Authority of Park Rangers in Proprietary Jurisdiction National Parks--Where Is It?* CALIF. WEST. L. REV. 126 (1976-1977).

Wiener, Norman J., *Uncle Sam and Forest Fires: His Rights and Responsibilities,* 15 ENVIRON. L. 623 (1985).

Wilkinson, Charles F., *The Public Trust Doctrine in Public Land Law,* 14 UCD L. REV. 269 (1980).

Wilson, David K.W., *Cabin Creek and International Law--An Overview,* 5 PUB. LAND L. REV. 110 (1984).

Wright, R. Michael, *Morne Trois Pitons National Park in Dominica: A Case Study in Park Establishment in the Developing World,* 12 ECOL. L. Q. 747 (1985).

Also of Interest

Abbey, Edward, *Desert Solitaire: A Season in the Wilderness* (New York: Simon & Schuster, 1968).

Albright, Horace M. and Cahn, Robert, *The Birth of the National Park Service* (Salt Lake City: Howe Brothers, 1987).

Bartlett, Richard A., *Yellowstone: A Wilderness Beseiged* (Tuscon: University of Arizona Press, 1985).

Bean, Michael, *The Evolution of National Wildlife Law* (2nd ed., 1983).

Brokaw, H., ed., *Wildlife and America* (1978).

Brown, William E., ed., *Islands of Hope* (Washington, D.C.: National Recreation and Park Association, Inc., 1971).

Chase, Alston, *Playing God in Yellowstone* (Boston: Atlantic Monthly Press, 1986).

Coggins, George C., and Wilkinson, Charles S., *Federal Public Land and Resources Law* (2nd ed., 1986).

Connally, Eugenia H., ed., *National Parks in Crisis* (Washington, D.C.: National Parks and Conservation Association, 1982).

Conservation Foundation, *National Parks for a New Generation* (Washington, D.C.: Conservation Foundation, 1985).

Conservation Foundation, *National Parks for the Future* (Washington, D.C.: The Conservation Foundation, 1972).

Corbett, Marjorie, *Greenline Parks* (Washington, D.C.: National Parks and Conservation Association, 1983).

Darling, F. Fraser, and Eichhorn, Noel D., *Man and Nature in the National Parks* (Washington, D.C.: The Conservation Foundation, 1969).

Despain, Don, Houston, Douglas, Meagher, Mary, and Schullery, Paul, *Wildlife in Transition: Man and Nature on Yellowstone's Northern Range* (Boulder: Roberts Rinehart, Inc., 1986).

Everhart, William C., *The National Park Service* (Boulder: Westview Press, 1983).

Foresta, Ronald A., *America's National Parks and Their Keepers* (Washington, D.C.: Resources for the Future, 1984).

Fox, Stephen, *The American Conservation Movement* (Madison: University of Wisconsin Press, 1985).

Frank, Arthur S. and Rankin, Janna S., *The Law of Parks, Recreation Resources, and Leisure Services* (Salt Lake City: Brighton Publishing Co., 1982).

Freemuth, John, *The Politics of External Threats: Visibility, Mining, and the National Parks,* (unpublished Ph.D. thesis, Colorado State University, Political Science Department, 1986).

Garrison, Lemuel A., *The Making of a Ranger: Forty Years with the National Parks* (Salt Lake City: Howe Brothers, 1983).

Hartzog, George B., Jr., *Battling for the National Parks* (Mt. Kisco: Moyer Bell Limited, 1988).

Hays, Samuel P., *Beauty, Health and Permanence: Environmental Politics in the United States, 1955-85* (New York: Cambridge University Press, 1987).

Ise, John, *Our National Park Policy: A Critical History* (Baltimore: Johns Hopkins University Press, 1961).

Johnson, Ronald W. and Schene, Michael, *Cultural Resources Management* (Melbourne: Krieger, 1987).

Kitchell, Katherine Phelps, *A Needs Assessment-Based Review of the National Park Service Science Program in the Rocky Mountain Region,* (unpublished M.S. dissertation, Utah State University, 1985)

Machlis, Gary E. and Tichnell, David L., *The State of the World's Parks* (Boulder: Westview Press, 1985).

Mantell, Michael, ed., *Natural Resources Law and the National Park Service: Duties, Opportunities, and Tools* (Washington, D.C.: The Conservation Foundation, 1986).

Millemann, Beth, *And Two If by Sea* (Washington, D.C.: Coast Alliance, 1987).

Nash, Roderick, *Wilderness and the American Mind* (New Haven: Yale University Press, 1982).

National Parks and Conservation Association, *Investing in Park Futures--The National Park System Plan: A Blueprint for Tomorrow,* Volumes 1-9, (Washington, D.C.: National Parks and Conservation Association, 1988).

Natural Resources Law Center, University of Colorado School of Law, *External Development Affecting the National Parks* (Conference Proceedings, September 1986).

Nichols, Rosemary, *The Politics of Parklands: Resource Decision Making in the National Park Service,* (unpublished Ph.D. dissertation, Duke University, Department of Forestry and Environmental Studies, 1981).

van Oseten, Richard, ed., *World National Parks: Progress and Opportunities* (Brussels: Hayez, 1972).

Runte, A., *National Parks: The American Experience* (Lincoln: University of Nebraska Press, 1987).

Sax, Joseph L., *Mountains Without Handrails: Reflections on the National Parks* (Ann Arbor: University of Michigan Press, 1980).

Shands, William F., Hagenstein, Perry R., and Roche, Marissa T., *National Forest Policy: From Conflict Toward Consensus* (Washington, D.C.: The Conservation Foundation, 1979).

Shankland, Robert, *Steve Mather of the National Parks* (New York: Alfred A. Knopf, 1970).

Shanks, Bernard, *This Land is Your Land* (San Francisco: Sierra Club, 1984).

Sheridan, David, *Hardrock Mining on the Public Land* (Washington, D.C.: Council on Environmental Quality, U.S. Government Printing Office, 1977).

Swain, Donald C., *Wilderness Defender: Horace M. Albright and Conservation* (Chicago: University of Chicago Press, 1970).

Tilden, Freeman, *The National Parks* (New York: Alfred A. Knopf, 1968).

U.S. Department of Agriculture, *The Principle Laws Relating to Forest Service Activities,* Agriculture Handbook #453 (Washington, D.C., 1978).

U.S. Department of Agriculture, U.S. Forest Service, *A Citizen's Guide to the Forest and Rangeland Renewable Resources Planning Act* (1981).

The Wilderness Society, *National Forest Planning: A Conservationist's Guide,* 2nd ed., (Washington D.C.: The Wilderness Society, 1983).

Wilkinson, Charles F., and Anderson, H. Michael, *Land and Resource Planning in the National Forests* (Washington, D.C.: Island Press, 1987).

Wirth, Conrad L, *Parks, Politics, and the People* (Norman: University of Oklahoma Press, 1980).

Zaslowsky, Dyan and The Wilderness Society, *These American Lands* (New York: Henry Holt, 1986).

Index

Pollution
regional customary international law and,
161
at sea, 164
source, in different state, 94–95
source of, 300
transboundary, 158–159
Popular name indexes, used to find federal
statutes, 525
Precedent, 515
Preliminary injunction, 513
President of United States, political
accountability of, 49–50
Pre-trial conference, 514
Prevention of significant deterioration of air
quality. *See under* Clean Air Act
Priority toxic pollutants, 246
Private nuisance, 87
Production of documents, 513
Programatic Memorandum of Agreement
(PMOA), 284
PSD. *See* Clean Air Act, prevention of
significant deterioration of air quality
(PSD)
Public lands, definition of, 128
Public law, labeling of statutes and, 524
Public nuisance, 87–88. *See also* Nuisance
law
Public trust doctrine, 94, 96–99
Public Utilities Regulatory Policies Act of
1978, 450

Radioactive fallout, 143
Rainbow Bridge National Monument, 455,
456
Reagan Administration
deep-seabed mining provisions and, 150
regulatory reform efforts for coal industry,
476
valid existing rights proposals, 479
Record of Decision, 117–118
Redwood litigation, 77, 78, 79
Redwood National Park
cases involving public trust doctrine, 97–
98
Redwoods Amendments (1978). *See under*
National Park Service Organic Act of
1916
Redwood National Park Act, 98
Redwoods Amendments (1978). *See under*
National Park Service Organic Act of
1916
Regionalism, 200–202

Regulations
finding, 533–535
reading and understanding, 534
Remand, 517
Reparations, 156–157
Reserved rights doctrine, 262–264, 269
national forests and, 345
Reserved water rights. *See* Water rights,
reserved
Resource Management Plan (RMP), 118,
285
Restatement of Torts, 88, 95
Restitution of status quo, 146
Rights-of-Way, FLPMA and, 137–138
Rio Grande Wild and Scenic River, 152
Rivers system, wild and scenic, reserved
water rights, 267–268
Roads
improvement of, 180, 193–195
used for oil prospecting, 390
Rock Island Dam, relicensing of, 457
Rocky Mountain National Park
air pollution threat, 143
development outside park, 95
water rights, 265
*Rocky Mountain Oil and Gas Association v.
Andrus*, 405
Roosevelt Campobello International Park,
152, 315–316, 320
Ross Lake National Recreation Area, 450
Running Owl well, 201

Saguaro National Monument, 43
Salmon River basin, hydroelectric proposals
in, 459
San Juan Island National Historical Park,
152
Santa Fe Pacific Railroad Co., 132
Satisfaction, for international damages,
146
Sax, Joseph, 343, 354
Scotts Bluff National Monument, 299
Secretary of Agriculture, 138
Secretary of Interior
authority over mineral leasing, 396–397
duty to protect the parks, 75–78
FLPMA and, 130
jurisdictional authority over lands external
to parks, 79–80
limited options of, 80
National Park Service Organic Act,
implementation of protection duty, 78–
81

INDEX

Water. *See also* Wild and Scenic Rivers Act
of 1968
appropriation, under congressionally
delegated authority, 269–271
discharge effluent, standards for, 244–245
pollution, 94
of boundary waters, 152
use designations, for EPA, 245–246
Watercourses, international, non-navigational
uses of, 159–160
Water rights
Federal, for Wild and Scenic Rivers, 344–
355
National Park Service and, 261–262
for national parks independent of Wild and
Scenic River Act, 344
reserved for national parks, 264–266
adjudication of, 268–269
national monuments and, 266–267
in wild and scenic rivers system, 267–
268
in wilderness areas, 267–268
Waterton-Glacier International Peace Park,
161
Waterton Lakes National Park, 151
Watt, James, 132, 133
West Digests, 544–545
West Germany, bilateral environmental
cooperation treaty with U.S., 154
West Virginia Department of Energy,
enforcement of SMCRA, 470–472
Wild and Scenic Rivers Act of 1968
approval of nonfederal hydroelectric
projects and, 454
deficiencies in, 419–420
designated rivers, number of, 335
federal water right, 344–355
application of, 352–354
definition of scope of, 349–350
priority date for, 351
legislative reforms, 356–365
private right of action, 364–365
regulation of private activities, 356–358
statutory directive to protect park rivers,
358–364
overview, 332–335

Park Service and, 365–368
permissible and impermissible uses of,
338–344
protection against external threats, 366–
368
purposes and values of, 336–338
regulation of human uses, 340–341
significance for national parks, 336–355
type of right Act creates, 347–349
unappropriated water and, 351–352
Wilderness, designation and management,
131
Wilderness Act, 394
Wilderness areas, reserved water rights,
267–268
Wilderness Protection Stipulation, 400
Wilderness Society v. Hickel, 108
Wildlife
effect of oil and gas exploration, 391–392
preservation. *See* Endangered Species Act,
254
protection, multilateral conventions for,
151
Wilkinson, Charles, 345, 346, 347
Winchester Dam decision, 458
Winters Doctrine, 262–264
Words and Phrases, 531
World Heritage Convention, 147–148, 162–
163
World Heritage sites, 147–149, 426

Yellowstone National Park
adjacent lands
Beartooth Plateau, 410
development of, 442
industrialization of, 426
Washakie Wilderness, leasing proposals,
nearby, 408
bison in, 253, 254
oil and gas leasing, 392
thermal and biological characteristics,
425–426
thermal springs in, 427
wildlife in, 425
Yosemite National Park, 144, 449

Also Available from Island Press

Land and Resource Planning in the National Forests
By Charles F. Wilkinson and H. Michael Anderson
Foreword by Arnold W. Bolle

This comprehensive, in-depth review and analysis of planning, policy, and law in the National Forest System is the standard reference source on the National Forest Management Act of 1976 (NFMA). This clearly written, nontechnical book offers an insightful analysis of the Fifty Year Plans and how to participate in and influence them.

1987. xii, 396 pp., index.
Paper ISBN 0-933280-38-6. **$19.95**

Reforming the Forest Service
By Randal O'Toole

Reforming the Forest Service contributes a completely new view to the current debate on the management of our national forests. O'Toole argues that poor management is an institutional problem; he shows that economic inefficiencies and environmental degradation are the inevitable result of the well-intentioned but poorly designed laws that govern the Forest Service. This book proposes sweeping reforms in the structure of the agency and new budgetary incentives as the best way to improve management.

1988. xii, 256 pp., graphs, tables, notes.
Cloth, ISBN 0-933280-49-1. **$34.95**
Paper, ISBN 0-933280-45-9. **$19.95**

Last Stand of the Red Spruce
By Robert A. Mello
Published in cooperation with Natural Resources Defense Council

Acid rain—the debates rage between those who believe that the cause of the problem is clear and identifiable and those who believe that the evidence is inconclusive. In *Last Stand of the Red Spruce,* Robert A. Mello has written an ecological detective story that unravels this confusion and explains how air pollution is killing our nation's forests. Writing for a lay audience, the author traces the efforts of scientists trying to solve the mystery of the dying red spruce trees on Camels Hump in Vermont. Mello clearly and succinctly presents both sides of an issue on which even the scientific community is split and concludes that the scientific evidence uncovered on Camels Hump elevates the issues of air pollution and acid rain to new levels of national significance.

1987. xx, 156 pp., illus., references, bibliography.
Paper, ISBN 0-933280-37-8. **$14.95**

Western Water Made Simple, by the editors of **High Country News**
Edited by Ed Marston

Winner of the 1986 George Polk Award for environmental reporting, these four special issues of *High Country News* are here available for the first time in book form. Much has been written about the water crisis in the West, yet the issue remains confusing and difficult to understand. *Western Water Made Simple,* by the editors of *High Country News,* lays out in clear language the complex issues of Western water. This survey of the West's three great rivers—the Colorado, the Columbia, and the Missouri—includes material that reaches to the heart of the West—its ways of life, its politics, and its aspirations. *Western Water Made Simple* approaches these three river basins in terms of overarching themes combined with case studies—the Columbia in an age of reform, the Colorado in the midst of a fight for control, and the Missouri in search of its destiny.

1987. 224 pp., maps, photographs, bibliography, index.
Paper, ISBN 0-933280-39-4. **$15.95**

The Report of the President's Commission on Americans Outdoors:
The Legacy, The Challenge
With Case Studies
Preface by William K. Reilly

"If there is an example of pulling victory from the jaws of disaster, this report is it. The Commission did more than anyone expected, especially the administration. It gave Americans something serious to think about if we are to begin saving our natural resources."
—Paul C. Pritchard, President, National Parks and Conservation Association.

This report is the first comprehensive attempt to examine the impact of a changing American society and its recreation habits since the work of the Outdoor Recreation Resource Review Commission, chaired by Laurance Rockefeller in 1962. The President's Commission took more than two years to complete its study; the Report contains over sixty recommendations, such as the preservation of a nationwide network of "greenways" for recreational purposes and the establishment of an annual $1 billion trust fund to finance the protection and preservation of our recreational resources. The Island Press edition provides the full text of the report, much of the additional material compiled by the Commission, and twelve selected case studies.

1987. xvi, 426 pp., illus., appendixes, case studies.
Paper, ISBN 0-933280-36-X. **$24.95**

Public Opinion Polling: A Handbook for Public Interest and
Citizen Advocacy Groups
By Celinda C. Lake, with Pat Callbeck Harper

"Lake has taken the complex science of polling and written a very usable 'how-to' book. I would recommend this book to both candidates and organizations interested in professional, low-budget, in-house polling." — Stephanie Solien, Executive Director, Women's Campaign Fund.

Public Opinion Polling is the first book to provide practical information on planning, conducting, and analyzing public opinion polls as well as guidelines for interpreting polls conducted by others. It is a book for anyone — candidates, state and local officials, community organizations, church groups, labor organizations, public policy research centers, and coalitions focusing on specific economic issues — interested in measuring public opinion.

1987. x, 166 pp., bibliography, appendix, index.
Paper, ISBN 0-933280-32-7. **$19.95**
Companion software now available.

Green Fields Forever: The Conservation Tillage Revolution in America
By Charles E. Little

"*Green Fields Forever* is a fascinating and lively account of one of the most important technological developments in American agriculture. . . . Be prepared to enjoy an exceptionally well-told tale, full of stubborn inventors, forgotten pioneers, enterprising farmers — and no small amount of controversy." — Ken Cook, World Wildlife Fund and The Conservation Foundation.

Here is the book that will change the way Americans think about agriculture. It is the story of "conservation tillage" — a new way to grow food that, for the first time, works *with,* rather than against, the soil. Farmers who are revolutionizing the course of American agriculture explain here how conservation tillage works. Some environmentalists think there are problems with the methods, however; author Charles E. Little demonstrates that on this issue both sides have a case, and the jury is still out.

1987. 189 pp., illus., appendixes, index, bibliography.
Cloth, ISBN 0-933280-35-1. **$24.95**
Paper, ISBN 0-933280-34-3. **$14.95**

Federal Lands: A Guide to Planning, Management, and State Revenues
By Sally K. Fairfax and Carolyn E. Yale

"An invaluable tool for state land managers. Here, in summary, is everything that one needs to know about federal resource management policies." — Rowena Rogers, President, Colorado State Board of Land Commissioners.

Federal Lands is the first book to introduce and analyze in one accessible volume the diverse programs for developing resources on federal lands. Offshore and onshore oil and gas leasing, coal and geothermal leasing, timber sales, grazing permits, and all other programs that share receipts and revenues with states and localities are considered in the context of their common historical evolution as well as in the specific context of current issues and policy debates.

1987. xx, 252 pp., charts, maps, bibliography, index.
Paper, ISBN 0-933280-33-5. **$24.95**

Hazardous Waste Management: Reducing the Risk
By Benjamin A. Goldman, James A. Hulme, and Cameron Johnson for the Council on Economic Priorities

Hazardous Waste Management: Reducing the Risk is a comprehensive sourcebook of facts and strategies that provides the analytic tools needed by policy makers, regulating agencies, hazardous waste generators, and host communities to compare facilities on the basis of site, management, and technology. The Council on Economic Priorities' innovative ranking system applies to real-world, site-specific evaluations, establishes a consistent protocol for multiple applications, assesses relative benefits and risks, and evaluates and ranks ten active facilities and eight leading commercial management corporations.

1986. xx, 316 pp., notes, tables, glossary, index.
Cloth, ISBN 0-933280-30-0. **$64.95**
Paper, ISBN 0-933280-31-9. **$34.95**

An Environmental Agenda for the Future
By Leaders of America's Foremost Environmental Organizations

". . . a substantive book addressing the most serious questions about the future of our resources."—John Chafee, U.S. Senator, Environmental and Public Works Committee. "While I am not in agreement with many of the positions the authors take, I believe this book can be the basis for constructive dialogue with industry representatives seeking solutions to environmental problems."—Louis Fernandez, Chairman of the Board, Monsanto Corporation.

The chief executive officers of ten major environmental and conservation organizations launched a joint venture to examine goals that the environmental movement should pursue now and into the twenty-first century. This book presents policy recommendations for implementing the changes needed to bring about a healthier, safer world. Topics discussed include nuclear issues, human population growth, energy strategies, toxic waste and pollution control, and urban environments.

1985. viii, 155 pp., bibliogrpahy.
Paper, ISBN 0-933280-29-7. **$9.95**

Water in the West
By Western Network

Water in the West is an essential reference tool for water managers, public officials, farmers, attorneys, industry officials, and students and professors attempting to understand the competing pressures on our most important natural resource: water. Here is an in-depth analysis of the effects of energy development, Indian rights, and urban growth on other water users.

1985. *Vol. III: Western Water Flows to the Cities*
v, 217 pp., maps, table of cases, documents, bibliography, index.
Paper, ISBN 0-933280-28-9. **$25.00**

These titles are available directly from Island Press, Box 7, Covelo, CA 95428. Please enclose $2.75 shipping and handling for the first book and $1.25 for each additional book. California and Washington, DC residents add 6% sales tax. A catalog of current and forthcoming titles is available free of charge. Prices subject to change without notice.